THE LAST KAISER

THE LAST KAISER
William the Impetuous

Giles MacDonogh

Weidenfeld & Nicolson
LONDON

First published in Great Britain in 2000
by Weidenfeld & Nicolson

A CIP catalogue record for this book
is available from the British Library.

ISBN 0 297 817760

Typeset by Selwood Systems, Midsomer Norton

Set in Janson Text

Printed in Great Britain by
Butler & Tanner Ltd, Frome and London

Weidenfeld & Nicolson

The Orion Publishing Group Ltd
Orion House
5 Upper Saint Martin's Lane
London, WC2H 9EA

Contents

Illustrations

Between pages 212 and 213

The first Hohenzollern emperor, William I, 1880. *Bildarchiv Preussischer Kulturbesitz, Berlin*

William's parents at Windsor at the time of their marriage, 1858. © *Stichting Huis Doorn, Netherlands*

William with his sister Charlotte, 1863. © *Stichting Huis Doorn, Netherlands*

William, 1863. *Weidenfeld & Nicolson archives*

Georg Hinzpeter. *Ullstein Bilderdienst, Berlin*

The church of Alexander Nevski in the Russian colony in Potsdam. *Author's photograph*

William's bride, Augusta Victoria of Schleswig-Holstein, 1881. *Weidenfeld & Nicolson archives*

Portrait of Dona by Franz Lenbach, 1886. © *Stichting Huis Doorn, Netherlands*

Dona in later years with William. *Weidenfeld & Nicolson archives*

William with his English family at Coburg, 1889. © *Stichting Huis Doorn, Netherlands*

Fürst Otto von Bismarck, the creator of the second German Emperor. *Berliner Stadtbibliothek, Berlin*

William on a visit to Otto von Bismarck at Friedrichsruh, 1888. *Bildarchiv Preussischer Kulturbesitz, Berlin*

'The royal will is the supreme law', inscribed in the Golden Book in Munich town hall, 1891. © *Stichting Huis Doorn, Netherlands*

Cartoon in *Punch*, 1 February 1896, depicting William's impetuosity as threatening the stability of Europe. Punch *Library and Archive*

Hugh Lowther, 5th Earl of Lonsdale, at manoeuvres, 1899. *Imperial War Museum, London*

William, posing in a fine array of medals. *Bildarchiv Preussischer Kulturbesitz, Berlin*

William with his English crew on board his racing yacht *Meteor*, 1889. © *Stichting Huis Doorn, Netherlands*

William and Uncle Bertie at Queen Victoria's funeral, 1901. *Weidenfeld & Nicolson archives*

William and Edward VII, 1906. *Bildarchiv Preussischer Kulturbesitz, Berlin*

Acknowledgements

An apology needs to be made for adding yet another thick volume to the groaning pile dedicated to the Emperor William II of Germany, but after eighty years of recriminations it could be the moment now to strip away some of the prejudice which turns each new work into an indictment. William is a difficult subject, and I cannot guarantee an entirely new approach, but I have tried where possible to avoid malice of forethought, and I hope the result will help us to see Germany's last ruler in a light which is, if not ridiculously positive, at least a little more indulgent than that which has coloured attitudes in the past.

As usual I have had help from a wide circle in Germany. In Saulgau my friend Andreas Kleber introduced me to the Herzog and Herzogin von Mecklenburg-Strelitz, while in nearby Sigmaringen I had an interesting talk with Friedrich Wilhelm Fürst von Hohenzollern-Sigmaringen, the head of the Catholic branch of the Kaiser's family. The German National Tourist Board sent me to Coburg where I had fascinating discussions about the Coburg legacy with Prinz Andreas von Coburg and his son Hubertus, with the Bürgermeister Norbert Tessmer and Thomas Kahle and Waldi Gulder from the town tourist office. I also had considerable help from Hauptkommissar a.D. Jürgen Schmidt who took me to see Dr Rainer Hambrecht in the town archives. The same body allowed me the chance of a brief viewing of the Völkerschlachtdenkmal in Leipzig, possibly the greatest example of Wilhelmine art. Mario Scheuermann in Hamburg sent me details of the emperor's table; while Ernst Loosen in Bernkastel had something to say about his cellar.

KLM Exel facilitated a trip to Belgium and Holland. In Spa, Jean-Luc Troquette of the tourist office and the librarian Jean Toussaint were enormously helpful, the latter took time off to show me the various hotels and villas occupied by William and High Command. In Doorn the curator Dick Verroen showed me round William's last home; and André van der Goes gave me a similar tour of Amerongen. Van der Goes also kindly introduced me to Herr and Frau Wilhelm von Ilsemann. Ilsemann is the son of Sigurd, William's faithful ADC, and the emperor's godson. He was kind enough to talk to me about William's character over tea.

In Britain, thanks are due to Angela Bielenberg, Michael Bloch, Julian Brazil, Colin Clifford, Flora Fraser, John Graham, David Gray, Inga Haag, Russell Harris, Geoffrey Kelly, the Earl of Lonsdale, Gay McGuinness, Patsy Meehan and David Molyneux-Berry. Lucy Brazil also cast a careful oncologist's eye over the passages relating to the Emperor Frederick's fatal illness. I had a long conversation with Tisa von der Schulenburg a few years back, which also provided me with insights into the world of her father, the crown prince's Chief of Staff. At the *Financial Times*, my thanks to Julia Cuthbertson and Jill James for allowing me to put some of my ideas into print. Frederick Stüdemann of the *Financial Times Deutschland* also gave me the chance to air my views on the Kaiser.

Rebecca Wilson and Catherine Hill once again proved kindly editors at Weidenfeld & Nicolson. Douglas Matthews has produced another fine index.

The manuscript has been read by Angela Bielenberg and my agent David Miller.

I should like to thank the patient staffs of the British Library, the German Historical Institute, the Imperial War Museum and the Goethe Institute in London. Lastly I grovel before my little family for putting up with me during the agonies of composition.

Giles MacDonogh
London, 2000

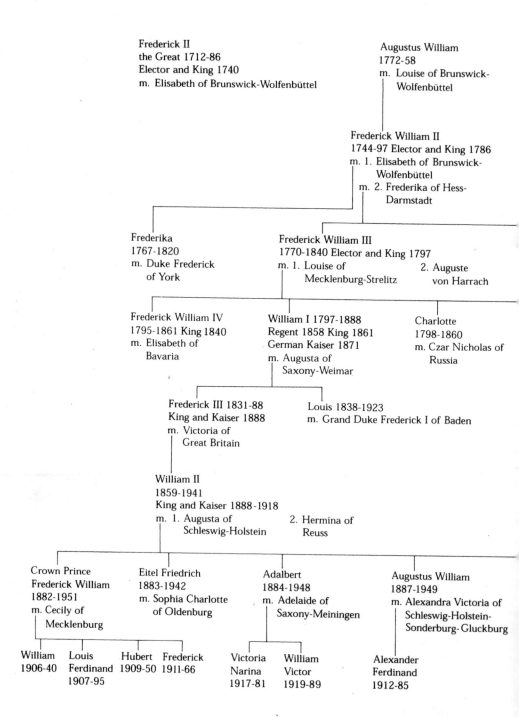

Frederick II
the Great 1712-86
Elector and King 1740
m. Elisabeth of Brunswick-Wolfenbüttel

Augustus William
1772-58
m. Louise of Brunswick-
    Wolfenbüttel

Frederick William II
1744-97 Elector and King 1786
m. 1. Elisabeth of Brunswick-
        Wolfenbüttel
m. 2. Frederika of Hess-
        Darmstadt

Frederika
1767-1820
m. Duke Frederick
    of York

Frederick William III
1770-1840 Elector and King 1797
m. 1. Louise of   2. Auguste
        Mecklenburg-Strelitz   von Harrach

Frederick William IV
1795-1861 King 1840
m. Elisabeth of
    Bavaria

William I 1797-1888
Regent 1858 King 1861
German Kaiser 1871
m. Augusta of
    Saxony-Weimar

Charlotte
1798-1860
m. Czar Nicholas of
    Russia

Frederick III 1831-88
King and Kaiser 1888
m. Victoria of
    Great Britain

Louis 1838-1923
m. Grand Duke Frederick I of Baden

William II
1859-1941
King and Kaiser 1888-1918
m. 1. Augusta of   2. Hermina of
        Schleswig-Holstein   Reuss

Crown Prince
Frederick William
1882-1951
m. Cecily of
    Mecklenburg

Eitel Friedrich
1883-1942
m. Sophia Charlotte
    of Oldenburg

Adalbert
1884-1948
m. Adelaide of
    Saxony-Meiningen

Augustus William
1887-1949
m. Alexandra Victoria of
    Schleswig-Holstein-
    Sonderburg-Gluckburg

William
1906-40

Louis
Ferdinand
1907-95

Hubert
1909-50

Frederick
1911-66

Victoria
Narina
1917-81

William
Victor
1919-89

Alexander
Ferdinand
1912-85

Family Tree

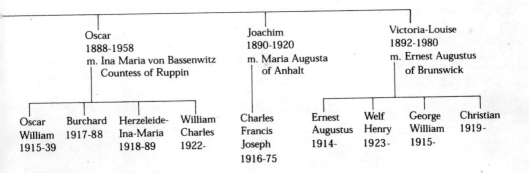

Ludwig
1773-96
m. Frederika of
   Mecklenburg-Strelitz

Williamina
1774-1837
m. King William I
   of Holland

William
1783-1851
m. Marie Anne of
   Hesse-Homburg

Charles
1801-83
m. Maria of
   Saxony-Weimar

Albert
1809-72
m. Marianne of
   Holland

Oscar
1888-1958
m. Ina Maria von Bassenwitz
   Countess of Ruppin

Joachim
1890-1920
m. Maria Augusta
   of Anhalt

Victoria-Louise
1892-1980
m. Ernest Augustus
   of Brunswick

Oscar
William
1915-39

Burchard
1917-88

Herzeleide-
Ina-Maria
1918-89

William
Charles
1922-

Charles
Francis
Joseph
1916-75

Ernest
Augustus
1914-

Welf
Henry
1923-

George
William
1915-

Christian
1919-

For Geoffrey Chambers
– who had never heard of the Zabern Affair.

Unter allseitigem, dreimaligem Hurra
Sagte ein Professor zu Kalifornia,
Man solle den Friedens-Nobelpreis dem deutschen Kaiser geben,
Denn trotz seiner grossen Armee lasse er alle Leute leben.

Er hätte so unzählig viele Menschen zum Schiessen –
Aber nichtsdestotrotz tate er kein Blut vergiessen . . .
Und überhaupt sei er ein Friedenslicht;
Er könnte wohl, aber er tut es nicht.
Kurt Tucholsky,
Logik, 1912

Introduction

'A howling cad!' was John Wheeler-Bennett's father's pithy condemnation of Germany's last emperor, delivered over the family breakfast table during the Great War.[1] It is an image which has stuck firm. William, with his feathers and bangles, occasionally in his curious cape and tweeds, but more often glittering with unearned medals in a uniform all covered in braid; with his steely gaze, his spiky moustache and his impotent left hand clutched permanently on to his sword hilt, was certainly no gentleman.

He earned that opprobrium even before he came to power as German emperor at the age of twenty-nine. His mother Vicky was the eldest daughter of Britain's Queen Victoria while his father was the dashing Fritz, crown prince first of Prussia, then Germany, and later briefly German emperor. She enjoyed the esteem of the British press and public for refusing to kowtow to the bullet-headed Junkers who apparently controlled her country of adoption. He passed for an English-style liberal, largely because that was what she wanted him to be. When relations between William and his mother grew strained at the end of his teens, the British took her side. When William showed signs of an impatient desire to assume the mantle of power, the press sharpened their knives on him. He arrived on the throne in June 1888 his copybook well and truly blotted.

Those same Junkers had helped him up. They were anxious to make sure that the next monarch would be cut in the old mould. They had no desire to see a 'liberal' empire used as a pretext for a ruler in petticoats. William, however, remained a mass of contradictions. He wanted to be a strong Prussian soldier, 'Another Frederick the Great, but different'; the very model of a warrior prince; yet he was born sickly and physically handicapped and had difficulty riding a horse. In all probability a manic-depressive, he had a fine mind and a fondness for many intellectual pursuits, and yet the Potsdam officers' mess on which he chose to centre his world had little time for anything but drinking and hunting. Prussian tradition dictated a need for good relations with Russia, her powerful eastern neighbour, yet William, by dint of his mother's teaching and admiration for her family, wanted only good relations with Britain.

As he himself always insisted that he desired Britain and Germany to be friends and allies, Germany would police the land, Britain the waves; but despite a quarter of a century of persistent attempts, he never managed to reach an understanding. In a Europe controlled in large part by his cousins he was unable to clear his mind of personalities in his pursuit of good international relations. Faced by his Uncle Bertie, or high-handed ministers such as Lord Salisbury or Sir Edward Grey, he felt the British put him down; they treated him as a grandson or nephew and not as the German emperor. Germany was never admitted to full membership of that board of great powers. He and his country were patronised, and he took it very personally.

If kindness could not win him that understanding, he believed he could achieve it by other means. Rough methods such as the sending of a telegram to Ohm Kruger in the breakaway Transvaal, to pledge his support at the time of the Jameson Raid, blew up in his face. So too did his attempt to shock the British into a realisation of Germany's new-found wealth and power by the construction of the powerful battle fleet that was both his favourite toy and his most important creation. Instead of leading Britons to ask whether it would not be wiser to listen to the German warlord, they decided he needed slapping down.

William had billed himself as the 'Friedenskaiser': the emperor of peace. After his grandfather had created the Reich (with a helping hand from his chancellor, Bismarck), William's self-appointed job was to consolidate it, make it healthy and to create its style in art, architecture, theatre and opera. Wilhelmine Germany breathed William. In that he had real success. His son, another William, could go to war if he chose and he was delighted to take him up on it; but once the crown prince began to rattle his sabre William grew jealous of his popularity and had him reined in. Some have argued that William allowed the war to happen because he was too readily accused of being soft. His son had stolen a march on him.

By 1914 William could record a startling success: Germany's economy had outdistanced that of Britain, and was growing faster than any other in the developed world. Directed by a circle of new men, bankers and industrialists carefully nurtured by the emperor himself and admitted to his intimate councils, Germany's trade had blossomed. A new merchant marine was taking German products and manufactured goods to the four corners of the globe. That, argued William, was the real reason behind his fleet. This trade needed the protection of the flag. From the American writer Alfred Mahan, William had learned that no world power had ever come about without first obtaining a fleet worthy of the name.

Sadly, the building programme triggered off an ugly arms race when Britain saw its naval ascendancy threatened by a fleet which sat taunting them from its harbours on the North Sea. For extra security Britain concluded 'understandings' with the two next most powerful European countries, France and Russia. The one still nursed its old grudge against Germany over the seizure of Alsace and Lorraine in 1871, coveted German gold reserves and maintained a giant, well-equipped army which seemed to be pointing east; the other had resisted all attempts to form an alliance with Germany after 1890 and, despite the setbacks caused by the war against Japan, was well on the way to overshadowing its western neighbour not only in numbers of soldiers, but also in equipment, guns and railway carriages. It looked to the Straits at the Dardanelles and to the power vacuum of the Balkans where William's Austrian allies were also hoping to mop up a territory or two.[2]

William increasingly felt that the 'Entente' powers were forging a ring around Germany in order to strangle it to death. The Entente grew stronger while his allies – a faltering Italy and an ailing Austria-Hungary – gave him less and less support. The latter even drew him into the increasingly precarious power struggle in the Balkans. He wanted to break the ring with its tightening grip by peaceful means but neither he nor his diplomats proved up to the task.

Catastrophe struck once William felt that Austria was honour-bound to exact revenge after the murder of the heir to its throne by Serbian-backed assassins. The response unleashed the mother of all wars. William swore to the end of his life that neither he nor Germany had any share in the guilt, while the Entente had it enshrined in the post-war Treaty of Versailles that Germany and its allies were alone responsible for the carnage. Their version is still accepted by most.

William signed orders and was shown battle plans, but it would be impossible to make out that he played the role of 'Supreme Warlord' between 1914 and 1918. The Englishwoman Evelyn Blücher set down the account of a friend who had returned from visiting the emperor in exile in Dutch Amerongen:

The Kaiser says he was treated as a nonentity by his General Staff; that they made a point of contradicting every order or command that he gave; that he was turned out of the room whenever the telephone rang at Headquarters, so as not to hear the commands and the real facts. He was never allowed to speak more than a few minutes alone with anyone who was likely to give him the truth of what was going on. He was never told of the true state of affairs at the front nor the strategy of his generals.

He was hustled backwards and forwards from the Eastern to the Western Headquarters so as to keep him 'out of the way', when his generals were especially occupied.[3]

It is significant that a book published on the 'Kaiser's Battle' – that is, the March Offensive of 1918 – contains fewer than half a dozen references to the emperor. He was not even present at the decisive planning meeting.[4]

For William, losing the war meant exile. He crossed to Holland, staying first as a guest of Graf Godard Bentinck at Amerongen until he was able to move into his own house at nearby Doorn in 1920. Here he suffered the slings and arrows of left and right. For the poet and satirist Kurt Tucholsky, he was the 'Deserter of Amerongen'.[5] Once he had managed to induce the Republic to release some of his money and a good selection of the treasures from his palaces, Tucholsky returned to the attack: William was nothing but a crook, and the European underworld were his new subjects.

Vor dem Schloss zu Doorn
– hinten und vorn –
tät sich allerlei Volks
  ansammeln.
Kaftane siehst du und Locken
  bammeln.
Pferdediebe aus Bukarest.
Galgenvögel aus polnischem
  Nest.
Ungarische Spieler. Lettische
  Schieber.
Marke: Pokern – je länger je
  lieber …
Und ein kleiner Jud aus der
  Krakauer Gegend
hebt die Hand.
    Oben, sich niederlegend,
auf dem Balkon, erscheint mit
  Gewackel:
ein Dackel.
    Unten die Menge lauscht.
Und ein Jauchzen durch all die
  Leute rauscht.
Oben auf dem Balkon, in
  schimmernder Wehr –:
ER.[6]

Outside Castle Doorn
– Aft and before'n –
The strangest beasts crawl out of their
  sets.
Men in kaftans with their dangling
  ringlets.
Horse thieves from some Romanian hive,
Gallows' birds from a rough Polish
  dive,
Hungarian sharpers and Baltic
  conmen.
Queer fish, haggling as much as they can,
  then,
A funny old Jew from somewhere near
  Cracow town
Lifts his hand.
    Upstairs, there, squatting down,
On the balcony, his tail on the
  jog,
A sausage dog.
    Below the masses hark.
From all their throats rise an exultant
  bark.
Up there, on high, the brightest of
  seraphim –:
HIM.

William would never have seen those lines. He had long since developed the habit of only looking at the cuttings from the press which had been selected for him. On the other hand the attacks from the right cut deep. To him, they represented the lies and ingratitude of those men he had promoted to positions of power at his court and in his army. Some, like Bismarck, Waldersee and Hohenlohe, came back from the dead to taunt him from the pages of their posthumous memoirs. Others such as Tirpitz, Bülow, Ludendorff, Hindenburg and Zedlitz-Trützschler either showed him up as an impotent fool, exposed the more ludicrous elements of court life, or cast him as the scapegoat for Germany's defeat.

It was all music to the ears of the Entente. It was convenient, to say the least, to have someone on whom one might heap the opprobrium for collective mistakes. The people wanted answers. They got them. There in Doorn was the guilty man. They made repeated calls for his extradition to face trial for war crimes: the first ruler in modern history to be threatened with such an indignity. They even wrote his guilt, and that of a thousand others, into the Treaty, but still the Dutch refused to be intimidated or to hand him over. In the circumstances, that was probably the best the Entente could hope for. Had William been tried, embarrassing details might have come to light.

So William sat it out in Doorn with his scaled-down court and a new, young wife. His eyes lit up every time the Republic dropped a stitch; every time he felt there was a chance to have his Empire back. When the Nazi Party began to gather strength they interested him too, but not half as much as they did the new empress, who chased after Göring and the other Nazi leaders and even had the former air ace invited to stay in William's Dutch Tusculum. William, however, sensibly decided that the Nazis were not going to restore him to his throne and cut off all contact with them in 1934. He died a courteous but profoundly embittered man in German-occupied Holland on 4 June 1941.

II

The Nazis had no desire to give William any credit that was due. With the exception of William's civilian son, Augustus William, or 'Auwi', after a brief, opportunistic flirtation the Hohenzollerns gave the Party a wide berth, and the heir presumptive, Louis Ferdinand, pursued his contacts with the German opposition. Post-war Germany had no time for them either, and when the historical machine began to work again, William was once more relegated to a shadowy role; over the years declining from a figurehead to little more than a hologram, while big business or the General Staff planned aggressive war against Germany's neighbours in order to stave off the fatal moment when democracy would bring in socialist government at home.

More recently historiography has taken another turn when it comes to William. It has focused on his unguarded scribblings and tempestuous statements, ugly things which were quite often contradicted on the next report or in the following breath. Some of these concerned the Jews and it is now postulated that William was a radical anti-Semite, so that the transition from him to Hitler was little more than a change of uniform.[7] William died six months before the Wannsee Conference which produced the first punctuation mark in the programme for the Final Solution. He was well aware of the persecution of the Jews in Germany, and in a strange, markedly incoherent letter written shortly before his death, he appeared to approve it; but it should not be forgotten that no Jews were persecuted during his reign, that not one Jew was killed on William's orders, with the exception of the very many highly patriotic and often extremely nationalist Jews who went to their deaths as soldiers in his armies. As Major Arnold says in Ronald Harwood's play about Wilhelm Furtwängler, *Taking Sides*, 'This man has made anti-Semitic remarks like you wouldn't believe, I got letters—'. The Jewish Lieutenant David interrupts him: 'Show me a non-Jew who hasn't made anti-Semitic remarks and I'll show you the gates of paradise.'

William's attitude to the Jews did indeed undergo a sea-change after 1918. During his rule he tolerated a group of rich Jewish businessmen whom he knew to be important in promoting Germany's trade and development. To one of these at least, he showed as much friendship as he showed anyone in his life. William – like both his parents before him – was not by nature a warm man. There had been periods in his youth when, under the influence of upper-class anti-Semites such as Waldersee and Philipp Eulenburg, he had expressed his distaste for the Jews in a language that one might have heard in ruling circles just about anywhere at the end of the nineteenth century.

During the war his close contact with Ballin and others like Walther Rathenau was interrupted. Members of his circle, such as Friedrich von Berg-Markienen, may well have encouraged his anti-Semitic rants and rambles. After the war, the 'internationalism' of the Jews annoyed the disgruntled nationalist in search of a scapegoat for defeat. In December 1919 he rounded on his Semitic former subjects:

The most profound and nastiest outrage that a nation has ever brought about in its history, the Germans have brought down upon themselves [when they were] seduced and [mis-]led by the race of Juda they hate so much, and who were enjoying their hospitality! That was all the thanks they got! No German must ever forget this and must not sleep until this parasite is swept from German soil and exterminated! This venomous toadstool on the German oak![8]

A few months later he was seen reading the immensely influential *Protocols of the Meetings of the Learned Elders of Zion* which must have appealed to him enormously, as it appeared to prove – until it was shown to be a sham – that the war and the catastrophe that involved had been engineered by a powerful clique of rich Jews.

There is another quotation which often surfaces when William's anti-Semitism comes up for discussion. On 15 August 1927 William wrote to his American childhood friend Poultney Bigelow. 'Press,' he said, 'Jews and mosquitoes ... are a nuisance that humanity must get rid of in some way or another. I believe the best would be gas?'[9] With the knowledge of the process of extermination carried out in Hitler's camps, the mention of Jews and gas naturally sends shivers down the reader's spine. William had no such information at hand, and the juxtaposition of the three elements – journalists, Jews and mosquitoes – would tend to imply that he was in a jocular mood. His sense of humour was ever cruel.

III

In his recent book, *Wilhelm II. Sündenbock und Herr der Mitte*, Nicolaus Sombart lists ten cases generally brought up against the emperor: the dismissal of Bismarck in 1890; the failure to renew the Reinsurance Treaty with Russia that same year; the hairpin bends of his foreign policy; the Kruger telegram of 1896; the 'Hun Speech' of 1900; the Björkö Treaty with Russia of 1905; the Morocco policy; the *Daily Telegraph* affair of 1908; the building of the fleet; and guilt at the outbreak of the First World War.[10]

In each case, Sombart argues most cogently, William can be said to have acted reasonably, and in some cases well. He had very little choice when it came to dismissing the *Reichsgründer*: Bismarck had not only become over-mighty, he failed to show his young master important documents and spent most of his time closeted on his estates. William would have argued that the Russians themselves would have scrapped the Reinsurance Treaty. He made repeated attempts to resurrect the Russian alliance, and Björkö, for all its amateurishness, was one of them. If he had succeeded in 1905, would there have been war nine years later? It is most unlikely.

The hairpin bends of his foreign policy certainly respond to the contradictory nature of his character which bounced back and forth from left to right, black to white, like a shuttlecock over a badminton net. On the other hand it might be said that some of the blame for these

U-turns lay with his ministers and officials. Until his dismissal in 1906, Fritz von Holstein operated his own foreign policy within the Wilhelmstrasse and successive chancellors and state secretaries fell in with it. The Kruger telegram is a case in point. The Boer cause was immensely popular in Germany where – as William said in his famous *Daily Telegraph* interview – very few people felt a shred of sympathy for the British. His advisers thought William's popularity – not great at the time – might receive a fillip. William may have suspected that the British would respond differently and become aware that their isolation would do them no good in the long run. The result was profoundly negative. It ended the annual family conferences William had enjoyed through his visits to Cowes and made the British public, increasingly driven by the Harmsworth press, deeply distrustful of the German emperor.

The attempt to use France's desire to create a protectorate in southern Morocco to drive a wedge between Britain and its new friend was also the work of Holstein and Bülow. William was extremely reticent about it and, to put it mildly, reluctant to make the stagy landing at Tangiers. When, in 1911, his Foreign Minister Alfred von Kiderlen-Wächter despatched a warship as a warning to the French that they might not proceed without compensating Germany elsewhere, William was again very loath to comply and snuffed out the flames lit by the warmongers in his entourage.

The 'Hun Speech' was delivered to his troops who were leaving as part of the international force sent to deal with the perpetrators of the Peking murders in 1897. It is gruelling stuff; a style William readily adopted when addressing soldiers. Many, however, thought it powerful and good. It was no different to the 'Give 'em hell!' that any general might utter in the circumstances. William's unvetted speeches were a cause of embarrassment to his ministers, not so much because of the language, which was often good, but because he tended to contradict their policies.

The interview he accorded the *Daily Telegraph* in 1908 can hardly be attributed to ignoble motives. Without consulting his chancellor Bernhard von Bülow, he told Colonel Edward Montagu-Stuart-Wortley how much he loved England (he never spoke of Britain), how much help he had given her, and that he hoped the interview would go some way towards restoring good relations. The article had no profound effect on the British, but for the belligerent, Anglophobic German middle classes it was dynamite. They certainly did not wish to know that William had provided a campaign plan to fight their friends the Boers. The explosion which followed nearly cost the emperor his throne. It is said that the fallout ended the period of 'personal rule' which had begun in 1900 with Bülow's chancellorship; but in reality personal rule had made its appearance before 1900, and there was life in the old dog even after Bülow bowed out.

The naval race was held against William as the single most important factor governing his poor relations with Britain. It was certainly one of the most important, but the British had been negative towards William since 1886 at the very least. Commercial rivalry figured large in the indignation of the Harmsworth press. That the British were not prepared to make reasonable concessions, and that William proved that he *was* at the time of the visit by the British Minister of War, Lord Haldane, is indisputable. 'Build no more ships and we will help you create a little empire, made up of cast-offs from Portugal or France.' That was the message. William did not think it involved sacrifices on both sides. And it did not.

Finally there is the issue of the First World War. As always William wavered over the preventative strike that had been advocated by his General Staff since 1888 and before. Each time he looked into the abyss he drew back in horror and countermanded his army chief's orders. He was in favour of giving Serbia a drubbing in July 1914 so long as it did not lead to world war. He was appalled by the killing of Archduke Francis Ferdinand. The military men were prepared to take the risk. Comparatively starved of funds by the Reichstag, the Chief of Staff wanted the chance to attack Russia before they had achieved military superiority – an event he predicted would take place in 1917 – but they were arming faster than even he knew. Once William heard that Serbia was prepared to accept almost all the conditions laid down by Vienna he was ready to call the war off. The army and the Foreign Office succeeded in confounding him. Right up to the last minute, when he finally understood which way Grey meant to jump, William endeavoured to stop war with both France and Russia; but the machine ran away with him and Europe slid into a conflict which cost millions of lives, the supremacy of European culture, and, last but not least, the cad his crown.

I

The Inheritance

The days were long in Dutch Doorn. A lonely former German emperor had plenty of time to reflect on his past and try to understand what went so wrong. By his own admission, his childhood often preyed on his mind: 'The darker the present the more my thoughts wander back and seek out the radiant sunshine of those happy years of peace and childhood.'¹ In this and all things his memory was selective. He skirted lightly over the ordeals he had faced as a result of his withered arm. He was mostly silent about the quarrels with his parents. The portrait was often idealised. Of his grandparents, for example, he said very little about Prince Albert who, in some ways, was the most important of all. His favourites were William I 'the Great', whose life and exploits on the battlefield pointed backwards to Prussia's more glorious past; and Queen Victoria who had had a special affection for her first grandchild in whose arms she died.

William was born in 1859 when the Kingdom of Prussia was about to enter the final, and most glorious, episode of its independent existence. Just eleven years later it would merge its identity with that of the new German Reich, and its austere virtues would be rewrought in the gaudy, new imperial colours. Not that Prussia was that old. The Margravate had emerged relatively strong from the Thirty Years War and had been begrudgingly granted regal status in 1701. As far as its reputation as a mini-superpower was concerned, that dated only from 1745 and Frederick the Great's victorious conclusion of the Second Silesian War. Frederick had succeeded in rounding off his scattered domains by acquiring some key Central European properties: Silesia, formerly one of Austria's richest provinces; Emden, with its useful North Sea port; and Great Poland with the Netze District, which provided him with what a later generation would call a 'corridor' to his distant territory on the Baltic, East Prussia.

With the Second and Third Polish Partitions, Frederick's successor, Frederick William II, greatly added to Prussia's extent. For a little over a decade, Warsaw was incorporated into the swollen state. Disaster loomed, however, when Prussia took on France's new, ideologically motivated, Revolutionary armies. Frederick William III's over-confident troops were routed at the battles of Jena and Auerstedt. In his old age, William blamed Frederick the Great's friend Voltaire for the defeat: the commanding generals had been infected with the spirit of the French Enlightenment, and it had diminished their will to fight.[2] What William failed to explain was why it was the French won, given that they were infused with much the same thinking.

Frederick William and his charismatic wife Louise fled to Tilsit in the farthest corner of their kingdom. Here the king considered abdication. There followed the humiliation of a seven-year occupation. Eventually Prussia threw off the French shackles at the Battle of the Nations at Leipzig. That was followed by a number of smaller defeats which drove the French emperor back to Paris, where he finally abdicated on 6 April 1814. It was in this campaign that William's grandfather first drew blood. With Bonaparte exiled to Elba, Prussia emerged from the conference table in Vienna in 1814 with its powers consolidated and with a policing role on the Rhine designed to keep both the French at bay and Germany's liberals under control. The Corsican's brief comeback the following year ended on the field of Waterloo. There was no further settlement. Prussia's destiny was unchanged.

Bonaparte had wound up the Holy Roman Empire in 1806, but Prussia was none the less meant to play second fiddle to Austria, which retained the presidency of the German Confederation. Prussia was content to play that role until Europe was shaken by a fresh epidemic of revolutions in 1848, which showed the serious chinks in Austria's armour. Russian armies even had to march into Hungary to restore it to the Habsburgs. Prussia's initial attempts to fill the power vacuum were checked in Electoral Hesse and by the degrading Punctuation of Olmütz in 1850. Revenge was not slow in coming. Austria lost Russian sympathy by failing to return the compliment for Hungary during the Crimean War. In the year of William's birth, Austria struggled to maintain its Italian provinces. Prussia, however, remained neutral, a few divisions tantalisingly mustered on the Rhine, while the French and the Piedmontese between them chased the Austrians out of Lombardy.

II

Had William been an automaton he would have been programmed from conception. He was to be a man with a mission; a fusion between Prussia's military might and Britain's parliamentary liberalism. The child's parents, Prince Frederick William of Prussia and Princess Victoria of Great Britain, had been brought together by a little love and a major dynastic experiment. Behind it stood two powerful Germans: the bride's father, Prince Albert of Saxe-Coburg-Gotha, who acted with the connivance of the groom's mother, Princess Augusta of Saxe-Weimar. It was a revolutionary match. For generations Prussian princes and princesses had rarely deviated from the practice of marrying the girl or boy next door: after an unhappy surfeit of Hanovers, that meant Anhalts, Brunswicks, and Mecklenburgs; those small states which could be more or less relied upon to raise a few regiments in the event of war.

In his several works of autobiography, William says very little about his maternal grandfather, except to recall his earliest memory of all. Some time between June and August 1861 at Osborne on the Isle of Wight, he was wrapped up in a towel and rocked by the prince consort.[3] Possibly he continued to associate Albert with the problems he had with his mother. It is also just credible that William had caught a whiff of the scandal which was meant to surround Albert's birth. It was persistently alleged that he was the illegitimate son of a Jewish chamberlain called Baron von Mayern. The proofs offered were that Albert looked nothing like his elder brother, and that his mother fell into disgrace after she had an affair with another courtier.[4]

Albert was a remarkable man who emerged from a dynasty only notable for its ability to marry above its station – the 'stud farm of Europe', as Bismarck called it. In an extraordinary series of alliances the children of Duke Francis Frederick Anthony and his wife Augusta Caroline Sophia were eventually to breathe new life into the royal houses of Britain, Russia, Denmark, Sweden, Spain, Portugal, Austria and Italy; while helping to create the new kingdoms of Romania and Bulgaria. It was a considerable achievement for a dukedom possessing just two small blocks of territory in Franconia and Thuringia, a few ramshackle palaces and small, homely country houses, and where the little princes and princesses did their French lessons with patches on their clothes.[5]

Albert was not even the eldest son. He could not even hope to inherit. Those slim pickings would go to his brother Ernest. What Albert did possess, however, apart from an unusually keen intelligence, was a powerful protector in the person of his Uncle Leopold. In an instance of the Coburgs' successful marriage-broking, Leopold had wed Princess Charlotte, the Prince of Wales's only daughter and heir to the throne of Great Britain. Sadly for Leopold the dream ended in childbirth. The German physician Christian Friedrich Stockmar attempted to save the mother at least but she expired five hours after the delivery of a dead child in 1817. In a rare confession of guilt on the part of an obstetrician, Sir Richard Croft, the English doctor who had bungled the birth, shot himself.[6] Leopold was deprived of his *raison d'être*, but he remained a force to be reckoned with by the British Hanovers until a throne was found for him in Belgium in 1830.

Another Coburger had gone to Britain. In 1818 Albert's aunt Victoria was married, second time round, to the brutal and unappetising Prince Edward, Duke of Kent. He was the fourth son of George III, and, after Charlotte's death, the next in line to the throne. For almost a generation he lived with his French mistress, amassing debts until he could be convinced that Britain badly needed an heir to the throne. That child, the future Queen Victoria, was delivered the following year. There can have been little more than that act of sexual congress between them: he spoke no German and she no English. A year later he died, leaving Victoria a widow for the second time. The future queen, her daughter, was neglected during her childhood, until the inevitability of her succession became clear to everyone around. Prince Leopold gave her what protection he could and the more he heard about his brother's second son back in Coburg, the more he drew the obvious conclusions.

Duke Francis had fought in the Prussian army, but his children's attitude was less indulgent towards the powerful north German state. Leopold's antipathy to Prussia went back to 1814 when he had hoped to win its support in extending Coburg territory in Thuringia.[7] Later his thinking was to evolve into the dynasticism which he was to communicate to his nephew: the Coburgs, through marriage, could control the destiny of Europe. Even more than the Habsburgs, *Bella gerant alii! tu, felix Austria nube!* marriage became their governing principle. Marriages and liberalism would keep Europe in check. William was fatally smitten with the first of these ideas. After some half-hearted early dabbling he was more or less indifferent to the second.

While Leopold continued to be more inclined towards Austria than Prussia (traditionally Coburg princes had sought preferment in the imperial army), Albert saw Prussia as the probable force behind German unification. In his mind's eye he envisaged Prussia transformed into a liberal, constitutional monarchy and wrote to Frederick William IV to that effect. Furthermore, Prussia could bring about Germany's unification by setting up the appropriate central, governmental bodies in Frankfurt which would eventually draw in the other German states, Austria included.[8] Even in 1847, however, it is unlikely that his hectoring impressed the Prussian king much. His brother and probable heir, Prince William, appeared to be more receptive. He had a firmer belief in German unity at least, and while he remained under the influence of his wife, Augusta of Saxe-Weimar, he showed occasional flashes of sympathy for the liberals who gathered in her salon.[9]

III

For Albert to have any influence on the course of world affairs he had to emerge from Coburg and find himself a powerful bride. At Bonn University he had imbibed some of the liberalism of the day. He had sat at the feet of August Wilhelm Schlegel, the historian Bethmann-Hollweg – the grandfather of William's chancellor, the younger Fichte; and like his grandson he joined the aristocratic corps, the Borussia.

The richest prize then on the marriage market for a Protestant prince was Queen Victoria, who had ascended the throne of Great Britain in 1837, aged eighteen. The eyes of numerous German princelings had turned to London as soon as it became clear that Victoria would inherit the British Empire. As Lord Palmerston put it sourly: 'A flood of German princes has descended on us. All of them have been gripped by a sudden desire to see England.'[10]

In deepest winter 1840 the Coburgs carried off the *coup* and Albert married Victoria. On the way to Britain he wrote to his grandmother that he 'would never cease to be a loyal German, Coburger and Gothaner',[11] thereby displaying a steadfastness or stubbornness (call it what you will) which would later be mirrored in his daughter's attitude when she departed for Prussia eighteen years later.

Father and daughter provide numerous parallels. Neither Albert nor Vicky was welcomed with open arms by their countries of adoption. If the British were just about used to their Hanoverian rulers after a century and more (they had latterly begun to see English as their first language), they were not ready to take some new strain of foreign interference on board. Albert had to struggle to do the good he evidently had in him. They found him over-educated and bereft of small talk. He was unmistakably German. For his own part he could not understand (like his daughter in Berlin a couple of decades later) why he could have no scientists or intellectuals at his table.[12] Despite his myriad talents, Albert was condemned to political impotence. Queen Victoria refused to accede to his desire for a peerage because a seat in the House of Lords would allow him to exercise just such a role. Initially she was extremely jealous of her position and determined to keep all power in her own hands.[13]

It was not just the queen: the political leaders of the day were not happy to have some German princeling threaten their authority in matters temporal. It was another foretaste of Vicky's reception in Prussia, only, unlike Vicky, Albert was eventually to succeed in convincing the British he had something to say, even if they continued to resent his German, prudish, holier-than-thou ways.[14] He had a thorn in his side with Lord Palmerston, just as Vicky was later to come up against the intransigent Junker Bismarck, but Palmerston had less power and could –

occasionally – be brought to book. Unlike Bismarck, Palmerston eventually came round to the prince consort and wept when he learned of
his death from cholera in 1861.[15]

If Queen Victoria was jealous of her power at first, there was no
doubting her physical attachment to Albert. Pussy, Vicky, or Victoria,
was not slow in coming. Eight months after the wedding William's
mother was born. She was carefully schooled. Albert had his eye on
Prussia from as early as 1844.[16] In his view, Prussia had to adopt the sort
of liberal regimen which had been introduced by the 1832 Great Reform
Bill in Britain. Once united under Prussia, there was to be a healthy
Germano-British duality to police the world. Just like his grandson later,
Albert envisaged the division of the toil: 'The invincible combination of
Germany by land and England by sea, inspired by the most exalted
ideals, would bring peace and prosperity to distracted Europe.'[17]

IV

When Vicky made her entrance into Berlin, her husband Fritz's father
was still prince of Prussia and heir presumptive to the throne. The
previous year Frederick William IV had suffered a stroke and occasional
bouts of insanity meant he could no longer manage the business of state.
William became regent, succeeding to the throne in 1861 when the
invalid king died. His grandson was already two years old. Young William
was to grow up hero-worshipping the first Hohenzollern German
emperor who represented for him all the finest Prusso-German traditions: 'He walked with firm steps in the paths ordained by God,'[18]
exulted William at Doorn, 'whether stony and beset with trials or bathed
in the sunshine of glory, and thus ripened into simple and unassuming
greatness.'

It became an article of faith that the first German emperor should be
addressed by his people as 'William the Great' after his death; but
despite all his grandson's efforts, the title never caught on. Most thinking
Germans probably had a shrewd idea that it was not the plodding
Prussian king, but his chief minister, Bismarck, who had brought about
the long-cherished idea of German unification. The earthiest Germans,
the Berliners, preferred to remember him as 'der Kartätschenprinz' – or
prince of bullets – from the time he ordered his artillery to fire into the
crowd in the course of the Revolution of 1848: an action which led to a
mercifully brief, albeit ignominious exile in London.

William married Augusta of Saxe-Weimar, the granddaughter of
Grand Duke Charles Augustus, Goethe and Schiller's patron, and the
force behind classical Weimar. Her mother was a Russian princess, Maria

Paulowna. The prince had been sniffing around those quarters for some time. In February 1827 he had even paid Goethe a visit together with his brothers, the crown prince, Frederick William, and Charles.[19] Two years later the wedding took place; it was a couple more before Frederick William, or Fritz – as he was known – saw the light of day.

William's relations with Augusta were not easy. She saw herself as a superior being, not least because she had been dandled on Goethe's knee and had, to some extent, benefited from the great man's teaching. She was cold, rigidly conventional and a plotter. Although autocratic in style, she was reputedly liberal. Under her influence and those of the Rhenish politicians he met in Coblenz, William too moved a little to the left while he was military governor in the Rhineland. She enjoyed pomp for all that, much like her son and grandson. She loved her palace in Trier too, formerly the bishop's, which she called 'grandiose'.[20]

In Berlin she kept a little circle of intellectuals to reinforce her feelings of superiority. The Hellenist Ernst Curtius, who taught her son, and the natural scientist Alexander von Humboldt attended her soirées. She was Anglophile, calling Britain 'the land of my dreams'.[21] This ran counter to the Prussian grain, as Prussia had long since been bound to Russia by emotional and dynastic ties. When the chance came to lock her only son into an 'English' marriage, she seized it with both hands. The product, little William would be a symbol of the Prusso-British dynastic alliance; or, as his later tutor Hinzpeter pompously put it, 'a blend of Guelph stubbornness slightly offset by energy and Hohenzollern self-will modified by idealism'.[22]

For Fritz growing up, there was the 'tortuous choice' between whether to follow the influence of Potsdam or of Weimar.[23] As a Prussian child, playing soldiers came naturally. Hohenzollern princes joined the army aged ten, and Fritz was happy to report to his father from the Potsdam guardhouse, 'All quiet at the watch and sentry posts.'[24] He became handsome, blond and serious. At Bonn University, however, away from his father and Potsdam, Fritz listed towards liberalism. Outwardly he could hardly have looked like a better match for Queen Victoria's eldest daughter. As an otherwise unsympathetic British writer put it, '... if Queen Victoria and Albert had been bidden to select any young prince from all the royal houses of Europe to be Vicky's husband, they would have chosen Fritz.'[25]

v

Although the marriage between Fritz and Vicky was arranged by Albert and Augusta,[26] it was William's job to bring round his Russophil brother

King Frederick William IV. Vicky and Fritz first met in 1851, when
Prince William and Augusta visited London for the Great Exhibition.
Fritz was nine years older than Vicky: at nineteen he spoke passable
English; at ten, she spoke fluent German. He was good looking and
dapper, posed a good deal, inclined towards the standard princely distractions, but of all things, he liked the army best.[27] He would do. Albert
could now begin to put his plans into action. Vicky 'must be in Germany
what her father had made himself in England ... virtually king and she
... must wield just such an enlightened supremacy over husband and
children.'[28]

In the autumn of 1855 Fritz went to Scotland accompanied by the
future Chief of the Great General Staff, Helmuth von Moltke. He
wanted to take a look at Vicky and see if she was the right bride for him.
She was just under fifteen. Vicky took to him, and he found her 'sweet,
natural, friendly and unaffected'. Probably more important than both,
Albert was impressed. With almost indecent haste Fritz told Queen
Victoria and her consort of his desire to wed their daughter. They were
happy, but imposed one condition: that she should not marry until she
was seventeen, and that there be no formal engagement until after her
confirmation, when she would be sixteen.[29] On 22 September Victoria
wrote to another fairy godfather, King Leopold: '*our* wishes ... *have*
been realised in the *most gratifying* and *satisfactory* manner.'[30]

It had worked a dream. The marriage was not just a successful alliance.
Like Victoria and her Albert, Fritz's marriage to Vicky was unusual in
being something like a love-match.[31] It was to be a long wait until she
was old enough to follow her heart. In the meantime Fritz went back to
Prussia and the army. In 1856 a rival attraction briefly distracted him as
the chance of war flared up over Swiss Neufchâtel, which was endeavouring to break loose from Prussian control. This time he was to be
thwarted in his desire to win laurels and glory.

To ensure the continuity of her father's ideals, Vicky went through a
course of training at the hands of her father and Stockmar. She was
schooled in the desirability of German unification and in Prussia's need
to adopt a liberal course. When the time came they were married in the
Chapel Royal on 25 January 1858, spending their two-night honeymoon
in Windsor Castle. Eight days later she left Britain, arriving in Berlin in
February 1858. 'The Englishwoman' was accompanied by Stockmar's
son Ernst, who became her private secretary and Coburg adviser. In
Frankfurt, the ambassador Bismarck warned, 'If the Princess can leave
the Englishwoman at home and become a Prussian, then she may be a
blessing to the country.'[32]

She could not and would not. From the first Vicky treated Berlin,
Prussia and the Prussians with a lordly disdain; nothing came up to

England. 'This smells of Prussia', she would say. In her treatment of the Hohenzollerns she mixed Guelph contempt with a superciliousness which echoed the British press of the period. Like *The Times*, she thought them a 'paltry German dynasty'.[33] Junkers were 'needy gentry'. There was more silver in Birmingham than in the whole of Prussia put together. Naturally the locals who heard these outbursts resented them.[34] English practices were set to continue in her household. Where Fritz's father still had a tub brought over from the Hôtel de Rome, she had bathrooms fitted in the Kronprinzenpalais.

Where the Prussians ate their Beeskow asparagus white, for Vicky it had to be green. It went with English food, English menus and English servants. She was 'Vicky', and her children were 'Willy' or 'William' and 'Henry'.[35] After her eldest was born she maintained that his arm might be treated by bathing in the English Channel, whereas a similar plunge in the Baltic would have no such beneficial effect.[36] For a young woman who was half Hanoverian and half Coburger, and whose DNA had not been refreshed with an ounce of English blood since the Guelphs landed the British crown in 1713, it was tiresome snobbery.

While she was contemptuous of any Prussians who came her way, she wanted her husband all to herself. To the Grand Duke of Baden, who had married Fritz's only sister, the Prussian crown prince had become the 'almost inert tool' of his wife.[37] Being a reigning queen's daughter she refused to see any problem in women ruling, even in a country where such a regime ran counter to Salic law. She told her husband she had every right to wear the trousers, and in no uncertain terms:

to govern a country is not a business that only a King and a few privileged men are entitled to do and that does not concern others ... It is on the contrary the right and sacred duty of the individual as well as of the whole nation to participate in it. The usual education which a Prince of Prussia has hitherto received is not capable of satisfying present-day requirements, although yours, thanks to your mama's loving care, was far better than that of the others ... You were not, however, sure of, nor versed in, the old liberal and constitutional conceptions and this was still the case when we married. What enormous strides you have made during these years![38]

Fritz's friend, the novelist and political liberal Gustav Freytag, summed up their one-sided relationship when he wrote,

His devotion and submission to his beloved wife was total. This love was the highest and holiest of his life and completely fulfilled his needs; she was the mistress of his youth, the guardian of all his thoughts, his counsellor. The layout of the garden, the decoration of the household, the children's upbringing, opinions of people or events, in all things he took the lead from her. If there was an occasion when he could not wholeheartedly follow her, or where his innate feelings contested her demands, he was deeply upset and dissatisfied with himself.[39]

Albert and Victoria, accompanied by three ministers, visited Vicky in Berlin in August 1858. Their daughter was waiting with flowers at the station. There were banquets and boat trips on the Havel. Stockmar and Duke Ernest came up from Coburg to show a little dynastic muscle. Albert visited the scholar Alexander von Humboldt and elsewhere alarmed the Prussians by looking as if he wanted to interfere with their internal affairs. Albert seems to have been unaware of all that: 'Parting was painful', he wrote in his diary. Leave-taking doubtless hurt Vicky too: Albert's voice was the only one she ever heeded. As one of William's recent biographers has put it, 'Vicky had an incurable tendency, one that experience failed to alter, to do exactly what she pleased and to speak her mind with arresting bluntness, indifferent if not oblivious to the consequences of her behaviour. She was charming and impressive but tryingly difficult.'[40]

2

Synthesis

Albert's synthesis was born at 2.45 a.m. on 27 January 1859. Regretting her inability to be present herself, and worried about the possible consequences of a fall Vicky had suffered in the fifth month of her pregnancy, Queen Victoria had been kind enough to send her midwife, Mrs Innocent, and her physician, Sir James Clark. He brought a phial with him: chloroform. Its use had already been sanctified by her mother, who had received a similar dose of anaesthetic during the birth of her son Leopold.[1] He made no use of it during Vicky's protracted labour: eight or nine hours of it during which the princess was in agony. Representing the Prussian side was Dr August Wegner, assisted by the midwife, Fräulein Stahl. Neither doctor was an obstetrician. Expert guidance was to be provided by the royal surgeon Professor Johann Lucas Schoenlein and Professor Eduard Martin.

Martin had arrived late as a result of Dr Wegner having entrusted his summons to the post. He would consequently take the blame for the injuries the child sustained in the course of the birth. According to records unearthed by his son, William had already been delivered by the time he got there. He found the other two physicians ministering to the child. The official report, however, says that he assisted at the birth. The child was in the breech position, and needed to be turned before he could be delivered. To get the process moving Clark gave Vicky a large dose of chloroform while Martin administered ergot – a uterine stimulant.[2]

William was not breathing when he emerged, but by 'continuous rubbing ... dousing in a hot bath and short, sharp slaps on his buttocks' Dr Martin and Fräulein Stahl 'managed to get the child to breathe' for which the latter, at least, later took the credit for saving the boy's life.[3] Those lost minutes and the absence of oxygen might have caused hypoxia, which could have resulted in slight brain damage. It has been suggested that this was the cause of the child's hyperactivity and emotional instability.[4] The first faint cries were greeted by those present with a huge sigh of relief. The prince regent pumped Martin's hand in gratitude, adding, 'But you don't hit a Prussian prince like that!'[5] Old Field Marshal Wrangel took it upon himself to inform the people. He opened the window and shouted out to the crowd gathered in the Linden below. 'Children,' he said, using Prussian military jargon for inferior ranks, 'it is a prince, and a stout recruit too.'[6] A 101-gun salute sounded off. The twenty-sixth spread particular jubilation among the onlookers: a princess received only twenty-five.

Three days later the midwife noticed that all was not right with the boy, that his left arm was slack. During the delivery it had been wrenched out of its socket and some of the muscle tissue torn. William's deformities were not entirely due to the clumsiness of the physicians who attended his birth. All his life he suffered from infections in his right ear which suppurated and often needed to be stopped up with cotton wool. He was also liable to throat infection and problems affected his entire left side. He may well have suffered from slight cerebral palsy. Later his midwife would put it about that he was 'not properly made by nature'.[7] Added to his other problems William possibly inherited Albert's propensity to depression. On the Prussian side, his great-uncle, Frederick William IV, was almost certainly a manic-depressive.

He was christened Friedrich Wilhelm Victor Albert on 4 March in the Kronprinzenpalais. The British minister's wife, Lady Bloomfield, reported that he was 'much taken up with the Prince Regent's orders and kept moving its little hands as if it wanted to play with them'.[8] He was called Willy until he was six. It was not to be the most joyful childhood, despite the rosy picture he painted in his autobiography. Very soon the treatments would start, to try to remedy the damaged arm: salt water, sea water and daily rubbing and binding. Until 1870 the lame arm was regularly galvanised by electric shocks. One of the oddest attempts to get it working was bathing it in the blood of a freshly slaughtered hare. He walked at six months, but at four he was observed to suffer from 'torticollis', his head drooping to the right. A device was made for him then which held his head in a sort of cage, which was connected to his waist by a bar running up his spine.

Later still there was surgical intervention carried out in the hope of rendering the royal child more normal in his appearance. Special exercises were prescribed with a view to lengthening the left arm. It none the less remained some three inches shorter than the right in the adult William. As far as the floppy head was concerned, the operation was partially successful even if he remained weak on his left side. The methods used by the doctors may seem barbaric, but even today treating a withered arm is rarely crowned with success. The fact that they were able to induce him to move the fingers of his left arm and lightly grip objects is an indication that they made considerable progress.[9]

William came to terms with his crippled arm. Although it was concealed from the public by careful posing for photographs, it was certainly no secret. He could hold an object in his left hand, but not lift it. The right hand compensated for the weakness of the left. Later his grip would be compared to that of the world champion boxer, John Sullivan.[10] At Doorn he confessed that the crude attempts to correct it had done more harm than good, in that he was subjected to intolerable pain, in particular by the electric shocks.

Medical science had not yet adopted modern othopaedic methods which would be used to treat such a condition today. Whatever the case I was treated in various ways which could only be castigated as unprofessional in the modern world. The only result was that I was in a painful way, greatly tortured.[11]

Historians continue to want to see William's deformity if not as the key, as an important clue to understanding his character. It is certainly the case that not only William, but all those around him, tried their hardest to make him overcome his handicap through physical and mental effort and that allowances were made in consideration for his gammy arm; but it is simply not true to assume that a disability of this sort – once the child has come to terms with it – will warp his character. In later life William made little fuss about his arm, which would have been obvious to any one of the many thousands of people admitted to his table. He would have taken it for granted that those people who came close to him would have been briefed in advance.[12]

II

Albert had gradually become aware that Vicky's mission had been blighted by the Hohenzollerns, who had never subscribed to the Coburg agenda. He had over-estimated his power to change them. For the little time he had left he would concentrate his attentions on Augusta.[13] In September 1860 Vicky took William to Coburg to meet her parents for the first time. They delighted in the company of their first grandchild.[14] Queen Victoria wrote:

He is a fine fat child, with a beautiful white soft skin, very fine shoulders and limbs [sic], and a very dear face, like Vicky and Fritz, and also Louise of Baden. He has Fritz's eyes and Vicky's mouth, and very fair curly hair.[15]

They met him again when he came to the Isle of Wight for the summer of 1861. Prussia was not behaving at all as Albert intended. Frederick William died on 2 January 1861 and Fritz's father acceded to the throne.

The new king showed that not even Augusta's influence could prevent him from adopting a reactionary course. The prince consort and Palmerston were confirmed in their worst fears by the speech William made at his coronation in Königsberg: 'Prussian rulers receive their crowns from God and therein lies the sanctity of the crown which is inviolable.' It was a long way from the liberal spirit of 1848, and gave Albert little hope that Vicky might succeed in her endeavours.[16]

William I already had his belly full of liberals. He faced opposition from the Diet over his proposal to increase the size of the army. For a while he considered stepping down and handing the job over to Fritz, but the latter was too indecisive to seize the moment. In the end he assembled a powerful team of ministers to guide him through the crisis. His Minister of War, Albrecht von Roon, strove to retain the army in royal hands, out of Parliament's reach. Otto von Bismarck, who took over as chancellor on 17 September 1862, was an even tougher nut. Once he had taken up office, Vicky's plans would be bedevilled for a generation. All she could do was to hold her husband in check, that 'hero in carpet slippers' – 'Please, please, man of my heart, listen to your little wife.'[17]

Fritz was not best suited to the fight proposed by Vicky. In Danzig he loudly washed his hands of the restrictive press controls published by Bismarck; a gesture which would have led to his being removed from his command had it not been for the new chancellor, who did not want him made a martyr. Bismarck rightly suspected that Vicky had been behind the stand, and marked her down as a political menace: the leader of the 'Anglo-Coburg' party at court. She was proud of herself: 'I did *all* I *could* to induce Fritz to do so.' The king, whose outbursts against the constitution and liberalism could be every bit as mordant as his grandson's were later, pushed his son farther and farther out of the nest. He no longer trusted his opinions. Vicky 'loved power and influence ... [but] with all her dazzling cleverness Princess Frederick was not wise'.[18]

Their young son was not a fast developer. He was notable for a degree of atavism in his earliest years, which made him a terror to those who were charged with the job of looking after him. He was twenty-two months before he uttered his first word, in German; and twenty-five months before he managed some English rhymes. In February 1861 he came out with his first sentences: 'Wilhelm heiss ich' and 'Soldat ist schöner Mensch.'* By the time he was three he was speaking a hodge-podge of English and German. Soon he learned to separate the two languages out.[19] He always spoke English in England, though his lan-

---

* 'I am called William' and 'Soldier is handsome person'.

guage was a little stilted and he never learned to correct the German failing of confusing adjectives with adverbs.

In March 1863 William was back in Britain for his Uncle Bertie's wedding in St George's Chapel, Windsor. William was dressed in a kilt for the ceremony. He admired the blue coats of the knights of the Garter and the music performed by the Horse Guards, the wedding march from Mendelssohn's *Midsummer Night's Dream*, and above all the drummers. By his own admission, however, the four-year-old found the service too long, and swiftly grew bored. When his uncles Alfred and Leopold – the latter was not many years his senior – tried to discipline him, William drew his skean-dhu and attacked. If that was not enough, he even bit Alfred on the leg. He was not allowed to live this tantrum down for the rest of his childhood.[20]

In September he went to stay at his Coburg great-uncle's *Jagdschloss* – the former Benedictine abbey of Reinhardsbrunn in Thuringia. In later life William could not recall the details of such trips. It is hardly surprising: he was constantly on the move. The intention was to let him get to know the country he would eventually rule. In July 1864 there was a holiday in Swinemünde and later he visited the Riesengebirge. In July 1865, the crown prince and princess chose the spa town of Oeynhausen in Westphalia and later Wyck on the island of Föhr off the east coast of Schleswig-Holstein.

Vicky wanted to mould her firstborn into a copy of her dead father. On 16 August 1864 she wrote to her mother,

How often I try to trace a likeness to dear papa in his dear little face, but as much as I wish it I cannot find it, but it may come perhaps – may he but remind me of him in mind and in heart and character.[21]

She was a cold woman, but she undoubtedly loved William as an infant. He was right to say later, however, that she had been hard on him. She saw his physical flaws as a reproach and it was hard for her to conceal the sentiment of shame, that she had given birth to a deformed child and he was to some extent a blot on her escutcheon. This feeling was wedded to a sense of guilt, stemming from the fear that she might have damaged the foetus at the time of her fall.[22] She did not, however, reserve this feeling of disappointment for William, and this needs to be stressed. His sister Charlotte's hands were bound at night and she was obliged to wear gloves to prevent her from chewing her nails; her daughter Victoria was castigated as 'stupid' and 'backward'; Henry as 'ugly' and 'lazy'. As more children arrived she was prone to transfer her tenderness to the latest boy; first Sigismund and then Waldemar. Sadly for Vicky both died in childhood. Sigismund, she thought, 'was going to be like Papa'.[23]

Living in Prussia meant venerating the army. William and his younger brother Henry loved to watch the Sunday parades down Unter den Linden in Berlin from a window in the Kronprinzenpalais. The infantry marched on the south side of the boulevard, the dismounted cavalry on the north. His grandfather was there to take the salute on the Opernplatz.[24] He was ever the simple soldier. With Bismarck's help he had been able to bring the army up to strength. In 1864 it was ready to fight the first of his wars, against the Danes, who had annexed the German-speaking duchy of Schleswig and imposed a new constitution on Holstein. The Prussians shared the laurels with the Austrians, who put up a creditable performance in the field contrasting starkly with their recent defeats at the hands of the French and Piedmontese armies in Italy.[25] Fritz received his baptism of fire riding beside the Duke of Württemberg and with the Battles of Düppel and Alster the Prussian army could boast its first real victories in the field since the Wars of Liberation.

It was an exciting time for a boy of five. The victors came home to Berlin and took their trophies through the Brandenburg Gate and along the Linden. In later life William remembered seeing his grandfather take the salute from his own 34th Royal Hungarian Regiment or 'Preusseninfanterie' 'in their glossy snow-white uniforms' and light-blue breeches. After the Prussians and Austrians annexed the duchies, Bismarck soon found a means of falling out with the Austrians over their support for the claims of the Duke of Augustenburg. Germany divided into camps for the last 'Brüderkrieg'. By his own admission, William's childish brain had the utmost difficulty in coming to terms with the fact that those soldiers he had seen turn to face the king on the Opernplatz were now the enemy.[26]

Once again William's father was in the thick of it. At a skirmish in Trautenau, Fritz was all but routed, but he brought his forces up to help save the day at Königgrätz: an action which earned him the highest military distinction – the *pour le mérite* – which the king his father awarded him the evening after the battle. In a rare moment of co-operation between Bismarck and the crown prince, Fritz succeeded in staying King William's hand, and prevented him from driving his victory all the way home to Vienna. The war was short, sharp and clean. It dazzled the liberals, removing their deep-seated opposition to Bismarck, and it dazzled the crown prince as well.

It even blinded Vicky to the contempt she normally felt for her country of residence: 'I feel that I am *now* every bit as proud of being a Prussian as I am of being an Englishwoman.'[27] A few years later Austria would be

Prussia's ally again and as such would drag her into war in 1914. Once again, for the now seven-year-old William the news of the Battle of Königgrätz and his father's role in it was enough to make his heart burst with pride.

While Fritz was away on campaign, William's little brother Sigismund died on 18 June at the age of twenty-one months. The next day Vicky wrote to her mother, 'my pride, my joy, my hope, is gone, gone ...' On the 26th she wrote again, 'he was so clever, much more than either of the others ...'[28] The crown prince joined the family in the Baltic resort of Heringsdorf. William had to recite his father a poem, in which there was a reference to his dead brother. The royal party travelled on to Erdmannsdorf in the Riesengebirge, where Vicky was running a field hospital. The king's grenadiers made their way back to Prussia that way, and Vicky crowned their banners with laurels. Once more little William had the chance to see his grandfather, father and the victorious Prussian army make their way down Berlin's *via triumphalis*.

For the time being Prussia and Austria went their separate ways. Austria was evicted from its German nest. The following year it would form the dual monarchy with Hungary, and concentrate its expansionist dreams on the Balkans. Prussia brought northern Germany together in a new Confederation, annexing those states, including the Kingdom of Hanover, which had taken up arms against her. Vicky must have felt the pain of seeing a monarchy abolished and exiled which had been the origin of her own house, and which had been so recently replenished from the other side of the Channel. England would now become the repository for Hanoverian hopes, such as they were. They certainly conditioned her brother Bertie's thinking.

IV

Until he was seven William's education was wholly in the hands of women. His first lessons were given by his governess, 'Dokka', or Sophie von Dobeneck, a 'big, gaunt lady'. He had the three 'r's' instilled into him by an appropriately named Potsdam teacher called Schüler. When the time came to properly shape the boy's mind it was decided to break with Prussian traditions and conduct William's schooling on 'humane, bourgeois' lines. Prussian princes were brought up for the army; Fritz and Vicky, on the other hand, decided that the humane arts should take precedence over the military. Not that he could escape the parade ground altogether. His grandfather for one would have taken a very dim view.

In 1866, to his immense pleasure, William was allotted a military governor in the form of Captain von Schrötter from the artillery guards, while a Sergeant Klee was detailed to teach him drumming, which he clearly enjoyed. Schrötter was no martinet, but a rather dreamy, poetic officer. William was in his charge for a bare year before being abruptly handed over to a first lieutenant of Irish ancestry, August O'Danne, who despite a fine singing voice, turned out to be an unreliable character who got into the bath with the small boys. He was later dismissed from the army for larceny. Worse was to come: he was spotted having sex with a young, male, factory worker in the back of a coach.[29]

William was already showing some of the character which would mark him out as an adult. Vicky told her mother he was 'very shy by nature and that often makes him look proud'.[30] By the time he had entered his teens, she had realised that the 'pride' she had noticed was not just a question of appearance; he was '*very* proud [and] extraordinarily self-satisfied and pleased with himself'.[31] Given his genetic make-up, these things were not particularly surprising, but William was lazy with it, something which – superficially at least – looked odd to the children of the assiduous King William I and Prince Albert.

He was a plucky child for all his physical disabilities. He enjoyed the gymnastics which were the province of a Captain von Dresky. He learned to swim and would go either to a private, family bathing place between Gaisberg and Caputh, or to the military swimming establishment on the Havel in the company of his father. William learned to scull, but his chief pleasure was derived from bigger boats. Shooting was another sport which he took on with alacrity. He bagged his first pheasant in 1872 at the age of thirteen. He had to wait for four more years before he killed a stag.[32]

The big change came with the arrival of the Calvinist Georg Hinzpeter in autumn 1866. He had formerly been the tutor to William's later friend, Emil Graf Görtz. He had been selected on the advice of the diplomat Sir Robert Morier and as the crown prince told him, he was to give his pupil 'the mental equipment of the intellectual cream'. William was to be a philosopher king and Hinzpeter Mentor to his Telemachos. His moral influence sank deeper than his lessons. William later admitted that Hinzpeter had had a 'decisive influence on my total intellectual development'. It is also significant that Hinzpeter despised Vicky and her husband, and possibly even mocked them in the company of his charges. Hinzpeter was a stern pedant: 'the rigorous upbringing of the Spartans' was his ideal; his motto, 'Prussian simplicity! – Denial! Toughening up the body and hard study!' The Calvinist in him sought to break the child's already notable will, turning, where possible, his head towards the good. He was totally committed to his pupil, but it is hard to imagine him smiling often – 'No praise was ever offered.' 'He demanded the impossible from his pupil, to permit him at least to aspire to the next level of perfection.'[33]

Hinzpeter clearly believed that he was being stern for the boy's own good. According to his own published account – written to introduce Germans to their new ruler – the child who was introduced to him was 'a wonderfully pretty, very girlish boy, whose delicacy was accentuated by the very awkward helplessness in his left arm which had made him weak'. Hinzpeter none the less claimed he admired the clay which had been given him to mould: 'Neither the physical nor the intellectual means were lacking.'[34] For years he stubbornly clung to the idea that he could make William into the perfect prince, but eventually despair set in when it became clear that although the future ruler was certainly above average intelligence, he was no phenomenon either.

In old age William came to see Hinzpeter's teaching as a slightly malign influence on his development. It certainly robbed him of a sense of pleasure. The world of this 'pedantic and austere man with his gaunt, hard expression on his parchment-coloured face who had grown up in Calvinism', was 'joyless'. Just as grim were his teaching methods and the 'youth through which the hard hand of the Spartan idealist led me'.[35] Yet, as others have pointed out, Hinzpeter's was not an easy task; his intentions, if not his methods, were always good, and his advice proved, in the long run, rather better than that offered by those who surrounded the Kaiser in later years.[36]

It was certainly a tough regime. Even these children had to put up with a twelve-hour day in the schoolroom: six till six in summer; seven till seven in winter. Frivolous subjects such as riding, swimming, fencing, dancing or modern languages had to be learned in their own time. For English William had Miss Archer, a 'fresh, endearing and funny' woman, and later a Miss Byng. Mademoiselle Darcourt taught him French, 'a charming, already mature, French lady' who married Hinzpeter in 1875. Hinzpeter taught him Latin, arithmetic, history and geography. He liked Latin, where he felt he had an advantage in the good memory he had inherited from his mother; but his favourite subject was always history.[37]

Hinzpeter's religious ethic allowed the boys no other sources of doctrine than the Bible and the Song Book. Relief came on Wednesday and Saturday afternoons, when he took the princes off to see ordinary Germans in factories. Here they removed their hats and asked the workers – carefully rehearsed – intelligent questions. William thought this had put him in good stead. Hinzpeter's teaching quickly led to a showdown with Bismarck after his accession, when the new emperor dallied with the notion of a liberal empire. He believed he understood the German worker and knew how to talk to him.[38]

William and Henry were taught from the first to deny themselves innocent pleasures. When his Meiningen cousins came to tea, William was allowed to offer them cake, but might eat none himself – although this may have been just an occasional test imposed on the princes to inculcate a sense of self-discipline. For breakfast they ate dry bread. The famous black broth of Sparta, wrote William later, would have been a good deal more appetising. When William's great-great-uncle, King Leopold of Belgium, sent them fruit from Blankenberge, the boys were not permitted to eat it: 'We were not to become sybarites.'[39]

Hinzpeter's brief extended to all domains not covered by the prince's military governor, even William's physical training.[40] No one other than his parents could interfere in his regimen, and sometimes they too seem to have been powerless in his hands. Vicky did not feel that her son was making sufficient progress. On 28 May 1870, for example, she wrote to her mother:

The poor arm is no better, and William begins to feel being behind much smaller boys in every exercise of the body – he cannot run fast, because he has no balance, nor ride, nor climb, nor cut his food, etc ... I wonder he is as good tempered about it. His tutor thinks he will feel it much more, and be much unhappier about it as he grows older, and feels himself debarred from everything which others enjoy, and particularly so as he is so strong and lively and healthy. It is a hard trial for him and for us.[41]

Young William was easily moved to tears. It made no odds with Hinzpeter, who was 'deaf to all pleading and crying'. William later maintained it was Hinzpeter who was detailed to teach him to ride. Without the use of his left arm, William toppled off the pony over and over again. The tutor 'pitilessly picked the endlessly plunging rider up again until at last, after a week of ordeals he achieved the hard-won balance'.

The tortures he inflicted, particularly when it came to riding the pony, were decided by my mother; she couldn't bear the thought that the heir to the throne was incapable of riding ... When nobody looked, I cried.[42]

Biographers have poured scorn on this account, however, and pointed out that William knew how to ride a donkey at two, long before Hinzpeter was appointed civil governor. Possibly the exile in Doorn had confused the stern Hinzpeter with his earlier trainer, Dresky; possibly some trauma occasioned by a fall 'had awakened the sense of helplessness'.[43]

Such methods managed to teach William to overcome his handicap, which was a considerable achievement. There was never a day in his life that he was not reminded of it – he could neither dress nor cut up his own food, although he did as well as he could with a contraption which doubled up the functions of knife and fork. He had prodigious strength in his right hand, and later evolved into 'an expert shot, good swimmer' and a 'capital oar'.[44]

It is clear that once the well-meant but agonising attempts to cure the problem had been abandoned, William simply accepted his deformed arm and compensated for it by increasing the strength in the right, which had to undertake three-quarters of the work.

His left is not entirely helpless as anyone can tell you who has seen him in the saddle handling his reins and wielding his sword simultaneously. But still the handicap is a severe one, and it speaks strongly for the Emperor's pluck and persistence that he has succeeded not only in being an excellent marksman but in doing so much work with one arm alone as he scarcely misses the other.[45]

The arm was none the less still seen by some as a stain on the Hohenzollern heredity. Prince Frederick Charles went so far as to say, 'A one-armed man should never be king of Prussia.'

Even in his twilight years William could not decide whether Hinzpeter was right or wrong,[46] whether he had made him happier or more miserable by his harsh training. There were more disappointments to come. By tradition Hohenzollerns had to learn a craft. At first bookbinding was dangled before him, but without strength in his left arm this proved impossible. Henry took it up instead and even survived some of the worst of inflation in the 1920s by binding books. William had no such lucrative talent.

He loved Potsdam most. He had few good memories of the long Berlin winter or of his room on the top floor of the Kronprinzenpalais, above his mother's studio, other than visits to the zoo, theatre, circus or opera; or the Easter egg hunts in the parks at Charlottenburg or Schönhausen (there was no proper garden at the Schloss); or the Christmas market.[47] 'How happy we were when spring announced our return to Potsdam.' Even in old age he still looked back on those years in 'silent melancholy'.[48] Here William and Henry inhabited a room in the mansard of the Neues Palais behind an *oeil de boeuf* window. In Potsdam he took his meals with his parents and had the chance to ramble in the park at Sanssouci. His father took him to the great Stadtschloss on the Havel, or to see the tombs of Frederick the Great and his father in the Garrison Church. There were expeditions to Bornstedt or Wildpark, up to the top of Pfingstberg or the Fuchsberge, or to his great-grandfather's love nest on the Pfaueninsel.[49]

There were members of the family to visit on the way. Old Princess Liegnitz, the morganatic second wife of his great-grandfather, lived in a villa at the entrance to the park at Sanssouci. William often had to take her flowers. Queen Elizabeth, the widow of the late King Frederick William IV, divided her time between Sanssouci and her apartment in the palace of Charlottenburg. She possessed a model of Jerusalem where you could lift the domes off the churches. It was one of William's favourite toys.[50]

He had his playmates too with whom he could knock about in the park at Sanssouci or farther away at Bornstedt. They were allowed to roam wildly; there was no etiquette on the romp, reported one later. He was a good sport, a 'plucky, hearty, unaffected lad, affectionate towards his parents, and full of consideration for the youngsters of his own age'. There was Mortimer von Rauch, von Rex, von Haenisch, the two von Bronikowski boys, Prince Georg Radziwill and Karl and Lothar von Bunsen. The Bunsens' father was later a member of the Reichstag and they had an English mother and grandmother. Perhaps for this reason Hinzpeter thought them not so much 'badly brought up as not brought up'.[51] William's best friend was more suitable: Eugen von Roeder's father had fallen in the great charge at Saint-Privat, which wiped out the cream of the guards. As good Prussian boys they played 'manoeuvres', but even then, it seems, William would not 'brook contradiction, was masterful of our children's games, insisted upon always commanding our toy armies, and always claimed, though he had not always achieved, the victory'.[52]

Apart from this coterie of Anglicised Prussian nobles, there was the American Poultney Bigelow, who was later to find a sort of vocation writing books about William: up to 1914 extolling his virtues; thereafter exposing his vices.[53] Bigelow's father was in the American diplomatic service and friendly with the Bunsens. His parents were frequent guests of the crown prince and princess. The young American had been sent to board with a Professor Schillbach who lived in a modest part of Potsdam. One day a royal coach was seen in the street. Shortly afterwards there was a knock at the door and Hinzpeter entered wearing a frock-coat and top hat.[54]

Writing just before America entered the war on the Allied side, Bigelow claimed he didn't take to William's tutor, 'a desiccated, school-masterly stripe of Prussian who prided himself much upon his frankness, learning and correctness'. The feeling was mutual. On his last meeting with Hinzpeter, the preceptor told the American, 'I never could under-stand why the emperor took such a fancy to you.' Bigelow was none the less carried off to play with William and Henry.[55]

… what was my delight when the elder of the two young princes came forward with outstretched hand and laughing eyes, welcoming me in good English and suggesting that we play Indians or indeed anything that furnished scope for rough and tumble.[56]

Bigelow had been selected because he had something to offer the young

Prussians: he knew all about the 'red savages of the wild west'. According to Bigelow, William's aristocratic Prussian companions had no taste for decent sport. William had read Fenimore Cooper and wanted to play some American games. They ended up by pretending to scalp the scions of some of Prussia's grandest families.[57]

No game interested him much that did not suggest war. Myself being fresh from America, I was credited, if not with Indian blood, at least with intimate knowledge of redskin tactics; consequently we talked much of Fenimore Cooper, the Deerslayer, and Chingachgook at our first meeting, and at our second I gave Prince William an Indian bow with gaudy tassels at each end and a bunch of arrows with blunt heads...[58]

The moment William II had these precious implements in his possession he radiantly suggested a war game on the Iroquois plan – and our victims were not far to seek. We elected ourselves exclusive members of the Ancient and Honourable Order of Red Men and declared all others to be palefaces; and as the outcasts were mainly of the much-drilled and very correct Prussian aristocracy we took youthful pleasure in chasing them through the bushes of the great park, seizing them by the hair, lashing them to trees, and then metaphorically shooting them full of arrows ... My poor young brain was heavily taxed to supply information regarding aboriginal custom on the Upper Missouri and the Rio Grande; but having once been placed in the chair of Redmanology I had to speak *ex cathedra*, for to have confessed that I had never seen an American Indian would have imperilled my palace prestige.[59]

In the park was a land-locked training ship put up to encourage Henry's maritime longings, and not just Henry's; sailing was English, after all: Vicky dressed her eldest in sailor suits and goaded him to love ships and the sea.[60] The boys could play in the rigging, or on special days there was a chance to go out on the *Ustan*, or the *Royal Louise*, a miniature frigate which had been a present from the 'Sailor King', William IV to Frederick William III. Bigelow remembered the vessel:

One of our chief amusements ... was to sail a toy frigate ... It was a perfect model of a full-rigged three master British man-of-war before the days of steam, and at a distance revived memories of battles under Rodney and Nelson.

For all its attention to detail, the boat was no bigger than a launch.

On this toy frigate we cruised after imaginary buccaneers, and under the guidance of an experienced petty officer of the navy we trimmed the little yards, flattened in the sheets of the head-sails, and manipulated the baby pieces of artillery with all the enthusiasm of boys playing at real war. William delighted in this work and it would not be much of an exaggeration to call this little British plaything the parent ship of his latter day navy.[61]

Sometimes the boys kicked a football around indoors.

In wet weather the great attic made a capital play-ground and many an imperial pane of glass was smashed by the blundering aim of one of the youngsters. The good Dr Hinzpeter would repeatedly whisper to take care not to hurt the prince's left arm, a warning I was apt to forget, particularly with one who was so clever with his right.[62]

On other occasions they played hide and seek in among the stage machinery in Frederick the Great's theatre in the Neues Palais. Bigelow did not believe that William wanted any special protection, and he was almost certainly right: '... the princes themselves were as much bored by Hinzpeter's henpecking as I was...'[63]

Bigelow reveals a slightly more pleasant picture of the crown princely family at home and of William's respect for his mother at the time. 'I can for my part bear witness only to his oft-expressed admiration for her talents', the American declared after being shown his mother's studio. William's face lit up at the sight of his mother, 'for the relation of parent to child could not be conceived in more happy form than in those days in the park of Sanssouci'. William's playmates were always offered tea before they were sent home. William took enormous pride in the cake his mother had made, which led to an argument with his American friend when he declared 'My mother makes the best pudding in the world!' Apart from this one outburst his manners were 'considerate and natural'. There was also a 'smile and a kind word' from Fritz and Vicky 'for each of their little guests'.[64]

Bigelow recalls that the younger children lost no opportunity to wind up their mother with her anti-German ways. On one occasion two of her daughters began to dip their cake into their tea-cups. 'The crown princess rose to the bait like a fish to a fly. "Now stop that, children!" she cried. "None of your nasty German habits at my table!"'[65]

v

In later life William recalled his relationship with his father in particular. In those days it had yet to be soured by Fritz's jealousy of his son or William's callous attitude towards his sire. Fritz took William and Henry to churches and introduced them to Prussia's mediaeval past in the monastic ruins of Lehnin and Chorin, and in the cathedral buildings of Brandenburg and Magdeburg. Fritz found Lehnin a ruin, and gave the orders to have it rebuilt. He also took William on an expedition to Rheinsberg to see the little palace Frederick the Great had built for himself as crown prince. On the way they visited the site of the Battle of Fehrbellin, where the Great Elector finally rid Brandenburg of the Swedes who had menaced it from the time of the Thirty Years War. After inspecting the tomb of Frederick the Great's best cavalry general, Zieten, in Wustrau, they arrived in Rheinsberg. Fritz discovered that the king's study had been painted over, and ordered a restoration. Little did he know that he was returning it to the form it had been given by Frederick's younger brother Henry.[66]

William liked the idea of venerating his famous ancestor, Frederick, but the practice was different. Later he would sell off the contents of Rheinsberg to pay for his archaeological digs at Achilleion on Corfu.[67] Fritz was behind the creation of a family museum at Schloss Monbijou in Berlin, the house which had had its heyday under Frederick the Great's mother, Sophia Dorothea, but it wasn't just Hohenzollern family history which intrigued him: he was enraptured by the idea that a new German Reich was just around the corner and used to show his son a book filled with lavish illustrations displaying the treasures of the Holy Roman Empire, then as now housed in Vienna.

He wanted the treasure brought back to Nuremberg. In 1870 Fritz had three of his friends make designs for imperial insignia. He liked those made by Graf Harrach the best. They were most in keeping with the mediaeval idea he favoured. On his accession he wanted to be called Frederick IV to continue the tradition of the mediaeval emperors. It was his idea to bring up the coronation throne from Goslar for the first session of the united German Reichstag in the Weisse Saal of the Berlin Schloss: a stunt which appalled his friend, the writer Gustav Freytag.[68]

It was Fritz – with Vicky's help – who foisted the dreadful new cathedral on Berlin: an ostentatious building which is often ascribed to William and which replaced a church designed by Karl Friedrich Schinkel – though admittedly not his most inspired. He was notoriously vain, and very anxious that his adoring public should not learn the truth of his unimpressive five foot eight inches.[69] In all things he liked pomp and parades, baubles and uniforms; and he would bequeath this taste to William. His character was also contradictory: he was snobbish and anti-Catholic, but philo-Semitic. Outwardly he passed for a liberal[70] but he poured scorn on the minor German princes, and let it be known that he would scrap their territories when he became emperor. It is questionable how much Fritz would have been a 'liberal' at all had he not married Vicky. As the journalist Maximilian Harden pointed out, 'He loved splendour, and had to appear solidly bourgeois; he was very proud and had to be affable and engaging.' He was her creature.[71]

Under the influence of his wife Fritz advocated an English alliance to replace the traditional Prussian preference for Russia, but his son doubted he would have been able to maintain that stance had he lived.

He was not a strong-minded man. It was typical of their marriage that Victoria should provide him with reading matter – John Stuart Mill and Adam Smith, for example, to make sure his thought travelled in the direction she had in mind. Even William, who ascribed a tremendous role to his father in later life, admitted that he was 'delicate and soft'.[72]

Vicky was much brighter. In his most balanced portrait of his mother he described her as a more complex person than his father:

very clever, very quick witted, not without a sense of humour and equipped with an extraordinarily good memory. She had a great general knowledge and a wide-ranging education. Her character displayed unbending energy, great passion and impulsiveness, and a questioning, argumentative inclination; it cannot be denied that she possessed a great love of power.

As far as fitting in with Prussia was concerned, she was not prepared to compromise. Things came to a head later, when William took it upon himself to champion Prussia above all else, while she remained unflinchingly wedded to the British idea.[73] Later, in more mellow years, William admitted that this difference of opinion led to scenes between mother and son which might have been avoided.[74] It is clear from his portrait of his mother, if nothing else, that William inherited a great deal from her too.

She was fond of spouting lapidary phrases: 'Any style is good, so long as it is pure', 'Politics are only the business of those who have seen the world'. These bossy generalisations were to become a trademark of her eldest son. So was a certain contrariness. It was her brother Bertie who famously recorded, 'When Vicky was in Germany she praised everything English, when she came home there was nowhere like Berlin.'[75] Her son could not make up his mind about his mother either. Interviewed at the end of his life he became excited and in his excitement he would become bitter about her. At other times he spoke with exaggerated politeness. She was a 'unique woman', or 'the great empress'.[76]

William always complained that Vicky was hard on her three eldest children, although there is no evidence of lovelessness on either side at that stage. She differed from her father in her approach to education. Albert treated his children as equals.[77] Vicky, on the other hand, kept them at a distance, at least at the beginning. Like Hinzpeter, she was more than sparing when it came to praise and encouragement. The strict approach she adopted for William, Henry and Charlotte was dropped when it came to the last three daughters. It was only much later that 'she found the way to the nursery'.[78] Her two favourites – Sigismund and Waldemar – were the sons who were taken away from her but that too might be an indication of the sort of woman she was: never happy with her lot.

William liked to see his mother as his cultural inheritance, while his father represented the military Prusso-German strain. She collected paintings, and brought together the Kaiser Friedrich Museum – now the Bode Museum – in her husband's memory. She also painted well, a little after the manner of Winterhalter, the artist who had been favoured at her parents' court. William had affectionate memories of his mother at her easel in her airy studio. It was on the first floor of the Kron-prinzenpalais, on the corner of the Oberwallgasse, overlooking Schinkel's guardhouse or Neue Wache. William read her English stories while she painted – 'mother didn't care for other languages'. They were selected from the shelves of her library-cum-living room in the arch which connected the palace with the Prinzessinnenpalais next door. Their favourite was F. E. Smedley's *Frank Fairleigh*, with its tales of a British private academy, buckets on doors, lost trousers and other slapstick.[79]

She had her coterie of intellectuals too: the pathologist Virchow, the mathematician Helmholz, the historians Geffken, Treitschke and Ranke, the philosopher Zeller, Gustav Freytag and the archaeologist Curtius – Fritz's tutor at Bonn. She met many of them at the home of her friend Mimi von Schleinitz at Wilhelmstrasse 73, a freethinking, liberal oasis. Later Curtius was to inspire William's love of classical archaeology. The man himself was absent-minded. While still a subaltern William accosted his father's friend in a Berlin street. 'Oh, my good lieutenant, to what do I owe the pleasure? Pray what is your name?'[80]

VI

On his tenth birthday William was commissioned in the army. Naturally there was training to go through first, and the boy threw himself heart and soul into his new, military life.

Like any private I had to get up in the morning when it was still dark and go to the 'Lange Stall', the drill hall of the First Foot, where rifle drill and marching were practised. People might laugh about it today, but they were good means of instilling discipline, which has to be if order is to reign. I can still see my sergeant with his thick notebook tucked in between the buttons at the top of his tunic. He called me up and inspected my kit to see that no blanco from the white belt had come off on my blue uniform, or any greasy pomade had been smeared on the red stripes through the buttonhole. I can remember the smell of this 'Amor-Pomade' to this day. Then I had to be kitted out with a tall tin hat; they were all too big, with the result that one had to be specially made ...
It is another Potsdam tradition, that there should be no sparing Prussian princes once they are in the army. Like every other grenadier I had to shoulder arms

and stand at ease on Bornstedt Field and take part in the usual storming of Angermann's shed.[81]

Then the great day came. On his tenth birthday father and grandfather stood by as William was issued with the uniform of the First Foot Guards ('the first regiment in Christendom') and the Order of the Black Eagle, Prussia's equivalent of the Garter. The king bore the latter on a gold salver and passed it to the crown prince, who handed it to his son. William had to don his uniform immediately and report to the king. When he returned his father informed him earnestly that he was now a Prussian officer. 'The solemnity of the occasion impressed me deeply; it was as if I had been dubbed "sir knight" at the same time.' Vicky sniffed; in uniform, she thought young William looked like 'an organ-grinder's monkey'.[82]

The first duties of a guards officer were not simple for a ten-year-old. He had to pay attention and take giant strides to keep up with the long legs of the men. On 2 May 1869 William attended his first parade. It was the Sunday church parade from the Lustgarten to the Garrison Church. The music was the 'Präsentiermarsch'. His grandfather walked up and down the ranks and 'loud beat the boy's heart as his eyes too met those of his king . . . It was an unforgettable day.' Later that year William attended parades in Berlin and Stargard. He wrote to his grandmother Queen Victoria to air his pride – 'I marched before the king; he told me that I marched well, but mama said I did it badly.' Hinzpeter also poured cold water on William's martial enthusiasm. William wrote later that his tutor had 'naturally observed it all with mixed feelings'.[83] It is just possible that Vicky saw the cruelty of forcing a small boy to renounce childhood:

With my elevation to lieutenant youth was brought to an end. I could no longer enjoy Berlin's Christmas Market, had to put my tin soldiers away and had no more business attending the children's matinées at Renz's Circus.[84]

There was still the compensation of the annual trips to explore Germany in the company of his stern tutor. In 1867 William went to the Black Forest with Hinzpeter. A photograph shows him dressed up for a country hike with his cousin and contemporary, the Grand Duke Frederick of Baden. On this expedition he glimpsed Hohenzollern for the first time, the mediaeval castle of his ancestors, who had quit Swabia to rule a dour and untamed territory in the north-east of Germany at the beginning of the fifteenth century. William revelled in the rocks and waterfalls and the tall pines. Of course with Hinzpeter there it was not all boyish rambles: there was serious work to do too, and visits to a watch and a cigarette factory were arranged.[85]

The following spring William was back at Reinhardsbrunn, this time with his parents. The stay at the Coburg residence was significant for one thing: it was the first time he met 'Dona' or Augusta Victoria of Schleswig-Holstein, the woman who became his first wife. After the Danish annexation of the duchies, Dona's family had lived in exile in Gotha. On this occasion the trips to industrial sites struck him more than the young princess. He saw a copper hammer and a glassworks. 'The raging flames of the fire and the sooty, Herculean forms of the workers impressed us profoundly.' At the glassworks he and Henry were allowed to blow and take the results home with them.[86]

Early in 1869 Henry's poor health necessitated a cure at Rehme near Bad Oeynhausen in Westphalia. The advantage for William was that he could bathe his arm in the warm waters. Some of William's friends were allowed to join the party led by Hinzpeter: Mortimer von Rauch and the Bunsens. William was also permitted to play with some middle-class children. He wrote to his mother full of enthusiasm at the experience: 'Above all life with my friends appears quite new and pleasant, because I learn and play with them, and that pleases me greatly.'[87] They saw the castle of Wittekind of Saxony and visited a mine belonging to the Krupps where they were left to gather fossils. William and Lothar von Bunsen had a fight. The prince got the worst of it. Later there was a trip to Essen to see the famous Krupp works and marvel at the 1,000-lb steamhammer.[88]

Long before William entered his teens he was well prepared to become the man they mocked as the 'Reisekaiser' or peripatetic emperor. It was another legacy of his parents, who appear to have had the greatest difficulty sitting still. He was constantly on the move. In the summer of that year William went to Norderney off the North Sea coast for the family holiday. Fritz's friend Graf Harrach came along, as did the younger Prince Albert of Prussia. William was absorbed by the humorous books and cartoons of Wilhelm Busch, and reading *Max und Moritz*. On the royal yacht, *Grille*, they visited Heligoland which was then still a British colony, and were received by the governor, Lieutenant-Colonel Sir Henry Maxse, who was something of a pariah as far as the local population were concerned; in 1864 he had revoked Heligoland's constitution and abolished the island's lucrative status as an offshore gambling den a few years later.[89]

William would later do a deal with the British which won Heligoland back for the Reich. More impressive than the sight of the rock, however, was a visit to the new harbour installations at Wilhelmshaven, to see the nascent Prussian fleet. He boggled at the ironclads lying at anchor in the port, and sailed out to the frigate *König Wilhelm* in a launch. 'As we moored alongside, I marvelled speechless at this powerful ship towering high above us.' They returned to Berlin via Bremen.[90]

Later that year, Fritz went off to join the festivities to mark the opening of the Suez Canal in Egypt and Vicky spent two months in Cannes with her boys. A large party stayed at the Grand Hôtel de la Méditerranée: the Hesses, the younger Prince Albert of Prussia, and his adjutant, Graf Schulenburg, Prince Frederick and Princess Louise of Holland, and the Grand Duchess of Mecklenburg-Schwerin. Cannes was little developed then. It had been a fishing port until it was discovered by the British Lord Chancellor Brougham. The English still predominated in their villas, while there were a few hotels. As often as not they went to the English church on Sundays, although a German 'Betsaal' or prayer room had been opened.[91]

For William it would be the one and only time he had the chance to immerse himself in French culture. There is no evidence that it had much effect, but Mademoiselle Darcourt had taught him to speak the language well, if nothing else. After the crown princess left, the children were left at the Villa Gabrielle for another five months. There were other boys about: the children of Lord Brabourne, and the Duke of Vallombrosa. There were butterflies to collect and crustaceans in the fish market. William was struck by the luxuriant Mediterranean flora and the 'radiant skies of the south'. They ate oranges off a tree, presumably while Hinzpeter had his back turned.

William admired the French soldiers and joined the street children imitating their steps. He liked their music, especially the horns. When he became a battalion commander he introduced French horns into the regimental band.[92] Another seminal experience was a trip to the French fleet in Toulon with Hinzpeter. They saw the men-o'-war and also visited the 'bagnes' or prison hulks in the harbour. William was mortified by the 'horribly repulsive criminal faces' of the inmates, trailing their balls and chains and with their green or red caps betokening life sentences or those of a more limited duration.

During their time on the Littoral William and Henry made excursions to all the important places. He went out to the islands in the Gulf and on Sainte-Marguérite he saw the cell of the Man in the Iron Mask. The next year it became the temporary home of Marshal Bazaine, who was exiled for his part in losing the war, before he escaped to Madrid in 1874. He visited Antibes to see the simple monument which marks the spot where Bonaparte's foot 'first touched French soil' on the route to Waterloo, another emperor whose destiny led to banishment but one who made a brief but glorious comeback.[93]

Fritz returned from Egypt to Villefranche and the family was reunited on the quay when his boat *Hertha* docked. The boys could listen endlessly to his stories about Jerusalem and the Holy Sites, which he had visited in all his finery, complete with Black Eagle and Garter; about pyramids, sphinxes and mummies. They probably heard less about the fact that the Prussian boat had been pushed to the rear, behind the flotilla of French, imperial and Italian vessels. Later, *mauvaises langues* would say the crown prince contracted syphilis from a beautiful Spanish whore called Dolores Cada in Suez on 18 October, and that he was already undergoing treatment for it in Port Said on 16 November. Even if this did happen, there is no evidence that the disease had anything to do with the throat cancer which killed him.

William's parents went home after Christmas, leaving the two eldest boys with Hinzpeter, O'Danne and Dr Schrader.[95] 'Paradise' came to an end in the spring when William went home via the Rhone Valley. He stopped at Avignon to marvel at the palace of the Popes and arrived in Potsdam on 23 May 1870.

VIII

Events that year put paid to further holidays on the French Riviera. Following Prince Leopold of Hohenzollern's candidature for the throne of Spain, Napoleon III's government provoked Bismarck and Russia into war. Leopold was from the Catholic Sigmaringen branch of the family and was, incidentally, descended not only from Napoleon's Marshal Murat, but also from his stepson Alexandre de Beauharnais. William remembered his father coming into the schoolroom in the middle of a French lesson – 'Ah mademoiselle! Vos compatriotes ont perdu la tête! Ils veulent nous faire la guerre!'[96]* To Bismarck's delight, the chance of a scrap with the old enemy did the trick and united all Germans behind Prussian leadership. Even Vicky could not resist shaking her fist at France and the French.[97]

Eight weeks after his return from France, William was summoned to his father's study to say goodbye. Fritz was already wallowing in imperial dreams as he made his way to join his army. An eleven-year-old William later remembered singing patriotic songs with his playmates: 'Die Wacht am Rhein', 'O Strassburg', 'König Wilhelm' and 'Prinz Eugen der edle Ritter'.[98] Once more Fritz was in the thick of the fighting, at Wörth and Weissenburg, and enjoying victories which his son would later attribute wholly to his father – reading his memoirs, you would hardly know the great Moltke had ever existed. Soon trophies began to arrive at the

---

* 'Ah Mademoiselle, your countrymen have lost their senses! They want to go to war with us!'

Neues Palais: a cavalry helmet, the Lützelstein flag, an eagle, and the keys to the great Lorraine cities of Nancy and Bar-le-Duc.[99]

Hinzpeter hung up a map in the schoolroom so that the boys could observe the progress of the united German armies. The news of Wörth provoked a giant pillow fight in the nursery, and this set a precedent for later victories. William and Henry went out on to the streets of Potsdam to collect *Extrablätter* announcing the success of German arms, and made them into light-shades. At the end of August they accompanied their mother to Homburg where she was running a field hospital. The boys were already in bed when they heard the 'jubilation and singing of a huge number of people mixed with the noise of a band . . .' Candlelight flickered across their ceiling. They rushed to the window in their night-shirts to observe the procession. It was Homburg's voluntary fire brigade bringing the news to Vicky of the great victory at Sedan. The princes were spotted at the window. The next day Hinzpeter reproached them for their unlicensed behaviour.[100]

Fritz was lodging in Rheims, in the offices of Veuve Clicquot champagne. The imperial title – his passion for so long – was now within reach. This new Empire would humanise the world and turn it away from its 'frivolous French direction' – thoughts which unsurprisingly mirrored those of his wife, who believed French defeat was the fruit of 'frivolity, conceit and immorality'. Bismarck was less impressed with Fritz's flights of fancy, and thought the crown prince would die of his 'imperial craziness'.[101] He was naturally the man to stage-manage his father's coronation in Versailles, which he planned with all the drama of a Wagner opera. Fritz in no way opposed the annexation of both Alsace and Lorraine or the imposition of hefty reparations. The new province was, in his view, to be administered by the Reich, without installing a dynasty. The natives were to be allowed an advisory council.[102]

Fritz was conscious of an important German mission which would take form once his reactionary father was no more:

Only for the evening of his days will my father probably enjoy its honours; but on men of mine devolves the task of setting our hands in true German fashion to the completion of the mighty edifice, and that on principles consonant with these modern times and free from prejudice and prepossessions.[103]

Fritz also derived satisfaction from the fact the Empire was to some extent an Anglo-Coburg idea, and that he had discussed it with his late father-in-law in the course of a walk in the gardens at Buckingham Palace.[104]

Years later William too dipped his pen in purple ink to celebrate the rebirth of the German Empire:

At last there was a German Emperor again. The German Empire had arisen rejuvenated from dust and ashes. Barbarossa woke from his long sleep. The Ravens of Kyffhäuser disappeared, and the Treasure of the Nibelungs, the Imperial German Crown, rose again out of the green waters of Father Rhine, into the light of the sun, newly-forged by German hands in the fire of battle, studded with the rubies of German blood and with the diamonds of German loyalty! The Prussian eagle and the old German eagle wheeled their flight together in the pure blue of God's heaven![105]

The Empire was created on 17 January 1871. A few days later it was William's thirteenth birthday. Vicky took him off to a panorama at the Schauspielhaus. In a letter to her husband she wrote to compare him to her elder brother, who had caused her father so much grief in his time:

I'm sure you would be very pleased with William if you were to see him – he has Bertie's pleasant, amiable ways – and can be very winning. He is not possessed of brilliant abilities, nor of any strength of character or talents, but he is a dear boy, and I hope and trust he will grow up a useful man. He has an excellent tutor, I never saw or knew a better, and all the care that can be bestowed on mind and body is taken of him. I watch over him myself, over each detail, even the minutest, of his education, as his Papa had never had time to occupy himself with the children. These next few years will be very critical and important for him ... I am happy to say that between him and me there is a bond of love and confidence, which I feel sure nothing can destroy.[106]

The crown prince was far less hard on his eldest son. He noted in his diary:

May he grow up a good, upright, true and trusty man, one who delights in all that is good and beautiful, a thorough German who will one day learn to advance further in the paths laid down by his grandfather and father for the good governance of our noble Fatherland, working without fear or favour for the true good of his country. Thank God there is between him and us, his parents, a simple, natural, cordial relation, to preserve which is our constant endeavour, that he may always look upon us as his true, his best friends. It is a truly disquieting thought to realise how many hopes are even now set on this boy's head and how great the responsibility to the Fatherland we have to bear in the conduct of his education; while outside considerations of family and rank, court life in Berlin and many other things make his upbringing so much harder. God grant we may guard him suitably against whatever is base, petty, trivial, and by good guidance train him for the difficult office he is to fill![107]

Paris capitulated the next day. Vicky exulted to her mother: 'It is the retaliation for the way in which the French treated Germany in 1806–1809 – from which we are still suffering. The town of Königsberg had not finished paying off the contribution levied by Napoleon I [before] last year.'[108] Meanwhile Fritz was revelling in all the possibilities for pomp which were presented by the new Empire. It was he who master- minded a great *coup de théâtre* by bringing up the mediaeval throne of the German emperors from the former imperial city of Goslar. Vicky – according to her eldest son – disapproved.[109] There was no question, however, about her pride in the Prussian achievement. On 13 June when the troops returned to their Potsdam garrison, the crown princess was waiting to hand out the laurels.

The great victory parade in Berlin took place in stifling heat on the 16th. William had his own role in the procession, once he had got through a ring of Berlin drunks. His father signalled him with his field- marshal's baton to join him and he rode behind on a small, dappled pony, alongside his uncle, the Grand Duke of Baden. As they emerged on the Berlin side of the Brandenburg Gate, there were sixty virgins lined up on the Pariser Platz to greet the emperor while Berlin's mayor and aldermen were standing under a baldachin at the beginning of the Linden. Trophies lined the route. Among the loud applause of the crowd one man bellowed, 'Wilhelmken, Wilhelmken, leben Sie mal hoch!'*

When the soldiers reached the Schlossplatz the new Kaiser felt the moment had come to celebrate: 'Hut ab zum Gebet!'† He had avenged his father for the defeats of 1806. At a signal from his sword there was a combination of cannon-shot, music and hurrahs and William's grand- father unveiled the new statue of his father, Frederick William III. He then took the captured French eagles and laid them at its feet. 'Never to my last breath shall I forget the expression on my grandfather's countenance as he stood gazing into the bronze face of the statue. To me it said "Father I have done my duty. The shame done to you, to my dear Mother and to our poor Fatherland is washed away. Germany has become one and greets you through me!" '[110]

The king and freshly-baked emperor probably didn't think anything of the sort. He was notoriously unkeen on that unified Germany which had been for so long the dream of the liberals. He stuck to Prussia. As he left the parade he went over to his grandson and put his hand on the boy's shoulder. Using the third person of Prussian royals he said, 'He will not forget this day either!' It was an accurate prediction. Nor would his grandson be outdone when it came to statuary. Among the thousands of monuments which were littered throughout Germany in the course of his reign, in 1906 and 1907 he erected a brace to those who fell at Jena and Auerstedt.[111]

---

*Long live little William!
† 'Hats off for prayer!'

IX

Soon after the dawn of the Second Empire William began learning Greek. He had his first lessons in the Wilhelmshöhe castle above Kassel, which had come as a part of Prussia's booty in the war of 1866. He took to the language immediately and after finishing the last of the eight books of Caesar's *Gallic Wars* in Wiesbaden, Hinzpeter had him make a start on Ovid. He confessed he preferred Caesar by far – 'the description of battles and skirmishes was much more gripping ... than the whole of Ovid put together.'[112]

He had only one quarrel with Caesar, and that was the fact that the Romans had a tiresome habit of winning hands down, and that the German and Gallic chiefs got the worst of it. He found the exception, the annihilation of Cotta's army, particularly enjoyable.[113] William began mathematics at about the same time. Infinitely more interesting to him was the history of Germany in the Middle Ages. He pored over the pages of Kohlrauch's *Deutsche Geschichte* and drew much inspiration from the figures of Otto I, Henry III and Frederick Barbarossa. Homer was another source of pleasure to the young William, together with Cornelius Nepos. Only French grammar appears to have given him an occasional headache.[114]

Hinzpeter conveyed the meaning of religion in a series of long walks, during which he instilled in William an abiding fear of hell. It was Vicky who taught him the rudiments of chemistry. Mademoiselle Darcourt was not thought to be up to teaching the French classics, and a Monsieur Fiévet was engaged. For English, William had a Mr Fox. Drawing and painting was another subject which interested the young prince, who had so often watched his mother accomplish a good likeness of flowers or people at her easel. There was a Professor Eichen and the painter Schlegel. The latter was deformed, and spoke of nothing but the joys of Italy, the land where he had studied from 1847 to 1874. The children nicknamed him 'Signor Schlegeliano'.[115]

Despite the high-flown stuff he examined in the schoolroom, by his own admission William's reading was a good deal more appropriate to a child of eleven: Bechstein's fairy tales; Becker's *Alte Welt*; *Robinson Crusoe*, Captain Marryat, Fenimore Cooper, Jules Verne, Walter Scott (in particular *Ivanhoe*), and Gustav Freytag (above all *Die Ahnen*). Hinzpeter also sought to edify him with some Theodor Fontane and Willibald Alexis. His tutor made sure he had a grounding in the modern classics, too: Schiller, Shakespeare, Kleist's *Prinz von Homburg*, Calderon and Grillparzer. Byron he liked, not least because he learned that the poet was crippled like himself.[116]

Such duties did not fall to Hinzpeter alone. His love of classical archaeology was fired by Professor Boetticher. He also learned from the poet, philosopher and aesthete Karl Weder, who had an ability to explain drama to him. He lived in a flat above the famous wine house of Lutter & Wegner in Berlin. When Weder died, William donated a headstone inscribed with a typically self-important legend: 'amico imperator'.

Vicky set much store by a practical knowledge of art and she herself attended a course at the Kunstgewerbemuseum with her sons in the winter of 1873. It was not much use entrusting them to Hinzpeter for art lessons or appreciation, as his approach was at best prosaic. William, however, failed to gravitate towards the notable treasures in either the royal or the public collections. He liked Anselm Feuerbach, and the Russian Aiwasowski, who painted his favourite things – sea pictures – and enjoyed his visits to the studio of Georg Bleibtreu, who specialised in naval battles.

Other minor figures who appealed to William were Knille, one of Vicky's mentors, who had executed a Tannhäuser cycle; and August von Heyden, who also drew his themes from the legends which appealed to Wagner. The artist had worked in the mines for a while, and William later made him one of his advisers on social questions. His affection for the sculptor Reinhold Begas began early. Begas was to be awarded most of the major commissions during William's reign. Another sculptor who made an impression was Friedrich Drake, who was responsible for the massive figure of Victory which crowned the Siegessäule monument on the Grosse Stern and reminded Berliners of an asparagus spear.[117]

Two major painters also figure on William's list. The first of these was Anton von Werner, who was the official painter of the imperial coronation in the Galerie des Glaces in Versailles and whose chief vocation was the glorification of the young Empire. Vicky was godmother to two of Werner's children and with Fritz's influence, no doubt, Werner won the commission to decorate the interior of Berlin's new cathedral. The only artist of real distinction who appealed to William was Adolph (later von) Menzel, above all for his paintings of Frederick the Great and his period. Menzel did some sketches of the young William but regrettably was never commissioned to execute a proper portrait.

x

In 1871 there was another visit to Britain. William went from Buckingham Palace to Windsor and Osborne. From the Isle of Wight he had a chance to admire the warships in Portsmouth Harbour, as well as visit Nelson's flagship, *Victory*. On a trip to Plymouth he looked over the naval yards in Devonport and had the treat of being submerged in a diving bell. Queen Victoria always made sure he was treated like all the other children in the house. Princess Beatrix was his closest in age, but he liked Louise, the later Duchess of Argyll, best. At Windsor he even had the run of a model farm where he could make butter and cream cheese. He revered Victoria to the end of his days: 'She was a proper grandmother,'[118] he wrote. In order to ensure that she remained one, he always remembered to visit Albert's mausoleum at Frogmore when he stayed at Windsor.

William stressed Victoria's continued Germanness. After four generations the Hanovers might have finally become more English than German, but Victoria had been brought up by one Coburg and had married another: 'Queen Victoria never denied her German origins. She was proud of the title "Duchess of Saxony" and placed her Saxon arms in the centre of the English royal standard. With the ladies and gentlemen of my suite she used only German on principle, of which she had a total command and spoke without an accent.'[119] Germanness affected many of her children too: the Duke of Connaught was ever happy to wear the uniform of the Zieten Hussars, although he was less tempted by the idea of becoming William's vassal as Duke of Coburg. The life of another of her grandsons, the Duke of Albany, who accepted the chalice rejected by his Uncle Connaught, was the perfect tragedy of a family rent in two by war.

After the visit, William's life returned to its usual rhythm, divided between the schoolroom and his travels around Germany. A holiday on Föhr later that year celebrated Henry's entry into the German navy, then still very much the junior service, but that was soon to change. Professor Christian Karl Magnussen was on hand to continue William's drawing lessons, chiefly studies of old women. William would have preferred to draw old ships. Otherwise there was the company of the brothers Hermann and Ernest von Salza. The excitement of the following spring was a parade for the visit of King Humbert of Italy at which the Tsar was present. William received a precious gift in the form of a regiment of grenadiers.

In 1873 William made his first trip to Vienna with his mother for the opening of the World Exhibition, leaving a frustrated Hinzpeter behind. Vicky was beginning to have reservations about her sons' tutor who was as high-handed with the parents as he was with the boys.[120] There was a stopover in Prague on the way, and William was enthralled by his tour of Hradschin Castle. He was taken to the window where the famous 'defenestration' took place which unleashed the Thirty Years War. In Vienna he stayed just beyond Schönbrunn, and apart from the pleasure of going to the exhibition daily, he got to know Crown Prince Rudolf who was just a year older than him. Together they walked and talked in the park of Francis Joseph's summer palace, explored the Wienerwald or climbed the Kahlenberg. More exciting still was his meeting with Sissi, the Empress Elisabeth. Vicky had told him of her great beauty, and he was looking forward to the chance of kissing her hand. He was to get more. On a walk with Vicky and the empress he was permitted to carry the latter's train.

That summer he was back on Föhr for the last time. On 1 September he was present at the stone-laying ceremony for the new higher Kadettenanstalt in Lichterfelde near Berlin. The cadets were being shifted from their old academy in the Neue Friedrichstrasse in the centre of the city to the distant suburbs. There was plenty to do for a military-minded prince. In Stettin on 22 November his mother launched the *Preussen*, the first ironclad built in Germany. 'At the time I was filled with pride that we were now at the point in Germany when we could build ships ourselves, and did not have to fall back on foreign firms.'[121] He makes no comment on the fact that it was an 'English' princess who sent the new vessel down the slipway.

XI

For all the travelling and exploring, there was also the hard work and the dour features of his unpitying tutor Hinzpeter. On 2 April 1873 William was tested in maths, Latin and Greek by Hinzpeter and the masters of the Joachimstaler *Gymnasium*, one of Berlin's best schools, to see if he were good enough to enter the *Obertertia* or fifth form of a 'Humanist' *Gymnasium*. Not only was he found to be at the necessary standard, his maths was considered superior to the level required. His performance earned him a trip to the opera. By the time he was fourteen, he was doing homework until seven or eight in the evening. At the same time he was being prepared for Confirmation by Pastor Persius, the son of the architect Ludwig Persius who had done so much to beautify Potsdam and Berlin.

In the summer of 1874, Hinzpeter took William to Scheveningen in Holland. Again there were excursions to leaven the heavy routine of study. He visited the Mauritz House in The Hague, the Rijksmuseum and the Frans Hals Museum in Haarlem; he saw paintings by Rembrandt, van Eyck and, of course, Hals. He had tea with his cousin, Queen Sophie, and wrote a report on the military situation in the Netherlands to edify his grandfather. William still had the ability to charm those with whom he came into contact. Lady Emily Russell, the wife of the British ambassador to Berlin, praised 'his naturally charming and amiable qualities, his great intelligence and his admirable education'.[122]

The old emperor was still William's hero. From the age of ten the Prussian officer had the chance to see him on his own and even eat with him at his palace on Unter den Linden. They lunched in his writing room, at a rickety whist table which required great care to prevent it from toppling over. They spoke of battles, and of old William's baptism of fire at the Battle of Bar-sur-Aube, fifty years earlier. With the roast came a bottle of champagne.[123] The emperor poured out two draughts – William received his in a sherry glass – and recorked it. He then held the bottle up to the light and marked the level with a pencil. He was an abstemious man; unlike his grandson he didn't even smoke but for politeness' sake he would light a cigarette in the mess after dinner and take a few puffs, just to let the officers know that they might do likewise.

William's grandmother also appeared to dote on Germany's future emperor. It was 'the most wonderful relationship that one could imagine between grandmother and grandson'.[124] Augusta had the reputation for being formidable, yet William assures us that she was kindness itself in small circles. She was already frail and could no longer manage the old-fashioned *Steh und Sprechcouren* which involved standing and moving about to receive guests. The etiquette was gradually transformed to a *Defiliercour* to suit her: guests filed past and she greeted them one by one. Later she would do this from a wheelchair. When William ascended to the throne he did away with the *Sprechcouren* altogether.

Augusta examined her grandson prior to his Confirmation, to see whether he had absorbed the lessons of Hinzpeter and Pastor Persius. The ceremony took place on 1 September 1874 in the Friedenskirche in Potsdam. Queen Victoria sent a large portrait of Prince Albert, but could not attend. She was represented by Uncle Bertie who, like everyone else at the time, was impressed by the boy. 'Willy went through his examination admirably, and the questions he had to answer must have lasted half an hour. It was a great ordeal for him to go through before the Emperor and Empress and all his family.'[125] There must have been an uncomfortable atmosphere for all that. Vicky thought her father-in-law's influence 'very hurtful' while Augusta disapproved of the Prince of Wales's presence. She called him a 'bon vivant'. William would inherit her dislike of his mother's eldest brother.[126]

Soon after his Confirmation, William was told that he was going away to school. It had been decided that he would attend the Lyceum Fridericianum in Cassel, and sit in a class with ordinary, middle-class Germans. It was Hinzpeter's radical idea to knock the princely stuffing out of him in this way, and one which has since been imitated by other courts, notably the British. Hinzpeter's project went back to 1870 when he had broached the subject with Vicky in Homburg. Later he had set out his views in a memorandum and sent it to Fritz in Versailles. The style gives earnest of the pomposity of William's tutor:

For the future sovereign, the leader of a nation, it seems to be of the greatest importance, that he understands the thoughts and feelings of his people, and that is therefore only possible if he has the same education the most learned of them undergo, if he is nourished with the same images and principles as them, if he also has the opportunity to achieve close contact with people in various ways who issue from different classes from those which will later form his entourage.[127]

It is hardly surprising that such a revolutionary idea of educating a prince should have encountered heavy resistance. William thought Hinzpeter's eventual success was due to his 'Westphalian doggedness'.[128] It was not until 1874 that the project was approved, and then a suitable school had to be selected. The ideal was a goodish-sized town so that English and French teachers could be found to teach subjects neglected by the 'Humanistischen', which specialised in Latin and Greek. All the better if there were a royal palace nearby where William might lodge. Homburg and Wiesbaden were two early suggestions. Eventually the interested parties agreed on Cassel, which had been the *Residenz* of the Electors of Hesse until they were ousted by the Prussians in 1866, and which even possessed a decent theatre, an opera house and a museum as well as 'light and air' for the healthy development of the boy.[129]

William was not thrilled at the thought of leaving the parental home, but he was to some degree consoled by the idea that Henry would come too. As his brother was to enter the navy he did not require the doses of Latin and Greek thought necessary for the future German emperor, and there were worries that he would not be able to keep up. He would go to the *Oberrealschule* instead, which offered a more modern curriculum. The brothers were to have their own household, with Hinzpeter as their 'civil governor' and Fritz's companion in arms, Major-General von Gottberg, who had replaced the disreputable O'Danne, as his military counterpart. Hinzpeter must have bitten his lip. He hated Gottberg for reasons which were not clear to William.

Before he started school there was to be a last excursion to the Harz Mountains with his friends von Rex and von Moser. After a good tour of the usual sites, including the highest peak, the Brocken, they went to Wernigerode for the night. Hinzpeter tried to procure rooms for them at the Stolbergs' vast castle above the town, but the porter took a dim view of the party in their rambling outfits and turned them away. The prince was obliged to sleep in a tiny room at the inn, and because of the large number of tourists in town, he was denied the chance to sample the famous local trout.

The episode was very nearly repeated when they got to Cassel. At the former electoral town palace or Fürstenhof the porter also failed to recognise the princes in their strange, scouting garb and at first denied them access. Then they were obliged to sit down in the rain outside a pub and take a meal of hard bread, salty butter and beer. William spent his time covering his jug to stop the rainwater from diluting the ale.

The traumas of the grammar school were very quickly soothed. William felt at home in the *Obersecunda*, 'as if I had never done anything other than take my lessons in a classroom'.[130] Hinzpeter reported: 'His fellow pupils very quickly discovered that despite a constantly proven tactful reserve which prevented any unnecessary familiarity, he could and would be a good classmate.' Formality was reduced to the minimum: pupils were allowed to address him as 'Sie' or 'Prince William', rather than 'Your Royal Highness'.[131]

They were a new sort of German for William: members of the proud, professional middle class. He recalled some of their names in later life: there was Adolf Wild who rose to become a general and Minister of War in succession to Erich von Falkenhayn. William would later ennoble him. There was Johannes Brauneck, who became headmaster of a *Gymnasium* in Hamburg; the future lawyer Ganslandt; and last but not least a small Jewish boy called Siegfried Sommer who also went into the law, and who became a close friend, much to the delight of William's philo-Semitic parents.

The prince's attachment to Sommer was remarkable, given his later reputation as an anti-Semite. He gave Sommer his hand and showed him many other marks of favour, discussed liberal politics with him and even plied him with questions about Jewish life. Sommer was one of the few boys invited to drink champagne at William's birthday party in the Fürstenhof. The friendship began to set tongues wagging, especially when it transpired that Sommer had been invited to spend the holidays at the imperial palace. That story was even mentioned in the newspapers, which led to a cooling-off in relations between the two adolescents.[132]

When there was time Hinzpeter took the brothers off to see his former pupil Emil Görtz at Schlitz. He was a mediatised count, his family had ruled their small territory until the Holy Roman Empire was wound up in 1806. Görtz was talented in many branches of the arts. He had a good singing voice and could finely modulate the ballads of Carl Löwe. He liked acting and dressing up, as he was later to prove when he became part of Philipp Eulenburg's circle at Liebenberg. Before anything else, however, he saw himself as a sculptor. As the Kaiser's friend he was rewarded with commissions. He would later portray William's ancestor Admiral Coligny in a full-sized statue outside the Berlin Schloss, and he was asked to model Ludwig the Roman as a tribute to William's forebears which stood on Berlin's Siegesallee.

The teachers were as ever a mixed bunch. There was the headmaster, Gideon Vogt, who taught classical languages, and the history master, Harting, both of whom merited praise. Professor Heussner was arid, and Scherre, one of the maths masters, was a better huntsman than teacher. The maths master whom William liked was Dr Auth, who loved wine and a warm classroom. The latter was assured since William was in charge of putting wood in the stove. His fellow pupils suffocated, but the master was pleased.

There was no relief from toil at Cassel. Work could go on for ten or eleven hours a day. In the summer he was up at five and started his prep by six. Then William left the primitive palace and climbed the steps which allowed him to enter the *Gymnasium* without going round by the road, and began his lessons. Morning school lasted from eight to noon, followed by a two-hour break during which he had to accommodate not only lunch but walking with Hinzpeter, fencing, swimming and riding. There were three hours more school in the afternoon before dinner at five, which was followed by at least two hours more work. Time had also to be found for the French tutors Beauvon and Ayme and for English lessons. This gruelling programme was fully supported by Vicky who was ever more impatient with what she believed was William's falling behind at school. She expressed her dissatisfaction with her son's English by returning his letters scored, underlined and crossed-out to Cassel.[133]

In 1896 Ayme published a book about the experience of teaching William. The adolescent was deeply impregnated with Hinzpeter's ideas, which seem to have been designed to check tendencies which were already noticeable in the boy: 'from very early on he had inculcated the notion that laziness, ire, vanity and vices in general are incompatible with the rank of one who would inherit the throne.' Ayme admired William's mentor. He thought him a man who could not be more highly praised; a 'true cenobite' whose only relaxation was a half-hour over a cup of coffee in the evening, Hinzpeter had realised that 'his pupil was to reign one day and it would be wise to prepare him for the role'.[134]

Ayme continued to be impressed by his former pupil when he had the opportunity to observe him from a distance as the German emperor:

I can ... demonstrate that William II practises logically today the doctrines he professed at the age of eighteen. His actions like his speeches, sometimes contradictory, all stem from the same unique principle ... He is extremely intelligent and is endowed with a great ability to work and assimilate. Without going to absurd limits, he can deal with the most diverse subjects in the field of human knowledge. He is a soldier, statesman, orator, musician; he could also be a philosopher, philologist, a man of letters or a scientist. Had he not been sovereign, his true vocation would have been that of a journalist ... I have often thought that if William had been king of France at a time when the monarchical spirit flourished, the century would have rivalled that of Louis XIV.[135]

Unlike Ayme, Hinzpeter was disappointed by his pupil. William did not measure up to his standards. 'I don't think he is clever,' he wrote; 'he has, however, an excellent memory. On the other hand he believes he understands everything, talks on any subject and makes assertions with such sureness and in such a self-opinionated manner that he effectively prohibits all contradiction.'[136] He was passionate about Greek for all that: 'I insist that there is nothing higher than the Greek tongue, and that there is nothing greater in Greek than Homer, and nothing better than his *Iliad*.'[137] His father encouraged this by giving him terracotta statues of Achilles and Patroclus. It was strange that the man who was later to demonstrate a talent for public speaking should lose interest in Cicero as a result of *Oratory*. He had enjoyed the *Tusculan Disputations*, but in *Oratory* 'I found nothing more than an endless crowd of sentences and phrases with a list of speakers and sophists who were of little or no interest to me.'[138] He derived some solace in Demosthenes.

Horace he found plebeian. He took comfort in the history of Germany in the Middle Ages. Early modern German history pleased him less, 'because the beginning of the decline of the German empire was already visible; on the other hand during the knightly period the wonderful Holy Roman Empire was so much at one with its strength and fullness and wholly at the summit of the civilised world as it was.'[139] William became increasingly critical of the narrow, traditional curriculum of the *humanistische Gymnasium* where he felt that the concentration on classical languages was excessive and that more modern history should be taught to make pupils aware of the reality of nineteenth-century Germany.

He felt that the *Humanistischen* created 'no self-confident Germans'[140] and compared badly with British public schools such as Eton: 'Young Britons, who dream of conquest in the colonies, of research expeditions to new lands, of the expansion of trade, of being their country's pioneers in the sense of "right or wrong – my country" [sic]; they learned far less Latin or Greek, on the other hand they were much more imbued with the idea of making Great Britain greater and stronger.'[141] Later William endeavoured to reform the German school curriculum along these lines, but in old age he admitted that his attempts had been a failure.

It seems a wonder that with such a full timetable William had time to read, but read he did. He confessed that he devoured first all the books on the sea which Queen Victoria sent Henry. He loved the archaeology novels of Georg Ebers, especially *Uarda*. Hinzpeter preferred to read him Dickens. In French his favourite works were Gobineau's *Renaissance* and Taine's history of the French Revolution. He admitted to having no ear for, and no talent for, writing verse and later accused Hinzpeter of killing poetry for him.[142] He attempted to write an epic about the story of the tyrant killers Harmonius and Aristogeiton. It was called 'Hermione', after the love-interest, but he abandoned it before long.

Cassel offered plenty of recreational opportunities if time allowed. The theatre produced Uhland, Schiller and Shakespeare. During the summer months William was up at Wilhelmshöhe, and could ride to school. When it was warm he swam in the Fulda; or went skating when it was frozen over. There were fencing and riding lessons from officers of the garrison and William got to know the local *Prominenten* at a series of what Hinzpeter described as 'appeasement dinners' arranged by the very relaxed and un-Prussian General Walther von Gottberg. The most interesting local worthy was Colonel von Oettinger who had escorted Napoleon III into captivity and could regale William with endless stories about his detention in Wilhelmshöhe. The mayor, chain-swinging aldermen, generals and other dignitaries were given a chance to make friends with the future sovereign, but they certainly interested the adolescent far less than the colonel.

The middle-class boys at the school supported the liberal politicians in the Reichstag. At this stage of his life, William saw no problem in following suit. The debates were re-enacted: the talkative Sommer played the role of Eduard Lasker, the future Kaiser that of Hermann Schulze-Delitsch.

XII

In the summer of 1876 William was back at Scheveningen with his parents. There were visits from the Dutch royal family, and the British minister, Sir Edward Harris, gave William the twelve or fourteen volumes of James's *Naval History*. With time he would read them all. In general the holiday was a relaxed one. His father had his military duties, and was often ill – some have suggested, from *la maladie des sphinxes*. 'It was so nice, that my father – in the unbuttoned atmosphere of a beach resort – far from the pressures of the court, could follow his inner nature and live with us wholly as a friend.'[143] In Utrecht they chanced on a waffle-seller and Fritz told his children, 'Scoff as many as you can.' 'Hinzpeter had to content himself with dark looks.'[144]

The only other time William saw his father in a relaxed mood was on the home farm at Bornstedt, where Fritz and Vicky went to take refuge from the world. Here he wanted to be seen as an ordinary mortal. He rode in the fields or was seen wandering around the vegetable garden with Vicky on his arm. He dressed in an open Litewka* and relaxed by smoking a pipe. Some writers have pointed out Fritz's resemblance to his grandfather Frederick William III. There was the kindness, generosity, and also a touch of melancholy which was even more pronounced in his uncle, the late king, Frederick William IV. His more marked characteristic was his indecisiveness, however, and the constant giving in to his intellectually superior wife.[145]

In January 1877 William took and passed his *Abitur*, the examination which allowed him to proceed to study at a university. He came tenth out of the seventeen examined in Cassel. On the 25th he left school, and Hinzpeter, his work completed, retired to Bielefeld with the former Mademoiselle Darcourt. Two days after that, Hohenzollern house law decided that he had come of age. As a birthday present from his grandmother he received the Order of Bath. William was furious: he wanted the Garter. After a scene, Victoria acceded to his wishes. William purred: the Garter was generally granted only to rulers or their heirs; he had it for being the queen's grandson. It remained one of his proudest possessions and, after his exile in 1918, he resisted all attempts to make him yield it up.

At the ceremony in the Schloss he was properly invested with his Black Eagle. The whole royal family was gathered to witness the event, as well as the most high-ranking generals in the Prussian army: Field Marshals Wrangel, Moltke, Steinmetz, Bitterfeld and Manteuffel. He was robed by his father and the younger Prince Albert and accompanied by them to the old Kaiser on his throne. He knelt down, his grandfather put the chain round the young man's neck. When he stood up the emperor kissed him and he had to swear an oath to honour the Hohenzollerns and maintain royal prerogatives.

After a suggestion that William should study at Balliol College, Oxford, was effectively shot down, it was decided that he should attend Bonn University where his father had been, and his maternal grandfather before him; Bonn was, after all, a Prussian foundation. There was six months to go before the beginning of his first semester and William went off to the army. His career had made slow progress since he became an officer in 1869 at the age of ten. In January 1873 he had been appointed to the 2nd Landwehr Guards, a territorial unit. In March 1876, when he was seventeen, he was promoted to first lieutenant. Now, on 9 February 1877, he joined Sixth Company of the First Foot Guards, Prussia's grandest regiment. At the same time he attended the

---

* Literally a Lithuanian jacket. It was worn by officers in undistinguished units of the Prussian army until 1920.

Kriegsschule. He went with his grandfather's blessing – 'Now go and do your duty, as you will be taught how to do it.'[146] It was his father's job to take him into the mess and introduce him to his brother officers.

XIII

William revelled in the army life. There was Graf Heinrich zu Rantzau, his battalion commander, and the pedantic Captain von Petersdorff, who had been wounded at Königgrätz, was his immediate commanding officer. He also became acquainted with 'Julius' – Helmuth von Moltke, the nephew of the field marshal, who was to be rapidly promoted under William, and end up Chief of the Great General Staff at the beginning of the First World War. On 24 March he had his first moment of glory when Sixth Company marched past the Kaiser in the Berlin Lustgarten. His grandfather lunched with the regiment after the parade. It had been his eightieth birthday just two days before and he was presented with a cake with the same number of candles.

On 1 April William acquitted himself well in exercises on Bornstedt field. Three months later he was tested on weaponry, fortress science, field manoeuvres and tactics. He was now able to hold his head up high with the other officers, who had taken the exam earlier on. He was present at the manoeuvres that year on the left bank of the Oder. It was to be his first meeting with another man who was to be at his side when Germany entered the Great War – Theodor von Bethmann-Hollweg, whose father owned an estate at Hohenfinow. Later he went to Kiel to be with Henry on his first night of active service in the navy. Henry had trouble with his hammock, lost his blanket during the night and ended up walking on his brother in his attempts to retrieve it. The next morning the two of them inadvertently ate Henry's commanding officer's breakfast.

There was a last holiday in Ostend before William went on to Bonn. With his parents he visited Bruges, Ghent and Brussels. In Ghent he particularly admired the statues of Charles the Brave and Mary of Burgundy. From Belgium he crossed the Channel to Cowes for the Regatta and stayed at Osborne. He returned to Ostend and travelled on to Darmstadt to stay with his cousins. A few more days were whiled away in Karlsruhe and Baden-Baden with the grand ducal family. In the autumn he was present at the unveiling of a National Monument in Niederwald in the Rheingau. Then he travelled on up to the Rhine by steamer from Rüdesheim to Assmannshausen to Coblenz to stay with Augusta, who gave a dinner in his honour at which he would have experienced the French etiquette she reserved for her Rhineland court. After such a journey Odysseus hung up his sword. The time had come to begin his studies in Bonn.

3

The Emperor as a Young Man

William was back in the classroom, but rid of Hinzpeter he could pick and choose from a wider academic menu, like his father or his maternal grandfather before him. He was billed to study law and government, the two subjects deemed most useful for him as a future monarch. It proved an opportunity to unlearn virtually everything Hinzpeter had sought to drive into him. He had his own small household: there was Major Wilhelm von Liebenau, who was later to become his court marshal; and his adjutant Captain Albano von Jacobi, a Pfälzer who knew something of student life from his time in Strasbourg. They set up house at the Villa Frank which afforded views of the Siebengebirge beyond the Rhine. William loved Bonn and its setting, 'directly on the vine-clad river, rich in German legends'. In his own words, he was possessed of 'unfettered youthful desire and full of longing to see, experience life and learn'.[1]

William dabbled in law, economics, politics, history, German literature, art history, physics and chemistry. The lectures were delivered in his own home. Certain dons impressed him: Professors Reinhard Kekule and Justi, for example, who taught art history. Kekule further inflamed William's passion for the antique. Much later he visited William at Achilleion, his home on Corfu, and advised the then emperor on the statue he was erecting of Achilles. William ennobled him for his pains. It was destroyed by the 'Franco-Serbian force of occupation' after the First World War.[2] There was also Professor Loersch who took him to see the site of Charlemagne's coronation in Aachen. Loersch's sister-in-law taught him how to make a salad. A history teacher, Wilhelm Maurenbrecher, was to remind him of Treitschke in his outspoken style and nationalist fervour. It was not always easy for William to concentrate on his studies. His inner ears continued to give him pain, with occasional swellings and discharges of evil-smelling pus which resulted in his physicians piercing his right eardrum.[3]

Another attraction of Bonn was the *Burschenschaft*. The 'Borussen' brought together the most aristocratic students from Prussia, with a scattering of rich middle-class Germans who aspired to the same. William's father had also been a member, but it was not felt right that the prince should participate fully. The *Mensur* or duelling was not permitted to him, preventing him from calling himself 'Satisfaktionsfähig', or able to challenge someone to a duel. He was to be a sort of fellow traveller or *Konkneipant*. The excessive drinking of the *corps* was shunned, although this may have had as much to do with William's distaste for alcohol as any stipulation from his parents. He believed drunkenness belonged to the 'shady side' of student life, and hoped that an enthusiasm for sport would eventually eradicate it.[4]

His circle was a reflection of the changing face of the *corps*. At the top were a couple of 'Regierende': members of other German reigning houses – his friend and fellow rambler, Grand Duke Frederick of Baden, and Duke George of Oldenburg. For the most part William consorted with noblemen such as the Silesian magnates Graf Viktor von Henckel and Freiherr von Seher-Thoss, later *Regierungspräsident* of Liegnitz; Graf von Thiele-Winckler, Freiherr Ernest von Salza whom he had got to know in Wyck; the son of the ambassador to London, Graf Münster; and a Herr von Sydow from an untitled noble family with estates in Pomerania and Sweden. Added to these were two Hamburgers: one Ohlendorff and Otto Ehlers, who was later to meet an early death in New Guinea. Whether the old guard liked it or not, German society was changing: there were even a few *Bürgerliche* in the Borussen.

Bonn's musical tradition attracted William's attention. He attended concerts in the Beethoven Halle, built to commemorate the town's most famous son. He heard Amélie Weiss, the wife of the great violinist Joachim, sing and Clara Schumann play. Also in Bonn, William heard Pastor Dryander preach for the first time. William frequented a few houses where he could find a decent social circle in the evenings. One of these belonged to Henry XIII of Reuss, from Thuringia, one of Germany's oldest reigning houses, even if their land encompassed little more than a castle and a few buildings scattered around it. Outside Bonn there were doors open to him too: by horse, steamer, boat or rail he could reach any number of sympathetic hearths, and there was the advantage of 'getting to know one of the prettiest parts of our Fatherland better'.[5] He would take the night steamer to Coblenz and sail back with Otto Ehlers, who being from Hamburg, was an excellent sailor. There was a chance to stop off at Schloss Argenfels for a short lunch. For protection they took along the Rhinelander Busch, a swimmer who had already saved twenty people from drowning in the Rhine.

There were no lectures at weekends, which meant that William could spend Friday to Monday away from Bonn. At Neuwied were the Wied family. One of the princesses went on to become queen of Romania, and became a published poet under the pseudonym of Carmen Sylva. In Coblenz was Empress Augusta. She frequently summoned William to her side. She possessed a 'lovely old Schloss there with a pretty garden and splendid views of the Ehrenbreitstein'.[6] More close relatives lived in Darmstadt, where the Grand Duchess Alice was another of Vicky's sisters. They seem not to have been too impressed by their cousin William, referring to him as 'the Unique', 'William the Impetuous' or 'Gondola Bill'. The family was beset by tragedy. In 1878, William's first cousin May died of diphtheria, and her mother, Alice, succumbed to the same disease soon after. One of the Hesse-Darmstadt sisters married William's brother Henry. William's special favourite was Ella, but she rejected his suit. She and her sister Alix both wedded Romanovs. They were murdered within twenty-four hours of one another in 1917.

The more Catholic aspects of the Prussian Rhineland did not appeal to William. There was the *Karneval,* which left him cold. Bismarck's *Kulturkampf* – an attempt to define the ultimate authority in the new Germany – was then at its height and the Catholics were feeling the weight of the chancellor's hand. William disapproved of the 'unholy struggle'[7] which proved so divisive and swelled the ranks of the hitherto insignificant Catholic Zentrumspartei (Centre Party). Later he went so far as to call it 'the greatest stupidity ever committed by a Prussian statesman';[8] yet he was snubbed as a Prussian, Protestant prince. At a meeting of the local hunt, many of the nobility refused to attend when they learned that he was to be of their number.

II

Royal duties tore him away from his studies at frequent intervals. In February 1878 his closest sister, Charlotte, married Prince Bernard of Meiningen. William's Uncle Bertie came too, still full of golden opinions of his nephew. 'It is impossible to find two nicer boys than William and Henry,' he told his mother.[9] On 11 May there was a first assassination attempt on the old emperor by Max Hödel. Less than a month later there was a much more serious attack by the socialist Karl Eduard Nobiling. On this occasion he was badly hurt and for the first time his son Fritz had to stand in for him while he recovered in Gastein. Fritz had demanded a formal regency, but this was refused. One of his first duties was to sign Hödel's death warrant, which gave him a sleepless night. The crown prince's biggest role was to play host to the Congress of Berlin, but it was Bismarck who was the real puppet master there. It was typical of both Fritz and the chancellor – Fritz 'did the honours, but Bismarck alone shaped policy'.[10]

There was work for William too: he had to sit in on the reports from the heads of the civil and military cabinets and 'help rule'. For the most part his assistance was essentially technical. William's memoirs make it clear that neither father nor son had much of an idea of what to do, and that their 'government' was chiefly limited to signing officers' patents. William then strewed sand over his father's signature. 'At the end of the reports every free table and all available pieces of furniture were covered with these documents; only a narrow passage was left free to allow access to the door.'[11]

Nobiling's attempt on the old Kaiser's life also led to William's first official duty: he was despatched to attend the celebrations marking the silver wedding of his Coburg cousin King Leopold II and Queen Maria of Belgium in Brussels on 22 August. William took Liebenau and Jacobi and joined up with the Austrian party on the border: Archduke Charles Ludwig (the father of the ill-fated Francis Ferdinand) and the aged Prince Windischgraetz. William rushed back from Brussels to be in Potsdam for the visit of Duke Frederick of Schleswig-Holstein, who was bringing his daughters, Dona and Lenchen.

Duke Frederick had served with Fritz in the First Foot Guards as well as having been a student in Bonn at the same time. William had already visited the family in their exile in Gotha at the beginning of that year. Dona had evidently replaced Ella Darmstadt in his affections. He found the opportunity to pay another visit to them in Primkenau in April 1879 after a capercaille hunt near Görlitz. In his memoirs William states that he had the total support of his parents in his choice, even if Vicky was pretty dismissive of Dona. It was a political match which was seen as a means of reconciling the Schleswig-Holsteins to the Prussian royal house, which had effectively ousted them from their land. The only thing which held up the wedding, William later wrote, was the death of Dona's father in January 1880, although they became secretly engaged over her father's coffin on 14 January 1880.[12] The engagement was finally announced on Valentine's Day that year.

William was seeking to conceal a good deal of sniffing about Dona's suitability as the bride of the future German emperor. Was she actually qualified by birth? One of her grandmothers had been a Hohenlohe, which was considered good enough; but the other was a mere Danish countess, and not really of the lineage required for a royal house.[13] It took the old emperor nine months to overlook the slight inequality of birth while the appropriate certifications were drawn up. Dona was taken to see Queen Victoria, who approved. Vicky had reservations about an early marriage and still hoped that her son would see something of the world first. The issue was raised in a letter from his mother to his grandmother. Once again Vicky put down her son with reference to her latest excursions in his company: '. . . he does not care to look at anything, took no interest whatever in works of art, did not in the least admire beautiful scenery and would not look at a Guide Book, or any other book which would give him information about the places to be seen.'[14] He was, in short, a philistine.

He was young for a prince, and Dona was even a little older. It seems fair to conclude, as some writers have done, that in his hurry to get married William was voicing his desire for an early break from his parents. It was already becoming clear that the generations were drifting apart. That summer Vicky complained to her mother that William was on the way to becoming a 'conceited Prussian'. 'Willy is *chauvinistic* and *ultra* Prussian to a degree and with a violence which is very painful to me.' A modern biographer of William has commented on the increasingly 'sour and self-pitying' tone of Vicky's letters. 'Surely few mothers can have been as relentless in criticising their children for not having measured up to exalted expectations. The Crown Princess was impossibly demanding and therefore inevitably disappointed.'[15]

III

There was naturally a sexual awakening. In his mid-teens William had revealed an obsession with hands; at that stage chiefly his mother's. He sent her letters from Cassel in which he dwelled on the erotic fantasies and dreams he had revolving around kissing her hands. He graduated from his mother to his mother's friends, older women such as Mimi von Schleinitz and Marie Gräfin Dönhoff. When he became involved with the redheaded Gräfin Wedel in 1882, her hands were clearly part of her attraction: 'Adieu chère adorée, je vous embrasse avec votre permission et je baise les belles mains de mon ange, ange [aux] cheveux rouges [sic].'[16]*

From Bismarck onwards, writers have tried to make a case for William being at least a repressed or 'closet' homosexual.[17] If it can be true that homosexuality is inherited, then William could certainly have pointed to several homosexuals among his forebears, and at least one of his sons was that way inclined. There is no evidence, however, that William himself ever indulged in a homoerotic act. One of the passages which is often quoted as evidence of this refers to his pleasure in being in Potsdam. The line about his mother, however, is left out: 'I never feel happy,' he wrote in bad English to Marie Gräfin Dönhoff, 'really happy at Berlin, only Potsdam that is my real "el dorado" *and that is where Mama most likes to live* where one feels free with the beautiful nature around you and

---

* 'Farewell my dear adored one, with your leave I kiss my angel's lovely hands, a red-haired angel.

soldiers as much as you like, for I love my dear regiment very much, those such kind, nice young men in it.'[18]

If there is nothing to prove that William was homosexual, there is plenty of evidence that he was not only heterosexual but also fairly highly sexed. Again if his parents and grandparents are anything to go by, there was every reason to feel that William might have inherited some of their mettle. His grandfather William I was well-known for his mistresses, in particular the Portuguese condessa Oriola, he and Augusta having long since gone their separate ways. He was also believed to be the grandfather of William's American admirer, George Sylvester Viereck. Bismarck claimed that he could detect the highly-charged sexuality of Vicky, and that it made shivers run down his spine. Fritz was devoted to Vicky. There were no mistresses, 'but there were whores and Dolores Cada was one of them'.[19]

The first indication of sexual experimentation comes from the man-oeuvres William attended in Alsace in the autumn of 1879. He slept with a thirty-five-year-old French prostitute who sported the evocative pseudonym of Miss Love. Her real name was more prosaic: Emilie Klopp. It cannot have been the experience of a single torrid night, for Frau Klopp bore William a daughter, who was later farmed out to live with her aunts in Barr. Now she had collateral and for the next ten years she made periodic calls on William's purse. In a letter to Waldersee, the Quartermaster-General, written in 1889 William denied having slept with Miss Love, but could reveal the names of several who had, including the chancellor's second son, Bill.[20]

The reality, of course, was different, as papers recently released by the Bismarck family archives have shown. William had been right to suggest that any number of high-ranking Prussian officers had slept with Miss Love, and Bill Bismarck as well. Where he had been less honest was in talking about his own relationship, and the effect that a tight financial rein had on his behaviour. After his first bouts of love-making, William had given Miss Love a signed photograph of himself and a promise to pay later. He had also written her several incriminating letters. When Miss Love began to threaten to make trouble for him in Germany, he moved her into a love-nest in the Russian Colony in Potsdam where he could make use of her some more, but still refused to give her any significant sum.

Miss Love had also written to Bill Bismarck complaining about Wil-liam's infamous behaviour. All three Bismarcks put their heads together to come up with a solution. The chancellor was not unduly worried about the story getting out. The fact that he had had a relationship with a prostitute was 'if not immaterial, then also not disturbing so long as the seduction of honourable girls was not involved'. His eldest son

Herbert added that the letters were the result of a disastrous habit 'inherited from his mother' of committing his thoughts to paper.[21] The Bismarcks resolved to let Herbert bring the matter up casually with William, and if that did not work, the chancellor himself would have to come up to Berlin for an audience.

Herbert had no luck. William admitted dalliance in Strasbourg but continued to deny vociferously the continuation of his relationship with Miss Love in Potsdam. Bill Bismarck thought William wrong to underestimate the consequences of the affair getting out, especially as there were indications of 'peculiar tastes'. The future emperor, it seemed, liked to bind his victims. William refused to comment further until Waldersee received his letter from Miss Love the following year. At that point he admitted that the prostitute had made a brief visit to Potsdam. Soon afterwards Herbert handed his brother Bill the sum of 25,000 marks and a 'chance' meeting was set up in the Frankfurter Hof hotel in Frankfurt. Miss Love signed a receipt saying that Bill was in possession of all the incriminating documents. She failed to honour her side of the bargain, however, making further demands until her death in 1893.[22]

Vienna was evidently a place to misbehave for William. In 1882 he was supposed to have fathered a dead child there by a Fräulein Caroline Seiffert, 'one of the late Crown Prince Rudolf's set'. The baby was born in August or September, just two or three weeks after his second son, Eitel Fritz. As the story goes, William's father knew all about it, and Caroline Seiffert demanded 100,000 florins for her silence. One thing which makes the tale suspicious is the idea that the baby was also allegedly born with a lame left arm.[23] More reliable were the stories put about by the Austrian crown prince who had to lend William money for his escapades and insisted on having a receipt. One of these has survived in the Viennese archives. William acknowledged a loan of 3,000 florins for 'charitable purposes' for an unspecified time. He was known to frequent the brothel of a certain Frau Wolf, a notorious madam reputed to offer some of the prettiest girls in Vienna.[24]

IV

For his first real vacation in 1878, William went to England with Johannes Heller, a young *Gelehrte* who was working on the *Monumenta Germaniae* and spent a few quiet days with him in the popular resort of Ilfracombe in north Devon. The big treat was an invitation to go to Balmoral to stay with his grandmother. He looked round the castle, with its 'small, comfortably furnished rooms'[25] and compared Scotland's climate to Norway's. He found qualities in its people not recognised by every casual visitor: they were 'a nice brand of humanity, very peaceable, modest and hospitable and unlike the English, they possess a sense of humour.'

Queen Victoria knew the way to William's heart. She gave him the complete Clan Stewart rig to wear. He had the green 'Hunting Stewart' kilt and the grey 'Balmoral', as well as a red one for the evening together with its accessories: a velvet bumfreezer jacket, a silver sporran, buckles for his shoes and a plaid for his shoulders fixed by a gold topaz brooch. Possibly even more exciting were the weapons which came with the uniform: a dagger topped by a gold topaz the size of a hen's egg, a claymore and a skean-dhu to remind him of the one he had once brandished at his Uncle Leopold.* The queen's gillie John Brown helped him dress up in his new finery and he was able to wear the green when he went stag hunting in the heather. As he left, Victoria reminded him of Prince Albert: 'My dear boy, never forget him! Your grandfather was the best man in the world. Try as much as you can to become like him. God bless you!'[26]

It is unlikely that the Queen's words had too much influence on William's behaviour. He did not have much time for the Coburgs, and Albert had been his mother's father which did not necessarily endear him to the prince. That autumn he progressed to Paris for the first and last time, where he was to attend the Great Exhibition. He enjoyed the sights: the galleries in the Louvre, the Musée de Cluny, Notre Dame, the Sainte Chapelle, and Saint-Cloud. He went to Versailles to see the Galerie des Glaces, where only seven years before the German Empire had been recreated at his father's instigation.

He sat in on a trial at the lawcourts and went up in a balloon in the Tuileries Gardens. He saw Sarah Bernhardt at the Théâtre Français. President MacMahon passed him in the street and he raised his hat. He dined with General Chanzy, who had led the campaign in the French provinces in 1870–1 harrying Moltke's armies from the rear. Despite so much excitement, however, Paris failed to work its magic on William: '... the feverish haste and filth of Parisian life I found highly repugnant ... I have never had any longing to visit the French capital again.'[27]

He rushed away without regret and proceeded to Kiel to say goodbye to his brother Henry who was off on a two-year, round-the-world cruise. He returned to Potsdam for his father's birthday before travelling on to Bonn for his third semester. He was back in England for the marriage of the Duke of Connaught to Louise Margaret of Prussia the following spring. His stay was marred, however, by the death by diphtheria on

---

* In 1884 William was photographed in all his Scottish glory. In his own hand he inscribed the legend: 'I bide my time'.

27 March of another of Vicky's favourite sons, Waldemar. William performed the vigil in the Friedenskirche, but even this act of family piety could not dispel the unflattering comparisons his mother made between her eldest and the recently departed apple of her eye. 'The grief my parents suffered at the loss of this magnificent son was indescribable.'[28]

Possibly it was on this visit that William and his parents stayed with the Prince of Wales at Marlborough House. In his idle moments William was able to explore the British Museum, the National Gallery, the Wallace Collection and the St John's Wood studio of the Dutch painter Laurence Alma-Tadema, whose large, erotic canvases were then in vogue. He went to Richmond, Hampton Court and Kew, and was received by Lord Beaconsfield at the Foreign Office.

More than art, however, William enjoyed the chance to witness some sport. Germany had yet to develop organised sports in the same way, and he revelled in the Eton–Harrow cricket match and the Oxford and Cambridge boat race. With the passage of time his memory of the race became clouded – not least in that he referred to it as a 'regatta' – and married the cricket match up with the boat race. He was amazed to see that everyone was wearing something in dark or light blue, even the ladies. 'There was a lively old lady standing behind me on a chair who noticed all at once my interest in the sport and the fact that I was a foreigner. She invited me to occupy the empty chair next to hers and taught me with astonishing expertise the different stages of the game.' Finally she cut off some of her ribbon and gave it to William to wear. What was it? 'Eton, of course! Now you look a full-blown gentleman, young man. Before you were only half one.'[29]

William left for his first journey to Italy with his still grieving parents. They went initially to Venice, where like ordinary tourists they saw the sights and enjoyed a night ride in a gondola. They then crossed northern Italy to Pegli a few kilometres outside Genoa, where they stayed at the Hotel Egli, the former Villa Lomellini. Again they led the life of idle, rich tourists. They inspected the Villa Pallavicini and the 'indescribable treasures' of Genoa and visited the royal family at Monza.[30] His family remained in Pegli. William went back to Bonn.

His studies were soon over. William said later that he had intended to make a world tour after Bonn, or at least see Egypt, but that this plan was vetoed by his comparatively stationary grandfather, who had none of the wanderlust of his son and daughter-in-law. He ruled that William must serve in the 'front line'. 'From now on Potsdam was to be my fate.'[31]

V

On 29 October 1879 the twenty-year-old prince reported for duty. His initial task was to train recruits for the First Company of the élite First Foot Guards, which retained the function of royal bodyguard. William already enjoyed a degree of independence from his parents. From 9 February 1877 he had had his own apartment in the Potsdam Schloss and acquired a new family in his soldiers. To Hinzpeter's and his parents' chagrin he revelled in the life of a subaltern in the Prussian *Residenz*[32] – a life that must have contrasted starkly with that of a guards subaltern in the contemporary British army, with all its high living and staggering mess bills. 'In circles of comrades dominated by the old Prussian spirit I have always felt unreservedly at ease,' he wrote much later. This may well have had something to do with his desire to cast himself adrift from his mother, seizing on the Prussian half of his inheritance: the army. By the time William rejoined the colours, relations had become so bad that even his sister Charlotte stepped in in an attempt to work a reconciliation between 'Nigger' – as his family called him – and Vicky. It was not to last long, and Vicky was not slow to bring Fritz in on her side.[33]

William liked the spartan simplicity which still characterised the Prussian army at that time: the midday meal of fried eggs and potatoes; or dinner at five – soup, one main dish, cheese and fruit. There was a pudding only on Sundays and holidays. *Sekt,* or sparkling wine, was served on officers' birthdays or after a parade. After dinner there were evening duties and eventually card games such as whist, piquet, skat, chess or billiards followed by a simple supper of bread and butter and beer. On one of these beery evenings he was introduced to the American writer Mark Twain. He did not impress William, who found him boring and not at all funny. For his part Mark Twain was probably mentally putting together his famous indictment of the German language.[34]

More than the routine of the regiment, it was the contact with the solid, Prussian Junker officers which appealed to William. For most of them the future ruler was an idol, and their worship naturally went to his head. One who was less easily smitten was Captain Adolf von Bülow, William's adjutant from 1879 and the brother of his later chancellor. Bülow was a seminal influence, keen to reshape the prince's mind and knock some of the stuffing out of it introduced by the high-minded Hinzpeter and the Anglomaniacal crown princess and turn him into a proper, Prussian soldier. Certain principles had to be instilled: the Crown was the ultimate authority and Parliament was not to be trusted; the army guaranteed order; and German diplomacy should secure firm links to the other northern courts: Vienna and St Petersburg. Bülow did not think he was successful in the long run, and believed his charge had the mind of an immature teenager.[35]

On 22 March 1880, soon after his engagement to Dona was announced, William was gazetted captain. A week later he was given his own company, the second. In October that year William went to Britain with Dona. He had been invited to Cumberland Lodge in Windsor Great Park and was to have the opportunity to get to know his future bride a little better. There were plenty of organised activities. At the theatre he saw Henry Irving, and Uncle Connaught took him to the Guards' Depot at Aldershot. Another treat was the chance to visit Portsmouth and his cousin General Prince Edward of Weimar, who was in charge of the garrison there. While in Portsmouth the party inspected the new Dreadnought, at 11,400 tons the biggest ship in the line. Back in Windsor he paid a visit to the barracks of the Scots Guards: 'The soldiers' quarters were very simple, one might even say, spartan, in the dormitory there reigned an exemplary order and painstaking cleanliness.'[36] He greatly admired their kit, and believed that before the Great War, the British army was the 'best dressed in the world'.

Unlike most Prussian officers who stayed festering as lowly lieutenants for most of their careers, William's promotions came rapidly, but he was still only commanding the Leibkompanie at the time of his wedding to Dona on 27 February 1881. The day before he brought his guards through the Brandenburg Gate to the applause of a crowd which had gathered to see his bride. The First Company of the Foot Guards were ready to present arms to their new 'mother' when her coach arrived in the Schloss courtyard.

At the ceremony 'Old Prussia rubbed shoulders with the new Germany'. The butcher's guild led the procession in morning coats and top hats, but unintentionally there appeared in their midst a perambulant float bearing an advertisement for Singer sewing machines. There was the traditional torch dance in the Weisse Saal of the Berlin Schloss, but instead of tearing up and handing out bits of the bride's garter, special pieces had been made and embroidered with the date together with the initials of the recipients.[37]

After their marriage William and Dona retained the use of an apartment in the Potsdam Stadtschloss and were given the Marmorpalais as a residence. Frederick William II's small but elegant palace on the shores of the Heiliger See was at a safe distance from his parents in the Neues Palais. He was his own man now. It was a comparatively modest building conceived long before any Prussian ruler dreamed of overseas empires. It had a succession of tiny rooms, nooks and crannies, and must have been only just big enough to accommodate the wedding presents. Some of these ended up in the Kunstgewerbe Museum, like the silver service offered by ninety German towns and cities.[38] On 16 September 1881, William was named major *à la suite* of the Hussar Guards, thereby incurring more jealousy from Fritz, who did not receive his coveted hussar's uniform until middle age.[39]

Prussia's new princess was chiefly notable for a certain high-Victorian prudery and priggery. She flexed her muscles wherever she smelled immorality, forcing the royal intendant to resign after an actress was allowed on stage indecently dressed. She had a little less success with Richard Strauss's *Salome*, but she categorised it as blasphemous for all that, and said the composer could not hope for royal patronage while William reigned.[40] William and Dona's first son was born in 1882. They baptised him William, which annoyed Vicky, who wanted them to show respect by calling him Frederick.[41] Dona was well selected when it came to breeding and playing the role of mother to the nation. She bore William six sons in succession, and followed up with a princess, who was the apple of her father's eye.

Soon after his own wedding it was the turn of the heir to the Austrian throne to marry. The ceremony took place in Vienna in May. William and Dona stayed in the Kaiserstöckl, a little baroque palace in the park at Schönbrunn and he was appointed colonel *à la suite* to the 34th, König von Preussen Regiment. He saw Sissi again – 'still lovely and majestic'. The formality of the occasion was clearly stifling and William's Uncle Bertie for one found it too much, although an informal note crept on to the gold service at the wedding feast when Francis Joseph's favourite, homely dish of braised beef was served up to the guests. It was William's first opportunity to talk to Francis Ferdinand, who became heir to the Austro-Hungarian Empire after Rudolf's suicide.[42]

William failed to recognise the enemy in Rudolf until it was too late. Until 1887 he continued to tell him confidences which the Austrian prince merely repeated as soon as he returned to Vienna. In the course of a visit to Berlin in 1883, Rudolf listened to some of William's more extreme ideas on statecraft. 'Despite his youth Prince William is a hard-baked Junker and reactionary. He speaks of parliament only as "that pigsty" and of members of the opposition as "dogs who should be taken out and whipped".' William also told Rudolf about a plan of his to have the liberal Eugen Richter beaten up by a half dozen NCOs.[43]

After showing his mettle at the manoeuvres in Holstein, William was transferred to the Hussar Guards on 22 May 1882. They were commanded by Colonel von Krosigk, and despite the relatively small number of officers, he found the regiment instilled with something of the same 'old Prussian spirit'. He made new friends too: one was Chelius, another was the baptised Jew, Major Walter 'Moses' Mossner, whom he later ennobled. Soon after he had settled in he had the task of demonstrating his new cavalry skills to his grandfather. As the old emperor could no longer ride much, they had to move around him. He was accompanied by the cavalry general Prince Frederick Charles of Prussia, who complimented his great-nephew fulsomely: ' "Bravo William, you did that well! Like a real hussar!" . . . On this day there was *Sekt*.'[44]

Prince Frederick Charles lived at Dreilinden near Potsdam, where he received his many guests – they included the novelist and Borussologue Theodor Fontane – in an informal manner for a Prussian prince.[45] William found the atmosphere strange but exhilarating: 'A few, mostly older gentlemen from different units and services, including the navy; from general and admiral downwards, discussed in perfect frankness the army's important strategic and tactical problems as proposed by the prince.'[46]

The Austrian court had attractions for William which St James didn't provide. True, he had more or less discarded the mask of friendship when it came to Rudolf, and the contempt was mutual. William didn't like the very clear satirical vein in Rudolf and his mockery of religion. Worse, he clearly disapproved of the new German Reich in general and Prussia in particular. On the other hand his relations with Francis Joseph were ostensibly 'close and warm' and the Austrian emperor was – in many ways – cut in the same mould as his grandfather. He was amazed by the emperor's linguistic abilities: he could manage all the languages spoken in the Empire – and that meant a lot. Once, when William attended manoeuvres, Francis Joseph noticed that his adjutant was having difficulty communicating with a Gallician. 'Da muss i amol selbst nachschauen,' commented the emperor in his own idiom, 'sonst kommt die Meldung nimmer an die Leitung.'*

What William appears to have enjoyed most was hunting with the old emperor at Mürzsteg or Eisenerz in Styria. Francis Joseph gathered an impressive collection of crowned heads for his annual chamois cull. There was the king of Saxony, Prince Leopold of Bavaria, the Habsburg grand duke of Tuscany in the royal camp, as well as the chief equerry, Prince Taxis, the chief court marshal, Prince Constantine Hohenlohe, and the much humbler Graf von Meran. William travelled down to Styria on the Semmering line, crossing the mountains which cut it off from Lower Austria. The whole party was kitted out in Styrian costume.

Early nights and mornings were the rule and the Austrian emperor expected his guests to scale perilous paths to lofty butts with the same ease as himself – Francis Joseph was an accomplished climber. Even with only one fully functioning arm, William managed, and enjoyed the

---

* 'I must go off and see to it, otherwise the report will never get through to the Staff.'

satisfaction of exterminating a few chamois bucks. Descent was – if anything – more frightening, with a youthful Prussian prince struggling to keep up with a mature Austrian emperor. Francis Joseph noticed the sweat dripping from William's brow when they reached the bottom: 'Es hat dich wohl a bisserl echauffiert?'*

After another visit to Vienna and Prague – where he stayed at the Hradschin – in May 1883, it was William's turn to get to know the third branch of the service: the artillery. He was posted to the First Field Artillery Guards on 1 July. On the old ranges at Tegel, near Berlin, he learned the essentials of gunnery and later had the chance to demonstrate his prowess to his father on the hill of Kreuzberg to the south of the city. He did not stay long with the gunners. 'Julius' von Moltke saw him in Hussar's uniform on 15 September, and commented on how well he was developing. In the autumn manoeuvres that year he was attached to General Blumenthal's staff. Despite his transfers, and his prospects, he was not yet familiar to everyone. Colonel von Werder, who was to command an army corps in the First World War, asked him who he was: 'Ordnance officer to the Commanding General, Prince William of Prussia, the grandson of the same person from whom I have the honour of delivering this order in cabinet.'[47]

On 20 October 1883 William came home to the First Foot as battalion commander. Soon afterwards he received an invitation to accompany his parents on a visit the king of Spain in Madrid. His request for leave was refused – possibly to his relief. The old Kaiser thought the idea frivolous: 'Just after receiving such an important command he wants to go on a pleasure trip to Spain!' William added, 'Despite everything I thought it my duty to swap the chance to look at beautiful Spain for the walls of the barracks' courtyard and the drill yard.'[48]

William continued to sink himself into the routines of army life, enjoying every moment of what he believed to be an utterly Prussian vocation. He used the Latin which Hinzpeter had so doggedly instilled in him to lecture his brother officers on Roman tactics. The Kaiser sent Waldersee along to listen in. The Quartermaster-General was impressed: 'He spoke very clearly and handsomely, and modestly too. It was a pleasure to see the young gentleman. What he undertakes he does keenly and thoroughly.' Waldersee was not the only one. The head of the Catholic Hohenzollerns, Prince Charles Anthony, thought he was a second Frederick the Great, but 'without the scepticism'. 'When he comes to the throne he will continue the work of his grandfather and without doubt destroy that of his father ... He could become the Henry

* 'Did [the descent] make you a bit hot?'

IV of his country.'[49] Henry IV united a France divided by religion. It was certainly William's later intention to unite all Germans behind the splendour of his empire.

4

Influences and Responsibilities

Although military and married life was providing William with most of what he needed, there was an aesthetic element that he appeared to crave too. From the mid-1880s this was to a very great extent supplied by Graf Philipp zu Eulenburg. William had met this East Prussian nobleman for the first time in 1871 and again in 1883, when he had been too young to take him in. He was twelve years older than the prince, and had served in the First Company of the Gardes du Corps during the Franco-German War. The army life was not for him, however. Even during his service days he had spent every free hour at the keyboard of a piano or painting at an easel. After the war he abandoned his regiment and took his *Abitur*. He proceeded to the universities of Leipzig, Strasbourg and Giessen, receiving his doctorate in law with an impressive *magna cum laude*.[1]

Eulenburg was especially well-connected when it came to getting close to William. He had befriended Kuno von Moltke, the future governor of Berlin, during his Kriegsschule days in Cassel. From his time as an ensign, Eulenburg knew plenty of people who could lead him back to the prince. The future Colonel von Kalisch; the later Generals von Kessel and Moltke; and Graf Richard von Dohna-Schlobitten, who was – like Eulenburg – to be made a prince once William had the chance to shower honours on his favourites at court. In his memoirs William was careful to stress that all these men valued Eulenburg highly. He mentioned Bismarck too, but his memory was failing him. Eulenburg was indeed a frequent guest of the Chancellor's family, and Bismarck may well have called him the 'Nordic bard Phili', but he called him a lot less flattering names besides; most memorably he said that the man's eyes could spoil a good lunch.[2]

Eulenburg joined the diplomatic service. He was not particularly ambitious; content to serve in a minor capacity while he dedicated most of his energy to composing ballads and plays, both of which enjoyed a small reputation in Germany at that time. For a while he was posted to

King Oscar's court in Sweden. Here he met the French diplomat, racial theorist and novelist comte Joseph Arthur Gobineau and became his friend. Gobineau was fifty-eight then, but he told the younger man, 'I lunch at eleven and dine at five, consider my house as your home!'[3] Some of Gobineau's ideas must have rubbed off on Eulenburg who betrays a marked tendency towards anti-Semitism in several places in his published papers.

He married a Swedish countess and attended Gräfin Schleinitz's Berlin salon where he performed his ballads to Richard Wagner's most fervent Prussian admirers. Eulenburg was posted to the consulate in Munich in 1881 and divided his time between the Bavarian capital and his house, Villa Cäcilia on the Starnberger See. His position not only allowed him to explore a richer cultural world in Bavaria; it afforded him the chance to examine his Starnberg neighbour, King Ludwig, from close quarters. Despite Gobineau and the fact that the great Wagnerian conductor was the son of a rabbi, Eulenburg moved in the circle of Hermann Levi in Munich. Like Levi he was 'overwhelmed' by Wagner's last opera, *Parsifal*.[4]

In 1886 Richard and Eberhard Dohna invited him hunting at Pröckelwitz in East Prussia to introduce him properly to William, who was to be at the same house party. Eulenburg was undecided at first whether he wanted to go: 'I am excited to meet my future lord, my children's king, in an intimate circle, but it is so far away and the mood so uncertain.'[5] Eulenburg arrived on 4 May and to his delight, found that the princely house-guest not only knew of his ballads, he could quote from them. Eulenburg did his party tricks, singing his 'Skaldenlieder' and playing the piano while William turned the pages for him. Later they discussed politics too. William was enchanted. Eulenburg remembered that 'I had to sing for him for hours each evening ... The young prince looked at me as if into a cup filled with a mixture of ingredients which tasted wonderful to him.'[6]

Eulenburg returned to Munich in time to witness King Ludwig's fate. He had been watching the comings and goings at Schloss Berg through a telescope, a little hampered by the incessant rain. On 14 June the railway inspector Hartmann told him that the king and his physician Gudden had drowned in Starnberg Lake. When he learned of the tragedy he rushed out of his house: 'Opposite the Villa Cäcilia stood the house of Ernst, the fisherman, his son Jakob had rowed me for years on excursions and fishing expeditions.' He woke Ernst and was therefore one of the first to see the king's corpse, the scratches on the physician Gudden's throat and the disordered reeds on the lake. He drew his own conclusions: the king had strangled Gudden and drowned himself.[7]

Eulenburg received an invitation to Bad Reichenhall where William was taking a cure with Dona and recovering from the latest infection in his ear. He wrote to a friend, 'For Prussia's sake I expect an enormous amount from him. His clarity, his energy and the richness of his indescribably individual existence make him a wholly extraordinary phenomenon.'[8] William met him at the station and put him up in his study where he had hung some big crayon drawings to illustrate his ballad on the subject of the disappearance of Atlantis. 'I was received like his best friend.'[9] They talked art, and Eulenburg played at the piano and sang to entertain the future emperor and his wife. William was particularly taken with *Atlantis*.

Since his friendship with Emil Görtz, William had known no one like Eulenburg. Not only was he an excellent raconteur, singer and pianist; he adored art and nature; and he was a diplomat with 'sound judgement'.[10] Eulenburg easily convinced William to go on to Bayreuth with him in August where he was an honoured friend of Cosima Wagner. William fell for the composer too then, if later he was to change his mind and dismiss him as a mere conductor. He liked *Tristan und Isolde*, but above all he enjoyed *Parsifal*. Eulenburg later took William round the studios of his artist friends in Munich – Franz von Lenbach and Karl von Piloty. William was excited by the huge evocative canvases of Piloty, who directed the academy there.

William recognised Eulenburg as the soul mate he had always wanted, and required his presence more and more. Above all this was to be the romantic friendship he had never had: close companionship with another man. He visited him in his Starnberg home and Jakob Ernst was recruited to row the two of them over to Schloss Berg where Ludwig had died. His visits to the Marmorpalais were eagerly awaited. He was, said William later, 'like a stream of sunshine [lighting up] our everyday lives'.[11] Eulenburg's colleague in the Wilhelmstrasse, Herbert von Bismarck, wrote to encourage his new intimacy with Germany's future leader: 'You must use this ... in order to work on him. For that certain romanticism which colours most of his views needs to be tempered so that the ideas of a Potsdam lieutenant are gradually replaced by the reflections of a statesman.'[12]

Unlike Herbert later on, there is every reason to believe that Eulenburg's friendship was genuine. He saw the impressionable young prince, destined to become the ruler of a powerful nation, as someone who required protection, even love – though not, it should be added perhaps, of a sexual sort. He was infatuated with the romantic notion of kingship into which he worked his own interpretation of Prussian statecraft, one that had nothing to do with the limited democracy which had been introduced since 1848. He wanted a return to the benevolent absolutism practised by Frederick the Great, only in this case he would be there to make sure that the ruler did not take the wrong path. Eulenburg later encouraged William to rule without taking heed of Germany's governmental organs, but his was certainly not the worst advice William received and he – possibly he alone – was able to *criticise* William. Even in the early days of their friendship, before he was allowed (but never used) to call his prince 'Du', he sent William a picture of a frog together with the legend: 'The frog's proud expression is classic, and expressedly teaches us to remain modest.'[13]

William was attracted to military men with aesthetic leanings, and he later found a means of promoting them to high rank in order to keep them within his entourage. As he grew older he developed a physical need to escape from the narrow bounds he had constructed for himself, while at the same time giving no indication that he had strayed from the military world. He was being a little like his mother and a little like his grandfather, all at the same time. He met the future General Oskar von Chelius on manoeuvres in the Brandenburg Mark. After dinner Chelius took his place at the keyboard 'and for the first time in my life I witnessed his musical gifts, his great technical mastery and extensive repertoire, which allowed him to sit down immediately and play any work of music he wished, without consulting the score.'[14]

Chelius had studied at the Conservatory in Leipzig, and although he had decided ultimately to follow a career in the cavalry, he still composed and his world abounded with singers and conductors. William thought him too much under Wagner's influence, so that the Master's leitmotivs had a habit of bubbling up in Chelius's compositions. He was one of the founders of the Berlin-Potsdam Wagner Verein. William and Dona were members and attended concerts in the Kriegsakademie building on the hill on the Babelsberg side of the Havel to the Potsdam Stadtschloss.* Another reason for keeping Chelius near to him was his trustworthiness – 'He was as steady as a rock.'[15]

Another artistic influence was Professor Paul Güssfeldt. It must have helped that he had won an Iron Cross at Mars-la-Tour before going on to explore Africa and South America. Güssfeldt's role in William's later life was to stage-manage the *Nordlandsreisen* or annual jaunts up the Norwegian coast towards the Pole. Another painter who came on the cruises was Karl Saltzmann. This Berliner had been one of Vicky's discoveries, but he was particularly interesting to William as a result of his genre: sea pictures and naval battles, which he could execute with astonishing speed. Saltzmann was engaged to give William lessons.

A pure soldier and much older mentor whom he met in 1879 when

* Now the Brandenburg Landtag.

serving with the guards and whose influence was paramount in the 1880s, was Alfred Graf von Waldersee. He fitted the bill: William's friends at that time had to be male, anti-English, anti-liberal and opposed to the crown princess.[16] Waldersee was all four. He was married to a pious American woman who became a close friend of Dona's, and the general and his wife were able to lure William into the world of evangelical Christianity which inhabited their salon in the General Staff building near the Reichstag. Waldersee was responsible for bringing William together with the Christian Socialist and anti-Semite Adolf Stoecker. While William and his wife joined in the movement to bring the Berlin working classes back to morality, Waldersee performed the role of middleman in William's tangled extramarital affairs.

Waldersee first expressed his admiration for the young prince in December 1882, after he had paid him a visit at the General Staff.

I have now seen the prince more often and have begun to form a picture. He has an unusually fresh approach and undertakes everything he can with thoroughness and conscientiousness. He seems to take after his grandfather a good deal. If his parents have set themselves the target of bringing up a constitutional monarch who obediently bends before the majority in the chamber they have had bad luck. On the face of it it looks as if precisely the opposite has been the case.[17]

The following spring William began to pay Waldersee frequent visits when he was ill and laid up in bed. They hunted together and their meetings began to put Waldersee's mind at rest. He had no time for the crown prince, whom he described as an 'extreme liberal', and feared what might happen when the emperor died. William was 'completely different' ... 'He is already a character and is forming distinctive views. He is unbending as the father is weak. Sadly the relationship between the two of them is nothing less than good. It would be better if they didn't live so close to one another.'[18]

II

With the old emperor now at an advanced age, and his heir still prey to the liberal, pro-British views of his wife, Bismarck thought it a sensible idea to educate William for government. The chancellor wanted William removed from his narrow circle of officers and brought up to Berlin, but he encountered opposition from the Hausministerium which was reluctant to make a palace available for him on grounds of cost. On 2 October 1882 an order in cabinet was issued appointing the prince to the Brandenburg Oberpräsidium in Potsdam, where he was to observe

Oberpräsident von Aschenbach during his morning sessions and learn what he could. The civil servant proved a good teacher and William was initiated into aspects of local government, of which he was most smitten with the intricacies of transport, laying new roads and railway lines and digging canals.[19]

In the spring of 1884 the so-called Battenberg affair rocked the Hohenzollern *ménage*. Prince Alexander of Battenberg's reign in Bulgaria had begun in 1879 when the Russians had backed his election as prince at the Diet in the old Bulgarian capital, Veliko Turnovo. A former Prussian officer, he had transferred to the Tsarist army for the war of 1877–8 when Bulgaria had been liberated from the Turks. He lost Russian support, however, when he began to take less heed of his patrons.

All this would have had little or no relevance to William but for two factors: his respect for Bismarck's foreign policy and the possibility that 'Sandro' would shortly become his brother-in-law. Vicky had set her heart on a marriage between the handsome Sandro and her daughter Victoria or 'Moretta'. Moretta had met Sandro first in Berlin in 1882 when she was only fifteen and still too much a child to be considered as a future wife. Moretta, on the other hand, instantly fell for the brave and dashing prince of Bulgaria. Vicky was possibly even more struck by Sandro's charm than Moretta. She was quite prepared to grant him whichever of her unmarried daughters he chose to name. In 1883 she had her way and Moretta became secretly engaged to Sandro.[20]

The potential match was all the sweeter for the knowledge that her mother had allowed the new Bulgarian ruler's brother Henry to marry her daughter Beatrice, sweeping aside any objections based on the dodgy Battenberg lineage.* There is also a suspicion that Vicky was out to make trouble; that her tenacious stance was influenced by her dislike of both Bismarck and Prussia's pro-Russian foreign policy. Other commentators raise the issue of Vicky's unhealthy obsession with the young officer. She was prepared to wreck everyone's lives, above all her own daughter's, to get her own way in this matter.

William was alerted to the problem by Prince Heinrich XVIII of Reuss. He was a minor German royal who had his eye on Moretta and who was jealous of her infatuation with Sandro. He asked William to help. Now the secret was out. It was Sandro's ancestors which put William off. He was the product of a morganatic marriage between Alexander of Hesse and a Gräfin Julie Haucke. The countess's father had been ennobled by the Russians as recently as 1829. Up to then the few *fleurons* on the family tree were made up of lowly Alsatian pastors and physicians.[21] Sandro was simply not *ebenbürtig* – not of their rank as

---

* The 'Mountbattens' were the result.

far as the German princely courts were concerned, with their rigid codes of family law. William's family divided down the middle over this issue. He and Henry, and his eldest sister Charlotte, were all opposed; the emperor and empress likewise.[22] Old William could recall the sacrifice he had made when the family decided that his first love, Eliza Radziwill, was not *ebenbürtig* either. With Fritz it was largely a question of whom he had spoken to last. If it was Vicky, then he was in favour of the match.

Bismarck considered the marriage project to be a piece of perfidious British–Polish* trouble-making designed to destroy the alliance and threatened to resign if it took place.[23] In an interview with Sandro on 12 May 1884 he expressed the hope that the rumours about the engagement were untrue. With the exception of Vicky and Moretta, the entire court was against it. Moretta, he thought 'would accept any other suitor, providing he were manly'.[24] He told Sandro to marry an Orthodox millionairess. She would be useful in providing the money he needed for the bribes he believed to be common practice in the Balkans.[25]

The weak link was once again Fritz. In the course of a dinner he furtively raised his glass to Sandro as 'The pioneer of German culture in the east'. Vicky had clearly worked on him in the meantime. Their eldest son was so furious that he threatened a complete break with his mother and father. Later William would claim that his objection to Sandro was based entirely on *raison d'état*, and that snobbery had nothing to do with it. William was cast as the villain of the piece who denied his sister the pleasure of a love-match with the dashing prince. 'That my relations with my mother were severely troubled by this, caused me great pain ... my country's well-being was at risk and all matters of personal taste had to keep mum.' He did not admit it in his memoirs, but relations with his parents had reached an all-time low. Nor did William enjoy the support of his father, who was still jealous of him. Fritz told Hinzpeter, 'I can't endure it! My father and my son clasp hands on top of my head and press me down.'[26]

Emperor William I had constantly maintained the traditional Prussian friendship towards its eastern neighbour. It was said that the old man still regarded himself as honour-bound by the oath sworn by his father Frederick William III and Tsar Alexander over the tomb of Frederick the Great in Potsdam. At the news of the assassination of his cousin, the Tsar Liberator, Nicholas II, the old Kaiser had silently wept. Bismarck was rather more pragmatic than his lord. He considered the Reinsurance Treaty to be an insurance against the anti-Russian, pro-British policies advocated by Fritz and Vicky.[27]

* Sandro's mother was nominally Polish.

In May 1884 while the Sandro episode was causing divisions in the family, young William represented his grandfather at the coming-of-age of the Tsarevitch, later Nicholas II. Before he went, Bismarck gave him a word of advice: 'In Russia anyone who wears his shirt over his trousers is a decent fellow; as soon as they tuck it in, and hang a medal around their necks, they are *Schweinehunde*.'[28] Suitably schooled, he travelled on 15 May 1884 accompanied by a little court composed of Liebenau, Major Gebhard von Krosigk, Captain von Bülow and General Graf von Waldersee.

William must have been thrilled to be greeted at the border by a squadron of Dragoons commanded by the Russian-German Brigadier-General Graf Lambsdorff. The German party was joined by the ambassador, General von Schweinitz, Herbert Bismarck – then a secretary in the St Petersburg embassy, and General von Werder, a Prussian officer attached to the Russian emperor's staff. They arrived at 8.00 a.m. on the 17th to be met by the Tsar and all the grand dukes dressed in Prussian uniform. William was able to introduce Waldersee to his cousin, the Russian emperor.[29]

The morning after his arrival, William went to the Peter and Paul Fortress to lay a wreath on the late Tsar's grave. He marvelled at Peter the Great's modest Dutch cottage, which had been reassembled there, rather than the cells stuffed full of political prisoners which captured Waldersee's imagination. His duties that morning included presenting the fourteen-year-old Nicholas with the Black Eagle. He discovered that he was improperly dressed – always a nightmare for a Hohenzollern. He had not been informed of his new colonelcy of the 85th Wiborg Regiment. It was not enough to destroy the glamour of the occasion: the bells at the church ceremony; the 301-cannon salute. Years later, in Doorn, he was still marvelling at the occasion:

the splendour of the Tsar's palace would be hard to describe. When I think of the party which marked my coming of age then the vision of that economical ceremony in the Knights' Hall of the grey Schlüter Schloss seems paltry by comparison ... The only thing which reminded me of Berlin were a few uniforms worn by the Russian guards regiments like the life guards which wore almost the same collars, breastplates and eagle helmets as we did in Potsdam.[30]

Tsar Alexander III had the reputation for being truculent, but William on the contrary found him 'uncommonly warm and friendly'. Waldersee too noted that William had pleased the Russian ruler.[31] He revealed that he was not overly keen on the form of Bismarck's Triple Alliance; that he would have preferred the pact to be directed against anarchy and democracy: the evils which he believed had been responsible for his father's death. Waldersee thought William was a natural diplomat. He gave every impression that he was not there for pleasure, but for his country's good, understood the important issues, and was particularly adept at concealing his own views on matters.[32]

William also had something to say about Sandro:

I assure Your Majesty that the German Reich has no interest in the prince of Bulgaria and his country, in whatever case not enough to let it disturb the cordial relations which exist between my Imperial grandfather and Your Majesty's house. Obviously there can be no question of marriage.[33]

The Tsar was grateful for reassurance. William 'pleased him enormously'. The Russian Foreign Minister Nicolai Giers thought that William had been an excellent messenger for Bismarck, as all that he said he had heard the German chancellor utter before.[34]

There was free time to visit St Petersburg, the picture collection at the Hermitage and the museums; and the navy at Kronstadt. On 22 May the Tsar took him to the station wearing Prussian uniform. The grand dukes were there to say goodbye, as well as his own – Wiborg – Regiment. William went on to Moscow as a guest of Prince Dolgoruki. The Muscovite showed him over the Kremlin with its many relics of the joint campaigns of the Russian and Prussian armies and the coffin of Ivan the Terrible. On the 25th there was a parting meal. The *zakuski* and the liqueurs were quite enough for the abstemious William, but the Russians were not content until they had swallowed a further twelve courses over the next two hours while gypsies serenaded them with songs. He left at midnight, his train drawing in to Berlin on the 28th. Waldersee concluded his examination: William 'would be the right man to properly maintain Germany's powerful position, possibly to expand it!' William was now seen as something of an authority on Russian relations.[35]

The Sandro affair had failed to die down in William's absence. Taking his cue from Bismarck, William now believed heart and soul that it was an English plot. On 25 May he wrote to the Tsar:

Can I ask you a favour? Don't trust the English uncle. Don't let yourself be worried by things that you hear about my father. You know him, he loves dissent and is in the hands of my mother, who is driven from her side by the Queen of England, who makes her see everything through English spectacles.[36]

On 19 June William wrote again. He had had an argument with his father who had called him names. He was 'Russophil', he knew nothing about politics, he knew nothing; whereas Fritz knew better. 'By fair means or foul,* the prince of Bulgaria has my mother in his pocket and that naturally means my father too ... But these English people have forgotten about me...'[37]

---

* In English in the text.

5

Duel to the Death

Relations with his parents had gone from bad to worse. Vicky knew that Fritz was a soft touch, and for that reason kept William away from him. Fritz, however, disapproved of his son's posturing and politics; there was a large element of jealousy as well. There was some evidence that ordinary Germans thought he would be a better ruler than his father. In the spring of 1885 Holstein noted, 'I am told that expressions such as the following can be heard among the ordinary folk lately: "The crown prince won't make a good ruler, we want Prince William; he'll be a second Frederick the Great." '[1]

William enjoyed the chance, whenever possible, to show off his battalion to his beloved grandfather. In September 1885 he led the First Foot in the autumn manoeuvres. That autumn he was appointed colonel of the Hussar Guards. Ever outwardly the prig, he reformed the NCOs' mess in order to stop them spending their time in the pub, providing it with edifying books and games, such as chess. His next step was to move against the vices of his officers. Like his austere ancestor, the soldier-king Frederick William I, William mounted a moral crusade. It was the Calvinism he had learned from Hinzpeter, and the former tutor heartily supported William's gesture.[2]

William was incensed that there was so much gambling going on among his officers and determined to put a stop to it, no matter how unpopular such an opposition would be in the eyes of the officer corps as a whole. His eyes focused on the aristocratic Union Club, 'the principal source of all evil' he called it. 'It cost many a highly promising young officer his uniform, his life even, and ruined more than one family.'[3] He promptly debarred it to his own officers. His friend Waldersee kept his distance, committing the events to his voluminous diary, but he approved, or rather his wife did: the teetotal daughter of a New England grocer.[4]

The reason was clear. Even the Quartermaster-General and number two in the General Staff would have been unwise to tackle such a powerful vested interest. William was warned to keep his hands off. The Union Club enjoyed support, not least from its patron, the Silesian magnate Herzog von Ratibor who asked him to reconsider his decision. Ratibor was even successful in appealing to the old emperor who acted as a guardian angel to the gambling den. 'It was one of my most painful experiences that for a while [the duke's] efforts were not without success.' The monarch took over the patronage of the club and tried to make him remove the ban. They were difficult times. When William became emperor he declared the club to be out of bounds to all Prussian officers.[5]

As William grew up, and above all as he was exposed to more and more key figures in the army, he was increasingly adopted by the right. The leader of this party was Waldersee, who found it hard to conceal his disgust for William's parents' *ménage*, and the way in which Vicky lorded it over her husband: 'She has transformed a simple, brave and honest prince cut in the Prussian mould into a weak man who doesn't trust his own opinions, is no longer open or honest, nor thinks as a Prussian.' The relationship between his father and mother was particularly difficult for William:

To his misfortune [William] thinks it wholly clear that his mother has not become a Prussian princess, but has remained an Englishwoman. He knows that she consciously works in the British interest against those of Prussia and Germany. This deeply upsets his thoroughly Prussian feelings and it is often hard for him to rein in his fiery temperament.[6]

William's pronouncements became increasingly anti-English. At the end of 1884 the crisis in the Sudan and the approaching fate of General Gordon who had gone to relieve the garrison in Khartoum seems to have given him a certain amount of malicious pleasure. Waldersee thought it all sadly natural: 'The prince has become strongly anti-English, for a large part a wholly natural reaction against the attempts of his mother to turn her children into Anglomaniacs.'[7]

It was undeniably true that Fritz and Vicky's views tilted at the Prusso-German foundations of the new Empire. Their liberalism ran counter to the Prussian authoritarian tradition, and their admiration for England questioned the basis of Prussian foreign policy. Matters were not helped by Vicky's complete inability to see herself as anything other than an English princess. She was highly partisan. She conspired to keep paintings from English collections out of German museums and supplied the British press with compromising material about Bismarck. She was capable of treason. On 30 December 1884 she wrote home to tell her mother to increase the number of ships in the Royal Navy in order to check Germany's colonial ambitions. 'It is a lesson for our own dear country to keep her eyes open. Three years ago we ought to have taken New Guinea.'[8]

William was having problems with his love life again. On 16 January 1885 he went to Waldersee to get him out of the mess. He made various confessions and took the general into his confidence. The only name he mentioned at the time was Elisabeth Bérard. Despite Waldersee's links to evangelical Christianity, he seems to have taken the confessions in his stride: 'The young gentleman is quite idiosyncratic, but he is already displaying a firm character, and that is the most important thing.'[9] Five days later the Bérard affair drove him to Waldersee again. The meeting was meant to be about the patent of Archduke Charles Salvator's repeater rifle which was being touted by the adventuress but there were undoubtedly other matters to discuss. William's extramarital affairs may have provided Waldersee with the means of getting him involved with Stoecker's Stadtmission, for on 5 February he was presiding over the mission bazaar.

Elisabeth Bérard was the estranged wife of Graf Hermann von Wedel, later William's Stadtholder in Alsace-Lorraine. She had had a sparkling career as a courtesan before she met William, her junior by ten years. In Potsdam she stayed at the Palasthotel opposite the Stadtschloss. Here William presented her with a diamond necklace. She was evidently a cut above the usual whores whose bills he tried to wriggle out of honouring.[10] The necklace was not enough. Waldersee had to find the odd 1,000 marks too. Eventually Gräfin Wedel moved into a flat in Charlottenburg where she continued to receive the prince until the end of the year. She too later successfully blackmailed William, and published revelations about their affair. She died a hopeless lunatic and occasional burden on the German taxpayer, some time after 1905.

The battle between William and his parents worsened. On 2 February Fritz maligned his son at dinner with the First Foot Guards. Before the assembled mess he described him as an 'immature man, lacking in judgement'. Waldersee thought they wanted to create a scandal which would lead to a rupture between the generations.[11] By now Waldersee received the young prince almost daily. His support was doubtless useful, as he never wavered in his condemnation of William's parents. On 6 April he wrote, 'The crown prince becomes weaker and more incapable of judgement with every day that passes. In reality he can have no other views than those of his wife, and she is in everything counselled in the worst possible way.'[12]

The squabbling led Waldersee to believe that – despite the justice of William's case – he should be banished to a remote garrison. 'Without doubt the parents bear the brunt of the guilt, but on the other side the prince is very uncircumspect, and particularly incautious in his utterances about his mother.'[13] Hinzpeter also thought Vicky was being unreasonable. He rather cheekily compared her to a mother duck who was uncomfortable about seeing her duckling take to the water. That was natural; what was not, was to accuse her young of degeneracy. Mixing his avine metaphor, he went on: 'Not even the pair of eagles themselves have the right to upbraid the eaglet for choosing its own flight path.'[14]

There was a brief respite occasioned by the Union Club business. Vicky and Fritz were happy to see their son out of sorts with the emperor, and over an issue with such a strong moral allure to it. The priggish Waldersee expressed his disgust at the gamblers and their methods: 'You see a hotbed of envy, hatred and nastiness in there which is horrifying ...' Dirt was thrown at William, an obvious target in the circumstances. It was clear that William's peccadilloes were no secret to the officer corps. 'To my regret I have to admit that certain circles are plotting heavily against Prince William; they are trying to warm up some old gossip and to discover some new stuff. It chiefly revolves around accusing him of extramarital infidelities.'[15]

William was beginning to make up his mind about the sort of friends he wanted in the future. He went along with Bismarck's alliances for the time being. In the autumn of 1885, together with other dignitaries, he visited Crown Prince Rudolf and his wife in Budapest to see the national exhibition. Dona and William stayed at the Hofburg in Buda where they met the statesman Andrassy: 'a Hungarian thoroughbred, [hair] as black as coal with a lock hanging down over his temples.' Uncle Bertie was there too. He took a dim view of the cheering which greeted the appearances of his nephew. Count Andrassy told him, 'He [Edward] won't have wanted to hear that! He is not happy about the Triple Alliance. Europe will undergo a few uncomfortable moments when he seizes the helm!'[16]

In February 1886 William made a second visit to hunt bears. He had been invited to Anton Radziwill's estate at Nieswiecz near Minsk. It was the first time he had taken stock of the Russian peasantry: the men doffed their caps to him as his sleigh passed through villages deep in snow and women held up their half-naked babies for him to kiss in temperatures five degrees below zero. The vision spurred William's host to philosophic observation: 'Everything that is weak, that cannot endure, dies out. Whatever survives is hardened in such a way, that they can endure anything.'[17] The moment came when William the avid huntsman was to face his first bear, equipped with a revolver in his pocket lest it come to hand-to-paw fighting. He was proud to report home that evening that he had stopped the bear with his shot. He killed two more bears on that trip, one of them a female. He was told that according to old Russian custom the killer of a female was obliged to take care of the cubs. He took two infants back to Potsdam with him 'where for many more years they gave my children pleasure and they themselves had fun nibbling off every button they could reach'.[18]

Waldersee's faith in William was wavering, possibly as a result of having to play go-between between him and his mistresses. 'I often have a lot of trouble,' he wrote on 11 February 1886, 'arriving at a calm judgement of his personality.' The general's loyalty was being severely tested with so much talk of William's taste for low-life. He thought the source of the gossip was Albedyll, the head of the emperor's Military Cabinet. This could have meant that the old emperor was aware of the stories too, although in reality he had nothing to reproach his grandson for there. He thought William spent too much time hunting to look after his regiment; and there was more hypocrisy with the prince banning his officers from certain noble households which had objected to his moratorium on gambling.[19]

Despite a gift of a bust of himself on Waldersee's birthday in April, the general had begun to find a number of William's ideas trying. He came to him with a scheme for dismissing the elder generals, which must have made Waldersee sensitive. He thought the idea 'absurd'. He also resented the growing influence which the earthy Herbert Bismarck exerted over his character. By October that year William was travelling up to Berlin twice a week to be with Herbert.[20] Herbert was a proper chip off the old block, and spent much of the day, and night, deep in his cups.

That year there were renewed problems with William's health. Dizziness, vomiting and severe earache laid him low for two months. He was treated by the leading ear, nose and throat specialist of his day, Riga-born Ernst von Bergmann, who advised against operating. Waldersee thought it was just a dietary problem, but others believed the ear infection could affect his brain. 'What great hopes would be destroyed if that were to be the case!' noted the general.[21] While he was incapacitated by the illness, he became for a short while closer to Vicky, who found him 'much more amiable, friendly and civil, also more cordial ...'[22] Soon after, William was forced to take a cure at Bad Reichenhall and diverted himself with Philipp Eulenburg.

II

In August 1886 William undertook his first diplomatic work when his grandfather invited him to join him in Gastein from his sickbed in Bad Reichenhall. The Bismarcks were there with Herbert and the elderly courtiers Grafen Perponcher and Lehndorf as well as Francis Joseph and Sissi. It sent Fritz into a predictable rage. He pleaded to have the mission stopped, claiming that William would do more harm than good: 'The lack of maturity as well as the inexperience of my eldest son when coupled with his tendency towards presumptuousness and conceit, makes it, in my estimation, *dangerous*, for him to become involved in foreign affairs.' To prove how unrealistic he could be, he put himself forward for the job. Vicky's tone was slightly less hotheaded, but the message was the same: 'I need hardly say that it would make endless mischief and do endless harm. William is as blind and green, wrong-headed and violent on politics as can be.' She went so far as to tell an Austrian diplomat how much she preferred the liberal Crown Prince Rudolf to her own 'barbaric' son.[23]

In the circumstances Bismarck was not impressed by Fritz and Vicky's ranting. William travelled to Brest-Litovsk to see the Tsar who was severely out of sorts with Bismarck and the alliance hung by a thread. Perhaps the latter was right to err on the side of caution when it came to Sandro. William reported that Tsar told him plainly, 'If he wanted to take Constantinople he would do so whenever he so pleased; he did not require the agreement or permission of prince Bismarck.' For the time being, however, he was prepared to uphold the Triple Alliance to keep the peace.

In the summer of 1886 the Battenberg business had resurfaced. On 21 August Prince Alexander's Bulgarian army had been incited to mutiny and deposed their leader. Russian patience had run out. In September 1885 Sandro had annexed Rumelia, which the Russians had also coveted. From now on he could no longer count on their support. More seriously, King Milan of Serbia clamoured for compensation and when none was forthcoming, declared war on Bulgaria. The Tsar responded by stripping Alexander of his rank as a Russian officer and provoking the mutiny.

Alexander was still popular with the Bulgarian people, however. When on 28 August he rode into Sofia, the crowd was jubilant; but he made the mistake of offering his crown back to the Russians, who accepted. Alexander's more glittering career had come to an end. The following year another German prince received the Bulgarian throne when Ferdinand of Coburg was elected in his stead. Bismarck told his friend Hildegard von Spitzemberg, the sister of Würtemberg's envoy Axel von Varnbüler, who set the conversation down in her diary:

There won't be war, the Bulgarian [Sandro] is riding back to Sofia, but only, this is the prince's [Bismarck's] conviction, to be thrown out a second time, and this time more thoroughly.

Bismarck was waiting for William to return and deliver his report on his meeting with the Tsar. Fritz was announced instead. 'Ceci est plus grave!' said Bismarck.* 'Quickly, give me a glass of champagne.' Baronin Spitzemberg commented, 'He was expecting a hard struggle over the Bulgarian.'[24]

The failure of Sandro's career as a ruler was only a temporary setback as far as Vicky – and by extension Fritz – was concerned. Together they dreamed up projects to put him in charge of the guards, the General Staff; the chancellorship of the Reich itself was even mooted. Another suggestion was viceroy of Alsace-Lorraine, a job which William briefly coveted for himself. The prince was so furious at the suggestion that he threatened to shoot Sandro. As far as Bismarck was concerned, the former prince of Bulgaria was still tainted by his having offended the Russians. Britain and Germany were at loggerheads over the latter's colonial policy which had begun to encroach on British interests for the first time. German–Russian relations were at their lowest ebb in years and war was indeed a possibility. Bismarck did not consider this to be the moment. He did not want the Russians offended and believed that any German support for Sandro would have precisely that effect.

William recalled that there was a growing call for a French alliance in Russia even at this time. With the benefit of hindsight he wrote:

Not for one moment would [the Treaty] have prevented a war between Russia and Germany; nor, had a war with France broken out at that moment, would it have guaranteed Russian neutrality. For me there is no doubt that the Treaty has been overvalued in many ways, it was no more than a prop in the extended game of the Great Chancellor.

In retrospect William did not have much time for Bismarck's continental alliances and felt he neglected the chance to forge a link with Great Britain. When the time came he would take up the Coburg method, and try to govern the world through family ties.[25]

A month later he became Herbert Bismarck's pupil at the Foreign Office; a relationship which was formalised by an order in cabinet in December. Herbert's approach was cynical. He befriended his pupil, drawing him into his hard-drinking world in as much as the sober prince would be led down that path. In private, however, he described William as a man who was 'as cold as a dog's nose ... heartless, superficial and vain.' He went to Geheimrat Raschdau too, who tutored him in trade and colonial relations. 'From ... Raschdau's briefings was I already aware of our independence from England, the cause of which lay principally

---

* 'This is more serious.'

in our failure to build a fleet and that Heligoland was still in their hands.'[26]

Herbert Bismarck had a wider brief. He was to sketch the characters of the leading practitioners and paint a larger picture of Prussia's traditional diplomatic relationships. In his memoirs, William is not entirely honest about his relationship with Herbert, dismissing his 'coarseness' and denying there was ever any friendship between them. This was not believed at the time, when it was widely thought that the chancellor's son and the prince went prowling together, preying on the actresses in the court theatre. In later life, however, William was prepared to admit Herbert's 'astonishing' ability in the diplomatic sphere. 'Without possessing the genial nature of his father, he was without doubt his most talented and most important pupil.'[27]

Bismarck used William at first. He was popular with his grandfather and a surefire means of baiting the crown prince and his wife. At first the chancellor had a high opinion of the young man, as he told his wife, Johanna:

I have spoken to Prince William almost daily recently and have got to know him well. From this I harbour the hope that one day he'll unite the functions of emperor and chancellor! In this there is a little bit of Frederick the Great in him, but he also possesses the aptitude to become a despot like him – it is a real blessing that we have a parliamentary regime.[28]

What William was quick to discover was that the Foreign Office, or Auswärtige Amt, was just a metaphor for Otto von Bismarck:

Foreign policy was shaped by the prince alone, who only took the trouble of informing his son what he was up to; the latter issued the chancellor's commands and had them drawn up as instructions. In this way the Foreign Office was just the office of the great chancellor; very unlike the General Staff under Moltke, independent-minded people who were happy to take responsibility received no training.

'The prince lay like a mighty, erratic block of granite on the valley floor: if one had tried to move him away most of what you would find would be composed of worms and dead roots.'[29]

William none the less worshipped the ground Bismarck walked on.[30] He was his grandfather's minister; the man who had redeemed Prussia in the dark days of 1862, who had dished the liberals. Up until then he had had little opportunity to get close to the great man. Bismarck did not attend social functions in Berlin or Potsdam. The world had to come to him, above all to his well-provisioned table. It was rustic food, accompanied by excellent wines, dispensed by the prince himself. As if to stress the fact that he was a law unto himself, after lunch Bismarck would stretch out on the *chaise longue* and smoke a pipe. It was there that young William met important foreign statesmen, including the future British prime minister, Lord Rosebery.

The fleet, or Germany's lack of it, was still an obsession. In 1884 William had been allowed to attend the naval trials in Zoppot near Danzig which were organised by General Georg von Caprivi. There was some commotion when a spy was caught observing the manoeuvres from a rowing boat, dressed in a grey top hat. On interrogation it turned out to be the local judge Tirpitz, who had come out to watch his son. At the time when William first came into close contact with Bismarck he had received a letter from Henry who had visited a clutch of German traders on his travels. They had informed him that there was no need to build a fleet when British vessels were happy to offer protection. William repeated the story to Bismarck. The chancellor hit the table in fury: 'This un-German attitude must finally cease!' 'It certainly will, *Durchlaucht*, as soon as *Durchlaucht* helps us build a German fleet!'[31]

Bismarck was not the only Prussian who could see no good in a navy. The army looked down on a service which was led by a general like Caprivi on secondment and where many of the officers had been recruited from the merchant marine. There was no officer corps worthy of the name. The War Minister Bronsart von Schellendorff, for example, thought a fleet a waste of time and money. What talent there was tended to be middle class and non-Prussian, although Tirpitz was an exception in that he was born in Küstrin on the Oder. Once William became emperor he tried to reform this unglamorous image by ennobling all officers who reached the rank of captain: Tirpitz was one, Müller another.

William's training in the business of state provoked a fresh attack from his father. Fritz took up his pen and wrote the chancellor an angry letter. Further fat was added to the fire in the Neues Palais. Waldersee noted the fury the order had provoked: '. . . they find [it] outrageous, pointless and Lord knows what else besides.' Waldersee thought Fritz jealous and his wife filled with hate against her son, and the iron will of the chancellor. The mood was exacerbated by the failure of her attempts to marry her daughter to Sandro.[32]

William visited Vienna in the winter of 1886–7 and once again ambled round to Frau Wolf's welcoming establishment. What he did not realise was that the brothel-keeper was spying for Crown Prince Rudolf, who was able to report back to his military attaché in Berlin, Colonel Stein-inger. According to Rudolf, William 'in his cups' spoke disrespectfully about Francis Joseph, comparing Rudolf to his own father as a 'vain, artistic, literary, Jew-loving [*verjudeten*], popularity-seeker, without char-acter or virtue etc.'. He predicted that the Austrian state would wither away and that Germany would mop up the German-speaking provinces, while the Habsburgs were left with Hungary. 'He said he liked hunting with us, we were all pleasant fellows, but useless, effeminate epicures.' He spoke ill of his parents and his wife and 'concluded this edifying conversation with two dirty females'. Rudolf added that he possessed the manuscript of a letter to Frau Wolf written five years earlier which revealed a similar lack of care and tact.[33]

William was still under the influence of both Waldersee and Herbert Bismarck, a curious blend. On the one hand it drove him to seek a confrontation with Russia; on the other it schooled him in the old principle of Prussian foreign policy which had reigned since the Great Frederick's time: to keep Russia on your side. Herbert's teaching also took the edge off William's incipient racialism, but the desire to win his spurs in war, as his father had done, tipped the balance against Bismarck and Russia. Waldersee reassured him that the expansion of the army which was then taking place would set the ball rolling again; it would provoke the Russians. This pleased William.[34]

6

Countdown

In January 1887 Fritz fell ill with an inflammation of the larynx. His hoarse voice began to cause concern. His own doctor, August Wegner, thought he was suffering from a cold, but symptoms persisted and he saw a specialist. Geheimrat Professor Karl Gerhardt thought he noticed signs of cancer and tried to remove the swelling with a wire loop.* In the acrimonious battle between the doctors which followed, the British specialist Morell Mackenzie accused Gerhardt of having turned the growth malignant. Sir Felix Semon, a German-Jewish throat specialist who had become a naturalised Briton, agreed with him. It was the inauspicious beginning of what must rank as one of the most vituperative medical quarrels in history.[1]

It was the man who had examined William's ears, Bergmann, now president of the German surgeons' association, who was called in. He was a political liberal, and passed for a friend of the crown prince. He was never, at any time, William's tool. He also thought the lump was cancerous, and proposed immediate surgical intervention. William maintained that Bergmann's initial suggestion was that his father should merely have a cordotomy, extracting the affected vocal cord, and not the entire larynx as in a tracheotomy. Bergmann was relying on recent advances in medicine: the use of the cannula had been discovered in the middle of the century, and the first tracheotomy coupled with an extraction of the tumor had been carried out by the German surgeon, Theodor Billroth, in Vienna, as recently as 1873. The patient was released three months later, but the cancer returned.

For the time being the story was covered up. Fritz was said to have a severe cold and went off for a cure. By 15 May it was clear to those close to the court that the spell in Ems had not helped and that something much more serious was wrong with the crown prince. Bergmann was sanguine. He thought he could remove the growth and that would

---

* Mackenzie said he used 'snares and a sharp spoon'.

suffice. The idea that Bergmann could have managed with just a minor operation seems to have been true, even if most specialists claimed that the entire voice-box would have to be extracted to give the best chance of success. It was and remains a risky operation.[2]

On 16 May the doctors involved on the case met and decided to call in Morell Mackenzie. The German-trained Mackenzie, who had the reputation of being the top European throat specialist, had compiled the standard work on diseases of the larynx. In Britain he was known to be a firm opponent of surgery, but this does not seem to have been communicated to Germany. The use of the Scotsman, it was thought, would be popular with the Anglophil crown prince and his wife. They were right. Vicky wrote a telegram begging her mother to send Mackenzie at once. She was still undecided as to whether to back the operation or not. The queen despatched her own physician, Sir James Reid, to Mackenzie's house at 19 Harley Street to alert him to the urgency of the case. The doctors also wired the physician, but did not tell him whom he would have to treat. Sir James's mission, however, must have made it abundantly clear and Mackenzie makes out that he knew who the patient was. On the same day both the emperor and the chancellor were informed of Fritz's problem. The omniscient Bismarck already knew all about it.[3]

Like Mackenzie, Bismarck opposed surgical intervention. He thought decisions were being made about the German crown prince by foreigners, who had no right to venture an opinion; he may have been referring to the Russian, Bergmann, or the Scottish Mackenzie. It was more likely, however, that he was referring to the crown princess.[4] Fritz's hoarseness had begun to set German tongues wagging. By the middle of 1887 it became clear to the court that William's father was seriously unwell.[5]

On 17 May Bergmann proposed carrying out a thyreotomy,* a new operation which involved splitting the larynx to stop the swelling. The German doctors agreed, and even Vicky was ready to give the go-ahead on the 18th. Mackenzie left London the next day, arriving on the 20th. He had forgotten to bring his instruments with him, but immediately countermanded the reigning view. Vicky had already set aside a room for the operation and a bed had been ordered to be brought over from the Charité Hospital, but Mackenzie literally 'took the knife out of the German doctors' hands'.[6] The Scot was able to present some statistics to show how risky Bergmann's course would be: from twenty-two case histories, 27 per cent had died on the operating table and 55 per cent had expired before two years had elapsed. Only two cases had lived for

---

* Equivalent to a tracheotomy.

longer. Bergmann disputed Mackenzie's evidence. He could find more examples of survivors.[7]

He examined Fritz, whose voice was reduced to the strength of a 'gruff whisper'. After borrowing the necessary tools, Mackenzie cut a small piece of tissue about the size of a split pea from Fritz's larynx and gave it to Wegner, who, resplendent in a general's uniform, took a *Droschke* round to the Pathological Institute and delivered it up to Rudolf Virchow's laboratory, a place of skulls and skeletons. Sadly the sample was not enough for the great man. Even so the rumour spread that Fritz had cancer from the very fact that the pathologist's advice had been sought. He needed more for his examination but suspected the problem was no more than pachydermia laryngis, a warty condition of the larynx.

On 23 May Mackenzie endeavoured to get Virchow another sample – this time with his own forceps, which had been posted from London – but was unable to dislodge any more of the swollen tissue. Bergmann was making no bones about his diagnosis, and the story of Fritz's cancer was now out. William went to see his father, remaining at his bedside until 11 p.m., 'profoundly shaken'. On 7 June Mackenzie went home having stifled all hopes of an operation. The German medical profession was effectively sent back to its kennels.[8] Almost immediately informed opinion in Germany turned against Mackenzie, marking him down as an 'artful swindler'.[9]

Mackenzie decided that Fritz was not suffering from cancer at all, but perichonditis. Vicky was triumphant: 'only perichonditis', she reported; but according to Mackenzie's own book, perichonditis left the patient completely without hope. It could not be healed, only palliated. Although it should be added that perichonditis is not a malignant condition. There was also a possibility that it was none of the above, but tertiary syphilis, the result of that fateful coupling in Suez.[10] There are indications that Mackenzie was well aware of the gravity of the illness, perichonditis or cancer. At the beginning of 1888 he told Fritz's marshal, Graf Hugo Radolinski, that the crown prince would probably die before the year was out. After the examination he was invited to Potsdam. It was clear that Fritz was going to appoint him his personal physician. It was now in his interest to prolong the crown prince's life, and that was only manageable if the operation were not carried out.[11]

William asserted that when Vicky and Fritz heard Morell Mackenzie's milder prognosis they accepted it because they wanted it to be the case. Fritz desperately desired to become emperor. Vicky had received a mild warning from her mother. The royal physician Sir William Jenner had told her that Mackenzie was a money-grubber, but had added that he doubtless knew his stuff when it came to larynxes.[12] Fritz had said himself that 'A Kaiser without a larynx is incapable of carrying out his office.'

There was some question as to whether he would be allowed to become German emperor. Bismarck was able to put his mind at rest. There was nothing in the constitution which stipulated that the ruler should be able to speak. Queen Victoria was playing a role behind the scenes. She was concerned that Fritz might not be able to attend her Jubilee. It was she who contrived to have Fritz treated in Britain. Not even Vicky knew the full extent of her machinations.[13]

Bismarck's interpretation of the case was far less charitable. He believed – or said he did – that Vicky refused to allow the operation to take place because she preferred the idea of being an emperor's widow to being the wife of a living prince. He thought he had the measure of both of them now. He had begun to recognise that neither really wanted power, just the outward trappings, 'and a little, and a little too much, the use of power'. It must have come as a relief after so many years. He knew he could deal with people like that.[14] The crisis pushed William yet further into opposition to his parents, whose court had become 'the epicentre of the plot'. He sided with Bismarck and Bergmann and the German physicians, although his tantrums made the former uncomfortable and there were renewed moves to have him banished to the provinces.[15] William thought Mackenzie was a charlatan and that his parents were deluding themselves. He maintained his low opinion of the Scottish physician to his dying day. He did not consider that Mackenzie believed his own diagnosis:

... the speed with which he got hold not only of his money but also his English title* – without first of all waiting to see if his treatment had had any success – speaks against him.[16]

Bergmann also thought Mackenzie was unconvinced by his own diagnosis. He suspected that the Scotsman knew that Fritz was incurable, but for various reasons had set about prolonging his life and trying, where possible, to alleviate his suffering. Failing to operate might allow him to rule – briefly; award him an empire without power and, this was important to Vicky at least, keep William away from the throne for as long as possible. If this is true, then Mackenzie's appointment was a political decision, about which Bergmann was ignorant. As one modern writer has put it: 'Mackenzie had no hope of preventing death from making his entry. He only wanted to ensure that it approached the invalid's bed wearing velvet soles.'[17]

Bergmann was also shaky on one or two medical points when it came to the throat, which gave the Scotsman and author of the textbook an

---

* Vicky asked her mother to thank Mackenzie by conferring a knighthood on him. William mistakenly thought this had something to do with *Adel* – nobility.

advantage. Bergmann was not going to be put out. He practised for the operation – on a corpse! The two rival groups of doctors divided over medical ethics. Mackenzie felt he was justified in not talking about cancer because Virchow had failed to prove that the growth was malignant, nor could he intervene until it was certain that there was cancer. The Germans took the opposite view: you could only do nothing if you were certain that the lump was benign.[18]

II

On 22 April Vicky wrote a long letter to her mother, in which she set out her current views on her eldest son. He had fallen in with a bad lot, such as his brother-in-law Ernest Günther of Schleswig-Holstein.

Vain and selfish they both are, and they both hold the most superficial rubbishy political views – rank retrograde and chauvinist nonsense in which they, in their childish ignorance, are quite fanatical ... William's judgment is being warped, his mind poisoned by this! He is not sharp enough or experienced enough to see through the system, nor through the people, and they do with him what they like. He is so headstrong, so impatient of any control, except the Emperor's, and so suspicious of everyone who might be only a half-hearted supporter of Bismarck's that it is quite useless to attempt to enlighten him ... I hope you will not take any notice of this when you see William and be as kind to him as usual – the reverse would do no good, he would not understand it, and only put his back up. I think and hope his visit to England may do him a deal of good, as he is fond of being there and has been far too little! He would be delighted to travel, see India, America, China and Australia, but the Emperor will not let him.[19]

William's relations with his rather less priggish grandfather were not permanently damaged by his moral crusade against gambling. In the spring of 1887 the Kaiser inspected his regiment in the Lustgarten: 'the friendly nod of his head expressed his total satisfaction.' That summer his grandson presented him with a new invention – a machine-gun. It was not the machine which had been peddled by Elisabeth Wedel, rather the creation of the 12th earl of Dundonald, called a 'galloping machine gun'. It had ten barrels turned by a crank.[20]

William was looking after his regiment hoping that way to keep his men out of low dives. He built the First Foot Guards a new mess in Potsdam, employing one of his mother's protégés, the architect Ernst Ihne, to carry out the plans. It was the first time William commissioned Ihne, whose ponderous baroque buildings would eventually litter the capital and earn him his entry into the nobility. The mess was uncharacteristically gothic, and William was able to garner presents of stained glass from his relatives to render a proper mediaeval tone. His Uncle Bertie was kind enough to donate a chimney-piece. It was typical that Ihne should add his sixpence to a barracks which had been up until then the work of two of the greatest architects in Potsdam: Ludwig Persius and Karl Friedrich Schinkel.[21]

Fritz and Vicky had picked up on the idea of banishing William to some distant garrison. 'Earlier this might have made a lot of sense,' wrote Waldersee, 'now it makes none, and besides, the emperor would never give his consent.'[22] It was old William's ninetieth birthday on 22 March. The Berliners showed their respect by lighting candles and setting them up between the panes of their double windows: 'the effect of this soft, white light everywhere was beautiful and unique'. The emperor's subjects put cornflowers in their lapels for the parade. Crown Prince Rudolf came up to Berlin for the celebrations and spent time with William as well as with his parents, deftly pretending to be the intimate of both. William poured scorn on everyone from Fritz and Vicky to Queen Victoria and Uncle Bertie.[23] Once again there was speculation as to what would happen when the old man died. Fritz's friend Franz Freiherr von Roggenbach told Waldersee that the 'imperial lunacy' had by no means abated: 'That the crown prince's imperium [would] start with questions of etiquette, such as names, coronations etc., and very quickly there would be arguments with the prince [Bismarck].'[24]

In May 1887 William received a controversial order from his grandfather to represent him at Queen Victoria's Jubilee, as his own father had been bundled off to Ems to take a cure and was apparently too ill to attend. Vicky was predictably furious. She wrote to her mother, making the decision look as if it had been entirely of William's making: 'I hope you won't be angry about William. I'm certain he didn't want to be impertinent. It is only his nastiness, his lack of consideration, tact and thought, which makes his say such stupid things.'[25] William was at his most Anglophobic. He thought it 'high time the old woman died' and told Eulenburg, 'One cannot have enough hatred for England.'[26] He was mad keen to go for all that. He summoned Bissing, Kessel and Hahnke and they crossed the North Sea on the torpedo boat *Blitz*, commanded by a certain Captain Tirpitz. The boat drifted up to Lowestoft on the East Anglian coast and had to be fetched down to the Thames by a pilot vessel.

With all the the in-fighting between the Hohenzollerns, William, Dona and another William – the first of Queen Victoria's great-grandchildren was to undertake his maiden voyage abroad in the company of his parents – were not put up at Buckingham Palace. Spencer House overlooking James's Park was rented for them instead. In the sumptuous

Palladian house they found a book in the smoking room setting out exactly what was due to take place over the next few days. As the Prussian general Hahnke pored over the instructions they were met by General McNeill, who was sent to liaise with the party: 'My dear Hanky,' he said, 'if you intend to go by this book, you will always be wrong, for everything will either be changed or has already...'[27]

McNeill had given wise advice. The organisation lacked a certain Prussian thoroughness. At a banquet William found that he had no seat as the original setting of oval tables had been replaced by one square one. He tried his best to square the circle and locate his new place. To his surprise – possibly horror too – he discovered he had placed himself next to the 'dark-skinned' sister of King Kala Kua of Hawaii. The king, it transpired, had paid him a visit in Potsdam. Later, in an obvious snub, Dona was placed behind the queen of Hawaii. William noted kindly in later life that small incidents of this sort failed to mar the unique flavour of the queen's Jubilee.[28]

William did not stay long at Spencer House. He lodged for a while with Lord Cadogan, then Lord Privy Seal. He met the German-speaking Chancellor of the Exchequer, George Goschen, whose grandfather had had a famous publishing house in Leipzig. Goschen's son Edward would be the unpopular ambassador to Berlin at the time of the outbreak of the First World War.

The great moment was of course the Jubilee celebrations. Queen Victoria came out of mourning for the first time since Albert's death twenty-six years earlier as she rode in an open carriage to Westminster Abbey flanked by horse guards and Indian cavalry. She was accompanied by thirty-two mounted princes, including Fritz, in the uniform of the Pasewalk Cuirassiers. It was the last time William recalled seeing his father on a horse. The surgeon Sir Felix Semon, noticed Fritz's deathly pallor as he rode by; not Lohengrin, he thought, more the Commendatore from *Don Giovanni*.[29]

The medical world was becoming involved in the crown prince's plight. On 4 June a throat specialist called Dr Butlin published a paper in the *British Medical Journal* in which he questioned the sagacity of coming to a conclusion on the basis of a single sample from the growth. Three or four would be required: '... there is still no proof that Dr Mackenzie is right and the German doctors are wrong.'[30] On 8 June Mackenzie did indeed cut away some more tissue, but without consulting Virchow he immediately put it about that there was no cause for alarm. The tissue was 'completely healthy'. Unfortunately Virchow's contribution to the debate was not much more positive. On 9 June he published his findings in the *Deutsche medizinische Wochenschrift*. The pathologist could find no cancer either and wondered whether the growth was not a pachydermia verracosa, or throat wart. He sat on the fence. The sample he had received had been benign. He left his judgement open.[31]

III

Vicky and Fritz did not return. They jumped ship. In Germany eyebrows were raised and the word 'desertion' muttered. They began a tragicomic 'vagabond life' which started in the Queen's Hotel on Beulah Hill in Upper Norwood in the south London suburbs – from there it was an easy distance to Mackenzie's surgery – and ended in the Villa Zirio on the Italian Riviera. In the meantime Vicky made arrangements with her mother to secrete away all her and her husband's papers in a strongroom at Buckingham Palace. The odyssey was sanctioned by Mackenzie, whom German officialdom was ever happier to write off as a 'quack' and who was equally hotly defended by Vicky. One writer has gone so far as to say, 'It is an impressive fact that the demon Coburger had enchanted him to such an extent that Fritz deserted his post.'[32]

Queen Victoria and Mackenzie had been determined to get Fritz out of Germany. According to Bismarck's friend, Lucius von Ballhausen, he told the minister Friedberg: 'I am not just convinced, I know for certain! If the prince came back with me into my surgery like any other mortal, he would be healed in four to six weeks.'[33] On 28 June he extracted some more of the growth and despatched it to Virchow in Berlin. The pathologist had an *idée fixe* about throat warts and persisted in seeing only benignancy in his samples. When Mackenzie included some pus after the twelfth examination, Virchow decided it was boiled egg, or porridge.[34] Still he said there was no cause for concern. He had not changed his tune on 8 August, after he had followed his patient to the Isle of Wight. Fritz stayed at Norris Castle, lent by the Duke of Bedford, Mackenzie at Carlton Villa in East Cowes. He upset etiquette by writing directly to the queen: it was still only 'a question of time' before Fritz made a full recovery.[35]

Accompanied by Doctors Wegner, Landgraf and the English surgeon Mark Hovell, the party went up to Braemar in the Highlands on 9 August, where the weather was anything but ideal for someone suffering from a disease of the throat. Virtually all the doctors who had any knowledge of the case were prone to condemn Mackenzie, his methods and his persistent optimism. Many – Sir Felix Semon included – thought that Mackenzie's continued refusal to accept the diagnosis of his German counterparts and his opposition to the operation, robbed the crown prince of any chance of longer life. On the other hand Queen Victoria, her eldest daughter and her husband clung to Mackenzie like drowning men to a life-raft. At Vicky's request, the queen actually knighted Mackenzie on 2 September. Fritz wrote to his mother-in-law to thank her, adding that the distinction 'will not be grudged ... except perhaps by those whose talent and experience were not equal to his own'.

It was quite clear that Fritz had put his faith in Mackenzie and Mackenzie alone.[36] On the following day, 6 September, they left England and travelled via Frankfurt to Munich where the staff of the Prussian consulate and the Bavarian princes were lined up on the platform to greet them. They stayed at the Vier Jahreszeiten hotel. Eulenburg, who was there, remarked that his clear opposition to, and supercilious attitude towards, the German princes did not make him popular with the Bavarian royal family. The next day they departed for Toblach in the Tyrol.[37]

With them came the faithful Götz von Seckendorff of the First Foot. He was an excellent painter and shared with Vicky a talent for languages and an interest in the arts. In his younger days he had been something of an adventurer, had travelled to India with the Prince of Wales and Abyssinia with Lord Napier.[38] There was already plenty of gossip about Vicky's relationship with her courtier, and the all-seeing Fritz von Holstein had a file on him. According to him, Fritz was not just a 'hero in carpet-slippers', he was also a cuckold. He may well have been correct.[39]

Once again the weather made Toblach an odd choice. In his *apologia* Mackenzie says he told them to go south if it got cold. When he arrived in Toblach himself he advised Venice for their next port of call. Near Toblach, in Innichen, Fritz saw the church of S. Candido which he thought would serve as a model for his mausoleum. The architect Raschdorff produced a pastiche of the building next to Potsdam's Friedenskirche not long after. Vicky and Seckendorff went up a mountain together and ended up having to stay the night in a remote hut. Naturally there were more scandals, and Holstein added another letter to his Seckendorff file. It is impossible to believe that they failed to reach William's sensitive ears. There were, after all, plenty of people around who were ready to fill him in. A propos, the courtier Graf Radolinski was discovered to be spying for the crown prince's enemies. There was very nearly a duel between him and Seckendorff.[40]

Fritz was reduced to a shadow of himself. He was entirely subject to his wife's whims and wishes, which involved dragging him from pillar to post across Europe without allowing him the time to repose. To occupy his mind he took to cutting out articles about himself from the papers and sticking them into his diary. Those who, like the doctors Landgraf and Wegner, disagreed with her or Mackenzie, were dismissed from the gypsy camp.

IV

Once he had returned to Potsdam, William held a dinner on 7 June for Eulenburg and Waldersee. He was still fuming about his treatment at the Jubilee, and Mackenzie, and questioning the need to employ a foreign physician. William complained of the distance between himself and his father, and of his mother's opposition to Germany. Eulenburg recognised a similarly indomitable will in William. He thought his father's coming to power would mean, in reality, rule by his mother, and that betokened the 'ruin of the Fatherland'. For her part she had told him that as soon as Fritz died she would leave Germany: 'I shall not stay in a country where I receive only hate and not a spark of love.'[41]

The younger generation of Hohenzollerns were once again up in arms over Sandro. The former prince of Bulgaria had retired to garrison life in his native Darmstadt where he had struck up an intimate relationship with a singer at the court theatre called Johanna Loisinger. It was Henry's turn to grill the former ruler. Sandro was not exactly frank. If his heart was elsewhere, his ambitions still lay with the idea of marrying into the imperial family. 'Princess Victoria', he said, 'is free to marry whomsoever she wants, I shall be the first to offer my congratulations when she becomes engaged to someone else.'[42] William was spreading ugly stories around the officer corps that Sandro had taken money from the Russians before biting the hands that had fed him. Sandro was at pains to refute the allegations. He was unnerved by Fritz's illness: he was aware that once William came to the throne there would be no question of his receiving Moretta's hand.[43]

The next day William and Eulenburg went up to his Prussian country seat, Liebenberg, together for the first time. They were going to do some stalking in the Uckermark woods despite Eulenburg's abhorrence of hunting. Eulenburg saw how difficult it was for William to shoot, as he needed to rest his shotgun on a servant's arm: 'Not every stag was prepared to do him a favour! The prince missed two stags and winged a third.'[44] Politically, both William and Eulenburg were convinced of the necessity of upholding the Russian alliance at the time. Eulenburg thought that there might have been something self-consciously old-Prussian about this Russophilia, that it derived from a reading of Frederick the Great's still unpublished Political Testament.[45] William expressed his fury at the way he had been received by his English cousins. He thought his mother was putting together a treacherous family league against Prussia.

Eulenburg had been offered the directorship of the theatre in Weimar, but William convinced him to remain in the diplomatic service. Perhaps he thought William might give him the job of intendant to the royal theatres, but he did not otherwise want a position at court. It was held by Bolko von Hochberg, who was hated in Bayreuth for his opposition to Wagner. William was prepared to back Eulenburg's candidature at that time. They returned to Berlin on the 11th, and met up with Herbert Bismarck 'and drank more than was good for them'. Herbert saw William as a trump card to be used in the event of the Liberal, South German element getting the upper hand in the Prusso-German Reich. Even then he tended to make noises about his addiction to old Prussia, without fully understanding what that involved. Once again part of the attraction was the fact that the 'Prussian idea' was anathema to his parents.[46]

In August William and Eulenburg again attended the Wagner Festival in Bayreuth and stayed on Starnberg Lake. Not everyone in Germany was as enchanted with Eulenburg as William was, and some people thought the friendship unhealthy. His interest in the supernatural was well-known and the belief that he was leading the prince into mysticism made him unpopular at court. He was also fey and prissy, and acutely hypochondriac; while his dilettantism meant that his excursions into the arts had little staying power and even less gravitas.[47]

On 7 September 1887 a new directive was issued. It prolonged William's service with the administration by a year and widened his training to include the Ministry of Finance. Here he was taught by the civil Servant Meinecke, whose briefings he found dry. He confessed later that financial matters never became wholly interesting to him until he appointed Johannes Miquel to the Ministry. Bismarck, worried about William's relative immaturity (although he noted with satisfaction that he was the same age as Frederick the Great when he came to the throne), and lack of perception, endeavoured to make sure that he enjoyed good counsel at all times. Two civil servants were attached to his household: the elderly Geheimrat Professor Rudolf von Gneist from the University of Berlin and Regierungsrat Hans von Brandenstein. To provide military advice William had the services of General Adolf von Wittich.[48]

Later that month William went on an extensive journey stopping off to do a little hunting in Hungary and Styria before joining his parents in northern Italy. In Mürzsteg he managed to have a meeting with two prostitutes which had been frustrated in Vienna by an over-protective sentry. They were Ella Sommssich and Anna Homolatsch. Ella had been William's mistress in Berlin and knew his tastes. She had procured Anna for the threesome, who had 'very beautiful hands'. They made a great deal of noise in a room at the inn, Zum König von Sachsen, disturbing the other guests. As once again William was not ready to give them the sum they desired, they stole his monogrammed cufflinks. Anna later claimed to have borne William another daughter. Eventually state funds had to be found to keep them quiet too.[49]

V

After a stay in Venice, the crown prince and his wife had moved to Baveno on Lake Maggiore where they took the Villa Clara. There they celebrated Fritz's last birthday. Queen Victoria had tested the house eight years before and planted two trees in the garden. William visited them there in October and there were a few moments of calm between him and Vicky. She talked to him about her admiration for the artistry of the Italians and together they went to Borromeo Island, where, said Vicky, Goethe composed his poem *Kennst du das Land wo die Zitronen blühn*. Another visitor was Mackenzie who arrived on 30 October. His boundless optimism must have been shaken by the sight of a growth on the previously unaffected right vocal cord.[50]

When Fritz and Vicky settled down in the Villa Zirio among the Ligurian olive groves above San Remo on the Italian Riviera on 3 November, the odyssey entered its antepenultimate phase. The Zirios drove a hard bargain. 'It is very expensive,' wrote Vicky, 'but new and clean and quite comfortable ...' It was another example of her own overriding optimism: there was no bathroom and no oven, but a small garden under the palms with an artificial grotto allowed Fritz to lie in the sun on his *chaise longue*.[51] The German press, with Bismarck behind them, had mounted a campaign against Mackenzie. When William arrived at the villa on 17 October it led to scenes.

Mackenzie made his first visit to San Remo on 5 November, by which time Fritz was coughing up lumps of tissue and the growth had got larger. Mackenzie examined him the next day. The lump 'had a distinctly malignant look'. Fritz asked him outright, 'Is it cancer?' 'I am sorry to say, Sir, that it looks like that. But one cannot be entirely certain.' So much for Mackenzie's vaunted unevasiveness![52] The larynx looked too angry to allow for another sample to be detached and Mackenzie was now sufficiently alarmed to seek a few more opinions. A Professor von Schrötter was called in from Vienna and a Dr Krause from Berlin. The three of them had a meeting in the Hôtel de la Méditerranée to discuss what to do. The news travelled swiftly back to Berlin. Hildegard von Spitzemberg noted, 'The prophecies of the German doctors seem to have been only too quickly fulfilled.'[53]

William was determined to get rid of Mackenzie. On 7 November a note of exasperation crept into Waldersee's diary: 'I don't think it's right that Prince William is going to San Remo. He certainly can't be of any help and against his mother's will he will never succeed in removing the English doctor; there will be angry scenes which will excite even more a father already deserving of pity.'[54] William returned to San Remo on the 9th, together with Professor Moritz Schmidt from Frankfurt, and convened another medical conference in the hotel. Mackenzie says he never learned what they discussed as he was called away, but it was almost certainly whether to go ahead with the tracheotomy. Schmidt was determined to believe that Fritz was suffering from an infection which he had had for many years and wanted to treat the throat with potassium iodide. Schrötter thought he was talking nonsense. Mackenzie may have believed that too. According to one of the journalists covering the story, he told Vicky the unpleasant truth, and she slapped his face.[55]

William wanted his mother to see sense and consent to an operation which might save his father's life. Both William and Schmidt had orders from the emperor to report back on his son's condition. His mother continued to be unsympathetic. She accused him of wanting to accelerate his father's death in order to come to the throne more quickly.[56] When William arrived, he was determined to see his father. Vicky tried to prevent him from doing so and stood at the bottom of the stairs to bar the way to Fritz's room. 'She treated me like a dog,' William said later.

She feared above all the collapse of the house of cards upon which she had based her hopes ... Standing at the bottom of the stairs, I was obliged to hear her reproaches at my behaviour and accept her decisive refusal to let me see my father; I was to leave immediately and continue my journey on to Rome...

Vicky said that his father's health had improved but 'I could see from the stony look on her face, which had completely altered since Baveno, that she was not telling the truth.' At that point William heard a door open and Fritz appeared at the top of the stairs with a smile on his face. William rushed to greet him and his father whispered his joy at seeing his eldest son. 'In the following difficult days we both came inwardly very close to one another.'[57]

Vicky's account of the famous meeting is slightly different. When William arrived,

He was as rude, as disagreeable and as impertinent to me as possible ... but I pitched into him with, I am afraid, considerable violence, and he became quite nice and gentle and amiable (for him) – at least quite natural, and we got on very well!

Vicky squashed his assertion that he was carrying out the emperor's orders, and told him that Schmidt was part of a general plot to spirit Fritz away to Berlin and subject him to the operation.

William is of course much too young and inexperienced to understand all this! He was merely put up to it at Berlin! He thought he was to save his Papa from my mismanagement!! When he has not his head stuffed with rubbish at Berlin he is quite nice and *traitable*, and then we are very pleased to have him; but I will not have him dictate to me – the head on my shoulders is every bit as good as his.[58]

William was still much taken up with his father's condition. He wrote to his former tutor Hinzpeter on 11 November, 'I would never have believed that tears could come as a relief, for I had never known them before [sic]. Today I felt they brought some relief from frightful pain. A blow, a bullet, anything would be better than this most horrifying of all diseases.'[59]

Fritz's friend General Loë thought William sensible in his attitude to his father and his illness. 'He recently spoke to Prince William in Basel in the course of his journey from San Remo to Berlin and had a very lively impression of the prince's deep unhappiness, his admiration for his heroic father, of his correct judgement of the situation, his reasonable thinking, and his own intentions.'[60] On the way back from Basel, William stopped in Munich to see Eulenburg, whose new play *Seestern* was opening in Berlin on the 25th.

He described his father as 'without hope' and told Waldersee as much on the 14th. Even an operation would only prolong his life by a few months. In Berlin old William consulted the doctors, who advised against an operation, saying it was now too late – the fault of the physician who had advised against surgery earlier that year. The problem had been Vicky. In the end William had parted from his father in peace. His mother was now associated in Germany with the 'English doctor' and the press were mounting a campaign against this 'unscrupulous man'. While he was in San Remo William had had an argument with his brother Henry, whom he had found to be under his mother's thumb. He had told Henry that it was 'highly questionable that a man who couldn't speak could be king of Prussia'; a statement which, though cruel, echoed Fritz's own earlier appraisal of the situation. In the case of his grandfather dying first, he wanted a regency.[61]

Eulenburg stayed in the guest-house at the Marmorpalais in Potsdam on the 22nd. William was still fulminating against Mackenzie who 'bears sole responsibility for this catastrophe'. 'The prince considers and reflects on everything down to the smallest detail, in order to be armed for every eventuality. No one can accuse him of lacking energy ...' Eulenburg sang, as usual. He had a way of calming William's nerves. At least, most of the time. On occasions the pathos reduced William to tears. The next day was the press viewing of *Seestern* by Ivar Svenson,

Eulenburg's *nom de plume*. He had lunch with William afterwards and when they had finished they walked round to the barracks of the Hussar Guards through a dark and wet Potsdam. 'I felt nothing of [the bad weather] because now that his fate was decided, the prince told me what he intended to do.'[62]

It looked clear that Bismarck, through the aged emperor, was set to give William powers to represent the Reich. William informed his father, who burst into tears when he received the news, threatening to go up to Berlin to sort things out. An official communication from Bismarck was confiscated by Vicky, who refused to show it to her husband. Fritz launched another strong protest. Roggenbach tried to step in and smooth the crown prince's ruffled feathers. 'He might have impressed magnanimity on the crown prince, but the crown princess was not the woman to take her hand off the reins of power a moment earlier than she had to.'[63] Fritz's blessing was withheld. There was never to be the peaceful takeover of power, and the fact that William had his own programme and was very keen to enact it, made the situation all the more galling for the inhabitants of the Villa Zirio.

The order became formal on the 18th, on the same day that William received the Tsar. Relations continued highly strained between Germany and Russia. There was talk of war. At Bismarck's suggestion William went to meet him on his train at Wittenberge, but the visit was not a success. William's soft touch with the Russian emperor was not enough to convince him to stay in the Berlin Schloss, and he elected to put up at the Russian embassy in the Linden instead. There had been a series of tit-for-tat actions at both courts: the Russians stopped the purchase of land by German nationals; the Germans ceased honouring Russian letters of change 'for fear of people making war on us with our own money'. The tension mounted but Bismarck would not give in to those like Waldersee who longed for a pre-emptive strike. Eventually the Russians backed down and the Tsar signed the Reinsurance Treaty, and William was once again praised for his diplomatic skills.[64]

The old emperor had asked Moltke to brief him on the situation, and what would be Germany's chances in the event of war. Moltke warned him of the danger of fighting on two fronts and pointed to the anti-German hue and cry from the Pan-Slavs. The emperor ordered a new railway network to be constructed in the east, to facilitate the movement of troops. On 3 February 1888 he licensed the publication of the Austro-German Treaty. The last word in the war scare of the 1880s came from the chancellor Bismarck when he stood up in the Reichstag on 6 February and declared: 'We have a desire for peace but we will also not shrink from a decision to take up arms if that is forced upon us. We Germans fear God, but nothing else in the world.' William and Dona were there to hear the speech.[65]

Life was accelerating for William, but there were still cultural distractions, and not all of them were orchestrated by Eulenburg. In the afternoon of 24 November 1887 Chelius played the Death March from *Götterdämmerung* on the piano. The next day William presented to Bismarck his controversial proclamation to the German princes, where he advanced the view that they should not be seen as vassals – as his father did – but as colleagues to be consulted.[66] It lay six weeks in the chancellor's drawer while 'the prince waited bootlessly for praise from his master'. Unlike Eulenburg, who believed the thoughts it contained were 'excellent, clear and simply expressed',[67] the chancellor took a dim view, and when pressed, told him to burn it.[68]

VI

The almost certain presence of cancer and Fritz's decision not to go ahead with the laryngotomy were reported in the official *Reichsanzeiger* on 15 November. It was tantamount to saying that he could not be saved. For his part, Mackenzie was still trying anything to avoid mentioning the fatal diagnosis. He left San Remo on 18 November but returned on 15 December. In January 1888 the crown prince developed a temperature and there were emissions of pus. His breath began to smell. When he coughed up a slough it was duly sent to Virchow, but again the pathologist could find no malignancy.[69] Fritz would not agree to the total operation, but he consented to the tracheotomy, if that was strictly necessary.

In that month of November 1887 William had further proof that not everything he chose to do would win Bismarck's approval. On the 28th he held a gathering in Waldersee's flat to promote the idea of Christian love as an alternative to socialism. He had thrown himself in with the movement around the anti-Semitic court preacher Adolf Stoecker and it proved both a stumbling-block to good relations and a battle of wills between his two demigods, the chancellor and Waldersee. Stoecker was a controversial and indefatigable evangelical pastor who had preached: 'The misery of Berlin cries out to Heaven and every Christian is called forth to take up the fight. Help me! I cannot do it alone!'[70] In an attempt to rid the working classes of their Godlessness and poverty he visited homes, prisons and hostels for drunks and lured the poor into his church by handing out bread rolls.

Stoecker would hardly have been seen as such a pariah had it not been for his attitude to the Jews. The Jews were Stoecker's political opponents in the Fortschrittspartei, or the Progressive Liberals. In 1879 he made a speech entitled 'Unsere Forderungen an das moderne Judentum' (Our Demands to Modern Jewry) in which he appealed for 'A little more modesty, a little more tolerance [and] a little more equality.' He was particularly opposed to the Jewish control of large parts of the press and a certain sort of unfeeling capitalism which, he believed, was a badge of their race. Some – respectable – commentators have said that Stoecker was not a racial, but a political, anti-Semite. He none the less became the undeniable focal point of racial anti-Semitism too, and that movement came to a head during William's flirtation with Stoecker in 1888.[76]

The evangelical theologian Friedrich von Bodelschwingh painted the Jews in rather more lurid colours, but the message was the same: 'Stoecker never attacked the Jewish religion, quite the opposite, [he attacked] irreligious Jews who had thrown out the beliefs of their fore-fathers and who, with alienated Christians, were united in hatred against the cross, throne and altar.'[72] It was Waldersee's American revivalist wife who was the most taken in by it all. She was close to Dona and it was William's wife who encouraged him to back the movement which she had supported since 1882. William remembered, in particular, a 'crushing description of the miserable life lived in Berlin's slums'.[73]

William was enchanted by Stoecker, who reminded him of Luther.[74] Bismarck was not so impressed. He thought him a hypocrite in a dog collar. William continued to attend the Stadtmission, causing loud pro-tests from the press, who were suing Stoecker at the time. Waldersee thought the press was entirely Jewish-controlled, so this did not matter. Under Stoecker and Eulenburg's influence, William became more and more outspoken about the Jews. On 8 December he told Minister von Puttkamer, in the course of a court hunt, that the Jewish press should be muzzled. Puttkamer replied in a matter-of-fact way that such an action would be against the law. William told him to scrap the law.

The press would not be silenced. By the 15th a scandal had erupted. Waldersee saw William at the hunt. He was being cornered by Herbert Bismarck who was endeavouring to convince him to drop his support for Stoecker. His court marshal Liebenau did the same. Waldersee was resigned to this new turn of events: 'Words don't help, so many people are influenced by the Jews.' Shortly afterwards Bismarck declared war on Stoecker through his paid 'reptiles' in the pages of the semi-official *Norddeutsche allgemeine Zeitung*. William was under direct attack. The chancellor's intention was to frighten William away from his new friend. He looked set to launch a new *Kulturkampf*, this time against the Luther-ans: 'The Protestant clergy are now the chief danger' ... 'We want no rule by women and priests.'[75]

William was hurt at being abandoned by Bismarck, who then conveyed his thoughts on the subject by the post: '... no greater disservice can be done to the imperial house than by letting yourself be made into a protector of one-sided party-politics and one, too, that has adopted this extreme path which public opinion has sought to stamp it with.' Bismarck counselled William to model himself on Frederick the Great, the states-man and the general. Stoecker was not compatible with Friderician traditions.[76] William resented being put down by Bismarck once again, whom he felt responsible for the bad blood which existed between him and his parents. William's little party were naturally delighted at the prospect of a fall-out with Bismarck. He was already thinking about dropping the pilot before he took over the ship of state. In December, at the same time as writing Bismarck a lengthy justification of his support for the good, monarchist Stoecker, he told the Minister of Finance, Scholz, that he would need Bismarck for a few years before his functions were divided up and reallotted. Bismarck's minister Karl Heinrich von Boetticher, thought William, would do as well. Stoecker claimed he had told him he would keep the old chancellor on for six months, 'then I'll govern myself'.[77]

The Stoecker problems refused to go away. On 27 December 1887 the 'scandal' press were attacking William for his plans to hold a pseudo-mediaeval parade to raise money for the Stadtmission. The papers called it a 'Stoecker Assembly' and described the court preacher as the 'chief of the anti-Semites'. Eulenburg noted that Stoecker was now the 'red rag which sets all the turkeys running'. William correctly suspected that Bismarck was behind the press campaign and was furious with Herbert. Eulenburg 'fought like a lion' for the reputation of his friend and colleague. At the end of the year he too warned William to distance himself from Stoecker. He suspected that the campaign was also directed at Waldersee, who was seen as over-mighty through his friendship with William. For his part William was furious and wanted to fight it out with Bismarck.[78]

William not only complained to Bismarck, he took the issue up with his grandfather. The emperor blamed Waldersee's wife Marie 'who goes a bit far in religious matters' and also had Waldersee under her thumb. She had stopped going to court although Waldersee claimed there were other reasons for this.[79] The crisis with Bismarck was a pointer to the future. William was not prepared to be patronised. The chancellor tried to remove Waldersee at the same time, who responded by encouraging William to seek a showdown with Bismarck. For the time being William toed the line. On 14 January 1888 he wrote to the chancellor to express the wish that 'not the shadow of a difference of opinion' should come between them.[80]

Eulenburg may well have hoped to keep William to himself, and shape his thoughts to protect the 'well-being of Prussia'. William's other 'bad' influence was Waldersee, who was driving him into the war party. Eulenburg was worried about the amount of trust William placed in the Quartermaster-General. Possibly he was unaware of the little services the soldier performed to clean up the mess after William dabbled in sexual affairs. Eulenburg also had problems with Herbert and his heavy drinking, which naturally meant the diplomat had to keep up. He complained that the whole Bismarck family were endowed with 'Altmark'* stomachs, after a session terminated at 2.30 a.m.[81]

William was showing himself as easily influenced as his father. By turns he was anti-British and anti-Russian. The first of these was particularly worrying to his parents. It had been noted, for example, that he had tipped off the Tsar about British troop movements on the North-West Frontier.[82] He felt snubbed. He claimed he had tried to inform his grandmother of his father's state, but she had not deigned to reply. He had told the British military attaché, Colonel Leopold Swaine, on 7 December that it was simply not true that he was anti-English. Nor was he anxious for war:

It would be monstrous if I in my position were to lead my country into war. I fully support the chancellor's policy and it is our intention to do nothing to provoke Russia or France ... As regards my feelings about England, for years I have believed that both countries should decide all political issues hand in hand, and because we are strong and mighty, we should reinforce the peace together; you with your strong fleet and us with our great army can do this, and when my English relatives give me the opportunity I would most like to tell them this myself ... But when they neither write nor speak to me when the opportunity presents itself, how can they know what my feelings are![83]

It was pure Coburg. William then burst into tears.

Ironically William's Russophobia was calculated to appeal to the Villa Zirio. Vicky saw a Russo-German war as a chance for her favourite, Sandro, to win back his laurels, and possibly the throne of Bulgaria too. Sandro, for his part, had rather more pacific intentions, which focused on the court theatre in Darmstadt. Fritz was possibly even more bellicose than his wife and wrote a memorandum in which he voiced his support for a war against Germany's great eastern neighbour. He told Waldersee that he wanted nothing less than 'a crusade against Russia'.[84]

There were further disappointments. The emperor had refused to grant his grandson a division and was deaf to Bismarck's entreaties. He 'seems still to see his not quite 30 year old [sic – he was not quite twenty-nine] grandson as a child'. William blamed the Villa Zirio. Waldersee

---

* The Altmark was the core of historic Prussia.

possibly agreed. He described Vicky as 'horribly selfish and uncircumspect'.[85] With Eulenburg, the intimacy was still just as great. Over the holiday season there were sleigh rides in the Potsdam snow. He had a seasonal, and restrained, letter from his mother: 'We had a lovely time [at Christmas] there was also no reason to be sad. Your father is well! The only sad thing is that your grandparents are so old!' William thought otherwise. He irreverently compared his father to the Cid, whose corpse they mounted on a horse before Valencia – to frighten away the Moors.[86]

The year 1888 opened with apprehension. It was to be the 'Dreikaiserjahr' – the 'greise Kaiser, der leise Kaiser und der reise Kaiser'.* Fritz's health was now the chief cause for concern. The crown prince's Catholic friend, General Loë, had an interview with Mackenzie and was able to report to Waldersee that the growth had reappeared: 'For the time being everything is all right – but the sword of Damokles! It has yet to be removed. This is the most important issue for our future.' Eyes turned to Vicky. Would she attempt to rule through her husband? After a talk with Bismarck, Lucius Ballhausen wrote: 'The crown princess is no Catherine [the Great] any more than the crown prince is Peter III. In the first place she is cowardly, she wants to be popular and to shine in conversation, but she has no real ambition to rule. She has artistic inclinations and will seek activities there. She wants to appear liberal, and embarrass people through paradoxes, but nothing more.'[87]

William's last appointment from the old emperor came in the blue promissory envelope on 27 January 1888. He was promoted Generalmajor (or brigadier-general) and transferred to Berlin to lead the Foot Guards. The idea of giving the prince his own brigade came from Emperor William's Military Cabinet chief, Albedyll. The emperor resisted at first, which hurt William, who had to pour his heart out to his friend Eulenburg. The old man could be talked round: 'But Albedyll, think about it, up to now the boy has commanded a regiment with something between twenty and five and twenty officers; now he will have three regiments all at once with three regimental commanders and be in charge of three officer corps and nine battalions! That is quite impossible!' 'He'll soon manage,' was Albedyll's indulgent reply.

It was his twenty-ninth birthday. In San Remo Vicky refused to raise her glass to her eldest son's health. There were consolations: William had been given the brigade he craved. Many still believed him to be too young, but Waldersee pointed out that his grandfather had commanded a brigade at twenty-one.[88] Berlin and Potsdam were still bickering. Dona

---

*The year of the three Kaisers: the aged Kaiser, the soft-spoken Kaiser and the travelling Kaiser. In some versions Fritz is described as the 'weise Kaiser', or the wise Kaiser, which is obviously more partisan.

had snubbed Herbert and the chancellor was angry. Waldersee was attacked in the *Deutsche Tageblatt* as the leader of the war party.[89]

When Morell Mackenzie appeared again in San Remo on 7 February the infection had made rapid progress. It was now vitally important that a tracheotomy be performed, and quickly. Kessel shouted at Mackenzie, and told him he would have him court-martialled: the crown prince could scarcely breathe. The operation finally took place on 9 February. Mackenzie was no surgeon, so the operation had to be carried out by Bergmann's assistant, Bramann. Bramann, on the other hand, was not allowed to examine the patient and Mackenzie refused to take responsibility for anything that happened. The whole process was strangely primitive. Fritz was put to sleep with chloroform and operated on in bed. Bramann performed the tracheotomy with a gun in his pocket; not – as one might imagine – to shoot Mackenzie if he made a fuss, but to dispose of his own life should anything go wrong with the crown prince.[90] When he made the incision slightly to the left of the trachea, Mackenzie was delighted to tell the world that he had bungled it.

On 21 February the Prince of Wales arrived to see his sister. On the same day Bergmann identified cancer cells in a slough taken from the crown prince. Waldersee was triumphant: he had 'torn up the whole tissue of lies [spread] by the English doctor'. Another cancer specialist called Kussmaul arrived and tested Fritz's lungs for secondary manifestations. Meanwhile Fritz's health was declining fast. When the British fleet appeared in the harbour in San Remo, the crown prince collapsed. Bergmann pronounced, 'This day counts as two on the way to the grave.'[91]

The war between the doctors in San Remo had become increasingly absurd. When Bergmann identified cancer cells under the microscope, Mackenzie refused to look. As it transpired, he had never used a microscope. There was a battle over whether the crown prince should be fitted up with an English or a German cannula. Fritz decided on one of German manufacture. Thereafter Mackenzie blamed all infection on the Teutonic instrument which he said had cut into the patient's throat and irritated his trachea. Bramann was given the Hohenzollernorden, which caused the newly knighted Mackenzie a fit of jealousy.[92]

Mackenzie scored a great victory in his turn when he managed to have Vicky dismiss Bergmann. Her order encountered opposition from the emperor, however; Bergmann was told to await instructions from William who was in Karlsruhe, where he was attending the funeral of his young cousin, Prince Ludwig of Baden. Later the old emperor rescinded the order and told the surgeon to stay put in San Remo until William's arrival at the beginning of March. Vicky thought her son had come to drag Fritz off to Berlin. Waldersee wrote: 'She is hardly capable of reason, so fanatically does she cling to the idea that her husband is not seriously ill.'[93] Virchow's assistant Waldeyer showed William the cancer cells under the microscope: 'So these little bodies I see here, they brought it all about?'[94] When William left, Vicky wrote to her mother:

Not one word of sympathy or affection did he utter, and I was distressed to see how very haughty he has become, and what tremendous airs he gives himself! It is no doubt the effect of being told so often that he may be Emperor in less than a year. His visit did not do any harm, and he did not meddle this time.[95]

On 4 March the old emperor summoned his son home. He must have been aware that he too had little time left. Mackenzie countermanded the emperor's orders. He was not to be moved before the arrival of the warm weather. He had not been so particular about this before. William was recalled on 5 March. His grandfather's condition had taken a turn for the worse.[96]

The prospect of William's rapid coming to power began to alarm elements of the old guard too. On 7 March Prince Hohenlohe, the future chancellor, had a talk with General von Heuduck about the probability of having to bury two emperors in a short period of time. Heuduck thought a clash between William and Bismarck inevitable: William had mustered certain conservative forces behind him which aimed to wrest power from the old chancellor. 'This would be unfortunate,' said Heuduck. 'The prince is, in any case, not popular in Germany, and will have to be very careful to turn public opinion in his favour.' Had Fritz been a Romanov, said William's old playmate Poultney Bigelow, there would have been a suspicion of foul play – so hated was he by the Prussian aristocracy.[97] General Stosch thought the first William too old and the second too young. 'How we will miss the link in the chain,' he told Waldersee.[98]

Waldersee naturally knew better. Less than a week before the old emperor's death he wrote to say how much opinions of the prince had altered for the better now that it seemed likely he would soon be emperor. 'He is apparently more serious, more mature and become Lord knows what other things besides; what strikes one is the speed. It is all a pack of lies. The same people who plotted against the prince can see that he might soon be emperor, and now want to win themselves good posts. The prince is exactly as he was, although he has learned a few things in the last few months.'[99]

When William returned to Berlin on 7 March, he was going from one deathbed to another. The emperor was in bed wearing a white jacket with a tartan shawl wrapped round his neck. He read William's report on his son's health. His own was failing fast. Later that day Waldersee went to the Schloss. William took him away from the crowd gathered in the antechamber and into the flag room: 'He was both moved and agitated.' Theodor Fontane described the scene on the Linden. Old William's impending death was not a shock. A man of nearly ninety-one could go any day. 'The rain dripped off their umbrellas and like cretins they stared across the way to the palace.'[100]

The next day the emperor spent in half-sleep. He saw Bismarck then, and uttered his most famous line, 'I have no time to be tired.'[101] To his grandson, who came to his bedside, he said, 'I have always been pleased with you, you have done everything well.'[102] 'Be considerate when it comes to the Tsar,' he told William. 'You know what he's like. Stick to the alliance with Austria, put your faith in it, for that is the stronghold of peace. Be careful to maintain it, but don't be frightened to go to war, when it is a just cause.'[103] It was not clear, however, whether he thought he was talking to William or his father. Whatever the case, he, and indeed Augusta, had long since transferred all their hopes to their eldest grandson.[104] William remained at his bedside, apart from a few hours' sleep, constantly tending his grandfather, while Augusta sat beside the bed in her wheelchair, holding her husband's hand.[105] The rest of the old Kaiser's utterances were largely mumbo-jumbo: 'That's nice . . . that's right . . . Amen.' He talked about the French army and failed to recognise members of his family.

He was given wine. Someone asked him if it were good. 'That I cannot swear,' said the emperor. At 7 p.m. on 8 March, old William asked for a glass of champagne. He ate a little soup and talked of Germany's preparedness for war, although it was not certain whether he was talking of the present or the Wars of Liberation in which he had taken part in 1814 and 1815. The press bungled the announcement of his death, running the story a day early. The emperor had appeared dead, but revived, saying, 'Give me a glass of beer!' When he was offered water he quibbled, 'What! You can drink that too!' In those last moments he had problems identifying those around his bed and addressed his chancellor with an informal 'Du'.[106]

His last intelligible words concerned German relations with Austria–Hungary and Russia. Life ran out at eight thirty on the morning of 9 March 1888. Waldersee saw Prince William with tears on his cheeks. The family filed past the corpse to kiss the hand of the first Hohenzollern emperor. Then it was the turn of the court, including Waldersee.[107] His great servant Bismarck was philosophic – 'Things are going to be very difficult now, but I hope to be able to lead them to a decent end.' With the first William old Prussia died too. Fritz and his son William would exchange the spartan tradition for 'boundless imperial splendour'.[108]

7
Ninety-Nine Days

At the same age as his father before him, Fritz was now king of Prussia and German emperor. As the latter he had made up his mind he would be Frederick IV, to carry on the mediaeval tradition. Bismarck was furious. He was having none of it and told the new emperor that he would merely offend the other princes.[1] The new German Reich had nothing to do with the Holy Roman Empire which had so fired Fritz's imagination in the 1860s. He was to be Frederick III, after the founder of the Prussian monarchy and Frederick the Great. 'What comparisons present themselves!' wrote Theodor Fontane. 'II and III, a victor, who triumphed over everything and – a dying man.'[2] His insistence was an indication that Bismarck saw the Reich only as an extension of the Prussian monarchy. In reality he was neither the Third nor the Fourth. As German emperor he should have been Frederick I.

Fritz's first act as emperor was to pin the Black Eagle on his wife and appoint Mackenzie royal physician, something which caused comment in the new court, divided as it was between the Victoria and Méditerannée hotels. He spitefully cancelled William's role as official representative of the Crown, thereby compounding his bad grace over the original appointment. Vicky coveted that one for herself. He sent his son a stiff telegram: 'In deep sadness over the death of my father, at which it was you and not me who had the privilege of being present, I utter my confidence at the time of my accession to the throne that you will be an example in all matters of loyalty and obedience.' Queen Victoria had been trying to prevent Fritz from going to Berlin. She thought he would be better off in the milder climate of Wiesbaden in the Rhineland, but Fritz could hardly ignore the fount of his new power and without him Germany was effectively without government.[3]

Fontane summed up the feelings of a traditional, yet liberal Prussian when he expressed his sadness at the passing of the old king and emperor and the arrival of the new. Fritz was 'full of goodness, refinement and distinction, only without force and without the lie! But from now on sowing confusion. Nations require decisiveness and commands. That "do what you want" is hardly desirable in private life, in politics certainly not.' On the day Fritz and Vicky returned to Berlin, there was an aggressive article in the *Vossische Zeitung*. Fontane thought it would make William pleased. He was certainly right.[4]

The bags were packed at Villa Zirio and the new emperor and empress headed north at 9 a.m. on 10 March. Eulenburg saw Kessel in Munich who told him that since Fritz had been given an English cannula he had entirely lost his ability to speak. Kessel added uncontroversially that William would succeed within the year. Eulenburg was able to catch a glimpse for himself, when the imperial train made a ten-minute halt in Munich Hauptbahnhof.[5] Johanna von Bismarck told her husband that William looked browbeaten. The old chancellor went to Leipzig to meet his new master's train. He cannot have been too anxious about this old bugbear – Bergmann had been even less generous than Kessel, telling the chancellor Fritz would not survive the summer.

It was Fritz's first meeting with Bismarck for eighteen months. He arrived in Charlottenburg at 10 p.m. on the evening of 11 March. In later life William could still remember the sadness in his father's eyes as he stepped out into a snow-girt Berlin. His appearance was a shock to all around. No one had seen him for a year. Now he looked like a dying man and not without reason – his windpipe was disintegrating. William kissed his father's hand. His mother turned away. 'It will be a frightfully short interregnum,' wrote Fontane, 'and that is all for the best.' He was taken to Charlottenburg Palace, as the Berlin Schloss was considered both too dusty and Vicky considered it too close to the people. There, in the centre of town, Fritz would have been 'a perfect prisoner'.[6]

The funeral was on the 16th. Fritz stayed in on doctor's orders. As the cortège took his father through frost and wind to his final resting-place in the mausoleum behind the palace, he wept quietly as he watched the ceremony through the window. The Berliners had done their old emperor proud. Possibly as many as half a million braved the cold to bid him farewell. On the city side of the Brandenburg Gate they had hung up a banner which read 'Vale senex Imperator', while on the Tiergarten side it was written in German – 'Gott segne Deinen Ausgang'.* The arch was flanked by two obelisks carrying portraits of the deceased's parents. William marched alone, 'firm and upright', behind the coffin, making the most of the opportunity presented by the absence of his father. He was followed by Henry and the kings of Belgium, Saxony and Romania. Old Moltke turned up and walked in the procession. Graf Perponcher carried his master's orders.[7]

---

* 'Fare thee well old emperor' and 'God bless your departure'.

Fritz's absence was noted. Hildegard Spitzemberg wrote in her diary, 'Soon we'll be burying the second German emperor.'[8] He had but a short time and little strength left to make his mark. His and Vicky's dream of seeing a liberal regime established in Germany was not helped by the fact that the party was in hopeless disarray and there was very little support for its programme. The National Liberals were too docile, and the Free Liberals too remote from power. There was no one to help Fritz. He made noises about broadening the educational base as early as 12 March, but Bismarck scoffed at Frederick's projects, undertaken in the unrealistic atmosphere of his retirement from the world, during his peripatetic life with Vicky. In practice such pipedreams would have disappeared 'like mist before the sun'.

Bismarck also reminded Fritz that he had made promises in 1885 when he had asked him to remain in office after his father's death. Bismarck had agreed (or so he says) on condition there were no 'parliamentary regime and no *foreign* influences in politics', by which he meant Vicky. Fritz had shaken his hand and said he had 'no thoughts' of either. Later he was to boast that he had never in his political life enjoyed so much freedom of action as he did during the ninety-nine days.[9] Waldersee was also unworried. At first he had feared old William dying before his son, but now he was certain that the new emperor and empress would create so much chaos during their reign that they would prepare the ground nicely for William's rule. The whole performance in Charlottenburg, he thought, was 'a comedy which cannot last long'.[10] He was worried, however, about Stoecker, who was told to busy himself with the cure of souls. Vicky was particularly keen to rein in the court preacher. William's role as the emperor's deputy was dangled before him, but the reality was different.

Vicky looked ready to confirm her son's cruel jibe about the Cid. To her daughter, Charlotte of Meiningen, she said, 'In a week everything will be all right again. We are going to Potsdam, and there the emperor will recover quickly.' Fritz did not have her rose-tinted spectacles. When the Finance Minister Scholz approached him for a picture to put on the new coins, he told the emperor that they might take a few months. 'I shan't survive that long!' was Fritz's honest reply.[11] Waldersee's judgment was more sympathetic than usual – 'The unfortunate, exhausted emperor is in need of rest and completely lacking in will in her hands.' There was much talk about Vicky having lost her senses; possibly she was simply going through the menopause. Bismarck enjoyed some of the new emperor's wine, but when he had stomach trouble afterwards he told his physician, Dr Schweninger, 'It was that horrid English wine.'

A monument to his father was decreed, but it was not until William had destroyed that rambling, picturesque tract of buildings before the royal palace known as the 'Schlossfreiheit', that one of his beloved Begas' most ambitious compositions saw the light of day. Even dearer to his heart was the chance to avenge Mackenzie by awarding him the same Hohenzollernorden which his father had granted Bramann. Orders were lavishly bestowed during his three-month reign. Minister Friedberg received the Black Eagle. Waldersee sniffed: 'Friedberg has been a friend for a long time, and in many delicate situations he has advised the crown prince and princess. He is seen, however, by the liberals as one of their own and he is of Jewish origin, I believe he was even once a Jew himself. The investiture must be a programme; they are revealing their effort to gain popularity among liberals and Jews.' Friedberg's elevation also sired a wry remark from the novelist Fontane: 'Jubilation in Israel!'[12]

The chancellor was offered a duchy and his son Herbert was to be made a prince. Bismarck refused both. As one of William's first biographers remarked:

The first wishes of the liberals were to create barons, counts and princes, so that Bismarck commented ironically, 'If he wants to stop the hatred between the nobility and the middle classes, the emperor should ennoble the entire population' ... Responding to the offer of titles for his own family, Bismarck quipped 'Yes, if I had two million thalers I'd have myself made pope!'[13]

Bismarck was able to cool the new emperor's heels over the Russian menace and stop him and his ministers from attacking Germany's eastern neighbour. Fritz agreed to sack Stoecker as a court preacher, but the final decision was left in the hands of the church authorities who did nothing. In the end it was his friend William who cast the preacher out. Bismarck's relations with Vicky improved too. After a little while he was boasting that he was like 'an old man in love'.[14]

Even Fritz's old friend Freytag agreed that it would have been better for Fritz's reputation if he had expired before his father.[15] While doubting he had the force to create a liberal Germany, writers sympathetic to Fritz maintain that he might still have succeeded in bringing about an alliance with Great Britain, which would have prevented war from breaking out in 1914 – had it lasted that long.[16] By 22 March there were already more widespread complaints of the new empress and her meddling in public affairs.[17] She was Lady Macbeth, he Hamlet.[18] William and Henry reassured Bismarck that they did not believe that the Reich should be directed by a woman, even when that woman was their mother.[19] She clearly had no time to lose. As soon as she could she revived the Battenberg marriage project, writing to Sandro to tell him it was now the moment to start the ball rolling. Sandro edged away from his potential mother-in-law by saying that he was of no interest now –

just an ordinary man. He was giving her every indication, but Vicky was not prepared to read between the lines.[20]

Vicky worked on Fritz and made him agree to appoint Sandro as commander of the Gardekorps. On 31 March Fritz told Bismarck that he had agreed to the marriage and summoned Sandro to Berlin. Bismarck had to go over the points once again: Sandro was 'deeply hated by the Tsar; the marriage would be morganatic; then he threatened to resign'. Fritz wrote two words on a slip of paper: 'Was tun?' – 'What must be done?' Bismarck replied that he must send a telegram and cancel Sandro's visit to Berlin.

At this moment Vicky entered the room crying. She said that her daughter's heart could not be broken for reasons of state. Fritz gestured to his wife to calm down. When this had no effect he ripped the cloth from his neck and tried to speak. The only intelligible word was 'Alleinlassen – leave [us] alone'.[21] Then he burst into tears. When, later, the chancellor claimed to have had Fritz entirely on his side he noted the invalid's undiminished pride, his 'Olympian sense of his own importance and majesty'. Fritz, according to Bismarck at least, agreed that the marriage was a *mésalliance*. Vicky seems to have worked him over later. When he came to write his will he consented to the marriage, and decreed that his successor, William, should make the necessary arrangements.[22] The crown prince, for his part, caused offence the next day by making a speech to celebrate Bismarck's seventy-third birthday in which he compared the Reich to a regiment where the general had been killed, the second-in-command badly wounded, and where it was vital that a junior officer take command.[23]

Bismarck was calm at first, believing that Sandro was a spent force. He changed his mind before a week had elapsed and threw a tantrum. On 5 April he once again threatened to resign if the marriage became law. William was no less adamant. He wrote to Battenberg: 'If you marry my sister I will see you as the enemy of my family and of my country!'[24] Sandro tried to shake Vicky off by writing directly to her mother. The queen told Vicky not to do anything without William's agreement, 'for he is the crown prince', and she would only end up by making both Moretta and Sandro unhappy. As Vicky had the bit between her teeth, she was not even prepared to heed her mother for the time being, and put pressure on Moretta. It was no longer important to her what her daughter felt. She wanted to legitimise her sister's marriage to Henry of Battenberg and deliver a slap in the face to Bismarck.[25]

It became clear that Queen Victoria herself was no longer so keen on the match, as she had been told of Sandro's liaison with the Darmstadt soubrette by his brother Henry. She almost certainly told Vicky too. Even if she did not, Bismarck did, but Vicky refused to believe him. It was then that Bismarck thought he had glimpsed something sinister in Vicky's eyes, a 'bottomless sensuality'. He thought she was besotted by the 'Battenberger' and harboured 'incestuous thoughts'.[26] For his own part, Sandro's passion had waned. He was now genuinely in love with Johanna and his conscience hurt him to pursue the matter further.

The resignation crisis was still smoking on 11 April 1888. To Hildegard von Spitzemberg, Bismarck compared working for the two Hohenzollern emperors.

My old master was well known to be dependent [on Augusta]. He used to say 'You help me, you know how much she wears the trousers!' And so we worked things out together. On top of it all this one [Fritz] is too proud, but he is dependent [on Vicky] and submissive in a way which is hard to credit, like a dog! ... He is a good soldier, but withal tied to the apron strings like some of the whiskery old NCOs I have seen scamper into mouseholes at the sight of their wives.[27]

Two days later the only person who could see no reason was Vicky. The British military attaché pointed out that the marriage no longer made any political sense. The British might once have had an interest in promoting it, 'but all that is past and he is now reported to have *ein zärtliches Verhältniss* [sic] with a member of the histrionic art.'[28]

William was also causing the old chancellor problems. He needed to remind both Hohenzollerns, father and son, that German policy since 1871 had been to maintain peace in Europe and to check the formation of anti-German coalitions. William was still anxious to take a swipe at Russia and noted in the margin of a report which advocated turning 'Russian power to ruins' an enthusiastic 'Yes!' Bismarck had to tell him that even a victory over the eastern neighbour would provoke ungovernable desires for revenge. On 10 May William backed down and told Bismarck that he believed that political arguments must always take precedence over simple military ones.[29]

Shortly afterwards, Fritz received a visit from his paladin in Alsace-Lorraine, Chlodwig zu Hohenlohe, who was to become William's third chancellor. Hohenlohe wrote: 'He did not look unusually ill, only thin and somewhat yellow, and the eyes were rather prominent. But on closer observation one notices the suffering expression of the eyes. ... He gave me the impression of a martyr; and, indeed, no martyrdom in the world is comparable with this slow death.'[30]

There were moments of normality for all that. On the first Sunday after his arrival, Fritz showed his son his plans for the new Berlin Cathedral as designed by Raschdorff. He and Vicky had instructed the architect to build one with a dome, after the Italian style. One thing stipulated by Fritz was that the new structure should honour his dynasty and its story. Above the sarcophagi in the crypt he wanted statues erected with inscriptions which married 'Imperial Roman terseness and German historiographical precision'.[31] The idea was clearly the ancestor of William's ludicrous 'Puppenallee', as Berliners called the collection of family portraits set in stone which lined the Siegesallee in the Tiergarten.

They had plans for a new palace too. On the Grosse Stern in the Tiergarten a great Schloss was to be built. Vicky was going to design everything from the doors to the doorknobs and a team of English designers was called in to rework the interiors of Knobelsdorff's Schloss Charlottenburg. On another occasion, Fritz approved a new uniform for the navy – an act worthy of his son. He fantasised about his coronation. He was to have a Prussian ceremony in Königsberg, and a proper German one in Charlemagne's Baptistry in Aachen.[32] Such positive, indeed, monomaniacal moments were, admittedly, few and far between.

Fritz's health began to fail on 12 April and his life expectancy was put at a week. It was believed that the cancer was making rapid progress as a result of the ill-fitting cannula and a new one was provided. Mackenzie and Bergmann were there together and fought over the patient. Mackenzie claimed that Bergmann had injured Fritz with the cannula and caused damage to his throat. Fritz's diaries do confirm his feeling that he had been roughly treated, but the pathologist Virchow failed to find the abscess alluded to by Mackenzie. Bergmann excused his brutality by stating that Fritz was on the point of suffocation at the time he arrived. It appears to have been milk which led to Fritz's demise, however. It got into his windpipe and caused an infection in his lungs.

'The Empress of Hindoostan' – as William called his grandmother – arrived in Potsdam on her way home from Florence on the 24th. Waldersee considered Queen Victoria's appearance 'untimely'.[33] It was to be a war of wills between her and Bismarck, who faced one another for the first and only time, but the wily Junker failed to give ground: there was not to be so much as an order for Sandro, Russo-German relations would not stand for it. On the other hand Bismarck seems to have admired the British queen. 'You can do business with that woman,' he said. They also spoke about the succession, Queen Victoria reported back to her daughter. She mentioned William's lack of experience, he had not travelled yet. Bismarck replied that though William knew absolutely nothing about the inner workings of the state, 'if thrown in the water, he would be able to swim, as he was certainly clever'. It was clear that he had confidence in William then and thought a 'difficult youth' had helped form his character. Bismarck charmed Queen Victoria at a dinner when he took up a sweet emblazoned with a picture of Vicky and – unbuttoning his coat – placed it next to his heart.[34]

Fritz had a last visit from his own, wheelchair-bound mother and collapsed sobbing beside her, unable to utter a word. Despite the signs of his imminent end, William was denied access to his father, whom he believed to be a prisoner of his doctors: 'The emperor is asleep and Her Majesty has gone for a walk.'[35] Unlike reporters from newspapers all over the world, William was never allowed to speak to him alone. When Fritz and the family moved to the Neues Palais William claimed he was shooed away by the flunkey on the steps who told him, like 'trained parrots', that his mother had a visitor.[36]

Like any number of people who were trimming their sails at the time, Waldersee could smell power for himself once Fritz was out of the way. William told him that he wanted him to be his general adjutant. Waldersee returned the compliment. On 24 April he praised William's soldiery when he led his battalion from Tempelhof Field to the Schloss and then reviewed them at the march past, without once turning aside to look at the admiring crowds.[37]

Waldersee sat next to Dona at a dinner on the 27th. They were both happy that William was less under the influence of Herbert Bismarck. On the possibility of reconciliation between William and his mother there seemed little hope. The stubbornness of both lay in their common blood. Despite a 'shower of honours' dished out to liberals and Jews, Vicky had few friends. Waldersee was contemptuous of the liberals who with their professions of loyalty 'were hunting for honours, promotions and patents of nobility'. 'People who up to now have been seen as confirmed republicans presently give the appearance of being the actual pillars of the realm.'[38] She admitted that even her entourage was against her. There was only Götz von Seckendorff.

Waldersee was rather paranoic about Vicky, believing that she now reigned in Germany. Bismarck would never have let that pass. The Quartermaster-General noted that Fritz could not listen to a long report, and declared him 'incapable of ruling'. In the end, however, a healthy emperor would have been bad news. 'How wonderfully things have turned out: everyone is looking hopefully at the crown prince [William]. Who would have believed that a year ago?'[39] The one formal occasion at which the new Kaiser was present was the short service which sealed the marriage of his second son to Irene of Hesse-Darmstadt on 24 May. He looked deathly pale in a general's uniform covered with 'every possible order'. He did not attend the wedding breakfast afterwards. 'I have never again attended a wedding the like, in which, instead of joy, all hearts were filled with sadness,' wrote William later.[40]

Vicky was constantly alluding to William's premature imperial airs. She took objection to his courting Bergmann, whom he even invited to dinner. William, however, arranged a last act of kindness for his father on 28 May. After exercises in Tegel, he planned to storm the bridge over the canal at Charlottenburg. Would it give Fritz pleasure to see his brigade along the terrace on the park side of the Schloss at Charlottenburg, so that he might view his old regiment in all its glory? 'No one knows anything of this ...'[41] Fritz was touched. He sat in an open coach by the side of the path and watched the troops file past. 'They were the first and last troops Frederick III saw as emperor.'[42]

On 31 May, Fritz visited the mausoleum in the park and took leave of his dead father. That evening he told Mackenzie, 'I shall go to bed early tonight. I feel tired.' It was arranged that he would travel to Potsdam the next day on board the yacht *Alexandra*. Again the fear of Berlin's dusty soil made it wiser for the emperor to travel by boat. As the steamer passed the Pfaueninsel, his grandparents' love-nest in the Havel Lakes, he began to cry. They docked below the Glienecke Bridge where carriages were waiting to take the party to the Neues Palais. The palace had been built by Frederick the Great to house his unwanted guests and therefore invested with a prosaic name. It was now to be re-baptised as 'Friedrichskron', or Frederick's Crown, to reflect the splendour of the later Hohenzollerns.

In those last days before he ascended the throne, Friedberg showed William a letter to his successors from Frederick William IV, who was forced by the revolution of 1848 to grant Prussia a constitution against his will. The letter enjoined them to scrap the constitution. It had been read by William I and by Frederick III. Both had returned it to the archives. William burned the document, writing: 'Contents read and destroyed' on the envelope and putting it back in the files.[43] It was typical of him: he wanted posterity to know that he had upheld the constitution, for all his bluster.

Their one great success was making Bismarck agree to the removal of his wife's cousin, the right-wing Minister of the Interior, Puttkamer, on 8 June, on the respectable grounds that he was guilty of electoral corruption. Even more exciting was the fact that he was another of Stoecker's men. That was universally seen as Vicky's handiwork.[44] Bismarck managed to offer Vicky a sweetener by doling out the 20 million thalers which the old emperor had left from his economies. It was another aspect of the Reich that was set to change. Economies were not the forte of Fritz or William.

The crown prince was still widely believed to be agitating for war against the Russians, whipped up by Waldersee. Hohenlohe was distinctly worried about what he heard and contemplated retiring in protest against the drift of German politics.[45] William believed such rumours were the result of a hate-campaign against him in the press, and that Mackenzie was in some way behind it. Later he named two journalists in particular, a Herr Schnidrowitz and Monsieur Jacques St Cere of the French daily *Figaro* – 'a German Jew' who came to a sticky end.[46] The idea was not perhaps as far-fetched as it seemed; Mackenzie prided himself on his ability to deal with newspapermen and editors and some of the worst reports on the new crown prince came from the foreign press. Waldersee also noted the antipathy of the Jewish press – the *Pester Lloyd* and the *Neue freie Presse*. Mackenzie claimed that he was the victim of the 'reptile' press too, and that Bergmann was behind it. They decided that the Scotsman was actually a Jew, who had changed his name from Moritz Markowicz.[47]

William was suspicious about the whereabouts of his father's papers, which had been spirited out of the country by Dr Mark Hovell. He warned his parents that he would surround the palace to make sure nothing left the building. He was true to his word. The Neues Palais was cordoned off on the night of 14 June. After Fritz's death Friedberg managed to calm him down and bring home to him what a poor impression his intended ransacking of the palace would have. By this time the papers were safely in England anyway, where they remain.[48]

Just four days before his death, Fritz gave vent to his frustration on a scrap of paper: 'I must get well, I still have so much to do!'[49] On 14 June 1888 Wilhelm von Doehring told Eulenburg that Fritz's neck was filled with pus, and that the food which went into his mouth was coming out through the other end of the cannula. Fritz could still summon up a bit of energy for the chance to pin on his medals to receive the king of Sweden on the 12th, but the gesture strained him greatly. One of his last acts was to recommend Vicky to Bismarck. He took her hand as she sat at his bedside, and laid it in that of her old bugbear, the chancellor. That night Moretta walked into his room to find he was dying.

Right up to the last moment Vicky denied her son access to Fritz, but William had been allowed to sleep at the palace and witnessed his father's death the next day. He scribbled his last words on a scrap of paper: 'Victoria, the children and I.' 'He was his old self with me ...' wrote William. 'Despite everything she had been making long preparations for my father's death, everything had been worked out with much reflection. There are, therefore, no written papers around, everything had been cleared away! Not even his last will or something of that sort,' William told Waldersee later.[50] Vicky wrote to her mother, 'No mother ever possessed such a son.'[51]

8

The Struggle with the Bismarcks

The interregnum was over. Bismarck had emerged victorious. He had rid himself of that 'egotistical, cold man ...' Frederick III: 'He had no heart.'[1] He could also kiss goodbye to the woman he cast as Fritz's meddling, power-hungry, Guelph-Coburg wife. He may have had little inkling at the time, but the son would be a tougher nut to crack. Bismarck's policy during the nearly two years he remained in control of Reich politics was to get his master into trouble so that he would learn to rely on his chancellor. It was not a successful ploy.

Germany's new ruler was not tall, but at five foot five or six, a reasonable height. He was superficially handsome, even if his face was slightly lopsided. His hair was dark blond, his eyes blue. With time the court barber Haby, whose job it was to shave the new emperor every day, trained his moustache upwards using a patent pomade to form a W; then made a fortune by selling it to every sycophant in Germany. The initial is supposed to have been purely fortuitous. In Germany moustaches of this sort were called 'Es ist erreicht!' – 'It has been achieved!' They were naturally very popular before 1918.[2]

William had long since got used to his withered arm. In his bedroom he had an oar which he used to exercise his right arm. Stories are legion which testify to the strength of his good hand, and to his nasty habit of squeezing guests' fingers when he greeted them.[3] Apart from rowing, he exercised by driving a break harnessed to a Trakehnen stallion the 28-kilometre distance from Potsdam to Berlin, a journey he covered in an hour and a half.

For the time being Vicky clung on to the Neues Palais and the model farm at Bornstedt, but William was anxious to turn her out as quickly as possible. Once installed in the palace it became his principal residence, the nearest thing to home for a man who was always on the move. His private rooms were on the first floor of the Schloss. His study looked out over the fountain and the park at Sanssouci. It was hung with green damask and some of the Watteaus which had been the favourite paintings of the youthful Frederick the Great, as well as a few Poussins. The furniture was also from the Great King's time. New bathrooms and WCs were installed behind baroque panelling to make them look like cupboards. Much was made of the fact that the room where Fritz died was used as a sort of corridor, but even the scandalmongers agreed that this was 'from necessity rather than irreverence'.[4]

Ursula Countess von Eppinghoven's *Secret History of the Court of Berlin* was first published in 1909. It was a mildly scabrous, warts-and-all portrait of the emperor's private life. It appears to have been the work of a disgruntled servant rather than the purported lady of the bed-chamber. It reveals some interesting details for all that, most of them hingeing on the very ordinary domestic life of the emperor and his bride. He had a hot bath after lunch to comfort him after an 'ablution of cold sea water'.[5] Perhaps this reminded him in some way of his childhood treatments for his arm? William slept in a nightshirt, had to be dressed and undressed by two valets, smoked in bed and kept a revolver in his bedside table.

His wardrobe demonstrated another odd imbalance. He owned six shirts with detachable cuffs and twelve pairs of socks, six yellow, six brown. His lisle underwear was embroidered with a W and a crown. He used no eau-de-toilette, only soap; and possessed a collection of sponges and scrubbing brushes. Two whole rooms, however, housed his uniforms. There were three hundred German regimental uniforms alone, and that did not include colonelcies and field marshals' kit from other countries, which he wore to receive guests on state visits. By 1898 William pos-sessed three Austro–Hungarian regiments, three Russian, one British and one Portuguese; he was also an admiral in the British, Swedish and Danish navies.[6]

He was ever abstemious. In the evening he generally contented himself with a small glass of beer. Both his sobriety and his uxoriousness were mocked in his regiment. He referred to Dona as 'the ideal German woman', although she had grown distinctly stout and matronly by 1889 and lost any of the youthful charm she had possessed at their marriage.[7] 'He just had to have females everlastingly swinging incense in front of him ...' wrote the English-born beauty Daisy Princess of Pless, but Dona 'successfully managed her volatile, clever, changeable, vain and unreliable husband ... [despite] innumerable mild flirtations'; and she had the advantage of her beautiful hands.[8] Bismarck thought William was highly sexed, and we have evidence to show that he was embroiled in countless little affairs as a prince. On the other hand there is little watertight evidence of extramarital sex once he came to the throne.

The *Secret History* agreed with Bismarck's evaluation of the emperor's sex drive, but Dona appears to have been the chief object of his lust, and he was prepared to sleep with her right up to her confinements. She was famously jealous and surrounded herself with ugly courtiers so that her husband would not be tempted to stray. When he sat for the coquettish painter Vilma Parlaghy – a Hungarian Jewess who had converted to Catholicism – Dona came too to make sure there was no impropriety. On the other hand, that may have been because William showed such an overblown interest in Frau Parlaghy, and stood patron to her exhibitions.[9] William found his wife socially dull, and could not be induced to remain with her a moment longer than he had to. After dinner he made directly for the billiard room where he could be in the company of his ADCs. The rumours never ceased. There were unconfirmed reports of his using the Holländisches Palais in Berlin for 'nocturnal poaching trips'.[10] Photographs of women he admired were displayed in his study. A Fräulein von Böcklin was exhibited for her bust and he was thought to keep a portrait of a naked Duchess of Aosta – née Laetitia Bonaparte, the daughter of 'Plon-Plon' – on his desk. The story did the rounds that she had been his mistress too.

William changed very little in the course of his long life. Many observed that he never 'matured' in the way that most adults do. His impetuosity and short temper were characteristics from first to last. Someone who knew him both as a ruler and later as a guest at Doorn was the diplomat Joachim von Reichel: 'Other people's judgements meant mostly very little to him; his own meant all the more ... although he often lacked knowledge or experience he felt himself within his rights to arrive at judgements and decisions ... Another disadvantage was that he could not listen, and that did not change later at Doorn either ...' There was a tendency to exaggerate; 'to indulge in superlatives, especially in letters, in which bombast and sentimentality sat cheek by jowl'.[11]

Like so many other commentators, Reichel stressed William's inferiority complex. That he suffered from one was hardly surprising. Much more serious for ministers reporting to him was the difficulty in getting a word in edgeways. You chose the right moment, and when there was no one else present:

Anyone who had to speak to him daily would be thrown into confusion by his interruptions. People let him speak waiting to leap in after a pause and then steadfastly maintained control of the conversation. Bülow, Eulenburg, Waldersee and Tirpitz too all used these tactics and achieved their aims by doing so.[12]

William's first appointments were uncontroversial. General von Wittich, Bismarck's choice for his military mentor, was confirmed in his role as Generaladjutant. Wittich survived for about three years until William had wind of the rude remarks he made behind his back, and sacked him. His father's friend Hahnke was named chief of his Military Cabinet, with responsibility for service appointments. Lucanus was the civilian counterpart. A commoner raised to the nobility, Lucanus was to William what Eichel was to Frederick the Great. He was as faithful as a rock, and saw in William someone who above all needed protection from the outside world. As he told Bülow, 'For God's sake, don't start right out upsetting the Kaiser. Where will that lead?'[13]

August Eulenburg also continued over from Frederick's court, and was the only minister to serve William without a break until he retired from the House Ministry in 1922. Philipp's cousin represented profound Prussian conservatism and remained fundamentally opposed to reforming the notorious three-tier voting system. There were a few changes in the structure of the military entourage. The *maison militaire* was replaced by a royal *Hauptquartier* under a general who had a permanent position in his suite. To the HQ were attached the serving ADCs who accompanied the emperor on his many journeys. The linguistic change is significant: William did his best to outlaw French from court. Where possible, German alternatives were found. This was also true of the royal cellars, where the stress was placed on German wine and *Sekt*.[14]

William needed to have his favourites around him, and since many of these wore the king's coat they had to be on hand as generals *à la suite*, general adjutants, and ADCs; the commander of the palace guard, the commander of the Kaiser's own *gendarmerie*, and the commander of his headquarters. The key positions were those of military and naval cabinet chiefs (the naval office was created only in 1889). All of these reported to the emperor alone, including the Chief of the General Staff. A minister was sacked for reporting to the Reichstag. With time this military entourage grew. In 1888 it totalled twenty officers. In 1914 there were more than twice as many.

There was a certain style about the ADCs. According to one modern writer, they had to be tall and good-looking to pass muster.[15] Perhaps more importantly, they had to be optimistic and keen on the same sort of things as William. Wittich was quickly jettisoned and replaced by General von Plessen, who remained at William's side until he went into exile. Plessen was clearly utterly devoted to his lord. Others such as Kuno Moltke and Chelius were there because they offered something else, in this case musicianship. It helped to be known to William – or at least to Eulenburg – to be appointed. It should come as no surprise that William preferred noblemen for his suite, and Prussian noblemen at that; but there were a few freshly ennobled ADCs, especially those representing the less socially exclusive navy. There were just three Catholics in thirty years, and one baptised Jew – Walter 'Moses' Mossner.

The politics of the entourage were conservative, but few members were actively interested in the workings of the state. Waldersee was quite exceptional for an army officer. Schlieffen was more typical, in that he had no interest in politics whatsoever. He was what was called a 'Nur-Soldat' – a soldier and only a soldier. Many of them doubled up as military attachés during the time when the army threatened to undermine the Foreign Office by operating their own diplomatic service reporting to the General Staff. As it transpires, however, no great diplomatic mishap can be attributed to their meddling. To some extent the ADCs were there to listen to William's interminable monologues on any subject imaginable. Some found this trying. Neumann-Cosel, who was later pointed out by Zedlitz-Trützschler as one of the most fawning toadies of the court, used to retire to his rooms at the end of each tour of duty, swear loudly two or three times and go to bed for twenty-four hours.

William retained the system of government by cabinet which had been introduced in Prussia after the death of Frederick the Great and which had worked reasonably well during the reign of his grandfather. Initially he was determined to work even harder than his grandfather had done. The first William had slept alone in a simple, soldier's bed, risen at eight and worked at a small table, and received the heads of his civil and military cabinets on alternate days three times a week at eleven for a one-and-a-half hour audience before lunch. In the afternoon the old emperor held more audiences and took a ride in his carriage before enjoying his late-afternoon 'dinner' with Augusta. He went to the theatre in the evening, then with Augusta he received his intimate circle before going to bed at eleven. He travelled rarely, and certainly saw little reason to explore beyond his native Prussia. There was the spring parade in Potsdam and the autumn trooping of the colours on Tempelhof Field, south-east of Berlin. A troop revue was fixed for the spring, while manoeuvres were held in the autumn.

William wanted to go one better. To this regimen, William added three more audiences, but after a very short time he began to grow lazy and failed to receive important members of his ministry. To some extent this was because he was not often there. The military cabinets were in a privileged position in that William was far more likely to see them. They came in threes, but had to keep the audience down to the shortest time possible. During the briefings William doodled or chain-smoked. This did not mean he was not interested, but it often looked like that. He was perspicacious: 'There are too many ifs and buts for my liking. I want to know the following.' He cracked jokes and lit another cigarette. He was easily sidetracked and wasted time, altering, for example, the position of the chimneys on a cruiser because they were unaesthetic.[16]

Correspondence was returned to the cabinet chief marked either 'Opened by His Majesty' or 'Unopened by His Majesty'. With William it was more often the latter, but to be fair, this might have been due to the sheer weight of correspondence in the files. Waldersee had made up his mind. Already by 1890 he wrote that William 'no longer has the slightest desire to work'. William, however, thought otherwise: 'According to him he is busy working from dawn to dusk.' The new emperor followed in his father and mother's footsteps and travelled as much as he could. By 1894 he was in residence in either Berlin or Potsdam for only 47 per cent of the year.[17]

From 1889 to 1895 he attended Cowes Week, which was later to be imitated by the Kiel Regatta. William raced aboard any one of five 'Meteors' which were constructed from 1886 to 1914. The first had been built as the *Thistle* in Glasgow, and the racing yachts continued to be built in British or American yards until *Meteor IV* of 1908. The name commemorated a naval action during the Franco–German War when Captain, later Admiral, Knorr disabled the French frigate *Aviso*. Dona had her own yacht, the American built *Yampa* of 1887, which was renamed the *Iduna* after the goddess who kept the life-giving golden apples.[18]

Hunting was another *sine qua non*. There were the many royal domains, even more of them since Prussia had annexed so much of northern Germany during the wars of 1864 and 1866. Some were deeply traditional: Königs Wusterhausen, for example, which was one of the favourite hunting grounds of the second Prussian king, Frederick William I, the father of Frederick the Great – who incidentally despised hunting. It was not all on royal land. In Silesia he enjoyed visiting the rich magnates such as the Plesses and the Henckel Donnersmarcks. He was not impressed by needy gentry, preferring the company of the 'well-to-do', even if the money was brand new. When it came to Cowes and Kiel he was as often as not in the company of American millionaires. It did not matter if the money had been made in an unglamorous way, as long as there was plenty of it.[19]

William stressed the formality of kingship. It was not a Prussian tradition, and if he inherited it from anyone it was Fritz. The monarch was the symbol of empire whose progresses were there to encourage the people through a constantly renewed pageant. His was a theatrical form of kingship meant to dazzle and impress and encourage worship from the people. Although 'Prussianism' was represented by his ADCs and in his circle by such powerful influences as Herbert, Waldersee, Philipp Eulenburg or even to some degree Holstein, William was happier to see its more austere features relegated to statements of intent. In his personal life he cannot be said to have been remotely 'Prussian' – he was too star-struck for that. Not for him that sober-minded austerity and simplicity, he wanted to shine.

Although William loved to dwell on the military glories of Prussia and the characters of its *two* 'great' kings, he did not strike observers as being Prussian either. Neither of the south Germans Marschall von Bieberstein or Alexander Hohenlohe thought he exhibited the austere features typical of the Mark; and the diplomat Graf Monts believed him as near to a Bavarian as a Prussian: 'For many years as consul in Munich, I had the opportunity to observe how Bavaria stood as close to his heart as Old Prussia, [and] how much trouble he took to read into the south German mind and how he really intended to be an emperor to all Germans.'[20] In his public utterances it was always Germany he extolled. He made an exception for specifically Prussian audiences, but, the Prussian agrarians often got short shrift. Like his father before him, he was happy to see the Prussian idea give way to the bigger, better notion of a united Germany. As he told the staff-officer turned writer Alfred Niemann in exile at Amerongen:

My grandfather felt himself above all to be the king of Prussia. Being emperor meant more to him as a title than for its content. I had no historical precedents to fall back on and was born to the position of German emperor. [I] had to spin new threads between the headship of the empire and the German people, in order to be true to my God-given German mission; [I had to] bring together all its diverse strengths and produce in every German a proud consciousness of *civis germanus*.[21]

It was forward-looking kingship for all that. William saw himself as the 'personification of the German nation' and with time the world would support that view. He used the court, newspapers and photographs to give himself a charisma which was intended to unify Germans behind the Crown.[22] Like his father he set enormous store by popularity, he liked to be admired by his subjects and he was prepared to alter his policy in order to gain their support. Given that they were flushed with pride over their flashy new Empire, and easily moved to bellicosity towards their neighbours, his populism had a dangerous side. He was nourished by their adulation; their disaffection literally wrecked his nerves. William's character was ambiguous enough, but his contradictory utterances were not helped by a desire to ride a popular wave.

The monarchy had to be updated because Germany was also changing rapidly. William I's Prusso-centric view could not be maintained for long. The rest of Germany needed to have a say in the Empire and be wooed by policies which the old Prussians treated with suspicion. The Empire was one of these. In 1884 *Punch* had published a cartoon of a German eagle flying over a tropical island, while natives and British lions looked on, worried. The Germans swiftly trounced the British with their fast-growing economy and there was a loud call for a powerful fleet to protect their commercial interests abroad. The great speed with which Germany expanded over those years inevitably brought about a raw Anglo-German commercial rivalry which was stirred up, above all, by the Harmsworth press.

William's natural inclinations often went against the grain of the German people. He liked to think himself at least half an Englishman, and felt he could transform his character as quickly as he changed his clothes, or as soon as he crossed the Channel. He was often shocked by his countrymen's reactions to England, and criticism from Britain cut him to the quick. He was an avid reader of the newspaper cuttings which were prepared for him daily – although he does not seem to have heeded Eulenburg's attempts to get him to read a newspaper, such as the *Kölnische Zeitung*, properly. He had inherited an idea from Bismarck that the press was there to be manipulated from above, and could not believe that articles in foreign papers – the British in particular – were not expressions of official policy.

He himself had two organs at his disposal: the *Norddeutsche allgemeine Zeitung* and *Wolffs telegraphisches Bureau*. On top of these he put pressure on the federal states to make their newspapers toe the line. His ability to censor the press was limited. The repeated charge was *lèse-majesté*, but it was hard to make it stick and William faced frequent criticism. One of his fiercest critics was the nobleman Graf Ernst zu Reventlow who wrote for the *Münchner neueste Nachrichten*. William could not close the Bavarian paper down. Instead he used the *Norddeutsche* to belittle Reventlow – 'This impertinent boy needs a good spanking.'[23]

III

Eulenburg continued to be the new Kaiser's best, and possibly only, friend. Hinzpeter told him, 'You are the first person who loves the Kaiser for his *own* sake.' William informed his old tutor that Eulenburg was his 'bosom friend, the only one I love'.[24] The feeling was clearly mutual. William kept a framed photograph of Eulenburg on his desk in his hunting lodge at Rominten in East Prussia. Eulenburg worked as a tonic after Vicky. Where she made him feel small, Eulenburg told him he was a god; that same Achilles with whose images he surrounded himself. It is needless to add that this treatment did nothing to help William's personality disorders.

In 1892 William went so far as to suggest that Eulenburg call him 'Du', but the courtier could not go that far, and stuck, respectfully, to 'Sie'. Despite all the accusations made later, much of his advice was for the good. He acted as a liaison between William and his ministers. It was Philipp Eulenburg, to some extent together with Holstein, who stopped the new emperor's most dangerous sabre-rattling, toning down his speeches and preventing him from appointing the worst hawks to positions of power. Eulenburg also tried to make William aware that it would not help him in the long run to adopt a Prussian pose by insulting the Bavarians and south Germans. Later Philipp Eulenburg attempted to define his role in the emperor's life:

I always had ... the duty to be 'something' spiritual and artistic to the emperor. It was my music and my poetical abilities until political work sank like a heavy dew on this world of flowers; later it remained my constant effort to preserve the emperor's spiritual ideals in the face of his more and more explosive passions as he turned to the question of his personal power ... My so-called influence was nothing more than the constant attempt to restrain the emperor's volatile and explosive temperament and to prevent the friend from taking rash measures. Any more than this for the most part I could not achieve. In that I calmed him down I occasionally did the fatherland some service. That was my influence.[25]

The chief accusation levelled at Eulenburg was that he encouraged 'personal rule'; not William utterly alone, but taking decisions with the help of benign advisers. It was this which sealed Eulenburg's fate; for it was not his homosexuality that worried the journalist Maximilian Harden, but his 'malign' influence on the emperor. He may have believed, as many right-wing Germans did, that a successful war could forestall the advance of democratic institutions and parliamentary democracy, but he was hardly to be seen as a warmonger in a world of Waldersees. He was aware of the problem of Prussia's survival within the Reich, and was convinced that it should continue to 'Prussianise', tactfully converting the rest of Germany to its ideals.

Eulenburg's cousins in East Prussia would have bent his ear about their agrarian interests, yet he stood aside from the pressure they later put on Caprivi's chancellorship, and William was not impressed by their whining either. Eulenburg advocated an Austrian alliance, which deviated from classic Prussian thinking which listed towards Russia, but then again many East Prussian Junkers had become anti-Russian when the huge state to the east had begun to undercut the price of their grain.

Eulenburg had his frivolous side too. On 31 August 1888, he convinced William to attend a seance. Later he told him ghost stories until

12.30 a.m. The emperor was present for another in September 1891, but evidence that Eulenburg was converting him to mysticism was not popular with the rest of the entourage and the emperor stopped going. Eulenburg also pushed William into making gestures towards the arts. It was he who encouraged the restoration of William's original family home – Burg Hohenzollern in Swabia. The 'Puppenallee' or 'Dolls' Boulevard' in Berlin may well have also been suggested by Eulenburg.

He introduced William to the Englishman Houston Stewart Chamberlain who was later to become a pioneer of the new racial thought. Eulenburg was very close to his own mother, and thought that the discord which Bismarck had sown within the imperial household was unforgivable. He must have concealed his distaste for the Bismarcks did not suspect him at first. His relationship with William in no way worried the chancellor's family. As Herbert told him on 15 May 1889, 'Your influence on His Majesty is excellent, and in fact is very dear to me.' When Eulenburg tried to quit the foreign service after his father's death in order to run his estates and devote the remaining time to art, it was Bismarck together with William who convinced him to stay.[26]

William continued to visit Eulenburg's country seat, Liebenberg, for long weekends, chiefly to hunt. Eulenburg gritted his teeth. He did not even shoot, and hated the idea of killing. Once in Bückeburg, when 116 stags were wiped out, Eulenburg complained that this 'butchery in the lovely wood is repulsive'.[27] It was typical of the man in which the Junker uncomfortably cohabited with the aesthete. Sometimes there was a little informal entertainment, farces generally, but even when these involved 'cross-dressing' it was never seen as being anything to do with sexual perversion and the keenest actors in these skits were often the least prone to homosexuality. Eulenburg, for example, never involved himself in the drag acts.

There was something in it for Eulenburg, but it does not seem likely that it was ever his intention to use his friendship for self-advancement. He disliked the Wilhelmstrasse and claimed that he generally drank a schnapps before he went in.[28] In 1888 William made him his minister in Oldenburg, which was not too far away if he was needed. His main occupation was still 'friend to the king'.[29] Two years later he was packed off to the Württemberg court in Stuttgart. In June 1891 he received the top job in Munich after jostling Bismarck's son-in-law out of the position. William wanted to send his friend to London as ambassador, but Eulenburg disliked the English and spoke the language badly. He eventually received the job he craved when William sent him off to Vienna in 1894.

Eulenburg had his henchmen in the business of endeavouring to keep the young emperor on the straight and narrow path: Fritz von Holstein was there from the start. Later they were joined by Bernhard von Bülow who would achieve an importance to transcend both. Holstein was a minor nobleman from the Brandenburg Mark who had taken refuge in the Wilhelmstrasse. Highly gifted, but lacking in any personal charm, he became Bismarck's dogsbody, even stooping so low as to spy on the latter's enemy, Graf Harry Arnim, when he served with him in the Paris embassy. His lowly conduct at the time was thought unbecoming, and 'Prussian high society avoided him like Judas'.[30] His only world was the salon of Helene von Lebbin, a politically engaged widow who gathered around her a crowd of bankers and civil servants. Holstein went there virtually every night.

Holstein became Eulenburg's nemesis, but for the time being the latter was still capable of showering the 'man with hyena eyes' with gushing flattery:

With the incomparable colour and perfume of musigny, I am writing your name on my grateful heart. I was a young third secretary, more taken up with poetry than diplomacy. I looked on you as a foreign body, inaccessible, permanently concealed. And now I can't imagine an existence without you.[31]

William had other cronies, but none was a friend in the sense that Eulenburg was. He had known Fritz Krupp since 1885 when he had first visited him in Potsdam. Both had inherited their empires at much the same time. Krupp had shrewd business reasons for keeping in with the future emperor. After William came to power there were annual, two-day visits to the Villa Hügel in Essen and Krupp was always his guest at Kiel where the firm had acquired the Germania yard.[32] Later William's racing yachts were built there. In 1896 Krupp told of an 'unforgettable evening' with William, when the conversation had ranged from 'x-rays, the Conservative Party and a few of its leaders, the Kanitz Bill, navy, the bad feeling vis-à-vis England and Stoecker'.[33] Admiral Hollmann (he was ennobled in 1900) was Krupp's man at court, part of an extended gang of officers who were on the industrialist's payroll. William listened attentively to Krupp, claiming to have sacked three ministers of war as a result of his advice, Krupp for his part saw no conflict of interest 'between patriotism and profit', but was careful not to expand into Britain, where he might have caused offence.[34]

In the first years of his reign, William also grouped his favourites into a small kitchen cabinet. One of these was Graf Hugo Douglas, a rich potash and salt mine-owner whom Vicky thought 'a great donkey'. He was of Scottish descent, was ennobled by William I and made a count by his grandson. At William's accession Douglas wrote a mendacious, air-brushed panegyric to introduce the new emperor to his subjects. William was a frequent guest in his house. Another was Geheimrat August von Heyden, a former mine official turned painter 'who', according to Bismarck, 'counted as a painter in mining circles and a miner among painters'. After Marschall von Bieberstein replaced Herbert Bismarck at the Foreign Office, William used to drop in on him, quite unannounced, calling for a simple bowl of soup. Later he shunned him, for he thought that as a south German Marschall had insufficient 'Prussian feelings'. Naturally William had his cronies among the hunting crowd, especially East Prussian noblemen such as the Dohnas. One of them even saved William's life after the horses bolted at Pröckelwitz.[35]

IV

The immediate aftermath of Frederick III's death has often been painted, and in all its sordid colours. Acting on plans laid as much as four months earlier William had the palace surrounded in an attempt to hold on to his father's papers, which had already been long ago spirited out of the country. He believed they were state papers and that they belonged in Germany, and he was almost certainly right. At the last moment Friedberg may have convinced him to moderate his behaviour, stressing its doubtful legality. In Doorn, after his abdication, William continued to defend his stance, pointing out that those very same papers were then being published in Britain and 'to the detriment of the German Empire'.[36] No one was allowed to leave until a search had been made none the less, but nothing was found. He countermanded his father's wishes over the Battenberg marriage and the autopsy. The latter proved that Bergmann had been right, Mackenzie wrong, all along.

In fact, even Mackenzie was careful to point out that the autopsy was required under Prussian law. The Scottish physician was woken somewhat abruptly the morning after Fritz's death and summoned to Bismarck and William who asked him to write a report in which he recognised the cause of death as being cancer. Mackenzie was present at the post-mortem. Most of Fritz's larynx had disintegrated.[37] The burial confirmed the feeling of many observers that Frederick's reign had been to some degree irrelevant. No foreign princes were invited to the funeral. According to Waldersee, this affront to the ruling houses was as a result of a spoken wish on Vicky's part.[38] Eulenburg described the scene as he had had it from Wilhelm von Doehring: 'The troops wonderful, the clergy laughing, Field Marshal Blumenthal with the standard over his back, staggering this way and that, talking. It was enough to make you shudder – In the circumstances the emperor [William] serious and worthy ... Only Moltke carried his marshal's baton.'[39] The procession made its way through the park from the Neues Palais to the

Friedenskirche. The court mourning was short. A week after his father's death 'Friedrichskron' became the Neues Palais* again and William gave his mother notice to quit.

Certainly William had decided to gloss over the ninety-nine days and to disregard any decisions made during that time. The pages of history were to be wiped clean. This was done on Bismarck's advice. The chancellor did not want a legend to grow up around Fritz, and took pains to stamp out any indications that one was about to arise.[40] His friends and the members of his military entourage were not entirely without pity for the late emperor. Julius Moltke examined his corpse and was saddened at the thought of a man being carried off before he had been able to make his mark. William did not think so: he told Eulenburg: 'God has not deserted Prussia in that he has removed the era of Frederick, husband and wife, from the annals of history.'[41]

Over the years William's treatment of his mother has gained her a permanent support lobby, and one which is even now spawning books. Many people, however, recognised the close similarity between Vicky and her son. One of these was her admirer Seckendorff, who once told Bülow, 'There are not two people who are more alike than the Kaiserin and her eldest son. The only difference is that the latter wears trousers and goes about with unbuckled sabre, while the mother goes around in long dresses wearing a veil.'[42] He had inherited her memory, her lack of snobbery, openness, vivacity, moodiness, over-estimation of her own importance, her cleverness without wisdom. William recognised the similarity better than she did. In 1889 he told the British ambassador Sir Edward Malet, 'My mother and I have the same characters. I have inherited hers. That good stubborn English [sic] blood that will not give way, runs in both our veins. The consequence is that, if we do happen to agree, the situation becomes difficult.'[43]

The largely English Marie von Bunsen who visited Vicky in her widowhood, thought she had no love left for any of her children. She virtually denied her consanguinity with William, pointing out his mad ancestors as his closest forebears: 'He has nothing of me, a great deal from Frederick William IV; he himself thinks he resembles Frederick the Great the most ... He certainly derives his character from Tsar Paul.'[44] Queen Victoria seems to have understood her grandson a little better than his mother did. After Fritz's funeral she wrote him a sympathetic letter which attempted to bring peace to the Hohenzollern household: 'Let me also ask you to bear with poor mama if she is sometimes irritated and excited. She does not mean it so: think what

---

* It was thereby saved from the rebuilding which Fritz and Vicky had planned for it. See Ponsonby, *Empress Frederick*, 319.

months of agony and suspense and watching with broken and sleepless nights she has gone thro', and don't mind it. I am so anxious that all should go smoothly, that I write this openly in the interests of you both.'[45] Victoria's understanding, such as it was, had its limitations. Like William she insisted on seeing international relations as family relations. William complained that he treated her as a grandson, not as the German emperor. The entire business, Fritz's death and a campaign against the new emperor by the British press which had taken Vicky's side, caused a frost between Britain and Germany.[46]

In one of his later apologia, William claimed that at the time of his coming to power he still 'honoured in the same way the mighty chancellor with all the vigour of my youth, proud that I had served under him and that from now on I could work with him together as my chancellor'. He was Bismarck's pupil and everything he knew about diplomacy he had garnered from the master.[47] It was less than the truth. He still bore Bismarck a grudge for the way he had treated him over Stoecker and the proclamation to the German princes. Eulenburg probably came closer to reality when he informed his friend Bernhard von Bülow that the relations between the two men were 'untenable'. He was right. Bismarck had run rings around his old master, and Fritz was in no position to stand up to him; but he could not reasonably expect this situation to go on for ever. For the new emperor it was clearly not going to work in the long run. Bismarck informed him of each new law after its promulgation, or greeted each of William's cherished ideas with biting sarcasm. Bismarck had been ill, and his recovery slow. Business was piling up. Important issues were despatched to Friedrichsruh or Varzin. Unimportant ones went into the 'Sunday file'.[48] Apart from Bismarck's increasing inadequacy as a minister to a thrusting young emperor, there existed powerful lobbies possessed of William's ear. One of the most important of these was Dona, who resented Bismarck's role in depriving her dead father of his duchy. Another was Vicky: William told Poultney Bigelow that he had never forgiven Bismarck for the troubles he had caused with his mother.[49] There was possibly further pressure from William's military entourage. The Prussian Junkers hated Bismarck because he had literally hounded one of their own – Graf Harry von Arnim – to death. Not for nothing was the Borussocentric Waldersee at the heart of the plot to unseat the chancellor.[50]

Johanna von Bismarck suffered clear trepidation at the onset of William's rule, much more so than her husband. 'I am terribly scared of his hotheadedness and his great *inner* youth, which is much greater than his years. Please may God not desert us!'[51] William also made a bad impression by delivering his first address to the army, rather than to his people. On the day of his accession he intoned, 'We belong together, the army and I, and we were born for one another . . .' His later apologists claimed Bismarck should have schooled him better.[52] With such statements Waldersee naturally believed his star was now firmly in the ascendant. He read the first imperial pronouncements with glee and noted that the liberals and Jews had been beaten on all fronts.

William's eagerness impressed his contemporaries. On 17 June Julius Moltke noted in his diary: 'The young emperor is constantly active and has been in conference all day, he has issued commands, signed orders. As [we] already expected the first cabinet orders were issued in the evening with the epiphet Imperator Rex.' Two days later he was blessing his 'young lord' for wanting to rule alone.[53] On the 22nd the press were sharpening their knives on Waldersee once again: he was the head of a camarilla, and was forming a war party with the intention of toppling Bismarck; Mary Waldersee had Dona in her pocket. William responded by packing Waldersee off to Vienna with a mission to explain some of the more bizarre aspects of his behaviour at the time of his father's death.

William met his viceroy to Alsace-Lorraine when he called on him for an audience at the Marmorpalais on the same day. Prince Hohenlohe had something to say about the last days of the late emperor: 'It seems that at the end the smell was terrible, so that death was a blessing, even for the attendants.' After his meeting with William he called on Vicky, who was still living in the Neues Palais. She was bitter and reproachful, chiefly against the Bismarcks, claiming that Herbert had put it about that her late husband had no right to rule. Her son was completely under Bismarck's thumb, and Waldersee 'a false, unscrupulous man who would not mind running the country to satisfy his personal pride'.[54]

On 25 June 1888 the Reichstag opened. Bismarck had talked William out of the idea of a coronation, stressing the cost. The chancellor also took a distinctly old Prussian view when it came to the fine robes of the Black Eagle. He refused to wear the red coat, saying 'This striking costume is uncontemporary, unpopular and politically detrimental.' For all that, he cut a dash in his cuirassier's uniform. He led in the members of the federal council like so many lambs. William still inspired a great deal of confidence – and not just traditional circles were 'enchanted and inspired' by him; he was young, vigorous and healthy, and much was expected of him.[55] His first speech was well-measured too: 'Our army should secure us peace, and, if this should be broken for all that, be in the position to fight for it with honour . . . Germany needs neither glory in war nor any form of conquest now that it has finally won the fight to be entitled to stand as an independent nation.'[56]

There were a few sops to the liberals, notably the appointment of Rudolf von Bennigsen to the Oberpräsidium in Hanover. In early speeches the new emperor also stressed his desire to help the oppressed, a sign that Hinzpeter's influence was still strong. In those first few months, William was popular with the workers so that when he rode through poor parts of Berlin they would cheer, 'Hail to the workers' king!'[57] In his speech from the throne on 27 June he remembered his father: 'The sceptre rested only a few months in my late father's hand, but long enough to recognise what a ruler the fatherland has lost in him. His lofty appearance, the nobility of his thinking, his glorious part in the recent history of the Fatherland and the heroic courage and Christian humility with which he fought against his mortal illness, these have erected a permanent monument in the hearts of his people.' Many more monuments were to follow; in stone.[58]

On the same day William sent the great Moltke his bust in plaster by Walther Schott,[59] with the promise of a bronze to follow. The general had been hoping to retire for some time: he could no longer ride a horse. Now his wish was to be granted. Waldersee was made Chief of the Great General Staff on 10 August, and Moltke, almost as old as the century, gratefully went into retirement. Waldersee was causing concern with the old guard. Bismarck's Jewish banker Gerson Bleichröder warned that the officer 'considered himself capable and fitted for anything'. Bismarck had plans to remove him from the General Staff and give him a command in Strasbourg. His anti-Semitism was seen as a bad influence on William too. Friedberg was also nervous of what would come to pass: 'He knows that the emperor does not favour the Jews.'[60] Hohenlohe came round to William then. On 3 August he saw his new master again and found he reminded him of Prince Albert, a view he maintained for some time. 'If he develops like his grandfather we may be content.'[61]

Waldersee, however, had fewer and fewer illusions about his new patron. On the 26th he noted feverish activity, but thought William was devoting too much time to military questions: 'There is hardly any time left for audiences, it is very hard to see the monarch.'[62] Waldersee still had access, however. After the parade in Berlin on 1 September William and his Chief of Staff smoked a cigar together in his apartment. On 1 October the new emperor was in Munich and stopped for lunch with Eulenburg whom he invested with the Hohenzollern Hausorden. Thirty days later his friend received his new posting to Oldenburg.

William's first state visit was to St Petersburg from 22 to 24 July. He had written to both Francis Joseph and Crown Prince Rudolf a month before and promised to visit Vienna in late summer or autumn. In his letter to Rudolf he revealed his hand. He wanted to prepare a new triple alliance to maintain peace. Rudolf promptly leaked it to the Quai d'Orsay.[63] The meetings between the two central European emperors were to take place once a year at the very least. William's grandfather's habit of staging the event in some German spa town was to be dropped in favour of a more showy state visit.[64]

William went to Peterhof with Bismarck's instructions in his pocket, and Herbert to hold his hand. As crown prince, William was still sporting a bellicose attitude towards the Russian court. Herbert was there to make sure there were no relapses. In Krasnoe Selo there was a parade of 60 battalions of infantry, 51 squadrons of cavalry and 168 guns. Herbert wrote to his father on the 25th from the *Hohenzollern*, to describe a meeting he had had with the Tsar.

Herbert was anxious to scotch any rumours that relations were worsening between the two courts. At first Alexander claimed that he had been uncertain that William would succeed to the imperial throne. He thought perhaps that the throne rotated through the different royal houses. Herbert put him right on the details of the imperial constitution. The Secretary of State noted that the Tsar put out his cigarettes: a sure sign that he wanted an extended chat. He was curious to know about William's relations with his mother. 'The faults are above all on the side of the dowager empress,' said Herbert. 'I have had the impression for some time', replied the Tsar, 'that the poor Emperor Frederick, of whom I was most fond, was no more than a malleable instrument in the hands of his wife . . .' He believed the English influence was too powerful from her side. 'It is clear that all agreement is impossible; it is a *petitio principii*.' The Russian ruler went back to the subject of Fritz: 'I very much believe that you must feel you have rid yourself of a nightmare since William mounted the throne.'[65]

v

On the return journey he dropped in on the kings of Sweden and Denmark. It was the first ever visit to the Swedish court by a Prussian monarch. While he was there his fifth son was born and he was named Oscar Charles Gustavus Adolphus as a result.[66] The priority granted to the Russians, let alone the Swedes and the Danes, was an intentional snub to the British, and was not missed in London, but he would have justified it by the worsening of relations with Germany's eastern neighbour.

France was now making loans and selling arms to Russia, and there had been a massive demonstration in favour of Pan-Slavism in Kiev.[67] It was the beginning of a restless reign. William believed in the maximum show, the absolute contradiction of the Prussian dictum that you should be 'mehr Sein als Schein' – be more than you seem. He seemed to be more than he was. When people complained that William travelled too much, he would reply that their attitude was short-sighted. They lived in the age of transport. As soon as cars were available William had to have them. As it sped through the streets of Berlin the horn of his approaching motor car made a distinctive sound: tatoo, tata, 'Bald hier, bald da' (Here today, gone tomorrow); as it passed, a second signal reminded Berliners of 'Ist unser Geld' (It's our money).[68]

The message put out to the European courts was still 'Our policy aims at the maintenance of peace',[69] but William's sabre-rattling was not all gone. At his brother Henry's wedding in May the Prince of Wales had not only made an ill-timed plea for compensation for the Cumberlands over Hanover; he had led William to believe that Fritz had promised to revise the Franco-German borders in order to return some of the less willing Germans in Lorraine to the mother country. No one knows whether this was true, or whether Edward was simply making trouble. It was, after all, Fritz who was largely responsible for their inclusion in the first place. He none the less repeated his suggestions to Herbert, who told William. The putative cession of territory formed the subject of William's hottest-headed speech to date, delivered at Frankfurt on the Oder on 16 August. The emperor made it clear that 'we would rather leave our entire 18 army corps and 42 million inhabitants on the field of battle than cede one single stone of what my father and Prince Frederick Charles won'.[70]

Uncle Bertie would continue to bother him, always for William the personification of perfidious Albion. Relations were more complex than they seemed. It was not just that Prince Edward was Vicky's brother, and therefore party to the feud which had grown up between mother and son; but he was also Alexandra's husband, and the Danish princess had never forgiven Prussia for the war of 1864. Even on the British side the Hanoverian issue was never clearly settled: Britain was still the natural home for the Hanoverian fronde. And then there was Dona, whose influence on William grew steadily after 1888. She detested the British. It was not just William who liked to reduce foreign politics to personal or family relations; it was Queen Victoria under Albert's influence who had established the precedent, and the Prince of Wales in no way diverged from his mother and father's teaching.

The military remained William's obsession during the first years of his reign. He held his first major review on 4 September and exulted to Eulenburg over the pleasure of having his entire, 30,000-strong guard under his command for the first time: '... what a feeling it is to call these troops *my own*.'[71] Waldersee took a dim view of William's insistence on being present at the naval manoeuvres at the beginning of October. He feared that money would be taken away from the land forces. The Chief of Staff was allowed to criticise the annual manoeuvres, which was one of the reasons for his fall. For the time being he felt he had extricated himself from a tricky situation extremely nimbly. He was still hoping to push William into making war on Russia. The parallel with Frederick the Great would have been too obvious to him. There was a great temptation to shower himself with military glory at the beginning of his reign.

Temptation was not enough, but William defended his later dropping the secret Russian treaty to the last: Bismarck did not trust the Russians either, and the Tsar certainly did not have any confidence in the Iron Chancellor. The situation in Russia had changed too. William later told Niemann at Amerongen that the French and the Russians had already become too close and the Pan-Slavs had managed to insinuate themselves into positions of power. There was also a fear of a revival of Kaunitzian principles which had governed Austrian foreign policy at the time of the Seven Years War: that the Danube Monarchy might turn away from Germany, especially if Crown Prince Rudolf were to accede. Even after Rudolph's untimely death William believed it was in Germany's interests to maintain Austria as a great power even if that meant friction with Russia.[72]

VI

In the third week of September Fritz's War Diary for 1870–71 appeared in the *Deutsche Rundschau*. Bismarck responded with the utmost ferocity. He had the editor, the historian, former Hamburg diplomat and envoy to London, Professor Geffken, arrested under article 92 of the Penal Code covering state secrets. The magazine was also prosecuted. Geffken had had some idea that publication was not going to be popular, and had briefly taken refuge on British Heligoland. The chancellor then issued a statement alleging that the diary was a fraud. Johanna knew better – '... the worst thing is that it is not spreading falsehoods around the world, but publishing a lot of troubling truths for the sake of pure evilness and against the young emperor and papa [Bismarck]'. William called it 'terribly poisonous'. Bismarck feared a surge of popularity for the dead emperor. His action certainly limited the diary's exposure in its uncensored state. It was more widely seen abroad than within Germany itself: an English publication came out within weeks.[73]

In his diary Fritz took most of the credit for the creation of the Reich, while the chancellor himself appeared deeply sceptical about the Empire, and the king, William I, wanted no part in it. The Bavarian king was belittled and Fritz also emerged as the man who had called for the annexation not just of Alsace but also the largely French-speaking Lorraine. It was a piece of mischief-making on the part of Vicky, who was finding it hard to come to terms with the fact that 'the aim and purpose of her life had perished' with her husband.[74] Poor Geffken was a member of her circle, and he had been a fellow student of Fritz's at Bonn.[75] On 16 October Morell Mackenzie's book *Frederick the Noble* was published, in which he criticised the German doctors who had attended the late emperor. Again Vicky had prior knowledge. She also commissioned a flattering portrait -'nothing controversial' – from the British diplomat Sir Rennell Rodd.[76]

In the end the revelations of Fritz's central role in the creation of the Reich seem to have had little effect. Hildegard von Spitzemberg noted that the subject was on everyone's lips. On 30 September Fontane wrote, 'Geffken! Who would have thought of him.' In Fontane's circle it was clear that the diary increased Bismarck's support and brought opprobrium for Fritz. 'He overrated himself, and did not wish to see that next to the great man he was only a dilettante.' Johanna Bismarck was extremely relieved to hear that Geffken had been locked up.

William was showing a marked interest in travel and for an extravagant emperor, going anywhere was a big business. Bags and trunks had to be packed and special uniforms, rings, watches and medals could not be left out. Throughout his reign William had the assistance of his valet Schulz, who was the only man to properly understand his requirements. Within Germany William had the court train at his disposal. It had dark blue carriages with ivory-coloured borders. His personal quarters consisted of a sleeping car, saloon and dining car. There was also a sleeping car for his suite, a kitchen, baggage wagon and two locomotives.

On 27 August he had been to Dresden for the start of a series of calls on the German princes. In September he went to Detmold, Stuttgart and Baden. William and Herbert went to Vienna together for the official courtesy visit, arriving on 3 October. Herbert's mother was kept informed and was alarmed to hear that William had changed his clothes eight times in one day. The new emperor wanted to cement relations with the younger generation of archdukes, notably Francis Ferdinand. Rudolf was clearly an enemy, but then his own father treated him with much the same lack of trust as William I had shown Fritz. Prior to his accession Rudolf had described William as 'an inexperienced Prussian officer, a hothead in charge of the German barracks, and God in Heaven knows what will happen ...' He predicted – accurately as it turned out – that under William Austria and Germany would 'sink in a sea of blood'.[77]

The older archdukes were still bitter about Königgrätz, but William was possibly surprised to see such a good turnout from Georg von Schönerer's German nationalists, who proclaimed William to be 'their emperor'. William's patronage of Stoecker had done him good in Austria, where Schönerer's men saw him as a saviour from the 'Jewish yoke'.[78] Herbert assured Francis Joseph that Fritz's reign had been no more than an interregnum, and that policy would return to the lines laid down under William I. Fritz's death had rid Germany of a 'bad nightmare'. Francis Joseph also condemned Vicky's behaviour. The publication of her husband's diary had, among other things, shown the reluctance of the Bavarian rulers, the Austrian emperor's wife's family, to enter a united Germany.[79]

One man who was not in Vienna to see William during the week he spent there was Uncle Bertie. William had had him banned, making it clear that he was to be the only prince received at the time. The German emperor had not forgotten Edward's trouble-making over Alsace-Lorraine. William was also aware that the Prince of Wales fed Rudolf's idea of a revival of the 1756 alliance against Prussia – or in this case Germany. Only this time Britain might come in on the side of the opposition. Rudolf's leaks exacerbated the feud between uncle and nephew and the archduke made a point of asking the English prince to join him hunting in the Siebenbürgen. Rudolf told his wife that the only reason he would invite William would be to organise an 'elegant hunting accident' to remove him from the world.[80]

William must have been aware of Rudolf's behaviour. Once he had returned from his journey he wrote to Francis Joseph to protest about the fact that Rudolf was Inspector-General of the imperial army, given that Austria was Germany's ally, and that her soldiers would fight shoulder to shoulder with Germany's. William suggested he be replaced by a proper military figure. The letter resulted in a scene between Rudolf and his father.[81]

From Vienna he travelled south to Rome, arriving on the 11th. The Italian press greeted the theatrical new German ruler with enthusiasm – he was 'il nuovo Cesare'. He had an audience, the first of three, with Pope Leo XIII, whose style impressed the young emperor, even if Herbert reported that he had found the Pontiff himself a boring hypocrite. On the 17th he was in Naples. There he visited the Museo Nazionale. For an entire minute he studied a bust of Caesar. 'I believe that I have a mission to crush the Gauls like Julius Caesar,' he intoned. He returned to Germany by sea. Waldersee not only thought all this travel was a waste of time and money, he believed William's ascent too rapid. The wags agreed. One joke which circulated in 1889 read: 'What is the leading firm in Germany?' '*Bismarck und Sohn*, because they have an emperor as a travelling salesman.'[82]

The Geffken case was closely followed by the Morier scandal. Sir Robert Morier was the British ambassador to St Petersburg and a close friend and adviser to Vicky, who had *inter alia* found Hinzpeter for

William. It was claimed that Morier had informed the French General Bazaine of German troop movements when he had been envoy to Darmstadt during the Franco-German war. Bismarck demanded Morier's recall. The diplomat fought back, publishing his correspondence with Bazaine to prove that he was not guilty. The episode caused Bismarck much embarrassment.

The third of Bismarck's anti-liberal tirades which occurred after William's accession was the action against the Swiss socialists. Social democratic literature was being written in Switzerland and carried across the border into Germany for dissemination. Bismarck planted a spy among them, and the Swiss authorities raised the matter in Germany. When the Swiss refused to do anything to curb the activities of German socialists, Bismarck prevented German tourists from spending their holidays in Switzerland and threatened to send in the army.

On 28 October Julius Moltke accompanied his uncle to the Marmorpalais. Here he renewed acquaintance with his former regimental comrade. 'My God, you are also already a major? It makes me feel old to think that I knew you as a little whippersnapper in the regiment. Well, I congratulate you.' Moltke and his uncle had lunch with the emperor and empress. Also present were the 'Hallelujah aunts', Dona's two ladies-in-waiting, Gräfinen Keller (Tante Ke) and Brockdorff, the later General Bissing and three of William's ADCs. From the small dining room there was 'a splendid view over the deep blue lake and the opposite bank'.

The royal children were brought out to meet the field marshal. There was some concern that the architect of Prussia's victorious campaigns in 1864, 1866, and 1870–1 might catch cold. Julius had to fetch his cap. Four little boys appeared wearing velvet suits and busbies, and little August Wilhelm in a white dress and with bare legs. Julius Moltke thought the eldest had his father's eyes. William smoked a cigar and looked on. 'It was a delicious family scene,'[83] wrote the younger Moltke in his diary. The real delight for the four Prussian princes was a chance to be drilled by the field marshal. Later they arrested one of the emperor's ADCs.

Eulenburg stayed with William in Potsdam in November, singing for his supper as ever. William's relations with his mother were discussed. In the Wilhelmstrasse they thought that the best solution was to drive Vicky away and thereby prevent open war from breaking out. On 5 November William took his friend to see his new apartment in the Berlin Schloss. Once again he turned the pages for Eulenburg that evening as he sat at the piano. They played William's favourites: 'Atlantis', 'König Eriks Genesung', 'Sängers Tod', 'Ingeborg' and 'König Alf'. William and Dona were still living in the Marmorpalais. Dinners were given in the small parterre saloon and followed a certain rule. There were always four courses, pudding, and red and white wine. German sparkling wine was served afterwards in the upstairs saloon. On this occasion Eulenburg sat next to Dona. The conversation, he records, was 'very relaxed'.[84] William was still obsessed by war and believed it very near. Eulenburg quotes a letter he received at the time: 'Dear Philipp, we live in strange circumstances. Any moment relations could change and throw us into war. An inward collapse in Russia or even France would be enough.' Once again he had received reports – presumably from Waldersee – that Russian troops were massing on the frontier.[85]

Despite Waldersee pushing him towards war with the Russians, William retained his own view of foreign policy. He was longing for that close relationship first mooted by Albert, and hoped that the British would soon see sense. Despite Bismarck's and Chamberlain's attempts, however, the alliance came to nothing. The German chancellor was left to rue his 'cauchmar des coalitions'. William believed that if Britain failed to ally with Germany in event of war, and if Germany were to be defeated, Britain would fall an easy victim to concerted action by Russia and France. The British, however, were being made increasingly aware of the rift between William and his mother, and unsurprisingly took the latter's side. On 15 November Vicky applied to leave for England, but expressed no desire to see William first. 'His mother accuses him of dishonouring his father's memory,' noted Waldersee.[86]

William responded by going to the station to see his mother off. Waldersee hoped she might stay away for a very long time. The austere Chief of Staff was shocked to find that William had engaged three court marshals to officiate at dinner that evening. These touches of un-Prussian luxury troubled him, and he thought one courtier would have been quite enough. There was something more sinister besides: 'It is strange how the emperor allows the influence of these gentlemen to grow, everywhere you hear complaints about their arrogance.'[87] Waldersee was witnessing the beginnings of William's Byzantine court.

To Waldersee's frustration he was not the sole influence on the new ruler. Herbert still had his ear. The Chief of Staff was distressed to find William to be anti-Austrian and attributed the sentiment to the chancellor's son. As it transpired, it may have had more to do with his growing contempt for Crown Prince Rudolf. William was also proving obstinate when it came to putting into practice Waldersee's cherished preventative war. Opening the Reichstag on 22 November he declared: 'To foist on Germany the suffering of war, even a victorious one, when it was not necessary, I could not reconcile with the duties I have taken on as Emperor of the German people and my Christian beliefs.'[88] Waldersee still retained the semblance of a relationship with Herbert's father, and watched him tippling Mosel wines after breakfast. Bismarck was aware that he had to spend more time in Berlin, rather than trying to run the country from his estates. 'I must go to Berlin soon', he told Waldersee, 'as I must see the emperor often; it is actually necessary that I speak to him twice a week.'[89]

The Chief of Staff noted two 'unpleasant events' to bring in the new year: the courts had thrown out the Geffken case, and the editor and publisher of Fritz's diaries had been released from prison. Hohenlohe dined with William in the new year, just a few days before his thirtieth birthday. Hinzpeter was also there. They discussed education. William was still smarting from his experience in Cassel. He was 'against the excessive demands of these institutions, while we defended them, making plain to him that only great demands could prevent a rush to them and check a learned proletariat'.[90] It was not to be William's last word on the subject, but he never managed to get his way. Later they pored over the plans for Berlin's new cathedral, which had been promoted by Fritz and Vicky. Over the holiday period, William also went to Liebenberg, and presented his friend Eulenburg with the first newly minted coin to bear his features.

VII

The new year brought in a new series of visits for the restless emperor. On 16 January William was in Bückeburg, visiting the Lippes. Over the next six months he made appearances in Oldenburg, Weimer, Brunswick, Saxony and Württemberg. Crown Prince Rudolf shot himself in Mayerling near Vienna on 30 January 1889. There was little or no pretence of friendship between him and William and he had lately taken to giving newspapers in Austria and France details of William's extramarital affairs. At the end of his life, William tried to conceal his contempt for Francis Joseph's only son – who had occupied a position analogous to Fritz at the Austrian court – but there was truth in his stressing 'how little inclination the crown prince had towards the German Empire and the alliance. Above all he hated the idea of Prussianism from the bottom of his soul.'[91]

One of the first tests of the new emperor's mettle was the Westphalian miners' strike in the spring of 1889, which took the civil authorities by surprise. It began in Gelsenkirchen and spread quickly. Soon Krupps had been brought to a standstill and workers were downing tools in Upper Silesia, Aachen and Saxony. It looked like turning into a general strike. William, who was still under the influence of Hinzpeter,[92] made noises about social justice and thought he understood the miners better than the Bismarcks, who were pressing for drastic measures. There was a strong difference of opinions during the cabinet meeting on 12 May. It was nothing to do with achieving popularity, he said later. He felt he could wean them off socialism with modern social legislation. It was worth having a go with a carrot before having recourse to the stick. Despite his later disclaimer, there is evidence that William's concern for the German workers greatly increased his popularity. He was much criticised for referring to the socialists as 'fellows without a fatherland', but he said he had been misinterpreted: many socialists were already talking of joining forces with their brothers across the French border.[93]

From his military commander in the region, the hussar colonel von Michaelis, William received a telegram which confirmed his interpretation of the situation. 'All is calm, with the exception of the authorities,' it read. William was determined to be the 'roi des gueux' – a king to the poor. 'To think consciously of society and to act in that consciousness, is my conviction from the quintessence of practical Christianity.'[94] This attitude led him to intervene contrary to his chancellor's advice. He went so far as to receive both sides in the Berlin Schloss, something which must have looked very revolutionary indeed at the time. The workers informed him that all they wanted was a return to the eight-hour day which had been the rule in the past. On 16 May he told the employers that he was there to understand both sides of the issue, and that the two sides should settle their differences before other Germans began to suffer as a result. William told them, 'If the firms do not raise wages immediately I shall withdraw my troops.' Bismarck countered: 'The owners are also Your Majesty's subjects.' The chancellor was all for wielding the stick, even if that meant gunning a few miners down. William objected that he did not wish to begin his reign 'stained with the blood of my own countrymen'.[95]

'I am not cross with my young master,' said Bismarck, 'he is fiery and full of life; he wants to make everyone happy; that is natural at his age!'[96] William's later attitude towards the socialists was such that few people give him credit for this flash of liberalism at the beginning of his reign. He did in fact free the party from the strait waistcoat put on it by Bismarck's anti-socialist laws. He would live to regret it. In 1891 the workers adopted the Erfurt programme, in which they chose to achieve power by parliamentary rather than revolutionary means. William opened a door which he was unable to shut. In 1894–5, he tried to curtail anti-democratic activities but the Reichstag refused to ratify an 'anti-revolution bill' which had been aimed at limiting press freedom. In 1897 William pressed for limits to the right to associate. These were also rejected by the Reichstag. A bill which proposed to stop strikes suffered a similar fate.[97]

In May William went hunting at Pröckelwitz. He told Eulenburg that he was out of sorts with Bismarck: 'I have had frightful difficulties with the prince.'[98] William later justified his behaviour on the basis of popular government. 'I was filled with a clear consciousness of my duty and responsibility towards my entire people, and that also meant towards the working class.' Eulenburg was already pulling the wires behind the stage. He was conspiring with Holstein to retain Bismarck as a figurehead, but to strip him of his powers. Possibly it was Eulenburg who advised William to thwart his chancellor by introducing his social welfare legislation in the Bundesrat, with the support of the king of Saxony.[99] William was worried about the constant presence of Gerson von Bleichröder at Bismarck's Berlin residence. He thought the old banker was loaning money to the Russians to finance a war against Germany.

Another of his complaints against Bismarck was that he ignored the non-Prussian parts of the Reich; he was 'too conservative and too Prussian'.[100] This difference of approach between the emperor and his chancellor was the 'actual reason for the rupture and earned me the enmity of Bismarck and for many years a large part of the German people too, in particular the civil service who were devoted to him.'[101] This William must have found galling, and it explains his persistent but reluctant attempts to bring about a complete reconciliation before the prince's death in 1898. William wanted to be popular and to unite his people. The feud with Bismarck stood in the way.

Two years later Waldersee made notes on the growing discord between William and the Iron Chancellor:

From then on the emperor only played games with the chancellor. At their meetings he was extremely polite and full of consideration; scarcely had the chancellor turned his back, however, than he complained and went as far as to mock him. Bismarck's approach was no different. During his audiences with the emperor he was always the faithful servant and subject who took the utmost pains about everything; afterwards he created immediate problems. Bismarck evaluated the relationship between the emperor and Herbert totally wrongly. The fault for this lay naturally with Herbert, who did not understand the emperor and gave his father incorrect information.[102]

Of course there was an element of sour grapes in this. The sententious Chief of Staff disliked the louche, heaving-drinking Herbert. He described the friendship between Herbert and William as 'an ominous mistake', and noted – certainly with pleasure – that the omniscient Holstein was deserting the Bismarck camp.[103]

Waldersee continued to detach new areas of power for the army and the General Staff. He had conceived of the notion of military attachés providing an alternative diplomatic service which compared favourably with the 'professionals' – a term used with a measure of distaste in his diary. On William's thirtieth birthday Waldersee was invested with a new advisory position on interior and exterior politics. Waldersee's ideas often conflicted with his master's, however. Like Bismarck, he thought the pursuit of African colonies of no importance. The next day Hinzpeter was in town. He met Waldersee, and they agreed in their judgements of William. The tutor told the Chief of Staff that his was the only voice William heeded. This was clearly untrue.

The Bismarcks were gunning for Waldersee. After a 'studenty' evening with Herbert that ended at 4 a.m. there were fresh attacks on Waldersee in the *Norddeutsche Allgemeine Zeitung*, 'Bismarck's personal organ': 'I have no doubt that there are plans to hunt me down again.'[104] On 13 February William warned Herbert to leave Waldersee alone. The attacks shifted to Stoecker. It was at this time that William decided that the preacher was a luxury he could no longer afford – especially as he was engaged in a messy squabble in the newspaper – and distanced himself from him. Both Dona and Waldersee waded in to protect Stoecker, but it was to no avail. Waldersee blamed the Jews for his downfall.

The 'Battenbergiade' finally came to a conclusion on the 25th, when Sandro married Johanna Loisinger of the Darmstadt Court Theatre. Waldersee noted maliciously: 'For the Empress Frederick it was a hard, but very deserving blow ... I have seldom seen the emperor look so contented.'[105] William was trying to recreate the 'tabakskollegia' of his ancestor Frederick William I. In the Sternensaal of the Berlin Schloss he brought together his hunting cronies: Waldersee, Prince Pless, Graf Asseburg, General von Arnim, and Herr von Meyerinck. True to the royal tradition they smoked, and drank beer or champagne.

In 1889 William made an important move towards the creation of a proper navy when he created the 'Oberkommando der Marine' or 'Reichsmarineamt'. Already an admiral, Alexander Graf Monts had replaced General Caprivi at the head of the fledgeling sea arm.[106] The sea and sailing were as important as ever – although William continued to suffer from *mal de mer*. On 30 June Eulenburg dined with Holstein at Borchhardt before his departure on the first ever *Nordlandsreise*. They were deep in conspiracy. They were worried that they might have to lose the chancellor, and yet they believed his presence to be necessary for the prestige of the realm.[107] Aboard the imperial yacht a group of William's cronies travelled up to the Arctic to enjoy the sea and landscapes of Norway and the northern lights. Eulenburg's fellow guests included a number of technocrats who could be guaranteed never to contradict His Majesty, as well as his favourite *farçeurs* and musicians: Waldersee, Adjutant-General Karl von Wedel, the later Cabinet Chief Lyncker, the adjutants von Scholl and von Lippe, Adolf von Bülow, the first head of the Naval Cabinet, the rabidly anti-British Gustav von Senden-Bibran, the diplomat Kiderlen Wächter, William's future theatre intendant Georg von Hülsen, and the artists Professor Güssfeldt and Karl Saltzmann. Waldersee was still at the top of his tree. Like Eulenburg he had the privilege of one of the best cabins: those flanking His Majesty's.

Eulenburg was not at his best. He never really enjoyed the *Nordlandsreisen* and usually needed to take a holiday to recover from the emperor's company. The renowned hypochondriac was suffering from rheumatism and shingles. As they crossed a glacier a large piece of ice crashed down at William's feet. Waldersee concluded, 'It became clear that when the shooting started, he would not bat an eyelid.'[108] Although Eulenburg was miserable with his ailments, he was obliged to make up a comic rhyme for Hülsen's birthday and sing his ballads again and again. William joined in the fun and squirted water at some of the company while they were quietly enjoying their game of skat. Later he disrupted a heavy drinking session which had continued until 1.30 a.m. by spraying the topers with champagne and soda water. The practical jokes were played on those who could take them. According to Marie von Bunsen, men such as Eulenburg, Court Marshal Hugo Freiherr von Reischach, Knesebeck or Seckendorff were always treated as gentlemen.[109] William was by all reports a very good host. On sea voyages, both in the north and in the Mediterranean, court etiquette was more or less put aside. Everything was done to make the emperor's guests feel comfortable.

They delighted in watching out for porpoises, hunted whales and shot seagulls. In Tromsö the news arrived that Queen Victoria proposed making William an admiral of the fleet, the naval equivalent of a field marshal. 'A distinction which had never been granted before and which could not fail to have a political effect ... The emperor was as excited as a child over his new honour ... In no way did William see the rank as a formality. He promptly sat down and began to fully reorganise the British fleet.'[110] In his idle moments, and there were plenty of these, Eulenburg encouraged William to read *Frithjof's Saga* by the Swedish poet Esaias Tegnér out loud. 'It was a joy to see him', wrote Eulenburg, 'enchanted by the beauty and the entire simplicity and plainness of his style.'[111] On Sunday William preached a sermon on the foredeck during the simple religious ceremony which took place on board. So was it to be every year until the North Sea excursions ceased just before the outbreak of war in 1914. A large trunk was covered with a flag emblazoned with a Prussian eagle and this served as an altar. The emperor wore his Black Eagle as if to emphasise the importance of the bird.

VIII

It was all go that summer. From 2–7 August William made the long-postponed first state visit to Britain when his squadron appeared off Spithead. On 5 August a grand naval review was laid on. From the Isle of Wight he went to Windsor. He attended manoeuvres in Aldershot on the 7th, where he had a chance to review his regiment, the Royal Dragoons. He was also given his official appointment as an honorary admiral of the fleet. The Prince of Wales refused to attend the festivities – he was still sulking after his banishment from Vienna. There was some serious work to do too. William was courting a British alliance and Herbert had put out feelers in March, using the Heligoland issue as bait. It was the old theme: Britain and Germany belonged together; 'sine Germania nulla sallus'. The British were anxious to lighten the German colonial portfolio of South-West Africa, which was more than Herbert was prepared to give. For his part Salisbury was still resisting diplomatic 'entanglements'. Splendid isolation had yet a little way to run.[112]

There was a return visit from Francis Joseph between 12 and 15 August, in the course of which William broke away from Bismarckian policy by assuring the Austrian emperor that he would join his country in war against Russia.[113] The visit had been planned in January, before Rudolf's death. The crown prince was supposed to make his peace with the German emperor. He would not co-operate, however, and had proposed to Russia instead.[114] The younger Moltke thought William looked uncomfortable in an Austrian uniform. The Austrian emperor had decided to honour the victor of Königgrätz with a regiment in the imperial army. The aged general misheard, and thought William was being granted yet another honorary colonelcy. When the Austrian military plenipotentiary congratulated him on being an officer in the Austro-Hungarian army, old Moltke recoiled in unconcealed horror. Once it was explained to him that *he*, and not William, had received the regiment he was deeply embarrassed that he had not thanked Francis Joseph properly.

On the 17th, William was in Bayreuth with Eulenburg. He wore an artillery uniform for the performance of *Die Meistersinger*, a reference perhaps to its bombastic style. What he donned for *Parsifal* is sadly not recorded. Hohenlohe discussed William with his uncle, the Grand Duke of Baden, on 24 August. He noted that there had already been a clash between the emperor and his chancellor. 'One must be prepared for the eventuality of the chancellor's dismissal. But what then? The emperor probably thought himself able to conduct foreign politics, but that was very dangerous.'[115]

On 12 December that year, Hohenlohe spent a musical evening with

William in the Muschelsaal of the Neues Palais. In the course of it, the Franconian prince received a better idea of the strange leaps and bounds made by the mind of 'Wilhelm der Plötzliche': William spoke to him about the speech he had made in Frankfurt am Main; using water to create electricity and its advantage to small traders; and his desire to have loopholes built into his Berlin Schloss in preparation for the attempted takeover of power by the Social Democrats. He was wrestling with the form of the monument to be erected in memory of his grandfather; he wanted a simple equestrian statue, but others proposed a lavish mausoleum: 'My father might have been put in such a mausoleum and surrounded with various things; he was for show. But my grandfather was not suitable for that.'[116]

Eulenburg's friendship with William made his presence in the Wilhelmstrasse vital from time to time, where his advice was called upon by Herbert, Kiderlen-Wächter, Lindau and Holstein. His job was to put out fires, and there were many. On 10 October he arrived at the Neues Palais just after Bismarck's audience. The chancellor was wearing the overcoat of his cuirassier regiment and carrying a white cap in his hand. Both Bismarck and Eulenburg had a hard job resisting the growing power of William's ADCs, whose terrible jokes appealed to the emperor. Dona's might was also increasing with time. At first William used to fulminate against the constraints of marriage, but 'the empress was victorious through her passivity'.[117]

William travelled to Athens on 27 October for the wedding of his sister Sophie to the Greek crown prince. He sailed into the harbour of Piraeus flying the pennant of an admiral of the Royal Navy. After a moment of shock the British naval captain Mark Kerr decided the best policy was to observe the etiquette in such matters and pay him a visit. His move was approved by the Prince of Wales. The officers were as struck by William's retentive mind as anyone else. He could recite the details of the British squadrons as well as the particularities of the engines in the latest class of vessels. He proposed a toast to Nelson and Howe. Herbert Bismarck told the captain, 'That comes from the heart.'[118]

It was decided to prolong the voyage by a visit to the Sublime Porte, the first ever made by a Christian monarch. Herbert Bismarck found the champagne glasses too small for his liking and called loudly for bigger ones. Poultney Bigelow, who was also there, described Herbert as a 'monumental eater and drinker. I never saw him drunk, nor yet sober.'[119] On 31 October the royal party travelled on to Istanbul where they were lodged in style at the Chalet Kiosk, which had been expanded to accommodate the German royal party.[120] William was still arming against the Russians, despite Bismarck's policy, and promised the Sultan

German help in warding off Russian attempts to take the Straits. The mission proved a success, initiating more than a quarter of a century of close Germano-Turkish relations.[121]

Eulenburg was still frequenting the Bismarck household. He was astonished by the food consumed at lunch. There was foie gras, smoked fish of all sorts and sizes, steaks, chops, vegetables and a heavy port wine, all placed on the table at the same time. Guests had to take something of everything, and comment on the foie gras – which Bismarck thought capable of curing his chronic indigestion. In the meantime the master of the house cut up little bits of meat and fed them to his famous dogs – the 'Reichshunde'. When Johanna criticised her husband for the amount of foie gras he ate, Bismarck replied with a line of Latin which his wife failed to understand. He translated it for her: 'What I have eaten, that I have. What I have achieved will be forgotten.'[122]

Bismarck told Eulenburg of his hopes for Herbert, whom he fully intended to succeed him as chancellor. 'I have unloaded all my experience on him. On no one else. The friendly disposition of the emperor's is fortunate for him, for he needs the kingdom for his life.' He talked about William too. 'He trusts in God as he trusts in fate allowing himself to be driven under the force of destiny with a little nuance of tragedy.' Bismarck observed his desire to surround himself with Hohenzollern memorabilia: 'Which path will the emperor take as he develops, however? For he is young, remarkably young, for his age.'[123]

Eulenburg came to the conclusion that both Bismarck and William wanted to pull the carriage of state, 'but one wants to go left, and the other right'. Bismarck's long absences were also contributing to the growing rift. The chancellor lived at Friedrichsruh near Hamburg or Varzin in Pomerania, where he received bundles of state papers and left the day-to-day business to Herbert. Bismarck may have thought William too young, but the emperor had begun to feel his chancellor was too old. He suggested senility and thought Bismarck's heavy drinking might be the cause. The waters were being muddied by William's Ober-hofmarschall von Liebenau who was feeding him with antipathetic reports. Eulenburg thought Liebenau largely to blame for the 'split which poisoned our country'. Liebenau wanted an ambassador's job and was running this way and that, telling stories to anyone who would listen.[124]

Waldersee found more things to rankle him in the new regime. William was showing a most un-Prussian tendency to squander money, and state money at that. A new royal yacht was to cost 4.5 million marks, a building by one of William's favourite architects – almost certainly Ihne – a further two million. It was the Tsar's turn to visit him at the beginning of October, but in the middle of November the emperor went off on another costly jaunt. Bismarck consented to these expenses, thought the general, because he was beginning to realise his job was at risk. Waldersee, however, took the high moral tone. Despite all he said, he did not think the new emperor a copybook Prussian either:

Very gradually a certain disappointment is developing: all those journeys, the restless activity, the various and different sorts of interests, have one natural consequence – a lack of efficiency. The Cabinet chiefs complain of the difficulty in obtaining an audience and that everything has to be concluded too quickly and with too little preparation. Ministers have the feeling that the emperor should speak to them from time to time about their portfolios, but he does that virtually never. He has regular briefings from the Minister of War and also very detailed ones from me, but way too much from Graf [Herbert] Bismarck.[125]

Liebenau was still rocking the boat. He was rude and tactless, and his master took the blame. He was hated for the spartan household he maintained. Even Dona failed to achieve the glass of madeira she craved after lunch. William resolved to sack his court marshal – 'They are already calling my court the Parvenu Court.' Worse still, he was suspected of spying for the Bismarcks. The chance came when William managed to offend the population of Elbing in East Prussia by not even appearing at the window to wave at an adoring crowd when his train went through the town on its way to his hunting lodge at Rominten or the royal farm at Cadinen. Liebenau had failed to warn William and was dismissed.[126] 'Radolin',* who looked after William's table and paid the household bills, did not have a much better reputation. The meanness of royal entertainment was at that time legendary.

On 5 December Hildegard Spitzemberg had a long talk with Bismarck in his coach at Friedrichsruh. Bismarck must have felt he had scored a victory in his fight against the socialists.[127] Despite all William's earlier noises, the chancellor had gone ahead and introduced a bill to extend the repressive anti-socialist laws on 25 October. The conversation was in French to prevent the coachman from understanding. It revealed that the old chancellor was in no way aware of how much the cards were stacking up against him.

He is sulking with me a bit, but that won't last. He is very Olympian, he is becoming carried away, less with himself or his rank, than with his position; in me he respects the statesman, his father and grandfather's counseller, the old man, but my successor will have a difficult time of it. The emperor has plenty of political judgement, he understands what is explained to him quickly; the problem is that he carries out immediately whatever comes into his head.

---

* He had Germanised his name from Radolinski in 1888.

Had he been a younger man he would have spent all day with William and wrapped him round his little finger. As it was the emperor allowed himself to be influenced by military men, above all his ADCs. The worst was the toady Waldersee, who compared him to Frederick the Great, 'and makes him even more Olympian'.[128]

Both Bismarck and William were unaware that Waldersee was losing faith. William's continued preference for the general and the rumours about the chance of his being made chancellor were beginning to make Bismarck nervous; especially as Waldersee persisted in seeing Russian troop movements as a pretext for preventative war. On 14 December, while William and his Chief of Staff were away in Hanover, he told Hohenlohe that Waldersee was no more than 'a muddle-headed politician upon whom no reliance was to be placed. He wanted war because he felt that he would be too old if peace lasted any longer … It was particularly stupid to believe that Waldersee could become imperial chancellor. Even as Chief of Staff he was unsatisfactory, and Moltke had only preferred him to Caprivi or [Hülsen-]Haeseler because he could do what he wanted with him.'[129]

Bismarck also underestimated the importance of Hinzpeter, whom he thought 'half-mad'. William was still writing to him and the former tutor put the world to rights in a letter to his pupil every two to four weeks. It was Hinzpeter who pushed William to carry out social reforms, to make him a 'roi des gueux'. William was also pleased with his work as a diplomatist. On 23 December he boasted to Waldersee of his relations with Russia as they went for a walk with a cigar. In fact, relations were worsening. Bismarck correctly believed that a Franco–Russian alliance was just around the corner. There was a pause for a family Christmas in the Neues Palais, which they had all to themselves now that Vicky had taken herself off to her new palace Friedrichshof which she was building in the west. The festivities on Christmas Eve were held in the Muschelsaal, the great grotto on the ground floor, facing Sanssouci. Every member of the family had his own tree. Dona did not meddle too much in politics at this stage. The church was her thing, and making sure lots of new ones were built in the expanding cities. There were thirty-two constructed in Berlin alone. Fifteen more garrison churches were built, but more on William's incentive than Dona's. She had an ally in her bigoted court marshal, Graf Mirbach.

On Christmas Eve William took a stroll around Potsdam in mufti, distributing alms to the poor. By tradition he went alone, but his private detectives were aware of the route. William was a pious man, and had no problem reconciling his faith with his occasional moments of bellicosity. He defied Hohenzollern tradition in later years by becoming rather more Lutheran than Calvinist. At home in Potsdam he attended the Sunday service in the Garrison Church, sitting in the royal box opposite the tombs of Frederick the Great and his father. As soon as he and his family arrived the organist started up. He took communion twice a year at Christmas and on Maundy Thursday. In Doorn he told a visitor, 'I am happy to be a believer. The believer has an easier time of it than one who denies God!'[130] It was a simple religion: 'Don't preach if you don't know where you are heading!' With Stoecker's demise he altered his perception of priests: 'Political pastors are an absurdity!' 'Pastors should look after souls, worry about loving your neighbour, but they should forget about politics, which is none of their business.' It might have been Bismarck.[131]

XI

William opened 1890 with a bloodbath. He went to stay with Graf Guido Henckel at Neudeck in Silesia, the richest man in Germany after William himself and Alfred Krupp. Henckel lived the sort of life William admired most: the entertainment was lavish, with caviar for breakfast, the count's serfs kissed the hem of the countess's dress as she passed and the game reserves were extremely well-stocked. In one single day's shooting William wiped out 550 pheasants.[132] Possibly it was the best sort of thing to put the emperor in the mood to deal with his over-mighty chancellor. The idyll, however, was cut short by the death of his grandmother, the Empress Augusta. He arrived in Berlin on the last day of Christmas. Augusta died on the 7th.

In the middle of January, William still had to make up his mind whether he wanted to sack his chancellor or not. Waldersee pumped the emperor's uncle, the Grand Duke of Baden, about this. The duke thought that he had resolved to keep Bismarck, but that he would demand a greater share in decision-making from now on. Waldersee did not believe him. He thought William was covering his tracks. He did not want the world to know that he was intending to drop the man who had been the architect of the German Reich. As Waldersee pointed out, Bismarck's position was extraordinary and by no means unassailable:

The chancellor wants to control everything and doesn't have the strength to do it any more. He is Minister for Foreign Affairs and meddles in every ministerial portfolio without any consideration for its heads; he is Minister President of Prussia and Minister for Trade and regards the other ministers as his juniors. On top of this he sits in Friedrichsruh and is therefore difficult to get hold of. Neither ministers nor heads of departments dare contradict him. They all complain of lack of instructions, uncertainty in taking decisions and especially about the chancellor's lying ... in times like the present when the

Reichstag and the Landtag are in session they often suffer from great embarrassment.[133]

Johanna was aware that there were problems afoot. She wrote to her son Bill on 20 January: '... it is really necessary that Papa comes [to Berlin] in order to put a stop to the confusion, excitement and cowardice.' William, she thought, was always so deep in his boyish visions that he could no longer differentiate black from white.[134] The two men were preparing for an almighty clash over the anti-socialist laws. Herbert stressed his father's 'experience', but Waldersee did not feel such arguments would count any more, William 'was not for turning'.[135] Bismarck arrived on 24 January for the ministerial and imperial councils after months of virtually permanent absence from his desk.

At the imperial council Bismarck threatened to resign if William continued to promote equitable social legislation in the face of the draconian anti-socialist laws he intended to bring in on 1 October. William was determined to offer his workers a better deal; Bismarck, 'to show them his teeth'. William was increasingly annoyed that the Bismarck press spoke of the 'chancellor's policy' and not the 'emperor's policy'. 'The ministers are not my ministers, they are prince Bismarck's ministers,' he complained. William none the less climbed down, thereby suffering a stinging humiliation which 'branded him an immature boy before the eyes of the Germans'.[136]

The chancellor was heading for defeat in the Reichstag the following day. He appeared to know what he was doing: he wanted to render Germany ungovernable again so that he could step in and emerge as a saviour. The ministers looked on in stupefied silence as the emperor and his chancellor fought it out.[137] When, next day, the Reichstag threw out Bismarck's repressive law, the chancellor thought the time had come to mend his ways a little with the young emperor. The Bismarcks began to flail about, blaming anyone they could for the worsening situation: Hinzpeter one moment, Boetticher the next, although it was unlikely that either of them was guilty of the charge. Hinzpeter was in Berlin in January and paid a call on Waldersee. They discussed the man who was to some extent a mutual pupil. Hinzpeter thought William had become more nervous, and more precipitate. He was pleased, however, at the way things were going with Bismarck.

Bismarck was still threatening to resign from some of his offices. When he was questioned more closely on this it was revealed that he was only thinking of the Ministry of Trade, which he ceded to one of William's closest advisers, Berlepsch. Two days later Bismarck backed down and began to give the impression that he would accept William's labour policy in return for tough anti-socialist laws later. That moment of weakness may have cost him his position. On 1 February William informed General Caprivi that he might need him in the near future.[138]

William's next move was to make the ministers report to him directly. But Bismarck was able to scotch that by citing a little-known cabinet order of 1852 which made it impossible for any minister other than the Minister of War to report to the emperor. No one, as it transpired, knew anything about this order, and the document itself was only located on 23 February. Bismarck's absences from the early 1880s onwards had made it imperative that ministers reported directly to their sovereign. To insist on such a law now was pure obstruction. Bismarck's high-handed treatment of his ministers earned him very little support at a critical time. They began to gather secretly at Boetticher's house.[139]

A meeting between Bismarck and William on the 3rd went badly for the chancellor, who, faced with an inauspicious silence, agreed to stand down from most of his offices at some later date, and the Minister Presidency on election day – 20 February. On 5 February, William held a reconciliation dinner for Bismarck in order to try to find a solution to the difference of opinion over social policy. Bismarck had the industrialists on his side, who were alarmed by the more radical suggestions put forward by the emperor. On the 8th Bismarck reiterated his suggestion that Caprivi should become Prussian Minister President while his son Herbert could retain his position as State Secretary at the Foreign Office. He would remain chancellor. William, however, had discovered that Bismarck had told him lies, and was out for blood. When Bismarck went back on his offer on the 11th, William must have felt smug that Caprivi was already waiting in the wings. Waldersee was watching carefully. He may have coveted the position for himself, but he was wise enough not to want the opprobrium of being the great man's immediate successor.[140]

Eulenburg and Waldersee made unlikely allies, but the former was able to report to the general and fill him in on the latest plots emanating from Friedrichsruh. On 16 February William and Waldersee were together in Potsdam. On the same day Eulenburg had a long talk with his sovereign in 'a tone of deepest mourning' in the park at Charlottenburg. William had initially decided to retain Bismarck and simply to curtail his functions.

But how difficult it is to get along with him! I always have to give in. I demand no more than that he examine the ideas that I hold to be proper, and when I cannot agree to his considerations – which up till now I have always fallen in with – that he once in a while give in to me, his king. He won't do it! For him his will is the highest law.* He can't bear it that there is also something that I

---

*Note, this is *suprema lex regis voluntas* (the king's will is the ultimate law): see below p.175.

want to see done ... I have already sacrificed my parental home to him. In the thought that I would one day be king, I have heeded all his advice and blindly followed him like a recruit...[141]

The previous day William had told Hinzpeter that Bismarck was to be removed. On 18 February Waldersee assessed the possibility of having General von Caprivi as chancellor. 'I don't think the emperor could make a better choice.' He was honest, respectable, and as Minister for the Marine had acquired recognition in the Reichstag.[142] William did not want a total break with the Bismarcks, and was anxious to hang on to Herbert at the Foreign Office. In the meantime the chancellor had predictably lost out in the election and was looking for allies. Waldersee noted with evident delight in his diary: 'The chancellor wanted to pay me a call! I couldn't believe my ears when I heard it.' Of course the ultra-conservative Waldersee was no more enchanted with the idea of William's social policy than his chancellor. He thought he was opening the floodgates.[143]

The last week of February introduced a distraction which may have delayed the *coup de grâce* which was being prepared for Otto von Bismarck. The new Reichstag refused to approve the military budget. Waldersee at once saw his chance to put an end to the universal suffrage which he thought an unhealthy consequence of the Revolution of 1848. He set about finding support among the right-wing politicians. Bismarck told him he was too old for such a move. He was clearly fobbing the general off as he was also meditating a coup! William was all the while hardening his position. Dealing with social democracy had become his affair. Bismarck was well and truly warned to step aside. On 5 March he told the Brandenburg assembly that he would 'smash to pieces' those who stood in his way.[144]

William was absorbing the necessary strength for the next round. He had received reports of troop movements in Kiev and decided that the Russians had designs on Austria. He wrote to Bismarck, who took his time about replying. He did not think it was worth worrying the Austrians with the news, which naturally incensed both William and Waldersee.[145] William had now determined that Bismarck was too Prussian, and that his presence inhibited his own popularity. William only wanted to be a Prussian in private, or in his rare attempts to court the Junkers who attended his Berlin balls. On 15 March the emperor held his international conference for the protection of workers in Berlin. Bismarck had been extremely unenthusiastic, and the meeting had been a flop.[146] The reasons were clear. Bismarck had done his best to sabotage it.

Bismarck had held talks with the Catholic Centre Party leader, Ludwig

Windhorst, on 12 March, in order to lift the blockade on his legislation in the Reichstag. The Centre was now the largest party in the Diet and Bismarck had the support of only a minority of members. He was planning his own *coup d'état* to introduce martial law and that way deal with the socialists. He needed the support of the Catholic Centre in order to arrest the Social Democrat leaders. The scheme was even more wide-reaching: William would stand down as emperor and the princes would bring out a new constitution which made no allowance for the antipathetic 'Reichsfeinde': socialists et al. Without Bismarck hearing of it Windhorst gave the story to the press, and William was therefore made aware of the negotiations on 15 March. He was not pleased and suspected, correctly, that the banker Bleichröder had also been involved: 'Jesuits and Jews have always gone together'.[147]

The emperor ordered his coach and drove round to Herbert's lodgings in the Wilhelmstrasse where Bismarck was sleeping. The Chancellor was still in bed. William burst in, and refused to allow him to dress. Throwing down his hat and gloves, he said, '*Durchlaucht*, what is going on with Windhorst?' Bismarck was taken by surprise. He had no idea that the Catholic leader would publish his account so soon. He gathered his bedclothes around him: 'I regret that I cannot give Your Majesty information on negotiations with party leaders which are still in progress and have not yielded any results.'

William expressed his anger that the talks had taken place in Bismarck's home. Bismarck replied that his sovereign's orders penetrated no farther than the doorstep of his wife's drawing room. 'Even when your king commands?' 'Not even then!' said Bismarck. William spoke ill of Bleichröder and the Jews. Bismarck responded that they formed a 'useful element in human society' and carried out important tasks, especially at foreign courts. William asked to see the cabinet order of 1852. Bismarck took his time before telling the emperor that he was not in a position to lay hands on the document. William then demanded his resignation.[148]

In later life William claimed that he had gone 'almost humbly' into that decisive meeting with Bismarck; begging for a little bit of the governmental cake to be pushed in his direction so that he might grant audiences to ministers and take a hand in ruling. 'I was young then and only wanted the best; above all to consider the new age which was not understood by the older generation. The survivors and the old-fashioned had to disappear. Anyone who failed to fit in with the changing times had to step back.'[149] Bismarck had all but lost his temper.

I sat at the table with a sabre between my legs smoking a cigar. The chancellor stood before me. In his rapidly mounting aggression, he made me increasingly calm. Finally he grabbed a large briefcase and threw it noisily down on the table. I was frightened he'd throw the inkpot at my head! I had my sabre of course! But I didn't think the prince would go so far as to lose all the respect due to his king. His megalomania and my calm made him furious. Then he suddenly began to cry. Then he became aggressive once again.[150]

Other versions of the story do not mention the emperor's humility. William was quite determined to release himself from the troubling subordination to prince Bismarck. 'Only one person can be lord of the land! and that is me – anyone who challenges me will be crushed!'[151] Waldersee was over the moon – at last his dreams were beginning to come true. 'The great crash has occurred!' William told him. 'I have just come from the chancellor. There was a violent argument that will properly put an end to things ... I told the chancellor that he has no authority to negotiate with Herr Windhorst at the present time, without first informing me of the fact. He immediately replied very aggressively that as a responsible Minister President he could receive whomever he pleased; besides he was cleverer than Windhorst and there was no one else capable of talking to him.'[152] William had conceded a little more than he made out. He had told Bismarck that he would have been happy had Herbert only informed him of the meetings with the Catholic Centre Party leader.

Apart from Bismarck's hobnobbing with the despised Catholic leader, William had a bone to pick with him about the 1852 cabinet order which allowed only the Minister President to brief the Prussian king. William wanted the order abolished – although he was to find it useful later. It was never repealed. William told Waldersee that he was hoping his chancellor would resign, as it would look better that way to the outside world. Waldersee added his own sixpence by informing the emperor that Bismarck had suppressed information on the danger of war with Russia and France.

Bismarck had clearly won a few rounds of the fight and is meant to have celebrated with a bottle of champagne.[153] He had shown William a letter from the Tsar which made it clear that the new emperor's proud boast that he got on with his Russian cousin was not entirely accurate. It said that William was 'mad, a boy who was badly brought up and had bad faith'. In consequence he planned to scrap a state visit. It must have been sweet music to Waldersee's ears. The general advised his emperor to sack Bismarck. At this point William took Waldersee's hand and said, 'Thank you, things will be all right soon', then, *Waidmannsheil! –* good hunting!'[154]

William sent for the offending order on the 16th. When Bismarck still failed to produce it Hahnke was despatched to ask for the chancellor's resignation. Waldersee saw William at the dedication of the Garrison Church in Spandau on the 18th. The Chief of Staff asked him if he had received anything from Bismarck – 'No. Neither the offer to resign nor the [1852] Order . . .' Lucanus was then sent with the same demand. Waldersee claimed that he did not have the vanity to want to replace Bismarck, but he would take up the appointment if ordered. When Eulenburg arrived in Berlin later that day, William explained that he had called for the chancellor's resignation: 'After the violent [behaviour] of the prince I can sadly expect no other solution'. He remembered the scene later. William bade him go to the piano: 'So that is enough, let's play some music. Now you will sing.' He was singing at the piano in the Schloss when Hahnke returned. Once he had received the papers William held up the letter triumphantly. 'Now I have his resignation'. 'And I had to sing some more,' wrote Eulenburg. William was pale and nervous.[155]

The Bismarckians were beside themselves. Hildegard von Spitzemberg wrote, 'It was to me as if a cliff had fallen on my head, I sat there in gloomy mindlessness with tears in my eyes and found it hard to swallow – the prince, Bismarck, dismissed like any old minister, it sounded like a bad joke!!'[156] Later she had to admit that Bismarck had it coming to him. 'A whole series of necessary laws simply fell by the wayside because they conflicted with the interests of his private estates or because he had no time to deal with them . . .'[157]

Old Moltke pronounced the story 'ugly', but there is certainly some truth in William's later assertions that he had no choice but to sack Bismarck, who was being insubordinate on a grand scale. Eulenburg suggested that a general should replace him. William called in Caprivi who was 'very astonished and horrified', but who – as a soldier – would obey a royal command.[158] Waldersee was informed the following afternoon that Bismarck had not produced the order, only his resignation. He also learned that the new chancellor was to be Caprivi. The Chief of Staff was sensible, and only had kind words to say about his rival.

The Bismarcks' clear belief in their indispensability makes sad reading now. Herbert was astonished at William: 'He knows not what he does.' William wanted to retain Herbert. Bismarck told him, 'My son is over twenty-one.' Herbert, however, resigned too; significantly, the only one of Bismarck's ministers to do so: 'I am used to serving my father and I could not stand there, with a briefcase under my arm, before another chancellor.' William regretted it. 'I had reckoned on keeping [him], I believed him clever enough to be able to properly appraise the situation.' The only one of the Bismarcks who seems to have reacted sensibly was Johanna. She wrote laconically on the 17th: 'The bomb has exploded and we will be celebrating the 1st [Bismarck's birthday] in Friedrichsruh rather than here.'[159]

Bismarck was determined not to be fobbed off. He refused to use the title of Herzog [duke] von Lauenburg which had been granted him, or the rank of colonel-general awarded on the 29th. He does not relate what happened to the 'life-sized portrait' which the emperor promised him at the same time.[160] He went pointedly to Emperor William I's grave instead, and laid some roses on the tomb of his old master. Then he packed up his belongings. The most important of these were his papers, 3,000 bottles of wine and some 300 boxes of cigars. When a squadron of hussars accompanied his carriage to the Lehrterstrasse station, he called it 'a first-class funeral'. There was a predictable public demonstration as he made his way through the streets. Hats and hand-kerchiefs were waved, flowers thrown. At the station he ran into Prince Max of Baden, a man who would eventually occupy the same hot seat, and at an even hotter period of German history. Bismarck told him that William would call him back.[161]

'The office of watch on the ship of state has fallen to me! We will ply the same course! Full steam ahead!' Despite the nautical metaphor William was bitter about the famous caricature in *Punch*.* The English magazine had already taken Bismarck's side the year before, when it warned the emperor against 'Caesarism', and he was sensitive to its sallies. When 'Dropping the Pilot' was published in March 1890, William was angry. Later *Punch* responded by printing a jingle in the style of *Struwwelpeter* called *Struwwelwilliam*

> Oh take that nasty *Punch* away!
> I won't have any *Punch* today![162]

Not all the press was pro-Bismarck by any means. The *Frankfurter Zeitung* suggested, 'The nation will soon add 18 March to the days that resemble public holidays.'

On the 21st Hohenlohe noted in his diary that the breach was 'unavoidable', but opinion was divided.[163] The reaction to Bismarck's fall was not all negative abroad, by any means. William wrote in jus-tification to Francis Joseph, putting a copy of the letter aside to be given to his son after his death:

The man I had idolised all my life, for whom in my parental home I endured the hellish tortures of moral persecution, the man for whom I alone, after the death of my grandfather, I stormed the breach to retain him, and for which I harvested the fury of my dying father and the inextinguishable hatred of my

* Not so Johanna von Bismarck, who hung a copy of it above her bed.

mother, [he] noticed not a jot of it and strode proudly away from me because I would not bend to his will! What a stab in the heart![164]

When William met the Tsar at manoeuvres in Narva later that year he displayed the sympathy of an autocrat. What, after all, was the fuss about. The Tsar told him:

I completely understand the line you took. Despite all his grandeur, after all the prince was nothing other than your employee or servant. The moment when he refused to obey your orders, you had to dismiss him. For my part I always distrusted him and I never believed a word he said or had conveyed to me, for I was certain that he was constantly making fun of me. As far as our own relations are concerned, my dear William,* the prince's fall will have the best of consequences. I trust you and you can rely on me.[165]

*William notes it was the first time he had addressed him thus.

9

The Liberal Empire

William claimed later that he had been stuck for choice, given that he had not planned to sack Bismarck. General Georg von Caprivi was a Prussian officer of Italian-Slav origin who had been head of the Admiralty at the time of William's accession. He was the last soldier to occupy this position, and the new emperor made it clear that from now on only sailors would hold senior ranks in the marine. Caprivi had shown how high principled he was by resigning from the post in protest at William's meddling in naval affairs. His name had been put forward for the position of Chief of the General Staff, but William had preferred his friend Waldersee. William thought him 'obstinate and not quite free from vanity', meaning that he did not wish to fall into the position of being a post-Bismarckian chancellor who simply rubber-stamped the emperor's decisions. For the time being William still ignored his ministers and relied on a kitchen cabinet composed of men in and out of government: General Verdy, Graf Douglas, Hinzpeter, Boetticher and, most important of all, Eulenburg – 'fantastic figures', thought the Bavarian envoy Lerchenfeld.[1]

Hildegard von Spitzemberg thought Caprivi's nomination 'the only consolation in this catastrophe; an unusually gifted man.'[2] He did not have an easy job of it. Bismarck's was a hard act to follow. His position was sadly summed up by the old porter at the Wilhelmstrasse, Manthey, who told visitors in a tearful voice, 'The new imperial chancellor is inside, in the old one's seat!' His free trade policy soon made him an enemy of the powerful Junkers in the east, who mocked his lack of land, dubbing him 'the man without straw or acre'.[3] He also had the job of fielding all the balls thrown at him by Bismarck over the next few years, and the distrust of those who regretted the old man's passing. He had to contend with permanent resistance within his own ministries or in the press, so that 'everything was declared to be bad, found risible or no matter what it was, mercilessly criticised'. For the time being, William had decided that Caprivi was to have a free hand. By the end of the year he was meddling again, however, and making appointments without informing him: a new bishop for the sensitive see of Strasbourg, an ambassador to Paris; he also dismissed diplomats and interfered in the choice of ministers.[4]

Caprivi represented a triumph of industry over the land and free trade over protection. He made a clean sweep when it came to some of his predecessors' more corrupt methods of government. The Guelph funds – the revenues of the Hanoverian Crown – were restored to their rightful owners, and no longer used for behind-the-scenes payments. He stopped manipulating the press and handing out bribes. On the other hand his lack of political experience could be quite alarming. He was a complete innocent in many fields and was not beyond saying, 'I really have no opinion of my own.' He left the field open for Holstein and Eulenburg. When William refused to ratify the re-election of Max Forckenbeck, the mayor of Berlin, because he had voted against the Army Bill, it was Eulenburg who had to convince the emperor to change his mind. Caprivi had not even helped on the drafting of the Army Bill.[5]

Eulenburg had played a very minor role in Bismarck's fall; he had even advised against sacking the chancellor. 'If Your Majesty has an argument with Bismarck,' he allegedly told William, 'the result will be the same as if you fired on the people.' He also told him that Bismarck's departure would be a national and personal disaster. William is said to have laughed.[6] His friend did, however, exert an influence when it came to choosing a successor to Herbert. At Holstein's prompting, the Badenese lawyer Marschall von Bieberstein was installed at the Foreign Office.[7] For a man who believed himself to be promoting Prussian interests within the Reich, it was a surprising choice. Eulenburg clearly thought it the wrong decision later and pushed forward Marschall's eventual successor, Bülow. William's fourth chancellor was very much Philipp Eulenburg's creation. It was Bülow who turned on the charm in what has been called 'the long-distance seduction' of Eulenburg. Bülow, for example, was at pains to fit in as snugly as possible with Eulenburg's thinking: 'I would regard myself as the executive tool of His Majesty, so to speak his political Chief of Staff. With me, personal rule – in the good sense – would really begin.' Eulenburg could then divest himself of a self-imposed role – 'the burden of holding the government together'.[8]

Before Herbert left the ministry on 21 March, the question of the renewal of the secret Russian treaty had come up. The 'Rück-versicherungsvertrag',* or Reinsurance Treaty, guaranteed Russian neutrality in the event of a war with France. It expired on 18 June. He wrote to William to say that the Russians would not sign the treaty under a

---

* Literally 'Back Protection Treaty'.

different chancellor. This was not exactly true. The ambassador, Shuvalov, merely demanded fresh instructions. William also seemed ill-informed. He minuted laconically, 'Warum?' – Why? On the 22nd there was a shower of Black Eagles. Giving one to Boetticher had been calculated to annoy the former chancellor, and it had the desired effect especially as Bismarck's minister had received the packet on the 8th at the height of the crisis. The Prince of Wales received his at the ceremony in the Weisse Saal. It provided an occasion for William to ask his advisers about the treaty. The ambassador in Petersburg, Schweinitz, was in favour of retaining it. Holstein was opposed. His view prevailed.[9]

Despite his decision to drop the treaty, William assured Shuvalov that he would continue to uphold Gemano-Russian friendship, which was the policy of his grandfather and himself. The Tsar would have been happy to renew the treaty. In the meantime he was anxious to know more about Caprivi; whether he, like Waldersee, was pressing for war. On 14 May William and the Tsar addressed this same issue. William told the Russian ruler, 'I want only peace without and order within.' 'That is exactly what I want,' said the Tsar. A coldness set in, however, and the frost did not melt until after Alexander's death. By that time Russia was firmly in the French camp.[10]

Old Moltke was at the *Ordensfest*, reduced to silence by the noise of two blaring bands. William appeared dressed in his British admiral's uniform in Prince Edward's honour and made a speech about comradeship at Waterloo, 'and expressed the hope that the English fleet, together with the German army, would maintain peace'. It was Albert's idea again, and one which remained close to William's heart. Moltke was not keen on the dual role and quoted Goethe on the subject of politics. Hohenlohe spoke to Caprivi, and found they got on.[11]

The refined Hohenlohe was in a position where he was able to talk to both parties and get to the bottom of the story. From Bismarck he heard that the former chancellor had been dismissed because William wanted to rule alone. From William he heard that his decision was based on the fact that it was clear that either the Hohenzollerns would rule in Germany, or the Bismarcks. Hohenlohe might also have been aware of Bismarck's unpopularity in south Germany, a point raised by his own patron, the Grand Duke of Baden. Bismarck was further suspected of being ready to drop the Austrian alliance and go over to Russia. This would have met with opposition from some members of William's kitchen cabinet, notably Eulenburg.

Waldersee may have been content to see the back of the Bismarcks, but William did not altogether please him either. On 21 March the Chief of Staff wrote that the emperor overrated his own military abilities and continued to express 'immature ideas'. 'My relationship with him is based on trust. If this is not fully to hand, then we must part.' William must have been aware that he had annoyed the general. That evening he asked him if he were still angry with him. Caprivi had been to see him. He was not convinced that he would last long in the job and faced the disagreeable task of trying to convince Herbert to remain at the Foreign Office.[12] It was not long before the former chancellor in the Sachsenwald began to make trouble for William and spoil the honeymoon he was enjoying with Caprivi. For his part, Caprivi was able to show the emperor just how much material Bismarck had suppressed. William was outraged by the way he had used the 'Guelph Fund' for his own dirty-tricks campaigns.

On 21 April William was received by the mayor of Bremen, and in a speech he chose to confirm his and his family's divine right to rule.[13] He was taxing his throat that day. He visited the Norddeutsche Lloyd ship *Fulda* and made another. In this he stressed his peaceful mission. '... My first concern, in every direction, as far as possible is to maintain the peace ... for ... trade can only prosper and flower when businesses possess sure protection and are properly looked after ... You may be assured that in many respects it is not as bad as it looks.'[14]

William liked the occasional cigar and Eulenburg did not smoke. On 24 April, under the influence of the fabulous old wines in the Bremen Rathauskeller, Eulenburg and Moltke both had to seek refuge from the fog caused by William and his entourage. The eighty-nine-year-old former Chief of Staff was more unbuttoned than usual. He thought Bismarck should mend his ways. 'Faced with a young and temperamental master, too much temperament is not a means for arriving at an understanding – and in this case an understanding is a pressing necessity.' Moltke none the less believed that William should have retained the services of the old chancellor.[15]

Eulenburg also had a talk with Waldersee in Bremen which emphasised the difference in approach of the emperor's two principal advisers. Eulenburg thought William would be fine providing he were properly nurtured. Waldersee was struck by worries about William's policies at home and abroad.

... what concerns me the most is the observation that the emperor still has no firm views. Fortunately no one in wider circles has noticed this. How often have I seen him oscillate between Austria and Russia! How many different views have I heard him develop so far about different personalities! Today someone can be excellent and a few days later he is worthless, or the other way round.[16]

The army were having their own problems with William. It was the one German institution still to take its lead wholeheartedly from Prussia and William was making waves, literally, by increasing the budget granted to the navy. Within the army itself, William doted on his guards regiments at the expense of the infantry and was rude to his senior officers in a way that would have been unthinkable in his grandfather's time. He wanted new blood and younger regimental chiefs. Waldersee took it upon himself to defend the army, attempting to push Caprivi about. Although a general, the army disliked the chancellor once he had been seconded to a civilian role. William was fond of soldier's games, 'particularly noticeable in the hourly alarms which serve no purpose, as we are prepared for every eventuality ...' He possessed 'great certainty in his judgement in matters that the gentleman had incorrectly perceived'. He also had a tendency to lord it over the views of more experienced officers.[17]

William intended to base his lasting fame on the creation of a proper German navy. This would also have the advantage of endearing him to the outwardly liberal, non-Prussian middle class. The navy had always been a minor consideration in Prussia and in the early days of the Second Reich. From 1871 to 1888 it was commanded by 'land generals':[18] Prince Adalbert of Prussia, Lieutenant-General von Stosch, and finally Caprivi. What real talent there was still lay concealed within the ranks of the service. Tirpitz, for example – a relative of Caprivi's – was busy creating a squadron of torpedo boats, which would be the first real claim to innovation. For the time being, at least, William's desire to see Germany equipped with a proper fleet produced no enmity in Great Britain. Indeed, as the emperor himself was wont to point out, in the early 1890s the British allowed the Royal Navy to run down.[19] William had also annoyed Waldersee through his desire to use criticism of the army to increase his popularity with the masses – presumably in the less military parts of Germany. He had weighed in to stop physical abuse of soldiers, and to countermand unpopular appointments.

II

In 1890 the *Nordlandsreise* took to the boats for its second outing. The emperor's ship stopped at Christiana to pay an official call on the king of Sweden. Eulenburg thought the dull little city which as Oslo, was later to become the capital of an independent Norway, 'prettily laid out'.[20] This year Emil Görtz was on board, a man of legendary clumsiness, and something of a clown. Eulenburg was able to tell William many stories of his behaviour at the newly Germanised University of Strasbourg. They went on expeditions to collect good-sized shells for the grotto in the Neues Palais. They met an English angler called Mr Byron who taught the emperor how to fish for salmon with a fly. There was a performance of Schweighofer's *Die Antisemiten*, which Eulenburg, who was one and the same, thought 'melodramatic nonsense'.[21]

There was occasional work to distract William. When the post came from Berlin he was obliged to add anything up to four hundred signatures to state papers which could not wait until his return. There were the usual farces too. Kessel's appearance in drag wearing a blond wig 'beggered all description' and caused a sensation on board. Such things appealed enormously to William's sense of humour.[22] The journey always involved painting and music. Sometimes the artist Willi Stöwer set up his easel on the deck while at the piano Eulenburg and Chelius improvised on Wagnerian and French *chanson* themes. The rest had their roles: Kessel listened, Löwenfeld told jokes, the ill-fated Hahnke – 'Chief Slurper' – thought about food and wine, Phili sang his 'Rosenlieder', Görtz – Chief Adviser on Accidents – imitated animals, Hülsen practised magic, Graf Eberhard von Danckelmann shot seagulls, while Wedel and Senden were the usual butts of the jokes. At one point Görtz and Kiderlen dressed up as a pair of Siamese twins, connected by an enormous sausage. In later life William rejected Eulenburg's accusation of frivolity – 'It wasn't like that. There were lots of lectures delivered by scholars invited on board, there were many serious talks and interesting debates were organised.'[23]

Sometimes the court minstrel Eulenburg reported back to Dona to set her mind at rest. 'The emperor's speech rings like some sort of beautiful music,' he enthused. 'There is never a sentimental word. The strength of [his] expression is imbued with the noblest spiritual ideal.'[24] Waldersee was more sober-minded in his estimation of William's character. The emperor was beginning to resemble his father. That summer he scrawled his bitterest judgement to date.

In no domain has the emperor views of his own and he doesn't know what to do; sadly he is putty in the hands of clever people and makes surprising leaps all over the place. One thought decides everything he does: his interest in his own personal standing, the desire to be popular! On top of this is a concern for his own personal security and a rapidly growing vanity. I thought the Emperor Frederick was a very vain gentleman who really enjoyed dressing up and posing. The present ruler, however, overshadows him by far. He fishes directly for applause and loves nothing better than a cheering populace. As he is very convinced of his own capabilities (something which is based on an annoying delusion) he finds this flattery very pleasant. He loves to play the Maecenas and scatters money about without the slightest care. This has all developed so rapidly that I stumble from one state of incredulity to the next.[25]

When two days later Marschall praised the emperor's understanding and cool judgement, Waldersee commented, 'From my heart I hope he continues to harbour the same views in six months' time.'[26] William had decided on another tack in his objective to stamp out socialism: he was going to build more churches and schools. It was to some degree the legacy of Stoecker. Hinzpeter's influence was wearing thin again. That month William was inclined to adopt Bismarck's methods for dealing with striking workers. The stick had replaced the carrot. Waldersee recorded his overreaction to some civilian unrest. He wanted to send an entire regiment to put it down.

On 10 August that year William had a chance to right one apparent wrong, and complete the unification of Germany begun by his grandfather: he acquired the rocky island of Heligoland, in exchange for Witu in Kenya and Zanzibar. The island had been a part of Denmark until 1807, when it had been occupied by Britain. British possession of this Gibraltar of the North had been confirmed at the Peace of Kiel in 1814. William took over the island from the last British governor, Arthur Barkly, and was greeted by a bevy of local women in the colourful *Tracht*. After assuring those islanders who wanted to become Germans of his loyalty, he outlined the rock's new role in Germany's life: 'The island is ... called upon to become a bulwark in the sea, [affording] protection for German fishermen, a support for my war fleet, a refuge and shelter in the German sea from any enemy who might prey upon her, or who shows her sails up on it.'[27]

His use of two pieces of Germany's fledgeling empire to round off the country's borders was much in keeping with Bismarck's policy of employing them as bartering counters to improve relations with Britain. Waldersee had agreed with the former chancellor on this point, and had been alarmed in May when William had become excited about acquiring more chunks of East Africa. In a contrary spirit the former chancellor mocked the exchange as 'a trouser button for a whole suit!' Bismarck thought Heligoland was nothing but 'old, barren cliffs'; but there could have been an element of sour grapes in his comments. He had brought up the subject with the British himself in 1884. In 1889 Joseph Chamberlain had included Heligoland in his offer of an alliance, but he had wanted the rather more substantial German South-West Africa in exchange. Other observers were less negative, seeing the acquisition as 'the first sign of a new age'. That Germany was annoying Britain at the time is clear from Hohenlohe's diary. On 19 June he wrote, 'We have been treading on the corns of the English in our colonial policy in quite an unusual manner. We are thus exposed to the danger that England might join France and Russia, which would have been very dangerous for us.'[28]

The agreement went further than a mere exchange of territories, it settled a number of disputed points as well. It confirmed Germany's borders in South-West Africa and ended her claims to Uganda. Under Bismarck there had been little impetus to do anything about Heligoland, but with William it was different. It was a 'pet project' he had cherished from the time of his first visits as a child. Even Bismarck noted that William was always 'fire and flame' when the subject came up. The former chancellor's only stipulation had been – get it cheaply, it means nothing to Britain.[29]

On 18 August William was in Narva and Reval to meet the Tsar. Despite the growing likelihood of a Franco-Russian alliance, William claimed that the Russian ruler was in favour of a revival of the monarchy in France, and that the Republic represented a danger to European peace.[30] The Chief of Staff was increasingly impatient with the emperor at the autumn manoeuvres which took place in Silesia that year. He had got away with a degree of criticism the year previous, and his success had gone to his head.[31]

I am convinced that the monarch has a certain understanding when it comes to drilling a regiment on a parade ground, not, however, for actually leading a body of troops. He has no experience of warfare, from which also derives his uncertainty over the limited usefulness of cavalry. The emperor is extraordinarily uneasy, chases about the place and is too far forward in the battle line; he meddles in the operations of the generals, issues countless, often contradictory orders and scarcely lends an ear to his advisers. He always wants to win and therefore he takes ill any decision awarded against him.

Waldersee may well have exaggerated William's incompetence. William often impressed officers. He learned the map by heart, knew the position of every village. One General Staff officer described him as 'enormously clever'. When Marie von Bunsen asked him if the emperor would make a good general, he was not so sure. His knowledge was too fragmentary, as a result of having done so many other things. He also agreed that no one dared beat him in the war games. Waldersee's criticisms did him no good in the long run. William gave him a 'wounded and later a very serious look'. That evening he blamed all his mistakes on Waldersee himself.[32]

Waldersee had overstepped the mark. His treatment of Caprivi also failed to impress the emperor. He was offered Eulenburg's job as envoy to Stuttgart, together with the Black Eagle. He refused it. William '. . . is beginning to feel military and as a result he doesn't want to look dependent on me. And for all that, what a dilettante in military matters! If he wanted to take command in a war, and not simply formally like his father and grandfather, what a misfortune that would be.'[33] Waldersee came to the terrible conclusion that possibly the Social Democrats were right in their views on the emperor.

In September 1890 William was in Munich. Eulenburg had had cause to warn him about the style of his orations, and had endeavoured to temper them a little. On 8 September he wrote *suprema lex regis voluntas* in the golden book in Munich town hall. Some of his apologists have hastened to point out that the assertion that a king's will was the ultimate law was merely a relatively witty response to being asked to sign the book by the Bavarian prince regent. That other favoured Latin tag, *Sic volo sic jubeo*,* actually came from the ceiling of the Ministry of Religion, Education and Culture in Berlin. Less generous souls recalled that two Bavarian kings had gone mad shortly before; and that for a Prussian to write such a thing was an affront to the federal princes. Caprivi believed it was a joke which misfired – the emperor was trying to be 'dashing and student-like'. There is no denying the outrage caused in Bavaria and that William was quite capable of making appalling gaffes.[34]

III

Waldersee had hung on to his position for the time being. His next task was to deal with the emperor's desire to rejuvenate the officer corps by retiring many of the senior generals. 'He decidedly came to the throne too early.' Yet the Chief of Staff was able to table some of William's qualities in the midst of so many indictments. He was intelligent; had a quick grasp of what was happening; an excellent memory; was kind, too, and showed a good heart towards those who had served him well; and he was extremely adept in his handling of people.

The general was still exasperated by his emperor and his contradictory nature, however. He had become lazy and showed not the slightest desire to work. His views changed more often than the moon:

The emperor is totally unpredictable. He approaches one party today and another the next, he criticises the Jews, then, however, he lets people of Jewish origin in; at one moment he promises his support to the agrarians, the next day, however, he looks set to ruin them; he shows an interest in heavy industry, then treats them with hostility in a destructive manner; he dismisses Bismarck, partly because he has been talking to Windhorst, then he sits calmly by while Caprivi strikes up a close co-operation with the Centre; he declares the nobility to be the most distinguished of his subjects, yet threatens to crush the rebellious gentry (and no one knows who they are); one moment he is filled with hatred and contempt against Russia yet despite this he pays them court, so that they

---

*Juvenal, *The Sixteen Satires*, trans. Peter Green, Harmondsworth, 1967, VI, 224. Green's translation reads:

This is still my wish, my command:
Warrant enough that I will it.

even laugh about it themselves; the Austrians are sometimes miserable people, sometimes loyal and excellent allies. Is he a truly pious man and god-fearing Christian, or does he merely pretend? Is he a reliable man or isn't he? We don't know.[35]

Like Bismarck, it could have been sour grapes, but Waldersee's criticisms now fell thick and fast. On 4 October he wrote that William's 'distractions, be they army games, or chiefly naval ones, travelling or hunting, are more important than anything else; so that he has, in fact, hardly any time left for work.'[36] He read only the cuttings prepared for him by his staff; wrote only the marginalia which he copied from Frederick the Great and thought the best briefing was the shortest. 'It is truly scandalous how the court circulars mislead the greater public over the activity of the emperor; according to them he is hard at work morning noon and night!' He was amassing debts too, another practice he appears to have inherited from his father.[37]

One reason for Waldersee's fury with his former protégé was his treatment of Stoecker, whom he had dropped like a hot potato. Indeed, it was suggested that the reason William had pushed Stoecker out of the nest was due to the sums of money he had borrowed from the Jews – a story, it should be added, that William found funny. On 4 November, the preacher was induced to retire from his position at court. Waldersee thought he had been hounded out by Lucanus and the Jews. Three days later William accepted his resignation. On 16 November Stoecker preached in the cathedral. William pointedly drove past the building and attended the service in the Garrison Church instead. The emperor had shown good sense. A few years later the socialist newspaper *Vorwärts* published some letters belonging to the discredited former editor of the right-wing *Kreuzzeitung*, Wilhelm von Hammerstein. They revealed how Stoecker had been involved in a plot to bring down Bismarck.[38]

William's sister Sophie – now Duchess of Sparta – had undergone instruction in the Greek Orthodox rite to abide by the conditions set by the Hellenes. Spurred on by the priggish Dona, William took umbrage. Vicky, however, told him it was none of his business. William was bitter about his mother. He told his Chief of Staff she had been 'in Berlin ... to sow discord around him and to damage him. He had made her ample provision, given her various castles, and set her up, above all, in such a way that she can do or not do whatever she pleases. There was [evidently] no question of gratitude.'[39]

One issue which spurred William to activity was the narrow syllabus of the *Gymnasien*. He wanted it broadened to stop pupils from suffering as he had done in Cassel. It was an issue close to his heart, but one which demonstrated that he did not possess absolute power, for he never wholly succeeded in reforming the syllabus taught in German secondary schools, with its strong emphasis on the humanities, although some *Gymnasien* altered theirs – a bit – to comply with the emperor's wishes. For the time being, however, he took up the challenge with verve. As he told an audience on 4 December:

the most important thing is that we seize on the spirit of the matter and not the simple form ... we must construct German foundations for the *Gymnasium*; we must produce nationally-minded young Germans and not young Greeks and Romans; we must depart from the principle which has reigned for centuries, from the cloistered upbringing of the Middle Ages, where Latin was of overriding importance with a little Greek thrown in. It is no longer of overriding importance; we must lay the foundation on German.[40]

Waldersee had failed to observe the golden rule with William, and that was to tell him how clever he was. The emperor even fished for compliments on the subject of his oratory. On 2 January 1891, Waldersee knew that his star was fading. He blamed Caprivi; but he knew there were other reasons such as criticising his extravagant plans for German fortresses. William did not approve of the network of military attachés Waldersee used in order to bypass diplomatic channels. He was scornful of a portrait that William had commissioned for the Paris embassy showing the young ruler in the uniform of the Gardes du Corps with a black breastplate, a purple cloak and carrying a long field marshal's baton. Waldersee wondered what it was all supposed to mean.

When Hildegard von Spitzemberg saw William and Vicky officiating at the anniversary of the founding the Reich on 17 January, she noted how fat and plain he had become. On William's thirty-second birthday a few days later, Waldersee received the Grosskomtur cross to his Hohenzollern Order and was informed that he was shortly to be given a district command. It was Altona; not, on the face of it, a sensitive spot where sudden movements on a border might necessitate fast decision-making, but he was given the idea that one special function would be to spy on Bismarck in nearby Friedrichsruh. William tried to sweeten the pill by telling the man who had extracted him from so many sexual embroilments that his new position was not a demotion. The General Staff itself was less important to William than the regional commands: 'For me the Chief of Staff should be only a sort of amanuensis, and for that I need a younger man.' Waldersee commented bitterly, 'he wants to be his own Chief of Staff! God help the fatherland!'[41]

Caprivi and Marschall were doing surprisingly well by comparison. William wrote to his surviving grandmother at Christmas to tell her: 'I think he [Caprivi] is one of the finest characters Germany ever produced.'[42] Even Marschall was hugely in favour for the time being. It was generally believed that Waldersee had sealed his fate by criticising William's leadership during the annual manoeuvres, although to Eulenburg he justified allowing William to win, just as others had let him win at games as a child. His successor was the 'nur-Soldat' Graf Alfred von Schlieffen. The new Chief of Staff made it clear from the outset that he had no objection to William receiving the laurels for conducting the war games.[43]

The 'Caprivi Treaties' were based on the Chancellor's belief that Germany had to export either goods or men. Caprivi's toughest job to date had been the promotion of his Russian trade treaty in face of furious opposition from the East Elbian landowners. William hoped this would appease Alexander by letting him ship in cheap grain, and make him popular with the workers by bringing down prices. Bismarck could sneer, in the still secret knowledge that Caprivi and William had allowed his Reinsurance Treaty to lapse. The Bismarcks refused to let up. Many had gone over to their side, including Hinzpeter. On 26 January 1891, the day before William's birthday, another bombshell exploded in the *Hamburger Nachrichten*. Hohenlohe believed that it would go on for a year or two longer, then peter out. The problem was Bismarck's popularity, especially among students. The very nationalist University of Strasbourg held a giant 'Kommers' that year, all in the former chancellor's honour.

Now that Vicky was living near Wiesbaden, distance improved their relationship. Bismarck's departure had also led to a slight defrosting of William's relations with his mother, to the degree that she agreed to do a little diplomatic work for him in Paris. She arrived on 19 February with her daughter, Margaret, and a large suite, ostensibly to thank those artists who had promised to submit paintings to a forthcoming Berlin exhibition. William had thought that by making her descent official, he could test the strength of anti-German feeling prior to an attempted rapprochement. For a few days, Vicky was able to visit studios without trouble, then the extreme Boulangist party organised a demonstration. The press followed suit, and the protest became tumultuous. Vicky made a hurried retreat to London.[44]

Vicky used hers and William's favourite architect Ernst Ihne to design her new tribute to Fritz, Friedrichshof. William was impressed by the building, which incorporated a few Tudor details in what was otherwise a heavily German design. A servant remembered the delight on Vicky's face when she received a letter from William: 'Oh, -, I have just had such a splendid gift from His Majesty! Just think, he has given me the old Cronberg fortress to restore as I like. Now I must get busy!'[45]

William's tongue was getting carried away with him again. On 20 February that year he addressed the Brandenburg assembly:

Now Brandenburgers! Your margrave is speaking to you. Follow him through thick and thin down every path he leads you! You may be assured that it is for the salvation and greatness of our Fatherland.[46]

But the bluster did not always add up to a firm commitment to change. Despite all the noises he had made about investing in a proper fleet, nothing had happened so far, perhaps because William was aware of the opposition which this would provoke in traditional army circles. He had not forgotten about the navy, however. His own desk had been a present from the Royal Navy, and was emblazoned with his hero Nelson's famous line: 'England expects every man to do his duty'. In the spring William met some of the younger naval officers at the Schloss in Kiel. 'Now I have listened to you, as you have been arguing for an hour. In principle the chaos must come to an end, but not one single one of you has come up with a positive suggestion.' Senden-Bibran encouraged Captain Tirpitz to speak out. William was not pleased with his words. The following day all the officers who had been present were given punishment duties.[47]

The navy took up much of his time in the first half of 1891. He was keen to design a new ensign, and ended up adopting his own flag as captain of the yacht club. There was the question of whether the light cruisers' funnels should rise perpendicular to the deck, or obliquely from it. When he saw the designs for his new yacht, this led to a revision of the guest list for that year's *Nordlandsreise*. He vetoed Waldersee and Bronsart because they might spoil the fun. The navy wanted one or other of them to go for precisely that reason.[48]

Hildegard Spitzemberg saw Bismarck on 5 March, when the former chancellor was quite candid about the problems he was causing William through the articles he 'inspired' in the press. He was naturally pessimistic about the future; less because of domestic issues than because he saw the possibility of war with Russia in two years or so, when they had equipped their army with the necessary munitions. 'The most terribly dangerous part of the emperor's character is that he is always open to any interest at any given time, and brings everything instantly to reality so that there is no consistency at all.' The next day Bismarck told his friend why he had been so unceremonially dumped a year before: 'A phrase of his chief flatterer Versen expressed it; he said to him, if Frederick the Great had had or had inherited such a chancellor he would never have become the Great, and he wants greatness...'[49]

There were lots of speeches: spurred on by the unveiling of a monument to his grandfather among others, William was happy to perorate. On 18 April he struck a Bismarckian pose as he reminded his audience that it was the army, and not Parliament, which had united the Reich.

The general who had played the major role, Helmuth von Moltke, died on 24 April and was given a state funeral on the 28th. William attended the ceremony which started at the Siegessäule: 'Only one man was missing – Bismarck!'[50] On 7 May in Bremen, William told his audience, 'I would like it to be so, that European peace lay in my hands. I would look after it on every occasion, and make sure it was never disturbed.'

His assurances that he wished to keep the peace or make his people happy and rich were treated with scepticism by journalists. He tended to be carried away by his own tongue and no one could call him to order. He flatly refused to submit his speeches before he delivered them, and his ministers were reluctant to show him the criticism they provoked in the press. Not even Eulenburg had the courage, and instead sent cuttings to Marschall to place on William's desk. Sometimes the fury seems a little exaggerated. Word for word, the speech 'I shall lead you to glorious days' is a fine piece of work.[51]

IV

The *Nordlandsreise* for 1891 began in Britain after the emperor had attended the wedding there of Mary of Holstein to Prince Aribert of Anhalt on 9 July. William made a state visit to Holland first and Eulenburg had to make his own way there to join the voyage. He was unimpressed by London – 'a grey sea of houses with chimneys and tasteless public buildings'. His Anglophobia was given full rein in his diary. The man who had served in Munich and lived on Starnberg Lake did not have anything good to say about English beer either, which 'tasted like rubber mackintoshes smell',[52] but there was the consolation of seeing his friend Raymond Lecomte, who was serving at the French embassy to the Court of St James. He would later be a central figure in the homosexuality scandal which racked the imperial court.

On the 10th there was a dinner at the Guildhall in William's honour and a similar party at Buckingham Palace the following day. Eulenburg was in the crowd to watch him in his Garde du Corps uniform: 'I hid from him, as I wanted to get to know London completely incognito, and any official invitation would have got in the way.' Eulenburg had plenty to think about. He was busy conspiring against Bismarck's son-in-law Graf Kuno Rantzau to obtain the top job in Munich.[53]

An all-male company assembled in Edinburgh. Eulenburg visited the Germanophile Lord Rosebery's estate on the banks of the Firth nearby and was particularly struck by its beauty. 'How enchanting the sight must have been', he wrote with bitter irony and unconcealed distaste, 'when his wife, Hanna Rothschild, with her long nose and amorous

Semitic leer, strolled under the beeches of this paradise – *c'est le revers de la medaille*.'[54] The party set off for the Arctic on 14 July from the port of Leith.

There were the usual farces. Görtz trod on the paws of either Lax or Dax, the imperial sausage dogs, and knocked over innumerable glasses. Eulenburg's sensitive nose was offended by the stench of drying cod in the Hansaviertel in Bergen. Adjutants Zitzewitz and Kuno Moltke performed duets on cello and piano while the emperor himself sang student songs from the *Kommersbuch*. Georg Hülsen and Görtz performed duets at the piano and the latter recited Goethe's 'Über allen Gipfeln'. Another member of the party then performed as an Italian tenor dressed in Nordic garb.[55] William donned his uniform as an admiral of the Swedish navy and there were hunts after whales and missions to capture polar bears for the little Norwegian menagerie in his house at Rominten in East Prussia. Eulenburg's secretary Kistler was there to record the trip on photographic plates, and made a famous picture of Georg Hülsen, Görtz and Kiderlen.

Eulenburg was impressed that William found time to work. There were audiences with the sailor Senden-Bibran, the soldier Hahnke and the diplomat Kiderlen. 'The emperor signed and settled hundreds of documents.'[56] William aired one of his favourite ideas on board: a *coup d'état* to allow him to dispense with the Reichstag. Kiderlen claimed that the emperor's new beard gave him might, perhaps the power to dissolve parliament: 'with a beard like this you could thump the table so hard that your ministers would fall over with fright and lie flat on their faces.'[57] There was plenty happening on the international scene which required William's closest attention. On 23 July the French fleet sailed into the Russian harbour at Kronstadt, and was rapturously received by the people. In August a formal alliance between the two countries was proposed. Bismarck's 'nightmare of alliances' was about to become reality.[58] It was at about that time that William noted presciently: 'European peace is like a man with a heart condition, he can live a long or a very long time. He can, however, suddenly and unexpectantly expire.'[59]

v

At the manoeuvres that year it was the king of Saxony's turn to criticise William's conduct. The king distrusted William's ability to lead in the field. He needed to act more like his grandfather, and take advice – 'He will never be a Frederick the Great.'[60] Waldersee continued to watch him from a distance, noting his many *bévues*; his fondness for the tag *suprema lex regis voluntas*; or his excursions into spiritualism with

Eulenburg, which reminded the historically sensitive Waldersee of Frederick William II and his general Bischoffswerder – a pair who were supposed to have let the side down in Prussian history. The general had a conversation with Dr Arendt of the *Deutsche Wochenblatt*: 'The question is apparently quite openly asked – in particular by doctors – whether or not some sort of mental disturbance has developed in connection with his earaches.'[61]

William caused further gasping by the speech he made in Erfurt on the day before the opening of the socialist conference there. He made a tough reference to Bismarck: 'I will suffer no one near me. He who is against me I shall crush.' It was not just the speeches. The naval officer Müller, who became an adjutant to Prince Henry in 1896, was appalled by the dirty jokes he loved to tell. He was particularly fond of mother-in-law jokes. There was an element of solid, bourgeois disdain in Müller's criticism of his master however. 'He does not do his duty, otherwise he would give over more of his free time to the serious tasks of his profession. He is not simple, but vain and extravagant, and inwardly he is not a pious man, else he would be man in everything he does. Let us hope he becomes one ...'[62] Müller was a bit of an oddball – one of the few middle-class men to make it as an ADC, and as such he was surrounded by often supercilious noblemen. He was surprised by William's fondness for personal chats often hingeing on small technical details of naval architecture and weaponry. On his trips he took the heads of his three cabinets with him. William read a lot on these occasions, and unusually fast, marking passages with a pencil.[63]

The younger Moltke had also been appointed ADC to the emperor. On 7 November he was with William when they visited Caprivi in the chancellor's palace. The sight of Bismarck's rooms provoked nostalgia in the emperor: '... as we drove away he spoke to me once again with great openness, he was full of bitterness and sorrow over his early experience [and Bismarck's] ... greatest ingratitude. He made me so sorry, for scarcely anyone understands how deeply the rift with Bismarck touched him and inwardly he feels the break.'[64]

In December William paid a visit to Alsace-Lorraine. He had acquired a new home in Gensburg. He discussed the continuing Bismarck affair with his viceroy, Hohenlohe. William thought all the trouble-making was on Bismarck's side and it was not his business to make the first move towards reconciliation. Were that to happen, Caprivi's position would have become untenable; and not just his. The Austrians were not at all happy about the prospect of Bismarck's rehabilitation and might easily withdraw from the Triple Alliance were it to come about. It was otherwise a relaxed occasion. Chelius played the piano and William expressed his desire to shoot grouse in the Reichs province. That month Caprivi was made a count to honour his trade treaties with Austria-Hungary, Italy and Belgium. The Russian treaty which had so aggrieved the East Prussian agrarians and their supporters, remained on the order paper.

Only a month later William told Waldersee that he was bored with Caprivi: 'I have already begun to have enough of the liberal era.' William told his chancellor of his plans to create a 'United States of Europe' which would be economically independent of the United States. 'It seems to me an attempt to guarantee eternal peace, which we will only enjoy once we make our entry into Paradise.' Caprivi had reversed Bismarck's protectionism in his desire to create a central European *Zollverein*. This formed the basis for William's frequent utterances in favour of a Common European Market.[65] William's liberal empire made further progress. He continued to question the two-year national service and cancelled orders to build up battalion strengths.

The liberal course was now represented by an eight-point plan: the destruction of the Social Democrats by improving the well-being of the workers and the launch of an international plan to that effect; school reform to broaden the curriculum and create more vocational training; moral reform; a strengthening of the German Empire at the cost of the individual states; a reconciliation with Russia; closer co-operation with Britain; friendly relations with Denmark; an improvement in the army. Waldersee scoffed at the likelihood of William having any success with his projects. The least successful of all, he thought, was 'the attempt to become a famous ruler, world respected and feared – and very popular to boot'.[66]

The theme of popular monarchy also underlay the speech William made to the people of the small town of Teltow in the Mark a few days before Christmas that year. He stressed the importance of these intimate occasions 'where the simple man of the people comes together with his ruler, not as a subject ... but feeling rather as the member of a family feels towards its head; that is a bond which exists only in Germany and which is especially possible in Prussia and Brandenburg ...'[67] At the end of 1891 William made a gesture towards reconciliation with Bismarck by sending him an album full of photographs of the late Kaiser William's apartment in the Berlin Schloss. Bismarck wrote back to thank his young emperor and told him how happy he was to be reminded of a ruler who was loyal and merciful to the end. That spring William sent no birthday greetings to Bismarck.[68]

In January 1892 William took a step forward in his desire to see a German navy worthy of the name. Despite their inauspicious meeting a year before, Tirpitz was made Chief of the Naval Staff and brought up to Berlin to elaborate a new strategy. He convinced William that they needed a battle fleet to protect Germany's new overseas interests: 'The fleet never struck me as an end in itself, but always as a function of our interests at sea. Without sea power Germany's importance in the world was like a mollusc without a shell.' It was the reigning view in Britain too, hence the rub.[69] Germany was expanding at tremendous speed. The population was growing by almost a million souls a year, the equivalent of an entire province. There was a practical need for trade and expansion. The problem was that a united Germany had arrived too late on the scene, when most of the world had already been carved up by the great powers. With the benefit of hindsight, Tirpitz asked the question whether this was not an artificial and untenable position; 'whether our rapid rise would not be followed by a terrible decline.'[70]

At the end of February William raised eyebrows when he expressed a desire to build a fortified tower in the vicinity of the Berlin Schloss with a commanding view over the Spree and its bridges, to protect him from the anarchists who were preying on European royalty. Another idea was to build a moat, or an artificial lake on the Friedrichstadt side, which would necessitate demolishing Schinkel's Bauakademie. The tower was never built but other elements of a 20-million-mark improvement package for the Schloss were adopted. Terraces were to be built to keep *hoi polloi* at bay and the Schlossfreiheit was going to be demolished, the inhabitants allegedly having too good a view of the royal apartments.

Also at this time William made a controversial speech at a banquet given by the Brandenburg provincial Landtag in which he spoke of Prussia's ally, God, who had fought with – the deist – Frederick the Great at Rossbach. 'I shall lead you on to ever more splendid days. I am taking the right course and I shall continue full steam ahead.' Neither Lucanus nor Caprivi had taken the trouble to edit the speech, which had been printed in the official *Reichsanzeiger* before he delivered it. It caused a predictable storm in the Reichstag. Hildegard von Spitzemberg thought the emperor was suffering from megalomania.[71]

In March the rumour that Waldersee might once again be up for the chancellorship must have encouraged the general greatly. Both Caprivi and the Education Minister Zedlitz offered their resignations because they had made such poor progress with William's cherished Education Bill. The sticking point was the emperor's desire to see more religious control of education in schools. The issue frustrated William so much he took to his bed with an ear infection for a fortnight. As it transpired, Caprivi survived another crisis by offering to stand down as Minister President of Prussia. The reactionary Botho Eulenburg was brought in instead. Waldersee thought him 'as slippery as an oiled eel'.[72]

A month later a further attempt to push through William's bill was causing heartaches for the chancellor. This time the Catholics were unhappy. Caprivi complained to Hohenlohe about William's style of government. He 'was continually talking to all kinds of people, which was an excellent habit in itself, but on these occasions he often contradicted his official announcements, and misunderstandings arose in consequence'.[73] Criticism was mounting on the right of the assembly. The Social Democrats and the Catholics were gaining ground and there were new fears of an alliance between the French and the Russians. 'A lost war will mean the Reich will fall apart.'[74]

Bismarck's trip to Vienna to attend Herbert's wedding to Gräfin Margarethe Hoyos occasioned new nightmares for William. On 9 June Caprivi sent his 'Uriah letter'; instructions to Ambassador Reuss not to offer him any more than 'conventional form'. He was even refused permission to attend the ceremony.[75] Not even the king of Saxony was allowed to receive Bismarck as he passed through Dresden on the way. Three days later William himself wrote to Francis Joseph asking the Austrian emperor 'not to make the situation at home more difficult for me by receiving this disobedient subject of mine before he has come to me and cried *peccavi*'. The battle was unpopular at home. As he passed through the streets, the public cheered, shouting 'Speech! Speech!' Bismarck replied, 'I am supposed to keep quiet! Keep quiet!' The public shouted back, 'If you keep quiet the stones will speak for you!' The National Liberals wanted a reconciliation, and – according to Philipp Eulenburg – Waldersee as chancellor. Bismarck was a stubborn enemy. 'I am and I remain the injured party,' he told Hildegard Spitzemberg.[76]

It was July and time for the journey to the north. Eulenburg stopped in Berlin on the way to talk to Caprivi, Holstein, Hatzfeldt and his cousin Botho whose political position preoccupied him at the time. Holstein was growing impatient with his king and emperor. It may have been then that he made the pointed remark, 'One day it will be possible to say that a man has told William II the truth; but I believe that this man will be the only man to have done so.'[77] Eulenburg did occasionally offer the emperor an honest appraisal, often in the course of a game of tennis. On 7 July Eulenburg wrote to his mother:

The Bismarck question becomes ever more acute, but I think his outrageous behaviour is gradually enlightening the people as to who is right and who wrong. The emperor is very calm, and plays a waiting game, apparently without rancour. Caprivi is in a difficult position regarding the prince's attacks.[78]

In August William learned that there was a surplus in the Alsatian treasury and suggested that they build him a ship. Hohenlohe wanted to see the palace in Zabern finished first. They talked about the rumour that William wanted to put the former chancellor in Spandau prison. The emperor denied it, saying he had no desire to make Bismarck a martyr.

On 14 October Waldersee noted the glorious reception William had been accorded by the Viennese: 'The [Austrian] newspapers are teeming with Byzantinism and celebrate him as one of the greatest monarchs; this boundless and senseless flattery does great damage to his self-consideration and awareness. Sadly it is much the same story here.'[79] The spectre of Waldersee had still not entirely vanished. In November that year there was once again a rumour that he was about to be made chancellor. He was vegetating in his provincial command in Altona where he had struck up an unholy alliance with Bismarck aimed at bringing down Caprivi. Bismarck, who had been elected to the Reichstag, intended to vote against the Army Bill in order to discredit the beleaguered chancellor.

V

In the autumn of 1892 the court was racked by the 'Kotze scandal'. For some time officials had been receiving anonymous pornographic letters complete with pictures where prominent courtiers were exposed *in flagrante delicto*. William's head was one of those most frequently gummed to a nude body. The suspicion was that he was having an affair with Gräfin Hohenau, the wife of his cousin Fritz Hohenau. Hohenau was the son of Prince Albert of Prussia by his morganatic wife, Rosalie von Rauch. Scandal fairly preyed on Albert's family, and his wife, a Dutch princess, had been discovered having a liaison with an equerry. Gräfin Hohenau was meant to possess beautiful hands, which would have recommended her to William. If the story is believable, the first of these poisonous letters showed William and the countess wearing nothing more than a few furs at the hunting lodge in the Grunewald near Berlin. They were described as 'Loloki' and 'Lotka'.[80]

At court it was generally believed that there was some truth in the idea of a liaison between the two. William's sister Charlotte is supposed to have remarked, 'and the best of it . . . my big brother escaped censure.' The Kotze scandal did not end there by any means. It carried on until the summer of 1894. An estimated 1,000 letters were delivered to the grandees of Berlin and Potsdam; 'nobody was spared', not even Dona or Charlotte. The letters came with the ordinary post at all hours of the day, postmarked from different parts of Berlin. The palace porters were alerted and told to put all suspicious envelopes to one side. They were printed with rubber type, 'or some queer writing machine'. At first a woman was suspected, but then the print gave way to a man's hand.[81]

The fact that the letters 'breathed an unrestrained desire for William's person coupled with a fiery hatred of any woman crossing his path' added fuel to the idea that a woman was responsible. 'Do not flatter yourself', read one destined for Dona, 'that the wiles you employ to be forever youthful in the boudoir are your secret alone, Imperial Messalina. Your baths and massages, your tinctures and perfumes – the meanest scullion in your palace knows their purpose. The Kaiser likes his Venus as she steps from the salubrious deep. But your servants also suspect that this is not the only requirement he imposes upon his charmer. That you hold him so well in hand as you do, and enchant him upon your couch one night out of six all the year round, proves your capacity for adaptation ...'[82] Gräfin Hohenau was supposed to be two-timing William with a Baron von R——. 'Now a guard lieutenant is poaching up the king's preserves. The smasher-in-chief knocked out by a masher-in-ordinary. And all for a silly harlot.'[83] About four hundred of the letters – presumably the least sensitive ones – were given to the police chief Freiherr von Richthofen. The theory now was that they were the work of a couple. One addressed to Dona showed the empress in the nude 'and at her side court chaplain Stoecker in *puris naturalibus*, save for his well-known clerical bib'. Dona, it seems, stopped receiving Stoecker after that letter.[84]

Now orders were given to open all outgoing mail from court. The move drove many sensitive courtiers away, including the Stolbergs, the Carolaths, the Sagans, Herr von Thiele-Winckler, the Maltzahns, the Perponchers and the Harrachs. Suspicion fell on one of William's court marshals, Leberecht von Kotze. He was '... a man after William's heart. In his agile and pleasing presence he combines von Hahnke's suppleness with von Plessen's devotion to duty and von Scholl's *bonhomie*. There probably never was an hour in his life, full of airy nothingness, when he would not have risked his soul for the king. He gave his services to the court gratis, and spent hundreds and thousands per annum to entertain His Majesty. In short he lived for the royal master only.' To show his attachment, he went so far as to wear a green cravat when William went hunting.[85]

A whispering campaign against Kotze was launched by his rival, Schrader. Schrader was able to locate a blotter in Kotze's office which, when held up to a mirror, revealed samples of writing similar to that used in the letters. William signed a warrant for Kotze's arrest on Potsdam station. He held up the blotter in triumph at dinner that night.Frau von Kotze went down on her knees to plead with the emperor to release her husband, but it was not until more letters arrived that he was prepared to countenance the idea that Kotze was not the author of the scandal.

The police now began to search high and low, even in Gräfin Hohenau's boudoir in the Bellevuestrasse. Kotze was still not at liberty. A graphologist examined his handwriting and decided he was not guilty, but he languished in the Lindenstrasse military prison in Kreuzberg until he was exonerated by a court martial at Easter. The only mercy William showed his old friend was to send some flowers and an Easter egg. The chief witness for the defence was William's own sister Charlotte. After his release there was a series of duels in which Kotze was maimed and Schrader killed. When William's conscience began to bite he finally sent some presents to Frau von Kotze.

After Kotze's release, fingers were pointed at Dona's brother, Duke Günther of Schleswig-Holstein. He left the country in the spring of 1893 'under a cloud of burned stationary'. When he returned, the correspondence started up again. Günther's accomplice, the marquise de Villemomble, was banished, and the duke was made unwelcome at court for a time. It was just possible that some of the letters had been written by Charlotte. Perhaps for that reason William prevented any further investigation from taking place. The decision was hard on Kotze, but understandable in the circumstances. Waldersee came to the informed conclusion that the culprit must have been a close relative.[86]

VII

With such problems in Berlin, William found solace in hunting. 'You often hear the expression "le roi s'amuse!" here. It is a clear reference to the uninterrupted series of hunting trips he has made since the middle of September. In the past between the end of October and the middle of December there was one hunt a week at the most, now there are always two, so that of the seven days at least four are devoted to pleasure. For ages the Socialists and the Progressives must have been keeping a book on just how much time the emperor gives over for audiences.'[87]

The shoots all offered different delights. In Potsdam he could shoot duck, pheasant, hare and deer; in Saxony, Baden, and on the Görtz estate at Schlitz the attraction was woodcock; on the Dohna estates at Pröckelwitz and Schlobitten in East Prussia he killed roebucks; at nearby Madlitz, with the Finckensteins, it was partridge; at Rominten on the Russian border there were harts; and on the Schorfheide near Berlin, red deer. William seldom stayed more than two days, but that could cost the noble proprietor of the estate 40–50,000 marks. William was very competitive and pleased with his prowess as a gun. In May 1895 he wrote a laconic missive to Dona from Pröckelwitz: 'Just shot a deer, Kessel missed. William.'[88]

It would be false to imply that William did no work on these trips. The telegraph had already begun the revolution in communications, and William's hand-picked ministers and advisers came with him on the hunt. William was staying at the hunting lodge in Göhrde on 18 November when a vital decision had to be made as to who should replace Bismarck's great ambassador to Petersburg, General von Schweinitz. The Tsar had expressed a preference for General von Werder. Werder was duly despatched: 'No small part of the [maintainance of the] peace of Europe lies in his hands,' wrote William.[89]

On 3 January 1893 William had recovered enough of his old self to wash his hands of the liberal Empire in no uncertain terms. Addressing the commanding generals he said, 'I shall get the [military] budget approved whatever the price. What does this house of civilians know of military matters? I shall not lose either a man or a mark and *I will pack that half-crazy Reichstag off to the devil if they oppose my will!*'[90] Hohenlohe witnessed William enjoying truffles *en serviette* with his Baden cousins in Karlsruhe later that month. He was beginning to know his ruler better. He had recognised the laziness, the reluctance to read reports. Eulenburg was with him and told Hohenlohe that he had too little ambition for the State Secretary's job, which had been dangled before him recently. He was no keener to be in charge of foreign policy than he was to take up the ambassadorship to London or replace his cousin August at the House Ministry; '... he was afraid that his relations with the Emperor, through his constant personal intercourse and audiences, might be disturbed; and yet it was just this friendly relationship which was very important and necessary to the Emperor, who was aware that he would never ask anything of him and give him only honest advice.'[91]

Eulenburg was keener than ever on the idea of Bernhard Bülow and more and more convinced that he should replace Caprivi. On 9 January Bülow wrote to Eulenburg in the sort of vein which appealed immensely to the artistically-inclined consul in Munich: 'All things considered we have the healthiest conditions of all European countries. We are healthy root and branch. We have a monarch who possesses qualities which cannot be acquired, and faults which are easy to banish.' This new course would have William himself designing the broad lines of policy with the detail left to Bülow, Philipp Eulenburg and his cousin Botho. Diplomatic appointments would be made by Holstein, Kiderlen and Eulenburg.[92]

On 18 February a new right-wing political party, the Bund der Landwirte, or Agrarian League, was formed to oppose Caprivi's trade policy. Waldersee noted – probably unhappily – that anti-Semitism had been dropped from the party programme. The general was now comparing his ruler to Frederick William IV, a king who by his reluctant acceptance of the 1848 Revolution and his inability to stand up to Austria, earned himself a bad name with hard-line Prussians. 'Both were idealists who began their work with plenty of pretty but poorly worked out plans and who quickly suffered a number of disappointments. They also have in common above all their moodiness and their rapid somersaults from one idea to the next. The greatest similarity with that period I find to be the general uncertainty and dissatisfaction, in particular with the aimlessness of the emperor.[93] On reflection Waldersee had to admit he was being unjust: William was no autocrat, and unlike Frederick William, he did not like to surround himself with clever or talented people.

Bismarck was a nuisance. William was aware that every one of the demonstrations of support he received when he left his estates or visited university towns was tantamount to a protest against his regime. William's conscience occasionally bit over Bismarck too. He wanted a reconciliation, yet he did not wish to lose face. One of those who endeavoured to bring the two together was Felix von Bethmann-Hollweg, the father of William's later chancellor Theodor, and a man whose judgement the emperor trusted. What stood in the way of such a reconciliation was the rumour that William was intending to return to the old course and would have to seek out his former minister, cap in hand. The idea that William should so humbly seek Bismarck out, had caused a 'wall to be built around him', from which there was, apparently, no way out.[94]

Eulenburg's routine mirrored that of the emperor. He was permanently on hand for the North Sea journey, even if he found all its slapstick pranks repugnant. In the summer of 1893 he once again reported first to the chancellor, Caprivi, who had just come from the Reichstag with a narrow majority for his military budget. It was a special year for the *Nordlandsreise*. The emperor's new luxury yacht *Hohenzollern* had been finished on 8 April.[95] William had shown an interest in every stage of construction. He had wanted to know about the comfort of the bathrooms and had effectively fought off Admiral Hollmann who had tried to exercise a modicum of financial constraint. He had been told that if the navy would not pay, he would dip into his own pocket. He objected, for example, to the idea that the silver might be reused from the old royal yacht.

That year there was a radical departure in that there were two females on board: Dona and 'Cilli' or Cecilie of Mecklenburg-Schwerin, the future crown princess. As a rule William did not enjoy women's conversation. There were exceptions, but Dona was not one of them. Dona was trying to assert herself by insisting on coming. William made her feel unwelcome and she soon backed down. Eulenburg put down some notes on the cast: Plessen was 'false', Lyncker 'amiable', Dr Leuthold 'excellent', Kiderlen 'sharp', Dietrich von Hülsen 'a Berlin lad', Seckendorff 'foolish', Kuno Moltke 'my music friend', Lippe 'clever and good', Senden 'efficient but half insane', Görtz 'in every way and in no way gifted, a comedian against his will', Georg von Hülsen 'nice and amiable, not as talented as he believes'.[96]

Eulenburg joined William at Cowes and was able to observe at first hand his emperor at home with his English relations. On 29 July, for example, William received the Duke of Connaught and the Prince of Wales dressed in his English admiral's uniform. There was a fear that war might break out between Britain and France at any moment. On the 30th, Eulenburg noted: 'As soon as the emperor arrived back on board the *Hohenzollern* we went into his saloon. He had completely lost his nerve.' He maintained that the strengths of the French and Russian fleets exceeded that of Britain while the German army was not strong enough to fight a war on both fronts. 'The French had skillfully chosen their moment.' 'The entire prestige of Germany will be lost if one does not take on the leading role – and if one is not a world power then one is just a miserable figure.'[97] Eulenburg was not impressed with William's idea of coming to Britain's aid. On 5 August he discussed the matter with him again over a post-prandial glass of beer. He saw no threat to German interests, but admitted he did not know how to soothe William's nerves.

It was Eulenburg's nerves that were tested next – by the sound of the bagpipes. The crisis died down, and there was a dinner the following day at Osborne where the party was served by four Scots and four Indians. Queen Victoria was dressed in black velvet. She rose and proposed a toast to her 'dear grandson'. The company raised their glasses to 'The German Emperor!' William returned the compliment with a toast to the queen. It was then that the Scots started up their pipes – 'a frightful screeching noise,' thought the sensitive and musical Eulenburg.[98] He had time to study the queen and the way William behaved with her. She spoke German like a native. In conversation with her he discovered that Vicky had told her all about him. William played the grandson for all that it was worth.

The *Hohenzollern* returned via Heligoland. William had begun to fortify the rock and a cannon had been installed that could fire a shell 15,000 metres. Eulenburg must have bitten his lip again. He had had a surfeit, and he found the naval talk 'unbearable'.[99] Back in Berlin Eulenburg was present at a lunch with the sculptor Begas which must have been more to his taste. He was working on the equestrian statue of the first Hohenzollern emperor which was to be erected on the site of the Schlossfreiheit with its jumble of restaurants and hotels.

William was also not being one hundred per cent frank. While he gave every impression of being concerned about his former chancellor's health, he was standing up in Bremen on 18 October and hailing his father as the true founder of the Second Empire. It was just the argument Bismarck had sought to avoid by having Geffken arrested. Now here was Fritz, 'with the German sword in his fist' winning 'the imperial German crown for his father'.[100] Politics continued to be a hotbed of plots and plotters. Caprivi was caught between two stools. Hahnke and the military party wanted to oust him. When William lunched with Waldersee on 3 December he expressed his dissatisfaction with the free trade policy which had lost him much support in Prussia. Eulenburg was flexing his muscles in favour of his cousin Botho. Waldersee was now worried about Eulenburg.[101] Hohenlohe was grateful that his own name had not been mentioned in the course of this fresh spate of intrigues.

In December the satirical magazine *Kladderadatsch* took it upon itself to disclose the powers behind the throne. They were 'Oyster-Lover', 'Spaetzle' and 'Graf Troubadour'. The first of these was obviously the gourmand Holstein – the inventor of the recipe for veal which still bears his name. The article alluded to the dirty work he had done for Bismarck in spying on the diplomat Graf Harry Arnim. The second was Kiderlen. *Spaetzle* are Swabian noodles, and Kiderlen was a Swabian – and, some would have maintained, a noodle. The last was naturally Eulenburg, 'beloved for his nordic ballads'. *Kladderadatsch* called Eulenburg 'Insinuans', Kiderlen 'Intrigans' and Holstein 'Calumnians'. The most dangerous was Eulenburg. The attacks were eventually traced to two Foreign Office officials, but there was something suspicious in the fact that neither Caprivi nor Marschall would consent to an official inquiry.[102]

Waldersee enjoyed the scandal the magazine caused on this occasion. He thought the worst was Holstein:

He won't allow himself to be seen and disappears even before the emperor. Kiderlen amuses the innocent monarch with stories in Swabian dialect which he tells with a straight face. His influence is so important because he accompanies the emperor on his travels and he alone briefs him; everyone who knows him, thinks him fundamentally false and malignant. Philipp Eulenburg is as ever very well in with the emperor ... and knows how to captivate him with poetry and song. He is basically a decent man whose character has however become dangerous through his dealings and the intrigues he gets embroiled with with the other two.[103]

Waldersee thought it was the moment to complain about Holstein to the emperor. William would not listen. 'I think that is quite impossible. I know Holstein very well, he is an excellent, honest chap, just as Kiderlen is totally devoted to me and totally in my control.' Waldersee transferred his distrust to Eulenburg, 'of whom I would not have believed before that he could have gone so far'.[104] *Die Zukunft* now joined in the attacks on the trinity, pointing out that Holstein had been behind the sinking of Harry Arnim. Both he and Kiderlen-Wächter reacted furiously to the attacks, accusing Henckel von Donnersmarck of writing the libel. Holstein challenged him to a duel and Kiderlen shot and seriously wounded the journalist Polstorff on 22 April. He was then packed off to Hamburg to lie low as Prussian consul. It was a foretaste of what would happen when Maximilian Harden decided to tilt at William's coterie, and Harden was not shaken off so easily.

In January 1894 there was talk of a rapprochement with the Bismarck family and further speculation about a change of ministry. Once more Waldersee's hopes were dashed. The story was put about that he would get the chancellorship, with Herbert as Minister President. Herbert was asked to the Honours Ceremony that year, but despite his waiting patiently for a chance to speak to William, the latter snubbed him. William was supposed to have been ready to recall Otto von Bismarck to allow his Commercial Treaty to be ratified by the Reichstag. This led to a 'violent scene' with his mother.[105] If nothing changed in Berlin William found Eulenburg a job he wanted, the ambassadorship to Vienna. It was not a popular appointment in many quarters. The man tipped for the job was Karl von Wedel. Neither the incumbent, Prince Reuss, nor the chancellor, Caprivi, was consulted, and Francis Joseph was also said to be unhappy.[106]

VIII

Bismarck had not let up. Cooler heads urged reconciliation, although it was arguable that the old man in the Sachsenwald would have accepted anything less than his old job back. William's cousin, Prince Albert of Prussia, told him, 'If Bismarck dies without you having made it up with him, what will posterity say?' In September William heard that Bismarck was ill and staying at Varzin in Pomerania. William seized the moment and sent him a telegram, offering him the royal Schloss of his choice in which to convalesce.[107] William also despatched Kuno Moltke with a letter and a bottle of wine from the imperial cellars – 'Lacrima Caprivi,' said the wits. The reconciliation wine was actually a hock from the royal domaine in Eltville: Steinberger Cabinett Goldbeeren Auslese 1862.[108] Johanna reported the news to her son Bill on 22 January: the letter had been 'as full of praise as could be deemed possible – H.M. had heard that Papa's convalescence was taking too long, for that reason he was sending a bottle of hock that was only to be found in his cellar. What do you believe, what do you think, what do you say, my little Billy!'[109]

Bismarck did not hurry to uncork his wine. It is said that he consumed it with Maximilian Harden, the editor of *Die Zukunft*, who was later to cause the greatest crisis in William's life prior to the abdication. 'Is it not true, Herr Harden, that you think as highly of the emperor as I do?' 'Never has a king's death been decided in a more ironic or subtle tone.'[110]

On the eve of William's thirty-fifth birthday the long-hoped-for reconciliation actually took place. The Russian Ambassador, Schuvalov invited Hohenlohe to witness Bismarck's entry into Berlin from his embassy near the Pariser Platz. Kuno Moltke had been given the commission to fetch the old chancellor up to town and Hohenlohe saw him sitting beside Prince Henry in the closed state coach as it made its way towards the Schloss. A bit of his face was visible, his hands and his white-and-yellow cap. He did not notice the enormous enthusiasm in the crowd despite cries of 'Hoch! Hoch!' Other accounts disagree. Marie von Bunsen observed the 'joyful excitement' on the faces of the older Berliners. From her position in the Lustgarten, she had an excellent view of William, accompanied by her friend von Lippe, inspecting the guard of honour.[111]

The younger Moltke had already noticed the crowds by the Brandenburg Gate, 'everywhere happy, expectant faces'. Later estimates put their number at between 300,000 and 400,000. There was tension among the guard at portal 5 of the imperial palace. A band was at the ready and a group of ADCs had been convened: the two Moltkes, Plessen, two Arnims – one army, one navy; Scholl, Kessel, Hahnke, Senden and the head of the Civil Cabinet, Lucanus.

A flower-filled apartment had been prepared for Bismarck at the Schloss. William was dressed in his Garde du Corps uniform. He was in a bad mood, 'visibly nervous and excited'. He decided that all the flowers should be moved to the antechamber, as 'the smell was too overpowering'. As Julius Moltke and the other officers waited for Bismarck's arrival, there was frantic activity, tables were being wiped, carpets beaten, 'chaos reigned'. The *mise-en-scène* had been carefully prepared so that William should not lose face. General von Plessen was to introduce the ADCs to the former chancellor and then Bismarck would enter the next room alone, where William was to wait for him. Moltke drew Graf August Eulenburg's attention to a discarded programme for a drama called *Der neue Herr* (The New Master), and decided it was inappropriate. It was hidden in a drawer.[112]

Bismarck was now proceeding down the Linden with Prince Henry in the gala coach. They received word that Bismarck had come with Herbert. Herbert was definitely not expected. His presence 'was clearly unpleasant for the emperor'. He ordered that Graf Herbert should remain in the antechamber and might not come to him with the prince. The court marshal's office was in great excitement as to how to deal with this unexpected *fait accompli*. Now they could hear the uproar from the

Linden. The band struck up. From the apartment the ADCs watched as Bismarck got out of the carriage and waved to the cheering crowd. William sat alone behind a closed door in the other room.[113]

Bismarck climbed back into the carriage which then drove into the courtyard of the palace. He came into the antechamber leaning on Henry's arm. 'We all bowed very low.' Bismarck looked pale. Plessen did the introductions. Bismarck waved at everyone, reserving his hand and a cutting remark for Kessel: 'Kessel? It seems to me that you have got smaller since those days.' There was more acid for Lucanus: 'I have already had the honour.' A servant took Bismarck's coat. He was tense and excited, and shaking a little. Henry salvaged the situation as best he could: 'Would *Durchlaucht* now like to go in to His Majesty?' Bismarck bowed silently.

William was in the middle of the room. He stepped forward quickly, offering his hand. Bismarck bowed low and took it in both of his. William bent down and kissed Bismarck on both cheeks. The doors closed and they were left alone while the others stood around in the antechamber. The ADCs could hear the jubilant crowd singing 'Deutschland über alles'. Ten minutes passed and the doors reopened. William ordered that his two eldest sons be brought to him and signalled to Henry to join him. The princes arrived and spent a further five minutes with Bismarck. William then dismissed the ADCs. 'His face was bright and cheerful. There was a gleam of great joy.'[114]

Bismarck ate with William, Dona and Henry. At lunch all political discussion was avoided. Bismarck spoke of his time at the Frankfurt Diet and of the old Empress Augusta.[115] William made him colonel of the 7th Cuirassiers. Hohenlohe saw William later at the Empress Frederick's and he was chuffed at the signs of support he had received in the course of his afternoon ride in the Tiergarten. The crowd had cheered 'Hoch! noble emperor!' 'Long live our generous emperor!' 'Hoch! beloved emperor!'[116] When William saw his ADCs again that afternoon he was in a very good mood. 'He spoke in a lively way and joked with us. He told us how he had served his best hock at luncheon and how Bismarck had savoured it. He was clearly deeply moved by the rapturous ovations he had received, and happy about the victory he had won over himself, the hardest that a man could manage.'[117]

At six fifteen there was another little meal in Bismarck's room at which Henry, Herbert and the ADCs were present. Moltke thought the conversation 'animated and unbuttoned ... friendly and untroubled'.[118] The hock was served again, to Bismarck's great pleasure. They were eating the roast when Bill Bismarck appeared. William called for another place to be set. After dinner the ADCs smoked cigars, William and Bismarck cigarettes. Again they talked of military matters. Politics were scrupulously avoided. 'It was no longer an imperial chancellor sitting at table, now only the colonel general.'[119]

William joined Bismarck in the gala carriage as he travelled under escort to the Lehrter station. He helped the old man up the station steps. On the platform he once again kissed him on both cheeks. Bismarck kissed the emperor's hand, his eyes wet with tears. William talked to Bismarck through the open window of his carriage: 'Now dear prince I hope you will sleep well after a stressful day. If I go to Wilhelmshaven in February I shall enquire in Friedrichsruh whether I may pay a call.'[120] As the train pulled out, Bismarck waved from the window. For Bismarck's many fans it was a day of rejoicing: 'The blackest stain in our history has been washed away!' wrote Hildegard Spitzemberg in her diary. William was certain he had triumphed. To some people he allowed himself a little more hubris: 'I am always a length ahead.'[121]

IX

Caprivi's Commercial Treaty was still proving a headache for William. He had wanted to incorporate some of his ideas for a United States of Europe by creating a super national customs union, but the Russians had threatened a trade war if they were excluded, and Caprivi was forced to drop his plans. The agrarians were blocking the passage of the Russian treaty because they feared they would be undercut by cheap grain. On 5 February 1894 William told Waldersee, 'I have no desire to go to war with Russia because of a hundred stupid Junkers!' On 12 March the emperor announced, 'The Commercial Treaty must pass, I have given Tsar Alexander *my word*!' Waldersee, who was on the side of the Junkers or, at least, desperate to fight a 'preventative war' with the Russians, was not sympathetic. When the bill was approved by a healthy majority on 19 March, William took much of the credit and Russo-German relations took a marked turn for the better.[122]

Nor were the Catholics doing everything they were supposed to. When their lay leader, Graf Hompesch, donated what was considered a paltry sum to the fund set up to erect a national monument to William 'the Great', William exclaimed publicly, 'If the fellow ever comes to the palace I'll have him thrown down the stairs!'[123] These none too private utterances flew in the face of his policy to try to make the Catholics feel welcome in his Reich. They had endured Bismarck's *Kulturkampf* and needed reassurance that they were not second-class subjects. William had a sneaking love of Catholic pomp, and visited Pope Leo XIII no less than three times. On the last occasion, the Pope was already ninety-three years old.

Under Bülow the Jesuits were finally allowed to return to Germany and William was an early protector of the Benedictines, presenting the monks of Maria Laach with an elaborate new altar. The monks had to play their part too. As William told the cenobites of Beuron: 'What I expect of you is that you support me and my efforts to maintain religion for the nation and that you increase respect for throne and altar. That way in these stormy days the thrones of Christian princes will be protected by Christ himself!'[124]

In February William made yet another of his rabble-rousing speeches to the Brandenburg provincial assembly, in which he stressed the sense of duty which had united all Hohenzollerns in their nearly-five-century rule in the Mark.[125] In March 1894 there were rumours that William was once again suffering from bad health. There was even talk of a regency.

At the end of the month William was in Abbazia (or Opatija) on the Croatian coast with Eulenburg, who had now taken up his appointment as ambassador in Vienna. It was a relaxed time, despite a visit from Emperor Francis Joseph. They played tennis and talked politics over beer. It was Eulenburg's new way of reaching William: he 'lets me say anything to him about politics *because* I play tennis with him and between flying balls and in the little periods of rest [I] have a well-disposed imperial ear within reach. That makes it possible to use his good humour to obtain consent in difficult matters. To sport for king and country! Crazy world.' The game was becoming one of William's new enthusiasms. During Berlin winters he played it on a covered court in Moabit; in 1895 a new one was constructed for him at Monbijou, across the Spree from the palace.[126]

The friends went on to Venice and stayed in the Palazzo Reale. The Italian king had taken over Scamozzi's Procuratie Nuove between St Mark's Square and the Grand Canal. Eulenburg found William and the king smoking cigarettes before luncheon. There was a meeting with his ambassador, Bernhard Bülow afterwards, and the party strolled along the riva degli Schiavoni together: 'The unbearable situation in Berlin hounded us like a growling mastiff.' Later the enthusiasm of the Italians was able to make up for the crisis at home. As William took a ride in a gondola with Eulenburg and the king, the people cried out, 'Eviva! Ecco l'imperatore.'[127]

x

On 29 April any delusion which William might have had about the universal popularity of his reign was shaken by the publication of *Caligula* by the Bremen-born historian Ludwig Quidde. Quidde later sat in the

Republic's Reichstag and was the recipient of the Nobel Peace Prize in 1927. William was compared to the Roman emperor; Vicky, naturally, to Agrippina. 'Caligula ... was still very young, he was not even a mature man when he was unexpectedly called to the throne. Dark and sinister were the events surrounding his elevation, sublime the earlier fate of his house.'[128] Caligula was popular at first, but that soon changed: '... the common characteristic of his measures was a nervous haste, which constantly sped from one task to another, volatile and often contradictory and thereby a highly dangerous addiction to carrying everything out himself.'[129]

Bismarck was compared to Caligula's ill-fated minister Macro. Madness was not slow in setting in, 'megalomania, rising to self-idolisation'. At the same time the Roman emperor showed an 'unbridled addiction to magnificence and extravagance ... they also had to adopt very questionable means to increase [his] income and to cover up [his] debts.' Caligula wanted ever more palaces constructed: 'Coupled with this building mania was a striking fondness for destruction. Buildings worthy of preservation were pulled down or refaced for no reason.' Quidde went on to detail other traits of Caligula-William's character: his love of bogus manoeuvres, and his diseased and exaggerated fondness for the sea. He also mentioned the fact that the Roman emperor had made his horse a consul, although it is not clear here which of William's ministers Quidde thought comparable – Caprivi?[130]

Quidde's *Caligula* was a great success, selling 150,000 copies and going into over a score of editions. Waldersee commented: 'Despite the many truly striking analogies, I should not like to believe that the development of our emperor must lead to a sad ending.'[131] At the time of his death he was not so sure. The general thought that William's worst side was his Guelph-Coburg inheritance – Albert's still present ideas as instilled in him by his mother in his cradle.

Quidde was indicted for *lèse-majesté* and served three months. It was a common charge and it carried some rough sentences; even if fortress detention generally proved more comfortable than an ordinary gaol. Only in the tiny principality of Reuss could one escape the charge. One source contends that there were 'as many years of imprisonment ... annually meted out as there are days of the year ... for the heinous crime of impeaching the Kaiser's aptitude ...' In 1895 the writer Friedrich Wilhelm Foerster received a three-month sentence for an article in *Ethische Kultur*. In Weichselmunde fortress near Danzig there were three other prisoners: a piano teacher who had said William was 'green', an anti-Semitic editor who had accused the emperor of being 'Jew-ridden' and a lawyer who had shot his opponent in a duel.[132]

William made periodic stabs at tightening the law. Anyone who mocked the name of the emperor or impinged on the dignity of the imperial grandfather was liable. In November 1898 three members of the staff of the magazine *Simplicissimus* were arrested for mocking William's pompous Palestine journey. There were nine months for the wife of a feudal landowner in Pomerania who had suggested William 'might kiss her foot'; four months for a prostitute for issuing a rather more general invitation; and nine for the Reichstag deputy Eugen Richter for accusing the emperor of 'running after an old sow'. William thought the three months awarded to Hedwig Jaede for calling the *Song of Aegir* 'rubbish' was too lenient; when, on the other hand, a sixteen-year-old girl received nine months for saying she wished to sleep with the emperor, he had the sentence quashed.[133]

The efficacy of such draconian methods may have been a little exaggerated. Modern research has shown how difficult it was to make the charges stick. Many of Germany's newspapers ran quite daring, oppositional copy. The socialist daily *Vorwärts* published leaked documents. The *Norddeutsche Allgemeine Zeitung* contained articles written by members of the government. Here censorship was rarely applied and, when it was, it was 'insignificant'. Foreign newspapers also enjoyed more liberty. The critic Alfred Kerr could be quite daring in his heavily ironic letters to the *Prager Tagblatt*. That was published in Prague, but he lived in Berlin, and not behind bars. The French periodical *Le Rire* also laughed at the Palestine trip, and was banned in Germany. With the legend 'Interdit en Allemagne' it was fairly freely available, but sold for a high price. The paper itself was generally held responsible for the infraction. This meant that if anyone was fined or went to prison, it was the editor, publisher or distributor. It is difficult to make a case for William's Germany being a tyranny.[134]

This was neither the first nor the last time the emperor was lampooned in print. A subtler portrait was the ruler in Ludwig Fulda's *Der Talisman* of 1892. In this case a tyrannical king has set his heart on a suit of parti-coloured clothes: purple and gold, with plenty of braid. Later, when his realm is no more, he learns the truth: that he was surrounded by yes-men.

Mein ganzer Hof nur eine Schar	My entire court was just a bunch
Von Lügern, wär' mein ganzes Königreich	Of liars, could it be true, my whole land
Gestützt von Schurken, ich ein blöder Thor,	Reposed on scoundrels, me a fool most cursed.
Der sich mit blindem Aug' und blindem Geist	Who with unseeing eye and blind wit
Aus allem Volk die Schlechtesten erkor...[135]	From all the nation chose the worst.

The realisation of his folly and the craven, fawning nature of his courtiers leads to the revelation: 'I am freezing in solitary greatness.'

Now that he had lost his own influence on the emperor, Waldersee was acutely aware that other people had his ear. In July he reported that Holstein's importance in the running of foreign affairs was bigger than ever. He was now thoroughly opposed to Philipp Eulenburg who he thought was behind Holstein's power. 'I never wanted to believe it, that Philipp Eulenburg could be so false; now I can no longer protect him. He has taken on a heavy responsibility. That the emperor should fall into such hands is a national disaster.'[136]

There were women on board for the North Sea trip in 1894 too. Once again Dona came as well as Fräulein von Gersdorff. It must have cramped the men's style a little. William spent a lot of time painting boats. There was a strict routine and the menus were by no means lavish. Breakfast was from eight to eight thirty: tea, coffee and two dishes; at eleven there was hot broth, sandwiches and madeira; at one, a three-course lunch; at five, tea and wine was served; and at eight, dinner comprised three or four courses with sparkling red and white wine.

Soon after William's return from his Arctic excursion, the generally supportive *Vossische Zeitung* ran a story on his absences during the previous year. The emperor had been away from Potsdam and Berlin for 199 days. Nor did a breakdown of this total do William much honour: 156 had been spent hunting, at sea or making visits; for 27 William had been with the army; and 16 more had been dedicated to official duties. The Berlin wits were saying that William excused himself with the line vaguely reminiscent of his grandfather's: 'I have no time to rule.' On 4 September William was in Königsberg in East Prussia, and took the opportunity to underline his desire for peace: 'The lasting maintenance of the peace forms the continual goal of my efforts.' Two days later it was time to unveil the new monument to his grandfather there. He made a speech as usual, in which he announced that 'his door was open to all of his subjects'. Waldersee thought otherwise: 'Those in the know are aware that despite all outward openness, the emperor is almost unapproachable.'[137]

There was a harder edge to William's Königsberg speech. He was in the nest of the agrarian opposition. 'Gentlemen!' he announced, forgetting that the Great Elector had had to decapitate one or two in his time, 'opposition from Prussian noblemen is an absurdity.'[138] It was a warning to the landowners of his most remote province to stop holding up legislation in the Reichstag. At the same time William's ADCs were urging him to summon Bismarck, but he never had any serious intention of re-employing the 'nasty old man' or the 'frightful' Herbert. Eulenburg consistently advised William against bringing them back and counselled Bülow not to give Herbert an embassy.[139]

There was a further significance to the second of William's Königsberg speeches: it rang the knell to the liberal course. William had been profoundly shocked by the murder by anarchists of the French president Sadi Carnot. He wanted to abandon any form of progressiveness and introduce tough, reactionary measures. He felt the German workers were ungrateful for everything he had done for them to date, and he went back to the idea of a *coup* again. Caprivi would not co-operate. In his frustration over his failure to see the Army Bill become law he told Botho Eulenburg that he was to be appointed chancellor and Caprivi tendered his resignation. William then went hunting at Liebenberg, where Philipp convinced him to change his mind. A new Army Bill was drawn up. He continued to wrestle with the problem of who should be chancellor. He liked Botho and he disliked Caprivi; yet Botho was universally unpopular. In the end they both offered to resign.[140] According to Philipp Eulenburg, William was confused by the desertion of both ministers: 'The emperor came to me with that certain pale, pinched face. I asked him if we should go on with the shoot and went with him to the butt. The weather was grey, everything seemed uncomfortable ... I have rarely seen him look so helpless. "Who can you advise me [to appoint]? I haven't a clue who I could summon. Do you know of no one?"'[141]

William and Eulenburg had other things to talk about at Liebenberg that autumn. On the same day that Caprivi finally lifted the ban on Russian credit – 24 October 1894[142] – William's *Sang an Ägir* was performed at the Opera. William put it about that he had composed it himself at the piano. He was rumbled by his sister Charlotte who turned on Kuno at the first performance: 'Since when does His Majesty play the piano?'[143] In fact the words were by Eulenburg and Moltke's piano score had been orchestrated by Professor Albert Becker. With its sub-Wagnerian, pseudo-mediaeval German, it is an indication of how good the body of Eulenburg's ballads were. They are now extremely hard to find:

O Ägir, Herr der Fluten,	Oh Aegir, Lord of the Waves
dem Nix und Neck sich beugt,	To you Nix and Neck bow,*
in Morgensonnen gluten	In the sun's warm morning rays
die Heldenschar sich neigt,	Favour to our squad show,
in grimmer Fehd wir fahren	Forward to furious frays

* Aegir is a Viking deity; Nix and Neck his subjects. Ellida was Fridthjof's boat; The Dragon refers to the effigy on the prow of their own longboat; The 'Maid' in the third verse is a Valkyrie. That the poem required such heavy textual machinery is an indication of its turgidness.

hin an den fernen Strand,
durch Sturm, durch Fels und
    Klippen
fuhr uns in Feindes Land!

Away to the far shore,
Through storm, rock and cliff we
    blaze
Lead us to our foe's door!

Will uns der Neck bedräuen
Versagt uns unser Schild,
So wehr dein Flammend Auge
dem Ansturm noch so wild.
Wie Fridthjof auf Ellida
getrost durchfuhr dein Meer,
so schirm auf diesem Drachen
uns, deiner Söhne Heer!

Place us under Neck's aegis,
If our shield should e'er fail,
Watch us with your fiery eye
While in the fight we flail.
Fridthjof on Ellida, why!
Assured your seas he won
Smile upon our dragon this
The army of your son!

wenn in dem wilden Harste
sich Brünn auf Brünnste drängt,
den Feind, vom Stahl getroffen,
die Schildesmaid umfängt:
dann töne hin zum Meere
mit Schwert und Schildesklang,
Dir, hoher Gott, zur Ehre
wie Sturmwind unser Sang![144]

When in the wildest clashes
Shield on target crash,
The foe with our steel we smite,
Our Maid lends might to thrash.
Our lay stills the sea's splashes
Our song of shield and sword,
Like the wind it lashes –
It honours Thee great Lord!

As a contemporary sneered, William's talents were creative 'only in giving work to others'. His cartoons were drawn by Professor Knackfuss, Chaplain Frommel wrote his sermons, and Saltzmann painted his marine views. It was not the last of William's attempts to break into literature. He collaborated on Ernst von Wildenbruch's truly awful *Willehalm*, which was performed as part of his grandfather's centenary celebrations in 1897. It quoted one or two of the more memorable lines delivered by his grandfather, including that from his deathbed: 'I certainly have no time to be tired.'[145] It was said that of the thousand invited guests, 750 had fled by the end of the play. Wildenbruch was a cousin, a Hohenzollern from the wrong side of the blanket, being descended from the dashing Prince Louis Ferdinand who was killed at Saalfeld in 1806. He not only possessed the benefit of blood, he moved in the right circles. Wildenbruch had served as a reserve officer in Potsdam in 1880 where he met William, and read him part of his epic, *Sedan*.[146]

William also worked on at least one play with his favourite playwright, the Rhinelander – and Catholic – Josef Lauff. Lauff broke into William's life on 16 May 1897 when the emperor attended a performance of his play *Der Burggraf* in Wiesbaden. The choice of subject – mediaeval Hohenzollern rule in Nuremberg – can hardly have been fortuitous. The young playwright had chosen well. From then on he was to enjoy unstinting patronage. Despite the very narrow range of the emperor's tastes, his seal of approval was important for a dramatist. Only three months after the first performance of the *Sang an Ägir* Alfred Kerr noted: 'It seems remarkable. But in reality, this is how things are in Germany now, the entire fate of an artist or a work of art may be greatly influenced by the amount of interest the emperor shows in it.'[147]

William claimed to love Goethe and Kleist; the latter possibly inspired him with the powerful Prussianism contained in *Der Prinz von Homburg*. He also made occasional forays into conducting. Music, like monumental art and sculpture, made a strong appeal to him. When a military band struck up 'Funiculi, funicula', William claimed the tempo was too slow and grabbed the baton to show how it was performed in Italy. Before Begas stole his heart, his favourite sculptor was Walther Schott, who designed the neo-rococo candelabra figures for the park at Sanssouci and the attractive stone benches along the Siegesallee in Berlin, some of which have survived. He continued to patronise the marine painter Karl Saltzmann. Eulenburg must have encouraged him greatly. At the beginning of November he toyed with the idea of taking on the job of Household Minister. As such, he could have run a salon where William might meet the greatest names in the arts, sciences and politics.[148]

William's first sally into music and poetry had not put his mind at rest. Caprivi was summoned to the palace. He entered while the emperor was eating lunch. William came out wiping his face on a napkin and ordered Caprivi to tender his resignation. Caprivi was bitter about it afterwards. For months he had expected the blow 'but on the day I was dismissed I was not expecting it at all.'[148] Two days later Hohenlohe was summoned to Potsdam. In Frankfurt he had learned of the resignation of both Caprivi and the Prussian Minister of the Interior Botho Eulenburg. On the 28th he agreed to become chancellor. He was seventy-five years old.

Uncle Chlodwig

Caprivi was the first and last of the soldiers. 'Uncle Chlodwig', the former Minister President of Bavaria and viceroy in Alsace-Lorraine, was at least an experienced statesman. He was also Dona's uncle, and through the Coburgs, a relative of the British royal family. As such he could call William 'Du', but he refused to do so, reminding him that 'kings have no relatives'.[1] He had one brother in the Prussian House of Lords, another a cardinal and a third a courtier in Vienna. This, William believed, would assure him of a modicum of respect all round. Eulenburg may have agreed to the choice, but it was William's uncle, the Grand Duke of Baden, who had put 'Uncle Chlodwig' forward. He had been in the best place to observe Hohenlohe's mild rule of the Reich's territories across the Rhine. Hohenlohe was peevish when it came to Eulenburg, claiming he had 'the cold gaze of a snake'.[2] He also occasionally expressed his frustration at the notion that important decisions had to pass through Phili's embassy in Vienna for ratification. On 19 May 1896, for example, he erupted, 'I am not a bureau chief in the chancellor's office, and am the Imperial Chancellor. I therefore need to know what I have to say.' He had inherited a much weakened chancellorship from Caprivi.[3]

Many saw Hohenlohe as an odd choice. Waldersee's name had come up again, and the War Minister Bronsart von Schellendorff. The reactionaries still wanted Phili's cousin, Botho Eulenburg. In contrast to the giants who had preceded him, Hohenlohe was dwarfish, an old man with his head permanently tilted to one side. Waldersee thought that he might inherit the Alsatian job, but that went to another member of the same princely clan, Hohenlohe-Langenburg. Shortly afterwards he was awarded the Black Eagle as a consolation prize. Hohenlohe was to some degree the compromise candidate. It was at this time that Holstein began to part company with Eulenburg. He wanted William to get into a mess from which he could only extract himself with difficulty, suffering the consequences of mass resignations. William had to be chastened to prevent him from ruling alone. It was to be the basis of his later co-operation with Harden, two very odd bedfellows indeed.

The new ministry marked a further shift away from the traditional Hohenzollern power base. The Junkers had been routed from the top jobs. 'A Catholic Bavarian Chancellor and Prussian Minister President, an Evangelical [Rotenhan] at the Foreign Office, a Badenese State Secretary [Marschall von Bieberstein] at the same, a Württemberger [Hohenlohe-Langenburg] viceroy – that will cause a pretty rumpus among the dyed-in-the-wool Prussians!' wrote another Württemberger, Hildegard von Spitzemberg. On the other hand the Junkers had their man at the Interior Ministry: Ernst von Köller was a thoroughbred reactionary of the Botho school, and a great favourite of William's.[4]

Eulenburg and Holstein were coming to the end of the line. Holstein had also lost patience with Caprivi's 'operetta government' and did not favour personal rule with Hohenlohe as William's puppet. Contemporaries were quite open about Caprivi's impotence. One light-hearted *Festschrift* published in 1898 said, quite unabashed, 'Caprivi occupied the Imperial Chancellor's office while the emperor was his own imperial chancellor.'[5] Holstein thought personal rule would lead to a return of Bismarck as a dictator or to a republic. In a candid exchange of letters he tried to impose limits on Eulenburg. Eulenburg fought back:

The king of Prussia has the constitutional right to rule *autocratically* ... If now the Kaiser steps forward as a personal ruler, *he has every right to do so*, the only question is whether the consequences can be borne in the long run. There is above all the question: *who will win the game?* I am afraid that only a successful war will provide the necessary prestige for this [domestic] conflict.

Further on in the letter Eulenburg returns to his romantic idea of kingship.

I believe in an intention of Providence in that elemental characteristic of the Kaiser to rule the kingdom himself. Whether she [Providence] wishes to ruin or help us I don't know, but it is difficult for me to conceive of the idea of the decline of the star of Prussia.

Such romanticism was unimpressive to Holstein. Prussia had merged into Germany and Germany – for all its faults – was possessed of a constitution. Holstein replied on 2 December: '*As for ruling with the Conservatives alone*, I had thought we had agreed long ago that the king of Prussia could perhaps, but the German Kaiser could never, rule on an *exclusively Conservative* basis...'[6]

On 5 December 1894 William finally opened the new Reichstag building, the foundation stone of which had been lain by his grandfather on a wet June day ten and a half years before. As soon as William had ascended to the throne he had begun to meddle in the plans of the architect, Paul Wallot.[7] He disapproved of the florid, classical style of the design and would have preferred the building to have been constructed in a German Romanesque idiom.[8] In April 1893 he had told the German artists' colony in Rome that Wallot's construction was 'the pinnacle of bad taste'. Probably its function upset him as much as the design. German public opinion disagreed, and quickly took the lavish building to its heart. William's opposition caused a stir: he was likened to Ludwig II of Bavaria.[9]

On the big day William delivered a speech from the throne in the Knights' Hall of the Schloss. Ihne was busy reworking the White Hall in a suitably grandiose style and it could not be used. No mention was made of the recent political changes and elsewhere the ceremony was notably military in its tenor. Hohenlohe and Levetzow, the President of the Reichstag, were in uniform, William wore that of the Garde du Corps. The *Berliner Tageblatt* noted that the deputies in their ordinary frock-coats assumed very much a secondary role on this occasion. William took the trouble to remind the assembly of the bloody beginnings of the new Empire. The whole ceremony was over in half an hour. On the 9th he described the opening of the 'imperial monkey house' to Phili. Wallot had been rewarded with a title, but William's opinion of him had not improved: he ... 'was swimming in contentment. He didn't disappear from my side once. He noted that I had neither punched in his top hat nor been rude to him ... He was so happy that, when I ordered him to escort the empress, because she got stuck in all the doors as a result of not knowing the way, he went off with the words "With His Majesty's special command" and offered her his arm in *coram publico! Tableau!*'[10]

William's belief that he had effected a reconciliation with Bismarck proved premature. When Johanna von Bismarck died at Varzin at the end of the year, the Reichstag refused to send official condolences. William wrote instead to say that the attitude of the politicians represented quite the opposite of that of the princes and the people. Bismarck wrote a frosty acknowledgement: 'I hope Your Majesty will accept the humble expression of my gratitude for the All Highest announcement with which Your Majesty made me aware of the up till then unknown act of unfriendliness on the part of my old political opponents, which has been transformed in me into an occasion for joyful satisfaction.'[11]

There were changes on the world scene. Alexander III of Russia died at the beginning of November 1894. Despite their allegedly close relationship in the past, William did not attend his funeral. Perhaps he had been cut by the rude comments which Bismarck had vindictively revealed to him. The Foreign Office now thought they could govern his successor, the weak Nicholas II, and the famous Willy–Nicky correspondence was the result. It began innocently enough. For Christmas William sent his Russian cousin a photograph album containing pictures of military parades in Berlin.

In the meantime Hohenlohe brought the tact of the *grand seigneur* to bear on the office. With William's consent he paid a call on Bismarck in Friedrichsruh on 13 January 1895. The latter was tender, Johanna had died less than two months before. They drank a few glasses of Mosel before lunch. Bismarck complained of the envy of the Junkers. They had not forgiven him for becoming a prince. As regards William, Bismarck warned Hohenlohe, 'The difficulty of my position lay in the sudden decisions of His Majesty.' The new approach was sealed by the appointment of Bismarck's second son, Bill, as Oberpräsident in Königsberg.[12]

William's leading advisers began to polarise. Kuno Moltke, August Eulenburg and Lucanus formed a Prussian bloc determined to get rid of the south German Marschall, who was suspected of excessive liberalism. They also encouraged William's innate distaste when it came to Catholics. William was beginning to rely on Köller to introduce the extreme right-wing legislation he now favoured. He wanted to pass a law which made it illegal to slander his grandfather. The other ministers thought he was going too far. In the Köller crisis later that year there was indeed a threat of mass resignation by the key men who were determined to see William's power curbed: Holstein, Marschall and Bronsart, as well as all Köller's colleagues. William's military entourage was of course the most extreme. They were gunning for a *coup d'état* which would suspend Parliament and introduce changes in government. Holstein managed to save Marschall for a while, but he was finally brought down by the Tausch affair which was fast approaching, and replaced by Bülow.[13]

On 7 February Holstein – and William – wrote to the Tsar. The letter appears to be in character, right down to the idiosyncratic spellings: 'My Reichstag behaves as badly as it can, swinging backwards and forwards between the socialists egged on by the Jews and the Ultramontane Catholiks [sic]; both parties being soon fit to hang all of them as far as I can see.' His message to his cousin – or that of the Foreign Office – was to keep the monarchical principle strong.[14]

Things were clarifying in Eulenburg's mind. William visited him in Vienna at the end of February, looking pale after a bout of flu. They must have talked about bringing in Bülow to take over at the Foreign Office. William was overjoyed with Eulenburg's nomination: 'Bernhard, what a splendid fellow! I adore him. God! What a difference from that south German traitor. What a joy to have to deal with someone who is devoted to you heart and soul, who wants and knows how to understand

you!'[15] Kiderlen thought Bülow an eel, but that may have been sour
grapes. While William was in Vienna, Eulenburg had the opportunity
to talk about an adopted Viennese, Houston Stewart Chamberlain, who
had married Wagner's middle-aged daughter Eva and was busy putting
together a voluminous work on race.

On 26 March William called on Bismarck in Friedrichsruh to return
his visit to him in Berlin. He brought the crown prince with him and
presented the former chancellor with a sword made to William's own
design and a new patent making him a Prussian field marshal. It was
decorated with arms of the duchy of Lauenburg entwined with those of
Alsace-Lorraine. 'Your Majesty will permit in all obedience to lay my
thanks at his feet,' Bismarck responded. 'My military position relative
to Your Majesty does not allow me to tarry when expressing my feelings.
I thank Your Majesty most obediently.' It must have been a chilly performance. William further endeavoured to disarm Bismarck by giving
him his grandfather's pen.[16]

On 1 April William returned at Friedrichsruh to greet his former
chancellor on his eightieth birthday. Bismarck spoke of politics and
William changed the subject. He wanted to talk about his wonderful
army. It was an uncomfortable meeting. The younger Moltke whispered
to Tirpitz, 'It is terrible!' Finally Bismarck cuttingly announced: 'Your
Majesty, as long as the officer corps is with you, you can of course do
anything you want; were that to be no longer the case then the situation
would be completely different.' There were some old accounts which
had yet to be settled. Bismarck refused to acknowledge Lucanus. When
Admiral Heeringen kissed the old chancellor's hand, Bismarck took his
head in his hands and kissed him on the forehead.[17]

In June William opened the Kiel Canal. Despite fears that the ministry
had not been able to provide enough money to finance the festivities
Borchardt's restaurant in Berlin – incidentally Holstein's favourite – was
able to lay on a meal of eleven courses and six different wines for 1,050
people, all served in fifty-five minutes flat.[18] It was a great occasion in
Germany, and naturally it was commemorated by the wits too. They put
it about that William had wanted to sail the *Hohenzollern* himself, to be
the first man through the canal. Not trusting William's ability to pilot
it, the navy disconnected the bridge. The control room was actually
downstairs. Later writers have wanted to see this as a metaphor of
William's reign.[19]

From this time dates William's relationship with the Jewish businessman Albert Ballin of the Hamburg-Amerika shipping line. They
had met in 1891, when William and Dona had come to Hamburg for
the launch of the fast steamer *Augusta Viktoria*. After the ceremony
William had told the businessman, 'Just take our people out to sea; there

the nation and our society will gather rich prizes.' That meeting had failed to lead to a firm friendship. Before the opening of the Kiel Canal Ballin stepped in with funds to make the occasion worth while.[20] In the wake of that generosity he was invited to a planning meeting in the Berlin Schloss to decide the order of the ships which were to pass through the canal on the day. It had been proposed that the *Hohenzollern* should be followed by a Lloyd vessel from Bremen, the Hamburg-Amerika ship coming third. Ballin naturally wanted to see his ship enter second. For such a convinced anti-Semite Waldersee's comment was remarkably affable: 'As you are going to be strung up under the Brandenburg Gate as a result, I suggest we have lunch at Hiller's first.'[21] The gastronomic theme continued on board the Hamburg-Amerika vessel on the day. The quality of Ballin's buffet set tongues wagging.

Ballin was particular about his food, and it was the Jewish shipowner who brought the German emperor into contact with the most famous chef of his day, August Escoffier. In June 1906 Escoffier was asked to design the kitchens for Ballin's ships and on this occasion William, who generally insisted on German menus and German food, gave his permission for a French approach. William was present for the maiden voyage of the *Amerika* and paid an unofficial visit to the kitchen. Here he spoke to Escoffier about his experiences as a prisoner in Mainz during the Franco-German War. 'I am only sorry I could not have been there ... I would have liberated you,' he told the chef. He then proceeded to lecture him on diet, telling him that he advocated a proper, English breakfast, a substantial lunch, but only a modest dinner.[22]

It was natural that William should take an interest in the 'HAPAG' or Hamburg-Amerika line. Such things were close to his heart – even as he had spoken out as crown prince to prevent the construction of important vessels going to British yards during the trials of the new royal yacht *Meteor*. It was essential that Germany should get more than the mere 'Cinderella work'. The Vulkan yard in Stettin was renamed 'Augusta Viktoria' in Dona's honour in 1888. The shipbuilding industry was hoping for rich pickings under the new emperor.

By 9 April Waldersee had seen enough of Hohenlohe – he was not up to the job and once again the imperial bark was being tossed this way and that for want of a proper captain. William continued to court the Tsar. His role was to defend Europe against the 'Yellow Peril' – those Asiatic hordes that William thought threatened her peace and security. On 26 April he wrote to his cousin: 'I shall certainly do all in my power to keep Europe quiet, and also guard the rear of Russia so that nobody shall hamper your action towards the far east!' When Russia carved up China, William hoped that Nicholas would find him a decent port. He proposed a quiet chat on foreign policy somewhere in the Baltic.[23] On

10 July William wrote to Nicky again. Asia was much on his mind: 'the defence of the Cross and the old Christian European culture against the inroads of the Mongols and Buddhism ...' By September the theme loomed so large that William had an engraving prepared showing the Archangel Michael defending the Cross against the heathen.[24]

There were crude attempts to break up the Franco-Russian alliance, which had been signed on 4 January 1894. William reported those 'damned rascals', the French, massing on the Lorraine borders. This bellicose behaviour would require him to increase the size of his army. 'God knows that I have done all in my power to preserve the European peace, but if France goes on openly or secretly encouraged like this to violate all rules of international courtesy and peace in peace times, one fine day my dearest Nicky you will find yourself – *nolens volens* suddenly embroiled in the most horrible of wars Europe ever saw.' History might even see Nicky as the cause!'[25]

Philipp Eulenburg travelled up with Kuno Moltke for the annual North Sea jaunt. Eulenburg was then at the height of his power and his advice was called upon at all times. As he wrote to his mother, 'I have a lot of heavy, political work, a lot of responsibility which weighs me down.'[26] This year Julius Moltke was also on board for a state visit to Stockholm and Drottningholm, the king's summer residence. Their appearance in the Swedish capital was the occasion for an unwitting farce on the part of the drunken Swabian, Kiderlen. After a heavy night he found a queasy stomach called for his presence in the lavatory. He was still there when the Swedish crown princess came aboard, and effectively blocked his retreat by occupying the neighbouring saloon. Although much amused by Kiderlen's discomfort, his friends none the less kept his spirits up by lowering glasses of schnapps to Kiderlen's porthole. William went blue in the face with mirth when he heard the tale later.

After his Arctic revels, William went to Cowes where he came up against the British premier, Lord Salisbury, anxious to regulate Anglo-German colonial rivalry as well as proposing new solutions for Turkey and the Balkans. William suspected Salisbury of wanting to destroy the Triple Alliance. He arranged a meeting with him on the 6th, but Salisbury failed to turn up, leaving William waiting for two and a half hours. The next day the prime minister left early for London. The sensitive German monarch decided the snub was intentional. Some have suggested that the Kruger telegram at the new year was William's response. Salisbury claimed it was nothing of the sort in his apology to Ambassador Hatzfeldt.[27] Although it was probably no more than an oversight, William was never to forgive the marquess and the lapse had the unfortunate effect of encouraging the Anglophobes in Berlin.

Waldersee was triumphant. It might have been on this occasion that William was denied the Highland regiment he coveted. Colonel Swaine, the military attaché in Berlin, wrote: 'This would never do, and he is an admiral. The queen thinks he is far too spoilt already.'[28] 'They clearly believe that they can deal with the emperor better if they treat him badly; they know quite correctly that he is very impressed by the English way of life, by wealth and luxury, and that they can easily fob him off with various pleasures. I have been able to observe for years now, how it is that he, who as a prince had nothing but contempt for England, has gradually turned into an Anglomaniac.'[29]

II

For once Waldersee's information was not wholly correct. As soon as he had left the troubled waters round the Isle of Wight William had had a wonderful time in England. He had been to Cumberland to see the man the British papers called 'William's English pal', Hugh Lowther, the fifth earl of Lonsdale. William had met Lonsdale through his uncle, the Hon. W. Lowther, who had been at the embassy in Berlin. They had struck up a firm friendship and Lonsdale was present at German army manoeuvres for many years as an honorary ADC. Partly at the suggestion of Queen Victoria, he advised William on cavalry charges and boat-building. The yacht *Meteor II* was built in Glasgow and launched by Lady Lonsdale. Once, in Coblenz, Lonsdale had seen a vase he admired. William had immediately bought it for him. It was set up in the flower-beds at Lowther Castle inscribed with the words from *Omar Khayyàm*: 'Oh moon of my delight'. After dinner Lord and Lady Lonsdale used to walk out to visit the promissory pot.[30]

The fabulously rich 'yellow earl' was England's most prominent sportsman: gun, foxhunter, boxer, yachtsman and champion of all other athletic pastimes. He was also a lover of 'beautiful women and unpopular causes'. William must have fitted well into the latter category. Lonsdale remained loyal to William through thick and thin. Although they never met again after 1914, the English peer always praised and supported him, saying that he had been 'admirable company', and they exchanged Christmas cards until 1939. Lonsdale maintained that William had two personalities, one official and one private – 'All sovereigns attract sycophants and the German Kaiser more than most.' Even during the Boer War, Lonsdale continued to champion his friend. When William came to visit his grandmother with Bülow in 1899 all official appointments had to be cancelled, and a planned trip to Lowther scrapped. William none the less had Lord Lonsdale invited to Windsor for a private dinner.[31]

Lonsdale had been to Kiel as William's guest that year and now he had the chance to return the favour. The 'acceptance of a private invitation from an English nobleman, and the rakish Lord Lonsdale at that, caused a considerable flutter, not least in Berlin, where the Kaiser's friendship with Lonsdale was not viewed in official circles as altogether a good thing.'[32] Lonsdale had been at Cowes too, and William and his party were invited to a ball aboard his yacht *Verena*, which had been converted for the occasion with 'flowers, shrubs and tropical plants'. Once the yachting was over William and a party of ten took the train north. 'The hospitality which awaited the Kaiser at Lowther ... was to make the lavish feasting aboard the *Verena* seem little more than an al fresco picnic.'[33]

They were met off the train at Penrith by the Quorn in full rig, a squadron of yeomanry in their colourful uniforms and two outriders in blue coats. It was rumoured that they had been polishing their kit for two months in preparation. In a dark-blue, open phaeton sat Lonsdale with his brother, Lancelot Lowther. They set off with another nine vehicles following, each drawn by two chestnuts and with a footman in Lonsdale livery on the back. That meant white waistcoats and breeches, yellow jackets with Lonsdale devices on their left sleeves and white beaver hats. Policemen had had to be drummed in from elsewhere to line the routes. There was massive enthusiasm for the emperor. In Penrith all the hotels were full, with people camping in the corridors or sleeping in the streets. The cavalcade was followed by every possible form of locomotive. William sat opposite Lonsdale watching the locals on roofs and in windows, waving the imperial eagle.[34]

Lady Lonsdale was waiting at the castle. The imperial flag flew from the mast and a special telegraph office had been set up so that the emperor could communicate with Berlin. William's entourage consisted of Kuno Moltke, Ambassador Graf Wolff-Metternich, August Eulenburg, Plessen, Chelius, General von Lippe, Admiral von Senden-Bibran, Major von Jacobi, his physician Dr Leuthold, and Colonel von Arnim, one of the many officers from that huge Prussian noble tribe. William had come to shoot, and the three-and-a-half-mile track out to the butts had been named the 'Emperor's Drive' in his honour. Lonsdale had been alarmed by poor reports of the game on his own moors, and had rented the earl of Strathmore's at Wemmergill – across the border in Yorkshire – too.* Of the 150 brace shot during the party, William bagged 60. As a surprise, Lonsdale took William out for a walk through

---

* There is still a 'Kaiser's Butt' at Wemmergill. Behind the butt proper is a second station. The story is still told in the region that William's bag was augmented by Lonsdale's men, placed at a discreet distance from the emperor.

William's grandfather, the
first Hohenzollern emperor,
William I in 1880.

William's parents at
Windsor at the time
of their marriage in
1858.

William with his sister Charlotte in 1863. It is unusual to see William exposing his malformed left arm and hand, even at this age.

William, 1863. He had a lifelong fondness for dogs.

William's stern, Calvinist tutor, Georg Hinzpeter.

The church of Alexander Nevski in the Russian colony in Potsdam. Near here young William concealed his Alsatian mistress, 'Miss Love'.

William's bride, Augusta Victoria of Schleswig-Holstein, or 'Dona', as a young woman in 1881.

Portrait of Dona by Franz Lenbach, 1886.

Dona in later years with William. She quickly became stout and matronly after their marriage.

Where it all began: William with his English family at Coburg in 1889.

Fürst Otto von Bismarck, the creator of the second German Emperor. William parted company with him in 1890.

William on a visit to the former chancellor, Bismarck, at Friedrichsruh in 1888. Bismarck is flanked by one of his feared and famous 'imperial dogs'.

William's most famous gaffe, 'the royal will is the supreme law', inscribed in the Golden Book in Munich town hall in 1891. It did nothing to help the poor relations between the Prussian and Bavarian royal families.

Punch, 1 February 1896. William's impetuosity is threatening the stability of Europe. He was cross with the English magazine, since the famous 'Dropping the Pilot' cartoon which was occasioned by the sacking of Bismarck.

THE STORY OF FIDGETY WILHELM.

(*Up-to date Version of "Struwwelpeter."*)

" LET ME SEE IF WILHELM CAN
    BE A LITTLE GENTLEMAN ;
    LET ME SEE IF HE IS ABLE
    TO SIT STILL FOR ONCE AT TABLE !"

" BUT FIDGETY WILL
    HE WON'T SIT STILL."

JUST LIKE ANY BUCKING HORSE,
    " WILHELM ! WE ARE GETTING CROSS !"

Hugh Lowther, 5th Earl of Lonsdale, at manoeuvres in 1899. The Kaiser's English friend remained loyal through thick and thin.

William, posing in a fine array of medals.

William with his
English crew on
board his racing
yacht *Meteor* in
1898. Even the
cook was English,
but political
pressure convinced
him to replace
them with a
German crew.

William and Uncle
Bertie at Queen
Victoria's funeral in
1901. William is
riding a specially
trained horse which
could deal with his
poor balance in the
saddle.

William and
Edward VII in
1906. The bad
blood between the
two of them was
a major factor
contributing to
war in 1914.

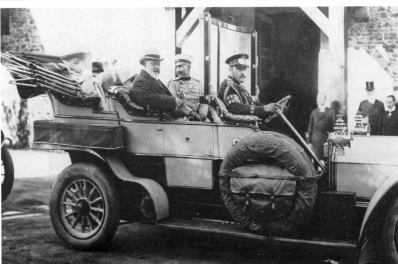

William posing for the portrait he gave the University of Oxford on his receipt of an honorary DCL in 1908. The picture still hangs in the Examination Schools.

Philipp Graf, later Fürst zu Eulenburg, William's best friend and the centre of the homosexuality scandal which bedevilled the court in 1908–9.

Achilleion, Easter 1908. William acquired Empress Elizabeth of Austria's villa on Corfu and went there to indulge his passion for archaeology every spring.

a wood on the estate, and told him to bring a gun, as he sometimes saw a rabbit pop out. Beaters were ready to drive scores of the beasts through the thicket on receiving the signal. A delighted German emperor picked off sixty-seven of them.[35]

In the evening there was a twenty-four-man band led by a Mr Hamilton. A special 'Emperor's Waltz' had been composed by the leader. The band also played 'Die Wacht am Rhein', 'Verena' – which had been specially composed for Lonsdale, the 'Song of Aegir', and 'Ever Welcome' which Hamilton had also written for the occasion. Lonsdale found William an 'easy guest' who went out of his way to make everyone feel comfortable. He had some fun at the expense of his ADCs who were making a hash of riding a bicycle on the terrace. August Eulenburg fell off a pony and hurt his head. The next day Lady Ethel rode the horse with no apparent problem. William made light of the occasion: 'Tell count Eulenburg that I am thinking of introducing a new uniform for my staff officers – a riding habit.'[36]

To show his gratitude William presented his host with a marble bust of himself, probably the new one by Schott. After his arrival it had been concealed behind some palms. The evening before he left, William silenced the band playing 'Heil Dir in Siegerkranz' and opened the box. Unveiling the bust he said, 'I can think of no better way of showing my regard for you personally and my appreciation of the hospitality you have shown me, than by asking you to accept this gift as a token of our great friendship.' Another story was told about the bust. The sculpture was taken out of its packing case while Lonsdale was absent from the castle, but no plinth could be found for it to stand on. An ADC, however, used his initiative and borrowed a stand from a Roman emperor. William wanted to know how he had solved the problem so efficiently. When he heard what had happened, and how a Roman emperor had had to make way for him, he laughed and said, 'Oh really! That was undoubtedly Caligula!' After the five-day stay the royal party rejoined the *Hohenzollern* in Leith. It was said that Lonsdale had spent a fortune on entertaining the German party, but he denied it. He was quite used to having sixty or seventy to dinner. Lonsdale was not famous for thrift.[37]

III

Hohenlohe had his hands full trying to put through the new provisions for military justice which had been drawn up by the Minister of War, Bronsart von Schellendorff. He had carried the new regulations concerning courts martial in Bavaria in 1869, but he encountered strong opposition in Prussia. Bavaria was only under the emperor's command in wartime, but even so, William's refusal to accept open justice in the army put his chancellor in an invidious position, especially as he was trying to befriend the Reichstag and had enough problems dealing with the excessive demands of the agrarians. Naturally the measure was opposed by Köller who leaked the draft to Plessen and Hahnke on William's headquarters staff, both of whom worked on William to have the measure dropped. Köller's action led Bronsart to challenge him to a duel.[38]

William was under the influence of his military household, but he was not wholly reactionary in military matters. He interested himself in tiny details such as uniforms, changing army dress thirty-seven times in the first sixteen years of his reign. He overhauled the messes, setting down how many courses and how much wine could be served. He wanted to rejuvenate the army and the navy. It was under his directives that the army became overwhelmingly bourgeois, even in the smarter regiments. William was sympathetic to the idea of putting an end to physical abuse of soldiers, saying that he was to be informed immediately of any 'slapping'. Later, however, he backed down. He would not scrap duelling – which was so important to the aristocratic student corps of which he was an enthusiastic member. To be 'capable of giving satisfaction' was the badge of a gentleman in Germany and society split in two: those who could duel and those who could not. William none the less allowed the law to be tightened up so that it was harder to get off scot-free. He wanted lighter sentences from the military courts: he was not the 'fantastic militarist which his enemies now want to accuse him of'.[39]

After the manoeuvres Lord Lonsdale visited William in Berlin. Lonsdale was not only credited with having introduced William to bevies of beautiful Englishwomen; the little party the month before was rumoured to have cost as much as a million marks. The Berliners were therefore surprised to find that the earl had been lodged at the Bristol in the Linden, rather than the royal palace. Later they learned that Lonsdale had been snubbed in this way because he had had the temerity to say that he was at the very least the equal of the king of Württemberg, having more 'subjects' than the south German monarch.[40]

In truth there had probably been no intended snub at all. The hotel was a great deal more comfortable than the Schloss. On 2 September Reuters reported Lonsdale driving down the Linden in William's carriage. He had been lent an imperial page and valet to look after him and the carriage had also been made available. He was a guest at the Tempelhof parade and also attended the opera with the emperor. That month

Lonsdale gave an interview to the *Berliner Tageblatt* in which he described his friend:

The Emperor is an extraordinary man in every respect ... his perceptive faculties, his energy, his grasp of everything that awakes his interest, but above all his foresight, are simply incomparable, and he possesses all these qualities in a degree only met with in geniuses ... He is just as excellent a naval expert as he is closely connected with all details of colonial questions. It is incomprehensible ... If he has a fault it is his youth, but in this respect he is improving every day.[41]

The Times grudgingly concurred – 'Kaiser Wilhelm is certainly an extra-ordinary man.'

IV

On 25 October 1895 the emperor and his advisers once again tried to drive a wedge between Russia and its allies and potential allies through William's supposedly private correspondence with the Tsar. France was not to be trusted. The French socialist orator Jean Jaurès 'sits on the throne of the king and queen of France "by the Grace of God" whose heads "Frenchmen Republicans cut off!"' The message was to stress legitimacy – 'We Christian kings and emperors have one holy duty imposed on us by Heaven, that is to uphold the principle *von Gottes Gnaden*.'* William switched his attention to Britain. He thought he could put the cat among the pigeons by telling Nicky that they were after the Straits. Meanwhile the Russians were threatening Germany with war if they did not 'knock down' in Africa. William suggested that Russia and Germany should exchange ADCs. He was prepared to send Julius Moltke, the future Chief of Staff.[42]

Officials believed that German trading interests were threatened by the British desire to make the Transvaal a protectorate. The German colony in British South Africa was growing. In 1857 the German Legion which had fought with the British in the Crimea had settled in the Cape, but the largest element had gone to Johannesburg where they were involved in the mines and banks. In 1913 there were 12,000 Germans living in the Transvaal and another 1,000 in the Orange Free State. A further 20,000 had settled in other parts of the colony.[43]

The British from their side thought the Germans were trying to muscle in, encouraging the Boers to revolt with offers of protection.[44] A few days before he wrote to the Tsar William had a heated discussion with the outgoing British ambassador, Sir Edward Malet, at Hubertusstock.

* The divine right of kings.

Malet had been invited for a last shoot along with Hohenlohe and Marschall. A private conversation with William was subsequently reported to Marschall.

Yes, he [Malet] went . . . so far as to mention the unbelievable word 'war'; and as a result of a few square miles of negroes and palm trees England threatened to declåre war on its one real friend, the German Emperor, grandson of Her Majesty the Queen of Great Britain and Ireland.

Colonel Swaine had endeavoured to defuse the situation by telling William that this had not been Malet's intention. William, however, was not to be put off his stride. Malet's 'tone' was the same as the British press.

Germany and the Triple Alliance were perpetually calumnied and teased, and a good part of my difficult seven-year task has been destroyed, to bring my empire and England together on the basis of common interests, to greater respect for one another directed at the solution of greater cultural missions.[45]

Such an attitude and Britain's 'selfishness and bullying' was bound to force Germany into the arms of France and Russia. When William learned later that day through Hatzfeldt that Salisbury had disowned Malet's warmongering, he seized the opportunity for a little Bismarckian *Realpolitik*. He told his diplomats to use the former ambassador's slip-up to press for a bigger navy on the basis of the 'need to protect increasing trade'.[46]

William paid another call on Bismarck on 16–19 December. He had come from Kiel and was going to Altona to visit the Blohm and Voss shipyard there. Naturally he lunched with Waldersee first, arriving at Friedrichsruh at five. Bismarck waited on the lawn. He wore no coat, just a military tunic and a helmet. William shook his hand warmly and told him to put on a coat. Inside Bismarck's daughter, Gräfin Rantzau, was waiting with her young son. William solemnly presented his former minister with a book on the German fleet. It was unlikely to have been greeted with great enthusiasm.[47]

It was then that William spent three-quarters of an hour alone with Bismarck. Waldersee was suspicious of this. It came at the time of a sea-change in William's foreign policy. They emerged in time for a relaxed meal with the usual collection of ADCs. 'The dinner was good, the wine excellent.' As the sparkling wine was poured, Bismarck recalled that Frederick William IV had complained that his ministers had drunk too little champagne. They lacked 'propellant'. Later a sweet, Italian wine reminded the younger Moltke of Château d'Yquem. The emperor, Bismarck thought, looked harassed: 'His Majesty might well be angry with his ministers. A king could live a much more peaceful life without ministers, but in the meantime it is quite good if there is going to be a flood, to have dykes.' After dinner Bismarck smoked an amber-tipped Meerschaum. William still wanted a few words with him about the Tsar. On the way to the train, Bismarck repeatedly kissed William's hand. As the engine shunted out of the station Bismarck returned to his military pose and salute.[48]

Despite the bad blood about German meddling in southern Africa William was trying to provoke Britain into closer relations, even if he was not going the best way about it. On 20 December he summoned Swaine, and accused Britain and Russia of trying to establish a condominium over the Straits. On 30 December occurred the famous raid on the Transvaal, when a group of 500 Britons led by Dr Leander Starr Jameson tried to unseat the government of Paul Kruger. William heard that the raid was planned on Christmas Eve and wondered whether the German response should be to send one cruiser or two. On the last day of the year, William was concerned enough to wire Hatzfeldt and tell him to find out if there were official government sanction for the raid. If it were the case, he was to demand his passport.[49] The immediate reaction was a plan to send fifty marines to South Africa to protect German interests. It was Marschall and Paul Kayser, the Director of the Colonial Department, who wrote and badgered William to send the famous Kruger telegram on 3 January 1896: 'an armed band which has swooped down on your land to disturb the peace'. Germany was prepared to 'restore peace and to defend the independence of the land from without'.[50]

Holstein was supposed to check it through, but he was nowhere to be found. He had gone to the restaurant Borchardt where he was consoling himself with a bottle of claret. It has been suggested that Holstein wanted the maximum amount of problems to result from the telegram: it would hit England, remove Marschall and prevent William from conducting his own foreign policy.[51] Hohenlohe is said to have been opposed to sending it. The question of sovereignty was, after all, a complex one. Britain still exercised a small control over the Transvaal's foreign policy according to the treaty of 1884.[52] The previous day William had covered his tracks by writing to the Tsar, 'I shall never allow the British to stamp out the Transvaal', lines also written in all probability by Holstein. That the message was sent largely against William's will is clear from Prince Henry's reaction to it. His brother was seen to be 'beside himself' with fury.

To Alfred Niemann he admitted that it had been an error: 'I only agreed because the imperial chancellor, Prince Hohenlohe [sic] and the Foreign Secretary, Freiherr von Marschall, urgently requested it. The temporary bad feeling which it provoked in British official circles, I only managed to remove with great effort and in the fullness of time.'[53] Lonsdale, who was in Berlin at the time, 'had no doubts about his blameless intent'. William told him that Kruger had appealed to him for help.[54]

In his memoirs William stated that he had become unpopular in Germany as a result of his suspected sympathy for Britain. His English grandmother and the 'Onkelei' marked him down as a 'half-Englishman' at the time when colonial and economic rivalry was at its worst. This must have been the reason why William was prepared to receive Leyds, the Transvaal's foreign minister, who was then in Berlin. For Hohenlohe it was essential that William show his people where his sympathies actually lay. In that the telegram was successful. Hildegard Spitzemberg noted that it had satisfied all the parties in Germany, and France too. Waldersee, for one, was as pleased as punch. As for perfidious Albion itself, 'They can only take it badly if they have a bad conscience'.[55]

They did take it badly. Queen Victoria found her grandson's telegram distasteful: 'The action of Dr Jameson was of course very wrong and totally unwarranted; but considering the peculiar position in which the Transvaal stands to Great Britain, I think it would have been far better to have said nothing.' William had thought Uncle Bertie directly involved, noting the massive investments made in the Transvaal by his German-Jewish friends Alfred Beit and Sir Ernest Cassel. Prince Edward denounced the telegram as a 'most gratuitous act of unfriendliness'. There was an upsurge of bad feeling against the emperor. German sailors and merchants were attacked in the streets. In Liverpool, German shops were wrecked and sailors beaten up on the quays. What must have affected the emperor most seriously, however, was the reaction of his own British regiment – the Royal Dragoons – who destroyed their colonel's portrait. William also received a quantity of hate-mail from 'ladies in English society', telling him they would receive no more Germans and would never set foot on German soil again. Hildegard Spitzemberg had little sympathy for them – 'It is just their wounded wallet which makes these shopkeepers so furious.' The *Daily Mail* was still calling for war in September.[56]

They also gave William's friend Lonsdale a hard time. 'I am also friendly with the Prince of Wales,' he told his critics. In a speech delivered at Whitehaven he said it was 'childish to imagine that the Kaiser had unfriendly intentions towards this country'. He condemned both Cecil Rhodes and Jameson for playing with their countrymen's lives to achieve their own aims and increase their profits. He thought both men should be given six months and 'twelve strokes of the cat!' Lonsdale's was a voice in the wilderness. William assumed the British would appreciate his refusal to join a continental alliance to attack when the country had its hands full. 'The English should be really grateful, rather than complaining about me,' he wrote crossly across one of his chancellor's memoranda. Hohenlohe summed up the episode wistfully – 'We achieved nothing, but we have prevented a good deal!'[57]

Waldersee was wedded to the old alliance with Austria, but he was nervous of the Franco-Russian coalition. He felt that the best might be a pact with Britain, but he knew that this would not happen and that the English were only 'interested in causing problems with our colonial policy'. There had been a desire to push Britain into an alliance, but that had clearly not worked.[58] For William's part, he was still in a very bad mood with the British. In January 1896 he was petulant. He would not visit his mother's country that year. There was talk of a 'continental league' against Britain, which was rather coolly received at the time, although the Russians revived the project in January 1897.[59] Ten days later, on 31 January, he struck on the idea of increasing the size of the German navy. An element of spite was evidently mixed in with the need to protect Germany's burgeoning colonial interests.

William will not have reached his decision entirely alone. In his memoirs Tirpitz takes credit for turning the emperor's ireful gaze towards the as yet unstarted naval expansion. The English outburst of 'hate, envy and fury' against Germany could be harnessed to inject some impetus into warship building. Tirpitz was categorical that the naval expansion was both innocent and not directed at Britain. He did, however, point out that the hysterical reaction across the channel was earnest that 'impotent German competitors would be crushed at the first opportunity.'[60]

In bitter reflection after the war, William summed up his feelings about Anglo-German relations at the time. The 'English' – William never referred to the British – saw themselves as 'God's chosen', feeling 'economic competition with Germany a sin, [Germany's] colonial activity as an interference in her rights, [and] the claim to a modest sea power as presumption'. 'Only an evil will could interpret a fleet capable of defending the coastline as an instrument of malign intention.' Germany had already been squeezed out of the possibility of an alliance with either Britain or Russia where they would be treated as equal partners. To add insult to injury, after Queen Victoria's death, Uncle Bertie tried to lure Francis Joseph away from his bond with Germany.[61]

v

To celebrate a quarter of a century of the new Empire on 18 January 1896, William had menu cards printed showing Werner's painting of the proclamation at Versailles; only he used the first state, where his grandfather, rather than Bismarck, occupied the centre stage. That evening he delivered a speech to announce Germany's admission to the club of world empires. All over the world were Germans, German estates, German knowledge and German business. It was a chance to reaffirm the need to protect them all with a powerful navy.[62] Ancestor worship went further that year when the thirty-seven-year-old William posed for the sculptor Joseph Uphues' statue of Frederick the Great as crown prince. The statue was destined for the so-called 'Puppenallee' in the Tiergarten, a celebration of Hohenzollern history in sculpture which excited considerable scorn and derision. Dressing up as Frederick the Great was an opportunity not to be missed. Twice in 1897 William stepped into his specially made clothes and surrounded himself with tall soldiers (actually more an attribute of Frederick's father): once for a costume ball on 27 February, and on another occasion at the Marmorpalais in Potsdam, to honour the painter Adolph Menzel who had done so much to bring Frederick's story to life.[63]

Hohenlohe was not proving strong enough to prevent William from endeavouring to steer the boat himself. For Marschall it was a seemingly hopeless task trying to govern imperial foreign policy. On 4 February he had an honest talk with Waldersee in Kiel. The Foreign Secretary thought William was already his own chancellor and that his ministers merely did what they were told (although by his own admission, William did what Marschall and Hohenlohe told him, over the Kruger telegram). 'It is unendurable,' said Marschall. 'Today one thing and tomorrow the next, and then after a few days something completely different.'[64]

In April 1896 William and Dona were guests of the king and queen of Italy and Eulenburg came down to join them from the embassy in Vienna. They went on the *Hohenzollern*. In Venice William and Eulenburg sailed together in a gondola. On 12 April Eulenburg complained of the discomfort of wearing his gold-embroidered ambassador's uniform. William had a lot on his mind with endless ministerial crises and intrigues. 'Also the unbearable Kotze affair'[65] had reared its head again. The emperor, however, amused himself in Venice, and dallied with the beautiful contessa Morosini. Eulenburg did not believe there was any substance to the rumours, but William paid her a call at her palace, and set many tongues wagging. There were several stories of this sort once William came to the throne. His name was linked with Fürstin von Fürstenburg, Herzogin von Ratibor, the Englishwoman Daisy Fürstin Pless, Fürstin Henckel von Donnersmarck, contessa Morosini, Gräfin Sierstorpf and the American opera singer Geraldine Farrer. William pooh-poohed all of these rumours and denied he had been alone with la Morosini. Equally, he poured cold water on the idea that he had had an affair with Geraldine Farrer. They were supposed to have enjoyed a *tête-à-tête* in the royal box. William pointed out that it would have been virtually impossible for her to have passed unobserved through the crowd. Her name was later linked with his son, the crown prince.

The empress would not have been pleased. William still paid her plenty of lip service in public, referring to her – at least twice – as 'the gem which shines at my side'.[66] In fact her power was growing while William developed another character trait which had been recognisable in his father before him: subservience to his wife. She was a prig, and called anyone she suspected of immorality 'Satan'. She had heard that Herbert had tried to procure her husband a mistress and ever after referred to the former chancellor's son as a 'drunk' and a 'roué'. She was even jealous of Philipp Eulenburg. Dona thought William was killing himself with so much travel and told Waldersee as much. '*Ach*, Excellency, these eternal trips! The emperor needs sleep and peace; he is just a bundle of nerves!'[67]

The excitement in the capital that spring was the big trade exhibition which opened in Treptow Park on 1 May. It was an occasion to muster all that was great and good, from chain-swinging aldermen, generals, professors in red gowns, courtiers with buckles on their shoes, down to journalists in frock-coats 'without Orders'. William and Dona were accompanied by Ferdinand of Bulgaria and William's cousin Prince Friedrich Leopold, who had been in disgrace only a few months before. He had beaten up his wife, Dona's sister. When William had heard this he had Leopold put under house arrest. He had been rehabilitated and 'looked very happy'. After the Trade Minister Berlepsch opened the exhibition, the emperor walked about beaming with pleasure to the repeated shouts of 'Hoch!' and verses of the national anthem, 'Heil Dir in Siegerkranz', which issued from the crowd.[68]

There was a crisis in confidence in Hohenlohe. A despairing chancellor had to take advice from Eulenburg: 'As long as we wish to be a monarchy we must take into account the king's own character.' William was 'knightly' and 'modern' all at once.[69] By mid-May Waldersee was convinced that William was being led by a modified trinity: Eulenburg and Kiderlen had survived from the old group. Now they had been joined by Ambassador Bülow. Once again the emperor did not realise how much he was being led. Nor was William containing himself within the constitution. Fortunately, thought Waldersee, the general public did not associate the increasingly autocratic remarks with any form of constitutional collapse. William, however, was more and more impatient with democratic forms. And there was no one around him who was interested in holding him back.

William's life continued its usual round of visits, peppered with ceremonies to unveil monuments the length and breadth of the new Germany. The autumn before he had inaugurated a statue of his father on the battlefield at Wörth. Now, in the late spring of 1896, he uncovered one of the most pompous of all, to the mediaeval German emperors who had so excited that same father, on the Kyffhäuser in Thuringia. It had taken all of five years to construct. Once again the purpose of Bruno Schmitz's monument was to glorify the Hohenzollern dynasty in general and William's grandfather in particular. A 75-metre tower was topped with a 6.6-metre representation of the imperial crown. On the terrace itself was an equestrian statue of William I by Emil Hundreiser.[70]

It was not just abroad where William had to reckon with unpopularity. Despite his attempt to shed the pure Prussian image of the Hohenzollerns, his high-handed treatment of the German princes led to serious complaints. In the summer of 1895 he had dressed down the Bavarian heir apparent for flying his own flag on entering Stockholm harbour. On 13 June Prince Ludwig made a speech in Moscow in which he criticised Prussian leadership. Ludwig had gone to attend Nicholas's coronation, and was invited to speak to the German colony. As a 'Hoch!' was addressed to Prince Henry – who was also present – and the emperor's 'representatives', Ludwig took offence and reminded the audience that he and the princes were 'not vassals but allies of the German emperor'.[71]

In Kiel on 28 June, William affirmed the peaceable intentions behind his naval programme. It was surely a bid to reassure Britain that no rivalry was intended. 'Seas do not divide, seas unite. The armed power which is gathered in the harbour should be seen at the same time as a symbol of peace, of the collective work of all civilised European countries in maintaining and upholding the mission of European civilisation ... Only in peace can world trade develop, only in peace can it prosper, and we will uphold peace.'[72] It was otherwise a painful summer. The Kruger telegram had cast a long shadow over William's holidays. He had planned another visit to Lowther, but it had had to be cancelled. Queen Victoria even withheld his invitation to her Jubilee the following year. On the *Nordlandsreise*, Eulenburg worked on him. Bronsart had to go, he was tainted by the courts-martial fiasco; Marschall had badly bungled the Kruger business. The cruise was cut short by another bout of ear trouble.[73]

Once again names such as Botho Eulenburg, Bronsart and Waldersee were put forward to succeed Hohenlohe but, remarkably, the chancellor rode the storm. William had to give in to public courts martial that autumn. Things were not going exactly his way. Another survivor, for the time being, was Marschall. The Secretary of State was bringing a libel action against the former imperial bodyguard and police inspector Eugen von Tausch for spreading malicious stories to the press to undermine the government and attributing them to Marschall. It proved a hugely popular trial and even if Tausch was exonerated, the clever south German lawyer Marschall emerged from it one of the most well-loved figures in the government. He had saved his neck, and delayed Bülow's return to Berlin.[74]

William was in Silesia for the autumn manoeuvres. On 5 September 1896 the emperor received the Tsar in Breslau, looking pale, in the uniform of the Alexander Regiment. 'Of course we had noisy music during dinner. Conversation was scarcely to be thought of.' Hohenlohe praised, however, William's speech on Russo-German relations. The Tsar spoke too, claiming, 'I sincerely share the traditional relations which unite our two countries . . .'[75] Two days later he made the acquaintance of the Englishwoman Daisy Pless who had married the prince and later duke Heinrich XV in 1891. In July she had heard that William was coming to stay with Dona's brother, Duke Günther, in Primkenau. William had evidently forgiven him, if it was indeed his brother-in-law who was behind the Kotze scandal.

Daisy was anxious that her husband should succeed at court. She told him, 'A great many men have to work under rulers with whose politics and mode of government they do not fully agree.' The pretext for Daisy's meeting with the German emperor was the unveiling of yet another monument to William 'the Great' in Breslau. William appeared wearing a breastplate and with an eagle in his helmet. For once, however, he forbore from making a speech. Daisy did not think much of the large, elaborate monument – 'a mediocre work, very high with steps leading up to it, and a great marble block on which stands the bronze equestrian statue of the old emperor.'[76] William, she compared to an actor – 'effusive, voluble, always striving for effect'.[77]

William's colonial rule over his Alsatians and Lorrainers was not bringing satisfaction to these reluctant subjects. Poultney Bigelow remembered his last meeting with William before the Great War. Although he had attended manoeuvres every year from 1888 to 1896, William had become cross with him as a result of reading his four-volume history of Germany down to 1849 – *The German Struggle for Liberty*. He was present as the emperor gave a speech in Metz: '. . . listening to William II making a speech to a people held only by the sword and praying each day for deliverance from its dominion. Never have I heard the Kaiser grind out his gutturals more snappishly; never have I seen his face and manner disclose so much malevolence, never have I seen him clutch the hilt of his sabre in a manner so suggestive of punitive purpose . . . "Germans you are," snarled the Kaiser at Metz,

"Germans you have ever been and Germans shall you ever remain – so help me God and my good sword." '[78]

On 17 October that year Hohenlohe admitted that his relations with his emperor were 'peculiar'. The business over the liberalisation of courts martial and the right to strike were giving him grief. He could not quite grasp that Eulenburg did not desire his job. He did not see the kingmaker in Phili.[79] Bismarck was preparing a new strike. On 24 October he published the secret Reinsurance Treaty with Russia, which William had allowed to go into abeyance. 'The emperor completely lost control, called all the officers present around him and solemnly informed them that he had just given orders for Bismarck's arrest on charges of high treason.' Nobody knows who convinced him to reconsider his move. Probably he thought better of it himself. Later he told his entourage, 'If people think I am going to send prince Bismarck to Spandau they are making a mistake; I am not thinking of making a martyr out of the prince so that people can go on pilgrimages!'[80]

There was alarm that the Austrians would feel that the leak was intentional, and that this meant a loosening of the Triple Alliance. William wrote to reassure Francis Joseph. Bismarck's action was an excellent demonstration of why it had been necessary to dismiss him.[81] The ill-will was poorly concealed. When someone referred to Bismarck as the 'imperial founder' William snapped back, 'That is not true, it was Grandpapa!' Bismarck's leak meant covering his tracks with the Tsar. William wrote again on 12 November: Bismarck was 'trying to make the people believe that I was and still am under *English*! influence – the clearer heads will begin to understand that I had reasons to send this unruly man with his mean character out of office.'[82]

William's relations with Great Britain were still soured by the effects of the Kruger telegram. On 25 October William wrote to Hohenlohe to find out whether it would be possible to make an arrangement with Russia and France to protect their colonies from British incursions. He was still unhappy about the strike power of his navy, which he compared to a 'handful of peas' against the great ships of the line across the Channel. 'Once again it becomes obvious how foolish it was to begin our colonial policy a decade ago without having a fleet. Our trade is locked in a life-and-death struggle with the English, and our press boasts loudly of this every day, but the great merchant marine which plies the oceans of the world under our flag must renounce itself to complete impotence before their 130 cruisers, which we can proudly counter with four.'[83]

William caused a storm in the theatrical world in mid-November. He interfered in the decision to award the annual Schiller Prize jointly to his cousin Wildenbruch and Gerhart Hauptmann. Wildenbruch won it outright for the second time. Hauptmann had upset the emperor by plays such as *Die Weber* of 1892 which realistically portrayed the Silesian weavers' revolt in the 1840s, and its heavy-handed suppression. William's gesture blew up in his face when Wildenbruch refused the money, and two members of the jury resigned in protest.[84] The cries against William's attempts to thwart the Reichstag were becoming louder. The press were aware of the Willy–Nicky correspondence and fingers were pointed at the ADCs for their influence over the emperor's policy-making. The manipulation of the press – a trick he had picked up from Bismarck – led William to suppose that such things were common policy in every country. He could not believe that the attacks on him in the British papers, which had begun with his allegedly rough treatment of his mother, were not government-inspired. On 3 December 1896, Salisbury was anxious to disabuse him of this. He wrote to the ambassador Sir Frank Lascelles to 'impress upon His Majesty that we are absolutely without the means of influencing or controlling the newspapers...'[85]

A new problem bedevilled the new year. The Cretan Christians rose up against the Muslims and declared their independence of Turkey. There was much bloodshed, and whole towns were put to the torch. William decided to intervene directly, issuing orders to blockade the port of Piraeus to help the Turks while the other powers did little to hinder the Greeks from taking control. William made it abundantly clear that he wanted to deal with this matter himself. Hohenlohe and Marschall demonstrated their impotence by calling on Eulenburg to get them out of the mess. Holstein thought the emperor had gone mad. Eulenburg did what was required of him, mediating between the two sides. He gently warned William off meddling in foreign affairs: 'It could happen that Your Majesty's actions might interfere with the working of the machine. I must repeat that unity between Your Majesty and the Office is a burning necessity.' In May Eulenburg faced the Wilhelmstrasse, and tried to deal with the individual complaints of the men who thought the time had come to muzzle the emperor.[86]

William was in Pless for his birthday. He had agreed to act as godfather to one of Daisy's sons, along with his Uncle Bertie. There must have been some substance, at least, behind the rumours of his relationship with the beautiful princess. 'He kissed my left hand one night, instead of my right, as he said: "I do not kiss a hand with a glove on," and then went straight up to the other ladies and kissed their gloved right hands.'[87]

The arts figured largely on William's agenda in February 1897. There was an exhibition in the old Reichstag building of the historical battle scenes of the Russian painter Vassily Verestshagin, that William greatly liked. He attended the rehearsals of Shakespeare's *Henry IV* and suggested changes. Effigies of Hohenzollern worthies were appearing thick and fast for his 'Puppenallee'. A Bismarck was commissioned, but it turned out to be only Claus, a sixteenth-century ancestor. He was also busy arranging the ball in the Schloss for the end of the month. As the dress was to be eighteenth-century he was working hard producing the exact replicas of the rifles used by soldiers of the time.[88]

In William's mind at least, Prussia had been largely reduced to a formal historical rôle. One of the favourite activities of the court during the short Berlin season was to attend costume balls using Prussian or Hohenzollern history as the theme. Sometimes, when they involved all the features of the – in truth *anti* – court of Frederick the Great, they were called 'Menzel festivities' after the painter. On 27 February, for example, there was a ball where guests were required to dress in costumes from a century before – the year which saw the birth of William 'the Great'. The previous day William had made a speech to his *Märker* in which he claimed that 'contact with the sons of the Mark is always an invigorating drink for me'.[89]

The ball came at the end of the short Berlin season, when the court flourished in a fairly dismal way. Most of William's chief courtiers were military men or ambassadors, their functions more or less sinecures. One whose office was rather more important to William was Fürst Pless, who organised the hunting. Otherwise Hermann von Hatzfeldt und Trachtenberg played the role of Oberstschenk, or imperial cupbearer, even if his diplomatic duties must have kept him at an inconvenient distance from the royal cellars. The Obersttruchsess was supposed to oversee the kitchens, but Fürst Radolin was the ambassador in Petersburg, which meant his role was merely formal. More active in all things was August Eulenburg, the Oberhofmarschall. Another was Graf Bolko von Hochberg who ran the royal theatres. He had studied music and composed, which came in useful for the opera programmes.

Other noblemen who played a real role were the Oberstallmeister Graf Wedel, who looked after the stables, the Oberjagdmeister Freiherr von Heintze-Weissenrode, who ran the game reserves, and the Ober-zeremoniermeister Graf Georg von Kanitz. Important contacts for those who would rise in Wilhelmine society were the house marshals, Frei-herren von Lyncker and von und zu Egloffstein, the chamberlains von Usedom and von der Knesebeck and the various *Schlosshauptmänner* who looked after the huge number of royal residences.

Rank was stultifyingly strict at the Prussian court, but military officers tended to figure more highly than elsewhere. There were sixty-two grades. After royalty came, in sequence, court officers, field marshals, the Minister President, and members of the Order of the Black Eagle, cardinals and the mediatised princes who had lost their principalities when the Holy Roman Empire was wound up in 1806, then generals, ministers, privy councillors, *Excellenzen* – the title was awarded – then officers according to rank, preachers, actors at the royal theatres, professors, with lieutenants at the bottom of the list. Nobles who did not possess court office were not automatically eligible nor were members of the Reichstag.[90] The status attached to quite humble officers influenced some of the restrictions on granting commissions: all officers were 'Hoffähig', and could attend court, and while it is simply untrue to say that the nobility predominated in the army under William II, there was certainly a reluctance to allow Jews to mingle with the great and the good, and they could not be granted commissions except in wartime.

VI

The Reichstag refused to support the emperor's plans for expanding the navy. So far the Germans had not been sufficiently prepared for the glories of owning a first-rate fleet. William dismissed Admiral Hollmann as Minister of the Marine and brought in Tirpitz instead. In his frustration William continued to toy with the idea of a *coup d'état*. He wanted to repeat Bismarck's strike of 1862, only this time the beneficiary would be the navy rather than the army. On 18 March he had met his industrialist friend Karl von Stumm-Halberg in the Tiergarten and told him to inform the Reichstag that if anyone tried to interfere with the naval budget he would dissolve the House, chase away the ministers and institute a *coup*. Like so many of William's hot-tempered lucubrations it was an empty threat. He could not rule without the Bundesrat, and the Bundesrat would not have approved the scrapping of the constitution.[91]

The grandfather's great day was not far off. On 22 March 1897 he would have been 100 years old. In the month or so leading up to the anniversary, William indulged in an orgy of grandfather-worship. On 3 March he made a speech in Brandenburg where he belittled Kaiser William's ministers – Bismarck, Roon, Moltke et al. – as industrious counsellors. He might also have called them 'pygmies and dogsbodies', but that has not been proven. The Berlin critic Alfred Kerr recalled that speech on the day itself. The streets and monuments were decked out with bunting for the occasion but he thought it a tasteless display, the magnificence of which contrasted strongly with the Prussian simplicity of the late emperor. It was raining and the public seemed downtrodden and unresponsive. This may have had something to do with the way they tended to be pushed around by the police on such occasions. It was the women who flocked to the parades, and stood about watching on the emperor's birthday, when the city was also illuminated.

Those Berliners who braved the rain placed simple cornflowers in their buttonholes or *corsages*. The Gardes du Corps impressed observers the most on the birthday parade – they looked as if they had been moulded out of bronze.[92] Begas had built a portentous national monument surmounted by an equestrian statue of the first Hohenzollern emperor. Bismarck's friend Hildegard von Spitzemberg agreed with Kerr. 'It is sad to see how the grandson, in his lack of understanding, twists the portrait of his grandfather ... the modest old gentleman would turn in his grave.'[93]

If the centenary was not enough, the theme came up again during the 'Imperial Days' festival in Wiesbaden in May, where William was to be seen riding daily, dressed in a green hunting costume of his own design. It was above all a theatre festival, run by the intendant Graf Georg Hülsen-Haeseler, who was to replace Hochberg in Berlin in 1903. The star attraction was Josef Lauff who had become the nearest thing to a poet laureate. Later that year he celebrated the renewed Italian alliance in a drama which was partly composed by William himself. Alfred Kerr poured scorn on the emperor's literary toady. He had read the historical scenes as they were printed in the press and averred that Lauff's work was not drama at all but simply making historical points. Kerr continued to mock the Rhenish author, calling him 'the festive Lauff'. Part of his secret was his ability to put up with William dictating his plots to him. He subsequently made up the rhymes.[94]

VII

The year 1897 was the high-water mark of Eulenburg's influence. With Bülow at the Foreign Office, Hollmann was replaced by Tirpitz at the Navy Office. Now a right-wing *Weltpolitik* predominated, together with Johannes Miquel's *Sammlungspolitik* which identified the interests of all the anti-socialists, industrialists and agrarians. William could rule alone with a good crew on hand to give him advice. It was a return to Bismarckian politics after seven years of failure. Eulenburg could now take the back seat again. He had put his policy into effect. With one exception – the advancement of his friend Kuno Moltke – he could say that nothing had been done for his own sake; rather for the promotion of personal rule. There had been rumours that he would replace the aged Hohenlohe, but other advisers valued by William were against it and the emperor himself said that Eulenburg was 'too gentle' for this office. Lucanus was ruder. 'He does not trust him enough,' he said.[95]

Before he handed William over to Bülow in June 1897 Eulenburg wrote him a good summary of the emperor's character.

This is my last word, my last request of you ... Only if you handle the Kaiser psychologically correctly can you be of use to the country. You are Kaiser Wilhelm II's last card. Wilhelm takes everything personally. Only personal arguments make an impression on him. He likes to teach others but does not like to be taught. He cannot tolerate boredom; ponderous, stiff, thorough people get on his nerves and achieve nothing with him. Wilhelm II wants to shine, to do, to decide everything himself. Unfortunately, what he does himself often turns out wrong. He loves fame and is ambitious and jealous. In order to get his approval of an idea, one must act as if it is his own. One must make everything comfortable for Wilhelm II. He will encourage others to be rashly vigorous but will let them lie in the holes they fall into as a consequence. Never forget that H.M. needs praise now and then. He belongs to those who become mistrustful if they do not hear recognition from important people ... Both of us will not step over the border of flattery.[96]

This was not totally accurate. In one letter to Bülow he told him: 'Above all don't forget the sugar.'[97]

It was otiose advice. As Bülow himself told his attachés, 'You must eat black broth with the Spartans and wear long robes with the Persians.' To Max Ratibor he gave advice on how to make progress in the diplomatic world – 'Never write how things are, only how they would like to see them in Berlin.'[98] Flattery was an important part of the new Foreign Secretary's armoury. His letters were coated with insincere gush. Writing to Eulenburg in 1898, Bülow said, 'I am more and more committed heart and soul to the emperor. He is so important! Along with the Great King and the Great Elector he is by far the most important Hohenzollern who has ever lived! He brings together in a way I have never seen before, the most real and original ingenuity with the clearest good sense. He possesses an imagination which soars above all pettiness, and thereby has a sober regard for the possible and achievable and – what vigour! what a memory! what speed and surety of grasp!'[99]

Bülow was not just a flatterer, however. He could be perspicacious when he wanted to be – or when it suited him. In August 1897 he declared of the emperor: 'It is as yet undecided whether his rule will amount to a shining or a dark episode in our history. With his individuality both are possible.' Bülow's approach to William was in some ways little different to that of Caprivi and Hohenlohe. Both had had their methods of dealing with the emperor's vagaries and rodomontades. Caprivi had to yield on some of his principles; Hohenlohe realised that his delaying tactics would not always succeed. Bülow was different only in that he was 'devoid of principles'. Nor did the outward appearance of German politics change that much under his influence. Foreign diplomats and statesmen still had to reckon first and foremost with William and his erratic moods.[100]

Waldersee's suspicions about Bülow were confirmed by the reshuffle on 16 June when the latter was brought back to Berlin and made Secretary of State. It was the culmination of four years of effort on Eulenburg's part. Hohenlohe would now stay on as an emasculated chancellor while William indulged his longings for personal rule. Waldersee had hoped that Bülow's arrival would put an end to Holstein's power too. For the time being, however, it merely enhanced it. Waldersee objected to the new style of government: personal rule vaguely steered by invisible (Eulenburg) or visible (Bülow) hands. William's utterances became increasingly outrageous. 'Larger and larger sections of the population are convinced that a fierce opposition should be mounted against the *sic volo* and *voluntas regis*. Did I not say the same years ago? Who, however, are the really guilty parties? Are they not the Caprivis, Marschalls, Boettichers, Hohenlohes and their handmaidens ... who always told him what he wanted to hear?'[101]

The Jewish businessman Albert Ballin also disliked the style of the new administration and complained to Waldersee about it: 'That cannot last long. The emperor is much too clever a man not to realise that Bülow is persistently showering him with flattery.' The general replied, 'I am of a completely different opinion: up to now the emperor has never been able to get enough.' Despite Waldersee's words, Ballin continued to see William as Bülow's victim.[102] Peace was still the message William was giving the outside world. Two days after Bülow's appointment William unveiled yet another effigy of his grandfather, this time in Cologne: 'It is therefore my wish that God will grant me the strength to carry on my grandfather's work and maintain peace in the world, which has certainly only existed since the revival of the German Empire...'[103]

The seeds of Eulenburg's terrible fall must have been visible too. William offered patronage to Kuno Moltke the musician. His march was performed by the band of the Life Hussars. That same year Eulenburg's brother Friedrich went through a nasty divorce, in the course of which his 'unnatural passions' were exposed before the court. He was obliged to resign his commission and the trial drove a cool wind between William and his friend.[104] To some extent the frost was mutual. Eulenburg had begun to believe that Germany needed a Reichstag. Perhaps like Bismarck before him, he realised that it was the only defence against inadequate autocrats. Imperialism was risky, and he thought William was mentally unstable and prone to telling inexplicable lies.

Despite William's sabre-rattling style, it was becoming clearer that he was not a Frederick the Great, or a Frederick William II, but a Frederick William III or IV, *ergo* a man of peace. The hawks were disappointed in him. On 4 July 1897 Waldersee summed up the views of the war party when he wrote, 'The emperor is, as I have known for some time, by no means a man to take the offensive.' This, thought Waldersee, was what Germany needed to make an impression on the world.

VIII

There was a nasty incident on the *Nordlandsreise* that year concerning one of the younger officers, the heavy-drinking naval lieutenant von Hahnke, son of William's former Military Cabinet chief. It is difficult to piece together the story now, as there was a massive cover-up. Moltke noted that William's eye had been injured by 'a falling rope ... that same afternoon, Lieutenant von Hahnke ... died.' Moltke leaves us with a cryptic remark: 'The sailors say, the whole unfortunate incident comes as a result of having a pastor on board.' The gossips told quite another story. Hahnke had, in a moment of drunkenness or tension, challenged William to a duel. When William had refused his request Hahnke had punched him in the eye. The lieutenant was imprisoned below-decks, given a revolver and told to take his own life. His death was disguised as an accident, and the body buried in Norway. In another version he either threw himself off a cliff in remorse or faked suicide before fleeing to America. William is supposed to have atoned by making lavish plans for a monument at the spot and heaping honours on the dead man's father. Despite all censorship the news of William's injury was already causing tongues to wag in Berlin before the *Hohenzollern* had returned to port.[105]

Apart from the many people for whom there was pleasure or an advantage to be derived from inviting the emperor to shoot on their estates, William had plenty of shoots of his own. In East Prussia there was Rominten, his principal lodge; two strange, wooden pavilions which looked more Russian than German. King Frederick William I's favourite estate at König's Wusterhausen was also a popular and William liked to organise a good, smoky 'Tabakskollegium' to round off the day. That year, 1897, was a jubilee for William: it was twenty-five years since he had downed his first bird. A calculation was made which might have made the basis for a new catalogue aria: William had killed 33,967 animals: 2 aurochs, 7 elks, 3 reindeer, 3 bears, 1,022 red deer, 1,275 fallow deer, 2,189 wild boars, 680 stags, 121 chamois, 16,188 hares, 674 rabbits, 9,643 pheasants, 54 capercaillies, 4 black cock, 65 grouse, 2 snipe, 56 ducks, 654 partridges, 20 foxes, 694 herons and cormorants, and 581 unspecified beasts. Two years later Alfred Kerr noted that two badgers had been added to the list and thought their paltry number contrasted starkly with the number of hares. He also questioned the 'unspecified beasts', but would not make so bold as to accuse the emperor of shooting dogs or billy-goats.[106]

There was little to show for it as yet, but the British were already becoming suspicious of the German navy. William had, in reality, never lost his passion for warships. He had drawn and designed them since his childhood. He procrastinated until 1897, and Tirpitz believed this wasted time had serious political consequences. The 'lost decade' pushed Germany's desire to own a fleet into a 'political danger zone'.[107] That year the Imperial Naval Office was created with Tirpitz at its head. Its main task was to steer the naval budget through the Reichstag. Tirpitz claimed that his dealings with Parliament gave him a rough-and-tumble approach to politicians.*

William had been much influenced by his reading of the American naval historian Alfred Mahan's *The Importance of Sea Power in History* of 1890. Mahan had shown that no country had ever achieved world power which had not at the same time possessed a powerful navy. The poor quality of the German navy had been apparent two years before when four Brandenburg Class 'ironclads' had made their appearance at the opening of the Kiel Canal. The embarrassment persisted. In 1897 William had to apologise to his brother Henry that the only thing he could send to Queen Victoria's Jubilee was the *König Wilhelm*, 'while other nations will shine with their proud warships'. 'I will not rest until I have brought my navy to the same high level that the army possesses.' In a rather more dramatic, inflated vein, he told Eulenburg that the navy was 'an instrument ordained by God through the divinely appointed House of Hohenzollern to bring Germany forth on the water'.[108]

One means of improving the navy was to design some impressive new ships. William set to work. An Italian admiral who saw one of these remarkable plans exclaimed, 'The ship which your Majesty has designed would be the mightiest, the most terrible, and also the loveliest battleship ever seen. She would surpass anything now afloat, her masts would be the tallest in the world, her guns would outrange all others. And the inner appointments are so well arranged that for the whole crew from the captain down to the cabin-boy, it would be a real pleasure to sail on her. This wonderful vessel has only one fault: if she were put on the water she would sink like a lump of lead.'[109]

If the British would not fall in with the Albertian idea that their sea power allied to Germany's land might could police the world, then Germany would have to build its own navy, and, if need be, police Europe with her existing allies. Even then, the fleet was not aimed at Britain, but at France and Russia. William was still up against the old Prussian distrustful attitude to the expanded navy. It was decided that the next warship to go down the slipway was to be named *Bismarck*. It

---

* 'Schlagschnauze' – what the French would call a 'tête-à-claques'.

was obvious that the government were courting popularity by invoking the old chancellor's name. Bismarck was aware of this too; he was also aware that for his eighty-second birthday he had received 3,200 telegrams amounting to 100,000 words, but not one of them from the emperor. Tirpitz wrote to him three times. On each occasion the letters were returned unopened because, as Bismarck told the admiral later, he did not accept any letter which did not bear the sender's address on the envelope. Finally Tirpitz went to Friedrichsruh to seek the elder statesman's blessing. Bismarck was cussed at first, slamming his fist on the table and shouting: 'I am not a tomcat which emits sparks when you stroke it.'[110]

William was anxious to surprise the man and Tirpitz was told not to reveal the name of the ship. Bismarck proved truculent again. He said he was too old to go out. Under the influence of a bottle and a half of champagne Bismarck cheered up at lunch. Tirpitz reminded him that plans had been made for a fleet as early as 1867, with the creation of the North German Federation. The admiral found him unreceptive – he was still living in 1864. Tirpitz tried to convince Bismarck how much the position had been altered by British aggression towards the Reich. Later they went out for a drive in the Sachsenwald. Bismarck armed himself with a couple of bottles of beer and spoke to the naval officer in English. This was to keep their conversation secret from the coachman. As a sailor, the former chancellor thought Tirpitz would understand.

It was taking time to bring German opinion round. The Reichstag opposed the expansion because the increased budget was associated with William and he had rubbed the point in by having drawings and texts in his own hand set up outside the chamber. In two letters to a sceptical Freiherr von Völderndorff in the autumn of that year, Hohenlohe set out the reasons why he personally approved the expansion of the German navy. It was couched in the language of a man who issued from a former ruling house.

It is always said the navy is a whim of the emperor's. And yet it cannot be denied that it is the German people's fault – or if you like, their merit – that we possess a navy. In the days of the Germanic Confederation we had a harmless, peaceful existence. We had no political (foreign policy) causes, few taxes, and we were spectators of how Austria and Prussia opposed each other in the Diet, in which the medium-sized states and the little states sided first with one, then the other. This, however, did not satisfy the German people; they wished to form a united whole, and play a part in the world . . .

Hohenlohe then gave his correspondent a potted history of Germany down to unification in 1870.

... it soon came to pass that there was no money to set up the state ... To obtain money ... Bismarck changed his tariff policy and renounced moderate free trade. In this too, the German people stood by him. We now obtained between 3 and 400 millions of money and the state could live. The policy of a protective tariff, however, produced a colossal development of industry. We ceased to be an agrarian state and became a manufacturing one. Owing to this our policy had again to be altered, and our aim directed to secure exploitation. Commerce developed so much that the government was called upon to protect it. That would only be done by a fleet.

Hohenlohe did not feel that the fleet needed to challenge that of the English in size, just big enough to break a blockade if it needed to. 'It is not to be denied that the emperor disturbs things by his impulsive nature. It is to be wished that he were more phlegmatic.' On the other hand it was quite wrong to reproach him for the fleet, which the Germans had desired for a century and a half.[111]

Other features of the emperor's rule were beginning to sadden the elderly chancellor. On 17 June 1897 William inaugurated the Bielefeld programme to protect production in the 'mighty Empire'. This involved a bid to curtail strikes by legislation. People who were found to have encouraged industrial unrest were to be sentenced to hard labour. The measure caused Hohenlohe to despair. He felt it was all too soon. 'Increasingly I am losing my desire to serve under this man.'[112] With personal rule, William's delivery became more and more outrageous, his outbursts frequently furious or boastful, particularly when he felt impotent to shape matters according to his will. In December, in the house of his minister von Hammerstein, William fulminated against the constitution and the Bundesrat which were preventing him from building the fleet of his dreams. It had been pointed out to him that he might have exercised supreme control in Prussia, but not in south Germany – 'If the south Germans want to spoil my plans, I shall simply declare war on them, Prussia has eighteen army corps, and they have only three or four, you'd soon see who would win.'[113]

IX

In autumn 1897 two German missionaries were murdered in Shantung. According to William, all of Catholic Germany cried out for revenge and Hohenlohe, who was among them, suggested immediate action. William saw it as the moment to win the support of the Catholic Centre Party which would give him a working majority in the Chamber. The cynics laughed up their sleeves at the suggestion of a holy war. Interrupting the winter hunting at Letzlingen in the Prussian Altmark,

Hohenlohe proposed sending a fleet under the command of William's brother Henry. The assembling of a European expeditionary force took time. William continued his progresses and unveiled yet another monument to his grandfather in Karlsruhe on 21 October.[114]

The murder led William to make fresh noises about the 'Yellow Peril'. This meant further encouragement for Nicky to proceed against the Asiatics. In the new year of 1898, the Tsar received a new picture showing Russia and Germany 'as sentinels at the Yellow Sea for the proclaiming of the Gospel of Truth and light in the East. I drew the sketch in the Xmas week under the blaze of lights from the Xmas trees!'[115] Much later, in the twenties, at about the same time as he was writing his memoirs, William increasingly saw Russia as a part of Asia, and thought it more likely that she would join forces with China to conquer Europe.

William acquired his own little piece of Yellow Peril on 6 March 1898 when Germany leased Kiao-chou or Tsing-tao for ninety-nine years, a treaty based on the British arrangement for the New Territories on the Chinese mainland. They had occupied it on 14 November the previous year, another decision in which Hohenlohe had played no part. Possibly German expansion in Asia was beginning to worry the stony-featured men in Whitehall. A fortnight later feelers were put out to the ambassador Hatzfeldt about an alliance. At last things were coming right. Tirpitz had finally won support from the Reichstag for his First Naval Law. The Kruger telegram incident had brought about a massive opposition to Britain, and now the German public was prepared to accept that it would have to pay a little more in taxes to cock a snook at the enemy across the water. After the wasted years the dream had come true; but Tirpitz was to have his drawbacks, not least in his aggressive nationalism and Anglophobia, sentiments which did not entirely match the emperor's own and which were to lead to severe personality clashes.

On 29 March the German ambassador met Joseph Chamberlain to discuss terms. William was keen at first, but later began to allude to the one-sided arrangement which had existed between Britain and Prussia during the Seven Years War, a century and a half before. Frederick the Great had ultimately been deserted by his Hanoverian cousins. The British also wanted the pact to hinge on colonial issues, whereas William's concern – as ever – was for Europe.[116] There had been some mild excitement at the beginning of the Spanish-American War when some diplomats had thought Germany might pick up a few crumbs off the American plate. William considered playing the legitimist card and calling for a European concert to protect Spain. Bülow thought the Austrians should decide whether they had an interest in saving the Spanish Empire. In Vienna, however, they were lukewarm. The lack of

European solidarity exasperated William. Britain's role was once again perfidious. 'England just doesn't want to belong to Europe ... but it wants to form an independent part of the world between the continent and America or Asia.'[117]

Hohenlohe's wife died at the end of 1897. The chancellor was a broken man, deaf and asthmatic. The political instability had gone, however, now that Bülow was in control. Eulenburg was satisfied: 'The matter is in the able hands of Bülow, whom the Kaiser thinks of as "*his* Bismarck".' In April naval expansion received a fillip through the creation of the Navy League backed by Krupp and Prince Wied. It was to become a runaway success. In 1906 it had a million members. A similar institution in Britain listed a mere 35,000 by comparison.

On 30 May William told Nicky about the moves to pull Germany into an alliance with Great Britain in April that year. He later claimed that he had rejected them because he had no intention of being used as a 'dry land weapon' against Russia. He attributed them to his grandmother, Queen Victoria. It was another attempt to show how things might be worked out within the family. What William really wanted, he said, was a Russian alliance. A month later he extolled the 'tradition in which I was reared by my beloved grandfather'. The British move was, said William, 'in real earnest and was sincerely made. Now as my old and trusted friend I beg you to tell me what you can offer me and will do if I refuse.' The mood had changed in St Petersburg. Nicholas's advisers were chiefly anti-German. The world had moved on since the time of the Germanophil Alexander II, who had a direct wire from his palace to the Berlin Schloss.[118]

At the end of March William's new contribution to Berlin was taking form. Along the Siegesallee, leading from the Brandenburg Gate to the Victory column in the Tiergarten, groups of statues had appeared to commemorate the rulers of the Mark Brandenburg since the Germans first asserted their supremacy over the Slavic Wends. In the *Prager Tagblatt* Alfred Kerr mocked: 'Victory Boulevard? Glory Way is the name of this street.' Kerr thought the statues spoiled the Tiergarten, but he admired the semi-circular benches, which reminded him of the paintings of Alma-Tadema.[119]

On 16 June William delivered another of his stinging attacks on the arts, or rather those artists who turned their back on the national mission. The speeches have a sad capacity to remind readers of a later German ruler. William, who liked to eat his dinner in the royal box, a practice which disturbed other theatre-goers, especially when the dining room was closed during command performances, addressed the actors at the royal theatre. He claimed that the stage should 'also play a role in the formation of the mind and the ennoblement of moral opinion. The theatre is also one of my weapons ... in continuing the fight against materialism and un-German behaviour.'[120]

Bismarck died during the 1898 *Nordlandsreise*. William was in Bergen when he heard the news. He directed the crew to make speed for Kiel and once he had landed he travelled straight to Friedrichsruh. William wanted there to be a state funeral, with Bismarck laid in the Hohenzollern crypt of the cathedral in Berlin or beside his old master in Charlottenburg. The will was unambiguous on this point, however: Herbert made it clear that Bismarck was to be buried on the estate. After the Iron Chancellor's death the Württemberg envoy, Eulenburg's bosom friend, Axel von Varnbüler, wrote to his sister Hildegard von Spitzemberg. He believed that it had been Herbert who had caused the problems all along: 'Herbert was the evil spirit who strengthened the old man in his brutal cynicism, in politics to treat the emperor like a puppet, like any other prince, but then along came one who simply was not one.'[121]

The excitement in August was the Russian call for a peace conference in The Hague. William thought the idea 'utopian' and hypocritical. 'We've got it already, there have been twenty-eight years of peace!' he minuted, followed by 'Dalldorf' – a reference to Berlin's main lunatic asylum.[122] Some progress was made on the colonial and diplomatic front when Britain and Germany signed the secret Treaty of Windsor on 30 August which gave Germany a first claim to Portugal's tottering empire. The following year the British issued a 'guarantee' to Germany, that they would receive the territories. As it turned out, the Portuguese Empire took a long time to fall, and only finally collapsed more than seventy years later.[123]

On 18 August William was annoyed by the attitude of the Catholic press in Austria and France to his projected visit to the Holy Land. They had labelled it a pilgrimage. Kerr went one better. He looked at the arrangements made for the royal yacht, and 'the requirements of our empress's toilette' and dubbed it a 'crusade in comfort'. Behind the *Hohenzollern*, with its orchestra, was a second ship filled with clerics.[124] On 20 October the emperor was in Istanbul, still crudely trying to whip cousin Nicky up against the British, who he suggested were anxious to annex Crete. William was on the side of the Turkish Muslim landlords and encouraged the Tsar to offer protection to the Muslims too. William and Dona reached Jerusalem on 29 October. The roads were lined with troops and German and Turkish flags hung from every pole. He was to go one better than his father twenty-eight years previously: while he was in the Holy City he consecrated the Church of the Redeemer. He wrote to Nicky from Damascus on 9 November that he had been appalled by the clutter in the Christian churches. Had he not been firm in his religion, the political activity of the Christians would have converted him to Mohammedanism.[125]

In contrast to Jerusalem, William enjoyed Damascus and Beirut with its 'lovely villas' which reminded him of southern Italy and Sicily. 'Never has a Christian ... monarch been so feted and received with such unbounded enthusiasm.' William offered his cousin a little wisdom on the subject of his ally, France, which was then in turmoil as a result of the Dreyfus case. 'The French are floundering about in their interior affairs, splashing dirt right and left till the whole of Europe reeks with the stench.' The letter took pains to stress French weakness: 'the ignominious retreat from Fashoda' – a reference to the French backing down before Britain in the Sudan, the last occasion when France and Britain came to the brink of war. Turkey, on the other hand, was a much better bet. It was 'very much alive, and not a dying man'.[126]

In his final years in Doorn William explained why it was he had renounced the old dream of bringing together Germany's land power and Britain's strength at sea just at the moment when an Anglo-German alliance was believed to be a possibility: 'All renunciations and disadvantages would have fallen on the German side, as our sea arm was then still so primitive that in terms of world politics and world economy we had to be satisfied with the carcase Britain patronisingly tossed us. At the same time, as a continental might we would have had to carry the entire risk that was implied in functioning as Britain's sword.'[127] In short, William was not prepared to take on the role played by Frederick the Great in the Seven Years War, and which Frederick himself bitterly regretted.

On 1 December, William indulged in a bit of theatre by riding into Berlin on a horse for the first time. More and more he wanted to show his people that he was the strong man, and especially at this moment when, after three years of stubborn resistance, he had approved the new code of military justice. Adversity had revived the Prussian in him. Hohenlohe was one of those south Germans who believed in the Empire, and who had to fight the Prussians to keep it afloat. Much of the time south Germans were far more ready to approve the third Hohenzollern emperor than the dyed-in-the-wool Junkers in the far east. There was a fair deal of liberalism in the south and west, and it was the liberals who had received the Empire with the greatest enthusiasm. On 15 December 1898 a despairing Hohenlohe committed the following to his diary:

As I laboured from 1866 to 1870 for the union of South and North, so I must strive now to keep Prussia attached to the Empire. For all these gentlemen don't give a fig for the Empire and would rather give it up today than tomorrow.[128]

Another German, as opposed to Prussian, cause was the fleet. Once again Hohenlohe was opposed to a direct challenge to the leading sea power. 'We must not expose ourselves to the danger of experiencing from England the fate of Spain at the hands of North America.' In a reply to the socialist Karl Liebknecht on 12 June 1900 he reiterated this belief: 'The history of the past century shows that the call for a fleet has inevitably arisen whenever the desire for the unification of Germany became prominent, or the realisation of this desire seemed possible or probable.'[129]

Alfred Kerr enjoyed the treat of a visit from the emperor just before Christmas. He lodged in the old West End of Berlin with the sculptor Eberlein who was meditating new wonders for the 'Puppenallee'. William walked straight past a sculpture of an elderly Bismarck to salute the landlord and 'Berlin's Michelangelo' – Begas. Little Willy was with his father. Kerr watched William use his famous iron grip on Begas and speculated on how much pain it gave. William 'looked exhausted, his face was yellow. Were the trials of travel to be read in these features? Was it the weight of government? Or fatigue from the last hunt?'[130] Waldersee predictably thought this fawning on the arts a rum thing: that Silesian dwarf, the painter Adolph Menzel, was given the Black Eagle in January. Not only was he an artist; he was – until his ennoblement the previous year – a commoner.

On 11 March 1899 William received a visit from Cecil Rhodes, who had come to talk to him about German co-operation with the Cape to Cairo railway. As this would cross German territory too, Rhodes had to talk him round. He did this, and William was impressed by the tall, fat, bright-eyed Englishman, calling him 'South Africa's Napoleon'. William and Rhodes made light of the Jameson Raid.[131] It was Rhodes who brought the audience to a close. Looking at his watch he told the emperor he had some people to entertain at dinner. William laughed. Later Rhodes would include Germans in his 'Rhodes Scholarships', which were created to allow men from the white, [Anglo]-Saxon world a chance to study at the University of Oxford.

X

On 9 May 1899 William made a new inflammatory Reichstag speech in which he appeared to be appointing himself the fourth member of the Trinity. Later that month he wrote Queen Victoria a long *cri de coeur* about the state of Anglo-German relations. He felt that he and Germany had been belittled by a number of small-scale international incidents where Britain might have shown his country rather more respect. He believed his old bugbear Salisbury was chiefly responsible, but he did not trust Chamberlain either: 'I of course have been silent as to what I have *personally* gone through these last six months ... the shame and pain I have suffered, and how my heart has bled when to my despair I had to watch how the arduous work of years was destroyed ... by one blow by the high-handed or disdainful treatment of ministers who have never come over to stay here and to study our institutions and people ... Lord Salisbury's government must learn to respect and treat us as equals.'[132]

Eulenburg was burgled in May. Thieves lightened him of 25,000 marks' worth of jewels while he 'snored alongside his wife'. Kerr imagined him dreaming 'of happy days after a *coup d'état*, when socialism would be kicked to death and the world ruled from Liebenberg'.[133] He was once again part of the entertainment for the *Nordlandsreise*. He was still one of the very few people who could tell the emperor the truth, even if his influence had already begun to wane. Personal rule had not improved William's position in the country and 'The German philistine is not in the position to understand the busy lifestyle of Your Majesty! There is a great ill-will against Your Majesty in the land!' In the course of the journey that year Eulenburg was able to expose the fact that there were moves to force William to abdicate. On his deathbed the chancellor's brother, Cardinal Hohenlohe had revealed that there had been an attempt to make William stand down on grounds of insanity.[134]

At Kiel Week, William invited Albert Ballin on board the *Hohenzollern* and had him sit next to him at lunch. Discussions were afoot to introduce a Plimsoll line on German ships and William evidently wanted an opinion. Since plans had gone ahead to increase the size of the German navy, Ballin had achieved a new importance for the emperor: quite conventionally, William believed that a prosperous merchant marine needed the protection afforded by a proper navy. The more men like Ballin raised the profile of German cruise and merchant vessels, the more the need for a new generation of battleships became pressing.[135]

William was causing concern even among the least critical members of his military entourage. On 25 August Moltke noted his excitement about some aspect of the Kiel Canal. 'I fear that he has already issued orders which cannot be rescinded.'[136] He provoked endless little conflicts with the Reichstag, but as Hildegard Spitzemberg gleefully pointed out, he had no Bismarck, no Roon to help him out of the mess. His fury against all forms of opposition led him to bar all those who voted against his policies from the imperial household. Eulenburg tried to stop William from making inflammatory speeches. William replied to his letter: 'Your frank words pleased me. I am particularly grateful to you for them. When you don't show me the proper course, who else will do it? I will therefore in the future keep my beak shut and only use it to eat, drink and smoke!' William's speeches up to 1900 alone fill four thick volumes. *Kladderadatsch* thought he was suffering from a disease called 'oratoritis'. As an English commentator scoffed later, '... the Emperor had no more bitter enemy than his own undisciplined tongue. No one, not even himself, could tell what it would say next.'[137]

The news that the Boer War was about to break out again gave William fresh hopes of coming to an understanding with Britain. He thought he could demand a high price for friendship. He had seen how the Russians had behaved in the past. On 20 December he issued instructions to the army. Germany was strictly neutral. This flew in the face of German public opinion, which was anything but. In the famous *Daily Telegraph* interview of 28 October 1908, William revealed his partiality for the British cause at the time: '... when the struggle was at its height, the German government was invited by the Governments of France and Russia to join with them in calling upon England to put an end to the war. The moment had come, they said, not only to save the Boer Republics, but also to humiliate England to the dust.'[138]

William sent telegrams of encouragement to members of the royal family. The German emperor wrote the Prince of Wales a 'eulogy' to Sir George Stuart White, who had defended Ladysmith against Boer attacks. On 7 March 1900 Uncle Bertie replied saying, 'All of us in England appreciate the loyal friendship which you manifest towards us on every possible occasion. We hope always to look upon Germany as our best friend as long as you are at the helm.' On 10 March, William wired his grandmother to offer to mediate between the Boer Republics and Britain. To Prince Edward William sent a series of 'aphorisms' which amounted to a plan of campaign, ending with an unfortunate comparison to the recent defeat in the test match with Australia which the Prince of Wales interpreted as a call for a negotiated peace.[139] William was suggesting nothing of the kind. He even thought he had made some progress with the anti-British sentiments of the German press: 'Bülow and I have slowly got the better of our press, swamped as it was with articles, roubles and francs from both sides, to create anti-British feeling which our neighbours harbour most themselves!'[140]

XI

In 1899 William showed how forward-thinking he was in educational matters by allowing the new technical universities to award doctorates, thereby creating the title 'Doctor of Engineering'. In a speech delivered to the professors and students at the Technische Hochschule in Charlottenburg on 19 October William reminded his audience that God had played a role too, but stressed the 'astonishing success of technology in our time, but this has only been brought about by the fact that the creator of Heaven and earth has given mankind the capacity and incentive to delve ever deeper into the secrets of his creation and to recognise ever better the strengths and laws of nature, in order to render service to the common weal.'[141]

The Boer War once again made some of those close to William aware that his sympathies were often at variance with those of the German people. On 23 October 1899 Waldersee recorded that the emperor was happy at the news of English success in South Africa. With a voice that might have been his mother's he said, 'What can we do? The English are so much better at it than us . . .' He was hopelessly out of touch and believed that the German press had been bribed by the Russians to write nasty things about the British. His circle thought differently. Hildegard Spitzemberg found herself in the company of a number of his ADCs on the 31st, who were revelling in the British difficulties at Ladysmith.[142] Waldersee also wanted the British humbled by defeat, an attitude which more accurately mirrored that of the man in the street.*

William was certainly severely taxed in his loyalties. Nicky knew this too. On 21 October 1899 he wrote to the Grand Duchess Xenia, revelling in British problems in the Transvaal: 'All I need is to telegraph an order to all troops in Turkestan to mobilise and to advance to the border. That is all! . . . Not even the mightiest fleet in the world can prevent us from hitting England where she is weakest . . . I intend to arouse the emperor's ire in every way against the English, by recalling to his mind the well-known Kruger telegram.'[143] Two weeks later the Tsar was in Potsdam to confer with William. The mood in Germany was still extremely anti-British. It was bad timing for the week-long visit which William and Bülow made to England from 20 to 27 November.

They went to Windsor as Queen Victoria's guests. A Second Naval Law was being drawn up, and the British were more than suspicious. William too. He had decided that the most he was likely to achieve in Britain was the sort of alliance which had proved so bitter to Frederick the Great. Germany was not to be treated as a poor relation. Bülow was not at all keen on an alliance, and in that he represented a truer picture of the German public which did not think the same way as its ruler. On the other hand, there was a hard core to the emperor's popularity. Like Hitler later, it was German women who admired him most. Waldersee recognised that it would be 'unjust not to recognise that in the main the emperor is a popular figure . . . For by the female half of the nation he

---

* In Erfurt in Thuringia there is a *Burenhaus*, decorated with the portraits of leading Boer generals and built at the time.

is perceived as a good husband and father who has chalked up seven children.'[144]

It was the new year and time to dish out the medals again. A record number of princes were created too. One of them was Eulenburg. 'The best criticism of the "new princes" are the faces you see when acquaintances talk about them,' wrote Hildegard von Spitzemberg in her diary. Kerr wondered whether Eulenburg had his reward for the *Sang an Ägir*.[145] 'Smiles, shrugs of the shoulders, a few mocking words, particularly when it comes to Phili Eulenburg the Graf Troubadour, who has little money, has performed scant service and who has lots of children, and is not even head of his family. Dohna was apparently very ambivalent: as for Hatzfeldt it is simply one more title; how Knyphausen responded I cannot say.'

Hohenlohe allowed his old, 'regierende' disdain to show. In a letter of 7 January 1900 he wrote: 'So many new princes. Soon I'm just going to call myself Mr Hohenlohe! ... It is fortunate that Axel [Varnbüler] is not Prussian; else he'd soon become a count, dirt poor, but well-endowed in children. It's strange, after '66 and '70 Bismarck became a prince and a few others were raised to counts. Since then, when we have really far less success to boast about, these elevations have increased in inverse proportion.' The Black Eagle was also becoming 'quite a common little beast'.[146] There was to be another honour shelled out too: after some unusually bashful reticence, William accepted a field marshal's baton for himself.

William claimed that both France and Russia were keen to attack Britain in February 1900, while she was busy with the Boers, but he refused to act.[147] On 6 May the crown prince came of age. At the ceremony in the Schloss he swore the oath of fealty to the Crown, and William kissed his son over and over again. Francis Joseph was present for the occasion, which gave William the chance to reaffirm the alliance in Austria. Fortunately Archduke Constantine of Russia was also there. The Boer War and the unrest in China called for important discussions.[148]

In May, William came under fire yet again over the Lex Heinze, which concluded a laudable attempt to reintroduce police-controlled brothels in the light of a notorious murder case involving a pimp called Gotthilf Heinze which had come before the Berlin courts. The idea was to attack the pimps who controlled so much of the underworld in the big cities. Such a far-sighted bill naturally came under fire from all sides. The Catholic Centre Party objected strongly on moral grounds, and the rising force of German feminism also played its part in having the bill talked out of the Reichstag.[149] Elsewhere the weight of censorship and the number of sentences handed out for offending against the imperial dignity was causing comment. Kerr complained that Germany was 'no playground for free men' and wondered if there were a policeman quartered in every hedge.[150]

On 14 June the Naval Law was passed and William was now heading for a clash with Britain over his plans to increase the size of the imperial fleet. Once again there was a cogency about his argument, even if it may sound unattractive to British ears. He felt that Germany was being belittled by its neighbours – chiefly Britain. On 3 July William launched the *Wittelsbach* in the presence of Prince Rupprecht of Bavaria:

The ocean is indispensable for Germany's greatness ... without Germany and the German Emperor no more great decisions may be made. I do not agree that our German people shed their blood for victory under the leadership of their princes thirty years ago in order to be shoved aside when it came to making decisions in the outside world. Were that to be the case then the world power status of the German people would be gone for ever, and I am not going to let that come to pass. It is my duty and my finest privilege to apply the toughest and most ruthless methods when it is proper and necessary. I am convinced that I have Germany's princes and the entire people firmly united behind me.[151]

The situation in China was worsening. In May there were disturbances, and on 20 June the German consul, von Ketteler, was murdered. On 27 July William made his famous 'Hun speech' in the harbour in Wilhelmshaven as he bade his troops farewell. He told them to show the Chinese no mercy.

Show yourselves Christians, happily enduring in the face of the heathens! May honour and fame attend your colours and arms. Give the world an example of virility and discipline. *Anyone who falls into your hands falls on your sword!* Just as the Huns under King Etzel created for themselves a thousand years ago a name which men still respect, you should give the name of Germany such cause to be remembered in China for a thousand years that no Chinaman, no matter whether his eyes be slit or not, will dare look a Christian in the face.[152]

'Then the reincarnation of King Attila descended from his pulpit, and with this benediction ringing in their ears his Huns set sail for China.'[153]

A horrified Bülow expurgated the text for the press, but at least one newspaper managed to get hold of the purple version and publish it. William was allegedly incensed by the changes when he read them on the *Hohenzollern* as he headed out for his delayed *Nordlandsreise*: 'You have struck out all the best bits ...' he told his Foreign Minister. The Russian ambassador had expressed concern about the tenor of the speech. Bülow summoned up all his diplomatic skills and wrote to William: 'I have replied to Graf von der Osten Sacken in great earnest that Your Majesty's speech in Wilhemshaven was the fully justified expression of All Highest indignation at the atrocious and impertinent murder of the All Highest representative...'[154]

Hildegard Spitzemberg agreed with the emperor for once. She thought it a very good speech.[155] The international peace-keeping force under Waldersee arrived in Peking on 14 August. His appointment had been a popular choice. Only a few days later he was at it again, informing his listeners of his 'rock-hard conviction, and the mission, which every one [sic] of My ancestors carried out'.[156] Later the Chinese sent Prince Tschun to Potsdam to humble himself as a gesture of reconciliation. The ceremony took place in the Muschelsaal of the Neues Palais.

Once William had returned from the North Sea, there was a monument to unveil to the Great Elector in Bielefeld.[157] Bülow had an attack of cold feet just before his moment arrived to be elevated to the highest political office in the land. On 23 August he informed Eulenburg, 'Even a courageous spirit like my own takes fright at the sight of such abysmal ignorance of the true facts, such unworldly thoughts, emotions, judgements, such illusions...'[158]

In September William used his joint army and navy manoeuvres as a bait to lure over the Tsar and make another attempt to break the Franco-Russian alliance. He could 'live on his Jacht [sic] ... as I do on mine'. Nicholas accepted. For a while there was detente in their personal relations at least. On 23 September William wrote from Rominten to tell Nicholas that he had been across the Russian border to the Lithuanian town of Wystitten to deliver relief after a fire had destroyed many of the houses. 'They took me for an exalted Russian general, as I wore the uniform of my Grenadiers of St Petersburg, maybe for the Governor-General himself!' In the same letter he gave his cousin details of the game that season: 'I was out hunting yesterday, but could get nothing as a wolf has come and is playing devil with the deer ... I am trying to collect materials for my dragoon uniform...'[159]

Hohenlohe was a forgotten man. He had not even been informed of the decision to send troops to China, nor did he hear about Waldersee's appointment until after it had been made. He resigned on 16 October. Bülow was waiting in the wings to bring on the glory days.

Bülow

William later put it out that Bülow's elevation was not a foregone conclusion, and that the idea came to him from the Bavarian envoy, Graf Lerchenfeld, who thought the chancellorship should not be occupied by another south German. Hatzfeldt's name had come up too; and that of Hohenlohe's cousin, Langenburg. Bernhard von Bülow was a Prussian, albeit of Mecklenburgian origin, but an unusually worldly one. He was youthful, at least compared to his predecessors in the imperial chair, and married to a glamorous Italian princess who had been a pupil of Liszt. He had a keen, if flashy intelligence. His fondness for peppering his writings and speeches with Latin tags was second only to the emperor's own. He was by no means a typical Junker.

Hildegard von Spitzemberg thought the choice was a good one: 'Bülow is not an iron man; he would not remain long as chancellor if he were, but would be quickly crushed.' He had undoubted qualities. Much like his friend Eulenburg it was said of him – and he would have been the first to say so himself[1] – that had he remained close to William, the war would never have broken out. He 'was the first and last chancellor intimate enough with William to prevent him from disruptive interventions in policy'. It was true only up to a point; but diplomats such as the later ambassador to Washington, Bernstorff, thought it was the case. Even William recognised it himself, admitting that for Bülow to have maintained the peace while all the while Tirpitz was expanding the fleet, was no mean feat.[2]

'With absolute certainty Bülow would have prevented the world war,' wrote an early editor of the chancellor's letters. The same source quotes Bülow on 6 November 1905:

If Russia combines with England [sic], this necessarily means a front directed against us and it would in a forseeable time lead to a great, international war. What would be the consequences? Would Germany emerge victorious from the catastrophe? In all probability ... Germany would be defeated, and the revolution would celebrate its triumph.[3]

Bülow was thought good at wriggling out of difficult situations – a talent which was considerably helped by his lack of moral scruple. Holstein, whose career was finished by him, believed he could keep Germany out of war too. King Victor Emmanuel also flattered the former chancellor in December 1914: 'If you had been in Berlin none of this stupidity would have happened.'[4]

Not everyone believed in his omniscience. One of Bülow's opponents was his successor in Rome, and very nearly in the chancellor's office, Graf Monts. For him, the chancellor 'ran after everyone and betrayed everyone. He had a disastrous fear of Russia, a besotted affection for Italy; these emotions were the foundations of his personal policy, into which Holstein, and from time to time His Majesty, allowed themselves to be drawn.' Monts did not believe that Bülow could have averted war if Paris and Petersburg were determined to pursue it. He was only interested in preserving his personal power.[5] There was some give-and-take between William and his chancellor. Bülow was prepared to fit in with the emperor's apparently contradictory policy when it came to keeping the peace. There was to be much waving and rattling of sabres, but basically William had learned his lessons from the Bonapartes: identify the enemies without and cultivate national glory, but he knew too much about the fate of Napoleon III to chance his luck on the field of battle.

William was overjoyed with his new chancellor, as he had been about each and every one of them in the past. In Bülow's case the honeymoon lasted longer. He had a key to the back gate of the chancellor's palace on the Wilhelmstrasse, and could drop in from the Tiergarten after his morning walk. William wrote to Eulenburg, 'I am giving Bernhard Bülow a free hand; since I got him I can sleep in peace.' Bülow was still working closely with Holstein, who was increasingly frustrated to see his policies countermanded by the emperor. He called William an 'impulsive, sadly completely superficial gentleman, who has not a clue about international law, about political precedent, of diplomatic history or how to handle people'. He told the British ambassador Sir Edward Goschen to treat him as a child or a fool. More than once he called for the emperor's removal, maintaining that the man was mad. He even went so far as to call him a psychopath. Some might have said the same of Holstein. William claimed that he warned Bülow against Holstein. That was certainly unnecessary. If anyone knew how to deal with the diplomat, it was Bülow. William would have been better off warning himself against the man who provided Harden with some of the sharpest darts in his armoury, but he apparently did know a thing or two about Bülow. Bülow's wife was supposed to have had a liaison with the Polish-born pianist and composer Karl Tausig, who had died aged thirty in 1871, and a casket filled with their love-letters had been for a short time in his possession.[6]

II

Anglo-German relations were at a low ebb. William did not help matters by his speech at the launch of the *Karl der Grosse* in Hamburg on 18 October 1900 when he talked of the 'bitter necessity for a powerful German fleet'. The Boer War was still smouldering. Across the North Sea there was still a strong jingo mood. Germany was suffering from a 'national sickness' and 'overheated admiration for the Boers'. At the end of the year the British seized two German steamers and brought them into harbour under escort. Both William and Tirpitz were beside themselves with joy. Now was the chance to pass the Second Navy Law. As William told the French ambassador, 'I am ... not in the position to step outside the strictest neutrality and I must first of all equip myself with a fleet. After twenty years, if it is ready, I shall reply in a different language.'[7] There was even a suggestion that the British commanding officer should be given a medal.

William's desire to see a fleet worthy of the name meant working closely with Tirpitz. Tirpitz was not an easy man, especially not for William: 'He has a Bismarck nature, and that doesn't work with me,' he said once. Tirpitz's goal was a fleet of thirty-eight ships of the line 'with supporting vessels'. The navy was becoming the enthusiasm of non-Prussian Germans. South Germans in particular flocked to the colours, and there were lots of Alsatians too. Tirpitz thought this was intentional, that William was using the navy to unite his countrymen.[8] The admiral, for his part, took a Prussian view of things. He complained about the influence of less responsible people who flattered the vanity of his master; a man who had a problem separating momentary successes from lasting ones. His – admittedly difficult – job was to keep him on the straight and narrow. Where he could, Tirpitz satisfied William's longings, as long as they lay within the bounds of financial possibility. He was less enthusiastic about the show, and less successful in stemming the endless tide of 'decorative events and speeches, festivities such as the Kiel Week and launching ships ... which the emperor thought useful for the German people, while I had their effect abroad more in view.'[9]

Tirpitz thought William's historical achievement was to bring the Germans back to a consciousness of their vocation on the sea; and for that he was prepared to tolerate the designs and drawings – which he handed out to all and sundry – just like the yacht races and the fanfaronade of Kiel Week. But there were drawbacks too. The RMA (Imperial Naval Office) had to humour him by working out the finer details of his designs which were often nonsensical when it came to naval construction. His pet project was 'Homunculus', a heavily armed torpedo boat. Tirpitz had some trouble convincing his sovereign that the design would not work. Finally he succeeded during a shoot at Rominten. Shortly afterwards William allowed his Naval Minister to shoot a stag. He wired back to the ministry in triumph to tell his brother officers that both beast and boat had bitten the dust: 'Hirsch und Homunculus tot'.[10]

Tirpitz had worked out how to manage William: always alone if possible, outside the reach of the all-powerful cabinet chiefs. When out shooting with William, he asked the gamekeeper to drive the animals away so that he could get his points across without distractions. The middle-class Tirpitz preferred the time spent at Rominten. There was less side to the emperor there; a more bourgeois feel to the life; and good solid food was served at a table suitably decorated with greenery. In the evenings the company read together, airing their favourite passages out loud. Sometimes they would invite the colonel from the Russian garrison over and tease him about what he would do to protect the game when the attack came.[11]

Tirpitz was an old-fashioned Prussian in many ways, and pro-Russian. He thought the war against Germany's eastern neighbour was the 'cardinal error of our foreign policy'. He hated Britain, and while he had the emperor's ear he must have often influenced William in some of his more outrageous outbursts of Anglophobia. In his post-war writings Tirpitz denied being an annexationist, but admitted a desire to see an independent Flanders and Zeebrugge under German control.[12]

III

While the South African war continued, William's relations with his mother's country had little chance of recovery: the Germans were pro-Boer and it was assumed that William, as their emperor, thought the same. In vain did William point out the enthusiasm which existed for Kruger elsewhere in Europe. The humiliation of Fashoda was still fresh in French minds when in November 1900 the Boer president visited Paris and received a rapturous reception from the government. Yet William refused to see him when he came to Berlin the following month, which hardly enhanced his popularity, and caused much sour comment in the press.[13] That William was not pro-Boer was only confirmed much later, and caused a storm of fury throughout Germany which very nearly cost him his crown. Brigadier Wallscourt Waters started his service as military attaché at that time. Soon after his arrival he was called upon to explain the workings of khaki to the emperor. The diplomat's wife and self-confessed gossip Lady Susan Townley tells of another incident during the war which demonstrates William's interest in British victory.

William paid an early-morning call on the long-serving and long-suffering ambassador Sir Frank Lascelles. He resisted all the attempts on the part of the embassy servants to retrain him and marched into the ambassador's bedroom to find him still tucked up in bed. 'Here was I . . . still half-asleep, unwashed, unshaved, and unfed . . . my bedroom slippers and my dressing gown were out of reach. My frantic desire was to find an excuse to open my window, for I became acutely aware that my room was stuffy.' Lascelles offered William a cigarette, but the emperor declined. 'He pushed me back on the pillows and advanced nearer, unfurling and placing before me a roll of documents and maps which he had brought with him.' It was a new campaign he had drawn up for the British in the war. On some pretext the ambassador managed to slip out of bed, open a window and put on his dressing gown, 'but the emperor declared that I would catch cold, and insisted on my getting back into bed before he would expose his plan of campaign'. When he had finished he told Lascelles to send the plans to London. William then got up to leave, Lascelles following him to the door. There was a bodyguard in uniform waiting for him outside in the Wilhelmstrasse. William gestured towards Lascelles – 'What a sight!' he said.[14]

It was the two-hundredth anniversary of the Prussian Crown that year. It fell on 18 January 1901. Shortly before, court mourning had been declared for the Grand Duke of Weimar. William had that cut short on the 17th in preparation for the big day when there was a predictably adulatory *Festspiel* planned at the opera house, scripted, as ever, by the 'Festive Lauff'. Then, on the 19th, came the news of Queen Victoria's illness. The Duke of Connaught, who had been attending the party, was summoned home. The emperor told Lascelles of his intention of going with him that afternoon: 'I have ordered my special [train] to be ready and shall accompany him. I have duly informed the Prince of Wales, begging him at the same time that *no notice* whatever is to be taken of me in my capacity as emperor and that I come as grandson.' William also saw the possibility of improving Anglo-German relations. The English were not overjoyed at the prospect. William thought it was the influence of evil women, probably Bertie's wife, the virulently anti-Prussian Alexandra, who had never forgiven the Hohenzollerns for the war of 1864: 'Those petticoats are at it again; they want a pair of trousers there!'

Despite a sunny day great waves made it a stormy crossing. William wired Bülow to tell him that it would not have been to his liking: 'A few gentlemen made themselves scarce. I let myself be buffeted by the sea air for six hours and was never better!' The train drew into Victoria Station. As the carriage door opened, an 'ordinary man' removed his hat and said, 'Thank you, Kaiser!' Uncle Bertie, who was there to meet him dressed in a Prussian uniform, added, 'That is what they all think every one of them, and they will never forget this coming of yours.' The emperor added in his memoirs, with ill-concealed bitterness, 'That happened for all that, and pretty quickly.'[15] Bertie wanted William to have a meeting with Lords Salisbury and Lansdowne before they took the train to Portsmouth the following day. 'Let God give me the right thoughts and words and that I know how to express them for the good of both countries ...' Chamberlain had said that 'splendid isolation' was finished and that Britain must either join the Triple Alliance or France and Russia. He hoped it would be the former. William told Bülow, 'Therefore it seems they are about to do what we expected.' He announced that he had no desire to hog the limelight, and would go back to London if that was desired. On 22 January the queen began to fade. William and her doctor, Reid, sat on either side of her, supporting her, William with his strong right arm. For two and a half hours neither moved. It has been suggested that the queen may have mistaken William for Fritz on her deathbed, but it was hardly likely she was ever conscious. She died at six thirty. As William wrote later, she 'softly passed away in my arms'.[16]

After his grandmother's death, Uncle Bertie had urgent business to do in London, and William was left in charge of things at Osborne: 'the only time a German sovereign had ever ruled ... even informally, over any part of England.' The emperor was ready to place Victoria in her coffin all by himself, despite his bad arm, but her children rushed in to help. 'I don't know what we should have done without him', one told Marie von Bunsen later. It was he who insisted that the coffin be placed on a Union flag, which he later took back to Berlin as a souvenir. It was William's birthday on Sunday 27 January and officials from the embassy joined members of the British royal family for a celebration on the *Hohenzollern*, which was now moored in the Solent.[17]

William caused concern by his reluctance to come home. He was oblivious to the opprobrium and outraged at the lack of a reaction to his grandmother's death in Germany. Hildegard von Spitzemberg thought this was responsible for the great unpopularity of William in Germany at the time. He had to take part in all the pomp surrounding the change of monarchs, 'while tact decreed leaving his uncle [to enjoy] his long awaited and desired place'.[18] He rode next to Uncle Bertie on a magnificent white horse. His role at Victoria's bedside had become known, and he was experiencing some rare rays of adulation from the London crowd. The Harmsworth press even referred to him as a 'friend in need' which did much to obliterate the effects of the Kruger telegram.[19] In Windsor the horses pulling the bier refused to budge. William earned the acclaim of the crowd by reharnessing them, then everything began to go smoothly.

William lingered in England until 4 February, thereby causing the Anglophobic Dona concern. He attended a lunch in his honour at Marlborough House where he replied to the health of the sport- and women-loving king, who, having chosen the name of Edward, had rapidly been dubbed 'Edward the Caresser'. William thought the moment had come to put in a bid for better relations:

I believe there is a providence which has decreed that two nations which have produced such men as Shakespeare, Schiller, Luther and Goethe must have a great fortune before them; I believe that the two Teutonic nations will, bit by bit, learn to know each other better, and that they will stand together to help in keeping the peace of the world. We ought to form an Anglo-Germanic alliance, you to keep the seas, while we would be responsible for the land; with such an alliance, not a mouse could stir in Europe without our permission, and the nations would, in time, come to see the necessity of reducing their armaments.[20]

IV

William's life was more turbulent than ever. There was, however, a pretty strict routine to his comings and goings. At the beginning of the year was the Berlin season: William moved from the Neues Palais in Potsdam to the vast baroque Schloss in Berlin. The chapter of the Black Eagle met, there was his birthday on 27 January, the *Grosser Defiliercour* followed by the winter balls. Court life was generally regarded as dull and William confessed he thought that, compared to London or Vienna, Berlin was a 'dowdy wasteland'.[21] This was partly due to the rigidity of the court, and partly to the novelty of Berlin as a national capital: many of the grander German families still kept away, and the Junkers who lodged in hotels for the short season were provincial bumpkins who hardly lent any glamour to the occasion.

William and Dona failed to make it easy for people to shine at court. Through her influence there was too much prudery and priggery. The latest American dances were outlawed and it was hard even to smoke, eat or drink. According to the strict etiquette, the emperor and empress were served first and everyone had to yield up their plates when they finished. Those who had been served last had often hardly touched their food. Children in particular, who were seated the farthest away from the royal pair, were left hungry, and had to cultivate good relations with the servants below-stairs in order to fill their bellies.[22] Unlike his uncle, William had no taste for gourmand pleasures such as oysters or caviar, and liked very simple food best. He scarcely drank, which meant he was intolerant of people who tippled too much, although he occasionally indulged a little drunkenness in his companions, especially on the Northern cruises.

The emperor was less prudish than Dona. Lady Susan Townley complained about the shortness of Victory's skirt on the Siegessäule, or Victory column, in the Tiergarten. Later William sent a message to her through her brother: 'Tell Lady Susan my Victory is now in fashion.' And yet he ruled his family with the proverbial rod of iron. One thorn in his side was Prince Joachim Albrecht, who had run off after an actress who had married a German baron in the unlikely setting of the London suburb of Brixton. William had him banished to German South-West Africa. The prince none the less returned without permission and married his love. He was expelled from the army as a result.[23]

William wanted to make something out of his capital. For that reason he had much of the old city pulled down. During a quarter of a century of peaceful rule, most of the old buildings in the centre of Berlin were demolished to make way for modern boulevards, tram-lines and exuberant neo-baroque, romanesque or gothic structures. A very large number of new churches were built, the most ambitious of which were the memorial buildings to Emperors William and Frederick and to Empress Augusta, as well as the new Garrison Church on the Südstern. There were also a great number of imposing public monuments. The Kaiser-Friedrich-Museum (now the Bode-Museum) was built by Ernst Ihne, as a monument to William's father, and with its striking site on the tip of the Museum Island has some claim to being the architect's best building. Ihne's other important commission was the new national library, completed just before the war.[24]

William took a particular interest in the development of palace hotels. He patronised Lorenz Adlon, whose new hotel he opened on 23 October 1907, and which lodged a large number of the guests who came for Victoria Louise's wedding on 24 May 1913. It took over the site of Schinkel's Redernpalais, but William is reported to have been unimpressed by any attempts to save the work of Prussia's greatest architect. Another hotel building in which the emperor took a personal interest was the Excelsior near the Anhalter Bahnhof, a luxurious place which was later to inspire Vicki Baum's novel *Menschen im Hotel* (*Grand Hotel*). William had the owner Kurt Elschner made a Kommerzienrat.[25]

Lady Susan Townley put her finger on it when she exposed William's frustration at the lack of glamour around him. His capital depressed him as much as the dowdiness of his female courtiers. 'He realised, I think, that there was between Berlin and Paris, or London, all the difference that there is between beer and champagne. He would have loved to top German thoroughness with a little naughty Gallic froth!' She then added about the man she went to jeer at the railway station in Maarn, 'Personally, I found him charming.'[26]

William missed the delights of the English house party, but he had plenty of *Schlösser* of his own, sixty-nine to be precise.[27] Even if he tried, he could not have managed a full week in each. Müller clearly found it all too much: 'The lodging changed from one castle to another. Today the special train, tomorrow a ship of the line or the Imperial yacht or a passenger steamer belonging to one of the two German lines [HAPAG or Norddeutsche Lloyd], London, Vienna, Venice, Lisbon, Tangiers, Naples, Genoa, Sweden, Norway or Finland all blend into one. There were relatively quiet days staying on Corfu, the *Nordlandsreise* or the Rominten weeks.' William sometimes literally did not know what day it was: 'What is the date today?' 'The 9th, if no other one has been ordered.' Müller, however, admitted that such moments of confusion did not occur often.[28]

The spring had its rhythms. After 1907 Corfu was the emperor's first port of call, and created a pretext for the Mediterranean cruise which had become the rule some years before. His new Schloss at Urville in Alsace beckoned later and then there was the rundown to Kiel Week. In summer July was fixed for the *Nordlandsreise*, then, when he was in favour in England, he would hop across to Cowes for the Regatta. The theatre festival in Wiesbaden was the next fixture and towards the end of August the family repaired to Wilhelmshöhe above Cassel, with its memories of William's schooldays. The autumn was dominated by the hunt. September was fixed for manoeuvres and then the call of the wild took him off to some magnate's land in Silesia to shoot. Later he travelled up to Rominten on the Russian border for a week before the fox cull began at Donaueschingen. He stayed in Potsdam and Berlin for the winter.[29]

William's 'Englishness' prescribed a fondness for sport. Another tennis court was installed at Wilhelmshöhe to add to those he already had and his yachting was performed in clear imitation of his Hanoverian cousins. The crew – even the cooks – of the *Meteor* was British until 1906, when middle-class German displeasure became so strong that they had to be packed off home. His withered arm prevented him from practising many other games and Dona forbade him to fly. He could not shoot from anything heavier than a 20-bore shotgun and horses could be a problem. They had to be trained to take him, he could not ride any old beast. One was always sent to England in advance of the emperor on his trips. The famous Berber horse in Tangiers had to rise up with him on its back and, lest it buck and injure its rider, it was led through the streets by two ADCs with a firm grip on the reins.[30]

William was a passionate card-player, mostly the German game of Skat which, Müller unkindly adds, he played badly. It was a way of filling up the evenings in his various hunting lodges and even during the war he was often found sitting down to a hand with Lyncker, Valentini and Müller. It might have also been a means of evading Dona, who generally accompanied him to Rominten or Hubertusstock, although her attempts to infiltrate the *Nordlandsreise* had petered out. At Rominten he was joined by his fawning friend Richard Fürst zu Dohna-Schlobitten, whose family was one of the oldest in East Prussia. Müller called him the 'Chief of the Hunting Cabinet'. He does not say whether he had a hand in the mechanisation of the shoot in William's remote Baltic estate. After a while the *Trakehner* made way for cars and telephones were connected so that the arrival of the game could be signalled to the hunters. Felt-covered steps provided a soft access to the butts.[31]

William's afternoon nap was of great importance if the emperor was to get through his routine. Müller provides us with two well-provisioned days in December 1904 when William was in Berlin. After breakfast on the 3rd there was a walk with the chancellor in the Tiergarten while William listened to the naval reports; then a visit to the English painter C. H. Cope in Monbijou. A baptism followed, then a visit to another painter, the Italian Vittorio Matteo Corcos. There was a break for tea; then a party for Landwehr officers in Tempelhof. At eleven he was back in the Schloss. The next day breakfast was followed by a visit to Gesundbrunnen to consecrate a church; it was a rough working-class district in the north of Berlin which William prudently visited under escort. He received the Cuban envoy at the Schloss and the marine painter Willi Stöwer. He lunched with Secretary of State von Richthofen, walked in the Tiergarten in the afternoon and dined with his theatre intendant von Hülsen. He went to bed at twelve thirty.[32]

Müller thought William's afternoon sleep was an imposition as far as the entourage was concerned. It meant that he was bright and lively for the evening session while his little court nodded off. Ambassador Metternich was notorious for snoozing, but Müller admitted that he sometimes did too. When there was nothing happening a simple bourgeois tea was served in the library of the Schloss after dinner. William read reports and newspaper cuttings out loud. The women – Dona in particular – knitted. Only William was allowed to smoke. It was on one of these occasions that Dona came up with the line, 'Are you not going to go to bed at all?' Which earned the rebuke, 'Well what else could I do, it is so incredibly dull here.'[33]

Anyone who was not careful could find their health damaged by this regime. Müller was a case in point. The naval officer found the long lunches hard to bear, especially once he became directly attached to the emperor, when he had to attend dinners and beer evenings too. It was not just food which turned Müller's stomach, but William's pranks, the physical jerks and the sermons of William's Byzantine chaplain Ludwig Göns. By the end of April 1906, Müller reported sick. In September the strains of the naval manoeuvres led to a further collapse. He came back to work too soon. The hunting season with the endless nightly games of cards meant crying off again. In January lunches sometimes drifted seamlessly into an early German dinner. During Kiel Week in 1908 William himself noticed that Müller's health was about to pack up. 'Christ! You look terrible. I am sending you home to have you fattened up.' The result was rather the reverse: Müller underwent an operation on his stomach.[34]

V

There were no famous artists or musicians at court, but it should not be supposed that William was a total philistine. He had the pianists Moltke and Chelius to play for him, and one of Dona's train – Fräulein von Gersdorff – had a pretty voice. William liked choral and orchestral music and conducted the band on the royal yacht. He had gone off Wagner after his initial enthusiasm, which may have had something to do with his mother's distaste for the composer of the tetralogy. Wagner did not pander to the people: William expressed the view that he had never heard a single street-arab whistle a Wagner *Leitmotiv*. He tried to commission an opera from Saint-Saëns, and had Leoncavallo compose *Der Roland von Berlin* based on the historical romance by Willibald Alexis. William clapped enthusiastically at the humiliation of the mayor. He had a weakness for loud, Italian opera.[35] He invited Edvard Grieg and the violinist, Joseph Joachim to perform at the Schloss. The wits said he always dressed appropriately for his visits to the opera house: as a Garde-Jäger for *Der Freischütz* and as an admiral for *Der fliegende Holländer*.

He admired Menzel, especially the history paintings. When the painter died in his ninetieth year, on 9 February 1905, William designed a magnificent funeral for him: the royal bodyguard in Friderician uniforms; the castle guard with banners; Joachim performed with his quartet in the Old Museum; the music-school choir sang a Beethoven cantata; and William, followed by his generals, walked behind his coffin – an honour only previously accorded to Moltke. He also commissioned portraits from the Hungarian László, who was fashionable all over Europe. Otherwise his taste was uncertain and he tended to take recommendations from friends. He bought cheap watercolours for Achilleion. His chief joys were marine views by Saltzmann, Bohrdt and the Norwegian Hans Dahl.[36]

Monumental art pleased him most and he would make plans and drawings during boring audiences, often on the back of envelopes and dossiers. His counsellors turned a blind eye. As Moltke said, 'We shouldn't spoil his fun.' This was not simply an inheritance from Vicky; his great-uncle, Frederick William IV, had done much the same and had a similar talent. He drew battleships, but also sketched out the form of the Coligny Monument for Wilhelmshaven. He patronised sculptors such as Wilhelm Haverkamp, Johannes Götz, Max Unger – whose 18-metre-high statue of Frithjof he donated to the new kingdom of Norway – and his old friend Emil von Schlitz-Görtz. Gustav Eberlein, he believed, had been rude to him, and he determined to starve him of commissions. Begas remained the clear favourite, but he believed the whole school of Berlin sculptors stood comparison with high renaissance Italy.[37]

Finally, in 1901, William formally unveiled his 'Puppenallee' in the Tiergarten. It contained a few concealed portraits of contemporaries. There was the emperor himself as Frederick the Great, and Eulenburg had been obliged to pose alongside William at Friesack for the knight Wend von Ilburg. The oddest was the artist Heinrich Zille, whose image peered out of the statue of Wendelin von Plotho by August Kraus.[38] The consecration gave William the chance to set out his jaundiced views on modern art. Art, he said, should serve the interests of the community:

The supreme task of our cultural effort is to foster our ideals. If we are and want to remain a model for other nations, our entire people must share in this effort, and if culture is to fulfil its task completely it must reach down to the lowest levels of the population. That can be done only if art holds out its hand to raise the people up, instead of descending into the gutter.[39]

William was aware of the tide of criticism mounting against the 'Puppenallee' but he defended his creation. 'When I went to Athens as a child with my mother ... and saw the deeds of the Greeks immortalised in their splendid marbles, I realised what a powerful stimulus to patriotism was the history of a country written in stone ...' Like the statues of Athens in its Golden Age, Berlin was to have its Alcibiades, or troops of them, who defaced the statues by night. Eventually a permanent police watch had to be installed in the park.[40]

'Rinnsteinkunst' or 'Gutter Art' became the war cry against those Berlin painters such as Skarbina, Baluschek, Liebermann or Leistikow who had introduced realism into the city's studios; while William stuck firmly to his favourites: Werner, Begas and Ihne. Werner in particular became associated with the emperor's battle. As director of the Berlin Academy, he discouraged his students from experimenting with avant-garde subject-matter.

Vicky had discovered Ihne, and in a rare instance of filial piety, William never abandoned him; even raising him to the nobility. Marie von Bunsen felt that Ihne was ruined by his 'pushiness'. William wanted always to influence his architects, which must have made their lives difficult. On one occasion Bülow advanced the view that you could not lay down the law to an artist. William replied, 'But you can prevent them from taking the wrong path.' He was a generous patron for all that – money was decidedly no object. When the question arose whether a museum building should be constructed of sandstone or limestone – the latter being the most expensive – William replied, 'It is meant to last for centuries, let's have the best.' Sometimes he was wholly confused by the architects' drawings. Seeing a star at the top of a sheet of paper bearing a design for the new Kaiser Wilhelms Gesellschaft, he insisted that it be built, even though others thought it looked silly.[41]

Being the supreme arbiter was not enough; William had to create too. He designed his own clothes and those of his wife. They were sometimes remarkable. He also took a hand in the form of public buildings, as Frederick the Great had done before him, and sketched the new monument for the working-class district of Friedrichshain in Berlin. Father Naumann commented: 'The emperor donates a design for a fountain to Friedrichshain. He is not just the Supreme Warlord, the Head of the Diplomatic Service, the Protector of the Board of Trade, Industry and Agriculture, the Highest Bishop of the United Evangelical Church, but also Supreme Promoter of Knowledge and Judge of Art. At his feet kneel Ares, Athena, Poseidon, Apollo and all the muses.'[42]

Belles-lettres were beyond him. Marie von Bunsen thought 'for German literature he did not do anything at all'. William hated Germany's greatest writer, Hauptmann, and preferred sentimental nationalists such as Gustav Frenssen, Jörn Uhl and Karl Schönherr. The latter was '*the* German writer of our time'. Müller believed that the only decent preacher in the emperor's retinue was Ernst von Dryander. William did not write his own sermons. The principal author was Ludwig Göns, the fawning cleric with a dislike of France and Britain, who combined a role at court with being padre to the Garde Korps. William was in two minds about Catholicism. While he hated the tenets of the faith, he admired the ceremonial and the loyalty it bred in children. Some of that pomp was written into the performance when Berlin's new cathedral was unwrapped in February 1905. The lavishness of the occasion shocked the pastors present.[43]

VI

One Catholic William more than tolerated was Max Fürstenberg, an Austrian prince who was gradually replacing Philipp Eulenburg in the emperor's affections. Fürstenberg used tactfully to absent himself from the *Hohenzollern* while everyone was still in bed, in order to attend Mass. He had no desire to excite the overwhelmingly Protestant sensibilities of the entourage. He had inherited his vast estates at Donaueschingen in Baden on the death of a cousin. They had met in Vienna in 1893, but William did not visit the estate until 1900. When he did, he found that a birthday greeting had been prepared for him in verse. A year later he allowed the prince to call him 'Du'. In the winter of 1904 Fürstenberg was given a formal office at court. It was a sign of unusual tolerance on William's part: Fürstenberg's set was Austrian or south German, and therefore principally Catholic, but there was something in the lavish lifestyle which appealed to William. Indeed, Max Fürstenberg was none too careful with money. He went spectacularly bankrupt in 1914.[44]

The same admiration for luxury led William to admit a large number of moneyed industrialists to his circle, mostly men with no claims to noble lineage, or at best very recent ones: Krupp, the Bohlen und Halbachs – who took over the Krupp firm after Fritz's death, the Stumm brothers with their massive concerns in the Saar, Gwinner and Helfferich at the Deutsche Bank, Max von Schinckel, and noble Silesian magnates such as Pless, Henckel-Donnersmarck and Hatzfeldt. Like Ballin, many of these men were interested in the idea of Mitteleuropa as an independent economic unit which would function apart from the American and British ones. Some, like William himself, toyed with the idea of going one further and creating a United States of Europe. The German emperor had first voiced his interest in this during Caprivi's chancellorship, and the idea had received attention in the *Frankfurter Zeitung* in 1895. That same year there were calls for an economic union of central European states both from the socialists and from the right-wing Pan-Germans. The later Weimar Chancellor, Gustav Stresemann was still talking about it in February 1913.[45]

On board the *Hohenzollern* in 1901 William told the French journalist Ségur of his plans to create a European *Zollverein* or customs union: 'a

customs line [of defence] against the United States'. William was equivo-
cal about Britain's participation in this 'common market'. He felt that
the islanders should decide whether they wished to play a role in central
Europe and fight against America or vice versa.[46] In August 1904 William
returned to the theme of 'les États unis de l'Europe' in one of his
marginal notes. Holstein scrawled alongside: 'Naturally under German
leadership.'[47]

VII

The industrialist and future Weimar Foreign Minister Walther
Rathenau made the emperor's acquaintance at this time. The Jewish
intellectual had some twenty meetings with William over the next thirteen years. He described his appearance, noting his small head, the size
of a child's: 'A youthful man in a colourful uniform bespangled with
strange symbols of his dignity, his white hands covered with coloured
rings; armbands on his wrists; delicate skin, soft hair, small white teeth.
A real prince; careful of what impression he made, permanently fighting
with himself, forcing his nature to gain control of his stance and strength.
Scarcely a moment when he was not aware; unconscious only – and here
comes what is humbly touching – of the fight with himself, clueless
against the nature he had formed himself.'[48]

Rathenau voiced a respect for the emperor's mind, but there were
gaps: 'The emperor had no consciousness of tragedy, even the unconscious feeling of the problem. He was not naive by nature, for an intellect
reposed on its foundations, but an undeveloped one. His thought
occurred by daylight, in the blaze of fact; he did not lack what the French
call *clarté*.'[49] Rathenau was amused as he was baffled by some of the
emperor's decisions. He appointed a 'blockhead' to command the foot-
guards. When another asked why, William had to explain that he was
obliged to sit next to the regimental commander once a year, and for
that reason he did not wish to promote anyone nasty.[50]

William could clearly overlook race or religion when he so chose.
The line 'I' bestimm' wer a Jud' is' (I decide who is a Jew) was not the
sole preserve of Viennese anti-Semites like Lueger. William was pleased
to hear that Rathenau was intending to stand for Parliament. Other Jews
besides Ballin and the Rathenaus, father and son, were admitted to the
emperor's circle: the Hamburg banker Max Warburg, Salomonsohn,
Robert von Mendelssohn and Carl Fürstenberg received friendly
encouragement. They were all assimilated Jews, their ideas fully in
keeping with German nationalism. It should be remembered that Max
Harden did not attack the emperor because he was too bellicose, he
censured him because he thought him too weak.[51]

William's consorting with Jews was not always appreciated by his subjects and it positively outraged his American dentist, Arthur Davis, who pointed to Berlin's richest man, 'a Hebrew coal-merchant [sic] named Friedländer. The Kaiser ennobled him and made him von Friedländer-Fuld. Another wealthy Hebrew [was] Schwabach ... he too was ennobled, becoming von Schwabach.' 'A number of wealthy Hebrews were honoured another way ... He visited their mansions ostensibly to view their art collections, but actually to tickle their vanity.'[52]

Ballin remained more than William's favourite Jew, he was a proper friend, in as much as William had such. He was punctilious about congratulating him on his birthdays and his sicknesses also caused him to worry. He was received at the important *Ordensfest* at the Schloss in January. When William was in Hamburg he lunched with Ballin in his home and office. Ballin came to family meals in Potsdam too. On 15 October 1903 he was there with Bülow and Metternich while the last preparations were made for the confirmation of his sons Oscar and Augustus William or 'Auwi'.[53]

William was not a snob about blood and titles. If anything impressed him it was wealth and style, and the lavishness of entertainment. He liked plutocratic Americans and one of the faces he was happiest to see at Kiel Week was Jonathan Ogden Armour, a wealthy Chicago butcher. A Mrs Galet – probably Goelet – came with her yacht *Nahma* and was received by the emperor. Other yachtsmen who entered the magic circle were two Britons, Sir Thomas Brassey, the liberal politician and future earl, and the shipbuilder and Quebec-born Ulsterman Lord Pirrie.[54]

VIII

The princes were now growing up. One by one they entered the army or navy, where, with the exception of Auwi, they remained. Having shown the usual Hohenzollern contempt for girls, William's heart melted when Dona's last child turned out to be one. Victoria Louise could do no wrong. With the boys he was 'friendly and loving in his way ...' wrote the crown prince later, '[but] only my sister succeeded from childhood onwards to win a warm place in his heart'. There was no spoiling for the boys: little princes had to show their 'military obedi-ence'[55] or face the consequences. They all entered the army on their tenth birthdays, as William had done, but there was to be no civil mentor of the Hinzpeter sort. The crown prince received lessons from a military governor in the form of the later general, minister and Chief of Staff, Falkenhayn. Then they were all packed off to Plön in Schleswig-Holstein to a specially appointed cadet school in the company of General von Gontard.

William's 'seventh son' was Charles Edward, the posthumous child of the Duke of Albany. Queen Victoria had had her grandson shipped out to Germany in 1900 as a sixteen-year-old Eton schoolboy, to be trained for the business of running the duchy of Coburg. The last duke in the direct line, Albert's brother Ernest, had died in 1895. He had been succeeded by the Duke of Edinburgh whose only son preceded him. William was quite particular as to which of his relations would take over the duchy. He wanted to be the master in his own house and would not tolerate being lorded over by his uncles. The first choice as successor to the Duke of Edinburgh fell on the Duke of Connaught, but he was not prepared to renounce his status and command in Britain, and nor was he prepared to accept a similar diktat for his son. At a stormy meeting on the Wartburg in 1899 it was decided that the succession should fall on Charles Edward, who was fifteen then, and ready to accept his German cousin's authority. William was adamant that Charles Edward should receive as German an education as possible. Field Marshal Lord Roberts also told him, 'Try to be a good German!' before he left. The boy did not speak the language, and a regency was declared until he came of age. He went to the new cadet school in Lichterfelde until he was commissioned in the First Foot and spent his weekends with the royal family in Potsdam.[56] Charles Edward married Victoria Adelaide of Schleswig-Holstein Sonderburg in 1905, a cousin of Dona's, and came into his duchy shortly afterwards.[57] The rest of his life was a tragic tug-of-war between his English and his German heritages. After burning his bridges to Britain in 1914 he became Hitler's first convert among the princes and remained a staunch Nazi until his death in the fifties.[58]

'Little Willy', as the English and his family called the crown prince, had come of age with the century and, as he entered adulthood, increasingly became a thorn in his father's side. He made his first political statement in Oels after the death of Krupp, when he attacked the 'miserable' socialists and earned their contempt for ever after. Following in the footsteps of so many crown princes, William became the focus of the opposition – not, on this occasion, of the radicals, but more the Pan-Germans of the extreme right. He was convinced that his father surrounded himself with the wrong advisers. His chief hates were the heads of the civil and marine cabinets, Valentini and Müller, who 'tightly pressed the emperor into their own points of view and harnessed him to them in all important issues'.[59]

The problem, thought the heir to the throne, was access, or rather the lack of it. Prince William was convinced that his father had surrounded himself with the sort of people who cut him off from his people. He remembered his own childhood when even he could only approach William after applying to his tutor or governor. Only the chancellor had the right to a personal audience alone with William; all the other ministers had to deliver their reports in the presence of the cabinet chiefs. In military matters this meant the ultra-conservative Plessen.[60]

William may not have wanted to see his eldest son, who disappointed him as much as he had saddened his own father. It was not just the crown prince's politics which caused concern, it was his lifestyle. Like his Great-Uncle Bertie he loved only sport and women. William forbade him all dangerous sports such as horseracing or drag hunting, but Willy defied the ban. Once when William heard that he had taken part in a race he enquired, 'I hope you won at least?'[61] The crown prince also disliked the stiff formality of his father's court; in his own world all this 'Kram' – junk – was 'as far as possible' suppressed.[62]

IX

There was an attempt on William's life on 6 March 1901. A mentally deranged worker called Weiland threw a piece of iron at him which cut a deep wound under his right eye. It was too deep to be stitched and was so close to both eye and temple that it could have been very dangerous indeed. Weiland was not a socialist, but the experience did not make him any better disposed towards the Left whom he referred to as 'enemies of the empire and fatherland'. There was a rumour that the attack threw the emperor into a depression. He was certainly even more jumpy than usual. By the end of the month he had recovered enough to make a fighting speech. He had read the papers, 'but nothing is more false than to pretend that my sanity has suffered in some way. I am exactly the same as I was; I have become neither elegiac nor melancholic ... everything stays the same.'[63]

William's attempt to arrange an alliance between Britain and Germany at the time of his grandmother's death came to nothing. To Lascelles, William dismissed His Majesty's Government as 'a pack of unmitigated noodles', which went back to London and offended Edward. His relations with Waters, the German-educated British military attaché, however, were good. On 27 May he boisterously slapped him on the back at the Neues Palais. Although William scarcely drank (he was virtually a chain-smoker) he wanted to drink a glass of Mosel with him. The bottle was brought and Waters told him how good he found it. William replied that there were still three or four bottles left of a yet finer vintage. Waters was wisely sceptical. 'A bottle was sent for. The Kaiser sipped some and even asked me for an opinion. It was something unbelievably superb even for that wonderful cellar.' Waters thought it might have been an 1864. Possibly it was the 'Versöhnungswein' he had sent to Bismarck.[64]

That same month William received two high-ranking French officers who had distinguished themselves in the suppression of the Boxer Rebellion. He made a speech in which he praised the 'gallant French army ... Of all the troops in China none were better than the French, who possessed every military virtue and with whom the Germans stood shoulder to shoulder not only in camp but also in victorious exploits in the field.' Later William made clear to Waters what was behind those kind words: 'Your policy of isolation will no longer do. You will no longer be able to stir up strife among the nations on the continent. You heard what I said at luncheon, and the continental nations mean to work for peace; and *you* ... will not be able to prevent us doing so. You have to join one side or the other.'[65]

William cut short the *Nordlandsreise* of 1901 when he heard that cancer was about to claim his mother too. In her declining years William had been more attentive towards Vicky. In the last year of her life he stayed at Wilhelmshöhe more often to be near her and was 'unusually considerate'. He had undertaken his North Sea trip thinking she would last out until the end of the year, but his sisters let him know she was sinking fast. He made it to Friedrichshof before the end and she was still conscious when he arrived. She died on 5 August. As he told the Tsar, 'The suffering was so terrible that one could look upon the end as a release.'[66]

His mother's death offered him the chance of a word or two with Uncle Bertie on 23 August. Both sides had dragged their feet since the good work William had put in in Britain. The pro-Russian Holstein had expressed the traditional Prussian view that Britain would shirk its obligations as it had done in the Seven Years War. On 6 April, the ambassador Hatzfeldt reported growing mistrust from the British end. William fulminated predictably: 'I cannot understand the British! Their lack of character is thoroughly monstrous. You can't do anything with these people!'[67] The sticking point now was that Germany should divest itself of its other allies before entering into a pact with Britain. On 23 August William was able to have things out with his uncle, Lascelles and Lansdowne at Wilhelmshöhe. It was time to have his revenge on Salisbury, who was about to retire as Prime Minister. William made the remark that there was an old school of politicians to which prince Bismarck had belonged in his time and which was now still composed of, for example, Lord Salisbury and a few old-fashioned gentlemen in Paris, St Petersburg and Vienna, who would like to see the task of politics as the grouping and regrouping of the individual states of the continent to play them off and stir them up against one another. This recipe is now no longer acceptable. Politics is now played in the world at large, European differences are paling. In recent years, and particularly since the Chinese expedition, the continental states have moved closer together. For example, who would have imagined it possible that French and German troops, under the command of a Prussian general, would have fought together against a third party? Bloodshed in common has worked wonders, and now we get on really well with our neighbours across the Vosges.[68]

William pushed his ideas of greater European economic co-operation at the British monarch. He still thought the purpose of alliances was to police the world; to keep the peace. He was courting the Tsar as well. They met at Danzig for the naval manoeuvres on 11 September. It went well and William wrote to Nicholas again in December to express his desire to show him over one of his new cruisers the following year.[69]

German trade was still affected by the Boer War. Ships lay loaded at anchor in Bremen and Hamburg, unable to sail. William threatened Waters: 'People cannot be held back for ever, and there will be intervention.' In his usual way he issued a tactless evaluation of the British army to its Berlin attaché: 'You had originally the splendid troops, officers and men, of the old army, but they have been worn out, and now you have only scum.' The British, he continued, were 'degenerate through too much luxury'. His ire was roused by an issue of *Simplicissimus* which depicted Queen Victoria, who had died nine months before, in a sea of blood, struggling to reach a shore where stood Ohm Kruger and Saint Peter. Yet William explained to Waters that he had abandoned trials for *lèse-majesté* because of the number of acquittals. The courts were loath to deal with them.[70]

At a lunch in Potsdam on 23 October, William made an attack on Joseph Chamberlain. He had previously expressed his opinion to Wallscourt Waters that Chamberlain should spend a night in the Veldt. This time the suggestion was more draconian: 'Chamberlain should be taken to South Africa, marched across the continent and then shot. A firing squad is what he wants.' Waters objected: 'Sir, ... many of our countrymen would like to see Mr Chamberlain prime minister of England; they positively adore him.' 'Ach was!' said William. 'They couldn't!' Two days later Chamberlain responded in kind, with an anti-German speech in which he excused the brutal behaviour of British troops in South Africa by pointing to the precedent established by the Germans when dealing with snipers during the Franco-Prussian War.[71]

x

William had been excited about the publication of the vast work by the colonial secretary's namesake, Houston Stewart Chamberlain's *Die Grundlagen des neunzehnten Jahrhunderts* (*The Foundations of the Nineteenth Century*). How much William read of this ponderous tome is unclear, but Chamberlain was certainly a seminal influence on his thinking. The principal message concerned Germany: the Germans were the one creative race to emerge from the ruins of the Roman Empire. Sections of the book are given over to the Jews. Chamberlain's contentions are not standard anti-Semitism. He thought the obsession with the 'Jewish question' missed the point: 'the Jew is no enemy of Germanic civilisation and culture.' Jewish influence was also exaggerated. 'Hand in hand with this goes the entirely ridiculous and outrageous tendency to make Jews the universal scapegoat for the vices of our age.'[72]

Chamberlain's theories on Christ's racial ancestry were eagerly taken up by the emperor. Jesus was no Jew. As the son of God he was not a man, and even if he were, Galilee was 'a heathen district ... marriages between Jews and Galileans were unthinkable.' Chamberlain thought that even if Christ were 'morally a Jew', 'there was not the slightest cause to assume that the parents of Jesus Christ were, from a racial point of view, Jews.'[73] Jews were not culturally welcome for all that. The Indo-Europeans had opened the gates of friendship to the Jews. 'Like an enemy the Jew tumbled in, stormed all positions and planted the flag of his eternally foreign nature, I shall not say on the ruins, but in the breach of our true individuality.'[74] The real problem was mixing blood, which led to racial degeneration.[75]

In October 1901 Eulenburg invited the author to Liebenberg to meet William. The emperor arrived on 27 October, and Houston Stewart Chamberlain the next day. His audience took place in the library of the Schloss. William fairly talked the adopted German off his feet, bubbling over with enthusiasm; he wanted the theologian Adolf von Harnack to join them. From a letter of 15 November 1901 from Chamberlain to the emperor, it becomes clear that the subject of their talk had been the creation of a 'moral world order'. He flattered William by telling him that all the old Aryan cultures were monarchies which offered unconditional loyalty to their rulers. The racialist Chamberlain also postulated that there was no progress to be made in knowledge, philosophy or religion 'except in the German language'. 'Today God relies on Germany alone.' It was a reflection of his ideas expressed in the *Grundlagen*: Germany was the saviour.[76] Germany needed to be protected from two evils, a 'Yankified Anglo-Saxondom and a Tartarised Slavdom'. Races needed to be kept pure.[77]

William replied to Chamberlain on New Year's Eve. He apologised for not having read the Hindu epics on which Chamberlain was basing much of his Aryan teaching. In the 1870s, when he was at school, no one had. The letter then rehearsed the familiar theme of the drawbacks of a classical German education: 'We were tortured by thousands of pages of grammar, we applied them, and proceeded with magnifying glass and scalpel to [examine] everything from Phidias to Demosthenes, from Pericles to Alexander and above all our dear, great Homer!' The Greeks, however, were not necessary for training German minds after 1870. Everything had been changed by the victories of his father and grandfather.[78]

While the *Grundlagen* purported to rise above mere prejudice, Chamberlain's reply to William's letter contained instances of more routine anti-Semitism: '... you only have to blink and the Semite emerges, or Semitic thought which is its derivative.' The Jews controlled Germany's universities, and Chamberlain felt put upon – 'two thirds of all dons and professors of philosophy in German-speaking countries are Jews or slaves to them.' As elsewhere in Chamberlain's writings there are contradictions. He points out Britain's inferiority to Germany in that only one in 5,000 young men attended a university, as opposed to one in 213 Germans; yet England offered a lesson to Germans: 'During the centuries of its rise not one single Jew was tolerated in the land.'[79]

Of all the anti-Semitic ideas William derived from the Englishman Chamberlain, the one which really went home was the notion that Christ was no Jew. It appealed to his piety, on the one hand, and his dislike of Jews in general on the other. On 16 February 1903 he was eagerly writing to his new correspondent to express the idea that Abraham was not a Jew either, even if he were a Semite.[80] William was not the only convert: two months earlier he had told Chamberlain that almost all the young officers of the brigade of guards were reading his work; indeed, the bulky book went through ten editions before 1912.[81]

XI

William did not believe it was his own fault, that relations had deteriorated between Britain and Germany. He wrote to his uncle at the end of December 1901 to say goodbye to a year which had seen the last of 'dear grandmother and poor mother ...' William wanted to express the community of interests between Britain and Germany at the expense of Britain's Celtic subjects, and Germany's Catholic ones. Britain was

the first world empire since the Roman Empire ... I gladly reciprocate all you say about the relations of our two countries and all our personal ones; they are of the same blood and they have the same creed and they belong to the great Teutonic race which Heaven has intrusted [sic] with the culture of the world . . .

Once again William showed how little he understood the independence of institutions in Britain which were more effectively muzzled on the continent:

The press is awful on both sides, but here it has nothing to say, for I am the sole arbiter and master of German Foreign Policy and the government and country must follow me, even if I have to face the musik [sic]![82]

There was a mild furore over the Prince of Wales's visit to Berlin which was due to coincide with William's forty-third birthday. Because of the press campaign against Britain in Germany, Edward VII told William that it was perhaps better that he did not come. William neglected to answer the letter. Bertie then put his foot down. He would not allow George to leave Britain until he had an assurance from William that no harm would come to him. The ambassador Lascelles broached the matter on the 22nd, the anniversary of Queen Victoria's death, when the German emperor made the extraordinary claim that he had not received his uncle's letter. William was clearly enjoying himself. Belatedly he reassured his uncle that George would be received in a way befitting a close relation; while he told Waters that his uncle had no comprehension of diplomacy.[83]

William was trying a new tack in foreign relations. He thought a reconciliation with France might be on the cards again. On 22 February 1902 Waldersee noted William's enthusiasm in his diary: 'It is . . . beyond doubt that the *revanche* idea has very few fanatical subscribers left.' William was aware however that a gesture might be necessary and that would have meant returning some, if not all, of Lorraine.[84] He wrote to the Tsar too. On 3 January he referred to his fleet as his 'peacemakers' and observed – this was Mahan's teaching again – that the Kuwait incident 'sets in strong relief the enormous advantage of an overwhelming fleet which cuts the approaches from the sea to places that have no means of communication overland, but which we others cannot approach because our fleets are too weak, or without them our transports are at the mercy of the enemy.' The British had established a protectorate over the oil-rich sultanate in 1899.[85]

He wrote again on the 30th. The Tsar's own ADC, Obolenski, was now a part of the imperial retinue. The Russian prince had 'accompanied me through the different functions of my birthday and will be able to tell you what a poor, overworked *Landesvater* has to go through before he is able to sit down quietly for a morsel of food and a cigarette!'[86]

On 16 June 1902 William was in Nuremberg celebrating the jubilee of the Germanic Museum. Being in an old Hohenzollern fief seems to have gone to his head and he 'fancied himself' still Burggrave. That night he had to address a banquet. Bernstorff, who had come up from the consulate in Munich, gained an insight into the way the emperor's speeches were written and how they were disseminated. He had recently caused a storm by speaking a little too freely at Marienburg, and Bülow was anxious to avoid a repetition. William dictated while Bülow wrote. The draft was then handed to Bernstorff to wire to Berlin. He kept it by him as the emperor spoke –

The fact that the Emperor delivered the speech with only the most trifling of alterations is a proof of his phenomenal memory. If the technique of preparation of this Emperor's speeches had always functioned as well as this, much misfortune might have been avoided.[87]

Three days later in Aachen, William made a speech he was proud of, in which he reaffirmed his desire to see a new sort of empire:

Broad and wide flows the river of our science and research, there is no work in the domain of new research, which has not been composed in our language, and no thought springs from science, which has not been tried out here first and been adopted by other nations afterwards; and this is the world empire after which Germany is striving.[88]

Peroration upon peroration issued from the emperor's lips. The following day William spoke again to workers in Krefeld, this time about the navy: 'I am firmly convinced that with every battleship which goes down the slipway, the security and inviolability of peace will grow, and with that the security of your work.'[89]

It was the Tsar's turn to entertain, and William and Nicholas joined up for the naval manoeuvres at Reval from 6 to 8 August. On 2 September he wrote glowingly to the Tsar that 'the souvenir of Reval is still vivid before my eyes'. There had been – apparently – talks which had meant disclosing secret plans of ships. 'The passion for the seas is inborn to us.' The alliance he was cultivating was based on a need to hold Europe in check: '... having decided that peace is to be kept, the world must remain at peace and will be able to enjoy its blessings.' Germany and Russia were 'peace powers' facing 'Christian-hating Jap officers ... In fact it is the coming into reality of the "Yellow Peril" which I depicted some years ago, and for which engraving I was laughed at by the greater mass of the people.' William signed off, 'Admiral of the Atlantic'. He appointed Nicholas to a similar position on the Pacific.[90]

On 4 September William made a speech in Posen. Bismarck's anti-Catholic and anti-Polish policies had destroyed any chance of the Poles acquiescing to Prusso-German rule. There had been a brief respite under the more tolerant Caprivi – who realised that Polish support would be needed to face an unsympathetic Russia – and the Catholic *grand seigneur* Hohenlohe; but with Bülow the Poles had felt a heavy hand again. William was keen to resurrect an independent Poland at the beginning of his reign and the idea occasionally resurfaced before 1914. Bülow would have strongly opposed it. The creation of just such a country during the First World War was, he felt, the greatest mistake made by his successor's administration, possibly including the war itself.[91]

The *Kulturkampf*, 'Germanisation', and extreme Pan-German nationalism inspired by the expansionist Hakata organisation had combined to excite Polish demands for independence in Great Poland, and the other regions in the east where a Polish-speaking population predominated. The centre of the trouble was Posen, where William was building a new administrative district to the west of the city, and a huge, chunky new palace for himself designed by Franz Schwechten, the architect of the Kaiser William Memorial Church in Berlin. The political purpose of the building was clear. He felt an occasional presence might help the Poles to know and maybe even to love their monarch. He toyed with the idea of detaching the areas from Prussia and turning them into a Reichsland on the model of Alsace-Lorraine.

There was little hope of peace with Bülow as chancellor. He had once advocated driving the Poles out, lock, stock and barrel. In 1900 and again in 1906 there were strikes when the Poles refused to send their children to schools where German was taught. Bülow supported the Hakatists' policy of colonisation: buying up the estates of Polish nobles and settling the land with Germans. The chancellor's stance was not uniformly supported in Berlin. As the Austrian ambassador put it: 'It is really unbelievable how openly his actions, and especially his *Polenpolitik*, are attacked in all circles, even among the high ranks of the nobility.'[92]

William made a small attempt to patch things up. He was fighting his old bugbear, disunity, which he realised was the inherent problem about his inheritance.

I regret deeply that some of My subjects seem to have difficulties with our relations. The reason is to be found in two errors: the first is the preservation of your worries about the infringement of your faith. Those people who claim that My Catholic subjects will have difficulties in practising their religion or will be forced to abandon the same, are guilty of a big lie. The entire history of My reign and My speech in Aachen prove how highly I prize religion and the personal relationship between every man and his God, and he defames the descendant [sic] of the Great King, who declared that every one must find salvation in his own way.

The second error comes from adding fuel to the anxiety that racial property will be eliminated through redistribution. This is not true. The kingdom of Prussia brings together several tribes that are proud of their earlier history and their individuality. That in no way prevents them, however, before everything else from being proud Prussians. That is how it should be here! ... Now I recognise only Prussians and I owe it to the work of my Prussian forefathers, to make sure that this province is indissolubly linked with the Prussian Crown and that it will always remain properly Prussian and properly German.[93]

Hildegard von Spitzemberg had a long talk with the former Foreign Minister Marschall von Bieberstein in Istanbul on 24 October. Marschall elaborated the several reasons why he felt the emperor's star was waning at home. The Badenese thought him 'too little king of Prussia and too much the German emperor, of which dignity he has constructed a completely false idea, false constitutionally, false because it doesn't take into account the feelings of the Germans.' He had lost the support of the princes and had been deserted by his Prussian subjects. Marschall blamed his playing with mystical, mediaeval ideas which were either dead or dying and made him look ridiculous or forced a large number of people into hypocrisy. 'For all that the emperor often still enjoys great prestige abroad, mostly by comparison with the miserable weaklings who sit on other thrones.'[94]

Waldersee observed an all-time low in Anglo-German relations on 3 November. *The Times* was at it again, spreading 'systematic hate and mistrust'. The British resented the German fleet and were seething after the German public support for the Boers. Waldersee noted, justifiably, that the French and the Russians were also guilty here. What the British disliked most, however, was the development of German trade.[95] William must have experienced some of this first hand: he was at Sandringham in the second week of the month.

XII

There was a personal blow for William on 22 November 1902. His friend Fritz Krupp was found dead in Essen. He had been spending less and less time at the Villa Hügel and more and more in France and Italy. His favourite retreat was Capri where he had purchased the Grotto of Fra Felice and used it to entertain young men from the island – 'fishermen, barbers and beggars' – who were enrolled into a bogus religious foundation. The order had a rather more earthy vocation, and sadly photographs were taken of orgies which were promptly retailed around Capri.

A scandal was not slow in breaking. The Italian press reported first and word came from Rome to Berlin that Krupp was now *persona non grata*.

Krupp's wife Marga took the story to William who refused to listen. When Krupp himself returned from sleeping it off in London he had his wife committed to a lunatic asylum. That week the *Augsburger Postzeitung* was the first newspaper to copy some of the stories which had been published in Italy. A month later the socialist daily *Vorwärts* took up the issue and printed a series of reports on 'Krupp auf Kapri'. The firm issued a disclaimer: Krupp was simply generous and liked giving money and presents to young men. Three days after the *Vorwärts* article appeared, Krupp asked for a private audience with William, but the meeting never took place. The next day Krupp was found unconscious in his bed. He died the same day from a stroke, but there were rumours of suicide and no autopsy was carried out. William showed solidarity with his friend and attended the funeral, walking alone behind the coffin. He used the occasion to make a speech, accusing the Social Democrats of having killed Krupp and asserting that all those who supported the party were morally inculpated in the crime.[96]

Krupp was never as close to William as Ballin. Where the emperor met the 'Cannon King' twice a year, he saw his Jewish friend from Hamburg a dozen times. Ballin was a port of call in Hamburg and a *sine qua non* when it came to Kiel Week. His conversation amused the emperor and he liked to look over the latest luxury liners produced by Ballin's yard. Ballin derived very little from the relationship and there were few in William's circle who were prepared to speak up for him; possibly only the Naval Cabinet chief, Müller. Ballin certainly kept his eyes open. During the war, when he was effectively held at a distance from his old friend, he wrote, 'We were all too weak toward the Kaiser. No one wished to disturb his childlike, happy optimism, which could shift at once into an almost helpless depression if anyone criticised one of his pet projects.'[97]

XII

On 12 November 1902 Bülow brought the emperor and Holstein together for the one and only occasion they met – a lunch at the Foreign Office. William claims he invited him many times, but on each occasion Holstein refused. As a special privilege he was allowed to come in a frock-coat, while all the other diplomats came in tails. Holstein's excuse was that he did not possess any formal attire. William is supposed to have made a joke at Holstein's expense so that all future invitations were refused. Another source tells us that William turned to his official and said, 'Now Excellency, as I know, you come from the Oderbruch; there are wonderful creek ducks there.' At which point he had turned and talked to someone else.[98]

Soon afterwards William left for England. He had told Nicky the purpose of the trip in a letter of 31 October. He had had an invitation to shoot at Sandringham and was going to tell his uncle that 'we [the Tsar and he] work for the maintenance of peace, and by this for the interests common to the continental natives, who wish to strengthen and develop their commerce and their economical positions.' It was a point of view he reaffirmed in a letter of 22 November. One of the guests at the house party was Joseph Chamberlain, but there were small consolations: Salisbury had stood down as Prime Minister and been replaced by his more sympathetic nephew, Arthur Balfour. Bülow thought matters might begin to improve. Balfour was better 'than his fat uncle whose arrogance and Gallomania made it so difficult for us to get on'.

William stayed at Lowther for the second time for the shooting and the sheep-dog trials from 15 to 18 November. The crown prince had been royally entertained by the 'yellow earl' the year before, but his arrival looked like taking place before the earl had been able to muster all his actors for the welcome on Penrith station. 'Shunt him!' said Lonsdale, and the prince was duly propelled down a side track until the driver of the train received the signal that he could proceed. A smaller house party had been arranged than on William's previous visit. He rode before breakfast, but his appearances excited the locals less: the Kaiser was decidedly less popular since the Boer War, despite his performance at Queen Victoria's funeral. He shot eighty-three rabbits and awarded his host the Hohenzollern Order 1st Class. He spent two uncomfortable days at Sandringham before leaving from Leith on the *Hohenzollern*, after a valedictory lunch with the Liberal politician Lord Rosebery.[99]

The progressive emperor gave a speech at Görlitz on 29 November when he endeavoured to define his age in Kantian terms: 'The new century will be mastered by science and technical concepts, and not like the last, by philosophy. That fits us to a tee. Germany is great in its scientific research, great in its capacity for discipline and organisation. The freedom of the solitary individual and the pressure for individual development, which is inherent to our race, is circumscribed by the subordination to the whole for the benefit of the whole.'[100]

On 11 December William lunched with Daisy Pless, who was cross with him for not coming to the second of her magnificent Silesian mansions, Fürstenstein. His eye was giving him trouble and he could not go to the Hatzfeldts at Trachtenberg to shoot. Daisy had learned some songs to please him and 'I had got a new shooting dress; but it serves me right for being such an idiot. I think he is much fussed about this new tariff bill; he told Zedlitz that if it were not passed he would dissolve parliament. We shall see.'[101]

On 14 January 1903 William wrote again to Tsar Nicholas. He had sent his eldest son to St Petersburg, and explained that his – that is the emperor's – sisters generally called him 'Little Willy' or 'Billy No. 2'.* The crown prince's reputation must have travelled before him: 'should he make any *bévues* you will kindly overlook them.' William was looking for a bride for the prince. His eyes had alighted on the Cumberlands. It would have been a means of reconciling the Hohenzollerns and the Guelphs, who had been dispossessed in 1866. They, however, wanted none of it. There was clearly an important mission concealed behind Prince William's journey: the emperor's manservant 'Father' Schulz had gone with him in order to show the Tsar how to put on his new cuirassier uniform. The sight of secret plans was not enough; William had given his cousin another regiment.[102]

On 29 January, Daisy Pless made a note of the blue velvet and sable she had worn for the emperor's birthday gala at the Opera. 'How I wish I had kept, or could keep, all the love letters I have received ...' When she saw William in Berlin he failed to give her his hand. He was 'terrified of measles ... he contented himself with smiling exaggeratedly from a distance and making ugly faces at me during dinner, which I did not think was very dignified.' If he was unhappy with his English friend, he should have revelled in the present he received from the Sultan. It was the entire first floor of Sassanides Palace from Mschatta in Syria. It ended up on the Museum Island.[103]

William might also have derived some solace from the chance of joint actions in the world after the hopeful precedent established with China. Early in 1903 Germany, Italy and Britain sent a punitive naval force to Venezuela after the government of that country had refused to honour its debts to foreign nationals. William had been nervous at first. It was not clear which way the United States would jump with its Monroe Doctrine, and Prince Henry was making an official visit at the same time. He was still unimpressed by his own naval showing and blamed the Reichstag, which – although it supported the idea of strong-arm tactics – made difficulties over funding William's hotly desired expansion. In Britain co-operation with the German navy brought forth attacks in the Harmsworth press.[104]

The future chancellor Bethmann-Hollweg was of the opinion that William was conducting a strong foreign policy. 'His fundamental idea is to break England's position in the world to Germany's advantage. For

---

* They called William 'Big Brother'.

this he needs a fleet and to have one of these, he needs lots of money, and because only a rich country can give him this, Germany has to become rich. That is the reason why he prefers industry to the detriment of agriculture.' The first Hohenzollern emperor had founded the German Empire with the army; William wanted to use the fleet to raise it to a mercantile and colonial power.[105]

Daisy Pless was still in favour. She was invited to Kiel Week and had a chance to race the latest *Meteor*. She noted the presence of the usual American plutocrats: the Goelets were there, and the Vanderbilts as well as Lady Ormonde, the daughter of the duke of Westminster. 'The Americans will be tumbling over each other to be the first to glow and swell, under the smile of royalty.' She was doing a little soliciting for her husband: 'I hope to see the emperor today; I have lots of things I want to say to him.' She wanted 'Hans' to be made governor of Silesia. At lunch on the *Hohenzollern* William and Dona were 'very charming and markedly so to me'. She was granted liberties rarely bestowed on others and criticised his beer evenings, where William pretended to drink. She had a bone to pick with Bülow, who had described her as a flirt. William thought that appropriate. It was not the same atmosphere when she went out with the ladies: 'I felt as if I were at a quaker meeting'.[106]

William's letter to Nicholas of 19 November 1903 is filled with the usual attempts to push the Slavic autocrat off course. He talked disparagingly of that 'arch-plotter' Ferdinand of Bulgaria before turning his attention to the main theme: the Orient. The Japanese were apparently arming the Chinese. The Japanese were 'sure to arouse Chinese hopes and inflame their hatred against the white races in general and constitute a grave danger to your rear in case you would have to face a Jap adventure on the seashore.'[107] Britain worried him too at the time. In a letter to Bülow written at the end of December he said, 'There is no denying that England is – surreptitiously – working at high pressure to isolate us from without ... we are to be gradually isolated and then clubbed to death.'[108]

Some wry comments were occasioned by Kuno Moltke's elevation to the headship of the historical section of the Great General Staff with the rank of general. Hildegard von Spitzemberg did not have any great faith in the artistic 'Tütü's' capabilities either. The Berliners were already calling it the 'musical section' of the General Staff: 'On the grounds that he would be later promoted to conduct the European Concert'.[109]

William was still dogged by ill-health. His ears were regularly treated with antiseptic or pumps were used to remove pus, even on the *Hohenzollern*. He was so susceptible to colds and flus that he banished people suffering from such ailments from his presence. Earaches continued to bring him low. On 16 November 1903 Waldersee heard the potentially alarming news that William had undergone an operation on the 7th for the removal of a polyp from his throat. His voice had become hoarse. There was always a natural suspicion that he might perish from the same disease as his father. The growth proved benign, and his voice recovered its force by Christmas time. He suffered a minor brainstorm at the time, which was discernible in his writing. For a while there were no 'e's: 'Fhlt dr Dgn! Soll gtrgn wrdn am Ldrkoppl' was an example. William had earned the reputation for callousness when it came to his own father. On the day of his operation, Little Willy used the opportunity to flout a ban and ride in a horse-race. William supposedly placed him under house arrest and stopped his leave.[110]

William was keen to encourage the Danes to take an aggressive stance against the British, and renounce neutrality. He wrote to Nicholas on 8 January 1904 in the hope that he would use his influence on the king – who was his grandfather. In order to put Nicholas in the proper mood, William enclosed some xenophobic cuttings from the British penny dreadfuls.[111] The next day there was more. Tension was mounting before the outbreak of the Russo-Japanese War on 5 February. 'May God grant that everything will come off smoothly and that the Japs may listen to reason; notwithstanding the frantic efforts of the vile press of a certain country, that also seems to have money left to sink it into the Japanese mobilisation abyss.' The Japanese attacked without declaring war, but Nicholas had the advantage of the plans of two cruisers which the British had sold them, and which had fallen into William's hands.[112]

William looked stressed at the Berlin balls. Daisy Pless saw him at one at the Bristol in the Linden. Dona was not with him, she was laid low with varicose veins. 'I do not think the emperor looked at all well, he was so pale.' There was trouble brewing over Daisy's friendship with Little Willy. 'The latest story (which I told him) is that the Empress requested me not to come to court because of him!' William deflated the rumour by seating her next to the crown prince at dinner. William had changed, however: 'The emperor has not been the same to me this winter, he seems shy.'[113]

William's application of pressure on the Tsar was having effects. With a war on his hands Nicholas acceded to William's new Commercial Treaty, which became law in July. On 11 February the *Morning Post* speculated that Bismarck's Reinsurance Treaty had been revived, a sure sign that the British thought the Tsar might well waver and climb into bed with his western neighbour. A helmet from the Alexander Regiment was despatched to Nicholas. Possibly William thought this old symbol of Russo-German co-operation from the time of the Wars of Liberation might help him in his unequal struggle. Prince Frederick Leopold was eventually sent too, as an observer; although his significance was less easy to gauge.

William was worried about internal enemies. Such a lot of kings and queens had suffered violent ends in the past two decades. Bülow tried to calm his fears: 'Emperor William I and the Great King [Frederick] never worried their heads about other people. The Great King had been entirely indifferent to the course Louis XV or Peter III might have adopted, provided he had secured his own ends. His Majesty was of the opinion that times had changed. There were neither socialists nor nihilists in those days to profit by the weakness of rulers.'[114] William left on a cruise on 12 March aboard the Lloyd vessel *König Albert*. His throat was still giving him trouble and a sea trip was thought to be beneficial. He was at Gibraltar on the 18th and Naples on the 24th. Two days later he met up with the Italian king. He wrote to the Tsar on the 29th, bound for Messina: 'What a pity you couldn't be there ...' He wanted Nicholas to push through the negotiations on the Commercial Treaty: 'A promise of a nice picnic in Siberia will I am sure do wonders.'[115]

On the journey south the *König Albert* stopped at Vigo where William had a meeting with King Alfonso XIII at which the Moroccan issue was brought up. France and Spain were currently seeking to divide up the country between themselves. William wired Bülow to tell him the fruits of the discussion. He had told the king: 'We wanted *no territorial acquisitions* there. Open harbours, railway concessions and the import of goods. He was very much put at ease and pleased about it.'[116] William was sowing discord again elsewhere. The Entente Cordiale was signed in April. As terms of the deal were to remain veiled, William tried to convince Nicholas that one of them was that France should not come to Russia's assistance: 'I would of course not have budged a finger to harm her; for that would have been most illogical on the part of the author of the picture "Yellow Peril"!' England, wrote William, was trying to annex Tibet. The German emperor told his Russian colleague that he would make Bertie lay off.[117]

The 'Yellow Peril' was on his mind at Kiel – 'the greatest peril menacing ... Christendom and European civilisation. If the Russians went on giving ground, the yellow race would, in twenty years time, be in Moscow and Posen.' There were prominent British guests: Lonsdale and Uncle Bertie; and Ballin too joined in the talks. On board Dona's yacht, the *Iduna*, William put his ideas on the Japanese and the Chinese to King Edward, aiming his darts at the British-Japanese alliance. The British monarch said 'he could not see it. The Japanese were an intelligent, brave and chivalrous nation, quite as civilised as Europeans, from whom they only differed by the pigmentation of their skin.' William also took the opportunity to quiz Edward about the Entente Cordiale. Bertie told him that it 'was not aimed against Germany. He had not the remotest idea of trying to isolate Germany.'[118]

William's friendship with Lonsdale may have been cooling down through Bülow's influence. The chancellor could not stand the peer, and had spent his time carping at him during their stay at Windsor. Lonsdale had the honour of a nasty remark in Bülow's memoirs. The chancellor referred to him as a 'frivolous' earl who had bleeding hearts and cupid arrows tattooed all over his body, and called him a bankrupt. When the book was published, Lonsdale read it: 'I'm tattooed all over but I can prove to whoever is interested that I do not have a single heart or arrow on my body!' William none the less made him a present of a watch, which was later stolen outside the Gaiety Theatre in London. On the eve of the First World War it was returned to Lady Lonsdale by the thief in person: 'I'm very sorry my lady, but I didn't realise it was his lordship.'[119]

The end was in sight for William's former guru Waldersee. At the close of his life he came back to the idea that the emperor was surrounded by flatterers. In his immediate entourage there were no exceptions 'and it is certain that there is also not *one* who would dare utter a little word that the emperor would take amiss'. The former Staff Chief died on 5 March 1904. His last written words have since become famous: 'I pray to God that I don't need to survive to see what is coming.'[120]

The newly ennobled Müller was on the *Nordlandsreise* in 1904. William popped the question: he wanted him to become one of his ADCs. Müller had mixed feelings about the promotion. His views were different to William's; he did not like the court and thought the rest of the entourage looked down on him as a 'poor officer of modest background'. They might think he was 'pushing in'. It turned out that they were wrong, and the emperor and his circle were very accommodating. He learned his new duties. He had to accompany William on his walks and trips and carry a Mauser in his pocket, as he doubled up as a bodyguard. He had to announce the arrival of William's council, and occasionally send an 'unpolitical greeting or telegram of commiseration' or deliver a verbal message on the part of the emperor to the imperial chancellor or one of his ministers. There were those meals to endure, but Müller denied the existence of a political clout on the part of the ADCs, or that they served to promote one another or their friends.[121]

Another of William's favourites on the journey was Julius Moltke, who shared his master's dislike of Catholics and 'yellow scoundrels'. In Trondheim they visited the yachts of some of his millionaire friends: Goelet, Drexel and Vanderbilt. William harangued Moltke over the manoeuvres: 'I must get a hold on Graf Schlieffen. More and more do I see how difficult it would be to inherit his position. That it should be so is certainly to a great degree Schlieffen's fault.'[122]

The fraternization between the German and Russian rulers continued apace. In August Nicholas asked William to be godfather to the Tsarevitch. The abstemious William sent an engraved goblet with the famous words of Luther:

Ein Glas Branntwein soll Mitternacht nicht schädlich sein . . .	At midnight a glass of brandy does no harm . . .
Im Wein ist Wahrheit nur allein Wer nicht liebt Wein, Weib und Gesang, der bleibt ein Narr sein Leben lang.	Wine is the truth, so pure and limpid Who loves not wine, women and song Remains a fool his whole life long.

They were at their closest then. On 28 August Nicky sent a message: 'Willy need not be anxious at all, he may go fast asleep [sic] at night, for I vouch for it that everything will come perfectly right.'[123]

XV

At the end of October William stepped in with a draft of a secret treaty which had been drawn up by him and Bülow, theoretically unknown to the Foreign Office in the Wilhelmstrasse: 'Let us stand together. Of course the alliance would be purely defensive, exclusively directed against a European aggressor or aggressors, in the form of mutual fire insurance.' It was to be a repeat of the treaty which William had allowed to lapse in 1890. He was translating the draft into English himself because Bülow's was not good and the emperor's French was too clumsy.[124] The treaty – 'to ensure the maintenance of peace in Europe' – would not have affected Russia's current obligations towards France. Nicholas asked whether that meant he could show it to the French, at which William said no. At that point Nicholas began to worry. He had cold feet, was 'weak-kneed' and 'limp' 'with regard to the Gauls'.[125]

William was still directing his wrath at Britain. He encouraged the Tsar to believe that the fishing fleet which his warships had pounded on

Dogger Bank on 21 October had actually concealed Japanese torpedo boats sold to them by the Royal Navy. Britain was Japan's ally after all. It was just one more example of British plots. He thought Nicholas should organise some demonstrations on the Perso-Afghan border to annoy the British and encourage their sense of vulnerability in Afghanistan: 'India's loss is a death stroke [sic] to Great Britain.' There was a war scare in Germany. The magazine *Vanity Fair* had published an article suggesting that the Royal Navy should steam into German harbours and sink its fleet while they still had the chance. 'Night and day Germany prepares for war with England,' it read. William minuted: 'A foul lie!' Believing that Britain controlled its press as effectively as he controlled parts of Germany's, he thought the government was behind the article.[126]

On 7 December William used the British refusal to allow Russian ships to use her coaling-stations to push Nicholas on the treaty again. He was most anxious that the Tsar should withhold his offer from the French until the ink was on the paper. 'Loubet and Delcassé are no doubt experienced statesmen. But they not being princes or emperors I am unable to place them – in a question of confidence like this one – on the same footing as my equal, cousin and friend.' If Nicholas were to tell the French, the offer would be null and void. William was also doing a little work for the German yards, telling Nicholas to buy the replacements for the warships sunk by the Japanese there. By the time William's birthday came round again on 27 January he had been forced to accept defeat on the Russian treaty – 'A wholly negative result after two months of honest work and negotiations.' He was going to try to come to an arrangement 'with the Bulgar ... He is coming for my birthday.'[127]

XVI

The naval race with Britain was a tinderbox. Graf Bernstorff, who served at the London embassy from 1902 to 1906, wrote: 'No one ... did not subscribe to the view that there would be war if the naval programme was maintained.' The British felt German animosity after the Dogger Bank incident. William had thought it a British plot, and had no sympathy either for the fishermen who lost their lives or for British compensation claims. Tirpitz, the Chief of the Naval Staff, had to face Sir Frank Lascelles. William told him: 'He still wants to talk to you about the business! Make the nastiest face you can when he comes and let him really squirm.' The naval rivalry was about to take off again fuelled by superciliousness of this sort. Tirpitz began the great acceleration in 1905 but acceded to pressure to slow down in 1908. Six cruisers were started in 1906.[128]

Further fat was added to the fire by an intemperate speech on 4 February by the Second Civil Lord of the Admiralty and former lecturer at the Woolwich Military Academy, Arthur Lee. Lee repeated the suggestion that the Royal Navy might like to imitate Nelson at Copenhagen, and send Germany's growing fleet down to Davy Jones's locker. The ambassador, Lascelles, was summoned to the Schloss. William was 'beside himself over this English threat'. The upshot was a stubborn call for the planned expansion to be enacted.[129]

Everywhere he went the German emperor faced the problem that despite the legitimacy of his hopes for alliances to secure the peace, no one wanted to deal with him. He had set up a meeting with the French President Loubet in Rome in May, but Loubet did not turn up. Hildegard Spitzemberg, always the first to condemn the man who had sacked her hero Bismarck, thought his tactlessness was at fault: it was grounded in a 'measureless overestimation of his own person, and all the slaps in the face he receives still won't allow him to recognise the fact that it isn't always *veni, vidi, vici.*'[130]

William was again having trouble with critics who increasingly placed their hopes on the crown prince. The Pan-Germans wanted a more forceful, acquisitive policy in the east. The Junkers expressed their dissatisfaction through the Bund der Landwirte, for whom – naturally – Waldersee had had a sneaking admiration. One of William's critics was Bismarck's friend, another Jewish nationalist, 'Paul Liman' or Saul Littmann. In March 1904 Liman published a character study called *Der Kaiser* which ran to many editions. Liman had fallen in with the Pan-Germans. He attacked not only the 'Byzantinism' of the court, but the lack of a tough, warlike stance. Liman wanted to write a different book, one which avoided the tone of those apologies circulated up till then. 'The emperor ... came to power young, before the foaming must could settle as clear wine.' Hildegard Spitzemberg found it all 'sadly true'.[131]

Another who joined in the attack on William's 'Byzantinism' was Graf Ernst zu Reventlow, the former naval officer turned politician and journalist who was later to join the Nazi Party. In 1906 he published *Kaiser Wilhelm II und die Byzantiner*. Like Liman he attacked from the right, using Bismarck as a stick to beat the emperor with. William's desire for flattery was a sickness which stood in marked contrast with the ways of his grandfather. Reventlow did not stop there. He lashed out against the emperor's faith in his divine right, bigotry, hypocrisy, and tastelessness. The author none the less gives some credit where credit was due: William was 'a born orator'.[132] He was also highly impressed by his ability to master difficult technical processes, and his modernity. On the other hand he was 'unwarlike' and squandered money. Reventlow told the story of a state visit by the king of Italy when William had ordered the gilding of the columns of the Brandenburg Gate. The gilt had to be scraped off after Humbert's return to Italy.[133]

XVII

Russia's war had metamorphosed into Russia's revolution. The proposed treaty had gone cold after it became clear that the French knew all about it after all. William wrote to Nicholas on 6 February 1905 to congratulate him on his guard: 'I am glad your soldiers showed themselves reliable and true to their sermon [sic – oath] to the emperor.' William then set about giving his cousin advice on how to reconstruct his country after defeat and revolution. He felt the most talented members of the *zemst-vos* – the district councils created in 1864 – should be co-opted on to the Imperial Council, and that he should steal the march from the workers by generous policy: 'Just like I did in 1890.' Much of this William had learned from his Russian specialist, Theodor Schiemann.[134]

William's motives were apparently sound: 'The emperor regards it as probable that the conclusion of peace after an uninterrupted succession of reverses would entail the loss of Russian military prestige and must involve the ruin of the kind-hearted and sympathetic Tsar, perhaps the fall of the monarchy as well and the transition to a democratic form of government, which in the case of Russia, where only about a fifth of the population is able to read, would be a very different thing from what it is in America.'[135] William continued to lecture his cousin in his letter of 21 February. He should be more of a father to his people. There should be open access to him. Had the Tsar appeared before them, and led his armies, possibly there would have been no bloodshed. William had a habit of letting it slip that he did not believe Russia was in Europe. 'On one point all seem to agree in Europe as by common "consensus" that the Zar [sic] personally is solely responsible for the war; the outbreak, the surprise caused by the sudden attack, the evidence of want of prep-aration is said to be his fault. They say that thousands of families who [sic] have lost their male relatives by the war, or must miss them for long months, lay the blood and their complaints at the steps of the Zar's throne.'[136]

Schiemann, who from 1906 was to become one of the *Nordlandsreise* set and a close friend of William's, brought a certain amount of Baltic thinking to bear on him. There had always been a sizeable German colony in the Baltic States, many of them noblemen and the descendants of the Teutonic Knights who had arrived in the Middle Ages. There was an important mercantile element in the towns and they had their own ancient university at Dorpat or Tartu. In the 1870s and 1880s, however, the Russians had set to work on Russianising the Baltic States, and suppressing German culture. Many Balts left for Germany where they

preached an attitude of aggressive hatred against the Russians. Schiemann was one of these. He had previously worked his magic on
Waldersee and Holstein. Another was General Friedrich von Bernhardi,
whose influential book glorifying war, *Deutschland und der nächste Krieg*
was published in 1912. Bülow thought Schiemann had become too
influential, and tried without success to have him shoved aside. He
dismissed him in a way that was typical. 'In our country', he told William,
'excited Pan-German professors occasionally make silly speeches and
retired officers write fatuous articles.'[137]

After the Russian Revolution of 1905, the authorities in St Petersburg
redoubled their efforts to Russianise the provinces. As many as 50,000
Baltic Germans and many noblemen abandoned their homes and headed
for Germany. Schiemann and the historian Hans Delbrück called for
military intervention to annex the provinces. The normally jingo Harden
thought they were going too far: he saw no excuse for a war to save the
reactionary Baltic barons. Questioned by Schiemann, William reassured
him that he would not leave the Baltic States in the lurch, but he did
nothing about it until his armies overran the region in the First World
War. Any gesture of the sort would hardly have helped him in his
strenuous efforts to woo his cousin in St Petersburg.[138]

Bülow was not much braver about telling William the truth than any
of his other chancellors, Bethmann-Hollweg included. He hated the
naval race, but he never told his emperor that. The chancellor also lived
in terror of William's speeches. As he told his successor, 'I had to use up
a great part of my time and strength clearing up after each gaffe or
indiscretion had taken place.' The language he used – gently tinged with
irony – was that of the consummate courtier. William made a thundering
speech in Bremen on the 23rd: 'I silenced the bayonets and cannons ...
bayonets and cannons need to be maintained sharp and efficient,
however, so that envy and disparaging looks from outside at the construction of our lovely house and garden should not disturb us within.'
'We are the salt of the earth, but we must also prove ourselves worthy
of it.' Which elicited the comment on 27 March, 'Here everyone is still
impressed by the powerful speech Your Majesty made in Bremen. I have
the feeling that Your Majesty has never spoken with greater depth and
force. I read the speech with total admiration.'[139]

XVIII

William undertook the Tangiers mission against his will. It was Holstein's idea, backed by Bülow. They wanted to be rid of Théophile
Delcassé, the virulently anti-German French Foreign Minister who had

been responsible for the Entente Cordiale and who was now rocking the boat in his desire to annex parts of Morocco. The Wilhelmstrasse aimed to put a spoke into the developing Franco-British alliance.[140] As the *Hohenzollern* was in dry dock, Ballin had placed the *Hamburg* at the emperor's disposal for a Mediterranean cruise and he had invited a party of 42 people along. They included Varnbüler, Professor Schiemann and Krupps' man, Admiral Hollmann. William was travelling as a tourist, which made it even more doubtful that he should go ashore as the Foreign Office wanted. The ship left port on 23 March, 'its political purpose somewhat shrouded in mystery'.

That William had extreme reservations about the landing is an understatement. He was nervous of anarchists, as ever. On 28 March he told Bülow that he would send Tattenbach – the ambassador to Lisbon – to check the place out. 'An Englishman had been half-murdered the day before.' He wired Bülow on 29 March that it would not be possible for him to go through the port on foot, and it was below his imperial dignity to ride a donkey: 'To mount a Berber horse without it having been tried out first by an equerry ... is at any rate dangerous because of my left arm.'[141]

In Tangiers, the consul, Richard von Kühlmann, was doing his best to accommodate his emperor. The consulate was empty, the furniture in store. Carpets were pinned to the walls and a light buffet lunch was cobbled together from the kitchens of the other foreign missions. A British secret agent had appeared to offer his services to protect his late queen's grandson. It had been a stormy night and the waters were still choppy. Kühlmann went out to the *Hamburg* to meet William. His parade uniform was drenched by the time he had reached the deck. William showed no inclination to land at all, and thought he had done enough when he pressed a Red Eagle into the hand of his envoy. Kühlmann, however, had a telegram from Bülow which indicated that the story of the visit had already been released to the press. William bit his lip. Kühlmann was told to go ashore and prepare matters then report back. The diplomat told the emperor, 'Your Majesty should not forget that all Africa is looking at you.' William replied, 'We are going to land.'[142]

William was in uniform, carrying a sword. He only managed to descend the ladder with the greatest difficulty and climb aboard the raft which was to take him to the shore. He was 'livid, his face haggard as if he had had a sleepless night'. It was clear to those around that he was frightened of losing face. After a long delay William was virtually carried up the steps on to the dock on 31 March. He was visibly shaking. Once on *terra firma* he was faced with a large crowd of flag-waving Arabs, concealing – or so his security man had told him – a body of Spanish anarchists. He may have exaggerated the dangers. According to a French diplomat who was stationed in Tangiers, there was great excitement among the Arabs when they heard that the 'one-armed Lohengrin' (as he called him) was going to dock in the port and they 'outdid one another in their enthusiasm in decorating the town, adding to the number of triumphal arches and great bunches of flowers'.[143]

William's pallor returned at the sight of the nag. Only with difficulty could he manoeuvre himself into the saddle. As he rode through the streets there were cries and whoops and shots fired into the air while the procession went off to the sound of a military band. No bombs were thrown, but he was hit in the face by a bunch of flowers. The horse was as nervous as predicted, and took fright several times at the flags and 'the spectators, who inspired little trust'. It became distinctly agitated at the sight of some mountain people doing a war dance, and very nearly threw its rider. It was a miracle, thought William, that they arrived at the Sultan's palace. William was on dry land for around two hours. Müller wrote that he was satisfied with the effect and thought it had been a success. Delcassé did indeed fall from grace.

He must have breathed a sigh of relief in Gibraltar where he went aboard HMS *Drake* and was received by the governor. His earlier discomfort was not obvious to the British naval officers who met him then. In June William sent the diplomat Friedrich Rosen to Tangiers to replace Kühlmann, receiving him on Little Willy's wedding day with 'the usual friendliness'. William was still 'extremely sceptical' about the business. Bülow was cheered in Swinemünde as a result of the international prestige which Germany had apparently achieved from William's unscheduled stopover. Uncle Bertie thought it 'the clumsiest bit of diplomacy he ever heard of, and an egregious blunder'; but then he would have done.[144]

XIX

Billy No. 2's marriage to Cecilie or 'Cilli' of Mecklenburg-Schwerin (a Russian on her mother's side) on 6 June provoked another effusion of theoretical statecraft from William to his cousin the Tsar. The letter is moderately revealing. Two themes emerge: you should be a popular monarch and avoid unpopular wars.

Is it compatible with the responsibility of a Ruler to continue to force a whole nation against its declared will to send its sons to be killed by hecatombs only for his sake? Only for his way of conception of national honour? After the people by their behaviour have clearly shown their disapproval of a continuance of a war? Will not in time to come the life and blood of all uselessly sacrificed thousands be laid at the ruler's door, and will he not once be called upon by Him the Ruler and Master of all Kings and men to answer for those who were placed under his control by the creator, who entrusted their welfare to him? National honour is a very good thing in itself, but only in the case that the whole of the Nation *itself* is determined to uphold it with all the means possible.[145]

At the end of the month William sat Julius Moltke down for a talk about the future. His name was already being touted as a successor to Schlieffen who was believed to be too old for the job at the General Staff. Moltke had told Bülow that he was not interested. Bülow and William were agreed that sooner or later Germany would be attacked by Britain. 'It is clear that this war cannot be localised; on the contrary it will lead to widespread European annihilation.' Moltke described his vision of a modern war. It would not be a small, glorious thing, but long drawn out and lasting until the national strength of one of the parties was broken. Even the victor would emerge exhausted.[146]

That year Müller went on the *Nordlandsreise* which travelled up the Norwegian coastline from Bergen to Odda, Balholm and Molde, before returning to Germany. Much has been written about the farces which took place in the course of the morning exercises which were conducted by the emperor in person. Müller quotes his American butcher friend, Armour, who said William was 'like a boy'. Braces were snipped; Admiral Senden-Bibran – evidently a man who worried about premature grey-ness – received the following telegram: 'Sorry cannot deliver hair dye you ordered before beginning of the month.' William told jokes in different dialects; his Saxon was particularly appreciated. Cards were played and newspapers tolerated. A few members of the circle were invited to drink Mosel wine with the emperor – who merely sipped – and were correspondingly called the 'Mosel Club'. The painter Gussfeldt was the president, Müller a 'corresponding member' because he stayed away.

There were edifying lectures on military history delivered by Colonel Gustav von Dickhuth-Harrach and Generalmajor Freiherr von Freytag-Loringhoven, but the long evenings were the worst side of the journeys. There was not enough work for Müller. In Bergen with its German church surrounded by the graves of the former Hanseatic traders, William met the people and made tactless remarks through an inter-preter, which hardly made him popular. He and half his party were entertained to lavish lunches by the consul, Conrad Mohr. Every year William told the merchant that his red wine was better than anything in the imperial cellars. The first year Müller went his neighbour jogged his elbow: 'Watch out, you are about to hear the line about the red wine.'

The other half of the party had to make do with the food at the Hotel Norge, which led Hülsen to quip:

Nur eines macht mir Sorge,	There's one thing that worries me:
Esse ich bei Mohr	Must I eat at Mohr's,
Oder esse ich im Norge.[147]	Or at Norge's – which will it be?

The great success of the *Nordlandsreise* of 1905 was the unscheduled stopover on 24 July in Björkö on the Swedish coast north of Stockholm, opposite the Russian province of Finland. Moltke, who was on board, found the emperor 'secretive and unscrutable' as they moored. Then he revealed his hand. He told them to change into parade uniform: 'In two hours you will stand before the Tsar.' Nicholas had in fact been contacted on board the *Polar Star* on 18 July and convoked for a secret meeting. On the morning of the 25th William wired Bülow, who was having his usual extended summer break on the island of Norderney: 'Treaty just signed by Tsar and me ... Tsar embraced me after signing.' He wrote at greater length the next day:

A work of rapprochement has been crowned by success ... During the past few days I have been thinking so hard that my head is still buzzing to be sure of setting about it aright, to keep the interests of my country before my eyes in equal measure with those of the monarchical principle in general. In the end I raised my hands to the Lord above us all and committed everything to Him ... And in the end I, too, breathed old Dessau's prayer at Kesseldorf ... I then felt wonderfully strengthened ...*

'The Czar embraced me and pressed me close to his heart as if I were his own brother, and kept on gazing at me with grateful, beaming eyes.[148]

After a deal of diplomatic foreplay – no changes in Alsace-Lorraine; the Tsar agreed that Uncle Bertie was a mischief-maker – there had been a dinner party on the *Hohenzollern*, during which the ice was broken. The Tsar did not leave until 3 a.m. The next day they had broached the Dogger Bank incident. Nicholas had said, 'The French behaved like scoundrels to me by order of England. My ally left me in the lurch.' At this William used the Prussian motto *suum quique* – To each his own – and suggested, 'What about having one of those little agreements?' He had the draft treaty in his pocket. They went into a private room where William coaxed Nicholas to put his name to it. According to William's later testimony, Nicholas said, 'That is quite excellent!' To which William responded, 'Should you like to sign it?' 'Yes, I will!' The Tsar told him, 'You are Russia's only real friend in the whole world.' Nicholas

---

* 'Lord God help me, and if you don't want to, at least don't help those rogues, our enemies, but watch over us while we fight. Amen. In Jesus' name, *march*!'

even gave William his word of honour that he would not sign a treaty with Uncle Bertie. William added that he must do something about the internal workings of his country by providing statutes such as Magna Carta and habeas corpus. It was a 'turning point in the history of Europe'; William was 'at last released from the hideous pincers of Gallo-Russia'.[149]

Moltke felt it was almost like a fairy tale. The arrogant Russians were as if transformed by gratitude in that still, lonely, distant spot. Heinrich von Tschirschky, who was also on board, recorded the genuine joy of the Tsar at the treaty and the chance to ensure a peaceful relationship between the two countries. Only a year before Moltke had heard William say, 'You don't attack Russia, it is not a state you declare war on, it is a continent...'[150] To the end of his days William considered it to be his greatest diplomatic achievement, a proof that the world could be run dynastically by talking to cousins in foreign courts, without having to rely on undependable 'pygmies and handmaidens'. William wrote to Nicholas when the *Hohenzollern* docked at Pillau near Königsberg on 27 July:

You were like a dear brother to me. The Alliance for mutual support in the case of need, which we concluded, will be of great use to Russia; as it will restore quiet in the minds of the people and confidence in the maintenance of peace in Europe, and encourage financial circles in foreign countries to place funds in enterprises to open up Russia, its vast stores of wealth yet untouched.

William played with the thought that Japan might be induced to sign a treaty too, which would

cool down English self-assertion and impertinence, as she is her ally too. The 24th of July 1905 is a cornerstone in European politics and turns over a new leaf in the history of the world, which will be a chapter of peace and goodwill among the great powers of the European continent, respecting each other in friendship, confidence and in pursuing the general policy on the lines of a community of interests.

He knew, however, that Japan would not yield any of the 'fruits of their military prowess around a conference table'.[151] In William's mind's eye the treaty was to become the basis of his latest common market: Holland, Belgium, Denmark, Sweden and Norway would attach themselves to a core composed of Russia, Germany, France, Austria and Italy. 'We'll be able to hold all unruly neighbours in order and to impose peace even by force, if there should be a power harebrained enough to wish to disturb it.' One 'European' country was very definitely not welcome. 'To use the metaphor of "marriage" again, "Marianne" must remember that she is wedded to you, and eventually [sic – from time to time] to give a hug or a kiss now and then to me, but not to sneak off into the bedroom of the ever intriguing *touche-à-tout* on the island.'[152]

XX

The problem was that William – and possibly Nicholas – was the only person who felt that the treaty was a triumph. For the diplomats on both sides it was a race against time to kill it. Holstein had been able to locate the draft of the previous year and send it up to Bülow in Norderney on 21 July with the advice to stop His Majesty.[153] They possibly had not reckoned with William's enthusiasm. Bülow worked on the idea of nullifying it by altering its territorial limits. Holstein poured scorn on the document: Russia would not have to attack India in the event of a war between Germany and the United Kingdom! After the Japanese war Russia was far too weak to be of use to Germany. On 4 August Bülow threatened to hand in his resignation. William agreed to change the treaty to make its scope worldwide. After pointing out how much he had done to please his minister, William wrote him some kind words, refusing to let him go.

Do not forget that you staked me *personally against my wish*, in Tangiers on the success of your Moroccan policy ... I went on shore to please you, because the cause of the fatherland demanded it, mounted a strange horse, in spite of my poor horsemanship, owing to my crippled left arm, and the horse was within an ace of costing me *my life that you had staked*. I rode through mobs of Spanish anarchists because you wanted me to and your policy was to profit by it ...[154]

You will no doubt ... let me off describing my state of mind to you. To be treated like that by the best and most intimate friend I have ... has been such a terrible shock to me that I have quite broken down, and have reason to fear a severe attack of nervous prostration ... And in the same breath you imagine you can answer for it to God ... for leaving your emperor and master, to sworn allegiance, who has lavished affection and distinctions on you ... in the lurch? A thing I cannot survive ... The morning after the arrival of your resignation would not find the Kaiser alive ... Think of my poor wife and children.[155]

For the time being Björkö was his one success. Elsewhere William was becoming aware of the failure of his and his government's policies. The Morocco crisis had failed to split the Entente as Bülow predicted and had merely gone to prove Germany's diplomatic isolation. Holstein had believed he could break the ring which was forming around Germany, but it was proving a tough bond to crack. Instead he was forcing Britain into the arms of Germany's enemies. Hildegard von Spitzemberg had called it 'one of the worst defeats of German politics since the dual alliance'. Germany needed powerful friends and only possessed mighty enemies. Staff Chief Schlieffen compared the country to Prussia at the beginning of the Seven Years War, when she was surrounded by countries keen to carve her up and make off with the booty.[156]

Tower, the British consul in Munich, saw William that August: 'The Kaiser's talk is ever of alliances and political combinations, and he gave utterance on the cruise to his cherished idea of being able to effect a combination between Germany, France and Russia, to the exclusion of Great Britain.' William's nervous, jumpy mind had set off in pursuit of a new solution to Germany's apparent problems. He thought about placating the French again. Could Belgium not be annexed and Alsace-Lorraine with its antipathetic population given back to France? Until then the Belgians had always believed the French were their principal enemies in the world; now the situation would change. Bülow had to warn William not to carry on provoking Britain with ideas of this sort. They were worried that Germany was building her fleet to attack them, and once that had been achieved that the Germans would make off with their colonies.[157]

The Russian Revolution had naturally provoked those warmongers who saw a chance of kicking the bear when he was down; or France, while her ally was unprotected. Schlieffen was all for it and Bülow had started out by supporting him. In 1887 he had written a minute stating that Germany should hit Russia so hard that it would take a quarter of a century before she could stand on her feet again. The memo had merited a famous comment from Bismarck: such thoughts should not be committed to paper. William could not be lured into war in 1905. He liked 'big words and warlike gestures, but was frightened of the consequences of an aggressive war on Germany's part, something which complicated the conceptions of his foreign political advisers and disappointed his military ones.'[158]

In early August William was still bathing in the roseate glow of the Björkö Treaty, and it was hardly the moment to talk to him about going to war with Russia. He wrote to Nicky from Wilhelmshöhe on the 22nd and congratulated him on calling the Duma. That 'arch intriguer and mischief-maker' Uncle Bertie had invited the crown prince to England. He was angry because he wanted every German to see the British fleet in the Baltic – where it was exercising at the time – so that they would understand the need to have one of their own. He wrote again two days later from the house his mother had built at Kronberg, where he had gone to help excavate the Roman remains on the Saalburg. 'Today, four weeks ago, "Björkö!",' exulted the German emperor. He was even more pleased to hear that King Edward had tried in vain to see a copy of the treaty.[159]

The mood persisted into the game reserves of Rominten, which lay snug against the Russian border. On 26 September William was still working out who could and who could not join his common market: 'The "continental combine" flanked by America is the sole and only manner to effectively block the way to the whole world becoming John Bull's private property . . .' Three days later William showed that he had an inkling he had failed once again. France was not happy with Nicholas's dalliance with the German emperor. William rebuked him: 'Your ally notoriously left you in the lurch during the whole war, whereas Germany helped you in every way it could without infringing the laws of neutrality.' For the time being he made a last gesture. At the end of the year he sent Jacobi to St Petersburg as his personal emissary to the Tsar.[160]

His anger with Uncle Bertie had not abated. Little Willy had not, in the end, gone to Balmoral. William was not surprised – 'first the father, then the son'. The crown prince received a carved walking stick as a consolation prize. Ballin had reported an interview with the 'notorious' German-Jewish businessman Werner Beit in the City of London. This led to a meeting between Bülow and Beit. The British felt that Germany was itching for war after the Entente Cordiale; which William thought 'rubbish'. Beit said that he had the impression Britain would go to France's aid. The City did not want war: 'it stuck to good relationships with us and didn't bother about the silly jingo press.' Besides press barons Moberly Bell and Harmsworth 'who His Majesty has now made a lord'. Sir John Fisher was also identified as a 'mischief-maker', and William complained that the 'court was terribly anti-German'.[161]

William claimed – possibly accurately – that his projects were dogged by conservatives as much as by anyone else. He was pulled this way and that by his advisers. Bülow and the Foreign Office would have worried the Björkö Treaty to death had it not been for Witte more effectively dishing it in Russia. He declared himself in favour of the Navy League, but Müller told him to disassociate himself from its policies. William was initially pleased with the landslide victory of the British Liberal Party in January 1906, for he believed them to be a force for peace. 'The emperor laid the greatest possible weight on peace with England, more than his occasional outbursts against the Island Kingdom, its monarch and its statesmen would lead one to believe.'[162]

England would not have been far from William's mind at Pless the previous month where he referred to his hostess as 'Daisy', 'my dear child'. Daisy wanted to regale him with some cuttings from the British papers, but Tschirschky warned her against it: 'For God's sake don't show them to the emperor, or goodness knows what he might do!' His English friend enjoyed the power she had over him. He was susceptible to women, as his father had been before him. In March she had obtained an assurance that he would have the sewers in the local Waldenburg cleaned up. That Christmas her father-in-law was made a duke.[163]

William must have been disappointed when Britain launched its first Dreadnought on 10 February 1906. It thereby became clear that they were going to meet the challenge and stay one step ahead of Germany. The British, however, inadvertently made it easier for the Germans to catch up, for the incredible Dreadnought now superseded all other ships and made them practically obsolete, and that went for the Royal Navy too. Strikes were one problem, the conservatives were another. Certainly they resisted the emperor's grandiose projects, as much on grounds of cost as for any other reason. Tirpitz tried to resign as Chief of the Naval Staff on 4 April in protest against the slowing down of the tempo in building warships. It was not just battleships which worried the conservatives. William wanted Berlin Cathedral to be magnificent, yet they grumbled at the expense. They effectively foiled his attempts to build a new opera house on the site of the Etablissement Kroll, opposite the Reichstag.

XXI

It was William's silver wedding on 6 March. Inevitably Daisy Pless attended. 'The Emperor sat up with the two ends of his moustache almost sticking in his eyes, and as I passed, seemed to say: "I allow you the honour of looking at me."' She was in Vienna when William arrived on 6 June. Later, before Kiel Week, William was at his Schloss Urville or 'Urweiler' in Alsace. Bernstorff had received a new mission and had to confer with his emperor. While he was there he became aware that William knew that he often bored his underlings. The two men stopped in front of a sofa. William pointed to it, and referring to his ambassador to London, said, 'Metternich went to sleep here one evening, and fell with his head on the empress's lap while I was reading aloud.' That Dona tolerated these things was unusual. She would not allow pretty women around her. Daisy Pless had already felt the chill wind. This policy was confirmed to her by William's sister, the Duchess of Sparta.[164]

There were radical changes afoot. Heinrich von Tschirschky arrived as the new Foreign Secretary and the communicating door between his office and Holstein's was sealed up. Bülow had set a course to jettison Holstein as a scapegoat for his disastrous Morocco policy. Tschirschky was quite happy about this; he was not going to be dictated to by the 'grey eminence' either. Eulenburg had just received the prestigious Black Eagle. Holstein drew his own conclusions: Eulenburg was back in favour and encouraging William to rule alone. He also thought he had made the government back down over Morocco. He decided the moment had come to go over to the offensive. The first thing he did was to submit his eleventh resignation, on 3 April. Bülow had replied that he wanted to discuss the matter but then suffered a spectacular fainting fit on the floor of the House and was declared unfit for duty. Not knowing what to do, Fürstin Bülow sent the letter on to Tschirschky, who agreed to Holstein's request. It went on to William, who also initialled it and sent Holstein a valedictory Red Eagle on 22 April. No one had ever even countenanced the idea of his going before.

There were also changes at the top level of military appointments in 1906. On 1 April Müller was made head of the Naval Cabinet and in July William appointed a new army Chief of Staff in Julius Moltke. It was not the most popular choice and Moltke was seen as being lazy and bigoted. Waldersee had preferred Hans von Beseler, but noted, as one who had been sacked from the job, that William did not feel he needed a Staff Chief: 'he could do it all by himself with his ADCs'. *Simplicissimus* also commented along these lines. Issue 41 showed William appointing Moltke: 'Now dear Moltke, don't worry! In wartime I am my own Chief of Staff, you will soon master the small amount of peacetime work!'

Moltke did not even want the job, and he imposed conditions which might have had disastrous results: William was not to interfere with the military leadership. He had his foibles: he was a cellist, a painter and a spiritualist; all three of which might have endeared him to William, but his wife was less appealing, in that she was a follower of Rudolf Steiner. In purely military terms the old *Generalstäbler* was able to stop William meddling with the Staff and bring it back up to the position it had enjoyed under his uncle. Later that year Hildegard Spitzemberg had a sleepless night after she heard a rumour that Moltke had been made imperial chancellor.[165] According to Müller, who was at pains to say how little he liked the emperor, William did not interfere unduly in military appointments. He was generally fair. He rarely had his own candidate, but even if he did, he was prepared to support the cabinet chiefs' views, even when they were not too kindly disposed towards his favourites.[166]

William visited Francis Joseph in Vienna at the beginning of June. Their relations were always respectful, although later that year William and Bülow agreed to ignore the Austrian emperor's ruling that Francis Ferdinand's wife might not become empress at his death. The Austrian heir had married Gräfin Sophie Chotek, a Bohemian noblewoman, but not of royal lineage, and the marriage was therefore morganatic. William always went out of his way to make her feel wanted, and sat her next to him when he entertained the couple in Germany.[167] His tolerance did not extend to his wayward subjects, who despite everything he did for them, still refused to resist the blandishments of socialists. In Breslau on 8 September William issued a dark warning to his critics: 'I shall tolerate no pessimists, and whosoever feels himself unable to put his shoulder to the wheel, then he must go, and if he wants, he may seek his fortune in a better land.'[168]

XXII

On 16 October that year there was a moment of light relief with the 'Köpenickiade'. Wilhelm Voigt, an habitual jailbird and sometime cobbler, had adopted the simple expedient of dressing up as a Prussian captain to extort money from the state. Having commandeered a detachment of soldiers in Plötzensee he took them to the working-class district of Köpenick, where he arrested the mayor, telling him he had orders to transfer him to the Neue Wache on the Linden. What he really wanted was a passport, which would allow him to pursue his trade again. Sadly, he had forgotten that the town hall was the wrong place to go. When he found out, he consoled himself with the petty cash. The whole episode pointed out how much Prussian society was subservient to the army. As Voigt told the mayor – who was a reserve lieutenant – if the authorities had really borne him ill-will, they would have sent a lowlier officer than a captain to arrest him.[169]

The next day Holstein wrote, 'I laugh very rarely, but as I took my coffee this morning, just for once I laughed out loud. And for all that it is a serious business.' Hildegard Spitzemberg compared the story to an operetta.[170] The emperor was apparently also amused by the tale. Voigt served only two years of his new sentence, and later went on to become something of a personality, dying rich in Luxembourg in 1922. Two days later William was visiting the cadet school in Bensburg. The Hauptmann von Köpenick might have accounted for his good mood, for he paid for a good deal of chocolate and cake. 'Get as much of it down you as you can,' he told the boys.[171]

The so-called 'encirclement' of Germany began in the new year. France, with its population of 39 million had an army the same size as Germany with nearly 70 million. Many people might have asked themselves the question at the time, who were the militarists, the Germans or the French? The clouds began to disperse, however, for a government anxious to adopt measures to counter pressures from without. First Bülow was successful at the polls. The so-called Hottentot Election of 1907 was named after the uprising in German South-West Africa. It halved the socialist representation in the Reichstag. The chancellor also won support for his colonial policy. In May a proper Colonial Office was set up under Bernhard Dernburg. Even better news came two years later when the Reichstag accepted the Naval Bill with a big majority.

XXIII

In 1907 William purchased the Empress Elisabeth's modest neo-Grecian villa on Corfu, where she had found a fleeting retreat from Francis Joseph and the Viennese court, and kept a bust of her son Rudolf. William had one set up of Sissi herself, which replaced that of Heinrich Heine. It is not known what happened to Rudolf's. William renamed it Achilleion as a tribute to his cult of the hero Achilles. A period at the villa now featured as a fixed part of the imperial year. Unlike the *Nordlandsreise* women could attend, although space was limited: only William, Dona, the Hofmarschall and a few servants could live in. The others found accommodation down the road. There were walks before breakfast, informal visits from the Greek royal family and squadrons from the British Mediterranean Fleet to divert the guests.[172]

William's presence was a mixed blessing for the peasants. They brought him flowers, and were compensated with the bars of soap which the ADCs had to carry about in their pockets. It was not a strenuous regime for the emperor. After breakfast he would sun himself on the terrace looking out towards Corfu Town through the olive groves. He tolerated the occasional report. After a modest lunch, and when there was no dig in progress, the imperial retinue went out in their cars to the extremities of the island equipped with a picnic tea. William liked the chauffeur to drive fast, thereby raising great clouds of dust which blinded the cars behind. This may have helped rid the island of pye-dogs. The Hofmarschall was on hand to compensate any islander who felt aggrieved at the loss of his pet.

From 1911 onwards William became excited about the archaeological digs on the island. The first was begun by the Greek government at Garitza in the suburbs of Corfu Town. Here they unearthed a pre-classical Gorgo figure that was to obsess William for the rest of his life, as well as part of a well-preserved frieze and sundry other figures from the temple. William was so enchanted with the idea of becoming an archaeologist that he equipped himself with a little spade and joined in the work. That meant his entourage had to follow suit. They were less excited about digging for pre-classical remains. One year they came up against the Greek Easter, which would otherwise have meant downing spades for five days. The Greek king, however, gave them a dispensation, allowing the Germans to continue.

On 8 May 1912 the king of Greece gave his permission for new excavations to be undertaken on a site which had been dug over many times and was now covered with brambles. 'His Majesty was delighted about it and had the presumption to exclaim "At last I have [found] something again on which I might concentrate."' And he did. For six to eight hours a day he immersed himself in the work. 'Neither the delicious landscape nor the reports from home interested him.' One day Müller left, claiming work to do at the villa. William turned on the others: 'Does perhaps one of the other gentlemen wish to leave me?' The next day William kept the company waiting for a quarter of an hour while he wired a professor in Berlin. This took place, adds Müller sniffily, while the people of neighbouring Albania were engaged in a bloody civil war. As William told Professor Georg Caro in a self-important way which was all his own: 'Although I am a layman, it is possibly very good that Providence has chosen me to show archaeology new directions.'[73]

Apart from the classical remains William was fascinated by a dance which was performed among the ancient olive trees by the women of the neighbouring village of Gastari. He set his heart on seeing it performed at the opera house in Berlin. In this he was supported ('sadly' said Müller) by his theatre intendant Hülsen. The entertainment *Kerkyra* was the result.

William still had constructive visions for the future in the moments between digs. At Kiel Week in 1907 he invited the French diplomat Raymond Lecomte on board the *Iduna*, which won the race that year. He was happy to expound on his vision of a united Europe: 'The great problems of the future, developing all over the world, called for a United Europe, and there France and Germany would come and go hand in hand ...' He told him that Germany was only prepared to make a *beau geste* in Morocco 'after France had concluded a fixed alliance with Germany'. 'I was now asking for their hand, or, better still, their arm.'[74]

A Sea of Troubles

Holstein's resignation was accepted. It proved a popular move and the press were jubilant. Now he had nothing to lose. It was the moment many must have feared. Even Bismarck had thought Holstein knew too much, and preferred to have him where he could see him, in Berlin. Eulenburg had said that he belonged in a kennel for vicious dogs. Holstein cast his 'hyena eyes' about. They settled on Eulenburg; *he* must have been responsible for the acceptance of his resignation. He wrote to Eulenburg on 1 May: 'I am now free, I need exercise no restraint, and can treat you as one treats a contemptible person with your characteristics.'

The man who distracted himself by firing a revolver on a pistol range was bent on a duel. When Eulenburg refused to rise to the challenge he went to Max Harden, the 'doctor of lethal irony'. Harden did not want to believe his story at first: 'What! You had to be perverted to make a career!' Eulenburg's sexuality did not seem particularly relevant to him at first. Indeed, he wrote to Holstein, 'Our position endangered by a few pansies? With all due respect I cannot support that opinion.' Holstein mentioned the French diplomat Raymond Lecomte, however, and the thought that state security might have been breached was enough to make the journalist sit up.[1]

Holstein was certainly not alone in providing Harden with information. There was once again a suspicion that William's sister, Charlotte of Meiningen, was involved. Many thought it was a well-planned operation on Bülow's part to remove the man who had made his political career and who might, in certain circumstances, have destroyed him. Holstein had found a description of Bülow and Eulenburg's former relations as 'sister-like', and had quickly lodged it in his files. Certainly William believed Bülow had been behind the discrediting of his friend, and not for the best of motives.[2]

The bomb had a slow fuse. It was not for a year that Holstein's campaign began to pay off. The first allusion to the prevalent homosexuality of the Liebenberg circle appeared in *Die Welt am Montag*. In an article entitled 'Die perverse Kamarilla', the newspaper accused Eulenburg and his friends of being responsible for Caprivi's downfall. An open suggestion of perversion was made in *Die Zukunft* on 27 April when Eulenburg was compared to such known homosexuals as Prince Frederick Henry and the Prince of Monaco. On 26 May 1907 Holstein's friend Hildegard Spitzemberg noted that 'Tütü' Moltke had handed in his resignation because of accusations of perversity, and that William's cousin Hohenau would soon follow suit. How long, she wondered, would it be until Eulenburg was uncovered? It was high time, she thought, that His Majesty did something about it. He was himself tarred with the brush.[3]

The crown prince claimed in his memoirs that the most difficult moment he had experienced up to then was having to explain the articles in *Die Zukunft* (which of course he had been reading avidly) and the truth about Eulenburg to his father. As a later commentator has put it, William 'seemed unconscious of the homoerotic basis of his closest friendship'.[4] William's son put it about that the decision to tell him had been his own, but a letter from Tschirschky to Monts of 18 April 1907 might indicate some gentle pushing. The head of the Military Cabinet, Hülsen, had refused. The crown prince was also the puppet of the belligerents, who wanted Eulenburg out of the way: 'Bülow does not wish to open His Majesty's eyes to Phili. Despite the pleas of the crown prince he has refused to warn His Majesty.'

The opportunity came in the course of a visit to the crown prince at the Marmorpalais. The younger man took the emperor for a walk in the garden: 'Never in my life shall I forget my father's despairing, horrified face.' The crown prince maintained – rather less convincingly – that William's 'moral purity' was such that he found the revelations hard to grasp. Of course it might be true that although he had plenty of experience of heterosexual diversity, he had never been exposed to open homosexuality. Even so, that seems unlikely in a world which was still dominated by all-male institutions: schools, universities, barracks and so on. Prince William reaped a reward for his forthrightness. He was cheered in the streets where his father was greeted with joyless silence.[5]

Eulenburg's homosexuality cannot have been that obvious either. He was hardly a 'screaming queen'. His life was outwardly normal. There had been a boy called Schere at school, and the joke ran that the two were 'inseparable' – *Schere* means scissors in German. He had built up a close circle of male friends during his student years, but by no means all of them were homosexual. One of these was Axel von Varnbüler, who knew him inside out, but who – when it came to brass tacks – could not say for certain whether it was true or not, although he suspected it was.

On his engagement to Augusta Sandels Eulenburg wrote to Varnbüler to say that it changed nothing in him: 'I am just as I was, completely calm and not at all silly.'[6]

According to Harden, Eulenburg was 'an unhealthy late romantic visionary'.[7] His friendships with men were conceived as something completely different to the business of marriage and fathering children. They were meant to rise high above ordinary sexuality. Just after the scandal broke he described something of this in a surviving letter to Moltke. The language is convoluted and probably intentionally cloudy –

In the moment when the freshest example of the modern age, a Harden, criticised our nature, stripped our ideal vision, laid bare the form of our thinking and feeling which had been justifiably regarded all our lives as something obvious and natural, in that moment, the modern age, laughing cold-bloodedly, broke our necks ... The new concepts of sensuality and love stamp our nature as weak, even unhealthily weak ... Family, art, friendship and all our ideals were completely divorced from sensuality and from that which we regarded only as dirt, even if it might have ruled us here or there in those reciprocal effects, which describe mankind ...

Sex was probably what he referred to as 'unconscious lapses', when he allowed the purely idealised, romantic love to turn into something less ethereal and downright earthy. The tragedy of Eulenburg was that the prosecution were able to show the sham of his romantic ideals. Instead of a series of beautiful, high-minded, artistic young aristocrats they led in a collection of 'rough trade' – those milkmen like Riedel and fishermen like Ernst who constituted the 'lapses' of the prince, courtier and best friend of the German emperor. After the story broke it emerged that Eulenburg had been 'a seducer of sailor boys' (one crew member on the *Hohenzollern* was deemed to be a part of his *caccia riserbata*) who figured on police files in Oldenburg, Munich – where he had been part of Graf Schack's circle of aesthetes – Starnberg, Stuttgart and Vienna. He had also pimped for friends, sending over obliging squaddies to satisfy their lusts. Holstein was thought to have rumbled Eulenburg and Moltke in a louche Berlin beer-house where they were dressed in sailor suits, and answered to the names of Krause and Hoffmann. When he wanted their undivided loyalty, so the story goes, he only had to say 'Krause' or 'Hoffmann' and he got it.[8]

The more overt homosexuals who were exposed after 1907 were not regular members of the Liebenberg circle: the Frenchman Lecomte, the emperor's cousin Wilhelm Hohenau, or Johannes von Lynar who had been William's 'adviser on matters of old vintages, champagnes, rare brandies and tobacco' and who later did hard labour in Siegburg gaol.[9] Eulenburg's friend Yan von Wendelstadt committed suicide when the

scandal broke. Homosexuality was not the dominant mood at Liebenberg. The men came to hunt by day and play by night. William was
molly-coddled, exposed to an artistic and literary world he craved when
away from the spartan life he had imposed on himself. The farces and
drag acts were never construed as being camp, they merely represented
a form of slapstick best calculated to please the ruler.

There were still those who would have believed that William too was
not immune. Many thought the same as the author of a book of court
tittle-tattle: 'If the charitable surmise is true, then William's faculties of
observation and for judging character and men must be sadly impaired.'
It is true that Eulenburg's sex life was already fuelling gossip as early as
November 1906. He was a 'person no decent *man* will talk to, and to
whose house no one will go! One can guess the reason – it seems horribly
prevalent in Germany,' wrote Daisy Pless. In Vienna the 'Uranus Brethren' claimed William as one of their own. According to one source, they
sent him a letter addressed to 'mon bon frère': 'We have searched the
records of history in order to further substantiate the belief that, like
your great ancestor and his immortal friend, Voltaire, you are one of us.'
'Quite naturally this letter upset the Kaiser.' 'Philanus' disseminated
some choice verses during the Kotze affair but what Daisy Pless said,
Germany was previously uncelebrated for this vice. In Spanish there was
a little jingle: 'En Espana, los caballeros; en Francia e Austria, los
grandes; en Alemania, pocos; en Italia, todos.'[10]

There had been a cooling-off in the relations between William and
Eulenburg. In the end he had proved a good ambassador to Vienna and
made friends with the right people, including Katharina Schratt, the
emperor's actress companion. Eulenburg had been blackmailed by a bath
attendant in 1901–2, and after confessing in his cups to both Holstein
and Hohenlohe he had thought it prudent to make a gradual retreat
from public life. He resigned from the Foreign Office in 1902. 'He was
politically a very gifted man,' wrote a colleague later, 'and at the close
of the century was undoubtedly of great use on more than one occasion
in smoothing matters down.'[11] Blackmail, ill-health and weariness have
been given as the reasons for his resignation.[12] William still came to
Liebenberg, but less and less. Graf Hülsen-Haeseler, who had become
chief of the Military Cabinet in May 1901 and therefore had William's
undivided ear, loathed Eulenburg, and may well have talked him out of
listening to his advice, although Marschall von Bieberstein thought
Eulenburg still leapt in when the opportunity presented itself and partly
blamed him for the Moroccan farce.[13] The last occasion was in 1906.
That same year Germany suffered a diplomatic defeat at the conference

in Algeciras and the nationalist Harden was out for blood and scapegoats. With Holstein's help his eyes fell on Eulenburg.[14]

Harden had named Kuno Moltke in the *Zukunft* articles. The general responded by suing the journalist for libel on 6 June. Harden was probably aware that Moltke was being blackmailed by one Axel Petersen, who claimed to have incriminating information relating to his time as military attaché in Vienna. After hearing some sensational evidence – much of it relating to his friendship with Eulenburg – from his scorned former wife, the court delivered its verdict on Moltke on 29 October. Harden was set free, and the former governor of Berlin was awarded costs. The next day Holstein was triumphant. Schiemann told Axel Varnbüler that William was taking the whole thing very badly. He was 'from time to time terribly sad, occasionally furious, and sometimes despairing!' There were periods when he appeared to be fainting.[15]

On 7 November 1907 another homosexuality trial came up in the high court. Bülow sued Brand, the editor of *Der Eigne*, a homosexual periodical, for accusing the chancellor of unnatural vices. The case cannot have been a strong one. Bülow's 'repugnance at anything in the least unnatural' was his later excuse for not abrogating the law against homosexuality.[16] Eulenburg was called as a witness. The case was thrown out and Brand was sentenced to eighteen months in prison.[17]

Now Harden began to sharpen his knife on Eulenburg. That same month *Die Zukunft* ran a series of articles warning Eulenburg of the consequences were he to use his influence on William again. Through a third party William asked Eulenburg what he was going to do about the charges. Eulenburg responded by asking the state prosecutor in the Uckermark, where he lived, to investigate his private life. Naturally he came up with nothing.[18] The Eulenburg case has a superficial resemblance to the Oscar Wilde trials which rocked late Victorian society. Wilde, however, was not a courtier and he was certainly a better poet than Eulenburg. The *Rosen* and *Skaldenlieder*, despite some 300 editions, have never been realistically compared to *The Picture of Dorian Gray* or *The Importance of Being Earnest*. The Wilde trials caused no political repercussions. The Eulenburg case together with the *Daily Telegraph* affair, which followed closely on its heels, brought down a ministry and altered the way the monarch perceived his role in government.

Bülow claimed that he advised Eulenburg against suing Harden. He had not seen him since he gave evidence in the Brand trial. Others claim that the trial gave him ideas, that it was only at this time that the rumours about Eulenburg, and Graf Hohenau, came to his ears. This was certainly nonsense, as Bülow had alluded to Eulenburg's proclivities in an internal memorandum several years before. He laid a false trail and blamed Max Fürstenberg for poisoning William's mind against his friend.[19] Another who believed that Bülow was pulling the strings was Graf Monts, the ambassador to Rome. That Eulenburg had 'certain tendencies' was not only well known, the press section of the Foreign Office had a file on it. According to him, Harden was also well aware that Bülow was behind the whole scandal as he felt that Eulenburg needed to be destroyed before the other destroyed him.[20] Zedlitz, the court marshal, thought Bülow solely responsible for the whole affair – '... he had personal motives to desire it. If at the time he had induced Eulenburg to stay abroad, there would have been no scandal. Since Caesar Borgia no such dangerous liar has ever lived.'[21]

Harden's case was based on events which had taken place in the 1880s. Even the industrious Berlin police could not come up with anything incriminating after 1888. Eulenburg had either become more cautious or changed his ways; indeed, if Bülow is to be believed, which is not always easy, only two of the 145 witnesses called by the prosecution damaged Eulenburg's case. They were presumably Jakob Ernst and Georg Riedel, therefore hangovers from his Munich days.[22] Riedel had been just nineteen in 1882. Eulenburg had fed him wine in Ernst's boat and then touched him intimately. Later, it was alleged, he tried to make him perform with a third person. Riedel's character made his evidence untrustworthy, but Ernst was much more convincing. A humble Starnberg fisherman, he had made three visits to Liebenberg and received a loan from the Prussian envoy and balladeer to the tune of 12,000 marks. There was no doubting the closeness of Eulenburg's relationship with Ernst. He had spent time alone with him and made a special visit to Starnberg when he learned that Ernst's father was ill with cancer. A third man also came under suspicion of having been Eulenberg's lover: his secretary Karl Kistler. He had been engaged in Bavaria in 1887. He was a good draughtsman and played the piano. Kistler also took Eulenburg out on the lake, sometimes with Ernst.[23]

II

William used the Moltke trial and Harden's acquittal as a pretext to wriggle out of going to England. He was finally persuaded by his entourage to spend from 11 November to 12 December 1907 there, a trip which combined rest with a few official duties. He had put it about that he had a 'complete collapse' although only suffering from a pain in his knee. He was entertained by the Lord Mayor of London at the Guildhall on the 13th, where he assured his audience that peace was 'a goal which would be unswervingly pursued. The most important exercise and the foundation stone of world peace is, however, the maintenance of good relations between our two lands.' Only a few months before he had churlishly observed that Britain was already allied to the rest of Europe; they only wanted to remain free of commitments to Germany.[24]

William may have been flogging a dead horse, but he persisted: 'The simplest solution is an understanding or an alliance with us ... That we are good allies is demonstrated by our relations with Austria.' He spent a 'harmonious' ten days with Bertie at Windsor, during which it was arranged that Edward would make his long-postponed state visit to Berlin in January 1908. When the time came, he cried off. Queen Alexandra was said to be responsible. As a Danish princess she still hated all thought of Prussia and Berlin and had still not forgiven the Hohenzollerns for the war of 1864. William was understandably cross.[25]

One of the guests at the castle was the Speaker of the House of Commons, Hugh Lonsdale's cousin, James Lowther. He reminded William of their days playing together as children at Charlottenburg. He referred to William's performance at the Guildhall: 'In the speech he made on that occasion the Kaiser was profuse in his protestations of his peaceful disposition and aspirations, and I have no doubt that at the moment he was sincere.' William went on to stay at Highcliffe near Bournemouth, a great French gothic fantasy built on the cliffs in around 1830, containing bits of old French masonry and the remains of an earlier, Adam mansion. The house was rather run down, and William took the opportunity to visit acquaintances who lived nearby: the Pembrokes at Wilton; the Malmesburys, whose young son and heir became William's godson; Lord Sturt – whose father had been MP for Dorset – who introduced him to the king's mistress Alice Keppel, whom William liked; and Lord Montagu of Beaulieu. It was there that he accorded an interview with his host Colonel, later Brigadier-General, the Hon. Edward Montagu-Stuart-Wortley, which together with their conversations at the manoeuvres in Alsace at the end of the year, constituted the foundation for the famous *Daily Telegraph* interview.[26]

In the meantime the Prussian government had waded in and ordered a retrial in the Moltke–Harden case. Eulenburg was called as a witness again. For the first, but not the last time, he denied having infringed Article 175 of the Criminal Code which dealt with homosexuality – 'I have never indulged in such filthiness,' he said. It may have been a legal nicety. It was hard to make a case stick under Article 175 if both parties had consented; also judicial authorities assumed that the paragraph applied only to *anal* intercourse, which was not even to every homosexual's taste. Moltke's wife's earlier evidence, however, was shown to be full of holes. On 5 January Moltke's honour was declared 'clean and without a stain'. Harden was sentenced to four months' hard labour.[27]

Harden appealed. His next move was an act of brilliance. A report appeared in the Munich-based *Neue Freie Volkszeitung* claiming that he had received a million marks to keep quiet about Eulenburg.[28] It was written by his friend Anton Städele. Now all he had to do was to launch a libel action against the paper in the much less antipathetic atmosphere of the Bavarian courts. It was here that he called his key witnesses, Riedel and Ernst. The Munich court awarded against Städele.[29]

Bülow reacted quickly. He ordered the arrest of Eulenburg on a charge of perjury, and Liebenberg searched. There they found some homosexual literature, which Eulenburg had inscribed with the name of another courtier in a clumsy attempt to disguise the evidence.[30] Hildegard Spitzemberg thought Eulenburg had it coming to him, not so much for his homosexuality, but because she, like Harden, perceived his political influence as being nefarious. She also credited Eulenburg with Caprivi's dismissal. In this she was probably echoing Holstein's views. Her brother Varnbüler thought on balance that Eulenburg was guilty, and that he would be convicted.

Meanwhile the second Moltke–Harden trial began in Leipzig in May 1908, ending with a reversal of the previous one. A third one followed, with a judgment against Harden, but behind the scenes moves were made to spare him the fine and the costs, which were paid out of government funds. When Eulenburg's trial came up on 29 June, the police were able to offer the court some impressive evidence of his delinquency: no fewer than 144 allegations of improper conduct. In a macabre way the court was impressed by the witnesses: 'about sixty of them including a smattering of aristocrats, but chiefly fishermen and peasants from the Starnbergersee.' His only hope lay in his wife, who had risen magnificently to the occasion and defended him through thick and thin. The scales were falling from William's eyes too. 'Why did he do this to us? Why did he not tell anyone about it?' Varnbüler claimed that William was 'deeply ashamed and disappointed by his friend'.[31]

On 17 July 1908 Eulenburg collapsed and was declared unfit to continue. A bail was imposed and a new trial was fixed for 7 July 1909. That one ended up being transferred to the Charité Hospital, with the defendant giving evidence from his bed. Eventually it was called off. Twice a year until 1919, Eulenburg was examined by the court doctors to see if he was fit enough to continue. He never was and the case was dropped. Bülow thought Eulenburg was guilty; otherwise he would have finished the case. He maintained contact with Harden throughout, but was careful to use that other nationalist Jew, Rathenau, as a go-between. Rathenau had written articles for Harden in the past, and his connection with the journalist prevented him from receiving the Red Eagle 2nd Class to add to the Kronenorden he had been awarded for his work in the colonies.[32]

William disowned Eulenburg once it became clear that he might be guilty. In doing so he was probably listening to Bülow: the chancellor had heard from Harden that William was acquainted with Ernst, who had rowed Eulenburg and him on the Starnberg Lake. William's tough line was encouraged by Hülsen too, whose fatal dance was to punctuate the crisis. It was, in many ways, an unfortunate decision, for whatever he was behind closed doors Eulenburg was a restraining influence on the emperor; his non-military voice had, in its time, counterbalanced the more bellicose noises issuing from the entourage. Some have postulated that with Eulenburg out of the way the personal regime became a military one. Bülow accused a military 'camarilla' of bringing about his downfall too, pointing the finger at Hülsen-Haeseler, Kessel and Plessen in particular.[33] Bülow was the only other 'dove' who had his ear. His influence was shattered and finally destroyed by the *Daily Telegraph* interview in November 1908. From then on Dona and the soldiers ruled the roost.[34]

The bedridden, chronically hypochondriac Eulenburg was taken back to Liebenberg where he died of old age in 1921. After the Great War he, and after his death his wife, published many books relating to his friendship with William, but none of these gave an honest appraisal of the case which brought him low. William, he said, had been 'the greatest disappointment of my life; I had all my hopes in him, and he lived up to none of them.' After the war he begged an important question: 'I am not unhappy that my official career finished twelve years before the war. But I remain tormented by the feeling that if I had still been ambassador to Vienna, the most terrible of struggles might possibly have been avoided.'[35] Apart from an occasional 'poor Phili', William scarcely mentioned Eulenburg after the trial. Only in Doorn did he drop his guard and sometimes defend his friend. One indication of how he felt, however, was the way in which he greeted the news of Holstein's death on 13 June 1909. He called Bülow's cousin, the diplomat Martin Jenisch over to him: 'Stop, I need to embrace you. Just think, old Holstein is dead!'[36]

III

A new fleet crisis was brewing. The ill-will between Britain and Germany reached its peak that winter. On 16 February 1908 William took the unprecedented step of writing to the First Lord of the Admiralty, Lord Tweedmouth, to explain the 'bogey' of the German naval programme. The navy, he said, was 'built for Germany's needs in relation with that country's rapidly growing trade'. By 1912 they would possess thirty to forty ships of the line. 'It is fair to suppose that each nation builds and commissions its navy according to its needs and not only with regard to the programmes of other countries ... [it was] very galling for the Germans to see theirs continually held up as the sole danger and menace to Britain by the whole press of the different contending parties, considering that other countries are building too, and there are even larger fleets than the German.'

William signed off his letter '... by one who is proud to wear the British naval uniform of an Admiral of the Fleet, which was conferred on him by the late Queen of blessed memory'.[37] The letter was not without humour, but it failed to reassure the authorities in Britain. King Edward was furious about William's breach of protocol in not writing to him. Bülow was no less disconcerted. He had only found out about the letter when he had seen furious allusions to it in *The Times*. Hildegard Spitzemberg wondered when he would learn to keep his mouth shut and leave his pen alone.[38] The German naval attaché in London, Captain Coerper, now pointed out that naval rivalry lay at the core of the poor relations between Britain and his country. Trading competition and the Kruger telegram had now paled into insignificance beside it. There was indeed a rage of tub-thumping across the Channel: King Edward's friend Lord Esher, who had been lampooned in the letter, demanded that two ships be built for every German one. The scout leader, Baden-Powell, said the Germans were about to invade. In March 1908 the First Sea Lord, Sir John Fisher, suggested once again that the Royal Navy should fall on the German fleet in its harbour and destroy it, as Nelson had done to the Danes at Copenhagen.[39]

In April William went to Corfu. The Royal Navy still observed the proper form despite the animosity at home. As the *Hohenzollern* came into view HMS *Implacable* and HMS *Formidable* fired a 21-gun salute to honour a British admiral. William knew Mark Kerr, the captain of the *Implacable*, of old, but he was able to confuse his colleague on the *Formidable* with his references to 'dry ships'. He meant it was about time the meeting closed and a glass was raised in the ward room. Kerr visited the island and William came aboard several times. He returned the favour and invited the crew to Achilleion. Kerr later remembered their talks in the smoking room. His 'schemes and dreams ... His great idea was to try and form an alliance between the English speaking and Teutonic races ... "If I were allied to Great Britain alone ... we would force the world to keep the peace."'

They spoke of many things. William expounded on the 'Yellow Peril' and on colonies. He expressed the view that Germany was not interested in colonial expansion: '... it is in the different parts of the British Empire that my merchants make their money.' A long time before he had asked Lord Salisbury where in the world he might have a little colony that would not be in Britain's way. The peer had replied discourteously, 'We don't want you anywhere.' When the Germans tried to gain a foothold in Delgoa Bay, and sent a couple of warships down, they were challenged by the Cape Squadron. 'Go to hell out of it!' [sic] they told the German commander. 'I realised unless I had a Navy sufficiently mighty that even you would have to think a little bit before you told me to "go to hell ..." my commerce would not progress...'[40]

William sat down and drew Kerr a plan of the new German navy as it would look in 1920: 'neither more nor less'. It showed that he planned a force of twenty-two ships of the line and twenty cruisers. Later, he told Kerr that he was welcome to send the paper to Fisher. 'I have kept the peace for over twenty years, and I have no intention of going to war if I can help it ... At present we are conquering the world peacefully.' In gratitude, Captain, later Admiral, Kerr sent William some lectures on British naval history. He also wrote out the duties of a British naval officer according to William's hero, Nelson: listen to orders; honour your king; hate the Frenchman as you would hate the devil. 'This regulation, which in its time was very proper and very reasonable, would be altered today and replaced by another nation. It would be unnecessary [Kerr had crossed the word out with a pencil and substituted 'unwise'] to say which.' William was furious, but the clever Kerr managed to convince him that he had meant the Russians. William was not put off his contacts with the Royal Navy. On the way to Norway that year the *Hohenzollern* ran into the British fleet on manoeuvres. It was only with difficulty that he was dissuaded from inviting the admiral to dinner.[41]

On 6 July William was in Travemünde, about to set off for the *Nordlandsreise*. Ballin reported to him from London that there was no longer a war mood. Four days later William minuted: 'It is mind-boggling [*hirnverbrannter*] nonsense to make out that we want to attack, ambush, or simply "push the English out of the way" out of competitive envy! The only thing we want from them is to be left in peace, in order to expand our trade undisturbed.' William had seen the figures. Britain now had seventy-four ships of the line to Germany's twenty-four. Any idea of a pre-emptive strike was 'lunacy!' 'The German fleet is not directed *against* anyone, not even England!'[42]

There is no denying that they are intriguing and girding against us from every hole and corner. I believe, as I have always done, that England, for financial and economic reasons, would be very loath to decide on war against us. I believe that Russia needs and wants peace. I believe, finally, that France, although it has not even today got over Alsace-Lorraine and the loss of 250 years of *prépondérance légitime* over the continent and has not given up its hope of *revanche*, would hesitate to run the calculated risks of war. But at the same time

I believe that it is in the interests of these powers to make us look nervous and unrestful.

That threat, real or apparent, explained French fortress building, British Dreadnoughts, and the Russians massing their troops on their eastern frontiers.[43]

Ballin had taken it upon himself to lance the boil which had grown up between Britain and Germany. On 20 June he told William of his informal talks with Edward VII's bridge-playing friend Sir Ernest Cassel. Cassel had expressed the king's view that Germany's rapid naval expansion was a threat to England's position at sea. Ballin compared the British attitude to the French humiliation at Fashoda, but he thought he might be able to mastermind a naval agreement for all that. Bülow also urged restraint in a letter to William on 15 July after he had spoken to Ballin himself: 'We cannot at one and the same time have the biggest army and the biggest navy. We cannot afford to engage in a Dreadnought competition with a far healthier England. The disparity between ourselves and England in battleships would probably remain much what it was for a considerable time.' Germany was indeed feeling the pinch. The Reichstag was keeping the fleet on a short leash by holding up funds. That winter it had to be kept in port because of the shortage of coal.[44]

Both sides understood the need for *détente*. King Edward arranged to meet his nephew on the way to Austria and Ischl, and the chancellor Lloyd George used the pretext of discussing social reform to visit Berlin with the journalist Harold Spender. He was entertained by Bethmann-Hollweg at Adlon's restaurant on the Zoo Terraces. Bethmann brought along J. L. Bashford, a British journalist resident in Berlin who did a little work for the German government. William saw the outgoing ambassador, Sir Frank Lascelles, on 11 August. He enjoyed good relations with Lascelles, and permitted himself to utter the line that the British were 'stark, staring mad'. They had entirely forgotten his Guildhall speech. England actually possessed the *three*-power standard. 'It is the navy ... ready to pounce like a tiger.' William was to suffer more of the same in the course of King Edward's visit to Wilhelmshöhe. The Permanent Under Secretary of State at the Foreign Office, Sir Charles Hardinge, tried to exert pressure on William to relent and cancel the arms race to prevent the 'grave apprehension' in England.[45]

William reported the conversation to Bülow. He had told the civil servant what he had always maintained: the fleet was being built to protect Germany's trade. 'If it is to protect trade, why is it always concentrated in Kiel, Wilhelmshaven or the North Sea?' The emperor replied pointedly: Because Germany did not have sufficient colonies or coaling stations, and no Gibraltar or Malta. Hardinge then suggested the fleet should get out and about more. That way it would cause less concern in Britain. William pointed out that he had indeed sent his fleet abroad, and that while the British were conducting their manoeuvres in the North Sea: 'an unmistakable indication of my readiness for peace and my trust in England.'

Hardinge admitted it had been a mistake to start building Dreadnoughts. William reminded him that the press had saluted the first off the line as 'the surest instrument for the annihilation of Germany'. Hardinge thought that an even greater mistake, but he made the point that at the present rate of expansion, Germany could have more Dreadnoughts than Britain by 1912. 'Absolute nonsense. Who told you that nonsense ... I am also an admiral of the English fleet which I know properly. I understand it better than you, a civilian, who knows nothing about it.' If William reported the conversation correctly – it is unlikely that Sir Charles made such grammatical mistakes – Hardinge told him, 'You must stop or build slower.' William was having none of it: 'We shall fight, for it is a question of national honour and dignity.'[46]

According to William, Sir Charles was red in the face. He realised he had overstepped the mark and calmed down. With Uncle Bertie's permission he gave him the Red Eagle. Hardinge was very pleased, and told William that he would treasure the medal. His grandfather had also been awarded one at the Battle of Ligny, where he had served under Wellington as an ordnance officer.[47] William refused to change the programme, even if he had the English authorities told that no further acceleration was planned. Hardinge put his view in a letter to a Berlin journalist: 'The German naval programme is the crux of the whole situation. Until this question is solved, the unrest, now prevalent on [sic] Europe is bound to continue.[48]

In William's account King Edward was far less flustered than his official at Wilhelmshöhe. He none the less went away disappointed with the conversation. William told him that the fleet was there to protect legitimate interests. His uncle replied, 'Quite so, quite so, I perfectly understand, it is your absolute right; I don't for one moment believe you are designing anything against us.' The visit was not exactly a success, and at the end of the year William was enjoying spreading a rumour that the Japanese were about to descend on India. As he minuted against a document during those difficult days, 'The British should be clear about this: war with Germany will mean the loss of India! And their position in the world with it.'[49] King Edward went on to Vienna, where he tried to convince the Austrian emperor to break his alliance with William. In June the following year Edward held discussions with the Tsar and his military advisers about the right method to contain

Germany. A few weeks earlier William had given his forceful view to officers at Döberitz: 'If it proves true that they are trying to encircle Germany, then I can reply to them: just come along, you will find us ready!'[50]

They probably were, but it was all bluff from William's point of view and that tended to frustrate the military men. Many civilians even, men like Professor Schiemann, felt that William should be tougher. Schiemann thought the emperor should merely style himself 'Supreme Warlord' and dispense with his other titles.[51] On 26 March 1909, Zedlitz recorded a talk with Lyncker, the head of the Military Cabinet. Zedlitz spoke of William's poor nerves and how they made him so difficult to deal with. Lyncker replied, 'I agree with you. Moltke is not frightened of the French and the Russians, but he is of the emperor.' Every time Germany had drawn back from the brink of war in the previous twenty-one years, it had been under the influence of William.[52]

IV

Internal problems also confronted William. Despite all his efforts to pose as the symbol of German unity his country was rarely behind him. On 31 August 1908 he spoke in the Catholic city of Münster: 'In the same way as I make no difference between the new and the old parts of my country, I see no difference between my subjects of the Catholic and Protestant churches. Both stand on the soil of Christianity and both make an effort to be loyal citizens and obedient subjects.'[53]

Colonel Stuart-Wortley had attended manoeuvres in Alsace that summer and with the fruits of his long talks with William set about concocting an article which would show the British public that the German emperor had always had their best interests at heart; to correct the 'stupid impressions concerning Your Majesty's feelings towards this country'. As the soldier was not necessarily a dab hand with words, he asked Harold Spender to give him a hand. On 23 September the draft was ready. It was typed on *Daily Telegraph* stationary at the insistence of Lord Burnham, Stuart-Wortley's friend and the newspaper's proprietor, and sent to William at Rominten for his comments. William recognised the words as his own and passed the article to Martin von Rücker-Jenisch with instructions that it was not to go to the Foreign Office but to be sent directly to Jenisch's cousin, the chancellor Bülow, on Norderney.[54]

Bülow was not keen to work during his holidays. He preferred to go for walks along the cliffs with his poodle, Mohrchen.[55] He must have leafed through the article but it is thought that he did not give it more than a cursory look before he countermanded his master's orders and sent it on to Wilhelmstrasse to be proofed, thereby saving 'strength and time'. He neglected to ask the diplomats for advice and the only men who actually read the paper confined themselves to mere technical work. Bülow received the document back from the diplomats Klehmet and Stemrich who had recommended changes in one or two places. They wanted to alter the passage about how unpopular Britain was in Germany. Instead of universal unpopularity, it was made to appear widespread among the middle and working classes. About the proposed concert of powers ready to attack Britain during the Boer War – a slightly doubtful story anyhow – (William: 'I refused point-blank') – a rather bland formula was made up which missed out the lively account of William's dramatic refusal to receive the Boer emissaries.[56]

Much controversial material was left in. The article reported that William's 'large stock of patience is giving out ... You English are mad, mad as March hares ... my heart is set upon peace.' William had said that his large fleet was partly necessary to deal with the Japanese. He spelled out for the first time how he had sent his grandmother tips on how to win the Boer War and finally issued the message: 'Germany is a young and growing empire. She has a worldwide commerce which is rapidly expanding, and to which the legitimate ambition of patriotic Germans refuses to assign any bounds. Germany must have a powerful fleet to protect that commerce and her manifold interests in even the most distant seas.' The message was thought useful enough for transmission to Britain. No one considered the effect this would have within Germany.[57]

Bülow approved the changes and the document was sent back to him. Once again he failed to read it, even if he made out that he had and that the corrections were his. It was then sent on to Rominten with the chancellor's authorisation to publish. When the catastrophe occurred and Stuart-Wortley's interview appeared on 28 October nobody wanted to take the blame. Their responses reveal much about the craven nature of William's court. Tirpitz, who had perused the paper by half-light at Rominten, maintained that he had advised William against publication. Neither Graf Eulenburg nor Müller had seen it, so they could not be accused, but they would surely have stopped its appearance if they had.[58] Bülow resolutely denied having read the interview. He had had problems with the handwriting on the *typed* document: 'I trusted my subordinates and therefore did not personally examine the *Daily Telegraph* manuscript.' Had he done so he would, of course, have advised against its release. He told Bodo von der Knesebeck – who had only recently *échappé belle* in the Eulenburg scandal – 'My first and only thought was to rescue His Majesty the Emperor and bring him safe behind the firing line.'[59]

On 30 October Bülow reported to William on the degree of fall-out over the article. William was to some extent hoisted by his own petard: he was too used to employing newspapers for his own ends. The British press was 'sceptical, critical and grudging'. Lord Roberts and the Foreign Secretary Sir Edward Grey had refused to discuss the matter with the Italians and the Russians. The Japanese were none too pleased. The effect was far worse at home. In Germany the government had been 'severely injured by the interview'. Many Germans were upset to learn that their leaders had passed up the chance of a scrap with the British during the Boer War. One deputy from the right, Liebermann von Sonnenburg, accused William of being 'un-German' and Ballin had to warn him to stay away from Hamburg, where his popularity had dwindled away to nothing.[60] Hildegard Spitzemberg stuck another pin in her wax effigy of the monarch: 'The emperor is ruining our political position and making us into the mockery of the world, and his son has had a patent drawn up for a new sort of cufflink. You pinch yourself – *man fasst sich an den Kopf* – uncertain whether you are not in a lunatic asylum.'[61]

William was still largely unaware what the fuss was about. On 4 November he was reported to be full of himself, with 'not a clue about the outrageous damage he has caused ... hopeless!' Bülow defended himself to his eventual successor, Bethmann-Hollweg, on the 5th: 'I knew no more of the statements of His Majesty in question beforehand than I knew about the letter to Lord Tweedmouth; of the objection raised to the candidature of the American ambassador, Hill;* of the dispatch from Swinemünde to the Prince Regent of Bavaria; of the telegram to the Prince of Lippe; of very many of the speeches, from the Hun Speech of the summer of 1900 down to the Pessimists speech of the manoeuvres of 1906.' It was only once Bethmann had the run of the Wilhelmstrasse that he learned that Bülow always told him something less than the pure truth.[62]

William was slow to take in the implications of his own actions. He sent his minister a cheerful note on the 6th. The next day Harden steamed in, firing his sixteen-inch guns: 'Will the king and emperor abdicate?' Holstein wrote to Bülow on the 7th suggesting it was now the moment to curtail the emperor's powers. The chancellor wrote back, 'I am operating in this sense. I will seek to make it so, that the events that have led to these days require a clarification which will act as a warning that it can go no further.' The press and the Reichstag were after blood. The emperor was cast as an Anglophil ruler to an Anglophobe nation. In some ways the reaction to the interview was surprising. The content was no worse than many of the things William had said in

---

* He had been vetoed because he lacked the wealth required of an American envoy.

the past.[63] On the 8th it was the turn of the liberal journalist Friedrich Naumann to call for help. In the mean time the American magazine *Century* published another interview with the emperor by William Hale – whom William had believed to be a clergyman – in which he had told the reporter how much he hated England and that the Americans and the Germans together should wind up the British Empire after it was inevitably pulled apart by the Indians and Chinese.[64]

The retired Holstein was more livid than ever: 'This situation must cease.' The abdication crisis followed. The princes threatened to stop the emperor themselves if the politicians refused to act. Bülow finally answered his critics in the Reichstag on the 10th. He stressed the unintentional effect which the interview had had in Germany and said that he now had the 'firm conviction that His Majesty will practise restraint, also in private conversations, which is completely indispensable in the interests of political unity and the authority of the Crown. Had this not been the case, then neither I nor any of my successors could have borne the responsibility.' That same day William received Graf Zeppelin to award him the Black Eagle. The arrival of the first airship was 'one of the great moments in the development of human culture'. He was distraught, and was making little sense and incensed that the newspapers had called the count 'the greatest German of the twentieth century'.[65]

Bülow's speech was reported to William at Donaueschingen on the 11th. He burst into tears, calling it judicial murder, with the man who was innocent becoming the victim. William never forgave Bülow for the mess caused by the *Daily Telegraph* interview. Philipp Scheidemann, who was to figure in Prince Max of Baden's government, said William 'hated Bülow ... as the devil hates Holy Water'. The emperor told Graf Friedrich Vitzthun that his chancellor had 'betrayed me at the time of the November Crisis. We stood shoulder to shoulder, and he ought never to have admitted in the Reichstag that he considered my behaviour unconstitutional.' William believed that the whole business had been arranged to damage his self-confidence and to allow Bülow to fill up the space left by the deflating of his master's ego. He felt he was in possession of the facts: Bülow wanted to govern as 'major domo'. In this he was almost certainly mistaken. Bülow was not being Machiavellian over the *Daily Telegraph* affair, just slack.[66]

William still did not let it spoil his hunting. He went to Eckardsau with Francis Ferdinand and shot stags, then stayed with Francis Joseph at Schönbrunn, before travelling on to see Max Fürstenberg. He was in an odd mood. He told Princess Norah Fugger's brother that he needed a bath. Later, at Donaueschingen, she had reason to remark on the peculiarity of his dress: 'The Kaiser in his self-designed hunting garb offered a rather unusual spectacle; he wore a tunic of a mounted chasseur, the heavy gold cords of an adjutant-general on his chest, at the opening of the collar a cross – a combination of the Order of Saint John and that of the Knights of the Teutonic Order – also his own design. No one but he was permitted to wear this cross. His boots, reaching up above the knee, were made of shiny yellow leather and equipped with gold spurs.'[67]

William had gone for the annual fox cull. Fürstenberg bred or bought the foxes to ensure they were there in sufficient numbers to please his All Highest guest. This was no easy matter. That year he notched up 84 of the total bag of 134. His evening dress was as strange as his hunting kit: 'green hunting dress – coat of the Fürstenbergs, black knee-breeches, long stockings and low-cut shoes; below the knee the English Order of the Garter; across his chest the ribbon of the Order of the Black Eagle; round his neck the Spanish Golden Fleece. In his shirt there were sparkling studs, richly set with diamonds, and similar cuff-links. On his fingers he wore a great number of beautiful rings.'

Princess Fugger was impressed by William's 'indefatigable loquacity. He delivered a spontaneous lecture on every subject he came to.' His discourse on wireless telegraphy 'could not have been improved upon by a university professor'. The princess watched him deftly wielding his eating implement. After breakfast he smoked a morning cigar and talked of the Poles: 'And it seemed to me that he did not think much of the Poles.' The south German woman was rather envious of the attention granted to a Gräfin Salm who was enjoying a *tête-à-tête* with the emperor, until she learned that he was lecturing her on Protestantism.[68]

The last straw occurred on the 14th when Graf Hülsen-Haeseler, as part of a series of drag entertainments for His Majesty, appeared in one of the princess's bright-coloured ballgowns complete with feathered hat and fan and did a flirtatious little dance to the music as he had done several times before. He was expressing a desire to distract the emperor in his misery. He cavorted around for a while, blowing kisses, then disappeared out of a side door amid great applause. Once he had left the room he stumbled noisily and died of a heart attack. The worst of it, reported a witness, was that the music continued while the doctor present certified the general's decease. William was stupefied. He suffered a nervous collapse which gave rise to a severe depression, and remained confused for weeks.[69]

He returned to Potsdam on the 16th. At his meeting with Bülow the following day he reluctantly agreed to the measures the chancellor proposed and signed a guarantee that he would cause no further trouble. Almost immediately he felt he had been humiliated. On the 21st there was Hülsen's funeral. William gave the impression of a broken man and was greeted by silence in the Berlin streets. He appeared to rally in his

Rathaus speech when he talked of 'rising clouds that will never cast a shadow to divide my people from me!' But for once the speech was all Bülow's work, and to make sure he toed the line, the chancellor handed it to him page by page.[70]

Very soon he changed his mind and again accused Bülow of betraying him and denying him before the Reichstag. It was all for nothing anyhow; only a new chancellor could have won such a guarantee. William had a proper mental collapse on the 22nd. For a while Prince William took over his father's functions. The emperor briefly even considered abdicating, but the princes had forgotten their protest and William eventually took it as a sign that they were happy with him after all. It is often said that the *Daily Telegraph* interview marked the end of the personal-rule phase in William's life, when he had been determined to be his own Bismarck; but there were plenty of other moments before 1914 when he made a move entirely on his own authority. On the other hand William's advisers, and his military retinue in particular, came more to the fore after 1908, 'while the emperor's own voice grew softer and softer'.[71]

The crown prince caught a whiff of power. In a fairly suspicious account, Bülow said he was reminded of Shakespeare's *Henry V* when Hal finds his father's crown and tries it on for size.* Prince William was itching to succeed. The prince asked the chancellor whether his father was still capable of reigning, or whether he should step down for a while. It was a situation all too familiar in recent Hohenzollern history. Bülow claimed that he reassured him, and that the prince left with a 'somewhat disappointed mien'. After that the chancellor made sure he saw no sensitive papers. Maybe Bülow cooked up the story later because he believed the crown prince had a hand in his dismissal, but others reported the growing strength of Little Willy's fronde. If he did cause the chancellor's fall from grace he would regret it: Bethmann-Hollweg was to give him a bellyful of grievances.[72]

v

While the *Daily Telegraph* interview had provoked a crisis which brought William to the brink of abdication, things had been happening on the international stage. The Austrian annexation of Bosnia and Herzegovina on 7 October that year once again brought the word 'war' to people's lips. Given the international situation and the problems with Britain, William was embarrassed about Austria's desires to expand in the Balkans. The General Staff was ready, as general staffs are supposed to

* Actually *Henry IV, Part Two*, iv.v.

be, for any reaction by the Russians who protected Slavic interests in the region. The following day there had been a revolt on the island of Crete, where the Greek-speaking population had rejected Turkish rule and declared themselves to be part of the motherland.

In October William cut Bülow dead at the Neues Palais. For the time being the chancellor stayed in power as a result of the advice of members of his entourage, and chief among them Dona, who was assuming an ever greater influence over her husband. The crisis had altered his appearance. In December that year Bernstorff came to see him before taking up his post as ambassador to Washington. 'You are much too young for an ambassador; your hair is not yet grey. Just look at me.' At this point Dona interjected: 'But Wilhelm, it is only in the last few weeks that your hair has grown so grey.'[73]

Daisy Pless was with Princess 'Mossy' – Margaret of Hesse – on 8 December. William's sister dwelled on his contradictory character. England, she said, was the only place she could breathe: 'I feel in his secret heart the emperor feels the same thing too though he fights against it; in his heart he is English but, politically, he is against us [sic]. I think he simply plays up to what he thinks are the feelings of his people … he has his country's best interests at heart, he works for her good; he means well … he will die of men the most disappointed, broken in spirit or in health – that is, if he doesn't lose his sanity and kill himself.' There was sympathy for William in certain quarters that winter. Some people remarked genuine suffering on his part. He put on a good show for his birthday.[74]

William took up his pen and wrote to Tsar Nicholas again on 8 January 1909. Germany had had no advance warning of the Austrian annexation of Bosnia-Herzegovina which had caused so much anger in St Petersburg. He thought it was worth trying to achieve an alliance again: 'I am even more firmly convinced than ever, that Germany and Russia should be as firmly united as possible; their union would form a powerful stronghold for the maintenance of peace and of monarchical institutions.' He reassured Nicholas about his ally. 'We here at any rate have not the slightest doubt that Austria is not going to *attack Serbia*', but he added that small states were an 'awful nuisance', 'quantités negligeables'.[75]

In the second week of February 1909 Uncle Bertie at last consented to make a state visit to Germany, eight years after ascending the throne as Edward VII. William informed him of the Franco-German accord over Morocco: 'I hope this agreement will be a stepping-stone to a better understanding between the two countries.' Edward nodded his head: 'May that be so!'[76] On the 9th William raised his glass to his uncle and saw the visit as 'a new guarantee for the further peaceful and friendly development of relations between our two countries'. 'I know', he said, 'how much our wishes for the maintenance of security of the peace tally.' Later King Edward wrote to William to express the view that he found the storm of anti-German abuse directed at the improvement of the German fleet in the British press 'ridiculous'.[77]

By his own admission, William cooled down his relations with Bülow and decided to deal with him only as much as business required. He was looking for a victim. Fingers pointed at Bülow, the person who had caused him so much heartache over the *Daily Telegraph* affair, telling the emperor that the chancellor had stage-managed the whole thing in order to clip his wings. The chief conspirators were a group of 'Kaisertreuen' around Kiderlen. They numbered the eternal plotter Elard von Old-enburg-Januschau and included a retired diplomat called Rudolf Martin who had been sacked by Bülow. Martin published a long indictment of the chancellor on 1 March called *'Fürst Bülow und Kaiser Wilhelm II*: 'The power of Fürst Bülow appears great, but in reality it is eaten-away and rotten. Fürst Bülow will never enjoy the trust of the emperor again.' Bülow's fate was sealed by the collapse of the 'Bülow Bloc' in the Reichstag. He was now expendable. It was finally possible for the 'Kaiser-treuen' to form an alliance with the Centre to bring the chancellor down.[78]

On 11 March the chancellor had requested an audience with his sovereign. It took place in the gallery of the Schloss 'among the portraits of my ancestors, the battles of the Seven Years War and the proclamation of the empire at Versailles ...'[79] The talk did Bülow some service: he remained a few more months in office. William agreed to eat with the Bülows in a gesture designed to reassure those who believed his end was nigh. The final act began in the garden of the imperial chancellor's palace. William had regained his self-confidence and wanted Bülow to say 'Pater peccavi'. Bülow pretended he could no longer recall the finer details of the affair. William was almost certainly already convinced that he would have to go, but not before he had put through the reform of inheritance tax, another levy, like that on German sparkling wine, which was to finance the navy. He wanted to humiliate Bülow as the chancellor had humbled him. The wheel had come full circle: 'The innocent monarch forgave the guilty chancellor.' 'I have had enough of Bülow,' William told Ballin at that time.

The Balkan fuse fizzled out again. On 3 April William wrote to Nicholas to thank him for not jumping in to protect Serbia: 'Europe has been spared the horrors of a universal war.' For his part he was off to Corfu, that 'paradise on earth' where there were 'no tourists' and which was 'easily reached from the sea direct'. On the way the *Hohenzollern* stopped in Venice where William had an interview with his ambassador,

Graf Monts. He told the count to put himself in readiness to become chancellor in succession to Bülow. Monts felt the time had come to make it up with the British. William thought the ratio of battleships should be three German ships to four of theirs; Monts told him it ought to be one to three. William, it seems, agreed. The next day Monts ran into Bülow in St Mark's Square. The chancellor informed him that William and he had made it up.[80]

On 20 April William saw King George of the Hellenes and told him not to think about going to war with Turkey over Crete. William was worried about his own interests in Asia Minor. He was once again convinced that Uncle Bertie was playing a shabby role in things, trying to spoil his relations with the Sultan. Bülow tried to soothe the situation by conferring with Hardinge. The mention of the Permanent Secretary's name did nothing for William's nerves and he immediately accused Britain of being high-handed again, when his dignity required him being treated as an equal. He eventually changed his mind about the Cretan business, and told the Turks that they would have to accept the loss of the island.[81]

He wrote again to Nicholas from Achilleion on 8 May. A revolution had broken out in Istanbul and shattered his tranquillity – 'We poor rulers it seems are not entitled to holidays like other simple mortals.' He was none the less enjoying the 'marble terraces in the shade of the fine palm trees'. He praised an 'excursion par automobile, tea, picnics in the country, quite delightful'. He returned two days later, stopping at Malta and Brindisi before he reached the north coast of the Adriatic where he met King Humbert at Pola.[82]

The chancellor's last act had begun. On 27 June Bülow was at Kiel on board the yacht of the Prince of Monaco together with William and the French chocolate king, Meunier. They talked about his successor. The day came soon after. The Reichstag rejected the inheritance tax and Bülow lost his *raison d'être*. The denouement took place in the small garden of the Berlin Schloss on 14 July. William kissed and hugged the outgoing chancellor on whom he had set his hopes. Later he showed a picture of the place to the king of Württemberg: 'That's where I drove the brute away!' he said.[83]

Bethmann-Hollweg

With the benefit of hindsight and fuelled by gall, Bülow claimed that in the course of his final interview in the Schlossgarten he had advised William against calling Theodor Bethmann-Hollweg and that such a minister would not have been able to stave off war. It is a testament to how prone William's fourth chancellor was to lies, that he had himself put Bethmann forward. There had been much speculation as to whom the emperor would appoint. Some said Tirpitz had been his first choice, but that he was worried about how he would go down in Britain. William had expressed a desire to appoint Prince Lichnowsky, his recently des-patched ambassador to London. He had also come close to taking on Monts, but Bülow naturally advised against this, as did the Civil Cabinet chief Valentini, who pointed out that the ambassador was a poor public speaker.[1]

William thought he could trust Bethmann-Hollweg in such a way that no one would have trusted Bülow. In that he was right. Bethmann was both upright and honest. He had known him for years, and sought advice from Theodor's father Felix long before the son ever offered him counsel. Their first meeting was during manoeuvres in 1877, when William was obliged to borrow clothes from his tall future chancellor as he had nothing to wear for dinner. His tailcoat was so immense that it hung like an overcoat on the prince.[2] Bethmann was not an altogether popular choice. There was something of the professor about him. He 'tended to put others down' and in a 'schoolmasterly way' lecture those who resisted his own conclusions.[3] After the war William was not alone in making Bethmann into a scapegoat for his own mistakes. He was a 'pacifist', but William acknowledged that his 'aims entirely accorded with my policy'. He prepared for audiences minutely, but despite all the work he put into them, he 'made mistake after mistake'.[4]

The new chancellor faced a well-entrenched war party which accepted the Bismarckian–Bonapartist view that a successful conflict was the only means of fighting the enemy within and restoring the prestige of the monarchy. War would end the call for reform, above all for Prussia's unjust three-tier voting system; and it was best fought while Germany still had the upper hand. The crown prince was a critic of Bethmann from the start. Later he extended his contempt to Kiderlen, Jagow and the head of the Civil Cabinet, Valentini. It was thought best to bundle Prince William off to the provinces. Instead of the Garde du Corps, he was given command of the Leibhusaren in Danzig-Langfuhr.[5]

II

The new chancellor had inherited a terrible foreign outlook. Powerful alliances faced Germany and the initiative to conclude a pact with Britain had been lost. Bethmann was slow and ponderous. Ballin called him 'Bülow's revenge'. The shipping magnate had had further talks with Sir Ernest Cassel at the latter's palatial Brook House on Park Lane. Cassel had told him that any understanding was now impossible: both the French and the Austrians were building ships. Cassel touched the root of the problem: 'Under the rule of Emperor William II, with a consciousness of goals which cannot be more highly praised, Germany has been taken into the world market and Germany's industry and merchant marine have developed to a previously unimaginable flowering [while] England has suffered immense losses in overseas trade. English trade is receding and it is undoubted that in the long run England will not be in a position to maintain free trade.'[6]

A second discussion between Cassel and Ballin exposed Cassel's view that the liberals were at fault. With their obsession with social questions, they had neglected the fleet. The British aggression towards Germany was the result. He suggested that further talks be held. William consulted Tirpitz, who thought the moment propitious: Britain was technically and financially behind. Bethmann was left with the job of organising things. He saw the fleet as no more than a bargaining counter designed to win concessions from Britain. He set his sights on taking Britain out of its alliance with France and Russia.[7]

Bethmann's appointment brought with it certain changes to the ministry. The man who took over religion and education was August von Trott zu Solz, whose career had been promoted by Bethmann-Hollweg from the outset. He was to prove William's most outstanding education minister.[8] It was Trott who, together with Friedrich Althoff, hit upon the idea of creating a 'German Oxford' in the Berlin suburb of Dahlem to celebrate the first centenary of Berlin University. This Kaiser-Wilhelms-Gesellschaft, as it was named, was a scientific academy of the first water, with departments teaching biochemistry, physical chemistry, biology, anthropology, cell physics and silicate research.[9]

The usual honeymoon period with his new chancellor passed quietly. At manoeuvres that year not only was William's old friend Lonsdale present, but so were General Sir Bruce Hamilton and Winston Churchill. Only in January did William almost conspire to cause an international incident when he slapped the 'long-nosed Ferdinand of Bulgaria on his postern gate'. The monarch was so furious that he left Germany at once and showed his anger once more when he ordered his new munitions, not from Krupp, but from a French firm instead.[10]

III

Germany continued its spectacular growth. Between 1900 and 1910 births rose to 866,000; the population of the country had grown by a third since 1870. Coal production rose by 218.1 per cent (in the United Kingdom it was 72 per cent), steel by 1,335 per cent, where Britain could muster a paltry 154 by comparison. In iron manufacture Germany's chief commercial rival lagged 50 per cent behind her. Germany had already offloaded capital abroad: German investments in French mines and steel works amounted to between 10 and 15 per cent, and Antwerp was already being called a 'half-German city'.[11] It was hardly surprising that the country talked of *Lebensraum*. The number of Britons had also increased, from 26 to 40 million in the forty years from 1870 to 1910, but they had the Empire on which the sun never set.

Its titular head, the 'encircler' – as his nephew called him – Edward VII died on 6 May 1910. Once again William dropped everything and went to London. Once again the British royal family was there to meet him at the station. He was taken to Westminster Hall on the 19th to see the body of his late, and not greatly beloved, uncle lying in state: 'The coffin was guarded by household cavalry, soldiers of the line and men from Indian and Colonial contingents, all in the characteristic pose of mourning, that is with bowed heads with their hands crossed over the rifle butts and the hilts of their swords ...' William stood by the bier holding George's hand. He was impressed by the way the light played with the gemstones on the coffin while the public trooped past the dead king and by the 'wonderful mediaeval setting for such a deeply moving scene'. At the funeral the two field marshals, William and Connaught, rode left and right of the king. William was chuffed to see that cousin Georgie was still only a lieutenant-general. The turnout was impressive, and the women cried. While he was in London William had a chance to talk to Cassel and President Roosevelt.[12]

William wrote to Bethmann from Windsor. The memories were bitter-sweet as he went through those same old rooms, 'where I played as a child, tarried as a youth and later as a man and ruler enjoyed the hospitality of Her Late Highness the Great Queen. [Memories] reawakened my old feelings of being at home ... which, a personal perspective of the political events of the last few years, has rendered it particularly hard to take. I am proud to call this place my second home-land and to be a member of its royal family.' In the streets William's appearance once again kindled a short-lived burst of popularity in Britain. 'Three cheers for the German emperor', the people cried; and William thought it a particularly good omen.[13]

Edward's death should have improved Germany's relations with Britain. While he lived there was little hope and much antagonism. Bertie was not above making quite personal remarks about William's deformities, which must have got back to him. William I. R., he quipped, 'Immer Reisefertig' – Always ready to travel, which was a little like the pot calling the kettle black. William described his uncle as 'Satan'. His epitaph was tinged with gall: 'An outstanding political personality suddenly disappears from the European stage leaving notable gaps. In such moments one forgets much. I believe on the whole there will be more tranquillity in European politics. If nothing else, that would be an advantage. Where the fires will no longer be poked, they will burn less strongly. His people will mourn Edward VII the most; besides them, Gauls and Jews.'[14]

William would have known King George not only from his visits to Windsor but also from the time in 1890 when he was attached to the First Foot Guards in Potsdam. Unlike his father and grandmother, his cousin 'spoke remarkably little German'; or any other language, apparently. William compared him to an 'English country gentleman without political interests ... whose sketchy linguistic abilities will incline him towards staying at home'. He thought that Britain's foreign policy would weaken and they would seek to become closer to Germany – 'but we shall not sell ourselves cheaply'. He was furious when the Russian Foreign Minister paid a call on King George: 'The swine Sazonov'.[15]

On 11 September Daisy Pless commented on the speech William had recently made in Königsberg which reaffirmed his belief in his divine right to rule: 'I see Myself as an instrument of the Lord. Without regard for the views or opinions of the day I go My way, which means the whole and sole well-being and peaceful development of our fatherland.' Like many other people who knew him, Fürstin Pless thought William a consummate actor, but one whose lines occasionally ran away with him: '... he *is* a constitutional monarch ... and the country is not ruled by him personally, but by the government. Well, he has the worst luck of any man living in that he is always in the glare of the world's footlights. He is much too much of an artist to come forward on the stage and

merely recite the words he has been told to speak, he must add the
expression of his own personal views, must dramatise himself ...' William's vanity was something else which Daisy Pless took pains to stress.
That winter he appeared at a shoot – probably at Donaueschingen –
wearing his yellow boots, gold spurs and real birds in his hat. 'Poor man,
he means so awfully well, and everything he does is intended for the
best, and still he is so completely destitute of tact that everything turns
out exactly opposite to what he intends.'[16]

In November 1910 the Tsar visited William in Potsdam. Bethmann
and Kiderlen took the passionate huntsman out in the forest, using the
opportunity to have a promising discussion with the Russian ruler. The
frustrations continued when it came to Britain. The British were not
prepared to provide anything more than a few scraps from their table
and the purpose of these even, as far as William could see, was only to
achieve a guarantee that Germany would stop, or decelerate, its shipbuilding programme. In March 1911 William minuted that this was no
longer possible, and he went so far as to say that if they had halted, as
Metternich and Bülow had advocated, four or five years earlier, there
would already have been a 'Copenhagen' war.[17]

IV

William went to Corfu in April and was alarmed at the sight of a British
naval annual which contained a picture of the German fleet over the
legend 'the enemy'. He complained bitterly to Vice Admiral of the
Fleet Sir Colin Keppel.[18] He wrote to the Tsar about the continuing
archaeological digs. Under the bramble bushes they had found the
remains of a wooden temple dating from the seventh or sixth century
BC, dedicated to the gorgon. William could forget the insult, and dig
with his little spade. Later he described as 'unforgettable, those hours
of tension' spent rescuing the treasures of the temple from the earth.
He had also spent several days 'baskin' (sic) in the sun. Rulers did have
holidays after all.[19]

Ballin had been over to see Cassel again soon after Uncle Bertie's
death and was congratulated on all sides by politicians over William's
appearance at the funeral and what a good impression that had made.[20]
William, the showman, performed well on such occasions. At the beginning of 1911 King George had invited William to Britain to take part
in the unveiling of the statue of Queen Victoria in front of Buckingham
Palace. William went on the *Hohenzollern*, accompanied by Dona and
Victoria Louise, arriving on 11 May and staying for just over a week. He
found the time to hold talks with the Minister of War Lord Haldane,

although they seem to have been of an unpolitical nature. Once again he made a strong impression on the London crowds. Ballin reported that he was 'today one of the most popular personalities in England', something which made the moment propitious for reaching an understanding. The *Panther* business put a stop to that.[21]

That summer William was thinking about the meaning of war. 'You would not consider it', he told Müller, 'if all your sons had to go off to the front.' 'War is not the greatest evil,' replied the Naval Cabinet chief.[22] War did not seem very far away. On 26 June Kiderlen noted laconically: 'Ship approved.' On 1 July 1911 a German warship sailed into the harbour at Agadir, allegedly to protect German interests in the southern half of Morocco, which was in fact about to fall to France. This show of force had been the Foreign Secretary's idea but he had clearly not thought the action through and the cool-headed Müller once again tells us he was not in favour. France and Britain were both taken by surprise, and German public opinion was delighted. The German ambassador in Paris demanded the Congo as compensation for the French protectorate in Morocco. William's interests in French Africa were faintly stirred before he went cold on the subject. Opinions vary as to whether William was happy about sending the *Panther* or not.[23]

William's popularity in Britain had been dissipated once again. He did not attend the coronation on 22 June, sending Little Willy and his wife instead. On 21 July the British chancellor Lloyd George made a warlike speech at the Mansion House in the City of London in reaction to the *Panther* incident. William was on his *Nordlandsreise* and heard about it when he stopped to recoal in Bergen. As war rumours went round the royal yacht he began to feel distinctly cold feet and imagined that Britain was about to fall upon Germany. He sought out Kiderlen, who was one of the *Stammgäste* on the Northern cruises. Kiderlen backed down. He said that Morocco would not suit German settlers and that Britain would side with France in any resulting war; and in that event Germany's allies were more or less worthless. 'His Majesty was very quiet, but agreed.' His lack of support exasperated the Foreign Office and Kiderlen threatened to resign. Any other solution than war would have been a defeat, thought the Foreign Minister. Tirpitz later compared the Morocco policy to the Punctuation of Olmütz of 1850, when Prussia was rudely humiliated by Austria for the last time before Bismarck turned the historical tables.[24]

Reventlow pointed out that neither the emperor nor his chancellor had been in favour of war. When the *Hohenzollern* docked at Swinemünde at the end of July, Bethmann was there to meet the emperor off the boat. William still put it about that he was nervous that Britain would fight on France's side and that Germany's present set of allies would avail her of nothing. He started by moderating the demands for the French Congo. In reality he did not want it to come to war, only that the pressure on Britain should be stepped up.[25] The *National Zeitung* thundered: The failure to strike has been 'much worse than Olmütz ... Has old Prussia gone to ground, have we become a race of women ...?' It did not mince words when it came to the imperial person either: William was 'Guillaume le timide, le valeureux poltron!'[26]

On 17 August William summoned his advisers to Wilhelmshöhe. A decision was made there not to push for war. Austria was not prepared to go along with it anyway. Germany was eventually compensated with 275,000 square kilometres in the Congo, an area beset with sleeping sickness. Germans had a sneaking suspicion that the French had fobbed them off with the wrong bit. Moltke was furious that he was not going to have a chance to field his army: 'If we are once again going to have to crawl away from the affair with our tail between our legs, if we cannot pull ourselves up to make an energetic challenge that we are ready to force our way with the sword, then I despair for the future of the German Empire, and I shall go ...'[27]

v

It was now that Little Willy became the principal focus of the warrior fronde. If the emperor was 'William the Peaceful' then the hawks would put their faith in the son and heir. The nationalists saw the crown prince as 'a central political figure and the most important lever above all to free the emperor from the influence of the "friends of England" and consensus politicians, and, as they were convinced, Jewish advisers.' At the rostrums that year the brief triumph of the right was dissipated. The Social Democrats won a resounding victory. Again the war party blamed the Jews.[28]

On 27 August, in a speech in Hamburg, William reaffirmed his desire to see Germany's trade develop yet further: 'We may not be astonished about it, the soaring success of trade in our recently united land has caused discomfort to many in the world. I am, however, of the opinion that competition in commercial areas is healthy. It is necessary for nations and peoples, to spur them on to ever greater achievements.' Trade meant battleships. That autumn at Rominten William was still braying for more cruisers. The fleet needed to be strengthened 'so that we may be sure that no one will dispute our rightful place in the sun'.[29]

There was a long sulk with Bethmann. At Hubertusstock, William's hunting box to the east of Berlin, he played second fiddle to Theodor Schiemann and Professor Reinhold Koser, the author of the standard life of William's hero, Frederick the Great. He was not invited to the shoot at Rominten, or to loll about among the Landseers afterwards. Later William irrationally grumbled that he had heard nothing from his chancellor and that Bethmann was complaining that he had not had the chance to talk to him: 'That's his fault. Why did he not come to Rominten? I don't exist for him. I have learned nothing about the way political negotiations are going. I said four weeks ago he should suggest a new ambassador for London. Still today there have been no suggestions.'[30]

Bethmann's exaggerated politesse let him down. He did not wish to disturb William on Sundays. From Hubertusstock William made it clear that was precisely when he wanted to see him. His other days were occupied: 'If the Imperial Chancellor knew how I live here he would grasp why I have convoked him for Sunday. I don't want a short audience with him, he is to talk to me about politics in the course of a walk. On weekdays immediately after breakfast and lunch I set off on the driven hunt.'[31]

The political crisis continued through the autumn of 1910. After nearly three weeks without so much as clapping eyes on his chancellor, William considered dismissing him and putting Field Marshal Colmar von der Goltz in his place. Bethmann was 'stuffed full of reflection and governed by fear of England, but I shall not let England dictate what I should and should not do. I have told the Imperial Chancellor that he should consider that I am a descendant of the Great Elector and Frederick the Great [sic – he was not], who would not have hesitated long about acting when it seemed to be the time.'[32]

The *Panther* incident convinced Tirpitz to fight for a larger fleet. He showed William anti-German articles which had appeared in the British press.[33] William was certain that a naval race would bring him greater popularity at home. He felt that Bethmann too should court the public's favour a little more, and not talk down to them. The chancellor was still upset over Agadir. Bethmann was certain that a naval race would end up with Germany at war with Britain. For Tirpitz, the trick was to up the ante: if the fleet were lethal enough Britain would be prudently neutral. Bethmann turned to Admiral Holtzendorff to plead his case: war would mean the destruction of the creation that was 'most the emperor's own – the fleet'. Bethmann won not only Holtzendorff's support but also that of the Staff Chief, Admiral von Heeringen, and the chief of the Naval Cabinet, Müller, who thought William was deluding himself about popular favour.[34]

On 26 September Tirpitz won William over to his point of view. The naval race was to be accelerated. William told Tirpitz to work on Bethmann to obtain his political support for a 2 : 3 ratio of ships, German to British, as quickly as possible. William erupted in fury against his ambassador to London, Metternich, on 1 November. He was angry that the count had tried to appease Britain once again by offering concessions over Germany's naval programme. 'Nonsense! We get slapped in the face and then on top of everything we are not allowed to build any ships!!! The usual Metternich advice. Simply don't build in Germany and you will put England in a good mood!'[35]

The crown prince had fallen under the influence of Elard von Old-enburg-Januschau, a right-wing frondeur and member of the Reichstag whose estates were not far from Danzig. Prince William decided that the Franco-German Understanding of 4 November was a national humiliation. Without obtaining the necessary permission, the prince travelled to Berlin to attend the debate in the Reichstag. From the imperial chair he applauded the opposition and sat with cool indifference when the chancellor and the government spoke. His gesture caused uproar from left and right. William thought Bethmann had been insulted and made a point of inviting the chancellor and his wife to dinner on the 9th when Prince William was due to be there. *Simplicissimus* ran a cartoon of the scene: 'Come on, give Uncle Imperial Chancellor your hand!'[36]

Prince William was sent packing back to Danzig after promising to behave. He was not a strong conspirator, no stronger than his father. Kiderlen saw his French opposite number and wrote the scene off as 'an annoying apparition'. The crown prince was upset to learn that his hotheadedness had made him unpopular in Britain, where as 'Little Willy' he was becoming a bad joke. He was mortified, as he had to a very real extent modelled his life on that of his great-uncle, Edward the Caresser. He assured Lord Glanville that he had nothing against Britain, he merely felt that Germany had been inadequately compensated for French territorial gains in Morocco.[37]

At the end of the year the emperor became heated about an unsigned article in the *Westminster Gazette* which maintained that Germany was bent on expansion in Europe. 'Unmitigated nonsense!' wrote William in English. 'Are twenty-three years of my government not enough as a proof that nobody here dreams of such nonsense?' Germany, said the writer, was backing the wrong horse. 'That is what England has been doing for the last seven years.' William blamed the Foreign Minister for this insuperable Teutonophobia in Britain; 'as long as Grey remains in office a really *political* understanding is *not* achievable.'[38]

Tirpitz had the backing of the Navy League, the Pan-Germans, and heavy industry. Naturally the army was not going to sit still and acquiesce if they did not have more men and arms too. The atmosphere in Germany was increasingly belligerent. In January 1912 the press baron and member of William's circle, Kommerzienrat Büxenstein, launched the Army League.[39] Britain's method was to fob Germany off with the offer of – other people's – colonies. William was not taken in. On 8 January 1912 he wrote: 'We have enough colonies! When I want something I shall buy it, or take it without England!' William believed that Britain was proposing territories which would lead his country into nasty colonial wars. It was a question of 'Beware of Greeks bearing gifts'. The point was that Britain had to 'recognise Germany's political importance and equal rights'. It was 'futile' throwing Germany scraps; colonial superpowers were also the owners of super fleets – 'without a strong fleet large colonies cannot be maintained.'[40]

A month before, when William had met his naval chiefs in the Neues Palais, Bethmann's policies *vis-à-vis* England came under attack. William wanted to 'cut the Gordian knot ... I must be my own Bismarck!' he declared. He then promised Tirpitz that he would have his ships and criticised his chancellor for his indecisiveness. Bethmann also wanted to play Bismarck. He used the *Norddeutsche Allgemeine* to push for an expanded army. Naturally it would not have been easy to win support for both army and navy in the Reichstag. William was angry. 'By publishing the Army Bill in the *Norddeutsche Allgemeine* the chancellor has betrayed me.'[41]

William was thoroughly out of sorts with Bethmann who was pleading for a limit to shipbuilding, or a restriction to smaller, defensive vessels. On 9 January there was an informal meeting of interested parties at the Neues Palais: Moltke, Solf and Zimmermann from the Foreign Office, the inevitable Schiemann, and the bankers Gwinner and Delbrück. The question was: should more ships be built or not? Or should Germany allow Britain to placate her with colonies? 'The same old song,' thought Müller. They were asked about the possibility of war with Britain. Delbrück puffed himself up and made warlike noises, but both he and Gwinner said that Germany was too poor. The consensus was opposed. They were for an understanding which would result in Germany founding more colonies after carving up the moribund Portuguese, Dutch and Belgian empires.[42]

The next day there was a supper at the Berlin Schloss, during which William occasionally railed at Bethmann for his cowardice and fear-mongering. William felt his chancellor did not help him at all, and decided that he would carry on his business with the War Minister, Heeringen, Tirpitz and Julius (Moltke). He reminded the company that he had been against sending the *Panther* because he feared it would create waves in Britain. Kiderlen rejoindered: 'So they scream. Whether they scream a little more makes no difference.'[43]

Britain was still resistant, chiefly through the intransigent Franco-philia of the Foreign Secretary, Sir Edward Grey. Not just Bethmann-

Hollweg but Ballin, too, was working to achieve some agreement between Britain and Germany over the navy race. He toyed with various ideas. He wanted to bring Tirpitz together with Jackie Fisher, the British First Sea Lord, but intriguing as such a meeting might have been, it never came to pass. According to Bülow, Bethmann stamped on the idea.[44]

VI

There was a joyful intermission in the high seriousness surrounding the quest for a British alliance and the business of achieving support for the Naval Bill. Three days before his own was the bicentenary of Frederick the Great's birth. William arranged another of his fancy-dress cele-brations and Josef Lauff was commissioned to do a play with incidental music written by the late king. Lauff does not seem to have shown great understanding for Prussia's most famous monarch. He made his crowning achievement the 'Fürstenbund' by which Frederick hoped to limit Austrian incursions into German territory at the end of his life. For the Rhenish poet, however, this was the blueprint for German unification. William must have had a hand in the script too. At one point Voltaire's friend, the freethinking king, exclaims: 'With God then: our great ally above!'[45]

On 29 January 1912 Ballin visited the emperor in the Berlin Schloss. William thought he had come to convey belated congratulations on his birthday two days before. He maintained that he was astonished to hear that Ballin had brought Sir Ernest Cassel with him, who wished to present him with an *aide-mémoire*. Bethmann was present at the dis-cussion. The gist of the note was that Germany should not increase the size of its fleet. British superiority was essential, but Britain would not stand in the way of Germany's colonial expansion.[46]

William wrote the reply rather than Bethmann, as it was believed that he had the best English. It was the work of an informal committee:

I sat at the desk in the ADCs' room, the gentlemen stood around me. I read a paragraph from the note and proposed a response, which was read out again. That was then criticised from right to left. Some thought it too accommodating, others too curt; it was remodelled, recast, improved and returned. The chan-cellor in particular with his philosophic examination and his deep, searching thoroughness weighed up every word ... [he] gave me a good deal of gram-matical and stylistic pain. After an hour's work the cast was finally finished. Once the note had gone from hand to hand a few more times and been read out half a dozen times by me, it was signed.[47]

On 7 February the Naval Bill was published. It prescribed three new ships of the line, to be launched in 1912, 1914 and 1916. William opened the Reichstag with a speech aimed at putting the British in the picture: he wanted two German warships for every British three, and if no alliance, at least neutrality in any continental war. The precious goal of peace 'required that the Empire remained powerful enough to protect and represent at any moment its national honour, its possessions and its rightful interests in the world. As a result it is my constant anxiety and duty ... to strengthen the defensive power of the German nation on land and on water.'[48]

On the following day the British Minister of War, Haldane, arrived in Berlin accompanied by his brother, the physiologist and philosopher John Scott Haldane, and Sir Ernest Cassel. Haldane's appearance caused excitement among the repositories of power in Wilhelmine Germany. The cerebral Bethmann seized on the fact that the minister was known as a Goethe scholar and expert on German philosophy; the military man, Tirpitz, recalled that Haldane had spent some time in the War Ministry under General von Einem as he prepared to create a British General Staff on the German model. William's meeting with Haldane occurred on the 9th. Tirpitz was present throughout, Bethmann only joining them at lunch. This was possibly a mistake: Haldane did not like Tirpitz, who opened the batting with a poor joke, calling himself 'the bogeyman of old England'. Haldane thought him dangerous, and William had to step in when their one-to-one discussions appeared to be leading nowhere. Haldane tried to tempt William with the promise of a Middle African empire. This, it later transpired, still belonged to Portugal, but Portugal, it was believed, was about to go spectacularly bust. When that happened her colonies might be bought for a song to allow her to pay her foreign debts. William was emphatic that he wanted a ratio of 3 : 2 ships, whereas Haldane stuck at the two-power standard – Britain should always possess a navy superior in fighting power to its two biggest rivals.[49]

William took Müller for a walk to tell him how things were going. 'Thank God I was there. Tirpitz's pigheadedness brought the conversation to a complete dead stop.'* Later Tirpitz complained that William's presence had inhibited the discussion; but it does seem more likely that the naval chief's intransigence wrecked the Haldane mission. Bethmann-Hollweg was hoping to wring an assurance of neutrality out of the British minister.[50] Haldane knew the political agreement was dead from the start. There was to be no neutrality because of British commitments to France. Tirpitz understood that the Anglo-French

---

* Sic; William's English expression.

alliance was not just a defensive one, although the British minister had assured them there was no such written treaty. There was a more relaxed dinner in the evening. Haldane left for home on the 11th with a bronze bust of William under his arm.[51]

William reported back to Ballin on 9 February saying he had made wide-ranging concessions: 'I believe that I have succeeded in everything which stands within My power!! I have performed My side of the bargain, Cardinal, do your stuff! Please inform Cassel, greetings, your loyal friend William IR.' He was prepared to halve the number of ships in the Naval Bill in his attempt to gain British neutrality, but when Grey and the British Admiralty tried to impose further conditions in exchange for a larger piece of – French or Portuguese – Africa, William's patience broke. Neither country, he thought, could be forced to part with their colonies. He was also being egged on by Dona, who had personally visited Bethmann in her attempts to convince him to implement the full naval programme. He told Metternich to inform Britain that he was only prepared to build at a slower tempo if he could have neutrality. He was cross with his ambassador, who he felt was on the British side. He, William, was the Supreme Warlord, and he decided. If Bethmann did not explain the situation to the Reichstag 'he would give the order to the Minister of War and State Secretary at the Imperial Naval Office to publish the Naval Bill. My patience and that of the German people is at an end.'[52]

There was a worry that William's attitude might lead to war. On 12 March the emperor minuted: 'Our programme is sufficient for our needs and I am indifferent to what England does about it. In any case it emerges that England does not want to make it into a reason for war, about which there has been great concern since November.'[53] Bethmann responded on the 7th by threatening to resign: 'I would hold it a sin against Germany to conjure up a war on our side when neither our honour nor life's interests are threatened, even if we could have a reasonable prognosis of total victory.' After soundly abusing his chancellor William backed down. He summoned him to a meeting in the mausoleum in the park at Charlottenburg. Over the tomb of Queen Louise of Prussia, Bethmann agreed to stay on.[54]

It was true to form, as Zimmermann had recorded earlier, 'When the situation gets critical, His Majesty can't see it through.' The next person to offer his resignation was Tirpitz. On 17 March Ballin wired: 'Your Majesty, I am bringing you the English alliance,' but the Haldane mission came to nothing and was officially declared dead the following day. The British worried it to death by imposing impossible conditions. Their proposal was to scrap the Naval Bill and they were not prepared to offer anything worthwhile in return. Grey was once again the stumbling-block on the British side. William did not appreciate Grey's attempts to do a deal with his ambassador: 'Grey has no clue who is actually the master here and that *I* rule ...' He 'negotiates like Shylock!' William blamed the whole fiasco on Graf Wolff-Metternich, who had failed to secure neutrality, and sacked him. Marschall von Bieberstein was sent to London in his place.[55]

Haldane had said that he spoke for the whole cabinet. At precisely the same time as Haldane was trying to make the Germans agreeable to a moderation of the naval race, Churchill made an inopportune speech in Glasgow, dismissing William's pride and joy as a 'luxury fleet'. As Tirpitz commented, that speech 'called the unity of the cabinet into doubt'. William wired Ballin on 19 March. The British press had called the speech a provocation, and that it was. 'The – agreement – is thereby broken by England – killed. Negotiations should be linked up on a different basis altogether. Where in the speech is the excuse for "luxury fleet?!" ' He went off to Corfu, dismissing the British cabinet as a bunch of 'scoundrels'.[56]

I hope that my diplomats will learn their lessons from this business, and in the future to listen more to their master, and heed his wishes and orders more than they have, especially when it is a question of bringing England into line, which they still don't know how to do; while I know it well! It was a *proper* English bluff directed against the budget and Naval Bill ... thank God that no part of the bill was sacrificed – that would not have been justifiable to the German people.[57]

VII

On 13 February William had a welcome discussion with the industrialist Rathenau and that other future Weimar minister Hugo Simon about the naval talks. Rathenau agreed with William about the need to obtain a pledge of neutrality from Britain. Haldane was becoming frightened by the fleet rivalry. William believed that his own personal influence would be enough to put things right. 'The Kaiser wanted to go to Cowes again, then he would settle everything. The king trusted him. His plan was: United States of Europe against America.' He thought both the Turks and the British would approve and would join it: 'five states, including France, could put something together.'[58]

On 27 February William launched the *Prinzregent Luitpold*. It was the moment to patch up the growing quarrel with the princes in general and the Bavarian Wittelsbachs in particular. Of all the former rulers, the Wittelsbachs resented Prussian domination the most. Germany was compared to a mosaic which 'seen from afar appears as a mighty whole put together from individual tribes, proud of their individualities and loyally dependent on their appropriate princes'.[59]

William was still thinking about his European union a month later. He wanted a 'defensive and offensive alliance' to include France. He went to Vienna in March on his way to a six-week holiday on Corfu. There he told the Foreign Minister Graf Berchtold of his desire to form a Triple Alliance with France and Britain, directed against the emerging world powers. He needed to make it clear to the islanders 'that the British had more serious rivals in the world than the Germans, particularly America and Japan'. That this was not just a flash in the pan, or impetuous loopiness on the emperor's part, was underlined by Kiderlen, who included similar ideas in an interview for the French daily *Figaro* that year. William asked Bethmann to develop the matter further. After 4 August 1914 the union was not forgotten; only Britain was to be pushed out.[60]

William was already having problems with Britain's ambassador, Goschen. He wanted him withdrawn. If he stayed, 'We shall be able to take our mobilisation plans out of the drawer, for then everything will be clear.' There was much head-scratching as to who would replace Marschall in London, who – if Bülow is to be believed – had taken to the bottle, the path Kiderlen was to take at the end of the year. Someone suggested Stumm-Halberg. William reacted in fury: 'No! He is too *afraid* of the English! And hates my fleet.' He wanted someone 'who has *my* trust, obeys *my* will, carries out *my* orders. With *one* instruction: when on arrival in London Grey asks him: "What have you got for us?", answer: "*Nothing*, I have come to hear what you are offering." '[61] In the event Prince Max Lichnowsky was sent to London as ambassador; he was anything but the blood-and-guts ambassador evoked in William's tirade and would receive a large part of the blame for the outbreak of war two years later. Bülow felt he was too little experienced for the post. Lichnowsky was detailed to bring home a guarantee of British neutrality. In this he failed. Later he would prove a critic of the risk-taking which allowed Europe to sink into war. Insufficient moves were made to preserve the peace, given the danger of a world conflagration.[62] Haldane had ended up by spreading a mood of doom and despondency. German domination of the continent would not be tolerated by Britain. In the circumstances Britain would side with France.[63]

William's absences from the fount of power were many and long. From Corfu he learned of the sinking of the *Titanic*. At seven thirty on the evening of 15 April 1912 he came into Müller's room: 'There has been a terrible accident, I am quite beside myself, the most frightful catastrophe that has ever happened. Imagine, the *Titanic* has gone down.' He ordered Müller to telegraph King George, the British government and the White Star line to express his sympathy. He wanted more reports and was so overwrought that he even read the telegram to the servants.[64] The *Nordlandsreise* lasted from 10 July to 6 August. On the way William had a meeting with the Tsar which he intended to be the crowning glory of his personal diplomacy: something it failed to become.

On the invitation of the president, Ludwig Forrer, William paid a state visit to Switzerland on 11 September. The Swiss were unprepared, and a carriage had to be borrowed from a Zurich man which seemed adequate for William's needs. William exercised his tact, or lack of it, by wearing the uniform of the Garde-Schützen, which had formerly been a Neufchâtel regiment. Neufchâtel had been a personal possession of the Prussian Crown until 1857, and William's father had had to be restrained from going to war to recover it. William asked the Swiss army corps commander what he would do if he sent in a force of 100,000 men. He received a factual reply. William then doubled the figure, to which the Swiss general answered that each of his men would fire twice.[65]

He was in the worst of moods at the naval manoeuvres that year, and rude to everyone around him. On 15 September he recovered his humour and in the mess that night spoke for two and a half hours about Queen Victoria and Edward VII at Osborne, 'showing what a good raconteur he was again'. There was splendid weather for the last day of the war games. The submarines were a great success, demonstrating that they could sink three large ships. 'His Majesty was very pleased [and gave] the now debased Black Eagle to the Commander of the Fleet [Holtzendorff].'[66]

VIII

The new eruption of the war in the Balkans caused another sea-change in William's thinking. He spent two hours examining the maps in a break from the hunting at Letzlingen. At first he was indifferent to the war, and simply wanted to keep Germany out of it. His treaty obligations to Austria rather required him to show an interest. A solution had to be found. Gradually he came round, or allowed himself to be talked round, to a greater commitment to the Austrian ally, who was hoping to pick up some more scraps from the retreating Ottomans. The success of the forces opposing the Sultan changed William's thinking utterly. He pledged total support, with the inevitable 'understanding' with Britain. If Francis Joseph declared war on Russia, William was 'ready, as I have already told the chancellor in Letzlingen, to carry out the *casus foederis* in the fullest measure no matter what the consequences'. He none the less wanted to find out what side the British were on. At the beginning of December he learned the truth: they would not tolerate French defeat.[67]

It was to be a full dress rehearsal for the war. In St Petersburg the Foreign Minister Sazonov expressed his indifference to the idea that Europe might hurtle into total catastrophe. On 3 December Lichnowsky had a conversation with Haldane in the course of which the British minister told him that Britain could not sit by while Austria walked into Serbia. The news that Britain was suggesting the Entente was a real alliance threw William into a fury:

Because England [sic] is too cowardly to leave France and Russia in the lurch on this occasion, and so deeply envious and hateful of us, for that reason other powers may not defend their interests with the sword, and despite all assurances given to Marschall and Lichnowsky they will proceed against us. What a proper nation of shopkeepers! They call that peace politics! Balance of power! In the final battle between the Germans and the Slavs the Anglo-Saxons find themselves on the side of the Slavs and the Gauls.

He was still fuming on the 8th. It was 'Jealousy, fear of our incipient greatness.' The matter concerned Germany's very existence.[68]

On 8 December 1912 occurred the famous War Council at which – according to historians of the Fischer school – Germany decided to launch its aggressive, annexationist war. Whether, however, these utterances on the part of the emperor represent war policy, will-power or simply anxiety that the doors were closing on Germany has not been adequately determined, and nobody has been able to prove that 'positive, concrete action' arose out of it. Clearly William's anger played an important role. It is also significant that it came to nothing, and that the events of July and August 1914 are only fortuitously connected. Present were Moltke, Tirpitz, the Minister of the Marine von Heeringen and Müller. William was still raging. He wanted allies: Bulgaria, Romania, Albania and Turkey were to be tested out. He was no longer prepared to wait patiently for an understanding with Britain. He wanted an immediate war with France and Russia. In his mind's eye he could already see the glorious feats of his navy: a U-boat campaign directed against British troop transporters to Dunkirk, mines in the Thames. Tirpitz was told to build more U-boats. Moltke was pleased with William's resolve: 'I regard a war as inevitable and the sooner the better ... we should, however, prepare better through the press for the popularity of a war against Russia in the sense of His Majesty's presentation.'[69]

Tirpitz was told to use his journalist contacts and a message was sent to Bethmann to prepare the public for war. The naval chief said he was not ready and needed another eighteen months, during which time the Kiel Canal would have to be widened to allow for the Dreadnought

Class ships to pass from the Baltic to the North Sea and when the new submarine base on Heligoland would be finished. That meant June 1914, which fits the bill, give or take a month. Moltke was disappointed that Tirpitz had put a dampener on the immediate prospect of war: 'The navy won't be ready even then, and the army will be in an even less favourable position; for the enemy is arming more strongly than us, as we lack the cash.' Müller agreed with Moltke, adding, 'That was the end of the conference. The result was this, pretty well nothing.' The army chiefs had achieved a far bigger budget for 1913 even so; and the General Staff went ahead with its wide-ranging plans of conquest. There was even one for Great Britain.[70]

As yet no thought had been given to the diplomatic position, but the Bavarian and Saxon military chiefs were informed. William had received secret reports that Britain intended to side with France and Russia and come in on the side of the alliance. They took their time about letting Bethmann know. Bethmann considered the matter of war: he thought it only possible if Britain were to remain neutral. That was still a possibility but it was foolish to provoke the British by building more ships. William was still bitter. Three days after the War Council he fulminated: 'England can't bear it that Germany is becoming the most powerful state on the continent and that [Europe] will unite under her leadership!'[71]

Britain was France's ally, therefore Germany's enemy. Bethmann was exasperated: 'Behind Kiderlen's and my back ... with his faithful from the army and navy, he holds a war council.' Haldane's words had been twisted out of all proportion. William went on to encourage Francis Ferdinand to strike while the iron was hot, but the Archduke did not believe that Germany's political leaders were with their emperor and took a cooler view. Rathenau was at Bethmann's country estate, Hohenfinow on the Oder on the 27 December. From the chancellor he learned the disappointing news about Haldane.

William exaggerated his abilities in times of crisis such as these. Müller and he had a conversation about high-ranking officers who had transferred money to Zurich to keep it safe in the event of war. William said, 'We live in remarkable times.' Müller added, 'And in times which must be extraordinarily difficult for Your Majesty.' William put on a brave face: 'Oh, that is my profession, I am quite happy, and I love tasks like these.' Müller was not certain that Bethmann was up to the job; he remained prudently silent on the subject of His Majesty.[73]

IX

A blow was the death of Kiderlen. Bülow was sulking in a well-appointed tent in Rome. He saw the Foreign Minister at the beginning of the year looking 'worn and puffy'. He was drinking heavily. He died of a heart attack on 30 December after drinking six glasses of cognac. The former chancellor thought this a 'misfortune'. He must have changed his mind. He once told Bernstorff that Kiderlen was a 'savage dog who ought to have been left on a chain in Bucharest'. What made the difference, apparently, was the fact he was not as 'stupid' as his successor Jagow; but then, Bülow had an animus against Jagow, as he did against anyone who was given power after his glorious reign came to an abrupt end.[74]

Müller travelled with Moltke from Potsdam to Berlin on Christmas Eve. Moltke was 'very anxious, in particular over our lack of war readiness, over the aimlessness of our, and even more, Austrian policy, over the impossibility of respecting Belgian neutrality, and over the unclear personality of the Austrian heir . . .' It did not please Moltke to hear that Francis Ferdinand favoured the Slavs and was presumed keen to create a semi-independent Bohemian homeland for the Czechs. Müller claimed it was the first time he had heard that there were plans to violate Belgian territory. Moltke was also worried about William, who he thought might try to take wartime decisions in the face of the Staff Chiefs. Müller tried to put his mind at rest. In his opinion William would stay out of it.[75]

Jagow carried on in the spirit of the War Council. He was to provoke war.[76] The emperor agreed, but soon went back on his word. Tirpitz dated this 'turnaround' 6 January 1913. By April the German military attaché was already reporting that William was not in favour of war, and nor was anyone else apart from the General Staff, which was convinced that it was unavoidable.[77] William's pacifism did not win him friends in the places he wanted to find them. He was facing massive attacks from the Right. In 1913 Graf Ernst Reventlow published *Der Kaiser und die Monarchisten*. 'The emperor and the king of Prussia possesses not only the human, but also the constitutional right to err. No German is justified in disputing or attacking this right, or in reproaching him because he is making mistakes; providing that he has not contravened the constitution.'[78] Liman published another edition of his *Kaiser* in the first half of 1913 in which he postulated that 'one might paint the history of this last quarter of a century on the gold background of Byzantium'.[79]

The last few months before the outbreak of war produced a bumper harvest of such works, many of them pushing the emperor and his government towards conflict and conquest. Alfred Class, the head of the Pan-Germans, wrote *Wenn ich der Kaiser wär* (If I were the Emperor) under the pseudonym of Daniel Frymann. Britain should either stand aside or fight. Harden and his nationalist ilk were preaching a racial war against the Russians. His co-religionary, Rathenau, wanted to see Europe under German hegemony, and to 'create an economic unit which would be on the same terms as America if not perhaps superior'. General Bernhardi called for war to win Germany new markets; and then there was Paul Liman, who had re-emerged as the crown prince's chief literary amanuensis.

Besides the journalists the Pan-Germans were pulling at William's sleeve. They wanted land, chiefly in the east. To William's annoyance they had focused their hopes on Little Willy. They had had reservations at first. Their leader, Class, thought Prince William should learn to work, like Frederick the Great, and not mess around with sport. After their conference in September 1913 the crown prince sent a telegram of congratulations to one of their leaders – General von Liebert. That summer the Pan-Germans and the Agrarians had concluded a formal alliance. Even some elements among German socialists were calling for expansion. The crown prince wrote the foreword to a Pan-German tract called *Deutschland in Waffen* (Germany at Arms) in which he spoke of the 'new warlike ideology'. Germany's place in the sun could only be won by the sword. Germany's army and navy had to be maintained at permanent readiness. That year the crown prince was riding the crest of the wave, and achieving massive popularity among the German right.[80]

William had unwittingly pointed the way forward for his son at the beginning of his reign. He had compared himself to King Frederick William I, the father of Frederick the Great, who created the Prussian army: 'My reign will be a boring age. My task will not be to make war but to consolidate the Empire ... My successor can go to war again.' He was jealous of his son in the same way that Fritz had been jealous of him – or indeed Frederick William had been of Frederick the Great. It was worse in this case, because William was aware of his deformities, whereas his son was a healthy, sporty, lusty young man. When General Plessen pointed out to him what a pleasure it was to observe Prince William on his horse, William replied, 'It is a real art riding, when you have two healthy arms.'[81] Prince William was something of a dandy. On one occasion he appeared wearing a new and fashionable hat. William growled, 'I have recently had an officer placed under arrest in Metz for wearing a hat like yours.' The next time he saw his son he was wearing non-regulation riding breeches.[82]

The crown prince's criticisms had been mounting since Algeciras. Germany did not enjoy equal prestige at the conference table. He would have liked to have seen a British alliance as much as his father did, but Bülow had convinced him it was not to be had. The enemy was France, 'a relentless foe'. He had had a brush with the bellicose general Bernhardi and he was far readier than his father to advocate war. Prince William had been drawn into the Pan-German camp. When one of their luminaries, General von Gebsettel demanded, among other things, the 'solution of the Jewish question' and the control of the Jewish press, going so far as to propose that the Jews should be deprived of their civil rights to encourage their emigration, Prince William sent a script to his father and Bethmann together with a covering letter to his father, which called for a chancellor who feared 'neither the death nor the devil'. William replied to his son through his Civil Cabinet chief, Valentini, defending Bethmann who was respected abroad, in particular in Great Britain.[83]

Early in 1914 Prince William published *Der Kronprinz. Gedanken über Deutschlands Zukunft* (The Crown Prince. Thoughts on Germany's Future), which was written for him by Liman. The book was a success, selling 22,000 copies. The crown prince's thought was firmly Pan-German. He wanted a *coup d'état* in order to restore the credentials of the monarchy and also called for Germany to expand beyond her frontiers. A rumour may well have come to William's ears that the Pan-Germans were planning to dethrone him and replace him by his more pliant son.[84]

The emperor was increasingly Slavophobic. Under the influence of Schiemann and Moltke, among others, he saw a war against Russia as part of a cultural mission: the final battle in a conflict waged over a thousand years, which had begun when the Saxons had put down the Slavic Wends in Brandenburg and continued two centuries later with the despatch of the Teutonic Knights into the Baltic. The Russians had become 'cocky', and their confidence threatened Germany. It was therefore 'a question of life and death for the Germans on the European continent'. This was a language which could be found elsewhere in contemporary Germany. On 8 March 1913 Maximilian Harden gave a lecture on the Germans and the Slavs in Munich, in which he brought up the life-and-death struggle which lay before Germany. The Jewish journalist also highlighted the issue of Britain's 'blood relationship with us'.[85]

x

Nineteen thirteen was a big year for the unveiler of monuments. It was the centenary of Germany's liberation from French occupation during the Napoleonic Wars. The emperor's message, delivered up and down the land, was not particularly bellicose. To Berlin University in February the dangers of foreign ways were highlighted. In Bremen on 5 March he spoke of the 'duty to learn and work for the Fatherland'. In Lübeck he exclaimed, 'I protect the merchant. His enemy is mine too.'[86]

War fever was spoiling William's well-orchestrated routine. On 18 March he still had not left for the Mediterranean. 'The damned Balkan muddle', he told Nicky – pointedly – 'has deprived me of the possibility of having my heavenly paradise of Corfu!' There was movement in the family, some bad, some good. On 20 May, Little Willy as patron of the Breslau Centenary Exhibition launched an attack on the Silesian dramatist Gerhart Hauptmann, who had written the festival's opening play. There cannot have been too much discord with his father on this point, and he succeeded in having the play banished. On the other hand he was causing problems over the marriage of his sister Victoria Louise to Ernest Augustus of Cumberland, the heir to the kingdom of Hanover which had been suppressed by Prussia after the war of 1866. The marriage was due to be celebrated on 25 May 1913. It was to some extent to be the symbolic reconciliation of the Guelphs and the Hohenzollerns. The crown prince wanted none of it. He behaved in a manner reminiscent of his father over Moretta and Sandro Battenberg. He wanted the groom to sign a legally binding document abdicating his rights to Hanover. William agreed a compromise: Ernest Augustus would not be granted Hanover, but he would be allowed to rule the smaller Guelph duchy of Brunswick instead.[87]

The wedding proved a useful moment to test out the Tsar and George V who had both come to Berlin for the ceremony. William was still receiving sound advice from Lichnowsky in London. He told the Foreign Office in Berlin that the moment that Britain would ditch Russia and France and collapse remorsefully in Germany's arms would never come. War with Britain was certain if Germany attacked France. The Wilhelmstrasse had to make it absolutely clear to the Austrians that Germany wanted war under no circumstances.[88] William's enthusiasm for Austria was cooling too. He found himself disagreeing about their expansion plans in the Balkans, even if he reiterated his support for the alliance. The attitude caused bitterness in Vienna. Germany had not come to their aid and Bulgaria and Serbia had managed to double their size. In the second half of September the Serbians went to war again to seize the border area of northern Albania. William promised help, but again none was forthcoming.

The new Army Bill added another 120,000 men to the colours, some 90,000 more than in 1912, but significantly less than the army leaders had wanted. It was the one positive outcome of the war scare the year before and William's frustration at the powers' refusal to admit him to full membership of the club.[89] The army had observed unpleasant signs of activity in Germany's neighbours: a trial mobilisation in Russian Poland, and a huge increase in the size of the French army. Moltke was pushed by Ludendorff at the General Staff to demand a similar augmentation. The Entente powers were still vastly better off when it came to arms and men.

The diplomat Friedrich Rosen found William in a determined mood when he met him aboard Ballin's yacht *Viktoria Luise* on 13 June. A month later, William was present for the maiden voyage of HAPAG's *Imperator*. Rathenau was there too, and had to put up with the emperor's dreadful jokes, including Irish ones 'in dialect'.[90] William had his second meeting with Escoffier on the morning following the launch party. Both the chef and the emperor expressed their keenness on maintaining the peace. It was the twenty-fifth edition of the *Nordlandsreise* that year. Despite the persistent fumes of the Balkan War there was not much talk of politics; although at one point William exploded against one of his advisers – probably Müller 'I have had enough of these utterances, I command and that is simply it. I am supposed to ask every Tom, Dick and Harry and then sign on the dotted line whatever the Maritime Republic thinks best. Now I have had it. Go to the devil. I am the Supreme Warlord, I don't decide, I command.'[91] William expressed a degree of *Schadenfreude* over the trials of his detested 'colleague' Ferdinand of Bulgaria who was supposed to have uttered, 'The Balkan War will put your pacifist emperor in yet another pretty pickle.'[92] William received a message relating to the Tsar's displeasure over the Liman von Sanders affair, which was set to trouble the 'good relations' between Germany and Russia. The note led William to make one or two unbuttoned remarks about Nicholas.[93]

XI

On 18 October the enormous, Piranesi-inspired monument to the Battle of the Nations of 1813 was unveiled in Leipzig; in its massive, imposing, self-confident way, the supreme expression of Wilhelmine art. The crown prince was in disgrace over his attempts to galvanise the opposition to the chancellor's attempts to keep the peace, and was conspicuously absent from the ceremony. He was sulking in his hunting lodge at Hupfrebe in the Vorarlberg. William once again assured the Austrian Chief of Staff that he could rely on Germany when the shooting started. He had been talking to Moltke again. He also felt that Austria was losing prestige by its refusal to act against Serbia. It was becoming unworthy of its great power status: 'I'm coming in with you. The other [powers] are not ready, they won't interfere. In a few days you will have taken Belgrade. I have always been a supporter of peace; but there are limits. I have read a lot about war and I know what it means, but in the end the position comes which a great power can no longer observe, but must reach for his sword.'[94]

In September William left Bad Salzbrunn, where he had been taking a cure, and on the 23rd went shooting with Francis Ferdinand at his estate at Konopischt in Bohemia. They had plenty to talk about. He was already changing his tune. The earlier enthusiasm for war had waned, like so many times before.[95] Three days later he was in Vienna where he sent his host a thank-you letter praising the garden and the pheasant shoot. William did not favour strong-arm tactics with Serbia unless all else failed to bring them into the Austrian camp: money, military training, favoured trading. If they refused to accept these civilised arguments, he told the Foreign Minister Berchtold, they should be attacked. At this point William touched his sword for emphasis.[96]

The discussion turned to Russia. Berchtold was in favour of reviving the Triple Alliance between Germany, Austria and Russia and bringing in the British for good measure. William said he had been brought up in that tradition, but he had been forced to recognise that since Alexander III's death it was another Russia altogether and that it was ruled by quite different people to the Tsar, people who were dedicated to Germany's defeat. William was not even worried about shaking the monarchical principle he held so dear. It did not matter how Russia went, as long as she went. William was surrounded by Slavophobes: Moltke, Jagow, Schiemann, even Bethmann, who famously refused to plant trees at Hohenfinow because he thought they would only be enjoyed by the Russians; and they were too, after 1945. Britain too felt this paranoia about Russian expansion at the time of the 'Great Game', when Russians seemed to be permanently threatening the borders of India.[97]

XII

On 28 October 1913 a new shock ran through political Germany which threatened to be the worst upset since the *Daily Telegraph* affair. Trouble was brewing in Alsace, where it was shortly to be revealed how much William disliked and distrusted the Alsatians.[98] In the notably *kaisertreu* town of Zabern in Lower Alsace, a twenty-year-old lieutenant, Freiherr Günther von Forstner, encouraged his men to employ their side-arms when they brawled with the locals. He also used the less than kind word 'Wackes' to denote the natives, which had been ordered to be removed from the vocabulary of soldiers serving in the imperial province, so offensive was it thought to be.[99] He was overheard by a local recruit. The upshot of a slip of the tongue was a campaign of civil disobedience during which a good deal of coarse insult was hurled at the officer whose drunken insouciance had earned him the epithet 'Bettschisser' – a name that was eventually celebrated in a Paris music-hall song. The military and civil authorities responded in a clumsy manner and arrested about fifteen civilians.

Despite its good German credentials, Alsace had somehow failed to gel as a German province after 1871. Part of the problem lay in the way the authorities in Berlin continued to treat it as a piece of conquered land, rather than pampering it as a special province as the French had done. There were too many soldiers in Alsace, about a sixth of the total German army, and they did not reflect the demographic picture of the territory, being largely Protestant and antipathetic. Their presence turned many of the region's towns and cities into gloomy garrisons.[100] One of these was Zabern, or Saverne, which had played host to a Prussian infantry regiment for twenty-five years. It was no worse than any other German garrison in Alsace, indeed, it was slightly better, but friction was rife.

Zabern calmed down fairly quickly. William, however, stoked up the fire again. Forstner's commanding officer, Colonel von Reuter, had chosen to retire on grounds of ill-health. William, however, countermanded his decision, and sent him back. Meanwhile, as the campaign stepped up against 'Bettschisser', the army was lashing out in an ever more clumsy way against anyone in town who might have played a part, using obsolete regulations to justify their replacing the civil police. More arrests were made, including a judge from the local court who had had the temerity to suggest that the army's actions were illegal. William, however, made it clear that he approved. Even when there was no legal basis for the way the authorities had behaved he believed that the military should be protected at all costs. Bethmann supported the provincial governor, Graf Wedel, who thought the army had gone too far: 'Even in the old provinces the most peace-loving population would have felt aggrieved.' He demanded Reuter's dismissal and a thorough spring clean prior to the Reichstag debate on the matter.

William refused to sack Reuter or even hold more than a routine inquiry. Typically, Bethmann backed down, even when he was convinced that the military's action was contrary to the constitution. He feared that Wedel would resign and that he would have to face the mounting criticism alone. Once again the crown prince waded in. He demanded Bethmann's resignation and sent telegrams of support to Reuter and the military governor, the African general Deimling. He complained of the 'impudence of the Zabern plebs' and suggested that 'an example should be made to remove the appetite of the natives for such incidents by making them taste nasty'.[101] Ludwig Frank attacked the crown prince in the Reichstag, and Bethmann was moved to defend him. William was furious with his son and relieved him of his command.[102] He said that he should thank Bethmann instead of constantly whispering that he needed another chancellor. Bethmann endeavoured to pass the Zabern affair off as a purely military matter: 'The king's coat must be respected at all times', but this would not wash with the Reichstag. Bethmann lost a vote of confidence; but, this being Germany, he held on to his position none the less.

Prince William's behaviour cost him his regiment. He was recalled to Berlin and the General Staff, where he might be better watched. His parting speech to his regiment was widely reported in the left-wing press. At the beginning of 1914 he was given a political adviser in the person of the Freiherr von Maltzahn, who was supposed to school him in the emperor's views. It turned out to be an unwise decision, as Maltzahn was a passionate opponent of the chancellor and merely strengthened the opposition of the emperor's son.[103] But if William disapproved of his son's courting the extreme right he had not forgotten the plans for a *coup d'état* he had hatched long ago. It is a central tenet of the Fischer thesis that William and his advisers launched the war in order to control the socialist menace at home. While that theory is difficult to prove, he certainly recalled Bismarck's plan to 'ally himself to the princes in order to chastise the Reichstag and eventually abolish it'. Several times in 1913 he threatened Bethmann 'that he would send one of his adjutant-generals into the Reichstag, if I am not tough enough[. This] constantly crops up in conversation with me.'[104]

On 6 November William tried to bring Albert of Belgium over to his side. He explained that war could be very close when the king came to see him in Potsdam. William had his Coburg cousin made Colonel of the 16th Dragoons in Lüneberg. The Belgian king held talks with both William and Moltke and both were keen to stress the dangers. They impressed on the military attaché, Baron Beyens, their belief that Britain would not come to their aid because widespread losses in the British fleet would mean the mantle of supremacy passing to the United States. They might well have been trying to frighten the Belgian monarch into accepting the passage of German troops through Belgium which had already been laid down in the Schlieffen Plan. Beyens thought William had fallen under the influence of his military entourage.[105]

On 15 November Bethmann delivered a salutary warning against the call for a 'preventative war': 'In no case has the honour and dignity of Germany been impinged by another nation. The man who wants war under such causes must have a national goal in mind which may not be achieved without war. For such aims and tasks Bismarck willed and made the wars of 1864, 1866 and 1870 ... A future war fought without a pressing cause throws not only the Hohenzollern throne but also

Germany's future in the balance. Certainly we must pursue a bold foreign policy, but in every diplomatic situation to rattle our swords when neither the honour, security nor future of Germany is at stake, is not only madly brave, it is criminal.'[106]

XIII

The outbreak of the First World War saved large amounts of the Berlin Schloss from destruction. The origin of the plans came from Vicky, who had discovered Ihne and dubbed him the 'modern Schlüter' after the great baroque architect who had given the huge building its outward form. A model was made and William set about reworking the Weisse Saal or White Hall. In this he encountered opposition from the architectural academy, which put pressure on the emperor to maintain its 'historic beauty'. Ihne none the less managed to alter the picture gallery and work was still going on halfway through the war. In the Second World War the entire, enormous building was gutted. Its ruins were blown up in 1950, as an unwelcome relic of Prussia's 'militarist past'.[107]

The refined Rathenau was fascinated by William's taste. 'Here in the land of duty everything served, therefore art had to serve [his] glorification; it was a dynastic, national, representative medium. Architecture delivered pomp; painting: decoration; sculpture, costume figures. The sickly-sweet macaroon and marzipan taste of these apparently baroque, Romanesque, Byzantine and Napoleonic things delighted the bourgeoisie of the day.'[108]

Wilhelmine art was also didactic. This was clear from a special exhibition held at the National Gallery in Berlin during the first half of 1906 when 2,000 works were exhibited from 600 lenders, illustrating the glorious events which had created the Hohenzollern Reich. In the years before the First World War the National Gallery filled up with pictures describing the events and, above all, the battles which had brought about German unification. Under its first director, Max Jordan, the Gallery had already bought 119 paintings by 69 different artists before 1903; they were intended to become 'the best means of education for the nation in the "national idea"'.[109] The painter Anton von Werner played a key role in this, acquiring the pictures after March 1908.

Not every director approved. Hugo von Tschudi, Jordan's successor, relegated the canvases to the second floor, and would have been happier if he had been able to get rid of them altogether. In this, however, he came up against the will of his emperor who approved the 'propaganda' value of the concentration on the achievements of his forebears. William's visits made it necessary to keep the collection together. He came on 13 April 1907 and uttered his approval for the new hanging. It was Ludwig Justi, when he took over at the National Gallery in 1909 who finally convinced William that the pictures did not belong in the National Gallery at all, which was for 'national art' rather than 'national history'. They might only be included if they were worthy of it as works of art. They were taken to the Arsenal on Unter den Linden instead.[110]

XIV

Bülow saw Ambassador Flotow on the emperor's birthday in January 1914. He told him, 'All the great powers are equally desirous of peace. All need peace.'[111] William was wrestling with other problems. Tirpitz argued that he should let the Jesuits back into Germany as a sop to the Catholic Centre Party, who might pass the Naval Estimates in gratitude. William proved resistant: 'As long as a Hohenzollern sits on the imperial throne there is no question of letting the Jesuits in. Why did Bismarck expel them in his time? I can't change everything that My grandfather created.' William was forgetting Frederick the Great, who gave the Jesuits their last refuge in Europe, after the Society of Jesus had been banned by the Pope.[112]

William was losing one of the linchpins of his foreign policy: Turkey. The French, it transpired, had longer pocket-books. The despatch of General Otto Liman von Sanders to Turkey to command an army corps, with a seat on the War Council, on 30 June was considered a great *bévue* in many quarters, but it was in response to a request from the Turks themselves. The decision went back to the famous War Council of 8 December 1912: William wanted a formal alliance with Turkey. He resented the presence of General Eydoux, a senior French officer in Greece, and there was already a British admiral advising the Turkish navy. George V had been *bon prince* about it, saying it was natural that Germany should want to play a role. The British were reshaping the Turkish police and gendarmerie. Bethmann was not told. Although William had informed the Tsar at Victoria Louise's wedding, the Russians were predictably furious. Quite apart from their interest in taking the Straits, their trade with the west had to pass through the Dardanelles. A Russian diplomat told Bülow that 'the final result has been destructive, and at St Petersburg they have the impression that chaos reigns in governing circles in Berlin.'[113]

William had more grandiose projects in mind than mere technical advice to the Sultan's armed forces. He wanted to see an eventual quiet Germanisation of the country's army. In return for German support for the Ottoman Empire in Asia Minor, he was anxious for a say in the country's foreign policy. The German mission should be sympathetic towards the Turks and excite their respect so that William might gain a strong army 'which obeys my commands'. 'You are in fact pioneers for the future and imminent partition of Turkey. Work calmly and diligently.' That William had high hopes of the Turkish alliance is clear from a light-hearted, if prophetic, remark he made when Liman von Sanders reported back to Berlin on 16 February 1914: 'Either the German flag flies over the fortresses of the Bosphorus, or I shall share the sad fate of the exile on St Helena.'[114]

Part of the general's mission was to re-equip the Turkish army with modern German gunnery. Soon long-range cannon were pointing out into the Straits, but the Turks themselves were already having qualms about the German presence. William continued to reassure the Russians that the mission was no different to the earlier ones. The German Foreign Office was not taken in: 'It is about our prestige in the world, which is severely attacked from all sides! So come on, stand to attention, put your hands on your hilt!' What lay behind the policy was the British fear of the Russians gaining control of the Straits. William still believed that Britain was backing the wrong horse. Once again his Turkish policy was an attempt to lure Britain into his bed.[115]

Some observers have noted a shift on the part of the emperor towards 'preventative war', but then again, these changes of mood were not new, and may simply have been a reflection on whom he had spoken to last. Already in November of the previous year the French ambassador thought he had detected a fresh, bellicose wind blowing across the emperor's features. On 10 March 1914 William informed the Badenese consul, Graf Berckheim, that neither the French nor the Russians were ready for war, 'but however the land lies, he, the emperor would never fight a preventative war'. It was to Lyncker's regret. The military chief thought he had seen a golden opportunity to move; and repeat the bold attack on the part of Frederick the Great which opened the Seven Years War, smiting a sea of enemies just waiting to pounce.[116]

On 26 February William wrote his last letter to Nicholas. Chelius was being sent to replace Dohna as his personal ADC at the Russian court: 'He is quite phenomenal as a musician and plays the piano as Rubinstein, d'Albert or any other great artist.' He was also 'one of my most intimate personal friends'.[117] He may have slightly exaggerated Chelius's talents, but all the rest was true, and further demonstrated how important William believed the post in St Petersburg to be.

He visited Vienna in March where he is said to have opened Francis Joseph's eyes to the Slavic menace on his borders. He had several meetings with the Hungarian leader, Graf Tisza, who impressed him much more than the Austrian Foreign Minister Berchtold, whose fears of the

Russians he none the less felt exaggerated. From Vienna William went to Venice and joined the *Hohenzollern*, which was moored on the riva degli Schiavoni, to receive the Italian king Victor Emmanuel. On the 24th he met up with Francis Ferdinand at his Schloss Miramar on the Adriatic near Trieste and was able to look over an Austrian Dreadnought. They talked about the possibility of war. William thought he had the Archduke 'wholly in his pocket'. It was important that the Russians should attack first; if not, the British were bound to come in on their side. The feeling that it was someone else's fault was also morally important to William. Jagow understood that: 'The emperor wanted to maintain the peace and would always back away from war and only countenance it if forced to do so by our enemies.'[118]

William then sailed on to Corfu on the 22nd. Bethmann joined him for a week on 6 April. Here he received his brother-in-law, the king of Greece, and administered a right royal dressing-down, telling him the holiday was over 'and the serious work for peace, which is your business, is about to begin'. The strong tone impressed the Greek prime minister, Venizelos, when he met him on a previous occasion: 'Now I understand autocracy when it is exercised by such a man!'[119]

As Bethmann left, the toady Lauff arrived. In a passage which gives an indication of both the man's style and his nature, he admired the flora surrounding the villa – 'Rose upon rose! In white, yellow and deep red cascades tumbling down the pillared hall and steps, leaping with curt gestures over dark blue crevices and ravines, staggering up again to reveal their full glory in the bright summer fire ... here was his life too. Work and effort, carrying out his duties as a ruler as on any other day, thinking about his people in passionate love and anxiety.' Lauff tripped around running into painters, sculptors and representatives of the arts and sciences; also generals. He admired the island's virgins who saluted the German emperor with cries of 'Heil Basileus!'. He returned on board the *Hohenzollern* with William who stopped off for a talk with the pro-German Italian Foreign Minister, marchese di San Giuliano, in Abbazia on the way.[120]

On the eve of war, William was still indulging his passion for archaeology. He invited Professor Dörpfeld out to Corfu to look at the dig, and Dörpfeld took up his Homer. Dörpfeld thought the nearby island of Levkas to be Homer's Ithaka and Odysseus's most probable home. With Dona and Dörpfeld they took the boat over to the island in order to see for themselves 'and visited one after another, the places identified in the *Odyssey*. Dörpfeld read the appropriate descriptive text out loud. We were surprised to have to concede that the place and the description completely fitted the bill.'[121] Later William would maintain that he was reading Homer while his cousin Nicholas was planning bloody war. At the beginning of the year he is alleged to have cancelled his holidays: 'Je resterai chez moi cette année, parce que nous aurons la guerre!'[122]

XV

William was fascinated by President Wilson's special envoy, Edward Mandell House. House was accorded an interview on Whit Monday, 1 June. He and the United States ambassador, James Gerard, paid a call on William in Potsdam. 'We must have made a wonderful sight when we were presented to the Kaiser; they sent the royal carriages for us with footmen standing behind in powdered wigs, outriders etc., though we must have looked rather dismal in our dress suits. In the glass carriages we must have looked like a funeral. The Kaiser is a much more majestic looking man than I expected.'[123]

House and the ambassador, Gerard, arrived in the middle of the traditional *Schrippenfest* when the garrison was treated to a stew accompanied by white rolls or *Schrippen*. They were decidedly underdressed: a 'grotesque sombreness quite out of keeping with the surroundings'. William compared them to 'two black crows'. William had to join in the Saturnalia and drink from a glass already used by a common soldier. He had not come across a 'Texas colonel' before, where rank was purely honorific. He explained that he had had a uniform, but he had given it to his 'negro butler, [who] wore it on solemn occasions, such as lodge meetings and funerals'. House's title intrigued the generals around the table too. Only the Chief of Staff Falkenhayn seemed to understand. William told the colonel that 'he wanted peace because it seemed in Germany's interest. Germany had been poor, she was now growing rich, and more years of peace would make her so. She was menaced on every side. The bayonets of Europe were directed at her.'

William told House of his plans for the coming year, predicting every move, right up to the *Nordlandsreise* and a trip to the Rhineland afterwards. Colonel House's visit to the Neues Palais depressed the Texan. Europe looked set for war. 'The situation is extraordinary. It is militarism run stark mad'; and yet he felt that William was saner and more far-seeing than his advisers. On 1 January House had discussed William with another American diplomat. 'He said the Kaiser had told him that the object in building a navy was not to threaten England, but to add prestige to Germany's commerce upon the seven seas. He had spoken of how impossible war should be between England and Germany, or, in fact, how utterly foolish any general European war would be.' Ambassador Gerard, who accompanied House to the meeting in Potsdam, also recalled the emperor's 'charm and nimble brain' once the war was behind him. 'He loved to appear in the martial array of the Black Hussars with the skull and cross-bones in the front of his busby; but that did not mean he loved war.'[124]

William thought that Germany, Britain and the United States had a community of interest, where France and Russia were 'semi-barbarous'. House told William that his navy was an impediment to an understanding with the United Kingdom. 'He replied that he must have a large navy in order to protect Germany's commerce in an adequate way, and one commensurate with her growing power and importance. He also said it was necessary to have a navy large enough to be able to defend themselves against the combined effects of Russia and France.'[125]

William and Tirpitz met Francis Ferdinand at Konopischt from 12 to 14 June. The Austrian did not share William's great admiration for Tisza. He distrusted the Hungarians in general and Tisza in particular, whom he suspected of wanting to set himself up as a dictator. Francis Ferdinand was in a warlike mood: 'If we don't attack the situation will get worse.' William was not enthusiastic. He thought the Russians were not ready and were unlikely to respond to an Austrian attack on Serbia. Some sources say he pledged his full support, but Francis Joseph later told Conrad, the Chief of the Austrian General Staff, he had done no such thing.[126]

A week before the assassination plunged Europe into bloody war, William had dinner with his friend, the Hamburg banker Max Warburg. 'In his view the Russian armament and the great Russian railway building programme were preparations for the great war which would break out in 1916 ... He complained that we would have too few railway lines on the Western Front against France. Beset by worries, he considered whether it was not better to attack rather than waiting.'[127]

14

The Slide into War

Francis Ferdinand and his wife Sophie von Hohenberg were assassinated on 28 June in the middle of Kiel Week. The most *mauvaise langue* of all, Bülow, held that William was reluctant to break off the merriment as he stood a chance of winning the cup; but he did.[1] That the young Serbians who had carried out the killings had had official military backing was never seriously doubted. Colonel Dragutin Dimitrijevic or 'Apis', the head of the *Crna Ruka* or 'Black Hand', was also the chief of the secret intelligence department of the Serbian General Staff. The man who had given Gavrilo Princip and his friends their bombs and pistols was Milan Cignovic, another member of Black Hand. The objective behind the murders was to unite all the south Slavs, half of whom lay in Austrian territory, in Slovenia and in the recently annexed provinces of Bosnia-Herzegovina.[2]

William later told a less than generous story about Francis Ferdinand and how his vanity had hastened his end. On their first meeting he had been impressed by the way the archduke's plump body had tautly bulged within his uniform, and the Austrian admitted that on occasion he had himself sewn in. This had been the case on the day of the killings. His aides desperately attempted to undo the buttons on his coat. By the time they realised they needed a pair of scissors, it was already too late. William was, for all that, 'the only person who had a spark of human feeling for the luckless archduke'; although the Tsar also ordered three weeks of national mourning. Francis Joseph did not even attend his nephew's funeral.[3] The shootings rang musically in the ears of General Conrad. It was a chance to deal with the Serbians once and for all. He wanted a punishment expedition, and he was backed by Graf Berchtold, the Foreign Minister.[4]

It has often been said that the Germans were keen to fight a war for European hegemony, but there was in reality no motivation, no planning, no programme of conquest beside that enunciated in the War Council of 8 December 1912; the only factor which pushed the High Command towards war was an unfortunate fatalism; an obsession that the Reich would go under unless it could bring home victory in a total war. Much was also motivated by the desire, foolish or wise, to preserve the power of their ally, Austria-Hungary, which led them to grant Graf Berchtold the 'blank cheque' he was longing for.[5] The General Staff naturally had its plans. Both its chief, Moltke, and the Military Cabinet chief Lyncker were in favour of fighting. There was a risk, but they thought they could win by superior technique. In 1913 they had increased the speed of the military timetables. It was important to get the fight over and done with before 1917 when the Russians were supposed to have perfected their military machine. They had reported on Russia's war readiness as recently as February and William had expressed the view that the 'Russian–Prussian relationship is dead once and for all!! We have become enemies.' Tirpitz was far from sanguine. As Moltke had predicted, his navy was not ready. He later postulated that had the war started in 1916 it would have been another performance altogether and Britain would have known how to keep the peace.[6]

Moltke was obsessed with the Russian railway network and continued to call for that preventative war which Bismarck had defined as 'committing suicide out of fear of death'. That being said, Moltke expressed no desire to acquire territory through war. He was also smitten with a deal of post-Darwinist thought about races and nations, thought which had infected the General Staff: war was a necessity, the Latin races were past their prime; the English wanted only material gain; Germany was the only cultural possibility remaining. Beyond the Chamberlainesque, wishy-washy theory, the central argument remained that the Russians were preparing to attack. William's ambassador in St Petersburg, Graf Pourtalès, thought this untrue. William voiced his contempt for his envoy in the margin of his report of 11 March: 'As a *soldier*, I hold the view derived from all my reports that there is not the slightest doubt that Russia is systematically preparing war against us, and I base my policy on that.'[7]

William still did not see the necessity for war despite all this. On 9 March the *Berliner Tageblatt* said the emperor was 'completely peaceful'. War frightened him. The bellicose marginalia he wrote at the time do not give an accurate picture of his way of thinking. According to Bülow – who was not out to defend his former master – they were intended to impress his officials just as his more menacing speeches were aimed to give foreign powers the impression that he was another Frederick the Great or Napoleon.[8]

The moment there was an actual danger His Majesty would become uncomfortably conscious that he could never lead an army in the field – in spite of the marshal's baton he loved to handle, of the medals and uniforms he adorned himself with, the pseudo-victories which, at manoeuvres, he counted on the judges to make him win. He was well aware that he was a neurasthenic, without real capacity as a general, and still less able, in spite of his naval hobby, to lead a squadron or even captain a ship. And neither Bethmann nor Jagow wanted war.[9]

William hopped this way and that over the assassination. 'In the critical days he flitted from recklessness to fear.'[10] The war party tried out their arguments: the Austrian alliance, now or never, *finis Germaniae* ...'[11] There were calls to arms from William's family, notably the crown prince, and Dona, both of them ever more gung-ho than him; Varnbüler, Eulenburg's friend and the long-serving envoy from Württemberg, was another warmonger. He felt the machine would rust if it were not put to work. He was not by any means the only influential civilian to think that way. Rathenau also believed in the use and inevitability of war.[12] General von Kessel and Adjutant-General Löwenfeld were annexationists and part of the anti-Bethmann fronde which gathered around Tirpitz. General von Plessen was also anxious that war should come, and above all against Britain, but William would not listen to him either. He had refused to commit Germany in the Balkans – 'non-intervention at any price' – and had even considered jettisoning the Austrian alliance. Only in December 1912 had he – briefly – committed himself to the war party, because he was incensed about Britain's determination to defend France.[13]

On 3 July William minuted: 'Now or never ... the Serbs must be done away with, and quickly.' It has been suggested that this new mood of William's stopped the diplomats in their attempts to cool the situation down. Austria-Hungary was the real 'sick man of Europe' and this was a last chance for it to prove itself. On 5 July it was maintained that William held an imperial council, something he denied to the end of his days. On that same day he offered the blank cheque to the Austrian ambassador Szögény, adding, 'As things stand today, Russia is in any case in no way ready for war, and will certainly need to reflect a while before they call [their people] to arms.' William was anxious to reaffirm the 'Nibelung loyalty' he professed towards his ally. To Bethmann he said that Francis Joseph must be made aware that Germany would not desert her in these serious times and that German interests required the maintenance of a strong Austria.[14]

It was the famous calculated risk: move quickly and Austria could recover its prestige before Russia could collect its forces. The same day Graf Hoyos arrived with Francis Joseph's note expressing the Austrian desire to eliminate Serbia. Francis Joseph was not at all sanguine about the course of events. To his Chief of Staff, Conrad, he voiced his uncertainty about the German ally. He had gone back on his word before.[15] On 6 July, at the Krupp works, William repeated that he would not back out this time. It was the Austrians who looked ready to do that, they were wavering.

'I don't believe we are heading for a great war,' William told Admiral Capelle the same day. 'In this case the Tsar's views would not be on the side of the prince's murderers. Besides this, France and Russia are not ready for war.'[16] On 7 July, Bethmann had a long talk with his secretary Kurt Riezler on his estate on the Oder: 'A distressing picture. He earnestly envisages the Anglo-Russian deal in the Naval Convention, [with a] landing in Pomerania ... Lichnowsky far too trusting, allows himself to be led down the garden path by the English. Russia's military power rapidly growing; with the strategic development of Poland the position cannot be maintained. Austria ever weaker and more cumbersome ...' That very day, however, House wrote to William from London. He had found no desire for war in Berlin, London or Paris.[17]

Bethmann filled Riezler in on the situation to date. It was the *casus foederis*, there was the old dilemma. Do you tell the Austrians to stop or do you encourage them. It was worse than the last time, in 1912. 'A move against Serbia can lead to world war. The emperor expects a war, to transform everything as it now stands. The future belongs to Russia, which grows bigger and stronger and lies upon us like an ever heavier burden.'[18] The chancellor and the responsible ministers were agreed that William should not cancel his North Sea journey: it would instantly give rise to the feeling that war might be about to break out. He questioned his military leaders first to ascertain their level of preparedness before he left for Kiel. Indeed, it was holidays all round: Tirpitz took a cure in Swiss Tarasp, and was told not to come back before time, as that might excite speculation. Moltke went to take the waters at Carlsbad and Bethmann-Hollweg disappeared from Berlin. Jagow went to Lucerne on honeymoon! The Quartermaster-General took himself off to bury an aunt. It has been claimed that all these holidays were merely a screen to cover Germany's malevolent intentions. The idea was challenged by the American writer Viereck: 'If the Germans had a talent for that sort of thing, they would have managed their entrance into the war itself with more ingenuity.' Bethmann prudently had a telephone installed so that he might run things from Hohenfinow. Tirpitz later claimed this was what caused the trouble.[19] In Britain, Sir Edward Grey went fishing.

William heard from House in Balholm. The Texas colonel had been rocketing around Europe trying to gauge the mood of the different capitals. He reassured William that he did not believe that the French were genuinely prepared to make war for Alsace-Lorraine. William, however, thought that the British had already given them an undertaking on that score.[20] Moltke had predicted that nothing decisive would happen before the 25th. On that day William heard the accommodating Serbian response while at Odde on the Utnefiord. He made a marginal note. He could not see what more the Austrians wanted. They had achieved a brilliant *coup*. 'It was a capitulation of the most humiliating sort. With it disappears *every reason for war*.' Plessen wired Moltke to that effect. Even Moltke had written on the 26th that 'if Russia undertakes no hostile act against Austria the war will remain localised'. William thought, however, that now Austria had mobilised a third of its army, they might as well occupy some territory to receive a pledge of future good behaviour. At that point, Tirpitz believed, the whole war scare could have disappeared if Bethmann and Berchtold had been sensible. The hawks had the impression that William was backing down. In Bülow's view, the 'carte blanche' or 'blank cheque' was awarded 'in sheerest apathy and indifference'.[21]

The last *Nordlandsreise* ended early. William ordered a return on 25 July against Bethmann's wishes. Serbia had mobilised and William was worried that the *Hohenzollern* and its escorts might be attacked by a Russian squadron. Müller expressed his policy on landing at Kiel at 7 a.m. on the 27th: 'Keep calm, make the injustice sit with the Russians and do not shy from war.' William arrived back in Potsdam at 3 p.m. He was still convinced that Austrian honour had been largely satisfied. 'Stop in Belgrade,' he told them. Unlike Bethmann, he was unaware that the Austrians had already answered the Serbians. He told the Foreign Minister Jagow to calm everyone down. 'The few reservations which Serbia makes to single points, can, in my opinion, be easily clarified through negotiation.' At this point the military leaders and Bethmann are believed to have conspired against their master. They thought he would back down as he had always done before and countermanded his orders. 'Stop in Belgrade' was never transmitted. Moltke thought it would be another two weeks before it was clear what was going to happen.

William was 'feverishly active' on the 28th, casting this way and that to keep the peace. 'He had no idea what the Austrians wanted. The Serbs had agreed to everything bar a few trifles. Since 5 July the Austrians had said nothing about their plans.' The initiative had already passed to the Chiefs of Staff. On the 30th Moltke wired Conrad in Vienna to ignore any further British attempts to uphold the peace and to accept his assurances that Germany would join them unconditionally. Bethmann, at least, did not desire a world war. Just a limited conflict which would bring some prestige to Austria and chasten Russia a little.[22]

William was still shocked by the enormity of the crime. It should be recalled that the Serbs had killed their own royal family in 1903. King Alexander Obrenovich and his wife were hurled from the windows of their palace. Alexander allegedly managed to hold on to the sill, but he fell to his death when one of the conspirators chopped off his fingers with his sword. Regicide was a heinous crime for one who believed in divine right and William considered the murders 'the first act in a new Pan-Slav Balkan policy'. If the world war was going to break out anywhere, William told Niemann later, it would have been in Serbia. He tended to see the Serbs as little more than bandits or a 'nest of assassins'. On Lichnowsky's telegram of 24 July he minuted: '... the fellows have caused agitation and murder and must be humiliated.' He thought the Austrians were windy and that their duty was to take control of the Balkans and drive the Russians out.[23]

Bethmann did not tell William what he was up to until the 27th. He was another who did what he could to stave off European war. 'What the world needs most is calming down', he allegedly told Bülow. To his critics that was simply not enough. Fear of yet another unseemly diplomatic defeat seems to have egged him on. On the 28th some news came from England. Stumm at the Foreign Office delivered the message that Britain would remain neutral; only if France were in serious danger would they throw their weight into the scales to secure peace.[24] On the same day Moltke delivered his report on the political situation. He spoke of Serbia's five years of troublemaking and voiced his gratitude to the Austrians for taking action. They had mobilised eight corps, enough for a punishment raid. Russia had responded by putting twelve on standby. What was to be the upshot? If Austria brought in more men war would become unavoidable. France would be dragged in too. 'It cannot be denied that the Russians have arranged things very smartly.'[25]

As the military position was becoming worse with every hour, and less and less to Germany's advantage, Moltke wanted to mobilise as quickly as possible. Bethmann gave in to the hawks, or as Bülow put it, 'He was the sacrificial lamb, who, in 1914, tried to assume the aspect of a wolf.' He was apparently taken aback by the Austrian ultimatum. When he saw the way things were going he tried to resign. William would not accord his wishes: 'You have cooked up this broth, now you are going to eat it,' he told him.[26] Bülow's attitude, however, was coloured by his annoyance that he was not called back to run Germany again at the outset of war.

The second crisis occurred on the afternoon of 29 July. There was no Imperial Council as such, just a series of small conferences with important generals, admirals and ministers: Bethmann, Falkenhayn, Moltke, Lyncker, Henry, Tirpitz, Müller and Pohl. The seven military advisers soon gained the upper hand over the one civilian. Berchtold was rapturous. 'It has worked!' he wrote from Vienna, and then enquired, 'Who is in charge – Moltke or Bethmann?' Bethmann, for his part was trying to apply the brakes, but without success.[27]

Despite all the warnings they had received from Lichnowsky they still wanted to believe that Britain would remain neutral. England's neutrality naturally reared its head on the 29th. Prince Henry had just returned from Britain where George V had given him an assurance that Britain would keep aloof. Tirpitz was sceptical – possibly he understood the British political system better than his emperor. William put him down: 'I have the word of a king, and that is enough for me.' Tirpitz maintained that there was no intention of annexing French land; Belgian and Dutch neutrality would be respected providing the other side did too. On the same day there was a report from Lichnowsky. Grey had made it abundantly clear: Britain could under no circumstances remain neutral if Germany attacked France. The next day William was informed both of Russia's partial mobilisation and of Britain's 'betrayal'. 'Miserable shopkeeper rabble', he called them. 'If we must bleed to death, then England must at least lose India.'[28]

The Royal Navy took up its position at Scapa on 29 July. The Russians did not mobilise until the 30th. The German emperor reacted: 'Then I must also mobilise ... the Russian Tsar therefore assumes the guilt ... My attempts to mediate have been a failure.' William later contended that the Russians had already begun preparations and printed the mobilisation order prior to that date. He believed until his dying day that he had circumstantial evidence that the Tsar had wanted war all along. The diplomats in the Wilhelmstrasse were clueless. 'Both they and their resistance had collapsed. They did not want to believe in war.' When William portioned out the blame, they earned a heavy responsibility for Germany's failure.[29] Bülow observed with interest that Botho Wedel, a high-ranking Foreign Office official, was still sunning himself on Norderney on 26 July. The assumption was that Britain would remain neutral and that the war would not take place.

In his *Ereignisse und Gestalten* (Events and Personalities) of 1922, William rehearsed the various points which proved that culpability neither lay with him nor with Germany. The Entente powers had begun hoarding gold in London from April onwards, whereas the Germans carried on exporting gold and grain, even to Entente countries. That same month the German military attaché in Tokyo picked up the scent of something he could not define: 'There is something in the air, like the commiseration for a not yet pronounced death sentence.' In March General Tcherbatcheff told the War Academy in Petersburg that the war had become unavoidable and would probably break out that summer.

'Russia would have the honour of launching the attack.'[30]

II

The Germans have spent eighty years examining their navels: from 1918 to 1933 denying and accepting responsibility by turns; from 1933 to 1945 refuting it utterly; from 1945 to 1961, they returned to the position under Weimar, and from 1961 onwards they have been keen to assume as much of the blame as possible. One of their own, however, has made the point that Fischer's theories have their limitations and that other countries share a responsibility for the war: 'Wilhelmine Germany was not the only country to possess a lunatic fringe.' War planning existed in every major European country. 'At no point did they have anything to do with the outright economic and financial preparation of war, to be unleashed by a certain date. The notion of a dead straight, one-way street, down which imperial policy consciously proceeded for years in advance towards the Great War, is unconvincing.'[31]

It was, says the same writer, the failure of William's sabre-rattling Bonapartism which to his chagrin unleashed a process of European alliances, the dreadful machinery began to roll, and the more containable notion of the 'calculated risk' failed. The fact that 'tendencies' existed proves in no way the will to bring about a war. To show the lack of forward planning, Wehler points to the fact that the gold reserves in the Juliusturm in Spandau fort contained just 202 million marks, enough for just two days of war. Nor had the Grand Fleet reached its stations. It was not assembled until the 31st, two days after Britain's.[32]

Only Germany's motives are questioned closely, and yet Russia's policy in the Balkans or France's in Morocco were every bit as reprehensible, as were the inflated numbers in their armed forces. Was Admiral Fisher any more justified in renewing and upgrading the Royal Navy than Tirpitz? Were, asks one recent writer, Sir Henry Wilson, Foch or Suk-homlinov 'any more virtuous than Ludendorff?'[33] It is hard to see why the German General Staff were so utterly convinced that Russia was bent on war, but two army reforms of 1906 and 1908 had made provision for a strength of 2.2 million men, which was a frightening prospect.[34] Even if no such plot existed, the idea that Germany was being encircled by enemies determined to destroy her, was very real to a very large number of people, some of them – like William himself – highly influ- ential ones. War was brought on by a European and American 'armament fever' exacerbated by the press, which saw fit to encourage the distrust that existed between the nations. There was no appreciable difference between the newspapers in Germany, Britain, Russia or France when it came to driving the people into a desire for vainglorious war. That the German emperor was best known for applying the brake is less disputed now than it was. He prevented anything coming of the war fever in 1905. He tried again, and failed, in 1914.

The Russians did not seem to know why they were mobilising against Germany. Chelius wired William from St Petersburg, 'I have the impression that they have mobilised from anxiety over coming events, and without aggressive views.' William minuted, 'Quite right, that is how it is.'[35] That day Bethmann told Tirpitz that he felt the emperor failed to understand the issues. Tirpitz wanted to know why William had not sent an emissary to St Petersburg. Instead the German emperor wired his cousin the Tsar: 'Our long proven friendship must with God's help succeed in preventing bloodshed ... you must give your troops an immediate order under no circumstances to make even the smallest violation of our frontiers.' Russia's war, however, had already started.[36]

William – and others – pointed out that the Tsar tried to apply the brakes. He ordered Yanushkevich to rescind the order. The general conspired with the Foreign Minister, Sazonov, to disobey his command. The minister told the general that Nicholas's order was nonsense, he was to go ahead and tomorrow he would see the Tsar and talk him out of the stupid telegram from the German emperor. Yanushkevich then told the Tsar that the mobilisation could no longer be halted. William, of course, took the credit for changing the warmongering Tsar's way of thinking. He recognised his 'monstrous responsibility' for the first time. That was why he tried to halt the engines of war and would have been successful had Sazonov not scuppered his plans.[37]

William was still desperately clutching at King George's statement. Despite all he said he knew about his mother's country, he had no idea where decisions were taken. 'It is my view', he told the State Secretary at the RMA, 'that from now on the only possibility of preventing a world conflagration lies in England, not Berlin; the English can't want it either.'[38] Grey's clarity has often come into question, but he was lucid enough to Sazonov in June 1912. He told the Russian Foreign Minister that public opinion would not tolerate an aggressive war against Germany, but the people would rally if Germany were to attack France. He also made it clear that Germany would not succeed in keeping Britain neutral.[39]

Britain might not have been so squeaky-clean either. There was considerable anti-German feeling, and not just from the Northcliffe press and its readers. Both the Foreign Secretary, Grey, and the diplomat Eyre Crowe were Germanophobes. There was no reason for going to Serbia's aid – such a move would have been unpopular anyway – but there were good, clear reasons for humbling Germany, as both Bülow and Moltke were at pains to point out. With Germany facing massive armies on both fronts, here was the opportunity to step in and 'reduce to impotence the most powerful continental state' which was 'also her worst economic rival'. President Wilson's special adviser, Colonel House, thought much the same: 'Whenever England consents, France and Russia will close in on Germany and Austria.'[40] The vindictive Bülow blamed the bad advice of Bethmann and Jagow for the outbreak of war, together with a seasoning of William's vainglory: 'Those who, in 1914, had the direction of Germany's policy were neither cunning incendiaries nor ruthless swashbucklers – they were fools.'[41]

Bülow felt that Moltke was inadequate too. The trick he had yet to learn was to make the others declare war on you. 'In 1866, in '70 even, Prince Bismarck had found means to leave his enemies the odium of declaring war. Appearances govern the world. They, as the Greeks already knew, decide more easily than reality.' Moltke too felt the declaration was premature. On 1 August Ballin asked Bethmann: 'Why such haste to declare war on Russia, Your Excellency?' Bethmann replied, 'If we don't we shan't get the socialists to fight.' They had to make the Tsar look responsible.[42] Jagow had even tried to talk Moltke out of applying the Schlieffen Plan in January. He feared that it would bring Britain into the war. Bethmann was not so sure. The French already had plans to violate Belgian neutrality in the event of war, which the British had asked them to drop.[43]

On 31 July William wired his cousins Nicholas and George:

It is not I who bears the responsibility for the disaster which now threatens the entire civilized world. Even at this moment the decision to stave it off lies with you. No one threatens the honour or power of Russia. The friendship for you and your empire which I have borne from the deathbed of my grandfather has always been totally sacred to me ... the peace of Europe can still be maintained by you, if Russia decides to halt the military measures which threaten Germany and Austria-Hungary.[44]

For technical reasons the mobilisation I ordered this afternoon had to be effected on the eastern and western fronts. The order sadly cannot be countermanded because your telegram arrived so late. However, were France to offer me her neutrality, which must be guaranteed by the British army and navy, I will naturally refrain from attacking France and employ my troops elsewhere. I hope that France will not be nervous. The troops on my borders will be immediately telephonically and telegraphically stopped from crossing the French frontier. William.[45]

Mobilisation for the next day was signed at 5 p.m. on 1 August. Gwinner later claimed he had to be talked into putting his pen to it, even then. Then came the news of Britain's guarantee of Belgian neutrality. The war was destined to be fought on two fronts and involve all Europe. William's feet caught a chill. He ordered Moltke to 'inhibit' the march to the west: 'We shall simply march the whole army eastwards.' Moltke answered that the work of years could not be altered. 'Your uncle would have given me a different answer.' Moltke replied that there would be nothing to protect Germany if France should decide to attack. For technical reasons the plan had to go ahead. He mentioned the French forts of Toul and Verdun being made over to Germany as guarantees. Moltke was in despair. He revealed that the 16th Division had been told to march into Luxembourg to secure it against a French strike. Bethmann told him that that must not happen, as Britain would not approve the violation of Luxembourg's neutrality either. William then instructed his ADC to telephone and order the 16th Division not to enter Luxembourg.

'I felt as if my heart was going to burst,' wrote Moltke. The order went out. 'It is impossible to describe the mood in which I came home. I was like a broken man and shed tears of despair.' At 11 p.m. Moltke received an order to report to the Schloss. 'The emperor received me in his bedroom. He had already gone to bed, but he had risen again and thrown a dressing gown over himself.' He showed Moltke a wire from King George. George knew nothing of any guarantee to prevent France from making war. Lichnowsky must have made a mistake. 'The emperor was very excited and said to me, "Now you can do what you like."' Moltke went home and telegraphed the 16th Division that they might now enter Luxembourg. 'I am convinced', wrote Moltke in November 1914, 'that the emperor would certainly not have signed the mobilisation order if the despatch from Fürst Lichnowsky had arrived thirty minutes earlier.'[46]

The Staff Chief was beside himself. His wife later admitted he had panicked at the assumption of responsibility for the leadership of the German army. 'His confidence was shaken. The relationship of trust between him and the emperor was destroyed.' Moltke in his frustration exclaimed, 'I can certainly fight a war against an exterior enemy, but not against my own emperor.' It was not a good start. For technical reasons the strike had to be continued. Not only the diplomats, but also the emperor, had to stand aside.[47] The English declaration had come too late.

The same day a second telegram came from Lichnowsky: Great Britain would remain neutral in a war between Germany, France and Russia. Müller recorded that William's good humour returned and he ordered *Sekt*. Germany declared war on Russia that day, France on the 3rd. Austria-Hungary waited a further week. The Germans appeared to have forgotten about the British and their fetish about Belgium. Then began William's nightmare again.

When war was declared on Russia on 1 August Ballin was profoundly shocked. 'Enormous stupidity!' he called it. Bülow thought Bethmann resembled the scapegoat in Holman Hunt's famous picture; using a nautical metaphor, Tirpitz thought he looked more like a 'drowning man'. For many he was to become just that after the war. Asked how this appalling situation had come about, he replied, 'If only I knew!'[48]

15

Into the Shadows

William had not wanted that 'mother of all catastrophes',[1] the First World War, but once again his mood did not correspond to that of his people. On 1 August they spilled out on to the streets in jubilation. After the war a severely disappointed Walther Rathenau tried to fathom the make-up of the crowds that clogged up Berlin's boulevards: 'just about everybody', he concluded. Many of them were now to be seen parading behind a red flag.

Who were those people who hung out the flag twice a week, who drank to the sinking of the *Lusitania*, who favoured the submarine war, and who joked about each declaration of war? There were a lot of good socialists among them.[2]

William was in his element. The actor came out. It was the moment to exercise his natural gift for oratory.

I thank you from the depth of my heart for the expression of your love and loyalty. In the struggle which lies before us I recognize no more parties among my people. There are only Germans, and those parties which have turned against me in the course of our differences of opinion, I forgive with all my heart.[3]

William's first move was to wire Francis Joseph to tell him that Serbia was no longer a priority. Austria would be compensated in Italy. Clearly the General Staff had told him there were bigger fish to fry, and a Serbian campaign would have made a nonsense of their strategy. William then tried to drum up allies among his family by sending a telegram to Constantine of Greece. The Greek king was keen to remain neutral. William was angry and later decided he should be treated as an enemy. The king of Romania was another – Catholic – Hohenzollern. He too was leaned on to come over to William's side. The huge disparity in men and arms between the Entente and the Central powers must have been an alarming prospect.[4]

On the 4th William delivered his famous Reichstag throne speech.

The Social Democrats were notable by their absence:

The world has been a witness of how, in the pressure and confusion of the last few years, we have stood in the forefront in our untiring efforts to save the nations of Europe from a war between the great powers.

 With a heavy heart I have had to mobilise my armies against a neighbour with whom you have fought together on so many battlefields.

All attempts at friendship with France had come up against the 'old grudge'. 'We are not driven by a desire for conquest, we are animated by the unbending will, to protect the place which God has given us, for us and for all our progeny ... With a clean hand and a pure conscience we reach for our swords.' The rest of the speech was delivered off the cuff:

Gentlemen, you have read what I said to my people from the balcony of the Schloss. I repeat, I recognise no more parties, I know only Germans and as a sign that you are firmly decided to join with me, without difference of party, class or religion and proceed with me through thick and thin, hardship and death, I call upon the leaders of the parties to come forward and to offer me their hands.[5]

When the last of the leaders had walked away William clenched his fist, raised it in the air then brought it down again, as if lashing with a sabre.

 Unity was briefly achieved. William had striven for a quarter of a century to put his entire population behind him. Now, on 4 August, the 'Burgfrieden' was assured: the Reichstag devolved its powers on to the Bundesrat composed of the princes. There would be no more problems with ratification of payments. Whatever William and the army wanted would be duly rubber-stamped. From the Schloss William pronounced, 'Now I commend you to God. Go to church and kneel down and pray for help for our soldiers!' The public would have to tighten their belts, however. A quarter of Germany's food had been imported before 1914. The blockade put paid to that and the best of what remained was hived off for the military. Prices inevitably soared.[6]

 On 5 August William had a final audience with the British ambassador, Sir Edward Goschen. He told him to inform George V that in consequence of what had occurred he would have to resign his positions as a British field marshal and admiral of the fleet. At 6 p.m. he appeared with Dona and Adalbert on the balcony of the Schloss. An hour later Prince Oscar celebrated a simple, wartime wedding to his morganatic bride, Ina Marie von Bassewitz at Bellevue. Adalbert was to wed himself, a more respectable bride, a few days later in Wilhelmshaven. The imperial pair spent the rest of the evening in the little Spree-side garden of the palace. It was to be the last time they lived in the vast old Schloss.

William was never comfortable there in the middle of the city. During the war it was constantly ringed by gawping crowds and he once again feared assassins. They moved to Schloss Bellevue in the Tiergarten, the erstwhile home of Frederick the Great's crapulous brother Ferdinand.[7]

George V kissed hands with the Austrian ambassador Graf Mensdorff. The king told him, 'There is not the slightest ill-feeling against Austria, we are only technically at war. I don't believe William wanted war, but he was afraid of his son's popularity. His son and his party made the war.'[8] Little Willy was indeed delighted. Once William had given up hope of averting the catastrophe he made his son commander-in-chief of the 5th Army. The other sons flocked to the colours too. Prince Eitel received the top regimental command: the First Foot. The crown prince for his part did nothing to alter his ways, maintaining his contacts with the Januschauer and through him, the Pan-Germans. His own goal, the removal of Bethmann-Hollweg, was once again uppermost in his mind. He even wrote to the disgraced warmonger Bernhardi.[9]

Life was busy in Berlin before William finally left for the front on the 16th. On the 1st a 'field altar' was set up in Potsdam's Lustgarten emblazoned with an iron cross for an open-air service. God was to be petitioned for his aid. Under brilliant blue skies which had come to be known as 'Kaiserwetter' – or imperial weather – there was an open-air service at the Bismarck monument on the 2nd and the 5th was declared a day of prayer. The first victory was announced forty-eight hours later with the fall of the heavily fortified city of Liège. The army was led by the middle-class General Staff officer Erich Ludendorff. He rapidly became a military and political icon. A number of underused royal palaces were turned into field hospitals: Strasbourg, Wiesbaden, Königsberg, Coblenz, Schwedt and the Orangery at Sanssouci. William's farm at Cadinen became a rest home. These were to be Dona's new babies, when she was not bending her husband's ear and meddling in politics.

On the 11th, William packed 700 Lichterfelde cadets off to war, counselling 'ruthless bravery, cold blood and a cool head'. They would take him at his word at Langemarck two months later, when in the course of the so-called 'massacre of the innocents' 50,000 uniformed men went to their death facing the superior rifle drill of the British Expeditionary Force. Two days later William paid a call on his dead father and prayed at his grave in the Friedenskirche. At 7 a.m. on the 16th he was ready to go. He received the Oberbürgermeister Wermuth and his ministers in the Sternensaal of the Schloss and boarded a fourteen-carriage train from the Potsdam station half an hour later. It took a roundabout route to confound attackers, arriving at Coblenz at 8.23 the next day. There William made his first GHQ, living in the Oberpräsidium until command transferred to Luxembourg on the 30th.[10]

II

There were other disappointments to come. The pro-German Italian Foreign Minister, the marchese di San Giuliano, was about to shuffle off his coil. His successor Sidney Sonnino had been equally pro-German initially, but after the Battle of the Marne he read the writing on the wall. Victor Emmanuel refused to come in on the side of the Central Powers because he saw no *casus foederis*. The Austrians had failed to consult him anyway, before they delivered their ultimatum to Serbia.[11] German diplomacy now proved a sorry failure. The Italians held out for some pieces of territory – Trentino or South Tyrol – before they would consent. William was even prepared to countenance giving parts of Frederick the Great's hard-won region of Upper Silesia back to the Austrians to make them agree to a cession of territory to their southern neighbours, but his diplomats proved unequal to the task of wooing the Italians.[12] Eventually it looked as if they might obtain what they wanted more easily by joining the Entente.

'We are in need, and necessity knows no law.' Bethmann admitted his tort in marching through Luxembourg and Belgium on the 4th. The Schlieffen Plan had always required a march through Belgium, because the defences of northern France were too strong. 'Germany desires nothing more than your friendship,' read the pathetic final message from the chancellor. 'Are you willing to shed rivers of blood, to bring untold calamities to the world, for a phrase, a technicality, a scrap of paper? Was there a war in which neutrality has not been violated?' The diplomats were aware of a secret clause in the Treaty of Vienna which allowed the Prussians to occupy Antwerp in the event of a war with France. The British were to land at Ostend.[13] Others pointed out that the French or British would have violated Belgian neutrality had the Germans not done it first. It was a pretext for the British anyhow, as their fleet had already arrived at its action stations by Scapa.

The main battles might have involved the French and the Russians, the Serbians and the Italians, but the real enemy was perfidious Albion. 'A word from England would have been enough.' William proclaimed there would be 'no peace before England is defeated and destroyed. Only amid the ruins of London will I forgive Georgie.' He told Bülow that Nicholas and George had planned the whole thing at Victoria Louise's wedding: 'History showed no greater perfidy ... God would punish them some day! ... The Tsar's ingratitude was revolting: he had always been the Tsar's close friend. As for "Georgie", all the emperor had to say was that Queen Victoria, their grandmother, must have turned in her grave at the spectacle of her English grandson flinging down the gauntlet to the German.' At the end of the year Ballin reported back to

Bülow: 'I have seen the emperor, whom I found full of confidence in the future, though also of wrath against England, and in this the empress encourages him. So that personal rancours and dislikes seem to play a considerable part in policy, and that appears to me very dangerous.'[14]

William's reasons for hating Britain were personal and dynastic, but during the war they married up neatly with some of the ideas propagated by the expansionists. A successful war could result in shunting the island off its position as the leading world power and Germany could take its place. That would mean more colonies. The Prussian school, however, pointed east, where Teutonic Knights and German settlers had already formed colonies in the high Middle Ages before they had fallen under the 'yoke of the Moscovites'. As William's war was increasingly successful on the Eastern Front, the cries for annexation grew louder.[15]

There were constructive ideas which emerged from the hatred. Once again William's mind turned to a future settlement in Europe. Bethmann wanted a bloc composed of Britain, France and Germany directed against Russia. The Anglophobic Tirpitz naturally disagreed. On 19 August he had a two-hour talk with William at HQ in Coblenz during which it was agreed to 'further develop' Germany as a world power with its weight in the west. William wanted 'France to be first of all totally defeated. Then he would offer the French [a deal], no territory would be annexed if they were prepared to conclude a defensive and offensive alliance with Germany. That would naturally be in France's interest.'[16] William was not an annexationist. In that he was supported by a business element composed, among others, of Rathenau, Gwinner, Thyssen, Erzberger (for the time being) and Naumann. They supported the creation of an economic bloc stretching from France to the Balkans.[17]

III

William was profoundly depressed as early as 6 August. His failure to keep the peace affected him deeply. One trusted servant who saw him in the first days of August reported that he had never seen him bear such a 'tragic and downtrodden' mien. 'Despite the proud speeches he forced himself to make, the emperor had an inkling of something that his diplomats and generals had failed to grasp: that the war would be the end of his empire ...'[18] Not even the fall of Liège excited him, he was too aware that the Belgian *démarche* had cost him war with Britain. Once again the rumour ran round that he had gone mad, but it was probably no more than bouts of manic depression. He became increasingly peripheral. He rubber-stamped orders. He fraternised with captured British officers until Plessen told him not to. Generals reporting to him noted his 'erratic thinking and impulsive behaviour'. As he had never accustomed himself to reading the newspapers, which were heavily censored anyway, he gleaned what he could from his visitors: 'What news have you brought from Berlin?'[19]

Bethmann thought William's importance was psychological. 'A king of Prussia, a German emperor who did not stay in the middle of his armies was an idea which would have been unbearable both to the emperor and the troops.'[20] A routine was set within the first month of the war and, except in moments of crisis, this was to remain William's life for the next four years. He travelled between the various fronts and reviewed his troops, encouraging them with speeches, consoling them with a homely 'Du', a slap on the shoulder and a medal pinned on their chests. The first of these was to go to Ludendorff, who won Prussia's highest military medal, the *pour le mérite*, for masterminding the seizure of the Liège forts. On 22 August Little Willy's army scored an initial victory in the battle for Longwy. William wrote to Cilli and gave his eldest son the Iron Cross, 1st and 2nd class. His little brother Oscar had to be content with the latter. To be fair to William, he was not the only monarch to suffer from medalomania; Francis Joseph literally sent him up a case of his highest award, the Order of Maria-Theresa, with instructions to William to take one each, for Moltke and himself.[21]

IV

On the 21st, before the disaster at the Marne told him the Schlieffen Plan would not work, the emperor found himself sitting alone on a bench. 'Do you already despise me so much that nobody will sit next to me?' Sometimes the mood was so bad that he was unable to get out of bed. But he was not called 'William the Sudden' for nothing. Bethmann's secretary, Kurt Riezler, saw him in Coblenz the next day and found him impressively fresh, at a high table also seating the king of Bavaria and Tirpitz. Riezler thought the latter a Renaissance personality, a Jesuit.[22]

Tirpitz believed William's constitution was not up to the 'pressure of responsibility'. His health collapsed increasingly often, a fact that worried his physicians. The Grossadmiral also thought that as he grew older he gave in to his entourage more and more.[23] But there were consolations in the east: after an initial setback where the Russians had laid waste to East Prussia, old Hindenburg had been called back from retirement to lead the armies. He swept up 8,000 prisoners at Gumbinnen on the 23rd and between 26 and 30 August a battle raged which was to become the first resounding victory of the war. It was promptly named 'Tannenberg', although it was miles away from the place where the Poles had trounced the Teutonic Knights in 1410. A few days later there was a further victory at Lyck, and Hindenburg, now promoted to Colonel General, also received the *pour le mérite*.[24]

Moltke modified the Schlieffen Plan himself. German armies were originally supposed to cross Holland as well as Belgium and the French were to be allowed to enter German territory. He did this to prevent Holland from coming into the war on the side of the Entente. He refused to strengthen his left wing at the expense of his right and weakened the spearhead. The changes Moltke made robbed the whole strategy of its 'revolving door effect'. On 25 August he launched a campaign in Lorraine, which was not mentioned in the blueprint, and Hindenburg and Ludendorff's great victories in the East showed that 'Schlieffen's vision had materialised in the wrong theatre'.[25]

On the 30th William moved to Luxembourg, which had been occupied since the beginning of the war. For the next four weeks William was billeted in the German consul-general's house. The following day, when he went to study his son's achievement at Longwy, he enjoyed his first lunch on French soil since his student days. He spent two days in France sleeping in the dining room of a house which had belonged to a French general. The pro-German Swedish explorer Sven Hedin went to visit William in his billet. William was living over the shop. Downstairs there was the chancellery which had been transformed into a map room, and he dined next door. It was a very tight squeeze.

Hedin met Generals Plessen and Gontard and Müller. The latter surprised him by speaking Swedish. Besides these were the usual team: Karl von Treutler, General Ulrich von Marschall, Maximilian von Mutius, Dr Friedrich von Ilberg, Pless and Arnim. William came down at one o'clock. There was a simple lunch: soup, meat and vegetables, pudding, red and white wine: 'I have rarely been so hungry as I was rising from His Majesty's table,' Hedin admitted. It was not the meal that was at fault: 'When the emperor speaks, I truly have no time to eat roast beef and vegetables. I listen and then order myself a sandwich when I get back to my hotel.' William had been visiting French prisoners and was expressing regret at the necessity for fighting France.[26]

Matters were coming to a head on the Marne. The German army had looked set to repeat its siege of Paris, which was only thirty miles away, but by the end of the first week of September it became clear that the strategy had failed. On the 9th the German advance was ordered to fall back and hold its positions. Prince Joachim received a slight shrapnel wound that same day: 'Now Hohenzollern blood has also been shed.' He was still oozing pride when Hedin saw him next on the 25th. He had a letter from a sergeant, giving the details of his son's gallantry in the field. In the other princely houses the losses had been worse: two Lippes and two Meiningens had already died.[27]

Moltke believed that the diplomats had caused the disaster. England's entry into the war made all the difference. Eventually the Chief of Staff suffered a breakdown, proving that his nerves were not much stronger than the emperor's.[28] Moltke's nightmare had been achieved: he did not think William had a clue what was going on. William heard about the failure of the offensive in his HQ in Luxembourg. 'He was not unmerciful, but I had the impression that he was not entirely convinced of the necessity of the retreat.' Moltke made way for the Minister of War, Falkenhayn, on 14 September. William did not have the heart to sack his old friend Julius and for the time being he retained the title of Chief of the General Staff. Falkenhayn none the less wanted to make it clear that Moltke was to stay out of it from now on. In the west the armies now dug in. It was the sort of war Moltke had wanted to avoid.[29]

Many had been aware that it was not possible to knock France out in six weeks: Valentini and Müller among the cabinet chiefs, Tirpitz, Pohl, Falkenhayn, Ballin, Gwinner and Helfferich. Too little credence had been given to England, and the arrival of the British Expeditionary Force prevented the Schlieffen Plan from working. The Germans had always poured scorn on Britain's 'contemptible little army'; now they were amazed by its fighting strength. As the Germans took stock of the stagnant war which faced them, they also played the atrocity card. William was told of the shooting of some doctors and that dum-dum bullets had been found. He made a formal complaint to President Wilson of the United States.[30]

Falkenhayn did not believe that Germany could win – the best that could be done was to make sure she did not lose. He wanted a massive offensive in the west (Verdun), submarine warfare aimed at destroying British commerce, and a separate peace in the east. He had important backing from Tirpitz and William and his entourage. They soon came up against Hindenburg and Ludendorff, the dynamic duo on the Eastern Front who were alone providing Germany with its triumphs. They wanted to play the Schlieffen Plan in reverse: beat the Russians resoundingly and then return to deal with the French. Apart from the running sore of Verdun, Falkenhayn proved himself a good general and Chief of Staff. The problem was the popularity of the Eastern Command. In 1915 they advanced 250 miles in contrast to a virtually static Western Front.

The crown prince visited William in Luxembourg in September. It was the same old song. Bethmann had to go. After Hindenburg's victories in the east he thought the old man would make a better overall commander than Falkenhayn. Young Willy was not impressed by his father either. 'With terrible clarity he recognised that the emperor was failing as Supreme Warlord.' Falkenhayn was depriving Hindenburg of troops. Prince William's desire to see Hindenburg placed in the top job was supported by Dona. The crown prince thought either Tirpitz or Bülow the best person for the job of chancellor.[31] Falkenhayn and Bethmann did not get on either. Bethmann thought the general had designs on the chancellorship and, early in 1915, looked at means of having him pushed out of the way. Bethmann also sympathised with the demands of the annexationists, but he needed the support of the socialists in the Reichstag, and could not make any public demonstration of keenness.

HQ moved again. On 28 September William installed himself in the three-storey villa of a rich industrialist in Charleville. It lay behind decorated iron railings, with a covered entrance up some steps. There was room for Plessen and an ADC, and the servants, who slept in the mansard. The great advantage for William was the large garden for his morning walk. From his new home he could reach the front and perform his official duties: pinning on medals and shaking scores of eager hands. Charleville became a Prussian garrison town – 'Klein Berlin' or 'Klein Potsdam'. An unfinished barracks building was turned into a chapel for Sunday worship. Chelius played the organ. Contrary to some reports, the emperor lived a very simple life. When guests came there was a slightly better menu, otherwise it was pea soup with sausages followed by fruit, with red or white wine in carafes. The soldiers smoked afterwards. His dachshund Senta whimpered at his feet. She was feeling deprived of the usual hunting at this time of the year. William's anxiety had grown so strong he often resorted to sleeping pills.[32]

William had an excuse for an excursion to the battlefield at Sedan and gave an old lady money to restore the house where his grandfather had received Louis-Napoleon. He posed for a portrait painter and handed out more Iron Crosses. Tirpitz was bitter. The loss of the cruisers *Köln* and *Mainz*, as well as a torpedo boat off Heligoland, was all the navy had had to say for itself so far. He did not get on with the cabinet chiefs, who he thought were there to keep William in a good mood.[33] The war was also not going according to his plan. He was in a gloomy, Anglophobic mood when he saw William in Charleville on 4 October.

This war is really the greatest lunacy ever committed by the white races. We are beating one another to death on the continent for the greater good of England, and at the same time England has managed to make the whole world believe that we are the guilty party. You could lose all faith in goodness. Of course we are not without guilt. The leadership in particular . . .[34]

As ever, William's temper swung this way and that. On 8 October Tirpitz found him near to nervous collapse. The next day he heard about the fall of Antwerp and was 'roseate': 'The cousins on the other side of the Channel will be cross, it is about to start again.' He gave orders that the historic centre of the city be preserved and was pleased too to hear that his son Eitel had distinguished himself in the fray: 'simple and good as always.' William had met a middle-class Frenchman in Charleville and talked to him at length. Now Tirpitz had to hear the Frenchman's views. The admiral was bitterly frustrated: 'Imagine his grandfather in this position! Then [we heard] details from the front.'[35]

William was still exulting in German arms the next day and ordered champagne served for the first time. He toasted Moltke, who had planned the operation, and General von Beseler, who had carried it out. Then he turned on Jagow and Bethmann and told them that they, the diplomats, should not lose what had been won by the German sword: 'embarrassed smiles from both.' The situation continued to frustrate the admiral. He could get little sense out of his emperor, and 'I have suffered and I still am suffering [from the realisation] that our whole policy in recent years has been nonsense, and that the entire imperial leadership – His Majesty excepted here – failed totally and continues to do so.'

William appeared out of his depth. Riezler thought he would be better off basing himself on the Eastern Front.

There they fight war the old-fashioned way. Here in the wake of a new refined killing machine, the incurable hatred of the population, the execution of Belgians and the blood-thirsty stories about them is possibly the worst [place for him]. Warsaw with all its talk about liberation would be much better.

Riezler's master, Bethmann, had just gone to Brussels to discuss the atrocities which were proving such a boon in the Entente press. On his return he told his secretary that William was a broken man, delighting in the image of the nation in arms because his peacetime life has been taken from him.[36]

On 25 October William had told a colonel how unhappy he was not to be able to wear the same medal that he was pinning on his chest. So far the crown prince and the Archduke Charles had them, but he had no Iron Cross. Tirpitz's frustrations were not diminished when he too received one on 17 November: 'I was "crucified" – *gekreuzigt* – yesterday.' He refused to wear it.[37] Two days later the king of Bavaria put William out of his misery when he awarded the emperor the Iron Cross, 1st and 2nd class in recognition of his role as 'Supreme Federal Commander'.[38] Hedin ran into William again while visiting the headquarters of the Bavarian crown prince. He dropped in with a cheery 'Good day, my dear Sven Hedin. You seem to like it here with my army.' Hedin observed the contradictory nature of the German emperor; his habit of blowing up and then becoming completely calm afterwards: '... he can certainly

Walther Rathenau. The Jewish industrialist formed an important part of William's circle of business advisers. William wanted to reign over a prosperous Germany.

William's study in 1913. Note the saddle seat and the portrait of his wife, Dona, on the wall.

William (left) in Norway, visiting the painter Hans Dahl. Note the dachschunds.

William (right) in Balestrand, Norway, admiring a projected monument to the Norse hero Bele. He looks uncharacteristically shabby in mufti.

William and his naval chief,
Alfred Friedrich von Tirpitz.

Below William with the younger Helmuth
Moltke in August 1914. Moltke wanted the
war to come, 'the sooner the better', but he
lacked the iron nerve of his more famous
uncle.

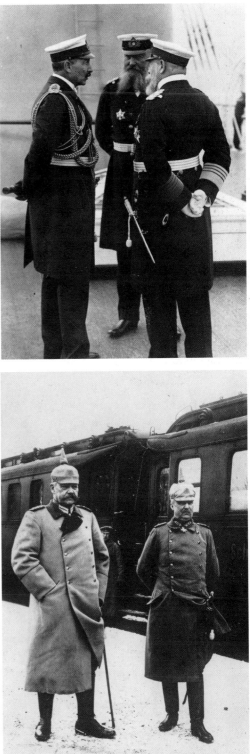

Right Field Marshal Paul von
Hindenburg, the hero of Tannenberg,
and his chief strategist Erich Ludendorff.
From 1916 onwards Hindenburg's power
within Germany exceeded William's own.
It was he who advised the Kaiser to
abdicate and seek asylum in Holland.

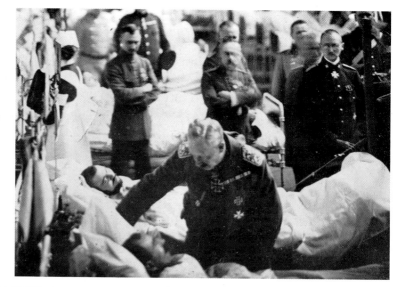

War work. William visiting the sick and wounded in Gleiwitz in 1917. He had ceased to have any role in the running of the campaigns.

William, an observer on the Western Front in 1917.

William and Dona at Amerongen in 1919. The *paparazzo* has caught them conferring with the *Hausminister*, General von Dommes.

Above House Doorn in the province of Utrecht, Holland. William's effigy still greets visitors to his Dutch 'Tusculum'.

Left Hermine of Reuss, William's second wife. She pushed William to try his luck with Hitler and Goering in the hope of achieving a Hohenzollern restoration.

Below Doorn: the woodshed. Every day the former emperor chopped and sawed logs for exercise and distributed the results both to the poor and his fans.

The Doorn Study Group. William is seated by the anthropologist Leo Frobenius and flanked by the other scholars who came to lecture on archaeology and ethnology.

Augustus William, 'Auwi', of Prussia. His fascination with the Nazis embarrassed his father.

Hermann Goering. Encouraged by Hermine, the Nazi visited William twice in Doorn but William set little store by his assurances of support for the Imperial cause.

William in exile.

William's seventieth birthday at Doorn.

William's funeral at Doorn. Hermine is covered by her veil. The crown prince stands near the 92-year-old Field Marshal Mackensen.

William on his deathbed.

William's final resting place at Doorn.

express his displeasure for the contemptible behaviour of the enemy with sharp words, but very soon he becomes sunshine and light again and laughs infectiously about some funny occurrence.'[39]

About this time William made a visit to the Vosges with Generals Falkenhayn and Gaede. He was received by Graf Rödern, the State Secretary in Strasbourg and started making forthright comments before leaving the station. All the important people had to be got out: 'the only thing that works here are firing squads. The Alsatians with their ugly pinched features are a great deal worse than the Lorrainers.' His comments continued over lunch: the Vicar-General of Metz should be strung up from the cathedral tower; and then again, after lunch: 'Now then, much more hanging and firing squads and no consideration is to be granted to clerics or members of the local assembly!' No one but Rödern took this speech seriously. The State Secretary asked Valentini, the Civil Cabinet chief, whether His Majesty was unhappy with his administration in Alsace. 'Oh, nonsense, the emperor just wanted to play the fool in front of his generals again.'[40]

V

The Eastern Front continued to reap the lion's share of the laurels. Hindenburg, now promoted to field marshal, mopped up another 80,000 Russians in the last weeks of October. On 29 November William visited this golden boy in Posen in the great new imperial Schloss. William did not stop to try the beds; he went on to Königsberg and Insterburg where the forester at Rominten reported on the damage caused to the game reserves by the Russian advance. On 3 December he was back in Berlin. On 1 November William had received a little fillip when a German naval squadron commanded by Admiral Maximilian von Spee sank two elderly cruisers off the South American coast. The Battle of Coronel was none the less 'the first British defeat at sea for a hundred years'. It was short-lived. On 8 December a British squadron commanded by Admiral Sir Doveton Sturdee cornered Spee off the Falkland Islands. Only one ship got clear and that had to scuttle the following year.[41]

William left Berlin on 20 December to spend Christmas in Charleville. A Lutheran service was held in the temporary chapel which had been 'very prettily decorated' with pine fronds. A long table had been set up, covered with presents: everyone, from the emperor to the lowliest grenadier, received apples, *Pfefferkuchen*, nuts, cigars and a pipe filled with tobacco, as well as a picture of William inscribed with the words 'Grosses Hauptquartier Weihnachten 1914'. Pastor Göns gave them a book of sermons and each of the officers received a leather letter-writing case from Dona. William and his commanding generals sat slightly higher at one end of the table. There was a small but attractively made crib and thirty Christmas trees covered with a thousand brightly burning candles and 315 packets of Christmas tinsel. Göns appeared in field grey. The company sang the hymn 'Ich bete an die Macht der Liebe', then Göns gave a short sermon. Plessen thanked William on the part of the army, and this was followed by cheers. William replied with a few powerful words then went joyfully around the room while everyone stood behind his chair. Finally there were three verses of 'Stille Nacht'. 'The whole thing was solemn and dignified.'[42]

At seven the tables were covered with flowers from the imperial greenhouses. The royal family opened its presents. Punch and dough-nuts were served until 11 p.m. On Christmas Day there was a service in the cathedral in Douai. William lunched with the officers of the First Foot. At the end of the year he could address his forces with the happy news that as 1914 turned into the great victory year of 1915, virtually the entire German army was camped on foreign soil.[43]

Tirpitz had already fallen from grace and found it impossible to penetrate the circle around William. He had nothing but contempt for civilians such as Treutler and Valentini who made it impossible for him to present his honest views. William, thought the sailor, 'will make no decision nor shoulder any responsibility'.[44] William's closest companions were indeed Treutler and Valentini. Müller was still admitted to the inner circle along with the Württemberger Reischach. They had the ear of the emperor on the routine afternoon walks which he took even in wartime. Tirpitz resented Valentini because he preached restraint. Müller records a telling exchange in Flanders in October 1914: William: 'Say Valentini, isn't this a beautiful country?' Valentini: 'I agree, but only when we have got out of it again!' William: 'I swear to you, I shall never leave this place.'[45] William was, however, showing signs of wanting to end the war as early as the end of 1914, when a letter from Chelius to Bülow mentions the chance of the Pope stepping in, come the spring, to end the fighting on the basis of the *status quo ante*. Like many of his military leaders, Tirpitz found that hard to accept. At the very least Germany should hang on to Flanders and Antwerp.[46]

VI

Bülow moved into a suite at Berlin's Adlon Hotel overlooking the Bran-denburg Gate. He bided his time, the ever hopeful, expecting to be called back to clean up the mess. There in the autumn of 1914 he claims he had a meeting with Walther Rathenau who had offered his services to the Crown at the beginning of the war. He asked the former chancellor:

Can a monarch of such arresting personality, so charming and human as a man, so utterly inadequate as a ruler, as the Emperor William II – with an impossible chancellor like Bethmann and a frivolous Chief of Staff like Falkenhayn, ever expect a triumphal return through that arch? If he gets it, history will have no meaning.[47]

In January Lichnowsky, the former ambassador to London, wrote a justification of his conduct on the eve of war in *Delusion or Design?*, in which he blamed the Foreign office for ignoring his repeated warnings about British intentions. Why had Germany gone to war for Austria, which sought to inhibit the national aspirations of the south Slavs?[48] William spent his first birthday in the field. GHQ was illuminated in his honour the night before and he was woken by an *aubade*. His chancellor had come to greet him and Chelius played the harmonium. William remembered his poets on his anniversary: both Gerhart Hauptmann and Richard Dehmel were awarded the Red Eagle.[49]

A certain joy for William was a new work of Houston Stewart Chamberlain who was now living uncomfortably at Bayreuth. It was called *England and Germany*, and compared the former unfavourably with the latter. In Germany the army was the backbone of the nation while Britain was, 'prey to brutal materialism and unscrupulous plutocracy'. Chamberlain had a kind word for the Jews: 'They are no longer in evidence as Jews, but are doing their duty before the enemy or at home as Germans.'[50]

William and Chamberlain had been corresponding again. At the time of the *Daily Telegraph* affair, he had seen fit to inform William that Stuart-Wortley's wife was his 'first cousin once removed'; but possibly for that reason they did not communicate again until November 1914. That month William detailed the men who had made Germany what it was: Luther, Goethe, Bach, Wagner, Moltke, Bismarck and his grandfather. Chamberlain's writings, published in English, were being used as propaganda against the Allies. For his services William made him a 'Knight of the Iron Cross'. Despite this high honour Chamberlain had reason to write to William's friend Chelius to complain about the heavy-handed treatment he was receiving from the Bayreuth authorities. As Wagner's son-in-law he enjoyed the protection of the Bavarian Ministry of War, but that did not allow him to write freely or to travel. Chamberlain saw fit to mention this to William's musical friend.[51]

When it came to Allied propaganda the gloves were off. Where before the war decorum prevented newspapers and magazines from mentioning William's withered arm, now it was aired in caricatures. In 1915 *Le Rire rouge* had William exclaiming, 'Where the devil has that arm gone?' The same periodical accused him of degeneracy. Worse things were to come. There were the *Hunnenbriefe* (the Hun Letters) concocted by the French lawyers Larnaude and Lapradelle as a justification for bringing the German emperor to trial. They were littered with calls for the killing of children, women and old people in the interests of a quick victory.[52]

In Britain the Department of Information was created in December 1916 from the earlier Press Bureau of the Parliamentary War Aims Committee. The adventure-story writer and future governor-general of Canada, John Buchan; the lawyer and Ulster Unionist, Edward Carson; and Lord Northcliffe were in charge. The third member of the trinity had probably done more to destroy Anglo-German relations than anyone alive. In February 1918 it was upgraded into a full-scale ministry. Atrocity stories were its stock-in-trade. The trigger-happy reprisals taken against sometimes imaginary acts of sabotage in Belgium provided a great deal of material for the department. Another great boon was the Bryce Report which gave pseudo-legal credence to the atrocity stories, although committee members carefully avoided verifying the evidence.[53]

The Belgian atrocity stories had provided such good copy by October 1915 that ninety-three German scholars decided to publish an open letter to justify the savage action taken in Louvain, where about one-ninth of the town, including the university library, was destroyed after a confused report of a Belgian counter-attack. The destruction of 230,000 books, 950 manuscripts and 800 incunabula proved 'a propagandist's dream'.[54] The signatories of the German justification included the German-Jewish nationalist and developer of poison gas, Fritz Haber, the playwright Gerhart Hauptmann, the musician Engelbert Humperdinck, Little Willy's collaborator Friedrich Naumann, the Nobel-prize-winning scientists Max Planck and Wilhelm Conrad Röntgen, the theatre director Max Reinhardt and the national economist Gustav von Schmoller.

It had proved the moment to reconcile William to Hauptmann who, in an open letter to the French author Romain Rolland, said that Germans would rather be seen as the sons of Attila than the heirs of Goethe – hence his Eagle. On the other side, professors were brought in to dissect Prussia – a possible 'throwback to some Tartar stock' and 'Prussian militarism'. William's speeches also fuelled the fires. Evidence of war-mongering and aggressive nationalism were ubiquitous in Germany:

German newspapers and periodicals, German government and military officials, German educators and authors, German leagues and associations, have been preaching these ideas and aims and policies far and wide to the German millions every hour of the day, both before, and especially since, William II came to the throne in 1888.[55]

German propaganda was pathetic by comparison, something which was observed and lamented by the young Joseph Goebbels. For William it amounted to telling the man in charge of his Opera, Intendant von Gerlach, to put on more German works by Wagner, Strauss and Schillings. He even commissioned an opera from his friend Chelius, but he must have wished he had not. It was not considered performable. After the war William voiced a horrified admiration for Northcliffe: 'Was für ein Mensch! [What a man!] If we had had Northcliffe we would have won the war.' He was his 'deadly enemy'. 'It is incredible,' said William at Amerongen. 'What Lord Northcliffe thinks today, England thinks tomorrow.'[56]

A bizarre bloodbath occurred in the spring of 1915: the slaughter of Germany's nine million pigs. The men from the ministry designated the porcine population as 'co-eaters' which threatened the supply of bread and decided that Germany could no longer afford to nourish them. This led to a momentary glut of pork, but it was short-lived and then there was a marked shortage of both meat and fertiliser. The following year it was the turn of sauerkraut to be regulated by the bureaucrats. Meanwhile the blockade was successfully whittling down resources and lengthening the food queues. How many people died as a result is still disputed, but at its worst the lack of subsistence may have reached famine proportions. U-boats threatened the British civilian population's supplies too, but more than twice as many German civilians died between 1914 and 1918 than they did in the United Kingdom. That was during the so-called 'turnip winter' of 1916–17 when the daily ration dropped to 750 calories (subsistence is 2,800 calories). The potato crop had been struck by phytophthora and was down by a third of its previous yield. An exhibition in Berlin-Charlottenburg showed housewives how to turn turnips into bread, coffee and jam. 'Ersatz' took over. By 1918 there were 11,000 Ersatz items on sale, including 800 sorts of vegetarian sausage.[57]

VII

Two small naval engagements at Heligoland and on the Dogger Bank had gone badly for Germany and the High Seas Fleet had returned to its bases to meditate a new strategy. For the time being Germany put its faith in undersea weapons. On 3 February William was in Wilhelmshaven. The next day Germany announced that from the 17th, it would begin to blockade Great Britain with U-boats. The sailors claimed they could bring Britain to its knees in six weeks. When this failed to happen, it was six months. Bethmann was sceptical and did not approve the political implications of the new war. British waters were declared a war zone, where enemy and neutral ships might be impounded. William had not been keen either, and he was encouraged in his reluctance by Treutler and Valentini. He was tugged in the opposite direction by Dona, and his son with whom Tirpitz was now in cahoots. The admiral was pleased: 'He sees things really clearly, the crown prince; sadly he has never learned to work.' There was now talk of the 'Crown Prince–Tirpitz Fronde' and frequent messengers sent between Prince William's HQ in Stenay and Tirpitz in Charleville.[58]

William was away in the east. He saw the Russian army from the heights of Szusczyn and went to Czestochowa where he gave the monks who looked after the Black Madonna 10,000 marks to grease her protecting hand. In the west Little Willy's behaviour grew so blatant that even Tirpitz became worried. The crown prince told his colleague Captain Hopmann about William's circle: 'These people who influence the emperor so much, you should look at them, Lyncker, Treutler, Müller, Valentini, all weak, spineless fellows, always trying to save the emperor from unpleasantness or difficult decisions.' Hopmann suggested that he, the crown prince, should take over. 'You are right there ... If I came to power I'd throw the whole lot of them out. I want to talk to people who tell me the whole truth. My father never does that; on the contrary he breaks off any discussion [of it]. Talking to him means he speaks and the other party listens.'[59]

In the three months of the U-boat campaign 37 German U-boats sank 115 ships at a loss of five of their own. Special medals were struck for the occasion with a picture of Tirpitz on one side and a submarine on the other above the legend 'Gott strafe England!'[60] Several American boats were sunk, ostensibly because they were carrying food or arms, and therefore breaking the blockade by which Germany hoped to bring Britain to its knees.

William had remained in Berlin and the east, where he had hoped to see the end of the brilliant eastern campaign. On the 7th he saw his new field marshal, Mackensen, in Lodz. He was a *Bürgerliche* who had been ennobled at the turn of the century. He went to the Radziwills at Nieborow, and was reminded of his bear-slaying triumphs in 1886. After a brief pause in the capital to receive emissaries from Turkey, he went back to Masuria to witness the last Russians driven off German soil. He delayed his departure twice in order to be there at the end. William thanked Falkenhayn with the *pour le mérite*. Plessen gave the emperor one too.[61]

The Gallipoli campaign had begun by the time Tirpitz's birthday came round on 19 February 1915 and William thought he could offer the admiral a present by telling him that two British ships of the line had been sunk. Tirpitz could scarcely control his indignation when he thought of his navy: 'There lies a fleet of forty ironclads, and more than half of them super Dreadnoughts, more than a hundred torpedo boats, rusting at anchor while Germany is engaged in a struggle for its existence ... I have experienced this aimlessness and the accompanying fanfares for more than two decades now and seen how every department works for itself, everything pushes its way to "him", the man who puts it about that he does everything himself ... Byzantium!'[62]

William returned to the west on 2 March. He lingered in Wiesbaden. He appointed General Bülow field marshal on the 15th and went exploring behind the lines. He took an interest in French architecture and looked at the ruins of Coucy-le-Château in the company of Bodo Ebhardt, who had restored the Hohe Königsberg in Alsace. There were further excursions to Châteaux Bouillon and Montcornet. Besides these cultural diversions he visited the sickbed of General Kluck to give him the *pour le mérite*. He had been wounded by shrapnel. 'Did I give you permission to crawl into the front trench?' 'I did neglect to ask Your Majesty's prior permission, that is true.'

VIII

The prescient Colonel House put down his thoughts on William and the war on 15 April 1915. Like the British themselves, he was confused about William's motives, but the rest was well understood.

It is clear to me that the Kaiser did not want war and did not actually expect it. He foolishly permitted Austria to bring about an acute controversy with Serbia, and he concluded that by standing firm with his ally, Russia would do nothing more than make a vigorous protest, much as she did when Austria annexed Bosnia-Herzegovina. The rattling of the scabbard and the shining armour were sufficient in that case and he thought they would be in this, for the reason that he did not believe that Great Britain would go to war concerning such a happening in the south east. He had tried England twice in the west and had found that he himself must give way, and there was not much danger of his trying it again where England was involved. But in this instance he thought Germany's relations with England had improved to such an extent that she would not back Russia and France to the extent of making war on Germany.

And he went so far in what might be termed 'bluff' that it became impossible at the last moment to recede because the situation had gotten beyond him. He did not have the foresight to see that the building up of a great war machine must inevitably lead to war. Germany has been in the hands of a group of militarists and financiers, and it has been to conserve their selfish interests that this terrible situation has been made possible.[63]

Tirpitz's U-boats were not idle. On 7 May they sank the *Lusitania* killing about 1,200 people, ten per cent of whom were American. This caused great waves of shock across the United States. Apart from the unfortunate Bernstorff most Germans were unrepentant. As Tirpitz put it, the ship was 'an auxiliary cruiser ... armed and heavily laden with munitions'. It broke up so quickly because the ammunition on board exploded. There followed a tough exchange of diplomatic notes, beginning on the 11th. The American ambassador, James Gerard, thought that diplomatic relations were about to be ruptured. The Germans replied that the ship was carrying munitions, which it was. In his reply President Wilson pointed out that no attempt had been made to inspect the ship's cargo.[64]

In the last *Lusitania* note of 21 July 1915 the Germans were specifically requested to voice their disapproval and informed that a repetition would be seen as a 'deliberately unfriendly action'. Some days later the American Secretary of State, Robert Lansing, asked Ambassador Bernstorff to come and see him. There would be no more notes. If another merchant ship were sunk 'war could not be avoided'. Gerard made it clear to House what sort of role William played in all this: 'The Emperor is at the front "somewhere in Galicia". They keep him very much in the background, I think with the idea of disabusing the popular mind that this is "his war" ...'[65] While the ambassador was consulting his government another American steamer, the *Arabic*, was torpedoed on 19 August. Bernstorff reacted quickly, offering 'satisfaction' to stave off the inevitable declaration of war. The Americans were temporarily palliated.

William moved into Schloss Pless in Upper Silesia on 5 May. It lay in a convenient position with so much happening in the east, and it was not far from Teschen, the base of Austrian operations.[66] Here the surroundings were a little more familiar to courtiers than they had been in Luxembourg or Charleville. Not everyone was at ease with Daisy's presence in the wings. William carried on fraternising with his English friend (who never learned German) until the summer of 1917. Tirpitz, for one, suspected her of being a British spy. There were presents in the form of medals for Mackensen and Falkenhayn – the latter received the ultimate accolade, the Black Eagle. Riezler caught a glimpse of William at Pless on 11 July. He was looking pale and serious among the splendours of the Schloss. 'Best of moods for the chancellor, fury at the tub-thumpers, Bülow in particular – and also at the annexationists. Valentini writes that Bohlen [Krupp], Hugenbergs are endangering their position at court.'

Bethmann and Valentini enjoyed a relationship based on trust. Riezler noted: '... Valentini makes a very good, concrete, reasonable impression, firm and decent with a pleasant wit.' Falkenhayn was at the height of his powers and could do no wrong. Riezler allowed himself to show a little intellectual contempt for the others: the circle was 'profoundly uneducated' if fundamentally decent. The only exception to this last was General von Plessen. 'What could a Silesian magnate such as Pless do if he were interested in art or literature? The education of all these people, however, stops at hunting.' Riezler concluded, 'Far too little to eat.' Putting the lie to the story that William stuffed his face while the nation starved.[67]

On 31 July William made a speech in which he reaffirmed his peaceable intentions and his guiltlessness over the events of the previous year. For ten years the Entente had been preparing to strike down a Germany which they believed had grown too big. Germany could not permit the humiliation of its Austrian ally. He repeated that Germany had no colonial ambitions in the conflict. He remained in the east where there was a mobile war. Warsaw fell to the Germans on 5 August, and on 4 September William enjoyed a few hours as a tourist in Crakow. In mid-September he had an enjoyable visit to the cathedral in Kovno.[68]

That summer Little Willy, while maintaining his opposition to greater democracy, put a little distance between himself and the Pan-Germans with their exaggerated demands for annexations in the east and west. According to his biographer, he became 'more realistic'. At the end of the year he supposedly produced a memo for his father in which he stated that the only way to win a peace which maintained Germany in its pre-war glory was to make a special deal with the Russians or to restart negotiations for an understanding with Britain.[69]

William went west on 23 September. He had refused to see the American ambassador, Gerard, because he could not forgive his countrymen for supplying Britain with arms and food. On 22 October 1915 Gerard managed to achieve an audience at the Neues Palais. William had come home for Dona's birthday and the celebration of 500 years of Hohenzollern rule in the Mark. He received him in field grey, standing over his map table. After a series of accusations, William apologised for the sinking of the *Lusitania*: 'no gentleman would kill so many women and children.' He showed, however, great bitterness against the United States, and repeatedly said: 'America had better look out after this war,' and 'I shall stand no nonsense from America after the war.'[70]

On 27 October he returned to Pless and remained in the east until the middle of December. He was in Brest-Litovsk on 9 November. The Russians had blown up the town on their departure. The ruins of the government buildings brought back memories, this time of the diplomatic mission which Bismarck had created for him in 1886. In those days it had been seen as essential to retain the old alliance. Nothing in the town remained apart from the Greek Orthodox church. On 29 November he visited Francis Joseph in Vienna for the first time since the beginning of the war. They could celebrate the fact that the Serbian army had been literally driven out of the country ten days before: 'The slaying of a prince in Sarajevo had been avenged.'

IX

There was no repeat of Christmas 1914. William spent the holiday at home in the Neues Palais with cellulitis. The cruiser *Bremen* added to his malaise when she went down on the 17th. It was reportedly a modest Christmas, even in the old home. Gone were the individual trees for the children and grandchildren. On 9 January the Entente finally evacuated Gallipoli and General Liman von Sanders received the oak leaves to his *pour le mérite*.[71]

William's armies in the west had failed to bring home those rapid victories. Instead German youth bled to death at the front. The more liberal elements in his entourage convinced him that he would have to make concessions. On 13 January, in his throne speech to the Prussian assembly, William promised to grant a fair suffrage. The crown prince had got wind of the move the day before and had telephoned Bethmann to voice his displeasure; he could do nothing, however, to stop the speech from going ahead. The plotter Oldenburg-Januschau then went to Hindenburg and Ludendorff and beseeched them to act. They claimed they were 'nur-Soldaten' with no interest in political affairs, so the Januschauer scurried back to the crown prince instead.[72]

William went off to Serbia on the 16th. There was a chance to gloat. In Nish the emperor and his retinue, together with Mackensen and General Seeckt, went over the second residence of the bandit king of Serbia. He even made his old enemy, the Bulgarian Tsar Ferdinand, a field marshal for his role in the defeat of the perpetrators of the catastrophe. On the 19th he had the chance to look round Belgrade.

William bobbed about in the waves created by the militarists but was prevented from drifting out to sea by the restraining hands of the civilians. Riezler sympathised. He thought it difficult for the emperor to reach a decision about whether to step up the U-boat war or scrap it. Could he veto something which the armed forces saw as the *ultima ratio*? He had become extremely apprehensive: 'I believe His Majesty will end up by following the chancellor. Despite everything he is very cautious and possesses a great sense of responsibility and you must reckon on considerable reservation whenever you talk to him.'[73]

'Fate had destined me for the part of Sisyphus in Washington,' the ambassador bemoaned. Just as everyone had calmed down over the *Lusitania*, Germany announced an 'intensified U-boat war'. Bernstorff's good work was undone. House went to Europe at this time. In Berlin he found a readiness to mediate, although William fobbed him off with the slightly unsatisfactory line that he would conclude peace with his cousins George and Nicholas when the time came. House had to ask Gerard if William had gone mad. He had earlier heard a story that he spent his time praying and learning Hebrew. Gerard reassured him that William had not been agreeable to the sinking of the *Lusitania*. The strongest opposition to peace House encountered was in France.[74]

In March 1916 it was the turn of the *Sussex*, which went down in the Channel killing a number of people, some of them American and including the Spanish composer Enrique Granados. The Americans issued a no-nonsense note telling the German government to cease its campaign against unarmed vessels. Bethmann went to Charleville on 7 March to deliver a memorandum calling for a halt to the U-boat campaign. The next day William told his chancellor that he agreed. He did not want war with the Americans, although he postponed the decision until 11 April. Once again he impressed the middle-class intellectual Riezler. He reacted well in a difficult situation and was cautious and sure in his judgement of men: 'When things become difficult he is always very clever. The gift of princes.' On 4 May the Germans acceded to American demands and brought the campaign within the bounds of international law.[75]

The *Sussex* claimed a further victim: not the chancellor, as Prince William had hoped, but the Grossadmiral who resigned on 12 March when William decided to call a halt to the sinkings. The crown prince appealed directly to his father to call him back, but without success. He called it a 'national misfortune'. Tirpitz made his way over to the right-wing opposition, where he was involved in founding the extremist Vaterlandspartei the following year.[76] The crown prince was also hauled over the coals. In June he had a meeting with his father which resulted in the dismissal of the prince's political adviser, Maltzahn. Valentini described the experience as 'shattering'. Maltzahn, however, continued to lurk informally in the wings.[77]

William transferred to the west on 24 February. Gerard had another audience with William at his villa in Charleville on 1 May 1916. He had been bidden to lunch, and found the emperor walking in the garden: 'Do you come like the great proconsul, bearing peace or war in either hand?' The allusion to Fabius and Hannibal was not lost on the ambassador. William upbraided Gerard for his country's accusation of barbarism in warfare. 'As Emperor and head of the Church, he had wished to carry on the war in a knightly manner.' He pointed to the other side, the French in particular: 'their officers, instead of being nobles, came from no one knew where. ... He then referred to the efforts to starve out Germany and keep out milk and said that before he would allow his family and grandchildren to starve he would blow up Windsor Castle and the whole royal family of England.' Before lunch both William and Bethmann denied the continued existence of international law, saying it was one law for the Germans and another for the British.[78]

Friedrich Rosen visited him four days later. Apart from Grünau he was the only non-officer present. He had been brought in to try to work on the king of Spain to secure an equitable peace between the belligerents. William clearly had too little to do. He went out into the forest where he chatted with the women gathering wood: 'Even though they called me *monsieur* they knew that I was the emperor.' Rosen complained about the food: eels with dill sauce and cucumber salad, peach pudding, butter and cheese and fruit – 'extremely plain and almost paltry', concluded the diplomat.[79]

X

William's toy, the fleet, was a serious bone of contention now. It had failed from the beginning, when it might have prevented the British Expeditionary Force from reaching France. Those who knew William's pro-British tendencies suspected collusion. William blamed Tirpitz. He had been earmarked to succeed Bethmann, but now he had fallen from grace: he had built the wrong sort of ships, which would be no use in war. Tirpitz blamed William, who he said was reluctant to let his creation put to sea and who he claimed was jealous of him. Early in the war William had expressed worries about the number of mines the Allies had laid. The fleet might also have some bargaining power when it came to the peace negotiations.[80] According to the bitter Bülow, part of the problem was that the navy really was a luxury fleet: 'His Majesty knew every battleship. On each he had his own luxurious staterooms, fitted out with special toilet apparatus by his faithful old body servant, Schulz. On the walls of each were portraits of his nearest and dearest. His heart sank at the thought of having to sacrifice even one of these toys ... The end of it all was Scapa Flow.'[81]

According to a modern observer, the Battle of Jutland or Skagerrak, as it is known in German, was an 'unambiguous defeat'[82] despite the fact that, in terms of sunken tonnage, the British came off worst. It was fought over two days from 31 May to 1 June 1916. William initially claimed it as a victory, but later in life he admitted it had been inconclusive, that was, as far as the Germans were concerned. From the British side, the consequences were clear: the High Seas Fleet never left port again, and the huge battleships which had been the pride of William and

Tirpitz were left to rust with their crews of increasingly mutinous sailors. After the war Sir John Fisher paid tribute to William's naval chief: 'Cheer up old chap! Say *resurgam*! You are the only German sailor who understands war! Kill your enemy without being killed yourself. I don't blame you for the submarine business. I'd have done the same thing myself, only our idiots in England wouldn't believe it when I told 'em.'[83]

William had been with Hindenburg in Kovno the day before the battle. On 4 June he made a special journey to Wilhelmshaven to visit his fleet. He thanked the navy for the great victory over the British. The German fleet, which had been for decades involved in 'peace work', finally came face to face with 'a powerful fleet [belonging to] the wave ruling Albion, that for a century since Trafalgar had cast a spell of maritime tyranny over the whole world ... And what happened? The English fleet was beaten! The first powerful stroke of the hammer has been made, and the nimbus of England's world rule has disappeared.'[84]

Little Willy had been given the opening role in Falkenhayn's deciding battle of Verdun. He subscribed to the view that France should be bled to capitulation. Despite throwing virtually everything they had at the French to break their line, the battle resolved nothing. By the middle of 1916 it was clear that it had all been a costly failure. The crown prince's continued opposition had prescribed a change in his Chief of Staff. Out went Schmidt-Knobelsdorff and in came an 'excellent soldier', Graf Friedrich von der Schulenburg, who was thought to be less addicted to extreme political views. A further setback for the prince was the decision to create a Polish buffer state by Germany and Austria, an idea which had crossed William's mind as early as 1889. The revival of the project, however, was down to Ludendorff, who valued Polish goodwill as a source of volunteers for the 'Hindenburg programme' as well as for the army. The move meant losing the chance of concluding a separate peace with Russia. Prince William had 'an impotent fit' when he heard the news. The new 'Kingdom of Poland' came into existence on 5 November 1916.[85]

The political situation at home had to be watched. The 'Burgfrieden' was collapsing. On May Day 1916 the left-wing socialist Karl Liebknecht stood up in Berlin and shouted, 'Down with war! Down with the government!' He was arrested and imprisoned for four years. But the strong arm of the law was not able to prevent a wave of political strikes. The first Russian Revolution in February the following year also removed one of the reasons for socialist support. In April Bethmann made the Easter Offer, in which he promised to reform the suffrage at the end of the war. Fear of revolution had led the chancellor to support the move. His was a difficult balancing act. On the one hand he had to tell the left that the war would destroy Russian despotism, on the other he had to inform the right that victory would mean the end of Britain's world hegemony. He also had to bring round William. This he claims he did: in the course of a walk in the park at Homburg he showed his monarch that after the war a soldier with the Iron Cross, 1st class, could not enjoy lesser rights than a moneyed skiver in the same village.[86]

If William did not have enough problems with the left and the end of the 'Burgfrieden', he was now facing demonstrations from the Pan-Germans on the right, who forced him to ditch Treutler on 5 July. William was ready to accept the Reichstag's peace note as a basis for negotiations. On 31 October he asked Bethmann to bring it to him and hold himself in readiness. Once again hopes of peace were scuppered by the right. The Bavarian Riezler pronounced the country an 'absolute madhouse. Everywhere the wildest rumours. The emperor melancholic, too weak, close to abdication. Demonstrations in Munich with inflammatory speeches ... The result takeover by the king of Bavaria; it is time for the Wittelsbachs to seize the moment.'[87]

In late June there was a further crisis in the command structure. More and more voices were raised against Falkenhayn, who was receiving a poor press despite his impressive performance as Chief of Staff. Over and over again he showed his mastery of the situation in the east. In the west, however, the costly failure of the battle for Verdun counted against him. One of the loudest voices was that of Bethmann, this time in alliance with Ludendorff. Bethmann resented Falkenhayn's dabbling in politics and supported the idea of replacing him with Hindenburg, whom he saw as a means of saving the Hohenzollern dynasty. Another who weighed in against Falkenhayn was Dona. William consented to enlarging Hindenburg's command at first. Ironically it was Valentini who first suggested that Falkenhayn be replaced by Hindenburg.[88] He was to receive the same reward as Bethmann.

The argument hinged on continued operations. Hindenburg and Ludendorff were easterners. They wanted a victory to be assured in the east first, before the final showdown with France. Falkenhayn had maintained the opposite. William was intransigent. He found Falkenhayn sympathetic. Hindenburg he did not, to say nothing of the rebarbative Ludendorff. In September, however, the decision of Romania to join the Entente forced William to relinquish his grip. The departure of his Chief of Staff reduced the emperor to tears. Falkenhayn fell from grace and Hindenburg became Chief of Staff with Ludendorff as his assistant – although he refused the title, styling himself Quartermaster-General. Almost as soon as Hindenburg had his feet under his new desk, High Command picked a fight with Bethmann.[89] Hindenburg and Ludendorff refused to confine their brief to military matters. The peace note was rejected with 'scorn'.

William had been defeated by Hindenburg and Ludendorff. It was, in effect, a half-abdication. From now on his role in the continuation of the war was less than merely formal. In November 1916 the crown prince wrote a letter to his father suggesting he rid himself of the 'worn-out bellyachers' in his entourage. The prince thought this group shed an unfortunate light on his father which led to his unpopularity. It was another attempt to unseat Valentini and Bethmann. William proved loyal once again. He refused to answer his son's letter, which he thought bore the marks of Hindenburg and Ludendorff. In December they also requested the removal of Valentini, who opened the letter in his capacity of cabinet chief. Valentini passed it to Bethmann without showing it to the emperor. The duo was incensed and now decidedly after Valentini's blood. It was a good moment for the crown prince to shut up. It had been suggested that he might be excluded from the succession were he to continue to harry his father.[90]

William was furious that the Americans were so obviously siding with the Entente when he visited the dentist that autumn. He asked Davis:

Why is it that your country is so unfair to Germany? Why do you persist in supplying munitions and money to the Allies? Why doesn't your president treat the European warring nations the same as he treated Mexico, by putting an embargo on munitions and letting us fight this thing out ourselves? You do not ship munitions to us. Why do you ship them to the other side?

'Dollars! Dollars! Dollars!' Each time he said the word he hit his right hand against his partially lifeless left.[91]

Bethmann's nightmare was the support for the U-boat campaign which, he felt sure, would bring America into the war. On 12 December 1916 Germany announced its 'readiness to discuss' peace. There were no takers. The High Command or OHL were clamouring for the renewal of the submarine war, and both William and Bethmann felt they had to abandon their resistance. William approved the measure on 9 January with effect from the first of the following month. Bethmann was not present at Pless when the decision was made. He was appalled and tried to resign, but reconsidered because he thought it would make no difference: the U-boat war was popular with the country, where it was seen to be effective in breaking the blockade. That explains Riezler's diary note of 31 January: 'William the Wholly Great or William the Last'?[92] Admiral Holtzendorff produced the old argument that Britain would be quickly starved into submission, and even if America were provoked into joining the Entente, their troopships would be sunk before they reached France. By the time they had landed enough troops to make a difference, the war would be over. All he needed, thought Holtzendorff, was a hundred submarines.

It was as Bethmann predicted. America entered the war on 6 April 1917. Hindenburg and Ludendorff were not satisfied. They let it be known that they wanted to see the back of Bethmann, who lacked resolution, and they informed Valentini that they could no longer work with the chancellor. William began to bend under the pressure from the right. On 7 April he started to backtrack over the reform of the Prussian suffrage, a proposal which found no favour with his leading generals. Riezler noted that William had wholly lost the support of the people who one might have assumed would back him the most: 'The emperor is terrifyingly unpopular among the upper classes, conservative and liberal. He has the most support among the workers, and that includes the Social Democrats.'

After 22 April Hindenburg and Ludendorff, like the giants Fasolt and Fafner, went directly to William in his new HQ at Kreuznach. The 'nur-Soldaten' had let their masks slip and were becoming decidedly political. They arrived with an article from the newspaper *Vorwärts* calling for peace. Bethmann was failing to keep the Social Democrats and the pacifists under control. Once again William hung on to his chancellor, complaining bitterly of Hindenburg's meddling in politics. Hindenburg and Ludendorff then went to Friedrich von Berg-Markienen, whom they hoped eventually to fit up with Valentini's job.[93] Little Willy joined in the fray in May with some new darts aimed at the chancellor. William responded by pointing out that Bethmann's departure would result in a general strike. The 'Burgfrieden' was threatened by the 'Siegfrieden' or Hindenburg peace, behind which the right hoped to stave off demands for reform and greater democracy.

William held on to Bethmann with extraordinary stubbornness and loyalty. There was a massive opposition growing up against him: Little Willy, a large part of the Reichstag, not to mention Hindenburg and Ludendorff; and yet he stuck with the chancellor until the Reichstag refused to work with him any longer and the two generals who had brought Germany Tannenberg and the Masurian Lakes threatened to resign. Riezler was not optimistic: 'It would be incredible if Germany were not to collapse as a result of its fantastic emperor, from the ignorance of its court circle, from the psychosis which has seized its intellectuals, and in particular from the blindness of its soldiers . . .'[94] William was losing control. On the 13th he ranted, 'I shall send a company up to Berlin and set them on the Reichstag. They are all rotten, blind and as clueless as those smitten by God.'[95]

XI

Both the Pope and the new Austrian emperor – Charles, who had succeeded Francis Joseph after his death on 21 November 1916 – were asking for peace. The papal nuncio, Pacelli (the future Pius XII), arrived at HQ on 29 June with his draft. There were secret negotiations with France through Emperor Charles's brother-in-law, Sixtus of Bourbon-Parma. He later denied having put out these feelers to William. His Foreign Minister Czernin none the less informed the Germans that Austria could not hold out much longer. The Austrians tried to enlist the crown prince's support. Czernin suggested that Germany should jettison Alsace-Lorraine and Austria would compensate her in Galicia. Austria would also give Italy South Tyrol. Prince William did not know if the German people would be prepared to accept this when her troops were still deep in enemy territory, but he promised to take the plan to his father and to the OHL. William was ready to alter the borders but the project received short shrift from Hindenburg and Ludendorff. They accused the crown prince of being the pawn of a 'bellyacher' and claimed that he had gone 'soft'.[96]

In his new role as a peace-broker, Prince William asked Valentini if he might have a meeting with his father. He also wanted to discuss the suffrage question and, of course, make a further attempt to secure Bethmann's dismissal. The cabinet chief arranged the talk for 11 July in Berlin. William had had his ears blasted by his wife, who as ever sided with her eldest son, and informed the chancellor of the talks. The crown prince also intended to seek advice from members of the Prussian assembly and the Herrenhaus. Dona stepped up the pressure on her husband to stop him from altering the Prussian suffrage. The emperor wavered and Bethmann offered his resignation that same day. William stood by his chancellor. He told his son that Bethmann's departure would cause grave problems, as he was the only man capable of concluding peace when the time came. He was prepared, however, to shelve suffrage reform.[97] The Januschauer was providing a possible compromise which did not undermine the dignity of the right. He suggested to Prince Eitel Fritz there should be no change before the troops came home. The Imperial Council issued a statement on the reform and William informed his chancellor over the telephone how well his discussion with his eldest son had gone. Little Willy was still opposed to suffrage reform, which he believed to be a step in the direction of a republic, yet he had agreed with his father that it was not the moment for Bethmann to go. There was a 'momentary truce'.[98]

Prince William was little more resolute than his father, however. From his meeting with the emperor he went on to hold talks with his adviser

Maltzahn and Colonel Bauer, the political muscleman at OHL. They succeeded in turning his mind. The two of them hand-picked a political lobby which could be relied upon to press for Bethmann's demise. The Entente powers, they argued, had no great respect for the chancellor. Prince William was convinced that he could return to attacking his father's minister. On the 12th he went on the offensive again. William and he had a walk in the gardens at Bellevue during the course of which the emperor thanked his son for a clear exposition of his views. William mentioned the peace proposal. The crown prince puffed himself up and described it as 'too soft', referring his father to Hindenburg and Ludendorff, and stressing their popularity with the masses. William spoke to Hindenburg on the telephone. The field marshal told him to delay electoral reform and to make no territorial concessions in any eventual peace: merely scrap the financial and political indemnities. It was the definition of the 'Sieg-' or 'Hindenburgfrieden'. To make things a little clearer in the emperor's mind, Lyncker brought the news that Hindenburg and Ludendorff were about to resign themselves: their 'patience was at an end'.[99]

The cabinet chiefs now took fright and asked William to intercede in order to convince the two officers to stay on. This was the crown prince's moment of glory. To lose Hindenburg and Ludendorff in order to retain Bethmann meant certain defeat. For good measure Little Willy also threatened to resign. William promised to summon the two military leaders and listen to their demands. On the 13th Prince William moved in for the kill with his political lobby. Bethmann could see where things were going and handed in his resignation. He did this before William's meeting with the generals as he did not want the emperor to be humiliated by having to accede to their pressure. Bethmann suggested the aged Bavarian politician, Graf Hertling, as his successor. When Hindenburg and Ludendorff arrived at Bellevue, together with the crown prince, William calmly assured them that Bethmann had already gone. What Prince Max of Baden described as the 'worst interior crisis since the foundation of the Empire', Little Willy called the best day of his life.[100]

Ludendorff then had the nerve to complain that no one had come up with a successor. High Command wanted Bülow back, and he was still waiting in the wings, lobbying all and sundry from his suite at the Adlon. William had neither forgiven nor forgotten his former chancellor's 'treachery' in 1908. He could also point to his unpopularity with the Austrians where his suggestions of territorial concessions to his beloved Italy had gone down badly. Tirpitz's name was aired too. Ludendorff's best suggestion was General Max von Gallwitz, a political officer, but Prince William was not keen. After the soldiers had decamped, Valentini tried Hatzfeldt and reminded William of Bethmann's own suggestion:

Hertling. When the meeting reconvened William threw his name into the ring. The crown prince received the suggestion like 'a stream of cold water over the excitement' he had felt at Bethmann's fall. He described the count as old, worn out and Bavarian. When it became clear that Valentini had backed Hertling it was decided that the cabinet chief would have to go too.[101]

Hertling did not want the job. All sorts of names came up again. One of the wisest was Bernstorff who had skilfully managed a difficult position as ambassador to Washington. He had the support of Bethmann and Valentini, but his role over the submarine war did not please High Command. Bethmann disowned his eventual successor.[102] Michaelis's nomination is explained in a vaguely trustworthy story of Bülow's. After Bethmann's departure the ADCs were sitting in the Marble Hall of the Schloss wondering who might make a good chancellor. No one was getting very far when in came Plessen: 'I've thought of a chancellor! I forget exactly what his name is – Michel, or something like that. He deals in bread supplies, and the other day he made a famous speech, saying he'd stick his blade through the carcass of anybody who barred his way.' Valentini had been listening. He got up. 'His name isn't Michel – it's Michaelis. And he doesn't deal in bread supplies either, he's Assistant State Secretary to the Prussian Civil Commissariat. He didn't say he'd stick a blade through anybody's carcass – all he said was that he had a legal weapon in his hand, and intended to use it ruthlessly if need be. It wouldn't be such a bad idea to make that man imperial chancellor ...' As it was, Michaelis was known to High Command, and they thought quite highly of him.[103]

William and Michaelis had met, but not to talk to. There was some initial reticence on William's part. He was his sixth chancellor and the first commoner. He was summoned to the palace where he impressed William as a sensible man. It was a strange recommendation for a prime minister.[104] The first thing Michaelis had to deal with was the growing call for peace.

XII

After Bethmann's departure William's significance underwent a further decline. He was no more than a shadow emperor. No one listened to him. In February 1917 he called for a war to break the power of the Jews and the freemasons, but he was ignored. 'The military and naval authorities always had the final word.' Bernstorff pointed out how much this conflicted with basic Clausewitzian thinking, which prescribed that war was an extension of diplomacy, and did not exist for its own sake.

Sadly a Ludendorffian *Lebensphilosophie*, which understood war in the post-Darwinian sense as a battle for racial supremacy, had its representatives at all levels. William, Bernstorff also stressed, was a 'Friedenskaiser'. He wanted a diplomatic solution, but he allowed himself to be overruled. 'His greatest mistake during the war was indeed that he did not personally intervene – but was too compliant with others and too ready to surrender the role of leader (though at the same time he wanted to keep its outward aspect).'[105]

In July 1917 William's British cousins adopted the name of Windsor, thereby discarding all connections with the land from which they came. The German emperor scoffed: he was looking forward to seeing a future performance of *The Merry Wives of Saxe-Coburg-Gotha*. A month later Charles Edward Duke of Coburg dropped his titles in the British peerage. The moment had come for the Pope to take action. He proposed a seven-point plan for peace without acquisitions. It was ignored by the French and British, who did not feel it was generous enough towards them. Benedict might have been swayed by a German offer to restore Rome to the Papacy after defeating Italy. Prince William did not take long to dislike the new chancellor. Michaelis was also 'too soft'. He was not opposed to peace, however, probably because he had begun to sense that prolonging the war might cost him his crown when the time came. He told his father that any attempt to shorten it must be examined. The Russians were the best bet.[106]

In autumn 1917 William paid a visit to Constantinople. He was met by Bernstorff who had taken over as ambassador a couple of weeks before. On the way up the Bosporus Bernstorff reminded him of his previous visit, and William had mentioned how opposed Bismarck had been to it. Turkish conduct in the war had shown what nonsense that was. 'And the Kaiser said with great vehemence that he would never forget how the Turks had stood by him when all his relations had declared war on him.' They put on a good show for the emperor, demonstrating the benefits of Young Turk rule. William also visited the battlefields of the Dardanelles in the company of Liman von Sanders Pasha. There was a tour of the old city. He was a little shocked by the luxury and the lavish meals. For the rest William objected to a crowded tea party at Germany's magnificent embassy and to a statue by Georg Kolbe at the summer residence in Therapia, before he went home.[107]

Tirpitz too pledged his support to a strange *galère* of annexationists in helping to create the Vaterlandspartei in September 1917. Prince William was keen, as it brought together his old Pan-German friends. It led to a fall-out with Hindenburg and Ludendorff, however. Prince William was still interested in peace. Unlike Ludendorff he could not accept that the choice was between winning or going under: he fully intended to succeed to his father's throne. He was encouraged by the Austrian Foreign Minister, Czernin, who wanted answers; and the Reichstag, which wanted an end to the war. He wrote a memo for Czernin which was seen by the emperor Charles and his wife Zita. That was unwise. The paper found its way into the hands of the French premier, Alexandre-Félix-Joseph Ribot.[108]

Brave or foolhardy, the crown prince took on the OHL. The 'silent dictatorship' was not prepared to listen. They created problems in his command. They turned nasty, pushed him around and tried to bully him into accepting their stance. When, on 20 August, Czernin wrote to Prince William about Alsace-Lorraine, the German heir had completely changed position again. Alsace-Lorraine was an integral part of Germany. He had tied his views into the government position: peace without cession of territory. This new Prince William was invited to the Imperial Council at Bellevue on 11 September. Despite Michaelis's determined opposition to democracy, Prince William did not like him. On 23 October he was agitating for his removal too. Once again Bülow's name was pushed forward, this time with Colonel Bauer's support. Once again both William and his allies objected.[109]

Valentini turned up the names of Hatzfeldt and Prince Max of Baden. Michaelis, continuing the bizarre practice of naming his successor, proposed Hertling again. This time the Bavarian count accepted the job. Once again there were objections from Little Willy and High Command. Valentini earned himself yet another black mark. Prince William seemed to be contemplating a palace revolution: he asked his old Bonn tutor, Zorn, to draw up a memorandum stating that the heir to the throne must be made party to the monarch's decisions. On 10 November there was a meeting at the Neues Palais at which the crown prince, Generals Plessen and Gontard, and Graf August Eulenburg were present. A long list of Valentini's sins was read out. He had given William bad advice and driven an axe between the emperor and his people. Plessen and Eulenburg agreed. Gontard remained silent. William accepted their points but failed to dismiss Valentini and refused the offer of his resignation. He had promised his son nothing, he said. Valentini tried again less than a week later. Again William was firm, even mentioning defamation.[110]

Encouraged by Colonel Bauer, Prince William lashed out at Valentini again on the basis of his refusal to countenance Bülow: the former chancellor was fresh and untainted by compromise with the socialists. Hindenburg gave him some support, as he was not happy with a Bavarian chancellor. William once again made it clear that he did not think Bülow was the man to steer Germany out of difficult waters and help her win the war. Despite the opposition of the crown prince and High Command, the new suffrage was placed on the agenda again. Prince William thought that Valentini and his father's continued isolation were responsible for both the wave of strikes and the disgruntled officer corps. On 22 November a truce with Russia was signed at Brest-Litovsk. Hindenburg was now rolling up his sleeves for acquisitions, encouraged by the usual crew including the 'frightful Schiemann'. Having missed their chance to make a generous peace in both east and west, the High Command then launched a campaign against the Foreign Secretary, Kühlmann.[111]

William had an abscess on his tooth in November. Despite America's entry into the war, his dentist was still in town. Davis was summoned to Potsdam. 'I can't fight the whole world, you know, and have a toothache!' He refused an anaesthetic as always. He never flinched in the chair. Davis had a chance to admire the rowing machine in his bedroom. William was interested in the American negroes. He told Davis that his brother Henry had enjoyed their singing.

Now's your chance to settle your negro problem – he declared half-facetiously, of course – If America insists on coming into the war, why doesn't she send her negroes across and let us shoot them down.[112]

In his wiser moments William was aware that Germany would not be the same after the war, even if they won it. He told his cousin Prince Max of Baden on 28 December that whatever happened the monarchy must emerge strengthened, and this might only be done by gaining the support of the people.[113] There were angry scenes at the Imperial Council meeting on 2 January 1918. Now the plots centred on the removal of Valentini, whom Müller had dubbed the 'German Rasputin', Kühlmann, and the rest of the Cabinet triumvirate. Hindenburg and Ludendorff played their trump card again – they threatened to resign. On 13 January the crown prince appealed directly to Valentini to go. The Civil Cabinet chief refused, saying there was no reason why he should take orders from the military. The next day Prince William went to his father and repeated his demand. Hindenburg and Ludendorff could not work with Valentini any more. Hindenburg came to Kreuznach with his resignation. Through the military chief, Lyncker, a frightened William asked Hindenburg to put his complaint in writing. The field marshal refused.

The crown prince wanted Berg to replace Valentini. Now he saw his chance. He had the backing of Dona. No one doubted that a direct choice between Valentini and the duo would result in the civil chief's departure. Prince William sent Colonel von Winterfeld to Valentini on a private mission to try to ensure his resignation. The choice was his: him or them. Valentini submitted his resignation. William reluctantly accepted. His pessimism had sealed his fate, 'to the immense sadness of the emperor'. 'Gegen Demokraten helfen nur Soldaten' (Only soldiers can help against democrats). William promptly had another nervous collapse and a triumphant Dona set to work ridding Germany of its Foreign Secretary, Richard von Kühlmann.[114]

Berg replaced Valentini as planned. No one was impressed. Kühlmann called him the 'gravedigger of the monarchy'. He had the backing of the right in that he was firmly opposed to any change in electoral law. William's increasing anti-Semitism was due to some extent to the influence of Berg. The army were still not satisfied. Two weeks after they had gored Valentini Colonel Bauer tried to incite Prince William to a *coup d'état* against his father: the emperor would neither act nor appoint a dictator to act for him. The crown prince made it clear that he would not rebel against the emperor.[115]

William attempted to reassert control on 23 January. He made a statement to High Command that it was the chancellor and not the army who ruled in Germany. He made it clear that he was not in agreement with Hindenburg and Ludendorff. He wanted a negotiated peace and to see Belgium restored at the end of the war. Queen Wilhelmina of Holland was to intercede on Germany's behalf. Now the generals turned on Kühlmann, whose job it was as Foreign Secretary to conclude the peace. William was not bowing to threats from his son. Young Willy had no influence on his choice of Prince Max as chancellor or on his decision to put forward electoral change to 30 September.[116]

It was into this world that Friedrich Rosen, William's envoy to Holland, slipped on 17 January. He had been invited to lunch at Schloss Bellevue. He was greeted by Dona, who was arranging the flowers, and who wanted him to get her rubber gloves in Holland for her hospital charities. William looked 'rather pale and exhausted'. A small round table was laid up, they were left in peace by the servants, and William rang the bell after each course. He had suffered from mental pain after the bully-boy tactics of Hindenburg and Ludendorff. He had tried to dismiss Ludendorff, but Hindenburg had said that he would go too. Later, at Amerongen, William added that he could not take the risk. People would have drawn a parallel with the dismissal of Bismarck and blamed him for every disaster from then on.

Lunch went on until 4 p.m. Rosen mentioned the current plans. Queen Wilhelmina was to call a peace conference in The Hague. Rosen was surprised when William said, 'There will be no such peace conference. Our enemies would not get involved at all. We must fight on until we bring them to their knees and then we will be able to dictate peace.' It was the spite of the old William. He was evidently frustrated by the failure of his diplomacy again, and putting out High Command's line. He showed Rosen a map of the sinkings around the British Isles.

'It looked like a thick swarm of flies around the islands.' William was putting his confidence in his submarines. Rosen thought him a little like Frederick the Great: 'From his youth he learned to show a different face to the outside world, to that which he revealed in private conversation.'[117]

Less than a week after High Command secured their sort of peace with Russia at Brest-Litovsk, William transferred his HQ from Kreuznach to Spa on 8 March. The old resort town was filled with luxury hotels which were ideal for housing officers and men. The General Staff took over the Hôtel Britannique. In the periphery and above all on the heights there were comfortable villas which could be used for the top brass. Hindenburg took the Château de Sous-Bois, Ludendorff 'Hill Cottage'. Even Hertling took over the mayor's house in the Château de Warfaaz. William himself requisitioned the Villa la Fraineuse, but on 21 April moved to the Château de Neubois, reserving La Fraineuse for his entertaining. The Norman French exterior of Neubois belied its rich rococo interior. An air-raid shelter with two exits was built in the cellar. Others were constructed downstairs in the Hôtel Britannique and in Hindenburg's residence.[118]

High Command established a forward HQ at Avesnes on the French side of the Ardennes. On 21 March Germany launched its great offensive in the west. The first serious attempt to recreate the mobile war since the Marne, the plan had been hatched at a meeting on 11 November at which William was not even present. He paid Hindenburg and Ludendorff a visit in Avesnes two days before the Germans went over the top. Several shells had fallen on Paris, but the brunt of the attack had intentionally fallen on the British lines. The idea was to smash Britain out of the war so that France would surrender. William pronounced the British defeated and ordered champagne at dinner. He went out in his car to inspect the long line of British prisoners. One of these remembered seeing him. He

had kindly features; he was benevolent, nothing like all the caricatures we had seen in the newspapers. He said, 'There is no need for you to be ashamed of being prisoners.' He congratulated us on the tremendous fight we had put up but said, 'My victorious troops are advancing everywhere and you will soon be home with your families once more.'

The celebration was naturally premature. Impressive at first, the attack ran out of steam and gave the Entente the chance to make up their reserves and counter-attack.[119]

Hindenburg was obliged to admit the failure of the offensive when Emperor Charles came to Spa on 1 May. Romania sued for peace a week later. A new Marne offensive started at the end of May. Progress was so rapid that William left Spa and established his base closer to the battle lines. On 1 June the crown prince's divisions were within 39 miles of Paris and Dona joined William in Spa.[120] In the second half of July the Entente counter-attacked on the Marne. With more and more fresh American troops arriving every day, the position became increasingly hopeless. The submarine warmongers had made a fatal blunder. From now on the German armies would be in gradual, followed by rapid, retreat.

The knives were out for Berg next. There were even a few voices heard advocating a return of Valentini. William seemed content with the idea of bringing in his cousin Max as chancellor, but there was unexpected resistance from within his own family – Dona steamed in once again. When Riezler returned to Berlin at the end of the first week of April, everything was misty: 'The military dictatorship hardly veiled any more.'[121] That month William's childhood friend Poultney Bigelow made his own contribution to the war effort. He turned on him with the publication of *Genseric, King of the Vandals and the First Prussian Kaiser*. America had entered the war against a man who had 'prepared a raid upon the trade-relations of the world, unparalleled for ferocity, for vastness, and for efficiency in diabolical details'. According to Bigelow, it had all been planned from the very beginning: 'William II did not drop his mask until he had been seven years on the throne; completed the North Sea–Baltic Canal; purchased the support of the Papacy in Reichstag elections, and had so drilled his people in hatred of England, that henceforward a declaration of war would be not merely welcome to his army, but also to his people as a call of God to a crusade for Kultur.'[122]

Bowing Out

There were minor changes to William's team at the beginning of August 1918. Captain Sigurd von Ilsemann was made an ADC and he was to remain at William's side until his death twenty-three years later. On that same day Alfred Niemann became William's General Staff officer and took up his duties in Spa. Plessen told him to take care of William's low morale. For the first time he had to dine with his sovereign, sometimes in the elegant surroundings of the Villa Fraineuse, a Little Trianon which had been built above the town by the rich industrialist Auguste Peltzer. Niemann was no art historian, but he described the interior as looking as if it had been made out of spun sugar, with its filigree decoration, its marble halls, the wide saloon looking out on to the garden with its lawns surrounded by woods. On either side of the main saloon were the dining and drawing rooms. Upstairs William's living quarters were 'English architecture'.[1] The guests were not inspired by the beauty of the place. The conversation was flat. People did not say what was on their minds.

On 8 August Germany suffered its blackest day of the war: the British advanced near Amiens, killing 20,000 and taking a further 30,000 prisoner. German morale began to collapse. It became an urgent priority to achieve an acceptable peace on the basis of the *status quo ante*. It began to dawn on William: 'Now we have lost the war.'[2] The terrible reverse showed on his face. He was nervous, and chewed his lip. He wanted a Cambrai-style counter-attack and told Niemann to inform the field marshal. Ludendorff reported a mutinous attitude among the troops. William thought the time had come to sue for peace through the queen of the Netherlands.[3]

There was an Imperial Council meeting on 14 August. It was thought that the moment had arrived to end the war. Secretary of State Hintze suggested that it might look better for peace if a few socialists were admitted to the government. Later that day Emperor Charles arrived with his new Foreign Minister, Graf Burian. Their advice tallied. A week later William went to Wilhelmshöhe. His nerves were shattered and to add to his problems, Dona had suffered a heart attack. The party entered the building through a side wing to avoid alarming the patient. As Niemann had not known William for long, he was struck by the paltry amounts of food offered at meals: the 'extremely limited diet belonged to one of the life-held habits of the emperor'. William appeared lonely. The ADCs tried to take his mind off things by talking to him about art and science. On the 16th there was another Imperial Council meeting, where once again the others tried to keep the truth from William.[4]

While William was in Wilhelmshöhe he received the Tsar of Bulgaria, who promised to stay firm and not conclude peace before Germany did. Ilsemann had to inform the emperor of further reverses as British tanks made their way towards Arras and Cambrai. The Siegfried Line had been pierced and William's Adjutant-General, Plessen, had come under fire at the age of seventy-six. William hit the table with his fist: 'Now we have lost the war, poor fatherland!' He took to his bed. 'Only the empress could help. She was the only one who really knew the inner life of the monarch, who with her woman's and maternal instincts would find ways and means to revive her husband's power to resist,' wrote Niemann in William's approved account of the events. She was very ill, but Niemann went to her. 'Tell me the truth! Is everything really lost? I can't believe that God has forsaken our poor fatherland!' Niemann impressed on her that she still had a role to play. 'I will help you,' she said.[5]

The aimlessness persisted. William went for walks in the woods around Cassel and picked white heather, telling Niemann that it was with such a flower that his father had become engaged to his mother. On 5 September the industrialist Ballin sought a last audience with William. He had been kept away from the emperor during the war years. Dona disliked him, and rightly suspected him of advocating a negotiated peace. After September 1914 they had been prevented from holding their usual informal discussions. Ballin thought William was told only what would make him happy. Berg had billed their talk as an audience in order to be present himself. William objected to this and changed the time so that he might see Ballin on his own. Once again he was thwarted by the new Civil Cabinet chief.[6]

William and Ballin talked for an hour and a half by the portico of the house. Berg-Markienen was with them, preventing them from talking freely. Ballin recorded:

I found the emperor very misdirected and in the elated mood that he affected when a third party was present. Things had been so twisted that even the fearful failure of the offensive, that had caused a severe depression in him at first, had been turned into a success. Now it was intended to fall back on the Hindenburg Line, and the offensive had achieved no more than the loss of the lives of around 100,000 valuable people. The whole thing was served up to the poor monarch in such a way that he had not noticed the catastrophe at all.[7]

Ballin wanted William to ask President Wilson to negotiate peace. The situation at home was deteriorating fast. He proposed sending Bülow across the lines. Time was being lost while High Command consolidated the front, and William was still hoping to use his cousin, the queen of Holland. The meeting was not a success. Berg told Ballin not to make William pessimistic. William – accurately – pointed out that this war would be followed shortly by another, the 'Second Punic War'. It was not just that Ballin was disappointed by having to talk in the presence of the unsympathetic Berg: William would not lunch with him, as was his wont in the past, but sent him off with the marshals while he ate with his ailing wife. Ballin concluded that William was 'a completely broken man' under the influence of Berg and the army leaders.[8]

On 6 September there was an exotic interlude when the Hetman of the new German puppet state in the Ukraine arrived for an audience at Wilhelmshöhe accompanied by a number of cossacks in colourful costumes. The Hetman was in some despair at the state of the armies in the east, especially the Austrians. William went on to make a speech to the workers at Krupp. He toured the works, wandering at will and speaking to people here and there, clapping them amiably on the shoulders; but even as a prototype for a modern royal walkabout it was not a tremendous success. His thirty-minute speech was half encouragement and half threat. And for once he delivered it badly. Ilsemann thought it contained much that was better not said. William asked Berg: 'How did you find my speech?' The cabinet chief was lost for words: 'Yes, I am aware, I can say whatever I want, but you will never be happy with it!'[9]

The emperor returned to Spa where he heard more distressing news about the Austrian attempts to conclude a separate peace. William was thrown into a state of nervous excitement. High Command had moved their Avesnes HQ, and now the war was being fought from Spa alone. On 18 September he visited his Alsatian Schloss at Urville near Colmar for the last time as he made a tour of inspection of Duke Albert's army. William seemed to recover at the sight of the troops and they took new force from a visit by their Supreme Warlord. Once he was back in Spa, however, bad news was once more there to greet him. The Turks had suffered setbacks in Palestine, and the Allies had broken through Bulgarian defences. On the 24th he went to Kiel to visit the shipyards, noting the 'many surly faces' among the sailors of his navy.[10]

He was still in Kiel inspecting torpedoes and mines when the Bulgarians collapsed on the 26th. Niemann took the news to him in the dining car of his train. William was profoundly shocked, and had to retire to his private quarters. He was beside himself with anger: had the Bulgarian Tsar not sworn an oath to him only a few weeks ago? Had this man lost his faith? William directed that they returned to Spa immediately. Over the next few days both the British and the Belgians made progress in their advance through Flanders. Niemann ran into General von Bartenwerffer on the steps of HQ in the Hôtel Britannique who told him that Ludendorff was pressing for a truce. The news was not popular with William, who believed a truce tantamount to capitulation. There was still talk of a final battle in the west followed by a *levée en masse* if that failed. This French Revolutionary last-ditch stand was forcefully advocated by Rathenau in the *Vossische Zeitung*.[11]

On 30 September Colonel von Haeften saw the outgoing Chancellor Hertling. Hertling asked the officer, 'What do you think of the military situation?' 'I should say it was catastrophic ... But, Excellency, what happens next if Wilson demands the emperor's abdication?' 'Last Sunday the emperor asked the same question and I replied – Your Majesty, I don't think he'll do it, but if he makes such a request then we will go back to battle.' Haeften asked if he thought the soldiers would fight. Hertling replied, 'I believe you are being too much of a pessimist.'[12]

II

High Command were in favour of Prince Max of Baden's appointment as chancellor to replace Hertling. Once again it forestalled a bid backed by Dona to bring back Bülow. Max was the nephew of the Grand Duke, and heir presumptive to the Badenese title. William played for time: he had to receive formal permission from the head of the family, the Grand Duke. Berg was not best pleased: 'You were not my candidate, but I didn't have another.' William went to Potsdam on 1 October, the day Max took office. He appeared to have accepted the inevitability of the parliamentary government which came with his Badenese cousin. A week later William was once again obliged to take to his bed. He was suffering from agonising sciatica which laid him low from the 4th to the 8th. He none the less gave audiences, and Max was able to prepare the ground for the sacking of the unpopular Berg. William must have liked the suggestion that he might have his friend Valentini back. 'You didn't come here to make difficulties for High Command?' William asked lamely. But he eventually acceded to the prince's will.[13]

William received Max in bed on 6 October. It was to be the only calm meeting they had. Max wanted to see the back of the Minister of War and the two generals. William squirmed. Max noticed that he did not possess the freedom to decide. In the meantime Berg was interfering in politics again, trying to keep Erzberger, the author of the Peace Resolution, out of the government. Max went for Berg again. William told him it was the emperor's business to choose the cabinet chiefs. Max replied that the High Command had not observed this decorum when they knifed Valentini. William was worried about which way the generals would jump. Max, on the other hand, had an assurance from Ludendorff that he would not interfere.[14]

On the 9th Max was back to square one in his attempts to rid Germany of Berg. Dona and the crown prince had worked on William to retain the Civil Cabinet chief and keep Valentini at bay. Questioned by Max, William could not tell him why Dona had such an aversion to Valentini, but he was obliged to support her view. There was a potentially nasty moment the following day when the crowd surrounded William's car in Berlin. Ilsemann reached for his revolver, but the people merely cheered and waved their hats. Ilsemann concluded that William should spend more time in Berlin. On the 14th Max received the princes Oscar and Adalbert. They had heard wild rumours about abdication. Adalbert asked the chancellor if he should go to his father and make it clear that this was necessary. His elder brother, however, made a 'dismissive gesture'. Max assured them that while he was chancellor he hoped that any attempt to force an abdication would fail.[15]

The second Wilson note arrived on the 15th. William handed it to Niemann: 'Read that! It aims directly at the fall of my house, and above all at the abolition of the monarchy!' On the same day Riezler noted in his diary that the only way to save the dynasty was for William to abdicate. Four days later he observed that the question had been shelved: Prince Max would not hear of it. As he told William's friend Max Warburg, that was exactly what he was trying to avoid.[16]

On the 17th William believed he had heard some good news when Ludendorff told him that he thought he could hold both fronts. William's eyes were radiant, and he dismissed his Quartermaster General with profuse thanks. On the very same day the Austro-Hungarian Empire began to crack up into federal states. America had already connived at the situation by recognising Czecho-Slovakia and Jugoslavia.[17] William agreed to appoint a new ministry which brought in moderate socialists for the first time: 'Now they can show me for once whether they can not just criticise me, but can also act.' On the 19th there was a meeting between William and Max at which the Bavarian envoy, Graf Lerchenfeld, was present. Max tried to make William stop the U-boat campaign. 'I didn't know you were an expert on naval matters,' said William superciliously. Lerchenfeld warned him of dangerous tendencies within the Empire. William knew all about them, and that there was a call for his abdication but, he added in deepest earnest, 'A successor to Frederick the Great does not abdicate.'[18]

On 20 October he received Friedrich Rosen again. The diplomat told William that everyone was discussing his abdication. The calls were louder from the right. William was probably not impressed, but there was plenty of support for the monarchy on the left of the Reichstag.[19] 'Then I must have it out with these gentlemen.' He asked Rosen what his opinion was. Rosen replied that William should take a lead in the reforms and tell the people: 'What you want is what I want. I also want a new organisation and want your support.' William did not appear to know how bad the situation was, although some of his sons (not the crown prince) had indicated that all was not right. Things were moving. That day both Philipp Scheidemann and Matthias Erzberger were received at Schloss Bellevue as State Secretaries. William impressed this collection of new men and his speech struck the right note when he said, 'The new age will represent the new order.' Despite all the efforts of the High Command, Germany was on the brink of becoming a constitutional monarchy. William would be bitter about this later: autocracy was the right system for Germany. If democracy had never been introduced there would have been no armistice and no Versailles *Diktat*.[20]

Wilson's third note came on the 24th. It talked of self-determination for Austrians and Germans: something which was notably absent from the Versailles Treaty. It also mentioned the need to stem Prussian militarism. More and more people realised that the Entente had no desire to make peace with the Hohenzollerns. Max consulted Haeften who thought that William could only abdicate of his own free will, and never as a result of pressure from the Social Democrats. 'If, however, His Majesty does not decide immediately it means rejecting the Wilson note, and the result of that will be – helmets off for prayers!'[21]

The next day the two giants of Prussian militarism, Hindenburg and Ludendorff, arrived in Berlin despite all attempts on the part of the chancellor to keep them in Spa. They wanted an end to the negotiations. 'We won't answer the fellow. Our army is unbeaten and occupies enemy soil. It may not surrender.' Wilson's note was having the desired effect. Talk of self-determination had led to trouble in the Landtag and the members who sat for the pro-French faction in Alsace, the Danes in Schleswig and the Poles in the east. There were calls from the right for a dictatorship, with the Januschauer once more encouraging Hindenburg to take a lead. The Foreign Minister, on the other hand, wanted to see the High Command's political power curtailed and that meant ditching Ludendorff. If Ludendorff would not stand down, Max, who was going down with flu, declared that he would resign.[22]

The new crisis came to the boil. Niemann tried to reassure William that the leaders only wanted the best for him. William replied, 'What is the use of goodwill, when negotiation leads to disaster?' William wrestled with his conscience in the park. There he met Niemann: 'He told me he would send the head of the Civil Cabinet to the chancellor and have him ask if he would rescind his call for [Ludendorff's] resignation if the High Command agreed in the future not to meddle in politics and that as a concession to this the Political Department would be abolished.' It was not enough. Max was adamant. The Bavarians were now asking for William to step down, and William had been informed that Hindenburg and Ludendorff were issuing orders without even informing the emperor. 'Ludendorff must go, he will cost me my crown.' William blamed the general for ridding him of Bethmann and Valentini: 'He mixed in all political affairs, and understood nothing at all.' He had an unpleasant, angry temperament. He had even once thrown a map at William's feet and he was now happy to blame Ludendorff for the approaching catastrophe.

William abandoned Ludendorff to his fate. At midnight on the 26th the ministers were sitting around the sick chancellor's bed when the news came from Haeften: 'General Ludendorff has been dismissed.' 'And Hindenburg?' 'He's staying.' 'Thank God!' they all said and jumped to their feet. He had saved face by mentioning bad health as the reason for his going and escaped from the scene of his humiliation in Hindenburg's car. After a number of other names had been suggested and rejected Ludendorff was replaced by the Württemberger Groener. According to Niemann, William was so overwrought his nerves 'vibrated'. On the way back to Potsdam in the car, Dona stroked her husband's hands to calm him down.[23]

On 25 October Ballin put down some last thoughts on William and the abdication issue:

I don't think the emperor would be very sad when he could now make a noble gesture and withdraw into private life. The war did not suit the character of the ruler, it had the effect of wearing him out so that in his own interest one can only wish that it be made possible that he retire into a comfortable private life ... With certainty the empress will strike up a hefty resistance. The appointment of his grandson as his successor and the naming of a regent in whom trust may be placed would remove much of the frightfulness of the present situation in Germany ... In my opinion the emperor never enjoyed rule. Whatever the case any joy that he might have had he has completely lost since this war has hung about his neck.[24]

On the 28th came more bad news from Austria. They had entered into direct negotiations with the Entente. William threw the paper on to his desk with contempt, biting his lip: 'Now we face the whole world alone ... So that is the reward for Nibelung loyalty?' Berg had been replaced by Clemens von Delbrück, but he had stayed on in an unofficial capacity. Berg lured him back to Spa, and persistently told him not to abdicate. Once again he had Dona's backing. William made the wrong decision to listen to him: 'the flight from reality became the flight from Berlin which decided everything.' Germany's first constitutional monarchy was abandoned in its cot. There was a massive conspiracy of silence. August Eulenburg, Chelius and Pastor Dryander all refused to tell him the truth. Müller went to see him at the Neues Palais, but William told him nothing about his intention to return to Spa.[25] He said nothing to his chancellor either, who learned only at 5 p.m. of his intention to flee back to the army. William was playing ostrich. When the diplomat Grünau brought Max the news he thought it was a bad joke. William had said that it was only for four or five days, but Max did not believe him. He thought the emperor would never return.

Max telephoned him. William said that decisions in war had to be taken quickly. Max tried to make him postpone the trip: it would make the most terrible impression. William said, 'You have had Ludendorff dismissed; now I must introduce Groener.' Max thought Hindenburg quite capable of performing that role. Could he possibly come round to see him? William said he did not want to catch Max's flu: 'Besides you must preserve your energy.' Max said, 'We are entering difficult days. Your Majesty cannot be absent.' Max threatened resignation but William ignored him. He had set his hopes on England now for peace. Despite entreaties from Solf, Delbrück and Eulenburg, the royal train left Potsdam-Wildpark for the last time on 29 October 1918. Dona took her husband to the station, and pressed a rose into his hand. It was a decision which was later compared to Louis XVI's fatal flight to Varennes. Dona's complicity in the William's departure may well have sealed the fate of the Hohenzollerns. William returned to Spa for the drama's final act at four o'clock on 30 October. The Château de Neubois had been cleared of its contents. William based himself on the Villa Fraineuse but until 2 November he slept on his train for added security.[26]

III

Increasing frustration with the conduct of war had led some of the more political officers in High Command to push for William's abdication too. The crown prince had refused to countenance the idea of a palace revolution. The other sons were also canvassed. They all said no. During the critical days in Berlin, the crown prince refused a summons to appear.

It was thought for a while that he might have been able to save the monarchy, had he acted quickly enough. Prince Max realised in time, however, that both William and his eldest son needed to go if the monarchy were to be preserved. Both President Wilson and Marshal Foch were insisting upon it.[27]

That was the view of many members of William's last ministry. Not only conservatives such as Friedrich von Payer and Wilhelm Drews thought that the throne might be preserved for a grandchild, Philipp Scheidemann would have gone along with that too. The crown prince realised this too late. On the 7th he tried to put himself forward, but the Social Democrats – those men he had reviled since his first intemperate speech at Oels – would hear nothing of it. Ebert, their leader, was prepared to entertain the idea of a regency under Eitel or Oscar, but not Little Willy. Groener thought the ideal solution would be a regency under Eitel Fritz until the young Prince Frederick William had come of age.[28]

The longer Prince Max left it, however, the longer William wavered, and the more the Germans heeded the Wilson notes with their promises of a better peace if Germany were rid of the Hohenzollerns. That was certainly Gustav Noske's view. The former Civil Cabinet chief, Berg, was a key to William's intransigence. Another was Plessen, who, over forty years, had seen it as his principal duty to prevent William from hearing bad news. No politician, he had pushed for war since the end of the previous century. Now, he refused to allow anyone to suggest that William should step down. The more intelligent officers, such as Ludendorff's friend Colonel Bauer, found the atmosphere at Spa 'unreal'.[29]

William had begun to saw wood in the mornings to let off steam. Ilsemann watched him at the Villa Fraineuse on 1 November. Drews came to see William. After a talk with the chancellor he had determined to tell William the truth. He wanted to convince him that he should abdicate and that the crown prince should renounce his right of succession for the sake of the dynasty, and so that Germany might receive more generous terms from the Entente. They went for a walk in the park at Neubois with Plessen. William's reaction was predictable. He would consider it only after total defeat: 'Now I am here with my army. If Bolshevism arrives at home, I shall put myself at the head of a few divisions and return to Berlin and hang all those who have committed treachery. Then we'll see if the masses stick to their emperor and empire!'

Prince Max tried to cajole Frederick Charles of Hessen into doing the job. The German prince told Max and Walter Simons that he would not oblige anybody to do something they did not wish to do. The jurist Simons hit the table: 'If the representatives of the monarchical idea fail at this time the republic will come!' 'Then let it come!' None of the other princes would take responsibility for telling William the truth either. When Max told Auwi that his father would have to go before the Reichstag took the decision for him, Auwi looked blank.

It was possibly the last chance of retaining the monarchy. By the time William reluctantly accepted to stand down it was far too late. The necessary papers for the abdication were already being drawn up. Max could do little either way. He was still in Berlin with raging flu. His doctor gave him a sleeping draught. He slept for thirty-six hours. Later that day William ran into Niemann, who was walking in the park. He fulminated against Hindenburg for putting himself before his master and praised the 'south German' Groener for telling the impertinent minister that the chief danger was not the enemy, but division and poor morale at home. That day Turkey capitulated.[30]

On the 3rd, Drews reported back. William had shown his unbending determination not to abdicate. Max turned to Haeften. He was an officer and said he could not tell William what to do: 'Do your own dirty work.' Max had no co-operation from William's sons at all. None of them supported the idea of a regency. William let his thoughts be known: 'If I go, then the army will break up and the enemy will fall unhindered on Germany.' By the 4th there were distinct signs that the revolution was about to break out.[31]

William continued his duties. He visited the HQ of Prince Rupprecht and General Sixt von Arnim, pinning medal after medal on the soldiers' chests. There was an air attack on the imperial train on the 4th and three bombs exploded nearby. The only things which landed close were propaganda sheets. Some civilians ran for cover including the cook in his hat and apron and the soldiers laughed. In Niemann's version William remembered his Shakespeare: 'Discretion is the better part of valour,' he spouted. Then he smiled and looking at the cowering civilians, uttered 'Toren!' – idiots – although the next day he prudently had the train armed with machine-guns. Falstaff's line was not enough. Now he recalled something from *Julius Caesar*:

> Cowards die many times before their deaths;
> The valiant never taste of death but once.
> Of all the wonders that I yet have heard,
> It seems to me most strange that men should fear;
> Seeing that death, a necessary end,
> Will come when it will come.[32]

It came to him in bed, nearly twenty-three years later.

Max Fürstenberg arrived from Vienna on the 5th. He brought with him an eyewitness account of the collapse of the house of Habsburg. It was the anniversary of Prussia's greatest victory over the French – Rossbach – and the Entente named their toughest general, Ferdinand Foch, to negotiate an armistice. Another general, this time the Dutchman Johannes Benedictus van Heutsz, arrived in Spa and stayed until the 9th. He was a former governor of the Dutch East Indies and adjutant to the queen. He ostensibly wanted to go to the front and inspect the German defences at Zeebrugge. He had also observed the exercises of the Rohr Battalion whose job it was to protect the emperor. William granted him a routine audience on the 8th. As one modern commentator has put it: 'That he neither knew nor noticed anything of William's flight plans seems little credible.'[33]

The next day William asked Groener to put out feelers for a truce. The new Quartermaster-General told Max that Germany needed to hoist the white flag. Max replied, 'Not for a week.' Groener said that was too long. The socialist leaders came to see the chancellor. Friedrich Ebert told him, 'The mood of the people pushes the responsibility on to the emperor, it doesn't matter whether they are right or wrong. The important matter for the people is that they can see supposed guilty parties removed from their positions. For this reason the emperor's abdication is necessary if the masses are to be hindered from going over to a revolutionary position.' Ebert suggested that William abdicate the next day – the 7th – with Oscar or Eitel representing him. 'The crown prince is not possible, he is too hated by the masses.'[34]

Groener told the men of the left that it was impossible to order the Supreme Warlord to abdicate. The socialist deputies Eduard David and Albert Südekum reassured the general that they were not anti-monarchical. Scheidemann, who had been on the telephone, brought them up to date with the news. 'The abdication is no longer the subject of the discussion. The revolution has broken out. Sailors from Kiel have grabbed power in Hamburg and Hanover as well [as Kiel]. Gentlemen, it is no longer the moment for discussion, we must act. We do not know whether we shall be sitting on these chairs tomorrow.' The socialists were tearful. Groener was told to have a last go at securing a regency. He said that the princes would have nothing to do with it. 'Under these circumstances any further discussion becomes otiose. Now things must take their course,' said Ebert.[35]

Groener stuck to his guns. There was no question of abdication. He revealed the situation in Spa. 'The emperor will offer up his life, or at least risk it, rather than standing down.' At that moment officers were working on the plan for a sortie on the 8th. Were William to die it would strengthen the monarchical idea. Groener and a number of other high-ranking officers were keen on this plan which was finally scuppered by Plessen. That afternoon Max decided that William should dissolve the Reichstag, call elections, then abdicate.[36]

On 7 November the delegation headed by Erzberger passed through Spa on its way to ask for peace and stopped, briefly, to confer with Hindenburg. Bavaria was declared a republic. The Wittelsbachs were chased from their palaces. It became imperative to ask Foch for a truce before the Federal Empire broke up. Ebert came to see Max in the garden of the chancellor's palace at the end of the morning. The chancellor feared a socialist revolution. Ebert told him: 'If the emperor does not abdicate a socialist revolution is unavoidable. I don't want it, however; the idea is as hateful as sin to me.' Max pointed to Prince Eitel. Ebert did not object. Later that day Max tried to resign.[37]

The next day the Rhine bridges were secured by forces of the German Revolution. Brunswick, Munich and Stuttgart had fallen. Cologne was teetering. In the course of the day Halle, Leipzig, Düsseldorf, Osnabrück, Lüneburg, Magdeburg and Oldenburg fell and William's Cumberland son-in-law stood down. Max called William. The emperor would not allow his chancellor to step down before the negotiations had been concluded. The chancellor had no confidence in the troops stationed in Berlin. Max received a telegram from Grünau. William had once again said he would not abdicate. Max called William again:

Your abdication has become necessary to avoid civil war in Germany and finally to fulfil your mission as the emperor of peace ... There are two possibilities: 1. Abdication, naming a deputy and calling a national assembly. 2. Abdication. The crown prince renounces his rights. Regency for the grandchild. If the abdication does not take place today, I can no longer work with you. I issue my advice as a relative of the German princes. Voluntary sacrifice is required to guarantee your [good] name in German history.[38]

William was aware that officially only the Bundesrat could unseat him. He told Max of another idea he had had: 'Unless you have something else in mind in Berlin, then I shall return with my troops after the conclusion of the armistice and I shall shoot up the town if that is required.'[39]

Having once again proved a stubborn determination quite worthy of Vicky, William went for a walk on Spa's heights with Fürstenberg. General Heutsz was due to come to lunch. Gontard asked whether, in the circumstances, he might be put off. William saw no reason to do so. At the meal he spoke to the Dutchman 'as if nothing had happened'. He was evidently acting again – William was very worried.[40]

The socialists were working on plans for a *coup d'état*. They had already made it clear they would take to the streets if William had not resigned by the morning of the 9th. They were egged on by the Independent Socialists, who were out for blood and had demanded a general strike. Max's nightmare returned the next morning when Scheidemann and Ebert appeared to ask if there had been an answer from Spa. When Max replied no, Scheidemann said, 'Then I really don't know how we are going to stop the people from taking to the streets.'[41]

v

In Spa it was cold, wet and misty on the morning of the 9th, typical autumn weather. William had breakfast with Fürstenberg, Ilsemann and his ADC Hirschfeld. Niemann ran into Groener and asked him whether William was aware of the gravity of the situation. The Quartermaster-General told him that they were expecting to hear any minute from the officers who had been sent out to canvass the opinions of different units as to whether they would continue to fight for their emperor. As soon as Groener had been informed he would take the results to William at the Villa Fraineuse. William was hanging about waiting for news. He told his suite that he would not go far, so that he could be briefed at any time. In the course of the morning Secretary of State von Hintze also told William that the army would not stand behind him if civil war broke out.[42]

Like Goebbels later, William was hoping that the Entente would break up from fear of Bolshevism and perhaps help him put down the revolution which was breaking out in Berlin. He wanted a chance to deal with the mutineers in the Rhineland. When Hindenburg and Groener arrived he went back into the garden saloon of the villa. Also there were Schulenburg and Plessen, General von Marschall and Hintze. No one seemed to know what Little Willy's Chief of Staff was doing there. He had suddenly turned up at the Hôtel Britannique. Hindenburg began inauspiciously by excusing himself for what Groener was going to say to him. William went pale.

Groener told William that it was pointless to go on. Schulenburg then asked to speak. He alone tried to rally the monarchy, reminding the emperor of Bismarck in 1862: 'You have all gone mad here!' There were still good elements in the army, they might be used to put down the revolution in the Rhineland. He is supposed to have told William, possibly disingenuously, 'Don't give in to the revolution at home, don't abdicate, take hold with both hands and restore order city by city! With this cry the army will fall in behind the emperor again and will preserve its discipline.' 'In that epic moment [Schulenburg] embodied the spirit of Prussia.' Groener told him that it was too late and the majority of the army would refuse to fight.[43]

William hesitated a while, then said that it would be better for Germany to sign a truce than that there should be civil war. Hindenburg also rejected Schulenburg's advice. Groener then drove the knife home: 'Calmly and in good order the army will march back home under its generals, but not under the leadership of Your Majesty!' William advanced on Groener, his eyes sparkling with anger and said in a high-pitched, trembling voice, 'Excellency, I want this statement from you in writing. All the commanding generals will receive it in black and white, that the army is no longer behind its Supreme Warlord. Did the army not swear an oath to me?' Groener: 'The oath ...? That is now just a fiction, Your Majesty!'[44]

Hindenburg recovered some of his courage and spoke. He told William that neither he nor Groener could take the responsibility. At that point there was a call from Berlin. The chancellor needed an immediate abdication if he were to preserve order, and save the monarchy. Schulenburg spoke a last line for Prussia: William should not jump to an immediate decision and destroy what centuries had built up. He and Plessen told William to jettison the Reich and retain only Prussia. The emperor strode into the park.[45] The crown prince arrived at the same time as Colonel Wilhelm Heye at around midday. He was anxious to know whether his father would abdicate. Heye had received the results from the various commands. He repeated that the army would not put down the revolution. When he heard the news from Berlin, Prince William quipped that that was what came out of enlarging the base of government. At Schulenburg's suggestion, William decided to abdicate as emperor while reserving for himself the title of king of Prussia. He would remain with the army. Paper was brought. Hintze, Grünau, Marschall and Schulenburg drafted the script. William also agreed to an armistice to avert civil war. This message got through to Berlin at about 1 p.m. Schulenburg and Hintze were to take the document there. Lunch was announced. There was no conversation. William just stared and bit his upper lip.[46]

In Berlin the army was refusing to act against the revolutionaries and the socialist ministers were threatening to resign *en masse*. The only possible way to save the dynasty was for William to abdicate. One of his telephones at the Villa Fraineuse was off the hook, the other permanently engaged. Prince Max made the decision by himself, informing only Simons. He saw it as his duty to make an announcement which appeared to have been approved by William, even though he knew it could not be official until he had spoken to the emperor. The message went out to the press agency at twelve noon.[47]

Back in the garden saloon at the Villa Fraineuse William was already changing his mind. Was it necessary to abdicate if Hindenburg and the army were ready to back him? He could face the situation with the sword. The issue was argued back and forth. William was worried that he might look cowardly: 'I will stay here and those loyal to me will rally round.' At about 2.30 p.m. General von Gontard broke into the room with a memo. He was breathing heavily and his teeth were chattering. He cried out, 'The emperor and the crown prince have been deposed!' 'Treachery!' shouted William. 'Treachery, shameless, outrageous treachery!'[48]

Where Schulenburg still felt that William should stay with the army, the others were now counselling him to leave for a neutral country. Schulenburg said he would be safe with his men. William lashed out at the navy: 'They have really left me in the lurch . . . my pride, my creation.' William compared himself to a captain abandoning his ship. Gontard and Plessen endeavoured to convince the crown prince to stand by his father. He would not. Without so much as an adieu, 'he got into his car and zoomed off'. Hindenburg was still trying to make things clear: 'I could not take responsibility were Your Majesty to be dragged back to Berlin by mutinous troops to be delivered as a prisoner to the revolutionary government.'[49]

VI

Things were moving fast in Berlin. Scheidemann had resigned from the government and Ebert had come to demand the chancellor's post for the socialists. Max suggested that Ebert should take over the position himself. He accepted: 'It is a difficult office but I shall take it on.' Max asked him if he were prepared to work under a monarchy. 'Yesterday I would have replied yes without condition, today I will have to ask my friends first.' Max thought a regency might still be possible. Ebert riposted: 'It is too late.' There was a little chorus behind him: 'Too late! Too late!'

They were still discussing the possibility of a regency when Scheidemann took it upon himself to proclaim the birth of the German Republic from the window of the reading room of the Reichstag. It was Scheidemann, fearing the introduction of Russian-style socialism by the Independent Socialists therefore, who administered the *coup de grâce*. Max only received William's message that he wished to continue as king of Prussia at two o'clock. The official message, however, had told the world two hours previously that he had abdicated both titles. Ebert made an attempt to have Max stay on in a presidential role, but the prince said he could not work with the Independent Socialists. 'Herr Ebert,' said Max as he bade him farewell, 'I am entrusting you with the German Empire!' Ebert replied, 'I have lost two sons for this Empire.'[50]

At Doorn William admitted he was in a quandary. He now seemed to regret the decision he had taken. There was no one there to give him the advice he sought. 'I was fighting a difficult inner battle, whether I should avoid the accusation of cowardice by not abandoning the more or less loyal parts of my army, but rather by dying fighting together with them.' Whether he seriously contemplated suicide is disputed, but he certainly thought about it after the event. 'If I had turned my weapons against myself would people not have said "What a coward! Now he is trying to evade responsibility?"' The Paris-based inquiry into war guilt, he thought, would have come to its own conclusions.[51]

Later William justified his refusal to die in battle to the American writer Viereck: 'Even had I desired to choose this path, you know that the rear of a modern battlefront is riddled with kilometres of shell holes, that it takes miles before anyone can reach the front lines. I might have broken my leg in a shell hole, but I could not possibly have established contact with the enemy . . .' Some others might have been killed. 'A king has no right to send his men to death to assuage his personal vanity. It would have meant the sacrifice of valuable lives, merely to provide me with a spectacular exit.'[52]

Another choice was to remain with the army and return to Germany. In retrospect William thought he had done the right thing, but he could never be sure. 'If I had stayed, the German people might have been forced to shameful compliance with the Allied demand for my surrender. I am responsible to God; I am responsible to my country; but I am not, and was not, responsible to my people's foes.' 'I had to choose between sacrificing myself and sacrificing my country. I sacrificed myself. It is not my fault that the sacrifice was in vain.' The fate of his cousin the Tsar swam before his eyes – 'the *coup d'état* of Prince Max left me no choice.'[53]

VII

William went up to his room in the Villa Fraineuse and collapsed in a chair, silently chain-smoking. He was concerned that Dona might be taken hostage. In his mind he was still the king of Prussia at least. That meant the treacherous navy had no more head, and the equally ungrateful Württemberger Groener was no longer his concern: 'I don't have anything to do with you any more,' he said petulantly. 'For the time being I shall stay in Spa. In the event of my present security troops proving disloyal, we shall drive to The Hague.' Niemann went down into the town. There were the wildest rumours flying about, that Spa was about to be taken by revolutionaries. When William heard these he announced, 'I have just at this moment abdicated. I have no desire to be strung up by some pack of eager fellows.' To his ADC Hirschfeld he said, 'I am not a coward, and am not frightened of the bullet, but I don't want to be nabbed here. Yes, who would have believed it would come to this. The German people is a bunch of pigs.'

'Children, arm yourselves, I shall stay the night here in the villa, we should not go anywhere unarmed.' At 4 p.m. William was still blowing hot and cold. He was looking for a way of dealing with Max's *fait accompli*. He fulminated against his people: '[God's] punishment will be frightful. There is no other instance in history of a universal act of treachery by a nation against its ruler.' At seven thirty Hintze and Plessen spent ten minutes alone with William upstairs. Half an hour later William agreed to go to his train. In the car he said:

Plessen and Hintze want me to go to Holland tonight. I can't say I agree with this proposal. I call the army to me, I tell them that I am going to remain with them as king of Prussia and then I flee before they arrive? And if I stayed back with a few loyal members of my train, with them I could fight to the bitter end when we would all be beaten to death – I have no fear of death! No I shall stay here ... [pause] The best thing would be for me to shoot myself.[54]

In Berlin the workers, promised gold, had broken into William and Dona's apartments in the Schloss and made off with the emperor's clothes. In Hamburg Albert Ballin took his own life.[55]

VIII

Dinner on the train was a silent affair. When Niemann saw William again, he found him restored. Niemann was told that William would spend the night on the train but that he had rejected any idea of going to Holland. At 10 p.m. Grünau needed to speak to him. The revolution was spreading from Aachen and Eupen to Spa and foreign troops were also converging on the town. Hindenburg and Hintze told him he should not lose a minute. Holland was his best bet and the most suitable for Dona too. 'So be it then. But not before tomorrow morning!' William then retired into his sleeping carriage.[56]

Plessen cried. Ilsemann was canvassed as to whether he was prepared to resign from the General Staff and go with William to Holland. He was. His colleagues gathered round him: 'Ilsemann, make sure our emperor gets safely over the border and look after him in Holland.' William's chauffeur, Warner, was placed at the ready. At four Ilsemann met William again in the dining car. He was still not happy with the idea of Holland: 'What happens if Bolshevism strikes there too?' At 5 a.m. the wheels began to turn, but the whole thing was a feint. There was a fear that Liège might have been taken over by revolutionaries. The train stopped in La Reid, just beyond Spa. Here the stationmaster led them through a pitch-dark station to starry night. The party transferred to a motorcade and drove the sixty odd kilometres to the Dutch border at Eijsden.[57]

While the train went on towards Liège, William, Ilsemann, Plessen and Hirschfeld got into one car; the soldiers Frankenberg, Zeyss, Niedener and the diplomat Grünau into another. They carried loaded carbines between their knees. William was 'extraordinarily excited'. He kept becoming agitated at the thought that the two cars would be separated. Then he worried that the first car was not driving fast enough and that the party would fail to arrive at the border by dawn. They saw a red flag, but it was just a control. They bluffed their way through. Then they saw the barbed wire of the border. It was patrolled by Bavarian Landwehr soldiers. They sniffed at the cars. Finding marks from where the imperial crown had been scratched off the paintwork they became suspicious. Frankenberg got out. 'General von Frankenberg with a few officers must get to Holland on important business!' 'The gates of freedom were opened,' Ilsemann wrote in his diary later. They had arrived on neutral soil.[58]

The flight was probably better orchestrated and planned than the emperor ever knew. At around 3 a.m. on 10 November 1918, William's man in The Hague, Friedrich Rosen, was woken by a lantern held to his face by a chancellery servant. Hintze had telegraphed the politicians in Brussels and Brussels had wired Rosen. An earlier message which might have explained what was happening failed to arrive until seven thirty. Once it had been decoded it was clear: 'The emperor and his retinue intended to cross to Dutch territory and I should ensure the hospitality of the queen.' The Foreign Minister Jonkheer J. A. van Karnebeek, as it turned out, was already on his way to see Her Majesty at Scheveningen. He had been alerted by Oskar von der Lanken, the head of the political section of the German General Government in Brussels. Many believed that George V had insisted that William be found asylum. He was not going to allow his cousin to face trial or be strung up like a criminal, no matter what noises his ministers were making to their electors. Van Karnebeek called Rosen at 8 p.m. The queen had already agreed to his asylum and wanted him to go to her summer residence at Het Loo.[59]

The Foreign Minister and Rosen agreed that this was a bad idea. Karnebeek suggested Huis ten Bosch, but the German envoy believed that was too near to The Hague and too hard to defend. He knew there was a danger of demonstrations. It was Karnebeek who remembered Godard Bentinck in Amerongen. The Foreign Minister proposed that Rosen accompany the official body which was going to meet him. He took with him the third secretary, Köster.

In Eijsden the civilian Grünau played the next card. He disappeared into the border post and the lights went on. William lit a cigarette. 'Children, you smoke too. You deserve it.' He asked Ilsemann about his family. Then the Dutch let the cars through. A Major van Dyl had been sent down from Maastricht to Eijsden on the evening of the 9th. At the border Sergeant Pierre Dinckaer recognised William's car. He called the garrison commander in Maastricht: 'The emperor is at the border.' Van Dyl arrived at eight. A Dutch diplomat came over from Brussels. He had left the Belgian capital at 11 p.m., having clearly been informed of William's plans while the emperor slept in Spa station. Van Dyl spotted the carmine stripes on William's trousers and transferred the party to the railway station. William stood around blowing on his fingers until the court train arrived at 8.28 a.m. It had passed through Liège without incident. A crowd of largely Belgian factory workers had appeared and were hurling abuse at William.[60]

William did not wish to be alone. He was comforted by his men. He was like a dying man: his whole life appeared before him on the train. A Dutch colonel arrived and two men from the German consulate in Maastricht. When the Dutch refused to eat lunch with the Germans, William took it as a sign that his asylum had been refused. The queen was said to be in conference with her ministers. Rosen, Köster and the Dutch party arrived at Eijsden just before midnight. 'As we finally arrived we saw the long, brightly lit imperial court train in the siding. The tiny station building lay behind.' Rosen and the others shunted into the station bearing the glad tidings. It was not until then that he knew asylum had been granted. William thanked the queen of Holland on the telephone and assured her that he was now a 'private person'.[61]

William was there with his cars, cooks and bottle-washers. For twenty-four hours the train served as his home. The Dutch lieutenant had wired for instructions as to whether to disarm the soldiers. Rosen and the Dutch party were led to William's saloon. 'His face shows signs of a severe mental battle over the past few days.' His eyes were sunken, the lids red and swollen. He was bitter about his cousin Max. When Bentinck was mentioned he cheered up and pointed to a picture of Middachten on the wall, then he fetched a *Gotha* and looked Godard Bentinck up. When Rosen tried to leave, William opened up: 'I am a broken man –

what can I do with my life now? There is no more hope, the only thing which remains for me is despair!' Rosen replied, 'Also for Your Majesty serious work will heal.' 'But what? What work can I do?' Rosen suggested that he should write a book – defending and justifying his reign. 'I shall start it tomorrow,' said William.[62]

IX

Graf Godard Bentinck van Aldenburg had just returned from a shooting party. He could not claim great acquaintance with William, although as a German Reichsgraf he had been presented at court in 1884, and met him then. The Bentincks were 'mediatised' and William addressed them as 'cousin' or *Erlaucht*, like minor royalty. The German emperor had stayed with Godard's brother Philipp at Middachten in August 1909 and both Amerongen and Middachten had been suggested as locations for peace talks, the Bentinck being to some extent Anglo-German. The two families were also connected through the Johanniterorden, a Protestant version of the Maltese Knights which was always headed by a Prussian prince. Bentinck lived at Kasteel Amerongen, a seventeenth-century mansion surrounded by a double moat. He had been selected because his castle was easy to defend.

He was telephoned by the governor of Utrecht, Graf Lynden van Sandenburg. Bentinck refused at the first attempt to make him offer William a bed. Much of the house was shut off. There was fuel for two days and the estate cars had not had an outing for two years. The castle staff were either away in the army or down with the flu. Bentinck did not think it was the moment to entertain royalty. Then Lynden van Sandenburg assured him that the government would pay. He was finally convinced by his eldest son Carlos or Charlie: 'The Bentincks took in the emperor in his glorious days. Now when he has been deposed, we cannot refuse him shelter.' The count reluctantly agreed to entertain William for just three days.[63]

Rosen had breakfast with William on the morning of 11 November – Armistice Day. The remaining food was shared out, and the German emperor served the entourage and his Dutch guests. At nine twenty the court train began to move. As it proceeded north through Holland there was a deal of whistling and heckling to be heard from the crowds which had gathered to see it pass. Clenched fists were brandished and the men made signs as if slitting their throats. 'It was completely disgusting,' wrote Ilsemann. It was assumed that some at least of the catcallers were Belgian refugees. The train arrived at the little station of Maarn at 3.20 p.m.

There was already a small crowd on the station shaking fists and shouting abuse. It might have been larger had it not been for the rain. One of them was Lady Susan Townley, who wanted to 'box the crown prince's ears', who she evidently believed was on the train. She had heard the news of William's arrival on her return from church, and full of love for mankind she drove down to Middachten where she assumed he was bound. There she discovered his real destination. She drove to Maarn: 'a lonely little country station, no one was present to see the arrival beyond a handful of Dutch officials, the ubiquitous reporters of the various journals and a few yokels attracted by curiosity.' As William was ushered to the waiting car it was discovered that the escape route was blocked by another behind.

He had to wait, 'exposed ... to the curious stares of all present, at what I suppose, was the most unpleasant moment of his life'. Lady Susan Townley claimed that the 'notoriously pro-Boche' government of Utrecht had planted men in the trees to cheer William's arrival, but these were drowned by the boos, which issued – presumably – from the 'yokels'. She was the only one to make a physical demonstration. Only with difficulty could Bentinck and the other Dutchmen prise her off the bonnet of the car and prevent her from attacking her old friend the German emperor. Her husband lost his job as a result. William was greeted by the Dutch count and Graf Lynden van Sandenburg, the queen's commissar. Together with four of William's men they drove the half-hour journey to a new life in Amerongen.[64]

17

Amerongen and Doorn

William's first words on arriving were 'Denn was sagen Sie dazu [so what do you say]; now give me a cup of hot, good, real English tea,' and rubbed his hands.[1] Upstairs he received a fillip to his imperial dignity: he was shown to a bedroom (and a bed) used by Louis XIV in May 1672. He excused himself to Bentinck's daughter Elisabeth: 'Honoured countess, forgive me for disturbing you, it is, however, not my fault.' When Bentinck laid on a grand dinner that night William repeated his innocence: 'The Lord God knows my conscience is clear, I never wanted this war.' Later that evening he fulminated against the navy:

Thirty years did I bear this mad responsibility, thirty years I have dedicated my entire strength to the Fatherland. This is now my success, this is the thanks. I should never have believed that the navy, my child, would thank me in this way. I never would have believed it possible, that my army should fall apart so quickly. They have all dumped me in it, those for whom I did so much! Ludendorff, Bethmann and Tirpitz are guilty for our losing the war![2]

Despite a trousseau of 158 bottles of wine and *Sekt* by his very nature he was to prove a difficult house guest. By all reports, Bentinck bore it all with saintly stoicism.

The Dutch Foreign Minister talked Bentinck into extending William's stay indefinitely. The Dutch government provided him with food and fuel, as well as fourteen policemen, various auxiliaries, and a detective. No one was allowed to pass Amerongen's tall, red-brick gates without Bentinck's prior permission. White cards were issued to approved visitors, and blue ones given them on leaving. The gates were secured at night and in the winter the ice was broken in the moats to prevent people from crossing. The authorities had convinced William to 'lighten his train', and the majority of those seventy-eight people who had entered Holland with him were sent back to Germany.[3] William had brought twenty-two of them to Amerongen, after the initial selection had been made. When Dona arrived two weeks later, she added another eleven.

There was no room for them all in the house and most of the courtiers were accommodated in Amerongen's small hotels.

There was a certain amount of anger on the part of William's retinue at the Dutch government's insistence on impounding their side-arms. Plessen's protest was most vociferous. He was the oldest officer in the German army. He had worn his sword continuously since 1864; it was a present from the old emperor, William's grandfather. The Dutch general in charge was not impressed. Rosen had words in The Hague and the side-arms were eventually returned to them.[4] In the meantime the crown prince had also thrown himself on the mercy of the Dutch. He had asked if he could return to Berlin with his troops but the new chancellor, Ebert, said he might go to Oels, but not with soldiers. He arrived two days after his father.

On the 12th Rosen came down to Amerongen to see the exiled emperor. He brought books. William had taken him up on his suggestion: he had begun the task of writing a justification of his conduct which would take up most of his twenty-three remaining years. As the two of them talked, Gontard and Ilsemann burst in: 'Your Majesty's life is in the greatest danger!' Two Germans had arrived to tell him of a plot to assassinate him. There would be a great many more scares of this sort, but no serious attempts on his life.[5]

And so began William's retirement, with the establishment of a routine which rarely altered. After the glamour of court, it must have been rudely dull. William rose at seven, dressed in mufti – a blue serge suit – and walked in the very narrow confines of the park wearing a Loden cape and hunting hat with a feather in it. He stopped for a talk with the gardener. At 8.45 a.m. there were prayers in the gallery, during which William read the lesson and Bentinck's daughter played the *Hausorgel*. Before lunch he sat with the letters in his study. Many of them were abusive, but his skin had grown thick with age. He also learned Dutch – which he assimilated remarkably quickly. There was tea at 4.45 p.m. at which he could enjoy the scones and buns baked by the Bentincks' Scottish housekeeper. Dinner was on the dot of eight.

After the lunch he set to work ridding the gardens of trees. By the time he left Amerongen he had killed some 14,000 of them and chopped them up into little bits. Most of these were distributed as firewood for the poor and needy. Every now and then there was an edition of signed logs, which were handed out like Iron Crosses of old. For the truly privileged, William had a supply of busts, photographs and the title of Hofrat, or court councillor, to award. When it rained he relived battles in the summerhouse.[6]

The tree-felling had begun during the war, to provide relief from tension and to provide exercise. It is tempting to believe it was done to spite Bismarck's memory, for the Iron Chancellor had detested the same destructive urge in British prime minister Gladstone. Bismarck regularly sent Gladstone messages through the Foreign Office to tell him that he was *planting* trees. Gladstone did it for exercise too. 'The forest laments that Mr Gladstone might perspire,' said Lord Randolph Churchill. If Hawarden's trees cowered at their master's approach, those at Doorn must have lived in terror. In one December week in 1926, William announced that he had destroyed 2,590.[7]

After his arrival in Holland William ceased to hunt and shoot and renounced the use of a horse. At both Amerongen and Doorn he was too circumscribed to be able to enjoy either, but there may have been something else besides, a desire to put aside his past life. At Doorn he developed a maniacal fondness for the ducks which quacked in his moat. Feeding them became an unshakeable part of his routine. Opinions about his finances vary. Certainly in Berlin it was believed that he had smuggled out a fortune. He possessed 650,000 marks in Dutch banks, but the exchange rate was not high, and for the time being the Prussian government released money in dribs and drabs until a proper settlement was made in 1925. At the first pretext, William sent a communication to Chancellor Ebert asking him to release his money and do likewise for the rest of the royal family.[8]

The bouts of fury continued. Prince Max was a natural target. He was accused of crawling into the depths of the Black Forest to evade his critics. A few days later William 'had visibly made a little recovery'. His features were smoother. He was mentally more balanced; his thoughts calmer. On the 28th, a delegation of sombrely dressed gentlemen arrived led by Graf Ernst zu Rantzau. They were bearing the formal abdication and an order to release the army from its oath of loyalty. William signed it at the Buhl writing desk in his room. It was a moment of 'fortitude and resignation'. William informed Bentinck of what had taken place under his roof. Ebert sent an acknowledgement on 3 December.

The same day as his abdication, William received some consolation in the form of Dona and Tante Ke and the empress's dachshund Topsy. Bentinck went to fetch them from the station. When they arrived William was alone on the bridge, standing to attention giving a military salute. For the first time ever, Dona hugged him. Now the royal pair were settled in a suite of four rooms on the *piano nobile*. Dona had experienced some rude shocks when the revolutionaries broke into the Neues Palais in Potsdam; now the dying empress had come to share his fate. Permanently indisposed, she ate her meals upstairs. William was still blaming everyone but himself: Ludendorff, Bethmann, Tirpitz – 'He was always shoved into the background and no one ever listened to him.'[9]

Plessen allowed himself a rare outburst of bitterness against his lord that day: William had no friends besides his wife. 'The emperor', Ilsemann jotted down the general's words in his diary, 'had a cold heart, towards everyone, even towards his children. He is ungrateful, had always acted, but never applied himself. He had never done any serious work.' William carried on entertaining the dinner table at Amerongen with his ranting against the German people, who had so lightly dropped him after thirty years of adulation, and against various figures in international politics. Wilson also came under fire. He had delivered the *coup de grâce*. William thought the American president a greater autocrat than even the Tsar of Russia. 'I call him Kaiser Wilson!' said Kaiser Wilhelm.[10]

'Vater' Schulz was still with him: 'Anyone who spent the days of mobilisation with him, as I did, would know that he was completely innocent of this war.'[11] On 7 December Lloyd George suggested he be hanged. He issued a formal request for the emperor to be arraigned before an Allied court. In more lenient moments Curaçao or Algeria was suggested as a place of exile. By 11 December calls for his extradition from Holland were beginning to mount. William felt that he would be executed if he were to stand trial in London or Paris. Among the entourage there were discussions as to how to disguise him best. The moustache would naturally have to go. His hair would be shaved off in part, and what remained could be dyed. The plans were put to William. He was ready to have his hair altered, but he wanted to keep his moustache. He would train the ends down. Even then, he said, he would be identified by his deformity. 'It was the first time I had ever heard him mention the arm,' wrote Ilsemann.[12]

He had plans to cross the border into Germany and hide on the estate of the Hereditary Princess Salm. He also talked of taking an overdose. Dona chipped in: 'William, then we'll go together into the beyond.' He worked off his frustration on the trees in the 'prison garden' as he called it. Then Rosen came down to tell him that he thought the Dutch would let him stay. They preferred him to remain at Amerongen for the time being. At Christmas, Rosen received a lithograph of William on his horse.[13]

The farce continued. William pretended that his ear problems had returned and affected a bandage around his head. He let his beard grow, and took to his bed to excite sympathy from the Dutch. He spent six whole weeks largely confined to his room. It was at this time that a group of eight American officers attempted to kidnap William. The plot had been dreamed up on New Year's Eve by Colonel Lucas Lia, who was based in Luxembourg. Under the influence of a surfeit of punch it was decided that he would make a present of William to Woodrow

Wilson. On 5 January they drove in uniform to Amerongen in two cars. They arrived late in the evening, informing the porter they had important things to communicate to the emperor. They were shown into the library by Graf Charlie Bentinck, who told them that everyone was in bed.[14]

Godard Bentinck had been dressing in the meantime. He looked at the officers' papers and decided they were suspicious. William also put his clothes back on. He said he would see the men if they gave him their word of honour that they came from the Peace Commission. Wine and sandwiches were served. While the Americans relaxed, Bentinck called for reinforcements. Colonel Lia looked out of the window and saw police and soldiers arriving at the castle. He realised that all was lost. He owned up to the purpose of the visit. The police escorted them to the frontier. One of them stole an object, generally reported as an ashtray – sometimes the emperor's cigarette end – from the library. William was amused. 'Outside ten policemen, and inside a robbery!' They were disciplined when they returned to the United States.[15]

II

On 23 January 1919 notes started to arrive in The Hague calling on the government to extradite William on charges of war crimes. The Dutch replied that they had a right to offer hospitality to whomsoever they pleased. The second note reminded them of the Dutch victims of the U-boat campaign. The Dutch leadership proved resilient to threats from the Entente, even if the upper house agreed to send him back for fear that he would be murdered in Amerongen. On 17 February the Entente menaced the Dutch with reprisals if they failed to render up the emperor.[16]

William had been busy writing his memoirs with a view to proving his innocence, Bentinck gave him a portrait of William the Silent on his birthday a few days later. Whether that was a hint or not, is not clear. Bentinck's son John had found a picture of the *Hohenzollern*, while his daughter Elisabeth made him a present of a lampshade decorated with a scene of a falcon hunt. A special tram had to be laid on to carry the flowers from the station at Dreibergen. It was still feared that William would not be able to tarry in Holland. In the next few weeks various countries were suggested. There was even a chance of him living in Germany – at Homburg or in the Marmorpalais in Potsdam. William liked the idea of Switzerland the most, but other destinations considered included Denmark or Sweden. William also looked at the estate of Princess Maria Christina of Salm, just across the border in Germany.

The uncertainty worried the sick Dona, who thought the Entente would come and take her husband from her.[17]

The archaeologist Dörpfeld came to Amerongen for a protracted visit. His conversation did not please the military men. It was about digs, and nothing but digs. A member of the entourage, Estorff went away to the crown prince on his island in the Zuider Zee, saying he would return when Dörpfeld had left. The household was up until midnight reliving days on Corfu. When the archaeologist left after six weeks there was universal rejoicing. At the Villa Plön, as the officers called their lodgings in town, there was a bonfire party where a huge gorgon was put to the flame. That night Tante Ke let the cat out of the bag when she told William about it. William was not pleased: 'So people are making fun of me and my archaeological studies?' It was an uncomfortable meal. Estorff thought his days were numbered.[18]

On 9 May the peace conditions were published. Ilsemann had to break them to William. They called for him to be delivered for trial. 'Ilsemann, it won't turn out as bad as it looks today,' said William. On 4 June 1919 the Allied Supreme Council in Paris renewed its call for him to be brought to trial. Four weeks later the Treaty of Versailles was signed. It not only contained a clause which laid the blame for the war squarely at Germany's feet; Article 227 demanded the extradition of a thousand or so war criminals. The Treaty came into force on 10 January 1920. Five days later twenty-six victorious nations demanded that the emperor be released into their custody. A dying Bethmann-Hollweg, who thought the aim of the peace was to enslave Germany, offered to stand trial before a neutral court in William's place. On 21 January and 5 March the Dutch again and again refused to give in to the Entente.[19]

William understandably argued that no court in the world had the right to try him but he none the less suffered from uncertainty and never knew if the Dutch would continue to stand by him. As he told Viereck later, 'I cannot conceive that any American president would permit any court composed of the enemies of his country to pass judgment on his official acts. If the shoe had been on the other foot, would the American people have allowed their president to accept trial at the hands of a court in Berlin ...?' When Karnebeek reported that there was no enthusiasm for his extradition in Paris, William thought he was going home and started sketching out appointments: Schulenberg to be Adjutant-General, Ludendorff to be Chief of the General Staff...[20]

The extradition issue still nagged. Bethmann, Hindenburg and the emperor's sons agreed to stand in the place of the alleged war criminals. There was more evidence that George V was staying Lloyd George's hand. The Pope also voiced his opposition. Later the crown prince incited his father's fury by offering to give himself up to release the others from their obligations: 'He wants to show the people that where the emperor is too cowardly, he will do it.' The emperor sent Prince William a 'rough' letter.[21]

III

On 16 August 1919 William bought Huis Doorn six kilometres away from his lodgings in Amerongen, the property of Wilhelmine Cornelia van Heemstra.* It was an eighteenth-century manor house with an earlier tower, but with nearly 60 hectares he had room to move around away from the public gaze. The village was a modest place then: 'a few delightful estates, a few charming villas, two inns, a number of shops, a post office, a bank [open two days a week]'. He and Dona decided to furnish it before they moved in. William designed a German gothic gatehouse with lodgings for his small, rotating court and other dependencies. The orangery was converted to house further guests, as there was precious little room in the house. He started converting the coach-house as a residence for his eldest son, but funds ran out, and the idea of having Prince William on the premises must have seemed a little bitter-sweet. Dona had an advanced heart problem and a lift was built to save her the stairs. With its central heating and mod cons, Huis Doorn was hardly an evocation of old Prussia.[22]

There was initially some worry that William would not be able to afford to buy himself a suitable house, but 69,063,535 Reichsmarks was recouped from the sale of various effects, including two yachts. Before the revolution he had, after all, been the richest man in Germany. The house became a home when William took delivery of twenty-three railway wagons, twenty-five furniture wagons, twenty-seven more containing packages of all sorts, one bearing a car and another, a boat. Doorn was filled to bursting-point with treasures from the imperial palaces: 'We are surrounded by busts, pictures and statues from the Great Elector, Frederick the Great, grandpapa and papa, just as we have pictures of the Prussian army from every period of its glory! Hohenkirchen and Leuthen, Hohenfriedberg and Königgrätz embellish the walls.' If he could no longer live like a king, he could live like a prosperous lord in the country with forty-six people domiciled on the estate, including twenty-six servants.[23]

There were five more wagonloads of medical equipment: William had donated a little wooden hospital with sixteen beds and an operating table as a present for the people of Amerongen whose lives he had turned upside down for eighteen months. The hospital china and linen were

---

* The actress Audrey Hepburn's grandmother.

marked with a W. Once he was installed in Doorn, William rarely left the house. In theory, conversations were governed by 'Doorn law', which held that no criticism might be made of Germany since the revolution. This was mere prudence. William was more than happy to lash out at his country's new rulers, but he did not wish to threaten the return of his patrimony.[24]

The crown prince had been passing the time working in a blacksmith's shop on Wieringen, a now reclaimed island in the Zuider Zee. He came to Amerongen for the first time on 3 October 1919. Ten minutes later William was to be seen walking in the garden with Hausminister Dommes. As Elisabeth Bentinck mused: 'Princes are therefore comical individuals, a puzzle for other beings.' William was now more like his old self. One poor man who was repeatedly teased by him, finally received a few digs in the ribs with the imperial cane, 'whereby to the enormous amusement of the emperor he squealed like a piglet'. A few days later William complained of the vanity of his children and the strangeness of their clothes. He does not seem to have been aware how strange his own were.[25]

On 23 November Max Fürstenberg visited William. William kissed him on both cheeks. Dona made little secret of her antipathy to him to Elisabeth Bentinck. When her future husband Sigurd von Ilsemann tried to go hunting, William would not let him. The man who knew him best, his valet Schulz, explained the reason why: 'The emperor is ever so; if he cannot be there himself he will allow no other man to have any pleasure.'[26]

On 13 March 1920 William heard about the Kapp Putsch in Berlin. For a short while elements of the Vaterlandspartei, supported by brutal Freikorps units, controlled the seat of government. They were brought down by a general strike. William was happy at the news and called for champagne as he had always done when he had news of a victory during the war. Ilsemann concluded that the Germans were not yet ready for a return of the monarchy. When he mentioned this idea to William, he did not wish to know. He was increasingly convinced that Germany needed a dictatorship.[27]

William and Dona were at last ready to move into Doorn on 15 May 1920. There were fears that the empress, terminally ill, would not live to warm her new house. At a final meal in Amerongen, William signed the menu. He gave his long-suffering host a bust of himself, and left something behind at the castle in the form of Ilsemann's heart. William told Elisabeth as the car prepared to leave, 'You must always remain grateful to me that I brought Sigurd to you.' Ilsemann carried on his duties at Doorn after their marriage. Of all William's aides, this buoyant apolitical, clear-sighted soldier remained the most loyal.[28]

There were family tragedies. Princess Charlotte of Meiningen was the first to go. On the same day a Dutch photographer disguised as a peasant on top of a hay-cart snapped the emperor in the garden at Amerongen. Of his immediate family Prince Joachim died first, on 20 September 1920. He was weak and epileptic.[29] There were attempts to withhold the fact that he had committed suicide from Dona whose death agonies began in November 1920. She clung to life until 11 April 1921 telling William as he sat at her bedside in January, 'I must live, because I cannot leave you alone.' William received over 10,000 messages of condolence. Naturally, he blamed others for his wife's death, those 'nasty people' who had forced her into exile, and who would not remain unpunished. 'It will be quiet in the house ... What a splendid person!'[30]

Her funeral was an opportunity to test the sympathy for the monarchy in Germany and plans had been laid months before her death. She had expressed a desire to be buried in Potsdam, but after the event his family thought it would be nicer for him to have her remains nearby. William was wedded to the propaganda mission. Her grave, like that of Queen Louise, would become a place of pilgrimage.[31] The republic had told the Hausministerium that they might have the Antikentempel in the park at Sanssouci, rather than in the Garnisons – or Friedenskirche; or the cathedral in Berlin where Hohenzollerns were more usually laid to rest. On 17 April William and part of his family said goodbye. Four of them in uniform kept watch on the coffin draped with pine fronds in the Prussian style. William followed it out to the gates of Doorn and then they drove to Maarn to see it lifted on to the train.[32]

As her coffin arrived at the station at Wildpark, there was a gathering of officers – especially those from her regiment, the Pasewalk Cuirassiers, *Korps*students and other figures from the right of the political spectrum: Hindenburg, Ludendorff, Tirpitz, ex-War Minister Karl von Einem, and Max von Gallwitz. Arrangements were made by the Potsdam son, Auwi, and the crown princess who was still living at the Cecilienhof, in the absence of her husband on Wieringen.

IV

Ilsemann noted that William's misery lasted only two weeks, but after Dona's death he was pathetically lonely. William always maintained that she had told him to remarry and after a few months it became clear that he was interested in finding a replacement. George Viereck, who visited William just before his second marriage, reported him suffering from 'ineffable grief'. 'Gloom rested upon House Doorn like a London fog. Gloom enveloped its master.' Viereck was particularly impressed by the 'little toy elevator' by which the late empress had ascended to the upper floors. And yet William had announced his engagement, which might render this story slightly incredible. He was as curmudgeonly as ever. When Berg's fellow plotter, the Januschauer, and Heinrich Dohna appeared to see him he was rude, and they had to eat at Amerongen.[33]

William was cross at the appearance of *Der König*, a lightly fictional account of the March Offensive by the Jewish writer Karl Rosner. Not only did it come out from Cotta in Stuttgart, the publishers of the third volume of Bismarck's memoirs which the Hausministerium had tried to prevent from appearing; it portrayed William as a weak man, jealous of his son 'who towered as high as a mountain over his father! The eternally recurring tragedy of the Hohenzollerns.' In the book William hated his son. Rosner also ghost-wrote the crown prince's autobiography, another book which had caused him annoyance. Despite all attempts, he refused to read it at first; indeed, that was his attitude to most critical accounts of his reign. Ilsemann pushed it at him, claiming that any bad bit was simply Rosner's invention. When he put it down he compared it to reading your own obituary written by your son. Had he done such a thing during the reigns of 'Papa or Grosspapa', he would have been put under fortress arrest in Küstrin.[34]

William constructed a shrine to Dona in her bedroom, which was held inviolate, her bed covered with a huge cross of flowers. 'Not a picture is changed, not a chair is moved. It is the largest and sunniest room in House Doorn.' At least once a week William repaired to his late wife's bedroom to commune with her soul. In the park Dona had her own rose garden. Here William liked to sit and meditate. With time it was joined by a Hermo garden. When his new wife Hermine arrived she had otherwise to accept a second billing and had to make do with two little, less-favoured rooms.[35]

William's mind had turned to women. He had little time for Cilli or the others. The one daughter-in-law he liked was Oscar's wife, who was not of royal blood. William decided that it was wrong to insist on royal lineage. He went back on this when his eldest grandson insisted he had fallen in love with a member of the minor nobility. William's new-found tolerance may well have been connected with a particular woman. The first to be tried out as a replacement for Dona was Frau von Rochow, who had been a childhood friend. He was enthusiastic, and said, 'Why should I not take a wife from our nobility? The whole business with the *Gotha* has had its day.' Daisy Pless thought she had been 'ignobly treated' by William, who 'besought in marriage his own niece, getting badly snubbed for doing so'. Another who offered to comfort William at Doorn was Fräulein Ittel von Tschirschky. She visited Doorn, but found her host embittered. Both of these made way for a young and flirtatious

Dutch noblewoman, Lili van Heemstra or 'Baroness Sunshine'. She was only twenty-five and too young. She was eventually settled on one of William's Hesse nephews instead.[36]

v

On 8 June 1922 Princess Hermine of Schönaich-Carolath stepped off the train in Amersfoort. Hausminister Dommes was there in the car to meet her. He took her to Doorn where she was received by William at the gatehouse in field grey with a bunch of red roses. He gave her a kiss and took her in to a 'simple but dainty supper'. Against house rules, she was allowed to stay in the manor itself. For the next few days William and she were seen in each other's company here and there around the house and park. It was as if they had known one another for years. Occasionally they fed the ducks in the moat. William told his guest, 'I look upon my fate as a tribulation, a trial, imposed upon me by God, which I must bear like a Christian gentleman.'

She flattered him by saying that as a child she had hung pictures of him around her bedroom. William claimed he 'instantly recognised that she was my mate [sic]'. William was like a young suitor: lighting her cigarettes, pushing chairs about, fetching cushions. Hermine herself wavered for three days before she gave in to William's ardent requests. 'Never had three days seemed longer to me. I actually trembled. At last she consented. My first kiss on her hand and our first embrace marked my first happy hour since the death of Augusta Victoria.' The only good fortune since he had heeded the 'ill-omened counsel of Field Marshal Hindenburg and his advisers, actuated solely by the sense of duty that has always inspired my family'. Hermine's decision to stay was nothing short of 'heroic'.[37]

William's family and entourage were originally at a loss to say where Princess Hermine of Schönaich-Carolath had sprung from. She was a Silesian neighbour of the crown prince, but he denied having encouraged her. The second suspect, Victoria Louise, denied all attempts at match-making. The story which William put about was that he had had a letter of condolence after Dona's death from Hermo's young son George. The letter read:

Dear Kaiser,
I am only a little boy, but I want to fight for you when I am a man.
I am sorry because you are so terribly lonely.
Easter is coming, Mama will give us cake and coloured eggs. But I would gladly give up the cakes and all the eggs If I could only bring you back.
There are many little boys like me who love you

George William
Prince of Schönaich-Carolath

According to William's account he had remembered having met the princess and his train encouraged him to check her out. He sent the boy his picture and an invitation to his mother to come to Doorn.[38] The last bit was certainly untrue. William's retinue assumed that the crown prince and Victoria Louise had been responsible. They were not even consulted.

Hermine had won the toss. She had many advantages apart from her relative youth: she was a rich widow, possessing two large estates in the Lausitz, and together with her sisters she was the last of the elder branch of the ancient house of Reuss, her only brother being a hopeless, catatonic lunatic. Her disadvantage was the possession of five young children, but they had their own money and it was decided that only one of them, the four-year-old Henriette, or the 'general' as she came to be known, would actually come to live at Doorn.

The decision to remarry not eighteen months after Dona's death predictably shocked the royalists. Dommes was the hardest. He said that William must wait three years from the time of Dona's death, otherwise he would do a disservice to the monarchist cause. William lied by saying that his family approved, and added that he was lonely – which was true. He had sacrificed everything to Germany; now he was exiled in Doorn, he was not going to renounce his happiness. A deputation of East Elbian Junkers came to see William to encourage him to put off his plans. William cited his great-great-uncle Frederick William IV who had remarried a Gräfin Harrach after the death of Queen Louise. The Junkers replied that it was fifteen years later, not one. William became angry and told them to mind their own business. Hermo was at least *ebenbürtig*, she was a 'royal highness' even if the principality was not much bigger than a pocket handkerchief.[39]

Much to the chagrin of the entourage, William was smitten. 'I hardly dared hope any more, to find a woman who would share my wretched loneliness. I have found it in her! My redeeming angel.' William told Ilsemann that he had become secretly engaged. When his ADC said nothing, he added, 'Aren't you going to congratulate me?' Ilsemann said something begrudging, but William took it for enthusiasm. Ilsemann thought she had a nasty mouth. His wife wrote, 'She is not pretty in any way, has a horrible figure; she looks best in profile.' Princess Castell said she had a reputation for being 'false and man-mad'; in her own family she went by the name of 'poison squirt'. Victoria Louise had decided she was a gold-digger. Auwi also turned up some nuggets from her past. William replied that Auwi was clearly jealous and wanted her for himself. In the meantime Hermo's picture had found a place in William's tower study, along with that of Dona, a sketch of William himself by Queen Victoria, William I and Frederick the Great. 'I have again someone to whom I can pour out my heart, who reads my thoughts and my moods,' William told Viereck.[40]

William drew his own picture of Hermo. Ilsemann was indulgent. The dress was not bad but the face 'completely and utterly horrid'. William decided he would send it to his beloved. 'She'll get a nasty shock,' wrote the courtier. A few days later Ilsemann described his master as behaving like 'a lovesick ensign'. When the story hit the press, however, on 14 September 1922, William caught fright and formally denied his intention of marrying Hermo. The result was a stinging letter from his *belle*. 'The princess has written to me in a language worthy of a lieutenant addressing his recruits! I have never received such a letter in my life! Her honour has been stained; I obviously want to palm her off, but there will be no question of that, she simply will not tolerate it!' It was her sixth letter that day. The previous five had been love-letters.[41]

Ilsemann thought the letter a timely warning, but naturally William did not see things that way. On 19 September court mourning was wound up. Four days later the faithful Schulz left him. He had been with William since his childhood. He said he did not possess the strength any more, but possibly the arrival of Hermo was tugging at his sleeve.[42]

A pilgrimage to Doorn was now an important diversion for Germany's monarchists or the simply curious. Apart from the immediate family came Prince Hohenzollern-Sigmaringen and his ten-year-old son, Hitler's fan Charles Edward of Coburg – 'a loyal prince and a loyal German', artists like Hans Dahl and Schwarz, and the Festive Lauff, 'the Kaiser's favourite playwright', who came twice, the last time in 1928. The Krupps visited in 1927. They all had to put up with William's abstemious, sometimes downright parsimonious regime. Hinzpeter's teaching was still the rule. He disliked foie gras or caviar, oysters or highly seasoned foods, although he had developed a strange affection for pilau. On Sundays there was only cold food, which was the rule in the evenings too, when cold meats were served. William did not eat beef or 'black meats'. Menu cards were used twice, recto-verso.

He ate a good deal of fruit: cherries, apples, strawberries, peaches and oranges. In that alone, perhaps, he resembled Frederick the Great. Pineapples did not agree with him. As ever he drank very little. There was a liqueur from Cadinen which his guests were obliged to sample, but which he never drank. He detested strong drinks such as whisky. He had a glass of port and a sandwich after a session sawing logs; apart from that the rule was German red sparkling wine. It was called burgundy, an allusion to the Pinot Noir grape which made his other favourite wine: Assmanshausen, which he drank cut with water.[43]

After dinner there were the hours of listening to William's stories, during which the men had to stand. Viereck all but toppled over and had to be given a cognac to fortify him. The women were luckier, but that meant it was easier to fall asleep. William did not easily forgive these lapses. When Gräfin Brockdorff nodded off William challenged her: 'You're not listening, countess!' She said she was. 'Then tell me the last sentence which I have just read!'[44]

The emperor had become a keen writer, although he was ever looking for someone to ghost-write his books. The first of these had been Rosen. His *Geschichtstabellen* came first. He compared the actions of the various governments in the build-up to war to show that the guilt lay on the Entente side with their gradual encirclement. It was not wholly objective. The *Panther* incident, for example, was left out; nor did he mention the encouragement given to the Austrians to fight the Serbs. *Ereignisse und Gestalten* came next, the memoirs of his reign, and a further justification of his conduct in foreign affairs. It was a considerable success, but perhaps less so at Doorn, where the entourage had to hear the entire book read out to them after dinner.[45]

The drudgery of the writer's life was not for William. He did not enjoy the long hours of composition and he was still keen on employing a ghost. The members of his train had to chip in a draft from time to time; Rosen was offered the chance to put together whole works, but refused. One who accepted was Karl Friedrich Nowak, a Bohemian journalist who had spent the war reporting from the fronts. The fact that he was a Jew does not seem to have worried William, even if the entourage seemed reluctant to have him in the house. He must have been an exotic figure. He travelled with his secretary, a 'Princess Sasha Dolgorucki'. Robert Bruce Lockhart had it that she was the daughter of the Russian anarchist Prince Kropotkin. If it was true, she must have been the strangest person to cross his portals. Nowak began an apologetic history of William's reign with the benefit of documents held at Doorn. Two volumes appeared, but it was never finished.[46]

In September 1922 William met George Sylvester Viereck for the first time. He was the grandson of the German actress Edwina Viereck who had given birth to George's father Louis amid a blaze of speculation. It was believed that a Hohenzollern had been the father, very probably William I. George himself was educated in Germany until he was thirteen, then went to the United States where he was to become about the most vociferous German apologist during the First World War. He made himself unpopular with the pro-Entente elements of the population by stating, for example, before it had left port, that the *Lusitania* was carrying arms and would, therefore, be sunk.[47]

Viereck remained in Europe for seven months, during which time he interviewed not only William, but also Little Willy and Hitler. Viereck immediately took on the job of improving William's reputation in the United States: '... because of the special confidence placed in him by the ex-Kaiser, Viereck was able to shed new light on William's personality and activities in the 1920s which helped dispel the opposite illusion built upon the wartime portrayal of Germany's leader as the "Beast of Berlin".' Viereck found William 'a radiant figure, simple, dignified, intellectual, with the physical buoyancy of an athlete and the mental elasticity of a neophyte paying his pristine devotions at the austere shrine of science...'[48]

William predictably ranted and raved against international free-masonry and capital, both of which were based in London, and about the encirclement of Germany before the war. He made a contemptuous remark about House, referring to colonels, who had never commanded so much as a couple of files. Viereck felt he loved Germany despite everything: 'He is a German before he is a monarch. He loves his country more than himself.' William and the entourage were suspicious of Viereck, who they thought was out to make money from his connections to William. William even jocularly suggested that Ilsemann should shoot him. In 1923 William still gave him carte blanche to fight his corner in America, and Viereck came to Doorn every year until 1930 telling his American readers, among other things, that only two things sustained the former emperor: a 'sense of duty' and a 'sense of humour'. 'No one knows the Kaiser who has not heard him laugh.'[49]

William also defined his 'divine right', saying: 'every labour is God anointed. The king as well as the humblest peasant is an instrument of God.' Another of Viereck's interviewees was Mussolini, who expressed an interest in William and asked the American whether he intended to make a comeback. Viereck replied that 'a man once schooled to rule could never be satisfied with a lesser part', and that the emperor in Doorn was no different from Napoleon at St Helena.[50] On 30 October 1922 Mussolini marched on Rome.

VI

William and Hermo were married on Rossbach Day 1922. The new empress arrived the night before with her sister and youngest child. William was waiting at the gate: 'The happy bride flew from the car into the emperor's arms, a few intimate kisses, then she called her little daughter to indicate "Papa Kaiser".' There was a disgusting meal of pilau and chocolate pudding.[51]

The next day William appeared dressed in the uniform of the First

Foot and Hermo in a velvet dress trimmed with ermine, and pink stockings and shoes. She wore a black-and-white hat with a broad brim and a feather. The guests assembled in the hall. The servants had on simple, black livery. The contract, which was signed at the 'Victoria Louise Residence' in the 'Frederick the Great District', among other things, decreed Hermo's right to two months' home leave in Germany every year. Holland did not agree with her health, and she needed to spend some time in German watering-places. After the civil ceremony a religious one was celebrated in the hall at Doorn by court preacher Ludwig Vogel of the Friedenskirche in Potsdam. It was 'the general's' job the strew the roses. The reception, grandly termed a 'Gratulationscour', was held in the Gobelinszimmer. A buffet lunch was served afterwards: salmon in aspic, ham with Cumberland sauce, chicken chaudfroid and Roman punch.[52]

If the ham dish was made to please William's one and only daughter it was wasted on her. She did not approve of the remarriage and did not come. The boys made a decent showing. Little Willy dressed in his Zieten Hussars kit, Eitel, Auwi and Oscar; and the head of the Reuss clan, Prince Henry XXVII, also made an appearance. A few days later Ilsemann reported that William had become less nervous and had stopped jogging his leg up and down so much. He dressed differently. Field grey was put away. He wore uniform in the evening with a simple embellishment of the Iron Cross, 1st and 2nd class, the *pour le mérite* and the golden Reuss Cross! The love potion was still working. On the 8th William exclaimed, 'How lovely the empress is, everybody must be jealous. Did she not look superb yesterday, and what enchanting clothes she wears!'[53]

Hermo seems to have valued her breaks in Germany, where she had her own cronies and a little salon composed of artists and literary types which included the painter Max Beckmann, a man whose works would certainly have been defined as 'gutter art'. William compared her optimistically with Frederick the Great's grandmother, Sophia Charlotte, who had plagued Leibniz with the 'warum des warums'. William stayed out of the business of bringing up Hermo's children, even if he did lay down the law when the same George who had played Pandarus to him and his mother, developed an affection for the Nazis. The great exception was 'the general' for whom William appears to have had a genuine affection. Henriette performed the role of resident grandchild, passing the sugar when coffee was served.

The new empress altered the fauna at Doorn by bringing her German shepherd dog, Arno, who now competed with William's three dachshunds and the Pekinese Wai-Wai for his affection, but Hermo's chief role was to replace Dona in the role of the mother William never had.

By dint of being there her advice was asked and frequently heeded, with terrible results. As she put it: 'The strongest man, in certain moods, is only an overgrown boy. Emperors are no exception.' She had few illusions about her new husband: 'What a big baby the emperor is! ... What sort of crimes have been committed against the poor man over the years, and how badly his first wife handled him! Now it is certainly too late! Oh it is really difficult!'[54] William admitted his dependence: 'I write no sentence in religion or politics or science, I decide no personal problem, without her advice ... She has X-ray eyes. She can see through a man or a woman in a few minutes.'[55]

On 9 November 1923 it was the turn of Adolf Hitler to seek to overturn the Bavarian government. William confined himself to complaining about Ludendorff who had also played a part in the plot. He was suspicious that the conspirators might have wanted to restore the Bavarian royal family rather than his own. The Hohenzollerns would not have been the first choice in Bavaria. When the leaders of the Munich putsch were arrested he exclaimed, 'Thank God, at least this ridiculous story has come to an end.' There was nothing wrong with the method, however. His ADC Admiral Magnus von Levetzow thought that a dictator was needed to restore the Hohenzollerns and William was hardly impressed by the German 'leaders'. The idea of a dictatorship was something which often found favour with him too. A year later Niemann published some conversations with William which revealed what he thought of the Nazis at the time, and where the common ground lay.

In Germany today there is a burgeoning nationalist movement. I see it not just as a reaction against the suppression of fatherland by the imperialism of wartime opponents, but also as a protest against the entire ideology of western materialism.[56]

The Germans did not want him back, not even those on the right. General von Cramon told Ilsemann, 'The father has no prospects, the oldest son damages [the cause] too much through his own faults, and his son is still too young ...' On 28 February 1925 Chancellor Ebert died. William thought he had a chance again. He put his faith in the army chief: 'Now Seeckt's moment has come.'[57] Instead Hindenburg stepped into the breach.

William was disappointed by Hindenburg when he won the presidential election in 1925. He must have hoped that the field marshal would bring him back. He was bitter and spiteful: Hindenburg was destroying Germany. 'The longer Hindenburg remained at the rudder the more difficult it would be for him later to impose some order on all this nonsense.' The Victor of Tannenberg was 'a rogue', Weimar a 'pig-republic'. One who would not come to Doorn was Schulenburg. The man whose son, Fritz-Dietlof, would later die on a Nazi gibbet for his part in the plot of 20 July 1944, was conspiring against the Republic. He wrote that he was 'committing high treason every day and it is enough that it costs him his own head, without drawing another into the [affair]'. He thought William finished anyway, and the crown princess the only man in the imperial family. William was more and more interested in a *coup*: 'I completely agree with this way out, the chaos is certainly about to begin.'[58]

In March 1926 the Swedish explorer Sven Hedin appeared, and had reason to admire William's bodily vigour and intellectual power. In June 14.4 million Germans voted to appropriate the Hohenzollerns' property in Germany. William's curt response was: 'That means 14 million *Schweinehunde*'. The vote went against outright dispossession, however, which encouraged William once again to believe he might stage a comeback. He possessed 250,000 *Morgen* in Germany (62,500 hectares) and two farms in South-West Africa. There was a share-out: the state took the main palaces, but left him the Cecilienhof in Potsdam, the English-style country house William had given his eldest son as a wedding present. They retained two palaces in the Linden and a number of villas in Potsdam. With Rominten, Cadinen, Hammelseck, Burgs Rheinstein and Hohenzollern, the wine estate of Schloss Reinhartshausen in the Rheingau, Oels and Schloss Schildberg in Brandenburg, the Hohenzollerns as a family remained the greatest landowners in Germany with 97,000 hectares.[59]

Ilsemann did not feel William had a sense of 'home' for all that. He had been just as happy in England or Corfu as he ever had been during his peripatetic life in Germany. Holland was the same. 'He does not feel real homesickness for Germany.'[60]

VII

William was to some extent still under the influence of his entourage: those ADCs who came and went after a brief period at Doorn. The retinue contained some firebrands, unrepentant men of the right who had done their bit in the counter-revolution following the abdication. As monarchists, most of them adhered to the DNVP (German National People's Party) which sat at the extreme right of the chamber. William gave the party no open support. 'Doorn law' must have been occasionally invoked. William was keen on anyone who wanted him and there were incessant flutters when he saw what he thought was a chance to take up his position again. The wise Ilsemann adopted a policy of silence on such occasions. William's sons had political ambitions and so did some of the rotating court marshals: Dommes, Schwerin, Rebeur-Paschwitz, Schmettow and Giese. Later some of these were lured over to the Nazi Party: Levetzow, Alexander Freiherr von Senerclans-Grancy and Leopold Kleist, for example. The former had played a part in some savage reprisals in Weimar in 1920.[61]

Hermo was very keen on bringing down the Republic. She thought the Nazis might be the ones to make her a real ruler, rather than the mere Empress of Doorn. In the late spring of 1927, she went to Berchtesgaden. Her visit was scooped by the *Berliner Zeitung* which believed it had rumbled a plot on the part of the Hohenzollerns to stage a comeback. In 1929 she took up an invitation to attend the Nuremberg Rally. At that period she made no secret of her admiration for the Nazis. The scales only dropped slightly from her eyes when Göring stood her up for lunch in Berlin.[62]

Many of the Hohenzollerns had a brief flirtation with the Nazis. The Brunswicks were keen and Oscar thought their policies had a lot to recommend them. Much was blurred later when organisations such as the old soldiers' Stahlhelm was decanted into a Nazi one and their members appeared with Nazi insignia. The real Nazi of the Hohenzollern family was the civilian son, Auwi, who joined the paramilitary SA in 1928, and the NSDAP or Nazi party two years later. He stuck to his guns despite his father's many attempts to force him to stand down. He eventually fell from grace with the Nazis themselves and died a broken man in 1949, after his experiences in an American internment camp.[63]

VIII

William had become an armchair archaeologist. His credentials were sound enough despite Müller's mockery of his spadework on Corfu. He had shown an interest in the subject since his Bonn days and in 1897 had promoted the rebuilding of the Roman praetorium on the Saalburg, which was dedicated to the memory of his father. As he could no longer travel beyond the borders of Utrecht province his favourite archaeologists were invited to lecture at Doorn. First of all it was the – non-Nazi – racial thinker Frobenius from the University of Frankfurt am Main, then Alfred Jeremias of Leipzig and Professor Vollgraf from Utrecht. The Spenglerite and cultural morphologist Leo Frobenius who had devoted his whole life to studying the rise and eclipse of African civilisations was to become an influence on William's thinking every bit as powerful as Chamberlain had been at the beginning of the century.

William weaved currently fashionable racial ideas into his archaeological research. He had decided that west and east had nothing in common, and that Germany now belonged to the east along with Russia, Scandinavia, Holland and Austria, while the Mediterranean teamed up with France and Britain. 'As soon as one impinges on the other there is a catastrophe. East is east and west is west!'[64]

From 14 to 17 June 1927 William held a proper conference in the house with lectures on Dionysos in Delphi, Zarathustra, the *Iliad* and the *Hesiod*. Frobenius went home with a cheque in his pocket for 10,000 marks to create a museum in Frankfurt which was to be called the 'Doorner Akademie'. The three-day conferences were now established. Over the next few years the gentlemen pondered the subject of 'the God', gothic and Celtic.[65] In 1930 William, the man his mother had branded a philistine, spoke on the subject of the nature of culture, thereby fleshing out some of Frobenius's notes. Old themes resurfaced: the hatred of materialism as enshrined in big, Anglo-American business. As culture degenerates society descends into a materialism which opposes the spirit. Fact and experience take the place of belief. Suddenly good memories of that terrible trip to North Africa surfaced: 'The Moors who received me in Tangiers had in their simple white burnouses infinitely more dignity, decency and bearing as the members of a one-time culture than the European diplomats who swarm around us in morning coats covered with stars and braid.' Smells too came to mind: the Frenchman was filthy, yet smothered himself with scent; the Englishman was a hygiene fanatic obsessed with Pears soap.[66]

In 1931 William created a formal Doorner Arbeitsgemeinschaft (Doorn Research Society) or DAG, to organise an annual symposium looking into the highly didactic aspects of antiquity which interested the emperor most. These were the study of the Gorgon, Babylon and the Bible; there were talks too on monads and symbols, of which the Aryan swastika loomed large. William's interest in sun symbols led him to want to examine the use of the swastika, which had been made popular as the calling card of the extreme right in the early 1920s, and adopted by Adolf Hitler.

The following year there was a clutch of new members: Julius Jordan, Professor Friedrich Sarre and Professor Kerenyi of Budapest. The minutes were taken by the retired Major-General Detlev Graf von Schwerin; another ADC, Major Freiherr Ulrich von Sell, also took an interest in the papers. The racial thinking of Houston Stewart Chamberlain resurfaced: 'We need without question, a healthy nationalism so that the *whole* German race stands decisively behind us and the negative, *antinational* spirit of Rome and Jewry once and for all abandons its disruptive handiwork. May God help us.[67]

IX

William's tolerance of the Jews and to some degree freemasons had turned a corner after the war. Before the war reduced her mind to physical violence against the German emperor, the hardly philo-Semitic Lady Susan Townley had a talk with William about his Jewish subjects. William was expressing the 'Treitschke view' – 'The Jews are our misfortune': 'The Jews are the curse of my country ... They keep the people poor and in their clutches. In every small village in Germany sits a dirty Jew like a spider drawing the people into the web of usury. He lends money to the small farmers on the security of their land and so gradually acquires control of everything. The Jews are the parasites of my empire. The Jewish question is one of the greatest problems I have to deal with, and yet nothing can be done to cope with it!' It is an indication of the trustworthiness of this account that Lady Susan informs us that William became *less* anti-Semitic with the passing years.[68]

When he was not too much under the influence of the rabid anti-Semites in his train – the Waldersees, Eulenburgs and Bergs – William could 'decide who was a Jew'. His views differed little from others – Germans and non-Germans of his time and world. Jews, especially the small-town usurers, the cut-throat middle men who ran the wholesale wine trade in the west, were distasteful people. On the other hand he, more than most of his class, recognised the uses of those Jewish magnates, who had promoted German trade during his reign and lifted German commerce to a position second to none. It is significant that the fatal last meeting with Ballin took place in Berg's presence. After the war, however, when most people were happy to blame him for their misfortunes, William too was on the lookout for a scapegoat. His eyes lighted on 'international' Jewry which is always despised at times of fervent national passion. In this he was greatly swayed by the publication of the *Protocols of the Meetings of the Learned Elders of Zion*. The first German edition of the work was published in Charlottenburg in 1919, but William would not have seen it before 1920. That year he was seen reading this elaborate fraud at Amerongen. He was impressed and recommended it to others.[69]

The *Protocols* appear to have been the work of the Russian, Sergei Nilus, a Tsarist police spy. They contained the purported minutes of a number of meetings of highly placed Jews who were determined to bring down the world and establish Jewish domination. The Elders outlawed morality in their politics, concluding that such considerations had value only in the kingdoms of the *goyim*. The *goyim* were ripe for destruction: 'bemused with alcoholic liquors, their youth has grown stupid on classicism and from early immorality, into which it has been inducted by our special agents – by tutors, lackeys, governesses in the houses of the wealthy, by clerks and others, by our women in places of dissipation frequented by the *goyim*.'[70]

In places you may read whole lines which later resurface in the writings of the former German emperor. 'Liberty, equality, fraternity ... these words are canker worms at work boring into the well-being of the *goyim*, putting an end everywhere to peace, quiet, solidarity and destroying all the foundations of the *goyim* states.'[71] The aristocracy had been replaced by an aristocracy of money, the Berlin financiers and the American butchers whose yachts he liked to see at Kiel; the Elders made it clear that the hated press was theirs: 'Through the press we have gained the power to influence while remaining ourselves in the shade.'[72]

The Elders had annihilated the aristocracy, which had been the only defence of the people. By fooling people with the notion of freedom they turned mobs into bloodthirsty brutes. They also undermined the power of kings:

In the times when the peoples looked upon kings on their thrones as on a pure manifestation of the will of God, they submitted without a murmur to the despotic power of kings: but from the day when we insinuated into their minds the conception of their own rights they began to regard the occupants of thrones as mere ordinary mortals. The holy unction of the Lord's Anointed has fallen from the heads of kings in the eye of the people, and when we also robbed them of their faith in God the might of power was flung upon the streets into the place of public proprietorship and was seized by us.[73]

Their similarity to Jesuits and freemasons was agreed. The Elders ran the masonic lodges too. Anti-Semitism was also useful to them 'for the management of our lesser brethren'.[74] Once they had achieved power the Elders would abolish the nation state. The worm lay in the liberal, constitutional state, which took the place of what was the only safeguard of the *goyim*, namely despotism, and *a constitution, as you well know, is nothing else but a school of discords*, misunderstandings, quarrels, disagreements, fruitless party agitations ...'[75] All will make way for the king of Israel who will become the patriarch of the world.[76]

The forgery was exposed in the British press in 1921. Lord Sydenham writing in the *Spectator* on 27 August pointed it out as a sham dreamed up by the Tsarist police to justify the pogroms. *The Times* also exposed it as a crib from Maurice Joly's *Dialogue aux Enfers entre Machiavel et Montesquieu*. Its effect was stupendous. As a political hoax it compares only to the literary fraud, *Ossian*, in the eighteenth century. The reason for its popularity was the Great War:

After many years of peace and prosperity the general optimism of Europe had been rudely shaken. To many the First World War came like a bolt from the blue; millions had died in a senseless slaughter and there had been unprecedented material destruction ... Many were looking for an answer, if possible a clear and easily intelligible answer, to their searching questions about the causes of these catastrophes and the unrest in the world in general.[77]

After the war many Jews surfaced in prominent positions. Members of William's circle like Walther Rathenau were identified as Elders. Many of the revolutionaries who had brought down the Russian and German monarchies were also Jews. The *Protocols* were a handy confirmation to the men of the right that they had not been responsible for defeat. The Jews became the scapegoat: 'An outside enemy – a solution that had psychologically much to recommend it.'[78]

William's anti-Semitism was far removed from Hitler's, however, chiefly in that it still strongly adhered to the Christian tradition. There were daily prayers at Doorn and William believed 'obedience and trust' were central tenets of Christianity. On the Feast of the Epiphany in 1926 William preached a sermon in which he made the Jews partially responsible for Germany's collapse. Germany was brought down 'from behind, from home, and by Jewish money'. 'While my generals and officers and the brave army at the front fought for victory under my command, the nation *at home* with its incapable politicians lost the war, lied to, corrupted and stirred up by the Jews and the Entente.'[79]

His apologist Viereck tried to explain away some of William's fury at the Jews. It was chiefly directed at journalists 'who had coquetted with radicalism and encouraged every subversive movement. But never has he permitted any prejudice to stand between him and those of his Jewish subjects who faithfully served their country, who were Germans before they were Jews ... While not encouraging mixed marriages, he did not, as he might have done, forbid them from becoming officers in the army.'[80] Sadly for Viereck there is enough evidence to show that the prejudice had put down deeper roots.

How virulently anti-Semitic William had become at the end of his life is clear from an exchange of letters with his friend Gräfin Alina von der Goltz. The war had already started again, and William was aware of Hitler's repressive measures against the Jews. The Final Solution, however, had yet to be enacted. The letters are so extreme and filled with hate that they call his sanity at the end of his life into question. Had the disease which killed him begun to affect his brain? He told the countess on 28 July 1940 that Satan's chief weapon was internationalism 'composed of Jews with help from freemasons which tempts the nations which have abandoned God with the catchwords liberty, equality and fraternity'. 'It is the same Antichrist today as it has always been since

Golgotha – *Jewry*, freemasonry, world Jewry and its *power of gold*. Since the disgraceful Peace of Versailles God has given them twenty years to come and go and reflect. Their answer – at Satan's behest – was the Second World War to create the *world empire* of the Jews, of the *Antichrist*! Then God interfered and crushed the plan! ... We must stand by Him in the struggle in order to *drive Juda out* of England, as it has already been driven from the continent...'

To her credit, the countess did not agree with William's appraisal and wrote back to say so. William wrote to her again. The Jews 'remain the enemies of all Christians ... I have had Jews at my table, I have given support to Jewish professors and helped them. The answer was scorn, mockery, world war, treachery, Versailles and revolution!' 'Jews through England, the slave of the Antichrist' had allowed the war to break out.[81]

X

William had to put up with the autobiographies of the main protagonists in his life drama. The third volume of Bismarck's *Gedanken und Erinnerungen* was held up for a while. When it appeared he was able to point out a few of the book's most glaring omissions. Bülow's must have been one of the most painful. As Joachim von Reichel reported after an interview with the ex-chancellor in Rome, everything *he* did was right, everything William did, wrong. William preferred the record to run the other way round. The three volumes of Waldersee's posthumous memoirs likewise incited him to wrath. William expressed a lordly contempt for the others. He none the less sent a wreath at Bülow's death, and similarly one to Prince Max's family. Books such as that of Zedlitz-Trützschler, whose anecdotes painted the emperor's court in all its Byzantine colours, were dismissed as 'ugly attacks' leading William to an 'access of fury'.[82]

He read Bethmann's less vindictive memoirs, and writings by and on Haldane, whom he admired. He wanted to know more about British wartime propaganda and found a volume called *The Secrets of Crewe House*. Behind that stucco-coated Georgian façade in London's Curzon Street, the press barons had wielded the great British campaign against Germany and its ruler. He liked anything which supported his views. Keynes's writings, for example, were a great boon to him just like those of the pacifist E. D. Morel who suggested in his book, *Truth about the War* of 1916, that it had been caused by Grey and the Russians.[83]

There was an innovation for William's sixty-ninth birthday. The cinema came to Doorn. After dinner the guests were treated to a screening of *Friedrich der Grosse*. The last scene in the film showed Napoleon standing by the Great King's grave in Potsdam – 'Had he been alive we would not be here'. William was thrown into a fury by the sight of the Frenchman: 'These pigs, the French, they must get away from the Rhine, yes, the time is coming when I shall throw them out!' The French had occupied the Ruhr and were treating the local population with unbridled brutality.[84]

In the summer of 1928 William saw an old friend in the form of the British Brigadier Waters, who was prepared to walk into the lion's den despite having lost a son in the war. William had written to Waters complaining of the British press, with its 'ocean of abuse, vilification, slander and lies'. When they met, William returned to the old themes: 'My whole life was filled with the hope to be able to bring about a better understanding between our two countries which in the end might lead to an agreement or alliance between Britain and Germany.' Instead he had been branded the 'archfiend, the Hun, Attila, etc.! ... and when she was on the verge of losing the unjust war she had for many years "engineered" against my country, she lied America into the fight, and *bought* the subversive part of my people with money to rise against their ruler who for four years had kept German soil from the heel of the invader.'[85]

William remembered that Waters was fond of German wine, and gave him half a dozen bottles from his cellar. Sir Frederick Ponsonby was preparing to publish the influential *Letters of the Empress Frederick*. William was very angry. He thought it the worst of the books to appear since his fall, although he claimed he would not read it, as he did not wish to spoil the image he had of his mother. The copyright was supposedly his, but his sisters had given Ponsonby permission to go ahead. He claimed that the letters had actually been stolen by King Edward's secretary 'after my mother's death *contrary to my special orders* ... The clandestine removal is theft.' William tried to prevent publication and sent Waters to parley with Ponsonby. As William wrote to Waters on 1 October 1928, he thought that not even his mother would have approved the publication after the fall of the Hohenzollerns: 'Imagine the *queen of England* as daughter of the German empress, placing the whole of her private correspondence with her mother behind the back of her son, the king of England, into the hands of a *German* court official.' When the book was brought out uncut in Germany, William wrote the introduction. The son contented himself with a little explanation of why his mother had been so negative, and advised that the letters be read with caution.[86]

Another Briton came in November of that year, the former secret agent Robert Bruce Lockhart. He was now a journalist and had not been accorded an interview. This was another 'Doorn law'. William was hidden somewhere and Bruce Lockhart was given a tour of the house and garden accompanied by Arno the German shepherd – 'a Dobermann'. 'The Kaiser is very frightened of journalists. He is very angry over the Ponsonby letters and also over the journalist (one of ours) who climbed into his garden. Everyone was terrified.' His guide let him know that 'The Kaiser is very hurt that no one in the English royal family sent him a word of sympathy on the death of the Kaiserin.' He also gleaned that William was still hoping for a restoration. Bruce Lockhart wrote his article. It was taken away and amended by William. Bruce Lockhart was not only poor on dogs, he could not tell the difference between a beech and a poplar. He sent over some photographs of himself, with Arno.[87]

The dogs must have had pride of place in Bruce Lockhart's piece: Arno and Wida, the latest in the dachshund series. His escort had filled him in on the little details of the former emperor's home life, right down to the 'claret mousseux' which William diluted with water, his taste for Turkish cigarettes and the occasional light cigar. Bruce Lockhart's conclusions were positive: 'Sooner or later history will have to revise the verdict, passed by Germany's enemies during the war, on the Kaiser's character.'[88]

On 27 January 1929 William celebrated his seventieth birthday in exile in Doorn. An enormous 'W' was set up over a baldachin and there were fireworks. The reception of the numerous important guests and well-wishers was a logistical problem to be worked out by his ADCs. There was never enough room in the house and its dependencies; poor Bentinck had to make Amerongen available, and there were rooms at the Hotel Cecil in the small town; others had to find a bed in Dreibergen or Zeist. The entourage had a new medal struck for William and the guests were entertained by sitting down to watch footage of the emperor touring the front during the war. To the pleasure of some, at least, Hermo was not there. She was laid up in bed with German measles.

Ilsemann thought the event must have looked very different to the *Defiliercour* in the White Hall. There were eighty-three to dinner in the house, with another twenty 'youngs' in the Orangery. The event was celebrated in one of the British Sunday papers with an interview with William, which the former ruler dismissed as 'a pack of lies'. A picture was taken of William with his court. In the next few months he put fresh vim into his tree-sawing so that a few celebratory logs could be sent out to the guests.[89]

Robert Bruce Lockhart had evidently done nothing to offend the sensitive ex-emperor. On 15 December 1929 he was back at Doorn, and this time with the promise of a meeting with William himself. It was a red-letter day: that morning he had felled his 20,000th tree since November 1918. He met the journalist in the drive. 'He was wearing a Homburg hat with a chamois beard in the back, a loose black cape. He carried a stick. His alsatian [!], Arno, was with him. We got out of the car. I was introduced. His Imperial Highness immediately took me by the arm, welcomed me to Doorn, and thanked me ...' It transpired that Bruce Lockhart had been helpful to William over the Ponsonby letters.

They climbed up to William's study in the tower, 'quite a small room, overloaded with knick-knacks'. The Austrian journalist Nowak was present. Bruce Lockhart observed the etiquette and refused a cigarette. William told a story about an Englishwoman 'in the days when Englishwomen could not speak French', who asked her guest 'Etes-vous un fumier?'* He spoke of his admiration for George Bernard Shaw and repeated the story about Isadora Duncan's brains and his legs – the dramatist rejected the dancer's suggestion that they should procreate. He feared the child might not be the prodigy she envisaged. They looked at pictures. A servant arrived to tell him it was a quarter to one. 'All right, I haven't committed any indiscretions yet!' Before they went down to lunch William gave his guest another of those teasing photographs: 'Nothing is ended finally, until it is ended rightly.'

William wore a miniature of Queen Victoria in his buttonhole in Bruce Lockhart's honour. At lunch were the duty courtiers. Ilsemann was away. There were the Grafen Hamilton (a Swedish-Scot) and Finckenstein and Hermo with her daughter. A simple meal was served, in the course of which William drank a glass of sparkling burgundy 'and talked the whole time. His versatility and range of subjects is amazing.' During his siesta-time William went through the written questions Bruce Lockhart had given him. The Scot left at six for Utrecht.[90]

In the summer of 1930 Brigadier Waters paid his second call on Doorn. William was still seething with fury about the French occupation of the Ruhr: 'We don't want any more wars. But, for one war we are ready to march tonight, and that is to strangle the French.' He was still convinced of the necessity for dictatorship.[91] In this he was not so different to Chancellor Brüning, who could only hang on to power and keep the country together by using his powers to rule by decree. As a democracy Weimar had already failed.

---

* 'Are you a dungheap?' *Fumier* is rude in French.

William and Adolf

Levetzow was the first of William's circle to go over to the Nazis. The subject was discussed at Doorn. William admired the energy of the national awakening and was keen to see an alliance of all the elements of the right which would be strong enough to achieve power. Naturally he hoped that such a grouping would ask him to return. In September 1930 he approved Alfred Hugenberg's move to tie up his DNVP with the Nazis: 'Although he has fought a good deal against the latter.' They worried him. Their socialistic tendencies seemed distressingly radical. He thought they aimed at abolishing private property. In 1930 he wrote 'Social = National! – Socialism = Bolshevism = antinational and international ... This socialism is therefore irreconcilable with the idea of the national.' There was no doubting his nationalism. When that November a retired captain, Detlev von Arnim, wrote to him expressing his hope that the day would come when 'we ride over the Rhine and fetch the Imperial Crown of the Hohenzollerns out of the blood and flames', William noted in the margin, 'We are working for this day.'[1]

On 17 January the Hausminister Kleist arranged for Hermann Göring and his first wife, Karin, to make the first of two visits to William at Doorn. Göring was announced as Döhring, the court preacher, to avoid possible leaks of the conversations. Hermo was excited; she was out to court the fat air ace. The food was decidedly more tempting: pheasant with cauliflower for lunch; Viennese roast and vegetables for dinner. Over the next two days the menus offered roast goose and snails. She even pressed a wad of banknotes on the Nazi, ostensibly so that he might take his sickening wife for a cure in Silesia. She died within the year. Hermo herself had met Hitler through Kleist's cousin Freifrau Marie von Thiele-Winckler. She was impressed. It was a period when the Nazis consciously flirted with the nobility, and tried to rid themselves of their more radical and plebeian image.[2]

On both evenings William and Göring sat up late discussing politics. The talks were reconvened at tea, with occasional diversions, when

William reverted to his favourite theme of archaeology. Göring was playing a game by making out he was a monarchist. On the other hand he was only interested in the Hohenzollerns, where William fought for the restoration of the entire princely brotherhood. The visit was not an unqualified success. Karin wrote to a friend that they had 'flown at one another'. 'Both are excitable and so like each other in many ways. The Kaiser has probably never heard anybody express an opinion other than his own, and it was a bit too much for him sometimes.' William managed to toast 'the coming Reich!' to which Göring rejoindered, 'The coming king!' But he was careful to leave matters vague, as there were several contenders.

Göring's stay may have ultimately helped in assuring William of an income once the Nazis achieved power and in a private deal William eventually sold Göring his hunting lodge at Rominten in East Prussia, thereby scooping up 700,000 Reichsmarks. After Göring's departure, Hermo was anxious to know whether he would receive some high office at the restoration. William was not prepared to promise more than the air force. He then told Kleist to stop making undignified advances towards the Nazis.[3]

On his birthday in 1931 William saw his first talkie: *Das Flötenkonzert von Sanssouci*. Once again the theme was Frederick the Great. After the last reel William appeared to glow with pride. More problems arose within his family. Young Prince William, the crown prince's eldest son, had become enamoured of a member of the minor nobility, Dorothea von Salviati. Despite all he had said when he was looking for a second wife after Dona's death, for the heir presumptive this would not do. It was contrary to 'house law'. 'Remember,' he told the prince, 'there is every possible form of horse. We are thoroughbreds, however, and when we conclude a marriage such as with Fräulein von Salviati, it produces mongrels, and that may not happen.' Young William accepted his grandfather's point of view for two years until love overwhelmed even the thoroughbred and he renounced the succession in favour of Dorothea. The new noble, Ilsemann, accused his master of 'Fürstenstolz' – disdainful snobbery.[4]

Mussolini with his Caesarian airs and his tolerance of the monarchy was always more palatable to William than Hitler. When his ADC Sell visited Rome in October, William sent the dictator greetings. He was snubbed. The *Duce* would not even receive William's man. When Frobenius arrived for the conference at the end of the month he expressed a hope that the lectures would take William's mind off politics. He was horrified to learn that the emperor was interested in the Nazis: 'Who is the criminal who drove the emperor down this path?' The answer, as if he did not know, was Hermo, together with Leopold von Kleist. His interest was opportunistic, but still Ilsemann thought he was deluding himself. Only 50 per cent of the Nazis had shown any interest in the monarchy.[5]

In May Göring paid a second call. It was even less successful than the first. He bragged, addressed the whole household like a public meeting and spouted propaganda. He was brimming with self-confidence after the Nazis' performance in the last polls. His 'highly spontaneous manners' also 'collided with court etiquette'. On one occasion he came down to lunch wearing plus-fours, which would not have been permitted even for the dandified crown prince, whose quarters he had endeavoured to take over, without success. Hermo held her husband back. She was angling to bring Hitler to Doorn next.[6]

The crown prince expressed a desire to stand for president in April 1932, hoping to use Louis-Napoleon's route back to the imperial throne. William was furious at the idea of his son swearing an oath to the Republic: 'If you do that . . . then you are finished as far as I am concerned, I shall disinherit you and throw you out of my house.'[7] Little Willy backed off, but like the rest of the DNVP, he was prepared to vote for Hitler in the second round. He was still flirting with the Nazis. Göring was invited to the Cecilienhof for his fiftieth birthday party.

After fourteen years in Holland, it was thought safe for William to stray outside the province of Utrecht. In June 1932 he and Hermo were seen on the promenade in the fashionable seaside resort of Zandvoort. A photograph shows the two of them, he in a raincoat and cap wearing pumps, and she in a sensible suit and a *châpeau cloche*. He had been having financial problems which required him to sell some gold. His porcelain factory in Cadinen, however, was doing good business and even turning out busts of Hitler, which much to his delight made a particularly good profit. Alfred Niemann, who was in Doorn that summer, thought William was making a great mistake by seeing hope in the Nazis.[8]

Brigadier Waters was back at Doorn in September 1932. There had been repeated calls for him to return the Garter, but he had refused. William was still keeping a beady eye on Hitler who had held talks with Hindenburg on 13 August. Hindenburg had told the Nazi leader that his 'conscience' had not permitted him to grant the Nazis full power, but he was prepared to see some ministers in a mixed administration. William had still not forgiven his field marshal. He was not sympathetic and he thought Hitler a fool.

It fills me with a deep sadness and concern to see what a groundless lack of *conscience* the demagogic Nazi leaders possess; that they should mindlessly squander the collected resources of national energy in their nationalist movement. As a result of this it is necessary to use all means to *support* the nationalist *movement*. The Nazi party disposes of strong *nationalist forces*; even today a few leaders and speakers must be pulled away from the irresponsible demagogic machinery and attached to a nationalist administration. Hitler's refusal [to accept partial power] was a frightful howler and a great disappointment to the nationalist minded elements in the nation. He doesn't have the slightest political 'flair' or any knowledge of history else he should have known: 'He who controls Prussia controls the Reich!' First make Prussia clean and lawful; provide order, enforce obedience and discipline and ensure her defences and the rest of the Reich will follow!' [9]

The letter was leaked to the Nazi hierarchy by a sympathiser at the Cecilienhof. William was furious and after accusing his daughter-in-law Cilli, had Kleist sacked for paying court to the Nazis. Kleist went on to become a deputy in the emasculated Reichstag of the Third Reich. By the end of 1932 the family was racked by violent arguments over the way forward. William demanded that Auwi and his son Alexander Ferdinand and Hermo's son Prince George, all leave the Nazi Party. George was particularly keen. He was attacked on a Dutch train for wearing a swastika. After he had called his assailants 'a bunch of Jews' he had to be taken back to Doorn under police escort. [10]

Kleist's sacking led to a more general witch-hunt. In December Admiral Levetzow wrote to William for permission to stand as a Nazi candidate for the Reichstag. William said no: membership of political parties was prohibited for those who worked at Doorn. Levetzow fought back. He wanted to defend the party. William expressed his contempt for Hitler, Göring and Goebbels in the margins. The 'monarchist thinking' alluded to by his courtier was no more than a 'screen'. [11]

The kings of Saxony and Württemberg were present for William's seventy-fourth birthday. Shortly afterwards Hitler formed his 'government of national renewal'. William still remained aloof, although it contained a number of traditional elements from the DNVP. There were calls for a restoration of the monarchy, but hopes were dashed by the Reichstag fire on 1 March which introduced rule by decree. In the interests of 'Gleichschaltung' many institutions which inclined to the monarchy were scrapped or merged into Nazi organisations. The crown prince was present at the Tag von Potsdam on 21 March, with his brothers and his sons, giving, as the Nazis intended, the occasion a little legitimist gloss. Hindenburg walked past the crown prince and bowed, then pointed to the emperor's empty chair with his field marshal's baton. The Nazis present responded with a 'German greeting'. William grumbled: 'Today in Potsdam is the celebration in the Garrison Church. This Friderician carry-on does not appeal to me at all, it is just to make the regime socially presentable ... it is high time that I became involved, above all to prevent a Nazi state forming . . . the swing to the Nazis must be exploited.'[12]

Like virtually everyone else on the right, William approved the reintroduction of conscription and the flouting of the clause in the Versailles Treaty which limited the German army to 100,000 officers and men. He knew already that the Nazis were merely using the monarchists and the monarchical idea in order to establish their credentials. When he understood this he began to give them a wide berth. Hermo continued to be the problem. As he told Ilsemann on 29 May 1933, 'As far as my wife is concerned, the barometer reads "storm". She is in an intolerable frame of mind! Politically she means well, things can't move quickly enough to get me back on to the throne, but we won't get there by her methods. She runs after the Nazis and everything she is able to do here or in Berlin she puts down in writing, which will sooner or later do us harm if it comes to light . . .'[13]

Waters's next trip to Doorn in late June followed a stay in Berlin with Hermo. The brigadier met a Graf Dohna at Doorn who had sung Hitler's praises. A positive mood was to be gleaned throughout the entourage. They 'were convinced that the National Socialist system and principles had come to stay in Germany'. William himself was surprisingly generous. 'Hitler has done marvellous things for Germany in my opinion,' he said, although he had reservations about the anti-Jewish crusade. He was both impressed by Hitler's refusal to draw a salary and by Göring's war record.[14]

Waters was in cahoots with Robert Bruce Lockhart. The latter had been in correspondence with Lloyd George on the subject of the man he had so vociferously wanted to hang. The former prime minister had changed his tune. On 9 July he wrote to him: 'The Kaiser had undoubted qualities. If he had not been Kaiser, he would have been a very great man. Kaisers have no chance from the start.' Bruce Lockhart had remained in touch. The socialite Lady Ottoline Morrell had been to see him too. After dinner he read P. G. Wodehouse to his entourage. Their English being less proficient than his, they were at a loss to know when to laugh. William adopted the solution of reading the funny bits twice.[15]

William's swelling English fan club was aware that there were political problems. Waters – who was a member of the Labour Party – identified Hermo as the source of the evil. He was bossed around by his wife who continued to court the Nazis in the hope of seeing him back on the throne, and her as empress beside him. It was soon to change, and both Waters and Bruce Lockhart were impressed by the grandson, Lullu, who was very anti-Nazi 'like the Kaiser'. Waters praised William's sound financial sense. He was keeping eighteen royal families, fifty families if you included the paid members of the entourage and the servants.[16]

On 24 March Hitler made a clear indication in a speech that he was not going to bring back the Hohenzollerns. On 9 May he had a meeting with Hindenburg in Königsberg with Berg in attendance. Hindenburg was anxious to go to his death with an assurance that there would be a restoration. Hitler let him know that he was in favour, but the time was not yet right. Hitler pointed to possible objections from foreign governments. Hausminister Dommes put his finger on it when he said in his letter to William, 'Clearly there is no positive desire to solve this problem.' At the end of the month Walther Darré, Hitler's agriculture spokesman and the only member of the team to have attended a British public school, accused William of cowardice in November 1918.[17]

Another Englishman William met and took to at first, was the twenty-three-year-old Randolph Churchill, the eldest son of the man who had lampooned his 'luxury fleet' and the future prime minister. He met him near Arnhem, and invited him to Doorn. Churchill arrived on 8 June 1934 and appalled everyone by his bad manners. He was a journalist – a species rarely allowed past the portals – and brought his secretary and a photographer with him. William did not seem unduly concerned about him at first, and sent him home with a pile of books for his father, whom he had met years before on manoeuvres. When an article appeared in the hated *Daily Mail*, William sang a very different tune.[18]

II

There was one good reason why William might have minded his Ps and Qs as far as the new regime was concerned. After Göring's visit the Nazi government agreed to provide William with an annual revenue. Doorn law was imposed once more, and this time a little more strictly than before. Kürenberg records the case of a countess who brought up the subject of the Nazis. William took 'the general' on his knees and picked up the menu card. 'Now, tell us what we are going to have for lunch! Duck? I hope the poor thing won't have been taken out of the moat!' The conversation then returned to normal.[19]

In September Dommes went to Hitler's secretary Hans Lammers with a whole series of complaints: the accusation of cowardice by his agriculture minister, the festooning of the royal Schlösser with swastikas, and repeated accusations that William was a 'freemason and a Jew-lover' loomed large. Lammers invited Dommes to a meeting on the 26th. These regrettable incidents were written off as 'flashes in the pan'. Dommes wondered if work could not be found for the princes. 'Schade nichts' – sorry, nothing, was the reply. Dommes wanted a meeting with Hitler himself. This was arranged for 24 October.[20]

After bathing the Führer in flattery Dommes broached the subject of his succession. Hitler started a long monologue which eventually began to focus on the Jews. 'I had the impression that Hitler was launching an indirect attack on Your Majesty; accusing you of being a Jew-lover. I interrupted him and recounted the words Your Majesty used in 1911 after lunching with Admiral Hollmann: "It is the duty of the sovereign to make use of the available forces in a nation. If we close the army and the civil service to Jews, then we must give them an outlet through which they may use their intelligence and wealth for the benefit of the people, and this is science, art and charity."' Hitler ignored Dommes and went back to his ramble in general and the Jews in particular. He then wound up the interview.

Dommes was to have a last chance. Once again it was occasioned by the words of the old King's School Wimbledon boy, Walther Darré, who had proclaimed that the emperor had betrayed the German peasantry. Dommes hinted at a duel: 'As an old soldier I deplore the fact that I may not take up arms for the honour of my slighted lord.' Hitler and he met on 27 April 1934. Hitler had prepared his answer in advance. He had not made the November revolution, but it had done one good thing in ridding Germany of the princes. They had poured scorn on him and his movement. 'He had his job to do ... and he wanted no one, not even the princes, to disturb him. He had nothing against the emperor. He had certainly made mistakes, but who hadn't?' Hitler finished with another rant: 'If Germany were ever again to become a monarchy, then this ... must have its roots in the nation – it must be born in the Party, which is the nation.'[21]

William had made up his mind that nothing could be hoped for from such a man and things calmed down again at Doorn. He took to having a two-hour nap in the afternoon, and encouraged his courtiers to do the same. That way, he said, they would not snore through his readings from books and papers in the evening. Films were shown and after the successful excursion to Zandvoort, a trip to the seaside was built into the annual programme.[22] It was not quite Achilleion, but it would have to do. William had friends there now, including a Baron van der Heydt, who had shown him his Japanese carvings.[23]

William heard about the Night of the Long Knives of 30 June 1934 on the wireless. He was shocked. At first he thought the bloodbath had been entirely aimed at homosexuals. What would people have said if he had done such a thing? He was most upset by the story of Frau von Schleicher's death. The wife of the former chancellor had been gunned down with her husband in the doorway of her home in Neubabelsberg. 'We have ceased to live under the rule of law and everyone must be prepared for the possibility that the Nazis will push their way in and put them up against the wall!'²⁴ After the Night of the Long Knives, Prince William's enthusiasm waned, but Hermo was still mixed in her opinions, thinking they might have shot a few more people.²⁵ Both the crown prince and Auwi were interrogated by the Gestapo and Prince William's former ADC, Major Ludwig Mülder von Mülnheim, was arrested.

In 1934 William's more arcane research gave rise to another book, *Die chinesische Monade. Ihre Geschichte und ihre Deutung* based on the lectures given at Doorn on 27 October 1933 before Professors Lommel, Naumann, Otto, Reinhardt, Sarre and Vollgraf. William was concerned with the symbols of life and God. He was at pains to show the universality of symbols from the Japanese yin and yang to the Chinese monad and the Aryan swastika. The Cypriots, for example, used the swastika as a symbol for the sun. The Corfu Gorgon naturally figured in the lecture: the 'oldest representation of the godhead'. The swastika, William went on, is above all a symbol of 'movement'. If the hooks turn to the right it means the movement of the sun: the sun, summer; the bringer of fame, luck, riches. When the hooks turn to the left it means *sauastika*: night, misfortune and death.²⁶

It was an emotive and contemporary subject and no one in that room was unaware of the Nazi use of the symbol. The swastika meant movement. The Nazis talked of their 'movement' too: 'The physically driving force in all cosmic and earthly happening. Behind the movement [man] sought [the swastika] as the driving force of the *Godhead*.' Not only was 'Doorn law' still in force, but William did not wish to make his message *too* clear: 'In the world of movements you saw frightening forces from a Godhead that was more feared than honoured. They knew nothing of the love of God, nothing of redemption.'²⁷

Waters made his fourth and last visit to Doorn on 5 May 1935. The old soldier was no longer nimble enough to dodge the German shepherd Arno, who savaged him on his arrival. There were more sad attacks on the Jews. 'I found out that Lee – who wrote the life of Edward VII and published lies against me in it – is really a Jew, Mr Lazarus, who quietly dropping his real name adopted that of Lee.' At the same time he said that he saw himself as no more than a pawn in the hands of God: 'He regards his present terrible trials as imposed by God for some inscrutable purpose of his own.'²⁸

On 15 November 1935, the former guards officer and diplomat, Joachim von Reichel, paid his first visit to Doorn. He was proposing to write a biography of William under his *nom de plume* of Kürenberg. William gave him a photograph with the legend written across it: 'War alles falsch?' – Was it all wrong? The visit offered the former emperor the chance to review the books that had already appeared. He was not impressed. 'I have seen little sign of justice so far. What has been written about me up to now has been for the most part distorted, wrong and silly, a lot of them even borrowing information from comic sheets [Witzblätter]!' The maddest was Emil Ludwig's, who 'without having ever met or spoken to me hurled bucket loads of rubbish over me. Now this fellow lives in lovely Switzerland; the fine confederates can only regret it!'

Reichel found the emperor more merciful, more understanding and nicer than he had been in the past, but also bitter. That last comment was typical. William had many times thought of transferring his exile to Switzerland himself. Reichel and he had their talks in the tower study. They were joined by Hermo. Tempers frayed and Reichel often had a frosty adieu which did not prevent William from sending over a friendly invitation to lunch, a walk or a chance to continue the discussion the next day. When Reichel's book was published in Switzerland as *War alles falsch?* William gave it grudging praise. It was an honourable attempt, and at least it set him properly and justly in his time.[29]

He told Reichel little that was new. Of the Bismarcks he was disdainful. They were like Pomeranian 'tenant farmers'. The servants pulled corks by putting the bottles between their knees and the old man fed the dogs from his plate so that they chewed the scraps on the carpet. 'The next day I might have had the same plate!' He stood by Eulenburg; and a little more openly than he had dared before: 'One of the most charming men I have ever known ... neither a hero nor a genius but this corrective should not give the impression that I am trying to back away from him; he was my friend, and will remain as such in my memory!' 'Whether certain accusations which have been raised against him are true or not I cannot decide.' He was more forthright in his unguarded moments. The Jewish nationalist Maximilian Harden, who had caused him so much grief in 1908, had not been forgotten. On 2 September 1927 he said Phili 'had fallen victim to judicial murder brought about by Holstein, Harden and international Jewry. It was the first blow to the monarchy, the introduction to the Revolution.'[30]

His attitude to Prince Max had become more reasoned, his perorations better turned, but his bitterness was exactly the same. William saw a cynical process starting with the former chancellor's spoken determination to protect the Empire, while pushing William out of all political decisions. This was followed by the abolition of censorship, which cast William to the wolves of the press. He failed to take the side of the monarchy in the abdication crisis and put pressure on William to voluntarily renounce the crown. He felt that Prince Max had become a pawn of Scheidemann and he transformed him into the 'destroyer of the Empire'.[31]

There were occasional silences, but mostly William was lively and rose to the bait. He received guests at tea, over toast and cherry jam. Lunch or a private conversation in the tower room was reserved for the privileged few. The meal was again not lavish: three courses with red and white wine. William drank red wine cut with Apollinaris water. Then coffee was drunk standing up. During the day he wore a grey suit with a gold tie pin and a miniature *pour le mérite* in his buttonhole.[32]

The publication of his lectures was now a regular event. In 1936 the German public saw William returning to the theme of his precious gorgon: 'The opposite to the beautiful image of the Greek God.' It was 'his' gorgon still. He mentioned the ill-fated reconstruction, three metres high, which had been burned in effigy by his entourage. He had chosen to forget that outrage.[33]

In May 1938 the heir apparent Louis Ferdinand, or Lullu, celebrated his marriage to a Russian grand duchess at Doorn and forty-four high dignitaries came for the ceremony. The Nazis had long since given up bothering to court him and his family; only Auwi stuck religiously to his Nazi guns. In June that year they would not allow Prince Eitel to celebrate the 250th anniversary of the First Foot. In April 1939 they arrested Hermo's son Ferdinand on his estate for disparaging the movement.[34]

George Viereck's imagined indictment of the emperor, *The Kaiser on Trial*, was published that year. Viereck had tried to enlist Lloyd George to write the preface, but the former prime minister who had swung from calling out 'Hang the Kaiser' to out-and-out appeasement, declined. His next choice was Ambassador Gerard, who now believed William to have been 'unjustly maligned'. In the end it was George Bernard Shaw who agreed to do the job. William was not pleased with the book and gave it to Hermo to read. On Reichel's last visit he dismissed it as 'amusing', nothing more.[35]

Shaw thought otherwise: 'On the whole William comes out of it pretty well for a man thrust by the accident of birth into a part which was not only extremely difficult, but to a great extent imaginary and flatly impossible.' Shaw thought William had 'some claim to be ranked as the best brain in the government in 1914'. William must have smiled at the playwright's dismissal of Britain's hated Foreign Secretary – 'In any sane country Grey would never have been trusted with any public office after his connivance in and defence of the Denshawai atrocity, and after his repeated proofs that he was incapable of telling the truth on any political subject because he never knew what the truth was: his brains being those of a naturalist, not of a diplomat.'

'The Emperor, having been the idol, was inevitably made the scape-goat. ... As to the withdrawal to Holland, it needs no apology any more than Louis-Napoleon's withdrawn to Chislehurst ... It was an admirable piece of common sense and a happy ending for a monarch who had done nothing to deserve an unhappy one.'[36]

William also produced a book that year: *Das Königtum im alten Mesopotamien*. The study of Mesopotamian kingship had naturally been inspired by the DAG, but William's interest was not just archaeological. There were lessons to be drawn too. 'Every [Mesopotamian] king is a servant of God.' Capitalism and corruption had destroyed Sumeria and there had been a suspicious involvement by the Semite Akkad, who had placed might before right. Hammurabi he compared to Frederick William I. The arrival of the Indo-Germanic Aryans brought with it the notion of the 'Supreme Warlord'. Their earthly world empire he compared to the theocracy of Charlemagne. This role was destroyed by the popes, who removed the Holy Roman Emperor's spiritual function. The Prussian kings, however, revived it. This was the achievement of Frederick the Great's father: his was the feeling of responsibility, he was the patron of law.[37]

The Kristallnacht of 10–11 November 1938 caused a rumpus at Doorn. 'What is going on at home is certainly a scandal. It is now high time that the army showed its hand; they have let a lot of things happen ... all the older officers and all decent Germans must protest.' One who did not was Auwi. William told Ilsemann, 'I have just made my views clear to Auwi in the presence of his brothers. He had the nerve to say that he agreed with the Jewish pogroms and understood why they had come about. When I told him that any decent man would describe these actions as gangsterism, he appeared totally indifferent. He is completely lost to our family...'[38]

There is some evidence that the German opposition began to flirt with William after the Kristallnacht. He was reported in *The Times* on 8 December as having described Hitler as, 'Having set up an all-swallowing state disdainful of human dignities and the ancient structures of our race ... for a few months I was inclined to believe in Nazi Socialism as a necessary fever. But the wisest and most outstanding Germans who were associated with it for a time he has got rid of, or even killed – von Papen, Schleicher, Neurath, even Blomberg. He has nothing left but a bunch of shirted gangsters.'[39]

William remained remarkably fit from his sawing and his regular walks. At the end of his life he had to put the saddle aside and bring in a comfortable chair. He even adopted the laid-back solution of working in bed. Fifty members of his family and other princes came for his eightieth birthday. It was a far calmer occasion than his seventieth. He was pleased to see the faithful Field Marshal Mackensen and Crown Prince Rupprecht of Bavaria's presence was a sure gesture of reconciliation. He must have forgiven Mackensen for taking up an appointment with the Nazis as well as for receiving a massive bribe from the party. The German press was forbidden to comment on the occasion.[40]

In August 1939, when the stench of war was already hanging in the air, William received a last visit from Robert Bruce Lockhart. He brought with him John Wheeler-Bennett, who had conceived an idea of writing a biography of the emperor as a sequel to his life of Hindenburg. It was Wheeler-Bennett's first and last meeting with the emperor. He made one or two assumptions which were false: chiefly that William's entourage was largely Nazi, which it was not. He found him 'weltering in self-pity' and imbued with a 'gigantic egotism', which was certainly correct. Otherwise he discovered a 'charming, humorous and courteous old gentleman'. He was particularly struck by his 'guttural but fluent' English which was spiced with such words as 'topping', 'ripping' – 'A damned topping good fellow'. He ranted about Hindenburg and Bülow and expressed his regret at dropping Bismarck. He had learned something after all. Overall Wheeler-Bennett was struck by William's dignity in exile.

Bruce Lockhart made a few notes:

Very simple luncheon: two courses only, beef – potatoes – red cabbage – strawberry tart (hot), red or white wine. In the front hall large map of the Far East with little flagged pins to mark advances. Tea with empress at 4.15. Again with Kaiser from 5.30 p.m. till 7 p.m. Just time to change for dinner – and again with Kaiser from 8.45 p.m. till 10.15. Tremendous day for him – and for us. At times, especially in the afternoon, seemed tired – small pauses – but laughed heartily – smile very attractive. Full of religion – now talks of Providence, not God – said he 'was eighty – next year; I may be called.'[41]

As they left, William came to say goodbye: 'Come back and see me again next summer if you can. But you won't be able to, because the machine is running away with *him*, as it ran away with *me*.'[42]

III

The war disrupted life at Doorn from the beginning. His ADCs were called up and Dutch troops were billeted in the house. William was a good host and took them over the rosarium. He had no quarrels with Hitler's war aims. Where he had stuck his head in the sand over Munich, he approved of the retrieval of Danzig and the Corridor. Ilsemann avoided call-up by falling ill and spending seven weeks in hospital. In the new year his staff was interned.[43]

Members of the family began to fall at the front. The first was his grandson Oscar on 7 September. The war impeded movement and only twenty-four guests were able to sit down to dinner for William's eighty-first birthday. On 10 May 1940 one of Winston Churchill's secretaries, R. C. S. Stevenson, wrote to the Foreign Office:

Mr Churchill wonders whether it would not be a good thing to give the ex-Kaiser a private hint that he would be received with consideration and dignity in England should he desire to seek asylum here.

The offer reached William via The Hague the next day. He declined. He was not slow to realise the propaganda aspect of the move. With characteristic acid he pronounced he 'would rather be shot in Holland than flee to England. He had no desire to be photographed beside Churchill.'[44] Queen Wilhelmina had always refused to see him, but she also thought about his well-being. She would have given him a refuge on a Dutch island if he desired. He stayed put. 'I shall never leave House Doorn!'

Here, on 14 May 1940, he was saluted by Colonel Neidtholdt of IR 322. Shortly afterwards a Colonel von Zitzewitz from the General Staff offered him the protection of the Wehrmacht. At four that afternoon he was photographed speaking to German officers at the gate.[45] On 23 May the crown prince's eldest son, that same Prince William who had been excluded from the succession, was shot in the French campaign and later died of his wounds. At his funeral in Potsdam some 50,000 mourners turned out, which was enough of a display of monarchical enthusiasm to disturb Hitler. He made up his mind from now on to stop the royal princes from serving at the front. Despite this family tragedy, the progress of German arms excited the old man. He felt that the jury had been appointed for the divine judgement of 'Juda-England'. When he sent his telegram to Hitler, it was published in the papers. William naturally thought it was *his* victory: 'The brilliant leading generals in this war come from *My* school, they fought under *My* command in the world war as lieutenants, captains or young majors.'[46]

When the Wehrmacht entered Paris on 17 June William was convinced to write a telegram to Hitler. It was a most grudging acknowledgement, but it was enough to damn him in the eyes of the post-war Dutch government, which impounded Doorn and its contents as a result. If anyone was actually praised, it was *his* army: 'In my profound emotion following the defeat of France may I offer my best wishes both to you and to the entire German army with the words of Emperor William the Great: "What things have come about through God's bounty." In all German hearts sounded the Leuthen Chorale sung by the victorious troops of the Great King at Leuthen: *Nun danket alle Gott!*'[47]

At first William received a 'guard of honour' composed of fifteen men.

Then came a ban on visits as the Nazis showed their sour attitude towards the old ruler. Finally the guard was withdrawn and replaced by a squad of ordinary soldiers. There were rumours that he had packed up and gone to Cadinen in East Prussia. Early on in the war Hitler had actually approved the idea of William going to the eastern part of Germany in the event of an Allied invasion of Holland.[48]

IV

Since 29 March 1938 William had been suffering from angina pectoris. On 1 March 1941 he fainted. Three weeks later he was complaining of pains in his colon. On 3 June an embolism was detected in his lungs. That day the nurse told him: 'Your Majesty, it is better above. With the Most Supreme Lord it is better for us than on earth.' William replied, 'I am ready. We will see one another again up there.' ... 'My end is coming, I am sinking, sinking!' He prayed out loud that day. On 4 June he lost consciousness and died. At eighty-two he was the same age as his beloved grandmother, Queen Victoria.[49]

A new codicil to his will, written on 25 December 1933, made it clear that he refused to be buried in the Republic, Nazi or otherwise.[50] That stopped Hitler's hopes of a state funeral with a chance to walk behind the coffin, as William had followed that of his grandfather. He had decreed a simple funeral at Doorn. Designs had already been made for a classical mausoleum. There were to be no swastikas. A coffin had been made by the sculptor Betzner as early as 1937. Five days later Hitler provided a special train to convey guests to the funeral as well as a battalion of honour. The sermon was preached by Doehring. Also there were Paul von Hase and Admiral Canaris, who were both later to perish on Hitler's scaffolds, and old Mackensen, still on his feet at ninety-two. The mourners sang 'Ich bete an die Macht der Liebe' and 'Jesu meine Zuversicht'.

Hermo had Doorn turned into a museum and retired to Silesia. She was caught by the Russian advance in 1944 and perished in poorly explained circumstances in Frankfurt an der Oder in 1949. She was the only one to be caught in the east, but both Auwi and the crown prince died, their spirits broken by their experiences of internment. There was to be no sympathy for the Hohenzollerns in post-war Germany either. Officially there is none today.

*   *   *

'William the Wholly Great or William the Last?' wrote Kurt Riezler in the middle of the submarine crisis which decided the fate of the war. It was a sensible question. Had William won, our attitude to him would be very different indeed. Reichel also felt that had William died, say in 1914, he would have been revered as a good if not a great ruler. Since Germany's defeat in the bloodiest of wars, the microscope has been turned on its leader and the disappointing side of his character amplified in the desire to make him the sole scapegoat for the catastrophe. In this the many accounts which appeared in Germany in the 1920s and 1930s were the most flagrant in their criticism, because they were written by those who also bore much of the guilt.

It has been open season on William from 1914, but in some places, notably Britain, he lost the sympathy of the general public before he even came to power. Once the documents were published after 1918 he was damned by his own hand and utterances: those marginal comments which both Tirpitz and Eulenburg apparently asked him not to make; those terrible fulminations which were published in the diaries of the major players, which no one was ever meant to hear. All we recall from his Uncle Bertie, after all, was the mildly derisory condemnation of a seaside resort as 'Bugger Bognor!' George V is not remembered either for the passionate bellicosity which so shocked Colonel House when he visited him during the war.

As far as William is concerned, the effect has been as total and as damning as the famous tapes which exposed President Richard Nixon. Yet of William, it must always be recalled that the German emperor was capable of saying one thing one moment, and the reverse the next. When speaking at least, he always fired before he took aim. The saintly Godard Bentinck who put up with him staying for eighteen months under his roof said with reference to his guest, 'People do not always mean what they say nor weigh their words when speaking in moments of intense pressure or excitement.'[51]

It is perhaps right that we condemn William, for if the First World War was not his personal undertaking, the finger of blame points over and over again to the failure of the German diplomacy in which he tried so hard to play a positive role. William saw himself as a major actor on the world stage, yet no one would act with him; and despite twenty-five years of attempts to maintain the peace by reworking Europe's system of alliances, he effected very little beyond reinforcing the convictions of those in power elsewhere; that the new Germany was an unwelcome bad element which exercised a malign influence on the old balance of power.

It is still not clear to what extent frequent illness and neurasthenia affected his mind and judgement. The bursts of anger, the rodomontades, the table-thumping and carpet-biting were not considered significant by those who saw the emperor daily. He could utter terrible threats, but despite the hard laws governing *lèse-majesté* Germany was not a tyranny. He threatened to wind up the constitution on countless occasions; but it is significant that nothing ever happened. He often called for someone to be shot too, but no one ever was; with the possible exception of Lieutenant von Hahnke. That sailor also died by his own hand, and the story seems to imply that William was oblivious of the decision to pass him a loaded revolver.

William was often sick with agony. In his last illness his coherence went once again. The composition of that terrible final burst of anti-Semitism would suggest a man who was physically tortured in some way. At Amerongen he proclaimed, 'The world says I'm mad ... but if it knew what tremendous difficulties I have to contend with it would perhaps be surprised that I am at all sane.'[52]

That William was a clever man was doubted by few people who met him. John Wheeler-Bennett thought he had a 'brilliant, if unstable intellect': 'The real tragedy of Wilhelm II is that he should ever have been emperor at all. Nature had designed him for a life of intellectual and artistic activity, fate destined him for a soldier and a sovereign.'[53] Bismarck also praised his intelligence, but he said that the young ruler lacked perception and staying power. Unlike Frederick the Great he could not be alone and dedicate himself to the hard job of ruling. The idea he liked, but the practice of power was too much like hard work.

William was a mass of contradictions. As he told his American admirer, George Viereck, 'I am afraid that the two strains in my blood make me a riddle both at home and abroad. The Germans claimed that I was too English. The English, on the other hand, complained that I was too German.'[54] They had said similar things about his mother, whom he resembled more than people were prepared to credit at the time. The British alliance for which he genuinely strove all his professional life, was almost an attempt to make a symbolic reconciliation between these two disparate elements in his own character. He failed in the one, and he failed in the other.

The mixed Hohenzollern–Guelph heritage explained his contradictory stance when it came to his mother's country. 'William's attitude toward England was a combination of admiration and envy, animosity and affection. Here is the explanation of apparent inconsistencies in his diplomacy and his character.'[55] The British also bear a portion of the blame. Very few of her statesmen were prepared to drop that supercilious pose when they dealt with the German emperor. Their refusal to accommodate him was also an important reason why catastrophe occurred in 1914.

The question remains whether there were positive achievements. Was the Wilhelmine Age all for naught? Clearly much more of it survived to give the tone of Weimar than is generally realised, but the continuation of the old laws and the old bureaucracy is not the side of Weimar which wins it friends today. Focus is always applied to the artistic effusions, which represented little in the long run, and almost all of which had their origins in the illiberalism of William's pre-1914 Reich. The official art of William's period has yet to find a large body of admirers, and yet it would be hard to make out that it was any worse than late Victorian academic work, or indeed its equivalent in France, Italy and Belgium.

In some ways William's Empire was a very modern one. In technology, cultivating the sciences, reforming schools and universities and in the proper evaluation of the role that business and industry may play in the creation of prosperity and financing culture, William needed no encouragement. He understood such things from the start. But that was just one face of Wilhelmine Germany. It had several others and in the long run they could not be reconciled. William failed and the Second Reich died of its own internal contradictions. Its ruler lost his crown because he was unable to tie up the two ends of the string. Whether another would have been more successful it is hard to say. Such men are precious rare.

Notes

Introduction

1 John Wheeler-Bennett, *Three Episodes in the Life of Kaiser Wilhelm II*, The Leslie Stephen Lectures 1955, Cambridge, 1956, 1.

2 William was apparently right to be frightened. See Norman Stone, *The Eastern Front 1914–1917*, London, 1975, 18, 35–6, 37–8.

3 Evelyn, Princess Blücher, *An English Wife in Berlin. A Private Memoir of Events, Politics, and Daily Life in Germany Throughout the War and the Social Revolution of 1918*, London, 1918, 319.

4 Martin Middlebrook, *The Kaiser's Battle. 21 March 1918: The First Day of the German Spring Offensive*, London, 1983, even has a close-up of the emperor on the cover.

5 'Frage und Antwortspiel', in Mary Gerold-Tucholsky, ed., Kurt Tucholsky, *Gedichte*, Reinbek, 1996, 283.

6 'Huldigung in Doorn', in Tucholsky, *Gedichte*, 342–3.

7 See, for example, Kenneth Rose, 'Churchill's Invitation to the Kaiser', *Tatler*, November 1999. I am grateful to John Graham for drawing my attention to this article.

8 J. C. G. Röhl, *Kaiser, Hof und Staat, Wilhelm II und die deutsche Politik*, Munich, 1987, 22.

9 Poultney Bigelow Papers in New York Public Library, Box 34A, quoted in Hannah Pakula, *An Uncommon Woman, The Empress Frederick, Daughter of Queen Victoria, Wife of the Crown Prince of Prussia, Mother of Kaiser Wilhelm*, New York, 1995, 456. It is quoted, without the reference to the 'press', in Kenneth Rose's *Tatler* article.

10 Nicolaus Sombart, *Wilhelm II. Sündenbock und Herr der Mitte*, Berlin, 1996, 143.

Chapter One: The Inheritance

1 Kaiser Wilhelm II, *Aus meinem Leben, 1859–1888*, 3rd edn, Berlin and Leipzig, 1927, Vorwort.

2 William II, *My Ancestors*, trans. W. W. Zambra, London, 1931, 101.

3 Wilhelm II, *Aus meinem Leben*, 3.

4 Hans-Joachim Netzer, *Ein Deutscher Prinz in England, Albert von Sachsen-Coburg und Gotha, Gemahl der Königin Victoria*, Munich, 1997, 153.

5 See Heinrich Pellender, *Ein Herzogtum macht Weltgeschichte*, Coburg, 1992; Giles MacDonogh 'A Small Town in Germany with a Right Royal History', *Financial Times*, 12 December 1998, 29, 83.

6 Netzer, *Deutscher Prinz*, 74.

7 Ibid., 72.

8 Ibid., 243–4.

9 Ibid., 244.

10 Ibid., 89.

11 Ibid., 160.

12 Ibid., 180, 182.

13 Ibid., 152, 183.

14 Ibid., 223.

15 Ibid., 322.

16 Lamar Cecil, *Wilhelm II, Prince and Emperor, 1859–1900*, Chapel Hill and London, 1989, 2.

17 Benson, E. F., *The Kaiser and English Relations*, London, 1936, 7–8.

18 William II, *My Ancestors*, 217.

19 Johann Peter Eckermann, *Gespräche mit Goethe*, Baden-Baden, 1981, 215.

20 Joachim von Kürenberg [Joachim von Reichel], *War alles falsch? Das Leben Kaiser Wilhelms II*, 2nd edn, Bonn, 1952, 15; Franz Herre, *Kaiser Friedrich III, Deutschlands liberale Hoffnung*, Stuttgart, 1987, 54.

21 Herre, *Friedrich III*, 60.

22 Thomas August Kohut, *Wilhelm II and the Germans, A Study in Leadership*, New York and Oxford, 1997, 30; Georg Hinzpeter, *Kaiser Wilhelm II. Eine Skizze nach der Natur gezeichnet*, 8th edn, Bielefeld, 1888, 4.

23 Herre, *Friedrich III*.

24 Herre, *Friedrich III*, 29.

25 Benson, *English Relations*, 1.

26 Sir Frederick Ponsonby, ed., *The Letters of the Empress Frederick*, London, 1928, 4, attributes the project to Augusta alone.

27 Michael Balfour, *The Kaiser and his Times*, London, 1964, 62; Herre, *Friedrich III*, 74.

28 Benson, *English Relations*, 7–8.

29 Hannah Pakula, *Uncommon Woman*, 66–7.

30 Ponsonby, *Empress Frederick*, 6.

31 Benson, *English Relations*, 2.

32 Ponsonby, *Empress Frederick*, 10.

33 Benson, *English Relations*, 4.

34 Kürenberg, *War alles falsch?*, 35; Herre, *Friedrich III*, 88.

35 Kürenberg, *War alles falsch?*, 16; Kohut, *Wilhelm II*, 28.

36 Kohut, *Wilhelm II*, 37.

37 Cecil, *Prince and Emperor*, 6.

38 Balfour, *Kaiser*, 67.

39 Quoted in Kürenberg, *War alles falsch?* 42–3.

40 Cecil, *Prince and Emperor*, 3.

Chapter Two: Synthesis

1 Netzer, *Deutscher Prinz*, 215.

2 J. C. G. Röhl, *Wilhelm II. Die Jugend des Kaisers, 1859–1888*, Munich, 1993, 28.

3 Ibid., 29.

4 Hannah Pakula, *Uncommon Woman*, 125n.

5 Letter from Geheimrat Professor Dr med August Martin, BPH Rep, 53, Nr 18–19, quoted in Giles MacDonogh, *Prussia. The Perversion of an Idea*, London, 1994, 65–6; Henry Fischer, *Private Lives of Kaiser William II and his Consort, Secret History of the Court of Berlin from the Papers and Diaries of Countess from Eppinghoven [sic], dame du palais to Her Majesty, the Empress-Queen*, 3 vols, New York, 1909, 8–9, suggests that Fräulein Stahl brought William to life. The 'Countess von Eppinghoven' of the book's title would appear to have been a disgruntled former servant who knew the court gossip well.

6 Kürenberg, *War alles falsch?*, 12. In some accounts Wrangel broke the window, e.g. Balfour, *Kaiser*, 73.

7 Thomas August Kohut, *The Politicization of Personality and the Personalization of Politics: a Psychological Study of Kaiser Wilhelm II's Leadership of the Germans*, Ph.D. thesis, University of Minnesota, 1983, 8; Fischer, *Private Lives*, I, 9–10; Poultney Bigelow, *Seventy Summers*, 2 vols, London, 1925, I, 81.

8 Ponsonby, *Empress Frederick*, 21.

9 Röhl, *Jugend*, 50, 54, 63–7; Pakula, *Uncommon Woman*, 130. The unequal arm-lengths are visible in William's uniforms which are displayed at Huis Doorn in Holland.

10 Fischer, *Private Lives*, I, 14.

11 Kürenberg, *War alles falsch?* 23; Wilhelm II, *Aus meinem Leben*, 31.

12 See Balfour, *Kaiser*, 74, who points out that the 1st marquess of Halifax had a withered arm, and that it did not appear to influence his personality. I am also grateful to Gay McGuinness for sending me the story of Arthur McMurrough-Kavanagh who rode, shot, fished and sat in the Victorian House of Commons, despite the fact that he was born without arms and legs.

13 Netzer, *Deutscher Prinz*, 304–6.

14 Ibid., 310–11.

15 Ponsonby, *Empress Frederick*, 24.

16 Netzer, *Deutscher Prinz*, 307.

17 Herre, *Friedrich III*, 90, 102.

18 Benson, *English Relations*, 7, 9.

19 Röhl, *Jugend*, 94–5; Kohut, *Wilhelm II*, 71–2.

20 Wilhelm II, *Aus meinem Leben*, 3–4; Pakula, *Uncommon Woman*, 184.

21 Quoted in Kohut, *Wilhelm II*, 31.

22 Röhl, *Jugend*, 51; Cecil, *Prince and Emperor*, 14.

23 Kohut, *Wilhelm II*, 39, 44, 46.

24 Wilhelm II, *Aus meinem Leben*, 4.

25 Jean-Paul Bled, *Franz Joseph*, trans. Teresa Bridgeman, Oxford, 1994, 135.

26 William II, *My Ancestors*, 230; *idem, Aus meinem Leben*, 4–5.

27 Ponsonby, *Empress Frederick*, 65.

28 Ibid., 60, 61.

29 Röhl, *Jugend*, 138, 195–6; Marie von Bunsen, *Die Welt in der ich lebte. Erin-
    nerungen aus glücklichen Jahren*, Leipzig, 1929, 27; Wilhelm II, *Aus meinem
    Leben*, 21–3, 30.

30 Kohut, *Wilhelm II*, 41.

31 Röhl, *Jugend*, 186.

32 Wilhelm II, *Aus meinem Leben*, 36–7.

33 Balfour, *Kaiser*, 76; Wilhelm II, *Aus meinem Leben*, 24; Marie von Bunsen, *Die
    Welt*, 198–9; Kürenberg, *War alles falsch?*, 16–17.

34 Hinzpeter, *Skizze*, 4–5.

35 Wilhelm II, *Aus meinem Leben*, 25.

36 Kürenberg, *War alles falsch?*, 17.

37 Wilhelm II, *Aus meinem Leben*, 29–30.

38 Ibid., 25, 27, 28.

39 Ibid., 23–4, 44.

40 Röhl, *Jugend*, 162–3.

41 Ponsonby, *Empress Frederick*, 68.

42 Kürenberg, *War alles falsch?*, 24.

43 Röhl, *Jugend*, 169; J. Daniel Chamier, *Fabulous Monster*, London, 1934, 3.

44 Poultney Bigelow, *The German Emperor*. Reprinted from the *New Review*, 1889,
    8; Emil Ludwig, *Wilhelm der Zweite*, Frankfurt am Main and Hamburg, 1968,
    26, says that in order to fire his rifle, William was obliged to rest the muzzle
    on a servant's arm.

45 Poultney Bigelow, *Prussian Memories 1864–1914*, New York and London, 1916,
    51.

46 Kohut, *Wilhelm II*, 44; Kürenberg, *War alles falsch?*, 24.

47 Wilhelm II, *Aus meinem Leben*, 34, 37, 40; for a description of the *Weih-
    nachtsmarkt*, see Theodor Fontane, *Die Poggenpuhls* (Ullstein Fontane
    Bibiothek), Munich, 1986, 26.

48 Kürenberg, *War alles falsch?*, 18.

49 Wilhelm II, *Aus meinem Leben*, 34.

50 Ibid., 34–5.

51 Bigelow, *Prussian Memories*, 40.

52 Poultney Bigelow, *German Emperor*, 12, 14; Kürenberg, *War alles falsch?*, 19;
    Cecil, *Prince and Emperor*, 22; James William Lowther, Viscount Ullswater, *A
    Speaker's Commentaries*, 2 vols, London, 1925, I, 3.

53 Wilhelm II, *Aus meinem Leben*, 38–9.

54 Bigelow, *Seventy Summers*, I, 63, 75.

55 Bigelow, *Prussian Memories*, 36, 39–40, 42.

56 Ibid., 39.

57 Bigelow, *German Emperor*, 13–14; *Seventy Summers*, I, 78.

58 Bigelow, *Prussian Memories*, 48–9.

59 Bigelow, *Prussian Memories*, 49–50.

60 Kohut, *Wilhelm II*, 69.

61 Bigelow, *Prussian Memories*, 47–8.

62 Bigelow, *German Emperor*, 7.

63 Bigelow, *Prussian Memories*, 39–40; *Seventy Summers*, I, 76, 80.

64 Bigelow, *German Emperor*, 11–12; *Prussian Memories*, 45–46, 50; *Seventy Summers*, I, 82.

65 Lady Susan Townley, *'Indiscretions' of Lady Susan*, London, 1922, 41.

66 Wilhelm II, *Aus meinem Leben*, 71.

67 William II, *My Ancestors*, 282–3.

68 Wilhelm II, *Aus meinem Leben*, 6.

69 Cecil, *Prince and Emperor*, 10.

70 Golo Mann, *Wilhelm II*, Munich, Berne, Vienna, 1964, 7; Herre, *Friedrich III*, 192.

71 *Die Zukunft*, 36, 1906, quoted in Kohut, *Wilhelm II*, 28–29.

72 Herre, *Friedrich III*, 210; Wilhelm II, *Aus meinem Leben*, 8.

73 Wilhelm II, *Aus meinem Leben*, 8–9.

74 Ibid., 10.

75 Kürenberg, *War alles falsch?*, 36–7.

76 Ibid., 38.

77 Netzer, *Deutscher Prinz*, 218.

78 Röhl, *Jugend*, 178; Wilhelm II, *Aus meinem Leben*, 9.

79 Kürenberg, *War alles falsch?*, 35; Wilhelm II, *Aus meinem Leben*, 10; [F. E. Smedley], *Frank Fairleigh; or Scenes from the Life of a Private Pupil*, London, 1850, 3, 9, 27.

80 Wilhelm II, *Aus meinem Leben*, 21.

81 Kürenberg, *War alles falsch?*, 21.

82 Wilhelm II, *Aus meinem Leben*, 40; Kohut, *Wilhelm II*, 69.

83 Kohut, *Wilhelm II*, 71; Wilhelm II, *Aus meinem Leben*, 41–2.

84 Kürenberg, *War alles falsch?*, 27.

85 Wilhelm II, *Aus meinem Leben*, 42.

86 Ibid., 42–3.

87 Röhl, *Jugend*, 171.

88 Wilhelm II, *Aus meinem Leben*, 42–3; Marie von Bunsen, *Die Welt*, 27.

89 Wilhelm II, *Aus meinem Leben*, 45; E. Lindemann, *Das deutsche Helgoland*, Berlin-Charlottenburg, 1913, 229–30; *Beschwerdeschrift der Helgolander Bürgerschaft wider den Gouverneur Maxse wegen Verletzung der Insel Helgoland garantierten Rechte und Privilegien*, Husum, 1866, 3.

90 Wilhelm II, *Aus meinem Leben*, 45–6.

91 Ibid., 47.

92 Ibid., 50.

93 Hannah Pakula, *Uncommon Woman*, 260, is inaccurate in many details of the Cannes episode; William II, *My Ancestors*, 177; *Aus meinem Leben*, 47–8.

94 Jean de Bonnefon, *Drame Impérial. Ce qu'on ne peut pas dire à Berlin*, Paris, 1888, 6, 8. According to the *Dictionnaire biographique française*, de Bonnefon 'took revenge' with his book for his expulsion from Berlin in 1888. On the other hand it was William he wanted to attack, not his father. Bled, *Franz Joseph*, 174.

95 Herre, *Friedrich III*, 164, 165–6; William II, *My Ancestors*, 273; *Aus meinem Leben*, 49; Röhl, *Jugend*, 172.

96 Wilhelm II, *Aus meinem Leben*, 52–3; Kürenberg, *War alles falsch?*, 28.

97 Herre, *Friedrich III*, 167.

98 William II, *My Ancestors*, 242–48.

99 Wilhelm II, *Aus meinem Leben*, 53.

100 Ibid., 54–5.

101 Herre, *Friedrich III*, 175, 178, 185, 190; Ponsonby, *Empress Frederick*, 90.

102 Henry Lucy, ed., *The Emperor's Diary of the Austro-German War 1866 and the Franco-German War 1870–1871. To which is added Prince Bismarck's Rejoinder*, London, 1888, 72; Ponsonby, *Empress Frederick*, 93–4.

103 Ponsonby, *Empress Frederick*, 105, quoting Frederick's *War Diary*.

104 Ibid., 106.

105 William II, *My Ancestors*, 278.

106 Ponsonby, *Empress Frederick*, 119–20.

107 Ibid., 118.

108 Ibid., 121.

109 Wilhelm II, *Aus meinem Leben*, 56–7.

110 William II, *My Ancestors*, 248.

111 Ibid., 148.

112 Wilhelm II, *Aus meinem Leben*, 60; the eighth book is the work of Caesar's friend Aulus Hirtius.

113 Book V, 35–7. See Caesar, *The Conquest of Gaul*, Harmondsworth, 1982, 120–22.

114 Wilhelm II, *Aus meinem Leben*, 61.

115 Ibid., 64; T. L. J. Verroen, 'Had ik dat talent gehad dan was ik geen keizer maar marineschilder geworden!', in W. G. Boven, ed., *Unsere Zukunft liegt auf dem Wasser. Herinneringen van Wilhelm II an zijn keizerlijke Marine*, Doorn, 1998, 31.

116 Kürenberg, *War alles falsch?*, 24.

117 Giles MacDonogh, *Berlin, A Portrait of Its History, Politics, Architecture and Society*, New York, 1999, 122.

118 Wilhelm II, *Aus meinem Leben*, 72.

119 Ibid., 74.

120 Röhl, *Jugend*, 208.
121 Wilhelm II, *Aus meinem Leben*, 88.
122 Ponsonby, *Empress Frederick*, 133.
123 Kürenberg, *War alles falsch?*, 22.
124 Wilhelm II, *Aus meinem Leben*, 104.
125 Ponsonby, *Empress Frederick*, 134.
126 Ibid., 135; Kürenberg, *War alles falsch?*, 39.
127 Quoted in Wilhelm II, *Aus meinem Leben*, 119–20.
128 Ibid., 120.
129 Kürenberg, *War alles falsch?*, 39.
130 Wilhelm II, *Aus meinem Leben*, 124.
131 Röhl, *Jugend*, 225; Wilhelm II, *Aus meinem Leben*, 124–5.
132 François Ayme, *Guillaume II, Une Education impériale*, Paris, 1896, 90; Röhl, *Jugend*, 232–9.
133 Röhl, *Jugend*, 247, reproduces an example.
134 Ayme, *Education*, 67, 90, 125, 121.
135 Ibid., 60–1.
136 Franz Herre, *Wilhelm II. Monarch zwischen den Zeiten*, Cologne, 1993, 26.
137 Wilhelm II, *Aus meinem Leben*, 128.
138 Ibid., 130.
139 Ibid., 132.
140 Ibid., 133.
141 Ibid., 133.
142 G. S. Viereck, *My Flesh and Blood, A Lyric Autobiography with Indiscreet Annotations*, London, 1932, 279.
143 Herre, *Friedrich III*, 205; Wilhelm II, *Aus meinem Leben*, 139.
144 Wilhelm II, *Aus meinem Leben*, 139–40.
145 Kürenberg, *War alles falsch?*, 42.
146 Herre, *Wilhelm II*, 32; Wilhelm II, *Aus meinem Leben*, 142.

Chapter Three: The Emperor as a Young Man

1 Wilhelm II, *Aus meinem Leben*, 157; Röhl, *Jugend*, 294.
2 Wilhelm II, *Aus meinem Leben*, 161; Cecil, *Prince and Emperor*, 39.
3 Herre, *Wilhelm II*, 33; Röhl, *Jugend*, 320–6.
4 Wilhelm II, *Aus meinem Leben*, 163.
5 Ibid., 166.
6 Ibid., 167.
7 Ibid., 170–1.
8 Kürenberg, *War alles falsch?*, 54.
9 Ponsonby, *Empress Frederick*, 168.
10 Herre, *Kaiser Friedrich*, 221–2.
11 Wilhelm II, *Aus meinem Leben*, 173; Kürenberg, *War alles falsch?*, 52.
12 Kürenberg, *War alles falsch?*, 56.

13 Röhl, *Jugend*, 352.

14 Ponsonby, *Empress Frederick*, 179.

15 Kohut, *Wilhelm II*, 52; Cecil, *Prince and Emperor*, 44.

16 Hannah Pakula, *Uncommon Woman*, 363–4; Cecil, *Prince and Emperor*, 58.

17 Nicolaus Sombart in J. C. G. Röhl and Nicolaus Sombart, eds, *Kaiser Wilhelm II, New Interpretations, The Corfu Papers*, Cambridge, 1982, 308; Herre, *Wilhelm II*, 39.

18 My italics; the line is excluded in Röhl, *Kaiser, Hof und Staat*, 27; and Cecil, *Prince and Emperor*, 46. Compare Kohut, *Wilhelm II*, 56.

19 De Bonnefon, *Drame Impérial*, 7.

20 J. C. G. Röhl, *Young Wilhelm, The Kaiser's Early Life, 1859–1888*, Cambridge, 1998, 455–7. The English edition has been revised to accommodate further information on William's love life.

21 Ibid., 459.

22 Ibid., 460–3.

23 Fischer, *Private Lives*, II, 309–10.

24 Brigitte Hamann, *Rudolf, Kronprinz und Rebell*, Vienna and Munich, 1978, 335.

25 Wilhelm II, *Aus meinem Leben*, 176.

26 Ibid., 179; Kürenberg, *War alles falsch?*, 50, has a slightly different version of these lines.

27 Wilhelm II, *Aus meinem Leben*, 180.

28 Ibid., 181.

29 Ibid., 253.

30 Ibid., 184.

31 Ibid.

32 Hinzpeter, *Kaiser Wilhelm*, 7.

33 Röhl, *Jugend*, 390.

34 Wilhelm II, *Aus meinem Leben*, 190; Kürenberg, *War alles falsch?*, 62.

35 Herre, *Wilhelm II*, 38; Cecil, *Prince and Emperor*, 60, 65.

36 Wilhelm II, *Aus meinem Leben*, 255–6.

37 Herre, *Wilhelm II*, 43.

38 Rudolf Vierhaus, ed., *Das Tagebuch der Baronin Spitzemberg, geb. Freiin von Varnbüler. Aufzeichnungen aus der Hofgesellschaft des Hohenzollernreiches*, 2nd edn, Göttingen, 1961 (hereafter Baronin Spitzemberg, *Tagebuch*), 200.

39 Cecil, *Prince and Emperor*, 61.

40 Herre, *Wilhelm II*, 44–5.

41 Kohut, *Wilhelm II*, 75.

42 Wilhelm II, *Aus meinem Leben*, 280–3.

43 Brigitte Hamann, *Rudolf*, 333.

44 Cecil, *Prince and Emperor*, 61–2; William II, *Aus meinem Leben*, 193–4, 202.

45 MacDonogh, *Berlin*, 160. See also Theodor Fontane, *Wanderungen durch die Mark Brandenburg*, 3 vols, Munich and Vienna, 1991, 1340–4.

46 Wilhelm II, *Aus meinem Leben*, 202.

47 Ibid., 206; Eliza von Moltke, ed., *Generaloberst Helmuth von Moltke, Erin-*

nerungen, Briefe, Dokumente, 1877–1916, Stuttgart, 1922, 113.

48 Wilhelm II, *Aus meinem Leben*, 206; Kürenberg, *War alles falsch?*, 61.

49 Heinrich Otto Meisner, ed., *Denkwürdigkeiten des General-Feldmarschalls Alfred von Waldersee*, 3 vols, Stuttgart and Berlin, 1925 (hereafter Waldersee, *Denkwürdigkeiten*), I, 234; Kürenberg, *War alles falsch?*, 63.

Chapter Four: Influence and Responsibilities

1 Reinhold Conrad Muschler, *Philipp zu Eulenburg, sein Leben und seine Zeit*, Leipzig, 1930, 60; MacDonogh, *Prussia*, 211.

2 William II, *Aus meinem Leben*, 227.

3 Muschler, *Eulenburg*, 91.

4 Ibid., 134.

5 Ibid., 151.

6 Johannes Haller, ed., *Philipp Fürst zu Eulenburg-Hertefels, Aus 50 Jahren: Erinnerungen, Tagebücher und Briefe aus dem Nachlass*, Berlin, 1923, 135.

7 Maurice Baumont, *L'Affaire Eulenburg et les origines de la guerre mondiale*, Paris, 1933, 16; Muschler, *Eulenburg*, 157; Philipp Fürst zu Eulenburg-Hertefels, *Ende König Ludwig II und andere Erlebnisse*, 2 vols, Leipzig, 1934, I, 100–11.

8 Muschler, *Eulenburg*, 162–3.

9 Ibid., 163.

10 Wilhelm II, *Aus meinem Leben*, 227.

11 Muschler, *Eulenburg*, 136; Wilhelm II, *Aus meinem Leben*, 228.

12 Muschler, *Eulenburg*, 168.

13 Herre, *Wilhelm II*, 64.

14 Wilhelm II, *Aus meinem Leben*, 233.

15 Ibid., 233.

16 Kohut, *Wilhelm II*, 74.

17 Waldersee, *Denkwürdigkeiten*, I, 222–3.

18 Ibid., I, 225, 231, 233.

19 Otto von Bismarck, *Gedanken und Erinnerungen*, Munich, n.d., 505.

20 Egon Caesar Conte Corti, *Leben und Liebe Alexanders von Battenberg*, 2nd edn, Graz, Salzburg, Vienna, 1950, 112, 130.

21 Corti, *Battenberg*, 7.

22 Ibid., 175.

23 Waldersee, *Denkwürdigkeiten*, I, 241.

24 Ponsonby, *Empress Frederick*, 202.

25 Corti, *Battenberg*, 176–7.

26 Ibid., 183; Wilhelm II, *Aus meinem Leben*, 317; Waldersee, *Denkwürdigkeiten*, I, 241; Cecil, *Prince and Emperor*, 69.

27 Kürenberg, *War alles falsch?*, 53–4.

28 Wilhelm II, *Ereignisse und Gestalten aus den Jahre 1878–1918*, Leipzig and Berlin, 1922, 12; Kürenberg, *War alles falsch?*, 58.

29 Waldersee, *Denkwürdigkeiten*, I, 236.

30 Kürenberg, *War alles falsch?*, 58.

31 Wilhelm II, *Aus meinem Leben*, 298; Waldersee, *Denkwürdigkeiten*, I, 238.

32 Johannes Lepsius, Albrecht Mendelssohn-Bartholdy and Friedrich Thimme, eds, *Die Grosse Politik der Europäischen Kabinette 1871–1914, Sammlung der Diplomatischen Akten des Auswärtigen Amtes* (hereafter *GP*); 40 vols, Berlin, 1922–7, III, 341; Waldersee, *Denkwürdigkeiten*, I, 238.

33 Corti, *Battenberg*, 185–6.

34 *GP*, III, 339; Corti, *Battenberg*, 186.

35 Waldersee, *Denkwürdigkeiten*, I, 238.

36 Corti, *Battenberg*, 187.

37 Ibid., 187–8.

Chapter Five: Duel to the Death

1 Kohut, *Wilhelm II*, 83. For the jealousy of his parents, see, for example, Waldersee, *Denkwürdigkeiten*, I, 242.

2 Herre, *Wilhelm II*, 38; Giles MacDonogh, *Frederick the Great*, 25–6; Hinzpeter, *Kaiser Wilhelm*, 13.

3 Wilhelm II, *Aus meinem Leben*, 211–12.

4 Cecil, *Prince and Emperor*, 63.

5 Wilhelm II, *Aus meinem Leben*, 216–17.

6 Waldersee, *Denkwürdigkeiten*, I, 239–40.

7 Ibid., I, 247.

8 Cecil, *Prince and Emperor*, 70; Kohut, *Wilhelm II*, 85.

9 Waldersee, *Denkwürdigkeiten*, I, 249.

10 Röhl, *Young Wilhelm*, 494.

11 Waldersee, *Denkwürdigkeiten*, I, 250.

12 Ibid., I, 255.

13 Ibid., I, 267.

14 Hinzpeter, *Kaiser Wilhelm*, 8.

15 Waldersee, *Denkwürdigkeiten*, I, 273.

16 Wilhelm II, *Aus meinem Leben*, 289.

17 Ibid., 307.

18 Ibid., 313.

19 Waldersee, *Denkwürdigkeiten*, I, 274.

20 Ibid., I, 280–1, 299.

21 Ibid., I, 292.

22 Ponsonby, *Empress Frederick*, 206.

23 *GP*, V, 55–6; Bismarck, *Gedanken und Erinnerungen*, 506; Kohut, *Wilhelm II*, 76; Kürenberg, *War alles falsch?*, 65; Corti, *Battenberg*, 305; Ponsonby, *Empress Frederick*, 207.

24 Baronin Spitzemberg, *Tagebuch*, 226.

25 Kürenberg, *War alles falsch?*, 64.

26 Herre, *Wilhelm II*, 58; Wilhelm II, *Aus meinem Leben*, 242.

27 Fischer, *Private Lives*, I, 95–6; Wilhelm II, *Aus meinem Leben*, 244.

28 Kürenberg, *War alles falsch?*, 55.

29 Wilhelm II, *Ereignisse und Gestalten*, 7; idem, *Aus meinem Leben*, 242.

30 Wilhelm II, *Ereignisse und Gestalten*, 3.

31 Wilhelm II, *Aus meinem Leben*, 244; idem, *Ereignisse und Gestalten*, 7.

32 Waldersee, *Denkwürdigkeiten*, I, 305–6.

33 Brigitte Hamann, *Rudolf*, 336–7.

34 Waldersee, *Denkwürdigkeiten*, I, 316, 321.

Chapter Six: Countdown

1 Michael Freund, *Das Drama der 99 Tage. Krankheit und Tod Friedrichs III*, Cologne and Berlin, 1966, 52; Sir Morell Mackenzie, *The Fatal Illness of Frederick the Noble*, London, 1888, 4, 40–1.

2 Freund, *99 Tage*, 48, 70–1.

3 Balfour, *Kaiser*, 109; Michaela Reid, *Ask Sir James: The Life of Sir James Reid, Personal Physician to Queen Victoria*, London, 1996, 88–9; Freund, *99 Tage*, 53–4; Mackenzie, *Fatal Illness*, 9.

4 Freund, *99 Tage*, 55, 57.

5 Friedrich Curtius ed., *Memoirs of Prince Chlodwig of Hohenlohe Schillingfuerst*, trans. George Chrystal, 2 vols, London, 1906, II, 371.

6 Freund, *99 Tage*, 78–9.

7 The case histories and their feeble survival rate are set out at the end of Mackenzie's apologia, *Fatal Illness*; Freund, *99 Tage*, 63–4, 66.

8 Freund, *99 Tage*, 97, 105–6, 111–13; Waldersee, *Denkwürdigkeiten*, I, 327; Mackenzie, *Fatal Illness*, 10, 12; Baronin Spitzemberg, *Tagebuch*, 230.

9 Waldersee, *Denkwürdigkeiten*, I, 328.

10 Freund, *99 Tage*, 65.

11 Ibid., 69.

12 Holstein thought so too. See Philipp Eulenburg, *Aus 50 Jahre. Erinnerungen, Tagebücher und Briefe*, ed. Johannes Haller, Berlin, 1923, 145.

13 Freund, *99 Tage*, 67; Herre, *Kaiser Friedrich*, 255; Michaela Reid, *Ask Sir James*, 89; Ponsonby, *Empress Frederick*, 234.

14 Freund, *99 Tage*, 46, 70.

15 Waldersee, *Denkwürdigkeiten*, I, 331.

16 Wilhelm II, *Aus meinem Leben*, 332.

17 Freund, *99 Tage*, 78.

18 Ibid., 49, 51, 77, 80.

19 Ponsonby, *Empress Frederick*, 215.

20 Wilhelm II, *Aus meinem Leben*, 219.

21 Ibid., 222; Bogdan Graf von Hutten-Czapski, *Sechzig Jahre Politik und Gesellschaft*, 2 vols, Berlin, 1936, I, 108–9; Georg Dehio, *Bezirke Berlin/DDR und Potsdam*, Munich and Berlin, 1983, 338.

22 Waldersee, *Denkwürdigkeiten*, I, 318.

23 Brigitte Hamann, *Rudolf*, 330.

24 Anon., *Recollections of Three Kaisers*, London, 1929, 98–9; Waldersee, *Denkwürdigkeiten*, I, 322.

25 Freund, *99 Tage*, 130.

26 Cecil, *Prince and Emperor*, 93.

27 Karl Rosner, ed., *Erinnerungen des Kronprinzen Wilhelm*, Stuttgart and Berlin, 1922 (hereafter Kronprinz Wilhelm, *Erinnerungen*), 31–2; Wilhelm II, *Aus meinem Leben*, 260.

28 Kohut, *Wilhelm II*, 90; Wilhelm II, *Aus meinem Leben*, 260–1.

29 Herre, *Kaiser Friedrich*, 249–50.

30 Freund, *99 Tage*, 136–7.

31 Ibid., 136, 139.

32 Ibid., 120. Beulah Hill had been a fashionable spa for some time, but its reputation was enhanced by the arrival of the Crystal Palace from South Kensington in 1854. See Ben Weinreb and Christopher Hibbert, eds, *The London Encyclopaedia*, London, 1995, 931–2; Ponsonby, *Empress Frederick*, 240. The papers have remained in Britain.

33 Freund, *99 Tage*, 128.

34 Ibid., 164, 166, 289.

35 Michaela Reid, *Ask Sir James*, 91.

36 Freund, *99 Tage*, 151; Reid, *Ask Sir James*, 92.

37 Eulenburg, *Erinnerungen*, 143.

38 Wilhelm II, *Aus meinem Leben*, 17.

39 Röhl, *Jugend*, 668.

40 Mackenzie, *Fatal Illness*, 55, 61; Kürenberg, *War alles falsch?*, 75; Dehio, *Berlin DDR/Potsdam*, 373; Freund, *99 Tage*, 204; Herre, *Kaiser Friedrich*, 229, 231.

41 Eulenburg, *Erinnerungen*, 136.

42 Corti, *Battenberg*, 365–7.

43 Ibid., 373.

44 Eulenburg, *Erinnerungen*, 137.

45 Ibid., 139. The *Political Testaments* were considered too 'hot' for public consumption. It was not until the Weimar Republic that they were offered for general consumption. See Giles MacDonogh, *Frederick the Great*, London, 1999, 235.

46 Eulenburg, *Erinnerungen*, 139. Was this just Eulenburg and the notoriously hard-headed Bismarck? William was renowned for his abstemiousness.

47 Baumont, *L'Affaire Eulenburg*, 25–6.

48 Cecil, *Prince and Emperor*, 101.

49 Röhl, *Young Wilhelm*, 485–7.

50 Ponsonby, *Empress Frederick*, 248; Kürenberg, *War alles falsch?*, 75; Wilhelm II, *Aus meinem Leben*, 11; Mackenzie, *Fatal Illness*, 63.

51 Kürenberg, *War alles falsch?*, 79.

52 Freund, *99 Tage*, 219; Mackenzie, *Fatal Illness*, 65.

53 Baronin Spitzemberg, *Tagebuch*, 234–5.

54 Waldersee, *Denkwürdigkeiten*, I, 322.

55 Mackenzie, *Fatal Illness*, 70; De Bonnefon, *Drame Impérial*, 11.

56 Mackenzie, *Fatal Illness*, 70; Kürenberg, *War alles falsch?*, 76; Freund, *99 Tage*, 116.

57 Waldersee, *Denkwürdigkeiten*, I, 333; Wilhelm II, *Aus meinem Leben*, 335; Kürenberg, *War alles falsch?*, 79.

58 Ponsonby, *Empress Frederick*, 256–7.

59 Wilhelm II, *Aus meinem Leben*, 389; Kürenberg, *War alles falsch?*, 80.

60 Freund, *99 Tage*, 246.

61 Ponsonby, *Empress Frederick*, 255; Waldersee, *Denkwürdigkeiten*, I, 332; Eulenburg, *Erinnerungen*, 147.

62 Eulenburg, *Erinnerungen*, 148.

63 Waldersee, *Denkwürdigkeiten*, I, 335, 338; Freund, *99 Tage*, 245.

64 Kürenberg, *War alles falsch?*, 72; Balfour, *Kaiser*, 113.

65 Waldersee, *Denkwürdigkeiten*, I, 335; Wilhelm II, *Aus meinem Leben*, 329; Kürenberg, *War alles falsch?*, 77.

66 Bismarck, *Gedanken und Erinnerungen*, 514.

67 Eulenburg, *Erinnerungen*, 149.

68 Bismarck, *Gedanken und Erinnerungen*, 515; Kürenberg, *War alles falsch?*, 78.

69 Mackenzie, *Fatal Illness*, 78–80.

70 Paul le Seur in *Adolf Stoecker, Erbe und Verpflichtung. Gedenkbuch zum 80. Jahresfest des Berliner Stadtmission*, Berlin, 1957, 12, and Otto Dibelius in ibid., 21.

71 Bishop Wurm, 'Adolf Stoeckers Kampf für Kirche und Volk', in *Adolf Stoecker*, 30; MacDonogh, *Prussia*, 347.

72 Quoted in Wurm, *Adolf Stoecker*, 32.

73 Wilhelm II, *Aus meinem Leben*, 341.

74 Bismarck, *Gedanken und Erinnerungen*, 508.

75 Waldersee, *Denkwürdigkeiten*, I, 339, 343; Freund, *99 Tage*, 251, 268, 272.

76 Bismarck, *Gedanken und Erinnerungen*, 517; Freund, *99 Tage*, 275, 280.

77 Adolf von Scholz, *Erlebnisse und Gespräche mit Bismarck*, Stuttgart and Berlin, 1922, 82; Lothar Gall, *Bismarck, the White Revolutionary*, trans. J. A. Underwood, 2 vols, London, 1986, II, 196.

78 Waldersee, *Denkwürdigkeiten*, I, 347; Eulenburg, *Erinnerungen*, 153, 157.

79 Waldersee, *Denkwürdigkeiten*, I, 352.

80 Bismarck, *Gedanken und Erinnerungen*, 522.

81 Eulenburg, *Erinnerungen*, 149–50.

82 Kohut, *Wilhelm II*, 87.

83 Freund, *99 Tage*, 264.

84 Ibid., 267, 293.

85 Waldersee, *Denkwürdigkeiten*, I, 336.

86 Eulenburg, *Erinnerungen*, 155; Kürenberg, *War alles falsch?*, 81.

87 Freund, *99 Tage*, 171, 173.

88 Herre, *Wilhelm II*, 69; Waldersee, *Denkwürdigkeiten*, I, 355.

89 Ibid., I, 358.

90 Kohut, *Wilhelm II*, 93.

91 Waldersee, *Denkwürdigkeiten*, I, 360; Freund, *99 Tage*, 318.

92 Mackenzie, *Fatal Illness*, 93.

93 Waldersee, *Denkwürdigkeiten*, I, 365.

94 Freund, *99 Tage*, 325.

95 Ponsonby, *Empress Frederick*, 279; Freund, *99 Tage*, 330.

96 Mackenzie, *Fatal Illness*, 121.

97 Friedrich Curtius, ed., *Memoirs of Hohenlohe*, trans. George W. Chrystal, London, 2 vols (hereafter Hohenlohe, *Memoirs*), II, 381; Bigelow, *Prussian Memories*, 70.

98 Freund, *99 Tage*, 174.

99 Waldersee, *Denkwürdigkeiten*, I, 365.

100 Theodor Fontane, *Briefe an seine Familie*, 2 vols, Berlin, 1905, II, 163.

101 Waldersee, *Denkwürdigkeiten*, I, 366; Freund, *99 Tage*, 326.

102 Freund, *99 Tage*, 330.

103 Corti, *Battenberg*, 388.

104 Marie von Bunsen, *Kaiserin Augusta*, Berlin, 1940, 264.

105 Waldersee, *Denkwürdigkeiten*, I, 366–7; Kürenberg, *War alles falsch?*, 82.

106 Baronin Spitzemberg, *Tagebuch*, 242–3.

107 Waldersee, *Denkwürdigkeiten*, I, 368–9.

108 Eulenburg, *Erinnerungen*, 161–2; Freund, *99 Tage*, 343.

Chapter Seven: Ninety-Nine Days

1 Waldersee, *Denkwürdigkeiten*, I, 370; Kürenberg, *War alles falsch?*, 83.

2 Fontane, *Briefe*, II, 162.

3 Waldersee, *Denkwürdigkeiten*, I, 370; Eulenburg, *Erinnerungen*, 164; Cecil, *Prince and Emperor*, 113.

4 Fontane, *Briefe*, 165.

5 Eulenburg, *Erinnerungen*, 164–5.

6 Mackenzie, *Fatal Illness*, 134; Herre, *Wilhelm II*, 70; Fontane, *Briefe*, II, 173; Ponsonby, *Empress Frederick*, 281.

7 Baronin Spitzemberg, *Tagebuch*, 245; Eulenburg, *Erinnerungen*, 166; Waldersee, *Denkwürdigkeiten*, I, 375.

8 Baronin Spitzemberg, *Tagebuch*, 245.

9 Bismarck, *Gedanken und Erinnerungen*, 498; Cecil, *Prince and Emperor*, 110.

10 Waldersee, *Denkwürdigkeiten*, I, 371, 377.

11 Kürenberg, *War alles falsch?*, 84.

12 Waldersee, *Denkwürdigkeiten*, I, 373; Fontane, *Briefe*, II, 168.

13 Ludwig, *Wilhelm der Zweite*, 41.

14 Kürenberg, *War alles falsch?*, 86.

15 Herre, *Kaiser Friedrich*, 238, 282, 299, 302.

16 Freund, *99 Tage*, 9.

17 Hohenlohe, *Memoirs*, 382.

18 Freund, *99 Tage*, 24; Herre, *Kaiser Friedrich*, 303.

19 Corti, *Battenberg*, 389.

20 Ibid., 390–1.

21 Ibid., 398–9.

22 Freund, *99 Tage*, 30, 369.

23 Balfour, *Kaiser*, 117.

24 Freund, *99 Tage*, 356.

25 Corti, *Battenberg*, 393–5.

26 Baronin Spitzemberg, *Tagebuch*, 249.

27 Ibid., 248–9.

28 I.e. a 'tender relationship', Ponsonby, *Empress Frederick*, 299.

29 *GP*, VI, 301–7.

30 Hohenlohe, *Memoirs*, II, 383.

31 Herre, *Kaiser Friedrich*, 226.

32 Freund, *99 Tage*, 173; Herre, *Kaiser Friedrich*, 286.

33 Herre, *Wilhelm II*, 73; Waldersee, *Denkwürdigkeiten*, I, 392.

34 Freund, *99 Tage*, 372–3; Baronin Spitzemberg, *Tagebuch*, 249; Ponsonby, *Empress Frederick*, 304.

35 Waldersee, *Denkwürdigkeiten*, I, 380; Reid, *Ask Sir James*, 95; Wilhelm II, *Aus meinem Leben*, 351.

36 Kürenberg, *War alles falsch?*, 86.

37 Waldersee, *Denkwürdigkeiten*, I, 392.

38 Ibid., I, 394, 401.

39 Ibid., I, 402.

40 Hohenlohe, *Memoirs*, II, 387; Wilhelm II, *Aus meinem Leben*, 353; Waldersee, *Denkwürdigkeiten*, I, 400.

41 G. S. Viereck, *The Kaiser on Trial*, London 1938, 57.

42 Wilhelm II, *Ereignisse und Gestalten*, 18.

43 Viereck, *Kaiser on Trial*, 63–4.

44 Waldersee, *Denkwürdigkeiten*, I, 380, 403; Eulenburg, *Erinnerungen*, 167–68.

45 Hohenlohe, *Memoirs*, II, 388.

46 Wilhelm II, *Ereignisse und Gestalten*, 18.

47 Mackenzie, *Fatal Illness*, 137–8.

48 Cecil, *Prince and Emperor*, 122.

49 Freund, *99 Tage*, 40.

50 Waldersee, *Denkwürdigkeiten*, I, 404.

51 Freund, *99 Tage*, 391.

Chapter Eight: The Struggle with the Bismarcks

1 Hohenlohe, *Memoirs*, II, 409.

2 Anon., *The Real Kaiser*, London, 1914, 60–1. There were reports in the British press in December 1999 that the 'Es ist erreicht' moustache was making a comeback among young Germans.

3 Interview with Friedrich Wilhelm Fürst von Hohenzollern, Sigmaringen, 14 May 1996. The prince had met his – very distant – cousin as a small boy in Doorn.

4 Fischer, *Private Lives*, 63.

5 Ibid., I, 40.

6 Arthur Brehmer, ed., *Am Hofe Kaiser Wilhelm II*, Berlin, 1898, 139.

7 Brehmer, ed., *Am Hofe*, 63, gives a series of photographs of the empress.

8 Kürenberg, *War alles falsch?*, 118; Daisy Princess of Pless, *What I Have Left Unsaid*, edited with an introduction by Major Desmond Chapman-Huston, London, 1936, 5; Moltke, *Erinnerungen*, 148.

9 Alfred Kerr, *Wo liegt Berlin? Briefe aus der Reichshauptstadt 1895–1900*, ed. Günther Rühle, Berlin, 1997, 22, 38.

10 Fischer, *Private Lives*, 41.

11 Kürenberg, *War alles falsch?*, 98.

12 Ibid., 99.

13 Cecil, *Prince and Emperor*, 127; Isobel Hull, *The Entourage of Kaiser Wilhelm II, 1888–1918*, Cambridge, 1982, 29.

14 Gordon Craig, *The Politics of the Prussian Army 1640–1945*, New York, 1964, 240. William favoured certain estates such as Robert Weil's in the Rheingau where he also possessed the excellent state domain. Information from Ernst Loosen of Bernkastel.

15 Hull, *Entourage*, 184.

16 Walter Görlitz, ed., *Der Kaiser. Aufzeichnungen des Chefs des Marinekabinetts Admiral von Müller über die Ära Wilhelms II*, Göttingen, Berlin, Frankfurt-am-Main, Zurich, 1965, 29.

17 Hull, *Entourage*, 33.

18 K. Lammerting, 'Iduna en Meteor', in Boven, ed., *Unsere Zukunft liegt auf dem Wasser*, 46–57.

19 Hull, *Entourage*, 40.

20 K. F. Nowak and Friedrich Thimme, eds, *Erinnerungen und Gedanken des Botschafters Anton Graf Monts*, Berlin, 1932, 143–4.

21 Alfred Niemann, *Wanderungen mit Kaiser Wilhelm II*, 2nd edn, Leipzig, 1924, 17–18.

22 Kohut, *Wilhelm II*, 103; Isobel Hull, 'Der kaiserliche Hof als Herrschafts-instrument', in Hans Wilderotter and Klaus Pohl eds, *Der letzte Kaiser, Wilhelm II. im Exil*, Berlin, 1991, 26–7.

23 Kohut, *William II*, 137.

24 Muschler, *Eulenburg*, 213.

25 Eulenburg, *Erlebnisse*, II, 322; idem, *Nachlass; mit dem Kaiser als Staatsmann und Freund auf Nordlandsreisen*, 2 vols, Dresden, 1931, 198.

26 Isobel Hull, *Entourage*, 80; Muschler, *Eulenburg*, 222, 223.

27 Muschler, *Eulenburg*, 213.

28 Ibid., 214–15.

29 Baumont, *L'Affaire Eulenburg*, 28.

30 Ibid., 70.

31 Ibid., 69.

32 Norbert Muhlen, *L'Incroyable famille Krupp*, Paris, 1961, 94, 96.

33 Isobel Hull, *Entourage*, 159.

34 Ibid., 168.

35 Brehmer, ed., *Am Hofe*, 570–1; Bismarck, *Gedanken und Erinnerungen*, 542; Ponsonby, *Empress Frederick*, 405; Graf Douglas, *Was wir von unserem Kaiser hoffen dürfen*, 4th Ed, 1888, see pp 9, 13, for some of Douglas's worst excesses; Cecil, *Prince and Emperor*, 134.

36 Kürenberg, *War alles falsch?*, 88.

37 Mackenzie, *Fatal Illness*, 180–3.

38 Waldersee, *Denkwürdigkeiten*, I, 407.

39 Eulenburg, *Nachlass*, 169.

40 Gall, *Bismarck*, 199. Gall also expresses doubt as to the possibility of a liberal course under Fritz.

41 Moltke, *Erinnerungen*, 139; Eulenburg, *Nachlass*, 170.

42 Kohut, *Wilhelm II*, 114.

43 Kohut, *Wilhelm II*, 118; in Marie von Bunsen, *Die Welt in der ich lebte*, 165, William delivers similar lines to Ambassador Lascelles – 'Wir sind uns ja so ähnlich, und das ist eine grosse Erschwerung.'

44 Marie von Bunsen, *Die Welt*, 165, 175.

45 Viereck, *Kaiser on Trial*, 58.

46 Ponsonby, *Empress Frederick*, 324.

47 Wilhelm II, *Ereignisse und Gestalten*, 21; Niemann, *Wanderungen*, 48.

48 Niemann, *Wanderungen*, 19.

49 Cecil, *Prince and Emperor*, 144; Bigelow, *Prussian Memories*, 47.

50 Baumont, *L'Affaire Eulenburg*, 46; Wickham Steed, in the introduction to Joachim von Kürenberg, *His Excellency the Spectre. The Life of Fritz von Holstein*, trans. E. O. Lorimer, with an introduction by Wickham Steed, London, 1933, xix.

51 Wolfgang Windelband, ed., *Johanna von Bismarcks Briefe, an ihren Sohn Wilhelm und ihre Schwägerin Malwine von Arnim-Kröchlendorff, geb. von Bismarck*, Berlin, 1924 (hereafter Johanna von Bismarck, *Briefe*), 76.

52 Friedrich Everling, ed., *Kaiserworte*, Berlin, 1917, 186; Karl Friedrich Nowak, *Das dritte deutsche Kaiserreich*, 2 vols, Berlin, 1929, 35. It should be recalled that Nowak was acting as William's literary ghost at the time of publication.

53 Moltke, *Erinnerungen*, 141, 142.

54 Hohenlohe, *Memoirs*, II, 390–1.

55 Kürenberg, *War alles falsch?*, 91; Moltke, *Erinnerungen*, 143, 145, 146.

56 Everling, ed., *Kaiserworte*, 167.

57 Cecil, *Prince and Emperor*, 133.

58 Nowak, *Kaiserreich*, I, 50; Everling, ed., *Kaiserworte*, 66.

59 This was done when William was still crown prince. See Brehmer, ed., *Am Hofe*, 66.

60 Hohenlohe, *Memoirs*, II, 390–1.

61 Ibid., II, 395.

62 Waldersee, *Denkwürdigkeiten*, II, 1.

63 Brigitte Hamann, *Rudolf*, 361.

64 *GP*, VI, 310–11.

65 *GP*, VI, 320–30.

66 Brehmer, ed., *Am Hofe*, 171–2.

67 Nowak, *Kaiserreich*, I, 44; Wilhelm II, *Vergleichende Geschichtstabellen von 1878 bis zum Kriegsausbruch 1914*, Leipzig, 1921, 10–11.

68 Kürenberg, *War alles falsch?*, 195.

69 *GP*, VI, 340.

70 Simon Heffer, *Power and Place. The Political Consequences of King Edward VII*, London 1998, 70; *GP*, VI, 331n.

71 Cecil, *Prince and Emperor*, 128.

72 Waldersee, *Denkwürdigkeiten*, II, 5, 7; Niemann, *Wanderungen*, 23–5.

73 Henry Lucy ed., *The Emperor's Diary of the Austro-German War 1866 and the Franco-German War 1870–1871. To which is added Prince Bismarck's Rejoinder*, 7, 8, 17–18, 19, 127, 136, 139; Johanna von Bismarck, *Briefe*, 78.

74 She had claimed her 'voice would be silent for ever!' Ponsonby, *Empress Frederick*, 320.

75 Benson, *English Relations*, 68; Lucy, ed., *Emperor's Diary*, 62.

76 See Rennell Rodd, *Frederick, Crown Prince and Emperor*, with an introduction by the Empress Frederick, London 1888.

77 Brigitte Hamann, *Rudolf*, 348–9, 353.

78 Ibid., 362.

79 *GP*, VI, 347.

80 Brigitte Hamann, *Rudolf*, 363.

81 Ibid., 366.

82 Fontane, *Briefe*, II, 189, 191; Baronin von Spitzemberg, *Tagebuch*, 254; Johanna von Bismarck, *Briefe*, 78; Nowak, *Kaiserreich*, I, 68; Cecil, *Prince and Emperor*, 129; Herre, *Wilhelm*, 90–1.

83 Moltke, *Erinnerungen*, 149.

84 Eulenburg, *Nachlass*, 202.

85 Ibid., 202–3.

86 Waldersee, *Denkwürdigkeiten*, II, 19.

87 Ibid., II, 21.

88 Everling, ed., *Kaiserworte*, 169.

89 Waldersee, *Denkwürdigkeiten*, II, 23, 25.

90 Hohenlohe, *Memoirs*, II, 398; Waldersee, *Denkwürdigkeiten*, II, 27.

91 Kürenberg, *War alles falsch?*, 237; Bled, *Franz Joseph*, 249.

92 See Hinzpeter, *Skizze*, 12.

93 Niemann, *Wanderungen*, 20–2; Gall, *Bismarck*, 202–3; J. C. G. Röhl, *Germany without Bismarck. The Crisis of Government in the Second Reich*, London, 1967, 36.

94 Niemann, *Wanderungen*, 66.

95 Wilhelm II, *Ereignisse und Gestalten*, 30, 32; Kürenberg, *War alles falsch?*, 92.

96 Kürenberg, *War alles falsch?*, 93.

97 Eleanor Tuck, 'Thwarting the Imperial Will: A Perspective on the Labour Regulation Bill and the Press in the Wilhelminian Empire', in Jack Dukes and Joachim Remak, eds, *Another Germany: A Reconstruction of the Imperial Era*, Boulder and London, 1988, 116.

98 Muschler, *Eulenburg*, 225.

99 Röhl, *Germany without Bismarck*, 35–6.

100 Wilhelm II, *Ereignisse und Gestalten*, 33; Muschler, *Eulenburg*, 227–8.

101 Wilhelm II, *Ereignisse und Gestalten*, 32.

102 Waldersee, *Denkwürdigkeiten*, II, 55.

103 Ibid., II, 56.

104 Ibid., II, 36.

105 Ibid., II, 40.

106 E. S. P. Blom and N. Wassenaar, 'Van driedekker tot Dreadnought, geschiednis van de Duitse vloot 1675–1919', in Boven, ed., *Unsere Zukunft liegt auf dem Wasser*, 21.

107 Röhl, *Germany without Bismarck*, 33.

108 Eulenburg, *Nordlandsreisen*, I, 38.

109 Marie von Bunsen, *Die Welt*, 190.

110 Eulenburg, *Nordlandsreisen*, I, 50–1.

111 Ibid., I, 55.

112 *GP*, IV, 405–9; Cecil, *Prince and Emperor*, 271; Heffer, *Power and Place*, 71–72.

113 Cecil, *Prince and Emperor*, 131.

114 Brigitte Hamann, *Rudolf*, 439.

115 Hohenlohe, *Memoirs*, II, 406.

116 Ibid., II, 407.

117 Eulenburg, *Nachlass*, 219.

118 Mark Kerr, *Land, Sea and Air. Reminiscences*, London, 1927, 61–4.

119 Bigelow, *Prussian Memories*, 173.

120 Philip Mansel, *Constantinople, City of the World's Desire 1453–1924*, London, 1995, 339.

121 Cecil, *Prince and Emperor*, 138–9.

122 Eulenburg, *Nachlass*, 205.

123 Ibid., 221–2.

124 Ibid., 225.

125 Waldersee, *Denkwürdigkeiten*, II, 76–7.

126 Ibid., II, 80; Fischer, *Private Lives*, I, 103, 106–7.

127 Gall, *Bismarck*, 204.

128 Baronin von Spitzemberg, *Tagebuch*, 264; Johanna von Bismarck, *Briefe*, 79, makes it clear that Bismarck knew that it was wrong to be away for so much of the time as early as 15 October 1888.

129 Eulenburg, *Nachlass*, 224; Hohenlohe, *Memoirs*, II, 408.

130 Kürenberg, *War alles falsch?*, 182.

131 Ibid., 183.

132 Cecil, *Prince and Emperor*, 147.

133 Waldersee, *Denkwürdigkeiten*, II, 95.

134 Johanna von Bismarck, *Briefe*, 82.

135 Waldersee, *Denkwürdigkeiten*, II, 96.

136 Gall, *Bismarck*, 206–7; Eulenburg, *Nachlass*, 228.

137 Cecil, *Prince and Emperor*, 154.

138 Baronin von Spitzemberg, *Tagebuch*, 192; Röhl, *Germany without Bismarck*, 37, 41–2.

139 Röhl, *Germany without Bismarck*, 43.

140 Waldersee, *Denkwürdigkeiten*, II, 102, note a; Röhl, *Germany without Bismarck*, 39.

141 Eulenburg, *Nachlass*, 230.

142 Waldersee, *Denkwürdigkeiten*, II, 103.

143 Ibid., II, 103–4.

144 Gall, *Bismarck*, 211.

145 *GP*, VI, 362–5; Gall, *Bismarck*, 214.

146 *GP*, VI, 371n.

147 Baronin von Spitzemberg, *Tagebuch*, 270; Bismarck, *Gedanken und Erinnerungen*, 562.

148 Hugo Graf Lerchenfeld, *Erinnerungen und Denkwurdigkeiten*, 2nd edn, Berlin, 1935, 362; Kürenberg, *War alles falsch?*, 104–5.

149 Ibid., 102–3.

150 Eulenburg, *Nachlass*, 230.

151 Kürenberg, *War alles falsch?*, 105.

152 Waldersee, *Denkwürdigkeiten*, II, 114.

153 Kürenberg, *War alles falsch?*, 95.

154 Waldersee, *Denkwürdigkeiten*, II, 115–16.

155 Baumont, *L'Affaire Eulenburg*, 47; Eulenburg, *Nachlass*, 236–7.

156 Baronin von Spitzemberg, *Tagebuch*, 270.

157 Ibid., 271–2.

158 Baronin von Spitzemberg, *Tagebuch*, 292–3. Hildegard von Spitzemberg had heard the story directly from Caprivi.

159 Eulenburg, *Nachlass*, 238; Waldersee, *Denkwürdigkeiten*, II, 118; Kürenberg, *War alles falsch?*, 109; Johanna von Bismarck, *Briefe*, 84–5.

160 Bismarck, *Gedanken und Erinnerungen*, 577.

161 Viereck, *Kaiser on Trial*, 86; Kürenberg, *War alles falsch?*, 107–8; Baronin von Spitzemberg, *Tagebuch*, 275; Bismarck, *Gedanken und Erinnerungen*, 581.

162 Friedrich Wendel, *Wilhelm II in der Karikatur*, Dresden, 1928, 16–17, 34, 40.

163 Hohenlohe, *Memoirs*, II, 409.

164 Kürenberg, *War alles falsch?*, 109.

165 Wilhelm II, *Ereignisse und Gestalten*, 15–16.

Chapter Nine: The Liberal Empire

1 Wilhelm II, *Ereignisse und Gestalten*, 43; Baronin von Spitzemberg, *Tagebuch*, 271.

2 Baronin von Spitzemberg, *Tagebuch*, 272.

3 Ibid., 272; Wilhelm II, *Ereignisse und Gestalten*, 45; Lerchenfeld, *Erinnerungen und Denkwürdigkeiten*, 351.

4 Wilhelm II, *Ereignisse und Gestalten*, 46; Röhl, *Germany without Bismarck*, 60.

5 Röhl, *Germany without Bismarck*, 66, 70–1.

6 Baumont, *L'Affaire Eulenburg*, 45; Muschler, *Eulenburg*, 230.

7 Röhl, *Germany without Bismarck*, 59.

8 Isobel Hull, *Entourage*, 88–9.

9 *GP*, VII, 3–4, 10; Georg Freiherr von Eppstein, *Fürst Bismarcks Entlassung*, Berlin, 1920, 65.

10 *GP.*, VII, 16, 20.

11 Hohenlohe, *Memoirs*, II, 410.

12 Waldersee, *Denkwürdigkeiten*, II, 120–1.

13 Everling, ed., *Kaiserworte*, 12–13.

14 Ibid., 36.

15 Eulenburg, *Nachlass*, 190; Waldersee, *Denkwürdigkeiten*, II, 104.

16 Waldersee, *Denkwürdigkeiten*, II, 125.

17 Ibid., II, 127.

18 Alfred von Tirpitz, *Erinnerungen*, Leipzig, 1919, 11.

19 Ibid., 28; Cecil, *Prince and Emperor*, 277.

20 Eulenburg, *Nordlandsreisen*, I, 76.

21 Ibid., I, 105.

22 Ibid., I, 111; Hull, *Entourage*, 69.

23 Kürenberg, *War alles falsch?*, 200–2; Benson, *English Relations*, 106–7; Ludwig, *Wilhelm*, 105.

24 Eulenburg, *Nordlandsreisen*, I, 108.

25 Waldersee, *Denkwürdigkeiten*, II, 138.

26 Ibid., II, 139.

27 Everling, ed., *Kaiserworte*, 298–30; Lindemann, *Deutsche Helgoland*, 42, 181.

28 Hohenlohe, *Memoirs*, II, 417; Tirpitz, *Erinnerungen*, 59; Kürenberg, *War alles falsch?*, 122–3; Manfred Sell, *Das deutsch-englische Abkommen von 1890 über Helgoland und die afrikanischen Kolonien im Lichten der deutschen Presse*, Berlin and Bonn, 1926, Vorwort, 35.

29 Sell, *Deutsch-englische Abkommen*, 36.

30 Wilhelm II, *Geschichtstabellen*, 13.

31 Cecil, *Prince and Emperor*, 130–1.

32 Waldersee, *Denkwürdigkeiten*, II, 145–6; Marie von Bunsen, *Die Welt*, 190.

33 Waldersee, *Denkwürdigkeiten*, II, 148.

34 Ponsonby, *Empress Frederick*, 427–8; Kürenberg, *War alles falsch?*, 160; Baronin von Spitzemberg, *Tagebuch*, 296; Hans-Michael Körner, 'Na warte Wittelsbach!', in Wilderotter und Pohl, *Der letzte Kaiser*, 37.

35 Waldersee, *Denkwürdigkeiten*, II, 152–3.

36 Ibid., II, 153.

37 Ibid., II, 153, 156–7.

38 Kerr, *Briefe*, 675n.

39 Balfour, *Kaiser*, 125; Waldersee, *Denkwürdigkeiten*, II, 167.

40 Everling, ed., *Kaiserworte*, 34, 160.

41 Baronin von Spitzemberg, *Tagebuch*, 284; Waldersee, *Denkwürdigkeiten*, II, 179.

42 Cecil, *Prince and Emperor*, 176.

43 Ibid., 130.

44 Ponsonby, *Empress Frederick*, 423–4; William II, *Geschichtstabellen*, 14.

45 Anon., *Recollections of Three Kaisers*, London, 1929, 127–8.

46 Everling, ed., *Kaiserworte*, 15.

47 Tirpitz, *Erinnerungen*, 40.

48 Görlitz, *Kaiser*, 31–2.

49 Baronin von Spitzemberg, *Tagebuch*, 288–9.

50 Ibid., 295.

51 Everling, ed., *Kaiserworte*, 187; Röhl, *Germany without Bismarck*, 73–4; Kürenberg, *War alles falsch?*, 161.

52 Eulenburg, *Nordlandsreisen*, I, 142, 146.

53 Ibid., I, 149; Röhl, *Germany without Bismarck*, 74–5.

54 Eulenburg, *Nordlandsreisen*, I, 162.

55 Isobel Hull, *Entourage*, 68.

56 Eulenburg, *Nordlandsreisen*, I, 188.

57 Röhl, *Germany without Bismarck*, 72.

58 Wilhelm II, *Geschichtstabellen*, 15.

59 *GP*, VII, 215.

60 Waldersee, *Denkwürdigkeiten*, II, 216.

61 Ibid., II, 228.

62 Görlitz, *Kaiser*, 36.

63 Ibid., 51.

64 Moltke, *Erinnerungen*, 161.

65 Waldersee, *Denkwürdigkeiten*, II, 230; Peter Marsh, *Bargaining on Europe, Britain and the First Common Market 1860–1892*, Newhaven and London, 1999, 182–3, 192–3.

66 Waldersee, *Denkwürdigkeiten*, II, 235.

67 Everling, ed., *Kaiserworte*, 23.

68 Baronin von Spitzemberg, *Tagebuch*, 296–7.

69 Tirpitz, *Erinnerungen*, 50.

70 Ibid., 51.

71 Waldersee, *Denkwürdigkeiten*, II, 233–9 n. 2; Everling, ed., *Kaiserworte*, 41; Baronin von Spitzemberg, *Tagebuch*, 296.

72 Waldersee, *Denkwürdigkeiten*, II, 237.

73 Hohenlohe, *Memoirs*, II, 430.

74 Waldersee, *Denkwürdigkeiten*, II, 237.

75 Ibid., II, 247 n. 3; Kürenberg, *War alles falsch?*, 119.

76 Gall, *Bismarck*, 222; Baronin von Spitzemberg, *Tagebuch*, 302.

77 Baumont, *L'Affaire Eulenburg*, 33.

78 Eulenburg, *Nordlandsreisen*, I, 212.

79 Waldersee, *Denkwürdigkeiten*, II, 266.

80 Fischer, *Private Lives*, II, 355, 358.

81 Ibid., II, 362, 367.

82 Ibid., II, 366.

83 Ibid., II, 371.

84 Ibid., II, 381.

85 Ibid., II, 387–8.

86 Ibid., II, 402–6; Ludwig, *Wilhelm der Zweite*, 100–1.

87 Waldersee, *Denkwürdigkeiten*, II, 269.

88 Fischer, *Private Lives*, I, 231.

89 *GP*, VII, 412, 416.

90 Waldersee, *Denkwürdigkeiten*, II, 274.

91 Baumont, *L'Affaire Eulenburg*, 35–6; Hohenlohe, *Memoirs*, II, 443, 440.

92 Röhl, *Germany without Bismarck*, 104, 106.

93 Waldersee, *Denkwürdigkeiten*, II, 287.

94 Baronin von Spitzemberg, *Tagebuch*, 312.

95 It is illustrated in Brehmer, ed., *Am Hofe*, 163.

96 Isobel Hull, *Entourage* 40; Eulenburg, *Nordlandsreise*, I, 259–60.

97 Eulenburg, *Erlebnisse*, I, 215–16.

98 Ibid., II, 219.

99 Ibid., I, 244.

100 Everling, ed., *Kaiserworte*, 65.

101 Baumont, *L'Affaire Eulenburg*, 53.

102 *Kladderadatsch*, no. 52; Baumont, *L'Affaire Eulenburg*, 53–4; Röhl, *Germany without Bismarck*, 108.

103 Waldersee, *Denkwürdigkeiten*, II, 300.

104 Ibid., II, 303.

105 Ibid., II, 305; Baronin von Spitzemberg, *Tagebuch*, 319–20.

106 Isobel Hull, *Entourage*, 79; see also Waldersee, *Denkwürdigkeiten*, II, 310–11.

107 Kürenberg, *War alles falsch?*, 120.

108 Goldbeeren Auslese denoted an immensely sweet wine made from healthy grapes which have turned to raisins. I am grateful to David Molyneux-Berry MW for explaining this to me. The term was suppressed with the 1971 Wine Law.

109 Johanna von Bismarck, *Briefe*, 91.

110 Baumont, *L'Affaire Eulenburg*, 50; Nicolaus Sombart, *Wilhelm II*, 184, 186; Cecil, *Prince and Emperor*, 223.

111 Marie von Bunsen, *Die Welt*, 137; Baronin von Spitzemberg, *Tagebuch*, 320–1.

112 Moltke, *Erinnerungen*, 165–9.

113 Ibid., 169–70.

114 Ibid., 170–2.

115 Baronin von Spitzemberg, *Tagebuch*, 322.

116 Moltke, *Erinnerungen*, 173.

117 Ibid., 174.

118 Ibid., 175.

119 Kürenberg, *War alles falsch?*, 121.

120 Moltke, *Erinerrungen*, 176.

121 Ibid., 174; Hohenlohe, *Memoirs*, II, 452; Baronin von Spitzemberg, *Tagebuch*, 321.

122 Waldersee, *Denkwürdigkeiten*, II, 306; Cecil, *Prince and Emperor*, 193.

123 Ibid., II, 307.

124 Kürenberg, *War alles falsch?*, 233.

125 Everling, ed., *Kaiserworte*, 14.

126 Cecil, *Prince and Emperor*, 178; Brehmer, ed., *Am Hofe*, 260.

127 Eulenburg, *Erlebnisse*, II, 22, 29.

128 Ludwig Quidde, *Caligula. Eine Studie über römischen Cäsarenwahnsinn*, 25th edn, Leipzig, n.d., 3; see also the spoof *Das Vermächtnis des Tacitus von Caligula Quitte*, Leipzig, 1896.

129 Quidde, *Caligula*, 6.

130 Ibid., 9, 10, 11, 15.

131 Waldersee, *Denkwürdigkeiten*, II, 313.

132 Herre, *Wilhelm*, 97.

133 Kerr, *Briefe*, 445, 722n; Fischer, *Private Lives*, II, 444–9.

134 Eleanor Turk in Dukes and Remak, eds, *Another Germany*, 118–19, 121; Kerr, *Briefe*, 497.

135 Ludwig Fulda, *Der Talisman. Dramatisches Märchen in vier Aufzügen*, 3rd edn, Stuttgart, 1893, III, 8.

136 Waldersee, *Denkwürdigkeiten*, II, 316.

137 Everling, ed., *Kaiserworte*, 34, 168; Waldersee, *Denkwürdigkeiten*, II, 320, 322; Fischer, *Private Lives*, I, 132.

138 Everling, ed., *Kaiserworte*, 136.

139 Baumont, *L'Affaire Eulenburg*, 51.

140 Cecil, *Prince and Emperor*, 206; Röhl, *Germany without Bismarck*, 114–17.

141 Ludwig, *Wilhelm der Zweite*, 97.

142 *GP*, V, 336–7.

143 Werner Kautzsch, *Hofgeschichten aus der Regierungszeit Kaiser Wilhelms II*, Berlin, 1925, 90.

144 [Wilhelm II], *Sang an Ägir, Dichtung von S. M. dem deutschen Kaiser, König von Preussen*, erläutert von P. Tesch, Berlin, Leipzig, Neuwied, n.d.

145 Ernst von Wildenbruch, *Willehalm. Dramatische Legende*, Berlin, 1897, viertes Bild.

146 Brehmer, ed., *Am Hofe*, 358.

147 Ibid., 361; Alfred Kerr, *Wo liegt Berlin?*, 20.

148 Fischer, *Private Lives*, I, 128–31; II, 460–3; Balfour, *Kaiser*, 143; Röhl, *Germany without Bismarck*, 131.

149 Baronin von Spitzemberg, *Tagebuch*, 327.

Chapter Ten: Uncle Chlodwig

1 Cecil, *Prince and Emperor*, 213.

2 Kürenberg, *War alles falsch?*, 153.

3 Röhl, *Germany without Bismarck*, 118.

4 Baronin von Spitzemberg, *Tagebuch*, 327.

5 Brehmer, ed., *Am Hofe*, 567.

6 Norman Rich, *Friedrich von Holstein, Politics and Diplomacy in the Era of Bismarck and William II*, 2 vols, Cambridge, 1965, II, 487–8, quoted in MacDonogh, *Prussia*, 78–9; see also Röhl, *Germany without Bismarck*, 127.

7 Michael Cullen, *Der Reichstag, Die Geschichte eines Monumentes*, Stuttgart, 1990, 200–1.

8 MacDonogh, *Berlin*, 125–6.

9 Cullen, *Reichstag*, 219, 228.

10 Ibid., 235–6, 241, 246.

11 Baronin von Spitzemberg, *Tagebuch*, 332.

12 Hohenlohe, *Memoirs*, II, 462.

13 Röhl, *Germany without Bismarck*, 137–8.

14 N. F. Grant, ed., *The Kaiser's Letters to the Tsar. Copied from Government Archives in Petrograd and brought from Russia by Isaac Don Levine*, London, n.d. [1920], 8.

15 Baumont, *L'Affaire Eulenburg*, 66.

16 Kürenberg, *War alles falsch?*, 121–2.

17 Tirpitz, *Erinnerungen*, 94.

18 MacDonogh, *Berlin*, 284.

19 Sombart, *Wilhelm II*, 152.

20 Bernhard Huldermann, *Albert Ballin*, 5th edn, Oldenburg and Berlin, 1922, 209.

21 Ibid., 277–9.

22 Timothy Shaw, *The World of Escoffier*, London, 1994, 58–59; Fondation Auguste-Escoffier, *Auguste Escoffier, Un des grands maîtres de la cuisine française*, Villeneuve-Loubet, n.d., 26.

23 Grant, ed., *Letters to the Tsar*, 10–11.

24 Ibid., 13, 18–19.

25 Ibid., 20–2.

26 Eulenburg, *Nordlandsreise*, I, 338.

27 *GP*, X, 20–5, 27; see also the highly unsympathetic account in Andrew Roberts, *Salisbury, Victorian Titan*, London, 1999, 612–14.

28 Benson, *English Relations*, 109.

29 Waldersee, *Denkwürdigkeiten*, II, 356–7.

30 Captain Lionel Dawson RN, *Lonsdale. The Authorised Life of Hugh Lowther, 5th Earl of Lonsdale, K.G., G.C.V.O.*, London, 1946, 153, 156; Douglas Sutherland, *The Yellow Earl. The Life of Hugh Lowther, 5th Earl of Lonsdale, K.G., G.C.V.O. 1857–1944*, London, 1965, 115.

31 Dawson, *Lonsdale*, 156, 162; Sutherland, *Yellow Earl*, vii.

32 Sutherland, *Yellow Earl*, 115.

33 Ibid., 116.

34 Dawson, *Lonsdale*, 158; Sutherland, *Yellow Earl*, 116.

35 Sutherland, *Yellow Earl*, 117.

36 Dawson, *Lonsdale*, 159–60; Sutherland, *Yellow Earl*, 118.

37 Dawson, *Lonsdale*, 161; Sutherland, *Yellow Earl*, 118; Baronin von Spitzemberg, *Tagebuch*, 386. The bust remained in the castle until after the Second World War, when it came under the hammer at one of the auctions which parcelled out the estate: letter from the earl of Lonsdale to the author, 24 September 1999.

38 Röhl, *Germany without Bismarck*, 142–3; Craig, *Politics*, 247.

39 Cecil, *Prince and Emperor*, 200–1; Görlitz, *Kaiser*, 43, 47.

40 Fischer, *Private Lives*, II, 471–2; Sutherland, *Yellow Earl*, 116–17.

41 Sutherland, *Yellow Earl*, 120.

42 Grant, ed., *Letters to the Tsar*, 24, 25, 26, 27, 28.

43 Robert Hoeniger, *Das Deutschtum im Ausland*, Leipzig and Berlin, 1913, 93–5.

44 *GP*, XI, 3–4, 6.

45 Ibid., XI, 9–10.

46 Ibid., XI, 12.

47 Moltke, *Erinnerungen*, 203–4.

48 Ibid., 203–10.

49 *GP*, XI, 15, 19.

50 Ibid., XI, 26, 31–2, 32n.

51 Kürenberg, *War alles falsch?*, 129.

52 *GP*, XI, 3.

53 Niemann, *Wanderungen*, 56.

54 Görlitz, ed., *Kaiser*, 15; Dawson, *Lonsdale*, 165.

55 Baronin von Spitzemberg, *Tagebuch*, 341; Waldersee, *Denkwürdigkeiten*, II, 364.

56 Cecil, *Prince and Emperor*, 288; Baronin von Spitzemberg, *Tagebuch*, 341; Wilhelm II, *Geschichtstabellen*, 21.

57 Sutherland, *Yellow Earl*, 122; *GP*, XI, 80; Kürenberg, *War alles falsch?*, 138.

58 Waldersee, *Denkwürdigkeiten*, II, 364–5.

59 *GP*, XIII, 3–4, 3n.

60 Tirpitz, *Erinnerungen*, 57.

61 Niemann, *Wanderungen*, 51–5.

62 Herre, *Wilhelm*, 172–3.

63 Dick Verroen, *Een tweede Frederik maar dan anders*, Doorn, 1995, 5–6, 8, 9; MacDonogh, *Berlin*, 122–3, 208.

64 Waldersee, *Denkwürdigkeiten*, II, 367.

65 Eulenburg, *Erlebnisse*, I, 260.

66 Everling, ed., *Kaiserworte*, 89.

67 Kürenberg, *War alles falsch?*, 116–17.

68 Kerr, *Briefe*, 149–50.

69 Röhl, *Germany without Bismarck*, 190–1.

70 Everling, ed., *Kaiserworte*, 52, 61; 'Dehio' – Stephanie Eissling, Franz Jäger et al., *Thuringen*, Munich and Berlin, 1998, 741–3.

71 Körner, in Wilderotter and Pohl, eds, *Letzte Kaiser*, 38–9.

72 Everling, ed., *Kaiserworte*, 126–7.

73 Benson, *English Relations*, 136; Röhl, *Germany without Bismarck*, 193.

74 Röhl, *Germany without Bismarck*, 201–2; Cecil, *Prince and Emperor*, 256.

75 Hohenlohe, *Memoirs*, II, 469; Moltke, *Erinnerungen*, 226–7.

76 Daisy Princess of Pless, *From my Private Diary*, ed. with an introduction and notes by Major Desmond Chapman-Huston, London, 1931, 44.

77 Daisy Pless, *What I Have Left Unsaid*, 158.

78 Bigelow, *Seventy Summers*, 76; *idem, Genseric, King of the Vandals and the First German Kaiser*, New York and London, 1918, 112–13. It goes without saying from the title and date of this book, that William's words might not be entirely accurately reported. Indeed, Bigelow admits he is quoting from memory.

79 Hohenlohe, *Memoirs*, II, 470–1; Baumont, *L'Affaire Eulenburg*, 61.

80 Görlitz, ed., *Kaiser*, 17 and n. 24; Kürenberg, *War alles falsch?*, 119.

81 *GP*, VII, 41–3.

82 Kürenberg, *War alles falsch?*, 119; Grant, ed., *Letters to the Tsar*, 38–9.

83 *GP*, XIII, 4.

84 Kerr, *Briefe*, 222–3, 694–5n.

85 *GP*, XIII, 11.

86 Ludwig, *Wilhelm der Zweite*, 144–5.

87 Daisy Pless, *Private Diary*, 50.

88 Kerr, *Briefe*, 244. Kerr neglects to tell us which part of *Henry IV*.

89 Everling, ed., *Kaiserworte*, 35.

90 Brehmer, ed., *Am Hofe*, 512; Isobel Hull, 'Der kaiserliche Hof', in Wilderotter and Pohl, *Letzte Kaiser*, 22; Sombart, *Sündenbock*, reproduces the order for 1903.

91 Baronin von Spitzemberg, *Tagebuch*, 353.

92 Marie von Bunsen, *Die Welt*, 196.

93 Kerr, *Briefe*, 253–8; Peter Fritsche, *Reading Berlin 1900*, Cambridge, MA, and London, 1996, 168; Baronin von Spitzemberg, *Tagebuch*, 352–4.

94 Kerr, *Briefe*, 270, 307–8.

95 Röhl, *Germany without Bismarck*, 10; Baumont, *L'Affaire Eulenburg*, 37.

96 Isobel Hull, *Entourage*, 107.

97 Baumont, *L'Affaire Eulenburg*, 30.

98 Monts, *Erinnerungen*, 146.

99 'Spectator', ed., *Fürst Bülow und der Kaiser. Mit einer Wiedergabe aus ihrem geheimen Briefwechsel*, Dresden, 1930, 40.

100 Spectator, ed., *Briefwechsel*, 40; Cecil, *Prince and Emperor*, 261.

101 Waldersee, *Denkwürdigkeiten*, II, 401.

102 Spectator, ed., *Briefwechsel*, 41.

103 Everling, ed., *Kaiserworte*, 144.

104 Isobel Hull, *Entourage*, 109.

105 Moltke, *Erinnerungen*, 230; Fischer, *Private Lives*, III, 530–2; Röhl, *Germany without Bismarck*, 29 n. 9; Anon., *Three Kaisers*, 150–3; Kerr, *Briefe*, 289.

106 Brehmer, ed., *Am Hofe*, 303: Kerr, *Briefe*, 557–9.

107 Tirpitz, *Erinnerungen*, 39.

108 Kürenberg, *War alles falsch?*, 134; Cecil, *Prince and Emperor*, 298.

109 Benson, *English Relations*, 145 – quoting Bülow.

110 Kürenberg, *War alles falsch?*, 138; Baronin von Spitzemberg, *Tagebuch*, 355, 362. Her account gives a slightly different feline metaphor: 'Ich bin kein alter Kater, den man erst hinauswirft und dann wieder herbeilocken möchte.'

111 Hohenlohe, *Memoirs*, II, 472–3.

112 Eleanor Turk in Dukes and Remak, eds, *Another Germany*, 123–4.

113 Baronin von Spitzemberg, *Tagebuch*, 362.

114 Everling, ed., *Kaiserworte*, 62.

115 Grant, ed., *Letters to the Tsar*, 45.

116 GP, XIV, I, 193–6, 212–7.

117 Ibid., XV, 5–7, 29.

118 Grant, ed., *Letters to the Tsar*, 49, 52, 53–4, 55 n. 1.

119 Kerr, *Briefe*, 371–3.

120 Everling, ed., *Kaiserworte*, 156–7.

121 Baronin von Spitzemberg, *Tagebuch*, 372.

122 GP, XV, 144, 149, 160.

123 Niemann, *Wanderungen*, 56; Friedrich Rosen, *Aus einem diplomatischen Wanderleben*, II: *Bukarest–Lissabon*, Leipzig, 1932, 149.

124 Kerr, *Briefe*, 427.

125 Grant, ed., *Letters to the Tsar*, 60–2, 66–7.

126 Ibid., 67–70.

127 Kürenberg, *War alles falsch?*, 142.

128 Hohenlohe, *Memoirs*, II, 474; Fürst Chlodwig zu Hohenlohe-Schillingfürst, *Denkwürdigkeiten der Reichskanzlerzeit*, Hsg Karl Alexander von Müller, Osnabrück 1967.

129 Ibid., II, 477–8, 479.

130 Kerr, *Briefe*, 458.

131 Cecil, *Prince and Emperor*, 327; Dagobert von Mikusch, *Cecil Rhodes der Traum einer Weltherrschaft*, Berlin, 1936, 234, 261.

132 Ibid., 325.

133 Kerr, *Briefe*, 493.

134 Kürenberg, *War alles falsch?*, 156.

135 Huldermann, *Ballin*, 284, 286.

136 Moltke, *Erinnerungen*, 238.

137 Kürenberg, *War alles falsch?*, 159; Benson, *English Relations*, 175.

138 *GP*, XV, 523.

139 Ibid., XV, 523–6, 553 ff., 557, 560.

140 Ibid., XV, 560.

141 Everling, ed., *Kaiserworte*, 150–1.

142 Baronin von Spitzemberg, *Tagebuch*, 389.

143 Viereck, *Kaiser on Trial*, 187.

144 Waldersee, *Denkwürdigkeiten*, II, 443.

145 Kerr, *Briefe*, 549.

146 Baronin von Spitzemberg, *Tagebuch*, 393; Baumont, *L'Affaire Eulenburg*, 62; MacDonogh, *Prussia*, 238.

147 Wilhelm II, *Geschichtstabellen*, 26.

148 Everling, ed., *Kaiserworte*, 95; *GP*, XVIII, 1, 4n.

149 Richard Evans, *Tales from the German Underworld, Crime and Punishment in the Nineteenth Century*, London and Newhaven, 1998, 192–3; MacDonogh, *Berlin*, 250–1.

150 Kerr, *Briefe*, 582.

151 Kürenberg, *War alles falsch?*, 141; Everling, ed., *Kaiserworte*, 128–9.

152 Kohut, *Wilhelm II*, 145. There are several versions of this speech.

153 Benson, *English Relations*, 174.

154 *GP*, XVI, 41.

155 Baronin von Spitzemberg, *Tagebuch*, 397; Benson, *English Relations*, 174.

156 Everling, ed., *Kaiserworte*, 14.

157 Ibid., 56.

158 Röhl, *Germany without Bismarck*, 268.

159 *GP*, XVIII, 1, 32–3.

Chapter Eleven: Bülow

1 Baronin von Spitzemberg, *Tagebuch*, 401; 'Spectator', ed., *Prince Bülow and the Kaiser. With Excerpts from their Private Correspondence Preserved in the Records of the German Foreign Office*, trans. Oatley Williams, London, 1931, 31, where he threatened an action for slander against anyone who accused him of following the same line as 'dear old Bethmann'.

2 Wilhelm II, *Ereignisse und Gestalten*, 101; Count Bernstorff, *Memoirs*, London and Toronto, 1936, 29; Hull, *Entourage*, 231.

3 'Spectator', ed., *Briefwechsel*, 27.

4 Ibid., 35.

5 Bernstorff, *Memoirs*, 43–4.

6 Kürenberg, *War alles falsch?*, 168, 172; Baumont, *L'Affaire Eulenburg*, 89; Kürenberg, *Holstein*, xxii. Given that Tausig had died thirty years before, it cannot have been exactly hot gossip.

7 Tirpitz, *Erinnerungen*, 104–5; Hermann Kantorowicz, *Gutachten zur Kriegs-schuldfrage 1914*. Aus dem Nachlass herausgegeben und eingeleitet von Imanuel Geiss. Mit einem Geleitwort von Gustav Heinemann, Frankfurt am Main, 1967, 137.

8 Görlitz, ed., *Kaiser*, 64; Tirpitz, *Erinnerungen*, 107, 127, 132.

9 Tirpitz, *Erinnerungen*, 132–3.

10 Ibid., 132–4. 'Homunculus' was the name of the test-tube baby produced by Faust and Helen of Troy in the second part of Goethe's drama.

11 Ibid., 138.

12 Ibid., 149, 150, 157.

13 Wilhelm II, *Geschichtstabellen*, 27; Baronin von Spitzemberg, *Tagebuch*, 404.

14 Lady Susan Townley, *Indiscretions*, 66–7.

15 Brigadier-General W. H.-H. Waters, *Potsdam and Doorn*, London, 1935, 28; Lord Newton PC, *Lord Lansdowne, A Biography*, London, 1929, 197; *GP*, XVII, 19; Wilhelm II, *Ereignisse und Gestalten*, 86–7.

16 *GP*, XVII, 19; Stanley Weintraub, *Victoria*, London, 1996, 634–6; Benson, *English Relations*, 177; Wilhelm II, *Ereignisse und Gestalten*, 87.

17 Weintraub, *Victoria*, 637–8; Marie von Bunsen, *Die Welt*, 190.

18 Baronin von Spitzemberg, *Tagebuch*, 405; Kohut, *Wilhelm*, 133.

19 Weintraub, *Victoria*, 639; Newton, *Lansdowne*, 198.

20 Benson, *English Relations*, 197, quoting Sir Sidney Lee, *Edward VII*, II, 11.

21 Cecil, *Prince and Emperor*, 273.

22 Information from the Duke and Duchess of Mecklenburg-Strelitz and Prince Frederick William of Hohenzollern-Sigmaringen, Saulgau and Sigmaringen, 14 May 1996. As small children, both the duchess and the prince visited William at Doorn.

23 Lady Susan Townley, *Indiscretions*, 46, 52.

24 MacDonogh, *Berlin*, 81, 83; Ronald Taylor, *Berlin and its Culture. A Historical Portrait*, New Haven and London, 1997, 165–7.

25 MacDonogh, *Berlin*, 294–6, 300–1; Hedda Adlon, *Hotel Adlon*, Munich, 1997, 6, 29.

26 Lady Susan Townley, *Indiscretions*, 43, 53–4.

27 Sombart, *Sündenbock*, 107–8, gives a list.

28 Görlitz, ed., *Kaiser*, 143.

29 Sombart, *Sündenbock*, 121, includes a useful diagram of the emperor's year.

30 Görlitz, ed., *Kaiser*, 178–9.

31 Ibid., 175.

32 Ibid., 143.

33 Ibid., 144; Robert von Zedlitz-Trützschler, *Twelve Years at the Imperial German Court*, trans. Alfred Kalisch, London, 1924, 102.

34 Bernd Schulte, 'Um Leib und Magen, oder "Wie im Kaiserreich regiert wurde". Eindrücke des Marinekabinettchefs Georg Alexander von Müller'. I am grateful to my friend Mario Scheuermann in Hamburg for sending me Schulte's article from the Internet.

35 Marie von Bunsen, *Die Welt*, 192–3; Taylor, *Berlin*, 203.

36 Görlitz, ed., *Kaiser*, 145; Kürenberg, *War alles falsch?*, 223.

37 Kürenberg, *War alles falsch?*, 223; Fischer, *Private Lives*, III, 527.

38 Baumont, *L'Affaire Eulenburg*, 11; MacDonogh, *Berlin*, 208.

39 Peter Paret, *The Berlin Secession*, Cambridge, MA, 1980, 17, quoted in Mac-Donogh, *Berlin*, 375; Everling, ed., *Kaiserworte*, 153–5.

40 Lady Susan Townley, *Indiscretions*, 47; Arthur Davis, *The Kaiser as I Know Him*, New York and London, 1918, 47.

41 Marie von Bunsen, *Die Welt*, 191–2.

42 Kürenberg, *War alles falsch?*, 228.

43 Görlitz, ed., *Kaiser*, 149–51.

44 Ibid., 151; Hull, *Entourage*, 151.

45 Fritz Fischer, *Krieg der Illusionen. Die deutsche Politik von 1911 bis 1914*, Düsseldorf, 1969, 27–30; V. R. Berghahn, *Germany and the Approach of War in 1914*, London, 1973, 134.

46 Fischer, *Krieg der Illusionen*, 72–3.

47 Ibid., 94.

48 Walther Rathenau, *Der Kaiser, eine Betrachtung*, Berlin, 1919, 26.

49 Rathenau, *Kaiser*, 45.

50 Hartmut Pogge von Strandmann, ed., *Walther Rathenau; Industrialist, Intellectual and Politician, Notes and Diaries 1907–1922*, Oxford, 1985 (hereafter Rathenau: *Notes and Diaries*), 126.

51 Rathenau, *Notes and Diaries*, 130; Fischer, *Krieg der Illusionen*, 42; in Görlitz, ed., *Kaiser*, 151, Müller denies any anti-Semitism on the part of the emperor.

52 Davis, *Kaiser*, 48–9. Davis's anti-Semitism did not help him in the long run. In 1925 Werner Kautzsch published *Hofgeschichten aus der Regierungszeit Kaiser Wilhelms II* (Berlin), in which he accused 'Nathan' Davis of being a Jew himself (208–9).

53 Huldermann, *Ballin*, 283, 286.

54 Görlitz, ed., *Kaiser*, 156.

55 Kronprinz Wilhelm, *Erinnerungen*, 5–6.

56 Rudolf Priesner, *Herzog Carl Eduard, zwischen Deutschland und England, eine tragische Auseinandersetzung*, Gerabronn and Crailsheim, 1977, 18–19, 222; author's visit to Coburg, August 1998; Rainer Hambrecht, 'Eine Dynastie – zwei Namen: "Haus Sachsen-Coburg und Gotha" und "Haus Windsor"' in *Historische Forschungen 63*; Hans Wiegand, 'Thron und Erbfolgestreit im Hause Sachsen-Coburg und Gotha 1914–1918' in *Coburger Geschichtsblätter* Mai–August 1998, 56–57.

57 Priesner, *Carl Eduard*, 23.

58 Giles MacDonogh, 'A Small Town in Germany with a Right Royal History', *Financial Times*, 12 December 1998.

59 Kronprinz Wilhelm, *Erinnerungen*, 8; Paul Herre, *Kronprinz Wilhelm, seine Rolle in der deutschen Politik*, Munich, 1954, 4–5.

60 Kronzprinz Wilhelm, *Erinnerungen*, 9–10; Herre, *Kronzprinz*, 9.

61 Ibid., 11–12.

62 Ibid., 16.

63 Kürenberg, *War alles falsch?*, 207–8; Baronin von Spitzemberg, *Tagebuch*, 407; Everling, *Kaiserworte*, 33.

64 Newton, *Lansdowne*, 247; Waters, *Potsdam and Doorn*, 38–9.

65 Waters, *Potsdam and Doorn*, 41–2.

66 Ponsonby, *Empress Frederick*, 468; Grant, ed., *Letters to the Tsar*, 75–6.

67 *GP*, XVII, 22–3, 50; Heffer, *Power and Place*, 134.

68 *GP*, XVII, 96.

69 Heffer, *Power and Place*, 135; Grant, ed., *Letters to the Tsar*, 74, 78.

70 Waters, *Potsdam and Doorn*, 57–64.

71 Ibid., 67–8; Wilhelm II, *Geschichtstabellen*, 28.

72 Houston Stewart Chamberlain, *Die Grundlagen des neunzehnten Jahrhunderts*, 2 vols, Munich, 1899, 17–18.

73 Ibid., 148n, 210–11, 214, 248.

74 Ibid., 1324.

75 Ibid., 1325.

76 Eulenburg, *Erlebnisse*, II, 322–3, 327, 331, 340–1; Houston Stewart Chamberlain, *Briefe 1882–1924 und Briefwechsel mit Kaiser Wilhelm II*, 2 vols, Munich, 1928, II, 131; Chamberlain, *Grundlagen*, I, 464.

77 Chamberlain, *Briefe*, II, 139, 149.

78 Eulenburg, *Erlebnisse*, II, 344–6.

79 Chamberlain, *Briefe*, II, 157, 151, 164, 158.

80 Ibid., II, 189.

81 Ibid., II, 167.

82 *GP*, XVII, 110–11.

83 Waters, *Potsdam and Doorn*, 70, 74, 76, 90; Simon Heffer, *Power and Place, The Political Consequences of King Edward VII*, London, 1999, 135–8.

84 Waldersee, *Denkwürdigkeiten*, III, 179.

85 Grant, ed., *Letters to the Tsar*, 81–3.

86 Ibid., 87.

87 Bernstorff, *Memoirs*, 47–8.

88 Everling, *Kaiserworte*, 123–4.

89 Ibid., 198.

90 Grant, ed., *Letters to the Tsar*, 90–1.

91 Waldersee, *Denkwürdigkeiten*, II, 81; Hutten-Czapski, *Sechzig Jahre* II, 145.

92 William Hagen, *Germans, Poles and Jews, The Nationality Conflict in the Prussian East, 1772–1914*, Chicago and London, 1980, 188, in MacDonogh, *Prussia*, 328.

93 Everling, *Kaiserworte*, 116–17.

94 Baronin von Spitzemberg, *Tagebuch*, 422.

95 Waldersee, *Denkwürdigkeiten*, III, 193.

96 Muhlen, *Famille Krupp*, 102–7; Isobel Hull, *Entourage*, 171.

97 Isobel Hull, *Entourage*, 173.

98 Wilhelm II, *Ereignisse und Gestalten*, 84; Baumont, *L'Affaire Eulenburg*, 75; Kürenberg, *War alles falsch?*, 172. Kürenberg maintains the lunch took place at Bülow's residence.

99 *GP*, XVIII, 67, 61, 68; Dawson, *Lonsdale*, 176–9.

100 Everling, *Kaiserworte*, 110.

101 Daisy Pless, *Private Diary*, 75.

102 Grant, ed., *Letters to the Tsar*, 92–3; Pless, *Private Diary*, 91.

103 Daisy Pless, *Private Diary*, 89; Baronin von Spitzemberg, *Tagebuch*, 431.

104 Görlitz, ed., *Kaiser*, 33; Santiago Perez Triana, 'The International Position of the Latin American Races', in *The Cambridge Modern History*, XII: *The Latest Age*, Cambridge, 1934, 695; *GP*, XVII, 241; Wilhelm II, *Geschichtstabellen*, 30.

105 Baronin von Spitzemberg, *Tagebuch*, 422, 428.

106 Daisy Pless, *Private Diary*, 106–7, 109, 153.

107 Grant, ed., *Letters to the Tsar*, 101.

108 Spectator, ed., *Bülow and the Kaiser*, 104.

109 Baronin von Spitzemberg, *Tagebuch*, 436.

110 Görlitz, ed., *Kaiser*, 163; Fischer, *Private Lives*, I, 16–19; Waldersee, *Denkwürdigkeiten*, III, 220; Huldermann, *Ballin*, 289; Kürenberg, *War alles falsch?*, 203–4 – 'Lacks a sword! Should be worn on the leather belt'; Pless, *Private Diary*, 121.

111 Grant, ed., *Letters to the Tsar*, 102, 104.

112 Ibid., 106–7.

113 Daisy Pless, *Private Diary*, 132–4.

114 Spectator, ed., *Prince Bülow and the Kaiser*, [*With Excerpts from their Private Correspondence Preserved in the Records of the German Foreign Office*, trans Oatley Williams, London 1931], 113.

115 Grant, ed., *Letters to the Tsar*, 114–15.

116 Waldersee, *Denkwurdigkeiten*, III, 229, 232.

117 *GP*, XVII, 363; XX, 1.8, 10.

118 Grant, ed., *Letters to the Tsar*, 118–19.

119 Huldermann, *Ballin*, 291; Spectator, ed., *Bülow and the Kaiser*, 114, 134–5.

120 *Memoirs of Prince von Bülow*, trans. F. A. Voigt, Boston 1931, I. 81–2; II. 171; Dawson, *Lonsdale*, 218–19; Sutherland, *Yellow Earl*, 131–2.

121 Görlitz, ed., *Kaiser*, 24–5.

122 Moltke, *Erinnerungen*, 296.

123 Spectator, ed., *Bülow and the Kaiser*, 137.

124 Grant, ed., *Letters to the Tsar*, 130; Spectator, ed., *Bülow and the Kaiser*, 143.

125 Spectator, ed., *Bülow and the Kaiser*, 144.

126 *GP*, XIX, 1.282, 2.353–6; Grant, ed., *Letters to the Tsar*, 134–5, 139, 141–2, 147–8.

127 Grant, ed., *Letters to the Tsar*, 150, 152, 156; Spectator, ed., *Bülow and the Kaiser*, 154.

128 Bernstorff, *Memoirs*, 2–3; Görlitz, ed., *Kaiser*, 21; Alfred von Tirpitz, *Wie hat*

sich der Staatsbetrieb beim Aufbau der Flotte bewährt?, Leipzig, 1923, 8–9, 14.

129 Görlitz, ed., *Kaiser*, 61.

130 Baronin von Spitzemberg, *Tagebuch*, 440.

131 Waldersee, *Denkwürdigkeiten*, III, 206–7; Paul Liman, *Der Kaiser, ein Charakterbild Wilhelms II*, Berlin, 1904, 7; Baronin von Spitzemberg, *Tagebuch*, 438.

132 Graf Ernst zu Reventlow, *Kaiser Wilhelm II und die Byzantiner*, 2nd edn, Munich, 1906, 29.

133 Ibid., 159.

134 Grant, ed., *Letters to the Tsar*, 160–61; Klaus Meyer, *Theodor Schiemann als politischer Publizist*, Frankfurt/Main and Hamburg, 1956, 130–1.

135 Spectator, ed., *Bülow and the Kaiser*, 41.

136 Grant, ed., *Letters to the Tsar*, 169–74.

137 Fischer, *Krieg der Illusionen*, 76, 78–80; Spectator, ed., *Bülow and the Kaiser*, 20.

138 Fischer, *Krieg der Illusionen*, 79, 81; Grant, ed., *Letters to the Tsar*, 225.

139 Everling, *Kaiserworte*, 125; Baronin von Spitzemberg, *Tagebuch*, 446, points out that the next line in the Bible is ominous; Spectator, ed., *Briefwechsel*, 42.

140 Spectator, ed., *Briefwechsel*, 46; Rosen, *Wanderleben*, I, 99, 129; Le comte de Saint-Aulaire, 'Guillaume II à Tanger', in *Les Oeuvres libres*, Paris, 1952, 81, 83.

141 Görlitz, ed., *Kaiser*, 61–2; Spectator, ed., *Bülow and the Kaiser*, 160, 169; Rosen, *Wanderleben*, I, 132; Mark Kerr, *Land, Sea and Air*, 160–1 – the *Drake* was an odd choice to send to Spain, where children are still frightened by the reproach 'Mira! Que viene el Drake!' Kantorowicz, *Gutachten*, 396: he uses the story of the horse as evidence of William's cowardice. Other sources do not necessarily back him up.

142 Richard von Kühlmann, *Erinnerungen*, Heidelberg, 1948, 225–30.

143 De Saint-Aulaire in *Oeuvres libres*, 83–6.

144 Görlitz, ed., *Kaiser*, 62; Rosen, *Wanderleben*, I, 132, 237; Kürenberg, *War alles falsch?*, 187; Newton, *Lansdowne*, 332; De Saint-Aulaire in *Oeuvres libres*, 87–9.

145 Grant, ed., *Letters to the Tsar*, 186.

146 Moltke, *Erinnerungen*, 305–11.

147 Görlitz, ed., *Kaiser*, 171–4.

148 *GP*, XIX, 2.435n; Spectator, ed., *Bülow and the Kaiser*, 174–6; Moltke, *Erinnerungen*, 326.

149 Spectator, ed., *Bülow and the Kaiser*, 176–83; Kürenberg, *War alles falsch?*, 178; *GP*, XIX, 2.460, 464.

150 Moltke, *Erinnerungen*, 329–30; *GP*, XIX, 2.454.

151 *GP*, XIX, 2.463; Spectator, ed., *Bülow and the Kaiser*, 15.

152 Grant, ed., *Letters to the Tsar*, 190–3.

153 *GP*, XIX, 2.435–9.

154 *GP*, XIX, 2.474, 481, 485, 489, 498; Spectator, ed., *Bülow and the Kaiser*, 194–5.

155 Spectator, ed., *Bülow and the Kaiser*, 44.

156 Fischer, *Krieg der Illusionen*, 98.

157 Newton, *Landsdowne*, 338; Kantorowicz, *Gutachten*, 132.

158 Berghahn, *Approach of War*, 52; Fischer, *Krieg der Illusionen*, 101; Kantorowicz, *Gutachten*, 292, contains a quotation from Tschirschky to the same effect.

159 Grant, ed., *Letters to the Tsar*, 198, 200–1; Rosen, *Wanderleben*, I, 163.

160 *GP*, XIX, 2.512–14, 526–7; Grant, ed., *Letters to the Tsar*, 209, 211, 216.

161 Spectator, ed., *Bülow and the Kaiser*, 206–7; Rosen, *Wanderleben*, I, 364, 365, 368.

162 Görlitz, ed., *Kaiser*, 64.

163 Daisy Pless, *Private Diary*, 175, 159, 177.

164 Bernstorff, *Memoirs*, 72; Daisy Pless, *Private Diary*, 184, 189, 193.

165 Waldersee, *Denkwürdigkeiten*, III, 225; Kürenberg, *War alles falsch?*, 292; Moltke, *Erinnerungen*, introduction by Eliza von Moltke, ix; Isobel Hull, *Entourage*, 248; Rathenau, *Notes and Diaries*, 181; Baronin von Spitzemberg, *Tagebuch*, 466.

166 Görlitz, ed., *Kaiser*, 42–3.

167 Spectator, ed., *Bülow and the Kaiser*, 214.

168 Everling, *Kaiserworte*, 112.

169 MacDonogh, *Prussia*, 137–9.

170 Baumont, *L'Affaire Eulenburg*, 179; Baronin von Spitzemberg, *Tagebuch*, 466.

171 MacDonogh, *Prussia*, 139. The story naturally lent itself to drama and at least five plays were written about it; a film was made too. The most famous adaptation is that of Carl Zuckmayer, *Der Hauptmann von Köpenick* of 1931.

172 Kürenberg, *War alles falsch?*, 202.

173 Görlitz, ed., *Kaiser*, 167–9.

174 Spectator, ed., *Bülow and the Kaiser*, 215, 219.

Chapter Twelve: A Sea of Troubles

1 Viereck, *Kaiser on Trial*, 135; Baumont, *L'Affaire Eulenburg*, 196; Kürenberg, *War alles falsch?*, 169; MacDonogh, *Prussia*, 222–3, 217.

2 Baumont, *L'Affaire Eulenburg*, 216–17; Kürenberg, *War alles falsch?*, 155.

3 H. v. M., *Enthüllungen, Bismarck, Bülow und Harden*, Leipzig, 1907, 8–9; Baronin von Spitzemberg, *Tagebuch*, 472.

4 Isobel Hull, *Entourage*, 21.

5 Baumont, *L'Affaire Eulenburg*, 201; Kronprinz Wilhelm, *Erinnerungen*, 13; Herre, *Kronprinz*, 8.

6 Isobel Hull, *Entourage*, 50. Dr Hull has pointed out that getting to the bottom of the scandal is complicated by lack of evidence. The correspondence between Kuno Moltke and Eulenburg was burnt in 1907. Lecomte destroyed his papers. In 1932 the evidence produced by the prosecution during the trial was also destroyed.

7 MacDonogh, *Prussia*, 217.

8 Kürenberg, *Holstein*, xxii; Fischer, *Private Lives*, III, 542–7, 549–550.

9 Fischer, *Private Lives*, III, 542–43.

10 Ibid., II, 314–16; III, 548–9; Daisy Pless, *Private Diary*, 200.

11 Kürenberg, *War alles falsch?*, 157; Bernstorff, *Memoirs*, 45.

12 Isobel Hull, *Entourage*, 118, 121, 124.

13 Ibid., 231–2; Baronin von Spitzemberg, *Tagebuch*, 473.

14 Isobel Hull, *Entourage*, 133.

15 Baronin von Spitzemberg, *Tagebuch*, 476–7.

16 Prince von Bülow, *Memoirs 1909–1919*, London, 1932, 27.

17 Sombart, *Sündenbock*, 175; Isobel Hull, *Entourage*, 138.

18 H. v. M., *Enthüllungen*, 5–6.

19 Baumont, *L'Affaire Eulenburg*, 231; Bülow, *1909–1919*, 24, 25.

20 Nowak and Thimme, eds, *Monts*, 183–5; Lamar Cecil, *Wilhelm II. Emperor and Exile, 1900–1941*, Chapel Hill and London, 1996, 113.

21 Spectator, ed., *Bülow and the Kaiser*, 63.

22 Bülow, *1909–1919*, 26.

23 Baumont, *L'Affaire Eulenburg*, 240–2; Muschler, *Eulenburg*, 185–6, 207.

24 Everling, *Kaiserworte*, 171: *GP*, XXIV, 87.

25 *GP*, XXIV, 87 and n.

26 Lowther, *A Speaker's Commentaries*, II, 51; Kohut, *Wilhelm*, 108–9; Kürenberg, *War alles falsch?*, 243; Görlitz, ed., *Kaiser*, 175. For Highcliffe, see *Victoria County History* for Hampshire, V, 84.

27 MacDonogh, *Prussia*, 225.

28 Baumont, *L'Affaire Eulenburg*, 238.

29 Isobel Hull, *Entourage*, 138.

30 Hans von Tresckow, *Von Fürsten und anderen Sterblichen: Erinnerungen eines Kriminalkommissars*, Berlin, 1922, 142–3.

31 Tresckow, *Fürsten*, 201–2; Baronin von Spitzemberg, *Tagebuch*, 479, 483–4.

32 Bülow, *1909–1919*, 28; Rathenau, *Notes and Diaries*, 76. See also Peter Berglar, *Walther Rathenau, ein Leben zwischen Philosophie und Politik*, Graz, Vienna and Cologne, 1987. Rathenau finally ended up with the Red Eagle 4th class, and was able to add the Star of the Order of the House of Orange, the War Merit Medal and the Iron Cross 2nd Class, before the war was out.

33 Bülow, *1909–1919*, 26; Baumont, *L'Affaire Eulenburg*, 96.

34 Isobel Hull, *Entourage*, 146, 237; Andreas Dorpalen, Empress Augusta Victoria and the Fall of the German Monarchy, *American Historical Review*, October 1952, 19.

35 Baumont, *L'Affaire Eulenburg*, 99, 273.

36 Görlitz, ed., *Kaiser*, 175; Baronin von Spitzemberg, *Tagebuch*, 506.

37 Tirpitz, *Aufbau*, 59–60; *GP*, XXIV, 32–5; also Asquith Papers in the Bodleian Library, Box 19f.249. I am grateful to Colin Clifford for communicating his transcript and notes.

38 Spectator, ed., *Bülow and the Kaiser*, 231; Baronin von Spitzemberg, *Tagebuch*, 481.

39 Huldermann, *Ballin*, 207–8; *GP*, XXIII, 1.

40 Kerr, *Land, Sea and Air*, 162–7.

41 Ibid., 168, 172, 177; Tirpitz, *Aufbau*, 65; Görlitz, ed., *Kaiser*, 66, 202.

42 *GP*, XXIV, 91, 96, 104.

43 Spectator, ed., *Bülow and the Kaiser*, 237.

44 Tirpitz, *Aufbau*, 67–8; Görlitz, ed., *Kaiser*, 73; Spectator, ed., *Bülow and the Kaiser*, 240.

45 *GP*, XXIV, 5, 122–3, 124.

46 *GP*, XXIV, 125–7. The full exchange is also in Tirpitz, *Aufbau*, 69–71; Fischer, *Krieg der Illusionen*, 103.

47 Tirpitz, *Aufbau*, 71.

48 Ibid., 100.

49 *GP*, XXIV, 128–9 and n. 132; Tirpitz, *Aufbau*, 100; Grant, ed., *Letters to the Tsar*, 236.

50 Kürenberg, *War alles falsch?*, 241–2.

51 Bülow, *1909–1919*, 92.

52 Fischer, *Krieg der Illusionen*, 106.

53 Everling, *Kaiserworte*, 113.

54 *GP*, XXIV, 167 and n, 168, 175; Wilhelm Schüssler, *Die Daily Telegraph-Affaire. Fürst Bülow, Kaiser Wilhelm und die Krise des Zweiten Reiches*, Göttingen, 1952, 14. Schüssler maintains that the journalist who cleaned up Stuart-Wortley's copy was called Firth.

55 Kürenberg, *War alles falsch?*, 244.

56 Schüssler, *Daily Telegraph-Affaire*, 13–14, 18–19.

57 *GP*, XXIV, 169–74; Schüssler, *Daily Telegraph-Affaire*, 14.

58 Görlitz, ed., *Kaiser*, 69.

59 *GP*, XXIV, 177–81; Bülow, *1909–1919*, 51, 60.

60 Spectator, ed., *Bülow and the Kaiser*, 252; Schüssler, *Daily Telegraph-Affaire*, 23; Viereck, *Kaiser on Trial*, 224.

61 Baronin von Spitzemberg, *Tagebuch*, 488–9.

62 Ibid., 491; Spectator, ed., *Bülow and the Kaiser*, 276, 279; Freiherr von Schön, *Erlebtes*, Stuttgart and Berlin, 1921, 92.

63 Schüssler, *Daily Telegraph-Affaire*, 40–3; Mann, *Wilhelm II*, 13; Kohut, *Wilhelm*, 134; Everling, *Kaiserworte*, 74.

64 Schüssler, *Daily Telegraph-Affaire*, 57; Cecil, *Emperor and Exile*, 142.

65 Schüssler, *Daily Telegraph-Affaire*, 57, 60, 61.

66 Cecil, *Emperor and Exile*, 137; Wilhelm II, *Ereignisse und Gestalten*, 98; Bülow, *1909–1919*, 48; Spectator, ed., *Bülow and the Kaiser*, 69; Schüssler, *Daily Telegraph-Affaire*, 37.

67 *The Memoirs of Princess Fugger. The Glory of the Habsburgs*, trans. J. A. Galston, London, 1932, 304–5.

68 Princess Fugger, *Memoirs*, 307–9.

69 Bernhard Schwertfeger hsg, *Kaiser und Kabinettschef, nach eigenen Aufzeich-nungen und dem Briefwechsel des wirklichen Geheimen Rats Rudolf von Valentini*, Oldenburg, 1931, 103; Cecil, *Emperor and Exile*, 138; Baronin von Spitzemberg, *Tagebuch*, 495.

70 Cecil, *Emperor and Exile*, 139.

71 Schüssler, *Daily Telegraph-Affaire*, 65; [Eduard Engel], *Kaiser und Kanzler im Sturmjahr 1908. Die Wahrheit nach den Urkunden*, Leipzig, 1929, 5. This book is often falsely attributed to William himself: Herre, *Kronprinz*, 17; Kürenberg, *War alles falsch?*, 249.

72 Herre, *Kronprinz*, 17–18; Baronin von Spitzemberg, *Tagebuch*, 497.

73 Bernstorff, *Memoirs*, 74.

74 Daisy Pless, *Private Diary*, 239; Baronin von Spitzemberg, *Tagebuch*, 498–9.

75 Grant, ed., *Letters to the Tsar*, 240–1, 245.

76 Wilhelm II, *Ereignisse und Gestalten*, 107.

77 Everling, *Kaiserworte*, 177; Wilhelm II, *Geschichtstabellen*, 44.

78 Schüssler, *Daily Telegraph-Affaire*, 69–73; [Rudolf Martin], *Fürst Bülow und Kaiser Wilhelm*, Leipzig-Gohlis, 1909, 5.

79 Bülow, *1909–1919*, 63; Wilhelm II, *Ereignisse und Gestalten*, 100.

80 Nowak and Thimme, eds, *Monts*, 145–6.

81 *GP*, XXVII, 1.25, 42, 99, 120; XXVII, 2.85, 89, 147.

82 Grant, ed., *Letters to the Tsar*, 248–54.

83 Spectator, ed., *Bülow and the Kaiser*, 44; Schüssler, *Daily Telegraph-Affaire*, 81–2.

Chapter Thirteen: Bethmann-Hollweg

1 Bülow, *1909–1919*, 11, 21; Fischer, *Krieg der Illusionen*, 107; Baronin von Spitzemberg, *Tagebuch*, 510; Görlitz, ed., *Kaiser*, 77; Nowak and Thimme, eds, *Monts*, introduction, 24–5.

2 Kürenberg, *War alles falsch?*, 257.

3 Wilhelm II, *Ereignisse und Gestalten*, 111.

4 Ibid., 112.

5 Herre, *Kronprinz*, 23.

6 Spectator, ed., *Bülow and the Kaiser*, 76; Huldermann, *Ballin*, 216–18.

7 *GP*, XXVIII, 205–11.

8 Wilhelm II, *Ereignisse und Gestalten*, 152, 166.

9 MacDonogh, *Berlin*, 340.

10 Baronin von Spitzemberg, *Tagebuch*, 517.

11 Fritz Fischer, *Krieg der Illusionen*, 18–19, 465, 479. Both the US, France and Russia had also massively outstripped Britain in steel production.

12 Wilhelm II, *Ereignisse und Gestalten*, 109; *GP*, XXVIII, 324–5, 328.

13 *GP*, XXVIII, 326.

14 Baumont, *L'Affaire Eulenburg*, 100; Kürenberg, *War alles falsch?*, 264; Kohut, *Wilhelm*, 150; *GP*, XXVIII, 321.

15 Görlitz, ed., *Kaiser*, 14, 78–9.

16 Kohut, *Politicization of Personality*, 18; Everling, *Kaiserworte*, 15; Daisy Pless, *Private Diary*, 266; *idem, What I Have Left Unsaid*, 59–60.

17 *GP*, XXVIII, 398–9.

18 Görlitz, ed., *Kaiser*, 83.

19 Grant, ed., *Letters to the Tsar*, 263; Wilhelm II, *Studien zur Gorgo*, Berlin, 1936, 11. He later changed his mind about the date of 'his' temple, saying it dated from the 8th century BC.

20 Huldermann, *Ballin*, 232.

21 Görlitz, ed., *Kaiser*, 83; *GP*, XXVIII, 415n; Huldermann, *Ballin*, 233.

22 Görlitz, ed., *Kaiser*, 88.

23 *GP*, XXIX, 152, 177–9.

24 Fischer, *Krieg der Illusionen*, 120–3; Görlitz, ed., *Kaiser*, 71, 86–7; Tirpitz, *Erinnerungen*, 182.

25 Fischer, *Krieg der Illusionen*, 130, 131–2.

26 Ibid., 131.

27 Ibid., 137; Görlitz, ed., *Kaiser*, 91; Fritz Fischer, 'Weltpolitik, Weltmachtstreben und deutsche Kreigsziele' in, Wolfgang Schieder, ed., *Erster Weltkrieg: Ursachen, Entstehung, Kriegsziele*, Cologne and Berlin, 1969, 83.

28 Fischer, *Krieg der Illusionen*, 142.

29 Everling, *Kaiserworte*, 180; *GP*, XXXI, 3n, 9–10.

30 Görlitz, ed., *Kaiser*, 96.

31 Ibid., 96.

32 Ibid., 97.

33 Tirpitz, *Erinnerungen*, 182.

34 Görlitz, ed., *Kaiser*, 90–1.

35 Tirpitz, *Aufbau*, 235.

36 Herre, *Kronprinz*, 26.

37 Ibid., 27.

38 Article and marginalia reproduced in Huldermann, *Ballin*, 233; *GP*, XXXI, 86.

39 Fischer, *Krieg der Illusionen*, 170–5.

40 *GP*, XXXI, 92, 94; Tirpitz, *Aufbau*, 270.

41 Fischer, *Krieg der Illusionen*, 178.

42 Ibid., 179; Görlitz, ed., *Kaiser*, 106.

43 Görlitz, ed., *Kaiser*, 106.

44 Bülow, *1909–1919*, 4–5.

45 Josef von Lauff, *Der Grosse König, zur Feier des 200 jährigen Geburtstages Friedrichs des Grossen*, introduction by Georg von Hülsen, Berlin, 1912, x, 40.

46 *GP*, XXXI, 97n.

47 Wilhelm II, *Ereignisse und Gestalten*, 125; Tirpitz, *Erinnerungen*, 186–7, confirms William's story.

48 *GP*, XXXI, 104; Everling, *Kaiserworte*, 174.

49 Tirpitz, *Erinnerungen*, 188–90; Görlitz, ed., *Kaiser*, 112.

50 Berghahn, *Approach of War*, 123; Tirpitz, *Erinnerungen*, 191; Görlitz, ed., *Kaiser*, 113.

51 *GP*, XXXI, 112–14.

52 *GP*, XXXI, 136–7; Fischer, *Krieg der Illusionen*, 188; Tirpitz, *Aufbau*, 317; Dorpalen in *A. H. R.*, 23.

53 Tirpitz, *Aufbau*, 325.

54 *GP*, XXXI, 157n.

55 *GP*, XXXI, 183; Fischer, *Krieg der Illusionen*, 188–9; Görlitz, ed., *Kaiser*, 117.

56 Tirpitz, *Erinnerungen*, 192–3; *idem, Aufbau*, 287; Huldermann, *Ballin*, 266; *GP*, XXXI, 205.

57 *GP*, XXXI, 209.

58 Fischer, *Krieg der Illusionen*, 195; Rathenau, *Notes and Diaries*, 146–7.

59 Everling, *Kaiserworte*, 104.

60 Fischer, *Krieg der Illusionen*, 201–4; Görlitz, ed., *Kaiser*, 118.

61 J. C. G. Röhl, ed., *1914, Delusion or Design?, The Testimony of Two German Diplomats*, with an introduction by Hugh Trevor-Roper, London 1973, 43.

62 Ibid., 51–2.

63 Ibid., 29.

64 Görlitz, ed., *Kaiser*, 169–70.

65 Kürenberg, *War alles falsch?*, 268.

66 Görlitz, ed., *Kaiser*, 166.

67 Fischer, *Krieg der Illusionen*, 225–30.

68 Ibid., 232; in Görlitz, ed., *Kaiser*, 123, however, William calls it an 'erwünschte Klärung', expressing his gratitude for the new clarity about British aims.

69 Dennis Showalter, 'Army, State and Society in Germany 1871–1914', an interpretation, in Dukes and Remak, eds, *Another Germany*, 13; Kohut, *Wilhelm*, 139; Görlitz, ed., *Kaiser*, 125, 212n.

70 Isobel Hull, *Entourage*, 262–3: Fischer, *Krieg der Illusionen*, 232–3.

71 Fischer, *Krieg der Illusionen*, 236.

72 Rathenau, *Notes and Diaries*, 173.

73 Görlitz, ed., *Kaiser*, 126.

74 Bülow, *1909–1919*, 87; Bernstorff, *Memoirs*, 82.

75 Görlitz, ed., *Kaiser*, 186–7.

76 Röhl, *Delusion or Design?*, 32.

77 Görlitz, ed., *Kaiser*, 128; Fischer, *Krieg der Illusionen*, 247.

78 Graf Ernst Reventlow, *Der Kaiser und die Monarchisten*, Berlin, 1913, 22.

79 Liman, *Der Kaiser*, 1919 edn, (reprinted from 1913), 7.

80 Fischer, *Krieg der Illusionen*, 360.

81 Görlitz, ed., *Kaiser*, 175.

82 Ibid., 196.

83 Fischer, *Krieg der Illusionen*, 404; Herre, *Kronprinz*, 12.

84 Fritz Fischer, 'Weltpolitik' in Schieder, ed., *Erster Weltkrieg*, 83.

85 Fischer, *Krieg der Illusionen*, 269, 278.

86 Everling, *Kaiserworte*, 47, 48, 134.

87 Herre, *Kronprinz*, 33.

88 Fischer, *Krieg der Illusionen*, 248–9.

89 Jack Dukes, 'Militarism and Arms Policy Revisited: the Origins of the German Army Law of 1913', in Dukes and Remak, eds, *Another Germany*, 22.

90 Rosen, *Wanderleben*, II, 168; Rathenau, *Notes and Diaries*, 179.

91 Görlitz, ed., *Kaiser*, 161.

92 Ibid., 129.

93 Ibid., 129.

94 Herre, *Kronprinz*, 35; Fischer, *Krieg der Illusionen*, 573.

95 Kantorowicz, *Gutachten*, 226.

96 *GP*, XXXIX, 325–7; Fischer, *Krieg der Illusionen*, 313–14.

97 Fischer, *Krieg der Illusionen*, 315. For the 'Great Game', see Lawrence James, *Raj, the Making and Unmaking of British India*, London, 1998, 81, 367, 378–9, 385, and the useful map showing Russian railway lines on 387.

98 Rathenau, *Notes and Diaries*, 182.

99 David Schoenbaum, *Zabern 1913. Consensus Politics in Imperial Germany*, London, 1982, 99; see also A. A. Löwenthal, 'Bettschisser, oder der Werdegang des Tunichtguts Forstner', in *Gesammelte Schriften*, VI, Tübingen und Stuttgart, 1971, 301–17.

100 Schoenbaum, *Zabern 1913*, 86.

101 Fischer, *Krieg der Illusionen*, 407–9.

102 Görlitz, ed., *Kaiser*, 198. Frank, a Jew, volunteered in 1914 and died the same year.

103 Herre, *Kronprinz*, 37; Karl Dietrich Erdmann, ed., *Kurt Riezler, Tagebücher, Aufsätze, Dokumente*, Göttingen, 1972 (hereafter Riezler, *Tagebücher*), 219.

104 Berghahn, *Approach of War*, 163.

105 Fischer, *Krieg der Illusionen*, 320–22.

106 Ibid., 382.

107 Wilhelm II, *Ereignisse und Gestalten*, 144; MacDonogh, *Berlin*, 57, 61.

108 Rathenau, *Kaiser*, 31.

109 Jörn Grabowski in *Anton von Werner, Geschichte und Bilder*, Ausstellung des Berlin Museums und des deutschen historischen Museums, Berlin Zeughaus, 7 Mai–27 Juli 1993, 91.

110 Grabowski in *Werner*, 99. The fate of these historical works after 1923 makes sad reading. They were banished to the Garrison Museum in Potsdam in 1923 before being stored in Frederick William III's Schloss Paretz in 1943, and disappeared after 1945. They probably went to Russia with so much else.

111 Bülow, *1909–1919*, 123.

112 Görlitz, ed., *Kaiser*, 131.

113 *GP*, XXXVIII, 195, 205, 219, 232; Bülow, *1909–1919*, 127–8. There is no obvious translation for the 'pots cassés' which signifies destruction in the text.

114 Fischer, *Krieg der Illusionen*, 486–8.

115 Ibid., 501.

116 Kantorowicz, *Gutachten*, 292. The moral justification for Frederick's attack was also seen as controversial, and has become all the more so since 1914 and 1939.

117 Grant, ed., *Letters to the Tsar*, 280–1.

118 *GP*, XXXIX, 336, 341; Fischer, *Krieg der Illusionen*, 584.

119 Görlitz, ed., *Kaiser*, 162; Baronin von Spitzemberg, *Tagebuch*, 544.

120 Josef von Lauff, *Spiegel meines Lebens*, Berlin, 1932, 352–6; *GP*, XXXIX, 351–

3; Denis Mack Smith, *Modern Italy, A Political History*, New Haven and London, 1997, 257–9.

121 Wilhelm II, *Ereignisse und Gestalten*, 170. The author has, quite independently of the present work, undertaken a similar study tour on Ithaca for which a rather stronger claim is made. The identification of a few spots with the story of the *Odyssey* is very popular with the islanders themselves. This is probably as true on Levkas as it is on Ithaca or even Kefallinia.

122 Ibid., 171.

123 Charles Seymour, ed., *The Intimate Papers of Colonel House*, 2 vols, Boston and New York, 1926 (hereafter House, *Intimate Papers*), I, 187.

124 James Gerard, *My Four Years in Germany*, London, 1917, 37–8; House, *Intimate Papers*, I, 225, 244–5; Viereck, *Kaiser on Trial*, xv, 265.

125 House, *Intimate Papers*, I, 256.

126 GP, XXXIX, 364n; Kantorowicz, *Gutachten*, 221.

127 Fischer, *Krieg der Illusionen*, 684.

Chapter Fourteen: The Slide into War

1 Bülow, *1909–1919*, 136.

2 Willibald Gutsche, *Der gewollte Krieg. Der deutsche Imperialismus und der I Weltkrieg*, Cologne, 1984, 14–19.

3 Kürenberg, *War alles falsch?*, 283; Viereck, *Kaiser on Trial*, 10–11.

4 Gutsche, *Gewollte Krieg*, 40.

5 Isobel Hull, *Entourage*, 249, 254; Roger Chickering, *Imperial Germany and the Great War, 1914–1918*, Cambridge, 1998, 12.

6 GP, XXXIX, 533–9, 545; Tirpitz, *Erinnerungen*, 231.

7 Kantorowicz, *Gutachten*, 388; GP, XXXIX, 554; Fischer, *Krieg der Illusionen*, 556.

8 Bülow, *1909–1919*, 148–9.

9 Ibid., 149.

10 Kantorowicz, *Gutachten*, 393.

11 Tirpitz, *Erinnerungen*, V.

12 Isobel Hull, *Entourage*, 260; Rathenau, *Notes and Diaries*, 153.

13 Isobel Hull, *Entourage*, 260–1.

14 Fischer in Schieder, ed., *Erster Weltkrieg*, 31; Kantorowicz, *Gutachten*, 295.

15 Kantorowicz, *Gutachten*, 221.

16 Ibid., 269.

17 House, *Intimate Papers*, I, 272–5.

18 Riezler, *Tagebücher*, 182–3.

19 Tirpitz, *Erinnerungen*, 210; Viereck, *Kaiser on Trial*, 13.

20 GP, XXXIX, 113–15, 126.

21 Moltke, *Erinnerungen*, 380–1; Bülow, *1909–1919*, 160; Fischer, *Krieg der Illusionen*, 703; Tirpitz, *Erinnerungen*, 214–15.

22 Fischer in Schieder, ed., *Erster Weltkrieg*, 43–4; Fritz Fischer, 'Weltpolitik' in

ibid; Kantorowicz, *Gutachten*, 267; Tirpitz, *Erinnerungen*, 237.

23 Fischer in Schieder, ed., *Erster Weltkrieg*, 38; Viereck, *Kaiser on Trial*, 12; Tim Judah, *The Serbs. History, Myth and the Destruction of Yugoslavia*, Newhaven and London, 1997, 53; Niemann, *Wanderungen*, 60–61.

24 Görlitz, ed., *Kaiser*, 140.

25 Moltke, 'Zur Beurteilung der politischen Lage', in *Erinnerungen*, 3–4.

26 Bülow, *1909–1919*, 138, 121, 161; Moltke, *Erinnerungen*, 6–7.

27 Kantorowicz, *Gutachten*, 305. Kantorowicz thought the Austrian Foreign Minister the man chiefly responsible for the war – see 379, 423.

28 Fischer, *Krieg der Illusionen*, 713; Kantorowicz, *Gutachten*, 261; Tirpitz, *Erinnerungen*, 238; Alfred von Tirpitz, *Deutsche Ohnmachtspolitik im Weltkrieg*, Hamburg and Berlin, 1926, 2–3.

29 Fischer in Schieder, ed., *Erster Weltkrieg*, 50; Wilhelm II, *Ereignisse und Gestalten*, 211.

30 Wilhelm II, *Ereignisse und Gestalten*, 213.

31 Hans-Ulrich Wehler, *The German Empire 1871–1918*, trans. Kim Traynor, Leamington Spa and Dover, NH, 1985, 193.

32 Wehler, *Empire*, 200, 202; Schieder, ed., *Erster Weltkrieg*, 3; Tirpitz, *Ohnmachtspolitik*, 5.

33 Dukes, in Dukes and Remak, eds, *Another Germany*, 36.

34 Fritz Fischer, 'Deutschland und der Ausbruch des Weltkrieges – In Erwartung des Blitzkrieges', in Schieder, ed., *Erster Weltkrieg*, 29.

35 Kantorowicz, *Gutachten*, 91.

36 Egmont Zechlin, 'Motiv und Taktik der Reichsleitung', in Schieder, ed., *Erster Weltkrieg*, 195; Tirpitz, *Erinnerungen*, 239.

37 Wilhelm II, *Ereignisse und Gestalten*, 217.

38 Tirpitz, *Ohnmachtspolitik*, 8–9.

39 Fischer, *Krieg der Illusionen*, 616.

40 Bülow, *1909–1919*, 84; Moltke, *Erinnerungen*, 10; House, *Intimate Papers*, I, 225.

41 Bülow, *1909–1919*, 64, 82.

42 Ibid., 162–4.

43 Fischer, *Krieg der Illusionen*, 567, 614.

44 Bogdan Krieger, *Der Kaiser im Felde*, Berlin, 1917, 3–4.

45 Kürenberg, *War alles falsch?*, 310.

46 Moltke, 'Betrachtung und Erinnerungen, Homburg, November 1914', in *Erinnerungen*, 19–23.

47 Viereck, *Kaiser on Trial*, xvi; Gerhart Ritter, *Staatskunst*, III, 20; Eliza von Moltke in Moltke, *Erinnerungen*, x.

48 Bülow, *1909–1919*, 145; Tirpitz, *Erinnerungen*, 242.

Chapter Fifteen: Into the Shadows

1 Golo Mann in the introduction to Prinz Max von Baden, *Erinnerungen und Dokumente*, neu herausgegeben von Golo Mann und Andreas Burkhardt, Stuttgart, 1968, 9.

2 Rathenau, *Kaiser*, 8.

3 Krieger, *Kaiser im Felde*, 9.

4 Fischer, *Krieg der Illusionen*, 722, 736.

5 Everling, *Kaiserworte*, 179–81; Krieger, *Kaiser im Felde*, 13–15.

6 Kürenberg, *War alles falsch?*, 313; Chickering, *Imperial Germany*, 41.

7 Krieger, *Kaiser im Felde*, 6–7, 10; Herzogin Viktoria Luise, *Ein Leben als Tochter des Kaisers*, Göttingen, 1965, 141.

8 Röhl, *Delusion or Design?*, 87.

9 Benson, *English Relatives*, 299; Herre, *Kronprinz*, 52, 54.

10 Krieger, *Kaiser im Felde*, 34–8; John Keegan, *The First World War*, London, 1998, 142–4.

11 Mack Smith, *Modern Italy*, 257–9.

12 Egmont Zechlin, 'Das "Schlesische Angebot" und die Italienische Kriegsgefahr 1917', in Schieder, ed., *Erster Weltkrieg*, 353.

13 Waldersee, *Denkwürdigkeiten*, II, 79; Moltke, *Erinnerungen*, 16; Viereck, *Kaiser on Trial*, 31.

14 Niemann, *Wanderungen*, 62; Isobel Hull, *Entourage*, 267; Bülow, *1909–1919*, 192, 198–9.

15 Fischer, *Krieg der Illusionen*, 69–70, 72.

16 Ibid., 760.

17 Ibid., 766–7.

18 Tirpitz, *Erinnerungen*, 243; Mann, *Wilhelm II*, 16.

19 Moltke, *Erinnerungen*, 24; Dr Paul Tesdorpf, *Die Krankheit Wilhelms II*, Munich, 1919, 5, 21–22; Görlitz, ed., *Kaiser*, 184, 185.

20 Theodor von Bethmann-Hollweg, *Betrachtungen zum Weltkrieg*, Berlin, 1919 and 1921, 20.

21 Krieger, *Kaiser im Felde*, 54.

22 Chickering, *Imperial Germany*, 33; Hull, *Entourage*, 267; Riezler, *Tagebücher*, 200–2.

23 Tirpitz, *Erinnerungen*, 135.

24 Everling, *Kaiserworte*, 76, 77, 78.

25 Chickering, *Imperial Germany*, 23–6.

26 Sven Hedin, *Ein Volk in Waffen*, Leipzig, 1915, 30, 46–7, 49, 52.

27 Krieger, *Kaiser im Felde*, 73; Hedin, *Volk in Waffen*, 136.

28 Moltke, *Erinnerungen*, 17–18.

29 Eliza von Moltke in Moltke, *Erinnerungen*, xi; idem, 25, 382; Rathenau, *Notes and Diaries*, 194.

30 Egmont Zechlin, 'Probleme des Kriegskalküls und der Kriegsbeendigung im erstes Weltkrieg', in Schieder, ed., *Erster Weltkrieg*, 154–5; Krieger, *Kaiser im Felde*, 79–80, 104.

31 Herre, *Kronprinz*, 55.

32 Kürenberg, *War alles falsch?*, 324, 350; Krieger, *Kaiser im Felde*, 84–5.

33 Kürenberg, *War alles falsch?*, 314.

34 Tirpitz, *Erinnerungen*, 413.

35 Ibid., 415–16; Hedin, *Volk in Waffen*, 279.

36 Krieger, *Kaiser im Felde*, 119–20; Riezler, *Tagebücher*, 217 and n1.

37 Tirpitz, *Erinnerungen*, 418, 426, 428; Krieger, *Kaiser im Felde*, 101.

38 Krieger, *Kaiser im Felde*, 118.

39 Hedin, *Volk in Waffen*, 470–1.

40 Ritter, *Staatskunst*, III.

41 Keegan, *First World War*, 233.

42 Tirpitz, *Erinnerungen*, 432; Krieger, *Kaiser im Felde*, 141.

43 Krieger, *Kaiser im Felde*, 146–53.

44 Tirpitz, *Erinnerungen*, 431, 433.

45 Görlitz, ed., *Kaiser*, 183.

46 Bülow, *1909–1919*, 208; Tirpitz, *Erinnerungen*, 440.

47 Bülow, *1909–1919*, 41.

48 Röhl, *Delusion or Design?*, 81–6.

49 Krieger, *Kaiser im Felde*, 170–1.

50 Houston Stewart Chamberlain, *England and Germany*, n.p., February 1915, 5, 9, 13.

51 Chamberlain, *Briefe*, I, 324–6; II, 224, 246, 250.

52 Wendel, *Wilhelm II in der Karikatur*, 70; Kantorowicz, *Gutachten*, 67.

53 Alice Goldfarb Marquis, 'Words as Weapons. Propaganda in Britain and Germany during the First World War', in *Journal of Modern History*, July 1978, 468–73; Trevor Wilson, 'Lord Bryce's Investigation into Alleged German Atrocities in Belgium 1914–15', in *Journal of Contemporary History*, July 1979, 378.

54 Mark Derez, 'The Flames of Louvain', in Hugh Cecil and Peter Liddle, eds, *Facing Armageddon*, London, 1996, 621–2.

55 John Horne and Alan Kramer, 'German "Atrocities" and Franco-German Opinion, 1914, the Evidence of German Soldiers' Diaries', in *Journal of Modern History*, March 1994, 1–24; The German Emperor, The German Crown Prince, Dr V. Bethmann Hollweg (sic), Prince von Bülow, General von Bernhardi, General von der Goltz, General von Clausewitz [!], Professor von Treitschke, Professor Delbrück, *Germany's War Mania. The Teutonic Point of View as Officially Stated by Her Leaders, A Collection of Speeches and Writings*, introduction by Lord Bryce, London, 1914, 15. See also Giles MacDonogh, 'Don't Let's Be Beastly to the Germans', in the *Spectator*, 4 September 1999.

56 Rosen, *Wanderleben*, III–IV, 63; Lady Norah Bentinck, *The Ex-Kaiser in Exile*, London, 1921, 63. Lady Norah's book was serialised in the *Daily Mail*.

57 Chickering, *Imperial Germany*, 41–5; for a dissenting view see Niall Ferguson, *The Pity of War*, London, 1998, 276–7. Some figures suggest that as many as 750,000 Germans died. Chickering (195) gives the figure of wartime deaths as 624,000 as opposed to Britain's 292,000.

58 Bethmann-Hollweg, *Betrachtungen*, II, 114.

59 Herre, *Kronprinz*, 57.

60 Tirpitz, *Erinnerungen*, 441–2, 462; James Gerard, *My Four Years in Germany*, London, 1917, 154.

61 Krieger, *Kaiser im Felde*, 186–92.

62 Tirpitz, *Erinnerungen*, 456.

63 House, *Intimate Papers*, I, 281–2.

64 Gerard, *My Four Years*, 168–9; Tirpitz, *Erinnerungen*, 352; Ferguson, *Pity of War*, 247.

65 House, *Intimate Papers*, II, 25.

66 Generalfeldmarschall von Hindenburg, *Aus meinem Leben*, Leipzig, 1943, 145.

67 Kürenberg, *War alles falsch?*, 327; Krieger, *Kaiser im Felde*, 248; Riezler, *Tagebücher*, 283–4.

68 Krieger, *Kaiser im Felde*, 270, 275, 292, 304.

69 Herre, *Kronprinz*, 59–60, 63–4.

70 Gerard, *My Four Years*; Krieger, *Kaiser im Felde*, 336.

71 Krieger, *Kaiser im Felde*, 359–60.

72 Herre, *Kronprinz*, 64–5.

73 Riezler, *Tagebücher*, 324–5.

74 House, *Intimate Papers*, II, 105, 137–9.

75 Bernstorff, *Memoirs*, 117–20; House, *Intimate Papers*, II, 139; Riezler, *Tagebücher*, 337–8.

76 Herre, *Kronprinz*, 66–7.

77 Ibid., 68.

78 Gerard, *My Four Years*, 245–8.

79 Rosen, *Wanderleben*, III–IV, 37–9.

80 Ritter, *Staatskunst*, III; Tirpitz, *Erinnerungen*, 398, 431; *idem*, *Ohnmachtspolitik*, 33, 229, 271.

81 Bülow, *1909–1919*, 178.

82 Chickering, *Imperial Germany*, 91.

83 Lord Fisher, *Memories*, 1919, quoted in Niemann, *Wanderungen*, 85–6.

84 'Der Kaiser an die deutsche Flotte. Dank für die Sieger vom Skagerrak', proclamation 5 June 1916.

85 Waldersee, *Denkwürdigkeiten*, II, 81; Chickering, *Imperial Germany*, 86; Herre, *Kronprinz*, 70–1; Hutten-Czapski, *Sechzig Jahre*, II, 275.

86 Bethmann-Hollweg, *Betrachtungen*, II, 185.

87 Schwertfeger, *Valentini*, 135; Bethmann-Hollweg, *Betrachtungen*, 152–3; Riezler, *Tagebücher*, 369.

88 Robert Asprey, *The German High Command at War, Hindenburg and Ludendorff and the First World War*, London, 1993, 248; Dorpalen in *A.H.R.*, 26.

89 Schwertfeger, *Valentini*, 140; Asprey, *High Command*, 251–2; Martin Kitchen, *The Silent Dictatorship. The Politics of the German High Command under Hindenburg and Ludendorff 1916–1918*, London, 1976, 28, 41.

90 Herre, *Kronprinz*, 76–7.

91 Arthur Davis, *The Kaiser as I Know Him*, 11–12.

92 Bethmann-Hollweg, *Betrachtungen*, II, 135; Riezler, *Tagebücher*, 404.

93 Herre, *Kronprinz*, 78–9; Schwertfeger, *Valentini*, 151.

94 Herre, *Kronprinz*, 81; Ritter, *Staatskunst*, III; Riezler, *Tagebücher*, 431.

95 Riezler, *Tagebücher*, 434.

96 Bethmann-Hollweg, *Betrachtungen*, II, 209; Herre, *Kronprinz*, 82–4.

97 Schwertfeger, *Valentini*, 160; Herre, *Kronprinz*, 87–8.

98 Herre, *Kronprinz*, 88–9; Bethmann-Hollweg, *Betrachtungen*, II, 222.

99 Herre, *Kronprinz*, 89–93.

100 Ibid., 94–6.

101 Schwertfeger, *Valentini*, 159; Herre, *Kronprinz*, 97.

102 Schwertfeger, *Valentini*, 167; Bernstorff, *Memoirs*, 126; Bethmann-Hollweg, *Betrachtungen*, 236.

103 Bülow, *1909–1919*, 259; Herre, *Kronprinz*, 98; Schwertfeger, *Valentini*, 168, confirms that Plessen dreamed up Michaelis.

104 Schwertfeger, *Valentini*, 160; Herre, *Kronprinz*, 99.

105 Bernstorff, *Memoirs*, 127, 130.

106 John Kelly (ed.), *Dictionary of Popes*, Oxford, 1986, 314–16; Herre, *Kronprinz*, 100–1.

107 Bernstorff, *Memoirs*, 151–5.

108 Herre, *Kronprinz*, 110.

109 Ibid., 116–18.

110 Ibid., 119–22.

111 Ibid., 123–8; Riezler, *Tagebücher*, 459; Prinz Max von Baden, *Erinnerungen und Dokumente*, 28.

112 Davis, *The Kaiser as I Know Him*, 214.

113 Prinz Max von Baden, *Erinnerungen und Dokumente*, 201–2.

114 Herre, *Kronprinz*, 105–6, 129–34; Görlitz, *Kaiser*, 183; Dorpalen in *A.H.R.*, 30–1.

115 Isobel Hull, *Entourage*, 288; Herre, *Kronprinz*, 137–8.

116 Prinz Max von Baden, *Erinnerungen und Dokumente*, 14; Herre, *Kronprinz*, 139–46.

117 Rosen, *Wanderleben*, III–IV, 132–7.

118 André Henrard, 'L'Année 1918 vue de Spa', in *Histoire et Archéologie spadoise*, June 1983, 50. All these properties are much as they were. The author was taken on a tour by the town librarian, M. Jean Toussaint.

119 Asprey, *High Command*, 384; Hindenburg, *Aus meinem Leben*, 264–5; Martin Middlebrook, *The Kaiser's Battle. 21 March 1918: The First Day of the German Spring Offensive*, London, 1983, 31, 123, 353.

120 Henrard, in *Histoire et Archéologie spadoise*, 52.

121 Riezler, *Tagebücher*, 459.

122 Bigelow, *Genseric*, v, 18–19.

Chapter Sixteen: Bowing Out

1 Alfred Niemann, *Kaiser und Revolution, Die Entscheidenden Ereignisse im Grossen Hauptquartier im Herbst 1918*, Berlin, 1928, 136. The author did not visit the upstairs rooms at the Villa Fraineuse, but the style is very classically French in the parts he was allowed to go into. It is now a sports club, and the gardens have been replaced by tennis courts.

2 Willibald Gutsche, *Ein Kaiser im Exil. Der letzte deutsche Kaiser Wilhelm II in Holland, eine kritische Biographie*, Marburg, 1991, 12.

3 Niemann, *Kaiser und Revolution*, 34–5, 39, 42–3.

4 Ibid., 66–8; Prinz Max von Baden, *Erinnerungen und Dokumente*, 286.

5 Niemann, *Kaiser und Revolution*, 71–3; Sigurd von Ilsemann, *Der Kaiser in Holland, Aufzeichnungen des letzten Flügeladjutanten Kaiser Wilhelms II*, hsg von Harald von Koenigswald, Munich, 1967, 2 vols, I, 16.

6 Huldermann, *Ballin*, 294–5, 375; Dorpalen in *A.H.R.*, 24.

7 Huldermann, *Ballin*, 375; Niemann, *Kaiser und Revolution*, 77.

8 Ilsemann, *Kaiser und Holland*, I, 16; Huldermann, *Ballin*, 375–6; Niemann, *Kaiser und Revolution*, 78; Hutten-Czapski, *Sechzig Jahre*, II, 502–3.

9 Niemann, *Kaiser und Revolution*, 80–1; Ilsemann, *Kaiser in Holland*, I, 17.

10 Niemann, *Kaiser und Revolution*, 83–5.

11 Ibid., 87–90.

12 Prinz Max von Baden, *Erinnerungen und Dokumente*, 332.

13 Ibid., 41; Ilsemann, *Kaiser in Holland*, I, 21, 22.

14 Prinz Max von Baden, *Erinnerungen und Dokumente*, 360–1.

15 Ibid., 385–6; Ilsemann, *Kaiser in Holland*, I, 23.

16 Niemann, *Kaiser und Revolution*, 95–103; Riezler, *Tagebücher*, 483–4; Prince Max von Baden, *Erinnerungen und Dokumente*, 40.

17 Niemann, *Kaiser und Revolution*, 104–5.

18 Ilsemann, *Kaiser in Holland*, I, 21; Prinz Max von Baden, *Erinnerungen und Dokumente*, 440.

19 Prinz Max von Baden, *Erinnerungen und Dokumente*, 359.

20 Niemann, *Wanderungen*, 31; Prinz Max von Baden, *Erinnerungen und Dokumente*, 446; Rosen, *Wanderleben*, III–IV, 211–13.

21 Prinz Max von Baden, *Erinnerungen und Dokumente*, 467.

22 Niemann, *Kaiser und Revolution*, 104–5, 108, 111; Prinz Max von Baden, *Erinnerungen und Dokumente*, 470, 474.

23 Ilsemann, *Kaiser in Holland*, I, 28; Niemann, *Kaiser und Revolution*, 116–19; Prinz Max von Baden, *Erinnerungen und Dokumente*, 475.

24 Huldermann, *Ballin*, 377–88.

25 Ilsemann, *Kaiser in Holland*, I, 30; Görlitz, ed., *Kaiser*, 207; Prinz Max von Baden, *Erinnerungen und Dokumente*, 501 n2; Dorpalen in *A.H.R.*, 35–6.

26 Niemann, *Kaiser und Revolution*, 122–5; Golo Mann in Prinz Max von Baden, *Erinnerungen und Dokumente*, 41, 497–500; Ilsemann, *Kaiser in Holland*, I, 30, 32; Maurice Baumont, *L'Abdication de Guillaume II*, Paris, 1930, 17; Henrard in *Histoire et Archéologie spadoise*, 54.

27 Herre, *Kronprinz*, 156–7.

28 Ibid., 160; Kürenberg, *War alles falsch?*, 370.

29 Baumont, *L'Abdication*, 68–9, 77; Oberst Bauer, *Der grosse Krieg in Feld und Heimat*, Tübingen, 1922, 257.

30 Prinz Max von Baden, *Erinnerungen und Dokumente*, 42–3, 506–7, 514, 527; Niemann, *Kaiser und Revolution*, 126, 128; Ilsemann, *Kaiser in Holland*, I, 31.

31 Prinz Max von Baden, *Erinnerungen und Dokumente*, 538.

32 Ilsemann, *Kaiser in Holland*, I, 32, does not mention the bombs or the Shakespeare. This may have been a little embellishment by Niemann. The quotation is from *Julius Caesar*, II.2.32–37.

33 Alfred E. Niemann, *Der Weg Kaiser Wilhelms II vom Thron in die Fremde*, Stuttgart, Berlin and Leipzig, 1932, 74; Gutsche, *Kaiser im Exil*, 25.

34 Prinz Max von Baden, *Erinnerungen und Dokumente*, 557–9.

35 Ibid., 560.

36 Ibid., 562, 565; Kitchen, *Silent Dictatorship*, 267; Wilhelm Groener, *Lebenserinnerungen*, Hsg Friedrich Freiherr Hiller von Gaertringen, Göttingen, 1957, 448.

37 Prinz Max von Baden, *Erinnerungen und Dokumente*, 567, 573.

38 Ibid., 581, 585, 588–90.

39 Ilsemann, *Kaiser in Holland*, I, 35.

40 Ibid., I, 36. Others put this meeting on the 9th, but it seems more likely that the Dutchman came to the villa on the 8th, as Ilsemann says. Henrard, *Histoire et Archéologie spadoise*, 55, says that William changed his lodgings again that night, staying at the 'Red Castle'.

41 Prinz Max von Baden, *Erinnerungen und Dokumente*, 593–5.

42 Niemann, *Weg*, 68; idem, *Kaiser und Revolution*, 136; Prinz Max von Baden, *Erinnerungen und Dokumente*, 595.

43 Herre, *Kronprinz*, 163; Kürenberg, *War alles falsch?*, 373; Baumont, *L'Abdication*, 88; Viereck, *Kaiser on Trial*, 330; Gutsche, *Kaiser im Exil*, 21; Niemann, *Kaiser und Revolution*, 137–8; Rudolf Olden, *Hindenburg*, Paris, 1935, 165.

44 Niemann, *Kaiser und Revolution*, 138–9; Kürenberg, *War alles falsch?*, 373.

45 Niemann, *Kaiser und Revolution*, 139; Groener, *Lebenserinnerungen*, 459.

46 Niemann, *Kaiser und Revolution*, 140; Niemann, *Weg*, 74; Ilsemann, *Kaiser in Holland*, 37; Baumont, *L'Abdication*, 107, 115–16, 120; Dr J. Charité's *Biografisch Woordenboek van Nederland*, S'Gravenhage, 1979, mentions nothing about Heutsz's role in William's abdication; Prinz Max von Baden, *Erinnerungen und Dokumente*, 597.

47 Prinz Max von Baden, *Erinnerungen und Dokumente*, 599.

48 Niemann, *Kaiser und Revolution*, 141–2; Groener, *Lebenserinnerungen*, 460.

49 Niemann, *Kaiser und Revolution*, 143; Ilsemann, *Kaiser in Holland*, I, 37; Baumont, *L'Abdication*, 129, 143–4, 152.

50 Prinz Max von Baden, *Erinnerungen und Dokumente*, 600–8; Philipp Schiedemann, *Memoiren eines Sozialdemokrat*, 2 vols, Dresden, 1928, II, 310–11.

51 Niemann, *Kaiser und Revolution*, 138; Kürenberg, *War alles falsch?*, 378–9.

52 Empress Hermine, *Days in Doorn*, n.p., 1928, 149–50.

53 Ibid., 150–1.

54 Gutsche, *Kaiser im Exil*, 22, 24; Niemann, *Weg*, 82; Ilsemann, *Kaiser in Holland*, I, 40.

55 Bogdan Krieger, *Das Berliner Schloss in den Revolutionstagen 1918*, Leipzig, 1922, 24.

56 Niemann, *Kaiser und Revolution*, 146; Baumont, *L'Abdication*, 157.

57 Ilsemann, *Kaiser in Holland*, I.41–43.

58 Ibid., 43–5.

59 Gutsche, *Kaiser im Exil*, 25; Rosen, *Wanderleben*, III–IV, 216; Wheeler Bennett, *Three Episodes in the Life of Kaiser Wilhelm II*, 17.

60 Kürenberg, *War alles falsch?*, 382; Gutsche, *Kaiser im Exil*, 26; Ilsemann, *Kaiser in Holland*, 45–6.

61 Ilsemann, *Kaiser in Holland*, 46–7.

62 Rosen, *Wanderleben*, III–IV, 219–21; Ilsemann, *Kaiser in Holland*, 47.

63 Lady Norah Bentinck, *Ex-Kaiser*, 1, 7–8; Niemann, *Weg*, 90, 93; Ilsemann, *Kaiser in Holland*, I, 53.

64 Rosen, *Wanderleben*, III–IV, 222, 238; Niemann, *Weg*, 90; Waters, *Potsdam and Doorn*, 191; Ilsemann, *Kaiser in Holland*, 48; Lady Susan Townley, *Indiscretions*, 282–5; Kenneth Young, ed., *The Diaries of Sir Robert Bruce Lockhart*, London, 1973, I (herefter Bruce Lockhart, *Diaries*) 316–17. Lady Susan says nothing about her own undignified behaviour on that occasion.

Chapter Seventeen: Amerongen and Doorn

1 Lady Norah Bentinck, *Ex-Kaiser*, 23; Kohut, *Wilhelm II*, 203.

2 Gutsche, *Kaiser im Exil*, 29; Ilsemann, *Kaiser in Holland*, I, 60.

3 Rosen, *Wanderleben*, III–IV, 237–8; Lady Norah Bentinck, *Ex-Kaiser*, 30.

4 Ilsemann, *Kaiser in Holland*, 49.

5 Rosen, *Wanderleben*, III–IV, 239–40.

6 Lady Norah Bentinck, *Ex-Kaiser*, 42, 51; Kürenberg, *War alles falsch?*, 384. Sigurd's son Wilhelm von Ilsemann also praised the housekeeper's baking abilities to the author.

7 Gutsche, *Kaiser im Exil*, 83.

8 Lady Norah Bentinck, *Ex-Kaiser*, 51, 53; Gutsche, *Kaiser im Exil*, 31, 36.

9 Ilsemann, *Kaiser in Holland*, I, 64; Gutsche, *Kaiser im Exil*, 31; Lady Norah Bentinck, *Ex-Kaiser*, 34.

10 Ilsemann, *Kaiser in Holland*, I, 67; Lady Norah Bentinck, *Ex-Kaiser*, 79.

11 Ilsemann, *Kaiser in Holland*, I, 69.

12 Ibid., I, 73.

13 Ibid., I, 74–9; Rosen, *Wanderleben*, III–IV, 243.

14 Kürenberg, *War alles falsch?*, 390.

15 Ilsemann, *Kaiser in Holland*, I, 86; Kürenberg, *War alles falsch?*, 392–5.

16 Gutsche, *Kaiser im Exil*, 36.

17 Ilsemann, *Kaiser in Holland*, I, 90, 95; Gutsche, *Kaiser im Exil*, 35–6; Lady Norah Bentinck, *Ex-Kaiser*, 36.

18 Ilsemann, *Kaiser in Holland*, I, 99–103.

19 Gutsche, *Kaiser im Exil*, 38.

20 Ilsemann, *Kaiser in Holland*, I, 105–6; Hermine, *Days in Doorn*, 166.

21 Ilsemann, *Kaiser in Holland*, I, 111, 144–5.

22 Gutsche, *Kaiser im Exil*, 41; Viereck, *Kaiser on Trial*, 352.

23 *Kaiserlicher Kunstbesitz aus dem Holländischen Exil Haus Doorn* (exhibition catalogue), Berlin, 1991, 13; Gutsche, *Kaiser im Exil*, 45.

24 Lady Norah Bentinck, *Ex-Kaiser*, 52; Kürenberg, *War alles falsch?*, 398.

25 Ilsemann, *Kaiser in Holland*, I, 118, 121.

26 Ibid., I, 129.

27 Ibid., I, 149.

28 Ibid., 150–5.

29 Daisy Pless, *Private Diary*, 475.

30 Ilsemann, *Kaiser in Holland*, I, 171, 173.

31 Ibid., I, 156.

32 Ibid., I, 177.

33 Hermine, *Days in Doorn*, introduction by G. S. Viereck, xi–xiii; Ilsemann, *Kaiser in Holland*, I, 178–9.

34 Karl Rosner, *Der König*, Stuttgart and Berlin, 1921, 63, 65; Ilsemann, *Kaiser in Holland*, I, 215–16.

35 Viereck in Hermine, *Days in Doorn*, xvi, 184.

36 Ilsemann, *Kaiser in Holland*, I, 186–7; Daisy Pless, *What I Left Unsaid*, 188.

37 Ilsemann, *Kaiser in Holland*, I, 218–19; Viereck in Hermine, *Days in Doorn*, xxii, 42.

38 Viereck in Hermine, *Days in Doorn*, xxi.

39 Ilsemann, *Kaiser in Holland*, I, 221, 223; Kürenberg, *War alles falsch?*, 418.

40 Ilsemann, *Kaiser in Holland*, I, 226; Viereck in Hermine, *Days in Doorn*, xviii.

41 Ilsemann, *Kaiser in Holland*, I, 232, 237–8.

42 Ibid., I, 242.

43 Hermine, *Days in Doorn*, 244, 252–6.

44 Waters, *Potsdam and Doorn*, 142.

45 Rosen, *Wanderleben*, III–IV, 245; Gutsche, *Kaiser im Exil*, 60–1.

46 Bruce Lockhart, *Diaries*, 73, n. 2, 3.

47 Neil Johnson, *George Sylvester Viereck. German-American Propagandist*, Urbana, Chicago and London, 1972, 8–9, 25; Viereck, *Flesh and Blood*, 237–9.

48 Johnson, *Viereck*, 122–3.

49 Ibid., 125–8; Viereck in Hermine, *Days in Doorn*, xv, 188.

50 Johnson, *Viereck*, 127; Viereck, *Flesh and Blood*, 278.

51 Ilsemann, *Kaiser in Holland*, I, 251.

52 Gutsche, *Kaiser im Exil*, 54; Viereck in Hermine, *Days in Doorn*, xxiii.

53 Ilsemann, *Kaiser in Holland*, I, 254.

54 Viereck in Hermine, *Days in Doorn*, xxiv–xxv, 169; Ilsemann, *Kaiser in Holland*, I, 266–7.

55 Viereck in Hermine, *Days in Doorn*, xxx.

56 Niemann, *Wanderungen*, 112.

57 Sigurd von Ilsemann, *Monarchie und Nationalismus. Der Kaiser in Holland II*, Munich, 1968, 15, 21.

58 Gutsche, *Kaiser im Exil*, 85.

59 Friedrich Wilhelm Prinz von Preussen, *Das Haus Hohenzollern 1918–1945*, Munich and Vienna, 1985, 40–1; Franz Mehring, *Historische Aufsätze zur preussisch-deutschen Geschichte*, Berlin, 1946, introduction by Fred Oelssner, x.

60 Ilsemann, *Kaiser in Holland*, II, 36.

61 Gutsche, *Kaiser im Exil*, 105–6.

62 Johnson, *Viereck*, 174.

63 Bruce Lockhart, *Diaries*, 348; MacDonogh, *Prussia*, 105–7.

64 Gutsche, *Kaiser im Exil*, 72; Hermine, *Days in Doorn*, 163.

65 Gutsche, *Kaiser im Exil*, 68–71.

66 Wilhelm II, *Das Wesen der Kultur*, Leipzig, 1931, 2.

67 Gutsche, *Kaiser im Exil*, 73.

68 Lady Susan Townley, *Indiscretions*, 45.

69 Lady Norah Bentinck, *Ex-Kaiser*, 107–8; Walter Laqueur, *Russia and Germany, A Century of Conflict*, London, 1965, 45, 93, 339, n. 49.

70 *The Protocols of the Meetings of the Learned Elders of Zion*, translated from the Russia by Victor Marsden, London 1948, I, 22.

71 Ibid., I, 26.

72 Ibid., II, 5.

73 Ibid., V, 3.

74 Ibid., IX, 2.

75 Ibid., X, 10.

76 Ibid., XV, 23.

77 Laqueur, *Russia and Germany*, 102–3.

78 Ibid., 102–3.

79 Gutsche, *Kaiser im Exil*, 75.

80 Viereck, *Kaiser on Trial*, 406.

81 Gutsche, *Kaiser im Exil*, 208.

82 Viereck, *Kaiser on Trial*, 90; Kürenberg, *War alles falsch?*, 408, 411, 413; Ilsemann, *Kaiser in Holland* II, 10.

83 Lady Norah Bentinck, *Ex-Kaiser*, 64; Prinz Max von Baden, *Erinnerungen und Dokumente*, 272.

84 Ilsemann, *Kaiser in Holland*, II, 84.

85 Waters, *Potsdam and Doorn*, 95–7.

86 Ibid., 154–7; Ilsemann, *Kaiser in Holland*, II, 106; Wilhelm II, introduction to Sir Frederick Ponsonby, *Briefe der Kaiserin Friedrich*, Berlin, 1929, x, xix.

87 Bruce Lockhart, *Diaries*, 73–4.

88 Ibid., 75–6.

89 Ilsemann, *Kaiser in Holland*, II, 111–17; Waters, *Potsdam and Doorn*, 161.

90 Bruce Lockhart, *Diaries*, 111.

91 Waters, *Potsdam and Doorn*, 172, 175.

Chapter Eighteen: William and Adolf

1 Gutsche, *Kaiser im Exil*, 125, 129; Johnson, *Viereck*, 174.

2 Gutsche, *Kaiser im Exil*, 130–3; David Irving, *Göring, A Biography*, London, 1989, 99.

3 Preussen, *Haus Hohenzollern*, 63; Gutsche, *Kaiser im Exil*, 211. The author was informed by some young Russian professionals in East Prussia in 1992 that Rominten had been Göring's house. They had no idea that William had been the original owner.

4 Ilsemann, *Kaiser in Holland*, II, 157, 165–7; Gutsche, *Kaiser im Exil*, 167.

5 Ilsemann, *Kaiser in Holland*, II, 173–6.

6 Viktoria Luise, *Ein Leben*, 267; Preussen, *Haus Hohenzollern*, 65.

7 Ilsemann, *Kaiser in Holland*, II, 199; Gutsche, *Kaiser im Exil*, 139.

8 Ilsemann, *Kaiser in Holland*, II, 200, 238; Gutsche, *Kaiser im Exil*, 142, 166.

9 B.P.H. Rep. 54 Nr 136, quoted in MacDonogh, *Prussia*, 93.

10 Waters, *Potsdam and Doorn*, 190; Gutsche, *Kaiser im Exil*, 151–2.

11 B.P.H. Rep. 53, Nr 168/1.

12 Ilsemann, *Kaiser in Holland*, II, 212–13, 215.

13 Ibid., II, 222; Gutsche, *Kaiser im Exil*, 10. Gutsche began his historical career in the DDR.

14 Waters, *Potsdam and Doorn*, 200–2, 207.

15 Bruce Lockhart, *Diaries*, 240, 261.

16 Ibid., 245–7.

17 B.P.H. Rep. 53 Nr 167/2; MacDonogh, *Prussia*, 98; Preussen, *Haus Hohenzollern*, 140.

18 Ilsemann, *Kaiser in Holland*, II, 261–3.

19 Kürenberg, *War alles falsch?*, 427–8.

20 B.P.H. Rep. 53 Nr 167/1.

21 B.P.H. Rep. 53 Nr 167/3, 4, 6.

22 Gutsche, *Kaiser im Exil*, 180.

23 Wilhelm II, *Die chinesische Monade. Ihre Geschichte und ihre Deutung*, Leipzig, 1934, 9.

24 Ilsemann, *Kaiser in Holland*, II, 264.

25 MacDonogh, *Prussia*, 96.

26 Willhelm II, *Monade*, 43–9.

27 Ibid., 49–55.

28 Waters, *Potsdam and Doorn*, 266, 295.

29 Kürenberg, *War alles falsch?*, 7–9, 398.

30 Ibid., 154, 157, 421; Gutsche, *Kaiser im Exil*, 77.

31 Kürenberg, *War alles falsch?*, 368.

32 Ibid., 423.

33 Wilhelm II, *Studien zur Gorgo*, 12, 36, 38.

34 Gutsche, *Kaiser im Exil*, 194.

35 Ilsemann, *Kaiser in Holland*, II, 298; Johnson, *Viereck*, 165, 167–8.

36 Viereck, *Kaiser on Trial*, introduction by GBS, xi–xii.

37 Wilhelm II, *Das Königreich im alten Mesopotamien*, Berlin 1938, 41–3.

38 Ilsemann, *Kaiser in Holland*, II, 313.

39 Richard Lamb, *The Ghosts of Peace 1935–1945*, London 1987, 98.

40 Ilsemann, *Kaiser in Holland*, II, 290.

41 Wheeler-Bennett, *Three Episodes*, 11, 15, 21, 22, 27; Bruce Lockhart, *Diaries*, vol. II, London, 1980, 40–1. Wheeler-Bennett was later involved in attempts to recover William's garter regalia. The PRO possesses three files relating to this: FO 370 1697 (L5824/2/402), FO 370 1698 (L6634) and FO 371 64347 (C4826/C13107/172/18). Wheeler-Bennett also seems to have been keen to track down a non-existent diary. Letter to the author from Patsy Meehan, September 1999.

42 Wheeler-Bennett, *Three Episodes*, 24.

43 Ilsemann, *Kaiser in Holland*, II, 318, 333, 335–336.

44 The letter was reproduced in the *Tatler*, November 1999; Gutsche, *Kaiser im Exil*, 200.

45 Ilsemann, *Kaiser in Holland*, II, 340, 342.

46 Gutsche, *Kaiser im Exil*, 204–5.

47 Ilsemann, *Kaiser in Holland*, II, 345.

48 Gutsche, *Kaiser im Exil*, 199.

49 Ibid., 213.

50 There have been recent moves to have William's remains reburied in Berlin. Presumably the instructions laid down in his will still apply. Roger Boyes, 'Call to end exile of Last Kaiser', *The Times*, 24 November 1999.

51 Bentinck, *Ex-Kaiser*, 58.

52 Ibid., 81.

53 Wheeler-Bennett, *Three Episodes*, 11–12.

54 Hermine, *Days in Doorn*, 272.

55 Viereck, *Kaiser on Trial*, 51.

Index